# HRM

NELSON SERIES IN HUMAN RESOURCES MANAGEMENT

W9-CEF-140

# Strategic Human Resources Planning

## THIRD EDITION

# HRM

NELSON SERIES IN HUMAN RESOURCES MANAGEMENT

# Strategic Human Resources Planning

## THIRD EDITION

**MONICA BELCOURT**
YORK UNIVERSITY

**KENNETH J. MᶜBEY**
YORK UNIVERSITY

**SERIES EDITOR: MONICA BELCOURT**

**NELSON** EDUCATION

# NELSON / EDUCATION

**Strategic Human Resources Planning, Third Edition**
by Monica Belcourt and Kenneth J. McBey

**Associate Vice-President, Editorial Director:**
Evelyn Veitch

**Publisher:**
Veronica Visentin

**Acquisitions Editor:**
Shannon White

**Senior Marketing Manager:**
Charmaine Sherlock

**Senior Developmental Editor:**
Karina Hope

**Permissions Coordinator:**
Nicola Winstanley

**Content Production Managers:**
Anne Macdonald/Wendy Yano

**Copy Editor:**
Karen Rolfe

**Proofreader:**
Erin Moore

**Indexer:**
Belle Wong

**Manufacturing Coordinator:**
Ferial Suleman

**Design Director:**
Ken Phipps

**Interior Design:**
Katherine Strain

**Cover Design:**
Maria Castelli

**Compositor:**
Interactive Composition Corporation

**Printer:**
Maracle Press Limited

COPYRIGHT © 2008, 2007, 2004 by Nelson Education Ltd.

Printed and bound in Canada
3  4  09  08

ISBN-13: 978-0-17-625245-8
ISBN-10: 0-17-625245-2

For more information contact Nelson Education Ltd., 1120 Birchmount Road, Toronto, Ontario, M1K 5G4. Or you can visit our Internet site at http://www.nelson.com

Statistics Canada information is used with the permission of Statistics Canada. Users are forbidden to copy this material and/or redisseminate the data, in an original or modified form, for commercial purposes, without the expressed permissions of Statistics Canada. Information on the availability of the wide range of data from Statistics Canada can be obtained from Statistics Canada's Regional Offices, its World Wide Web site at <http://www.statcan.ca>, and its toll-free access number 1-800-263-1136.

ALL RIGHTS RESERVED. No part of this work covered by the copyright herein may be reproduced, transcribed, or used in any form or by any means—graphic, electronic, or mechanical, including photocopying, recording, taping, Web distribution, or information storage and retrieval systems—without the written permission of the publisher.

For permission to use material from this text or product, submit all requests online at www.cengage.com/permissions. Further questions about permissions can be emailed to permissionrequest@cengage.com

Every effort has been made to trace ownership of all copyrighted material and to secure permission from copyright holders. In the event of any question arising as to the use of any material, we will be pleased to make the necessary corrections in future printings.

**Library and Archives Canada Cataloguing in Publication Data**

Belcourt, Monica,
  Strategic human resources planning / Monica Belcourt, Kenneth J. McBey.—3rd ed. Order of authors' names reversed on 2nd ed. Includes bibliographical refrences and index.

ISBN-13: 978-0-17-625245-8
ISBN-10: 0-17-625245-2

1. Manpower planning—Textbooks. I. McBey, Kenneth James II. Title

HF5549.5.M3B45 2006   658.3'01
C2006-902234-8

*To my son Marc, for his cool calm and engaging wit.*

M.B.

*With love to Betty-Anne, Robert, June, Roderick, and Donald.*

*Nulli Secundus!*

K.M.

# Brief Contents

*About the Series* xx

*About the Authors* xxi

*Preface* xxiii

*Acknowledgments* xxviii


**PART I   INTRODUCTION   1**

**Chapter 1   Strategic Management   3**

**Chapter 2   Aligning HR with Strategy   29**

**Chapter 3   Environmental Influences on HRM   61**


**PART II   HR PLANNING   89**

**Chapter 4   Job Analysis   91**

**Chapter 5   Information Technology for HR Planning   121**

**Chapter 6   The HR Forecasting Process   143**

**Chapter 7   HR Demand   167**

**Chapter 8   Ascertaining HR Supply   191**

**Chapter 9   Succession Management   223**


**PART III   STRATEGIC OPTIONS AND HR DECISIONS   257**

**Chapter 10   Downsizing and Restructuring   259**

**Chapter 11   Strategic International HRM   295**

**Chapter 12   Mergers and Acquisitions   321**

**Chapter 13   Outsourcing   351**

**Chapter 14   Evaluation of HR Programs and Policies   369**


**INDEX   405**

# Detailed Contents

*About the Series*   *xx*

*About the Authors*   *xxi*

*Preface*   *xxiii*

*Acknowledgments*   *xxviii*

**PART I   INTRODUCTION   1**

**Chapter 1   Strategic Management   3**

Chapter Learning Objectives   3

A Need for Strategic HRM   4

Strategy   5

Strategic Types   8

    Corporate Strategies   8

    Restructuring Strategies   8

    Growth Strategies   10

    Maintenance Strategies   11

    Business Strategies   11

The Strategic Planning Process   13

    1. Establish the mission, vision, and values   13

    2. Develop objectives   15

    3. Analyze the external environment   17

    4. Determine the competitive position   17

    5. Identify the competitive advantage   18

    6. Determine the methods for accomplishing the objectives   20

    7. Evaluate the performance   20

    Benefits of Strategy Formulation   20

Summary   21

Key Terms   22

Web Links   22

RPC Icons   22

Discussion Questions   23

Using the Internet   23

Exercises   23

Case: Aldo Shoes Limited   26

Endnotes   26

**Chapter 2   Aligning HR with Strategy   29**

Chapter Learning Objectives   29

Strategic HRM   30

    Theories of the Strategic Management of Human Resources   31

    Human Capital Theory   34

Strategic HRM    35

    The Importance of Strategic HR Planning    36

    Improved Goal Attainment    36

The Risks    37

Linking HR Processes to Strategy    38

    Corporate Strategy Leads to HR Strategy    39

    HR Competencies Lead to Business Strategy    39

HR Strategy and Corporate Strategy    40

    HR Becomes a Business Partner    40

Strategic Partnering    41

Ways to Become Involved in the Strategic Planning Process    43

    Membership in the Executive Team    43

    Review/React Linkage    43

    Integrative Linkage    43

HR Strategy by Division    45

    Characteristics of an Effective HRM Strategy    46

    Fit    47

    External Fit    47

    Internal Fit    47

    Focus on Results    48

The Strategic HR Planning Model    48

Summary    49

Key Terms    49

Web Links    49

RPC Icons    49

Discussion Questions    50

Using the Internet    50

Exercises    51

Case: A New Vision of HR    51

Endnotes    53

Appendix: HR Alignment with Two Strategies    55

HR Alignment with the Low-Cost-Provider
  Strategy    55

    The Employee    55

    HR Planning    55

    Selection    56

    Compensation    56

    Training    56

    Performance Evaluation    56

    Labour Relations    57

HR Alignment with the Differentiation Strategy    57

    The Employee    58

HR Planning   58

Selection   58

Compensation   58

Training   58

Performance Evaluation   59

Labour Relations   59

Endnotes   59


## Chapter 3   Environmental Influences on HRM   61

Chapter Learning Objectives   61

Environmental Scanning Sources and Methods   62

Sources of Information   63

Publications   64

Professional Associations   65

Conferences and Seminars   65

Professional Consultants   65

Methods of Forecasting   66

Trend Analysis   66

Delphi Technique   66

Impact Analysis   67

Scenario Planning   67

Challenges in Environmental Scanning   67

Isolating the Critical from the Insignificant   70

A Proactive Approach   71

Environmental Factors   71

Economic Climate   72

From the Industrial Revolution to the
   Knowledge Revolution   72

Globalization   73

The Labour Market   73

Political and Legislative Factors   74

Technological Factors   75

Demographic Factors   76

Social and Cultural Factors   77

Stakeholders   78

Shareholders   78

Customers   78

Suppliers   78

Governments   79

The Public   79

Unions   79

Employees   80

Top Management   80
Environment Scanning: A Case Application   81
Summary   82
Key Terms   82
Web Links   82
RPC Icons   83
Discussion Questions   83
Using the Internet   84
Exercises: The Nominal Group Technique   84
Case: Work–Life Family Balance   85
Endnotes   86

**PART II   HR PLANNING   89**

**Chapter 4   Job Analysis   91**
Chapter Learning Objectives   91
Introduction   93
Job Analysis   94
Job Analysis and HR Planning   96
Problems Associated with Job Analysis   97
The Process of Job Analysis   99
Output and Production Analysis   102
Current Job Descriptions and Specifications   102
Specific Job Analysis Techniques   107
Competency-Based Approaches   109
Summary   112
Key Terms   113
Web Links   113
RPC Icons   114
Discussion Questions   114
Using the Internet   114
Exercise   115
Case: Madness at Moosehead U   115
Endnotes   117

**Chapter 5   Information Technology for HR Planning   121**
Chapter Learning Objectives   121
IT and HRM   123
IT for HR Planning   126
Skills Inventories   126
Replacement Charts   127
Succession Management   127
Different IT Solutions for Different Needs   128

Selecting Technology Solutions for HRM   130
   Conduct a Needs Analysis   130
   Explore the Marketplace   130
   Request for Proposal   131
   Evaluate Vendors and Products   131
Implementing and Evaluating Technology   131
   Typical Implementation Process   131
   Business Process Re-Engineering   132
   Ensuring Data Security   132
Evaluating HR Technology   133
Emerging HR Technology Solutions   134
   Self-Service   134
   Web-Based HR   134
   Competitive Advantage   135
   Knowledge Management   135
   Enterprise Portals   135
Summary   136
Key Terms   136
Web Links   137
RPC Icons   138
Discussion Questions   138
Using the Internet   138
Exercise   139
Case: Building Talent at Cisco Systems   139
Endnotes   140

**Chapter 6   The HR Forecasting Process   143**
Chapter Learning Objectives   143
Forecasting Activity Categories   147
   Benefits of HR Forecasting   149
   Key Personnel Analyses Conducted by HR
      Forecasters   151
Environmental and Organizational Factors Affecting
   HR Forecasting   153
HR Forecasting Time Horizons   154
   Determining Net HR Requirements   155
Summary   161
Key Terms   161
Web Links   162
RPC Icons   163
Discussion Questions   163
Using the Internet   164

Exercise   164

Case: Sun Microsystems   164

Endnotes   165

## Chapter 7   HR Demand   167

Chapter Learning Objectives   167

   Index/Trend Analysis   169

   Expert Forecasts   170

   Delphi Technique   172

   Nominal Group Technique   174

   HR Budgets: Staffing Table   176

   Envelope/Scenario Forecasting   177

   Regression Analysis   180

   Simple Regression Prediction Model   181

   Regression Exercise   181

Summary   183

Key Terms   184

Web Links   184

RPC Icons   185

Discussion Questions   185

Using the Internet   186

Exercise   186

Case: Recruiting with Bells and Whistles   186

Endnotes   187

## Chapter 8   Ascertaining HR Supply   191

Chapter Learning Objectives   191

Skills and Management Inventories   195

   Succession/Replacement Analysis   196

Markov Models   200

   Linear Programming   203

   Movement Analysis   204

   Movement Analysis Exercise   205

   Vacancy Model   208

HR Supply and Retention Programs   212

Summary   213

Key Terms   216

Web Links   216

RPC Icons   216

Discussion Questions   217

Using the Internet   217

Exercise   217

Case: Ontario's Faculty Shortage Crisis   218
Endnotes   220

## Chapter 9   Succession Management   223

Chapter Learning Objectives   223
Importance of Succession Management   224
   Evolution of Succession Management   226
   Broader Focus   227
   Time Horizon   228
   Talent Pools   228
   Rating System   229
   Succession Management Process   230
Succession Management's Soft Spots   246
   Elitism   246
   Risk of the Spotlight   247
   Selection Bias   248
   Unpredictable Futures   248
Summary   249
Key Terms   249
Web Links   249
RPC Icons   249
Discussion Questions   251
Using the Internet   251
Exercise   251
Case: Acceleration Pools at PepsiCo   252
Endnotes   253

## PART III   STRATEGIC OPTIONS AND HR DECISIONS   257

## Chapter 10   Downsizing and Restructuring   259

Chapter Learning Objectives   259
The Downsizing Phenomenon   260
   Defining Downsizing and Restructuring   261
   How Common Is Workforce Reduction
     and Restructuring?   263
   Why Do Organizations Downsize?   263
   The Downsizing Decision   265
   Some Ethical Considerations   266
   Alternatives to Downsizing   267
Inplacement and Outplacement Issues   267
   Planning for Downsizing   267
   Adjusting to Job Loss   269

The "Survivors" of Downsizing    270
   Perceptions of Justice    271
   Survivor Reactions    271
   Impact on the "Downsizers"    273
Financial Performance and Downsizing    273
   Consequences of Downsizing    274
   Some Canadian Evidence    275
   Effective Downsizing Strategies    276
   Strategic Downsizing    277
   Effective and Ineffective Downsizing Strategies    278
   Summary of Best Practices    280
HRM Issues    280
   Managing the Changing Psychological Contract    280
   The "New Deal" in Employment    281
   Altering the Psychological Contract    281
   Downsizing and "High Involvement" HRM    283
   Labour Relations Issues    284
Summary    285
Key Terms    286
Web Links    286
RPC Icons    287
Discussion Questions    287
Using the Internet    288
Exercises    288
Case: A Downsizing Decision at the Department of Public Works    288
Endnotes    291

**Chapter 11    Strategic International HRM    295**
Chapter Learning Objectives    295
Key Challenges Influencing HR Practices and Processes within an
  International Context    297
   Workforce Diversity    297
   Employment Legislation    297
   The Role of the HR Function    298
   Flexibility    298
Strategic International Human Resource Management    298
Strategic IHRM Fits with Corporate International
  Business Strategies    299
   The Domestic Stage    299
   The Multidomestic Stage    299
   The Multinational Stage    300
   The Global Stage    300

Key HR Practices and Processes within an International Context 301
    Recruitment 301
    Selection 303
    Other Personal Characteristics 305
Pre-Assignment Training 306
Post-Assignment Activities 308
    Repatriation 308
    Career Development 310
    Performance Appraisal 310
    Compensation 312
Labour Relations 313
Summary 314
Key Terms 315
Web Links 315
RPC Icons 315
Discussion Questions 315
Using the Internet 316
Exercises 316
Case: An International Career Move 317
Endnotes 317

**Chapter 12   Mergers and Acquisitions   321**
Chapter Learning Objectives 321
Definitions 322
The Urge to Merge 324
    Strategic Benefits 324
    Financial Benefits 325
    Management Needs 326
    Merger Methods 327
    The Success Rate of Mergers 327
    Financial Impact 328
    Impact on Human Resources 329
Cultural Issues in Mergers 330
HR Issues in M&As 333
    HR Planning 335
    Selection 338
    Compensation 340
    Performance Appraisal 341
    Training and Development 341
    Labour Relations 341
Summary 342
Key Terms 342

Web Links  343

RPC Icons  343

Discussion Questions  344

Using the Internet  344

Exercise  344

Case: The City of Toronto—Courage in the Face
　of Chaos  345

　　Lessons Learned  346

Endnotes  347

**Chapter 13  Outsourcing  351**

Chapter Learning Objectives  351

Outsourcing  352

　　Outsourcing HR Functions  353

　　The Rationale for Outsourcing  355

　　Financial Savings  355

　　Strategic Focus  356

　　Advanced Technology  357

　　Improved Service  357

　　Specialized Expertise  357

　　Organizational Politics  358

　　Risks and Limitations  358

　　Projected Benefits vs. Actual Benefits  358

　　Service Risks  359

　　Employee Morale  359

　　Reduced Value  360

Management of Outsourcing  360

　　Selecting the Vendor  360

　　Negotiating the Contract  361

　　Monitor the Arrangement  363

Summary  363

Key Term  363

Web Links  363

RPC Icons  364

Discussion Questions  364

Using the Internet  364

Exercise  365

Case: Calgary Health Region  365

Endnotes  367

**Chapter 14  Evaluation of HR Programs and Policies  369**

Chapter Learning Objectives  369

Keeping Score  370

The Importance of Evaluating HRM   371

    Resistance   371

    Rationale   372

    The 5C Model of HRM Impact   374

    Compliance   374

    Client Satisfaction   375

    Advantages of Measuring Client Satisfaction   375

    Methods of Measuring Client Satisfaction   375

    Problems with Measuring Client Satisfaction   377

    Cost of Employee Behaviour   380

    Contribution   381

How HR Contributes to Organizational Performance   382

    Financial Measures   382

    Measures of Managerial Perceptions of Effectiveness   383

Approaches to Measuring HRM Practices   385

    Cost–Benefit Analysis   385

    Utility Analysis   386

    Auditing and Benchmarking   386

    The HR Scorecard   389

    Measuring the Worth of Employees   390

Challenges in Measuring the Impact of HRM   391

    Universality of Best Practices   391

    Separation of Cause and Effect   393

    Successful Measurement   393

Summary   395

Key Terms   395

Web Links   395

RPC Icons   396

Discussion Questions   397

Using the Internet   397

Exercises   398

Case: Measuring HR Impact at Wells Fargo   398

Endnotes   399

Appendix: HR Accounting Methods   402

The Human Asset Accounting Approach   402

    Limitations of Human Asset Accounting Models   403

    Intellectual Capital Approach   403

    Issues in Measuring Intellectual Capital   403

Endnotes   404


**Index   405**

# About the Series

More than ever, human resource management (HRM) professionals need the knowledge and skills to design HRM policies and practices that not only meet legal requirements but also are effective in supporting organizational strategy. Increasingly, these professionals turn to published research and books on best practices for assistance in the development of effective HR strategies. The books in the *Nelson Series in Human Resources Management* are the best source in Canada for reliable, valid, and current knowledge about practices in HRM.

The texts in this series include

- Managing Performance through Training and Development
- Management of Occupational Health and Safety
- Recruitment and Selection in Canada
- Strategic Compensation in Canada
- Strategic Human Resources Planning
- An Introduction to the Canadian Labour Market
- Research, Measurement and Evaluation of Human Resources

The *Nelson Series in Human Resources Management* represents a significant development in the field of HRM for many reasons. Each book in the series is the leading Canadian text in its area of specialization. Human resource (HR) professionals in Canada must work with Canadian laws, statistics, policies, and values, and this series serves their needs. It is the only opportunity that students and practitioners have to access a complete set of HRM books, standardized in presentation, that enables them to access information quickly across many HRM disciplines. The books are essential sources of information that meet the requirements for the CCHRA (Canadian Council of Human Resource Associations) National Knowledge exam for the academic portion of the HR certification process. This one-stop resource will prove useful to anyone looking for solutions for the effective management of people.

The publication of this series signals that the field of HRM has advanced to the stage where theory and applied research guide practice. The books in the series present the best and most current research in the functional areas of HRM. Research is supplemented with examples of the best practices used by Canadian companies that are leaders in HRM. Thus the books serve as an introduction to the functional area for the new student of HR and as a validation source for the more experienced HRM practitioner. Cases, exercises, and references provide opportunities for further discussion and analysis.

As you read and consult the books in this series, I hope you share my excitement in being involved in the development of a profession that has such a significant impact on the workplace.

*Monica Belcourt, PhD, CHRP*
Series Editor
July 2006

# About the Authors

## Monica Belcourt

Monica Belcourt is a professor of Human Resources Management at York University. Her research work is grounded in the experience she gained as director of personnel at CP Rail, as director of Employee Development at the National Film Board, and as a functional HR specialist for other organizations. Dr. Belcourt alternated working in HRM with graduate school, earning an M.A. in psychology, an M.Ed. in adult education, and a Ph.D. in management. She also holds the designation of Certified Human Resource Professional (CHRP). She has taught HRM at Concordia University, Université du Québec à Montréal (UQUAM), McGill University, and York University. At the latter, she founded and managed the largest undergraduate program in HRM in Canada and Canada's only executive-style Masters in Human Resources Management. She is the academic editor of the *Nelson Series in HRM*.

Dr. Belcourt is the founding director of the International Alliance for Human Resources Research (IAHRR) (www.yorku.ca/hrresall), a catalyst for the discovery, dissemination, and application of new knowledge about HRM. Under her leadership, IAHRR has launched The Research Forum, a column in the *Human Resources Professional*; the Applied Research Stream at the annual HRPAO conference; and the best theses awards program. She was the founding director of the Graduate Program in Human Resources Management at York University, where HR professionals can obtain an executive-style MHRM to advance their careers.

Professor Belcourt is active in many professional associations and not-for-profit organizations, and was the president of the Human Resources Professionals Association of Ontario (www.hrpao.org). She is a frequent commentator on HRM issues for CTV's *Canada AM*, CBC, *The Globe and Mail*, Report on Business Television, Workopolis, and other media.

## Kenneth M<sup>c</sup>Bey

Kenneth M<sup>c</sup>Bey is a professor of Human Resources Management at York University. His research and teaching draw on his earlier career as an infantry officer in the Canadian army, where he rose to the rank of Lieutenant-Colonel and commanding officer of the 48th Highlanders of Canada. Throughout his military career, Dr. M<sup>c</sup>Bey held a wide variety of command and staff appointments, including those in human resource–related areas such as recruiting, operations and training, and personnel officer (adjutant). This real-life testing of HR theories has proved invaluable to his work in the academic realm. Professor M<sup>c</sup>Bey earned an Honours B.A. in political economy and a B.Ed. from the University of Toronto, and an M.B.A. and Ph.D. in management from the Schulich School of Business at York University.

Professor M<sup>c</sup>Bey currently serves as the Graduate Program Director of the Human Resources Program at York University. He teaches a wide variety of courses, including Human Resources Planning, Leadership and Management Skills, Recruitment, Selection and Performance Appraisal, Training and

Development, Staffing Organizations, Organizational Behaviour, and Organizational Theory. He has been a visiting professor at the Graduate Programs in Human Resources and Management at the University of Aberdeen, Scotland; the Australian National University, Canberra, Australia; and the University of Otago, Dunedin, New Zealand.

Professor M<sup>c</sup>Bey is active in a wide variety of community and voluntary associations, and he serves on the boards of several not-for-profit organizations. He was awarded the Queen's Golden Jubilee Medal by the Government of Canada for making a "significant contribution to his fellow citizens, community and to Canada." Among Professor M<sup>c</sup>Bey's other honours and awards are the J. Reginald Adams Gold Medal from the University of Toronto, the Canada 125th Anniversary Medal for outstanding service to Canada, the Canadian Forces Decoration (C.D.), and appointment to the Order of St. John by Her Majesty Queen Elizabeth II.

# Preface

The fundamental premise of this text is that different organizational strategies require different human resources management (HRM) policies and practices. *Strategic Human Resources Planning*, Third edition, is designed to help human resources (HR) managers plan and make decisions about the allocation of resources for the effective management of people in organizations, within a given strategy.

HR planning should be more than just demand and supply forecasting; HR professionals should be business partners in strategy formulation and implementation and should be concerned with the implications of strategic decisions on HRM practices. A decision to expand internationally affects selection, compensation, and other functional areas. Strategic decisions to merge or downsize have HR implications beyond simple forecasting. All these strategic options will lead to questions about the best types of compensation, selection, and training to ensure the success of the chosen strategy. This text attempts to answer these questions, without neglecting traditional and important HR forecasting processes. It provides tools for HR planning and forecasting and matches corporate strategies with specific HR practices.

## Structure of the Text

The text is organized to introduce the reader to the concepts of strategy formulation and implementation, within an HR context. Part I outlines the fundamental building blocks of strategic HR with an introduction to the concepts and their links to HR planning, how trends and issues are identified, and how organizations determine if implementation of strategies, policies, and plans are successful. Chapter 1 lays the groundwork by introducing the concepts of both corporate and business strategies. We spend some time explaining strategic choices, because it is imperative that, as HR managers become business partners, they understand commonly used business terms. This will help them to participate fully in strategic discussions and to explain the impact of their HR programs on the organization. Strategy seems to imply that only corporate-wide plans are made, and these are used to manage and control the various units that exist within an organization. But many large organizations operate several businesses, each with its own strategy. For example, Bata operates two "divisions" or businesses, one that focuses on production and the other on retailing. Each has a different business strategy, although the overall corporate strategy is growth. Two types of business-level strategies are discussed. We have added a new section on the strategic planning process. Because most HR professionals are becoming strategic planning partners, and are playing a critical role in the development of mission, vision, and value statements, we have included new material on describing and differentiating these concepts. In the HR world, there is a growing understanding that human resources provide a competitive advantage. We describe what this means, and distinguish between tangible and intangible assets. We outline the benefits of strategy formulation. A model of strategic HR planning is introduced in this chapter to orient the reader and to provide the structure for the text.

Chapter 2 continues the introduction to strategy by embedding HRM strategy within an organizational strategic framework. A model of strategic HR planning is introduced in this chapter to orient the reader and to provide the structure for the text. As the field of HR develops, many are claiming that the discipline needs to have a theoretical foundation in order to test and validate new ideas about the best way to manage employees. New to this chapter are three perspectives, which may be in the embryonic stages of testable theories: the resource-based view, the behavioural perspective, and the "theory" of human capital. The rest of the chapter is focused on a description of strategic HR, the reasons HR planning is important, and the ways in which the HR function contributes to the strategic planning process. Finally we conclude with a section that outlines the characteristics of an effective HR strategy.

The environmental factors that influence strategic choice, particularly within an HR context, are discussed in Chapter 3. We look at the sources of information about the environment and the methods HR strategists use to scan the environment. In this chapter, we have introduced new information about the stages of environmental planning. We have listed the sources of information that are useful for environmental scanning. We have added additional material about the methods of forecasting, including scenario planning. New to the chapter are "expert" predictions about the future of HR including five mega-trends. We then describe changes in globalization, the labour market, politics and legislation, technology, demography, and culture that will influence the practice of HR. We conclude with a description of how stakeholders influence HR policies.

Part II focuses on the more traditional aspects of HR planning: forecasting supply and demand. A critical component of strategy is matching employee capabilities with organizational objectives. The ability to assess current skills is a fundamental part of strategic planning for human resources. Part II provides a comprehensive set of tools that enables the HR professional to develop the numbers and methods needed to support organizational objectives. The critical role of job analysis within a planning context is discussed in Chapter 4. We have written a new section, which describes the importance of job analysis to HR planning. Time is spent analyzing the challenges of job analysis. A new section describes an abbreviated method to deal with the time-consuming nature of job analysis. New to this chapter is a section describing how to use Canada's National Occupational Classification system.

Chapter 5 has been completely rewritten by a new author and expert in HRMS (Human Resources Management Systems), Professor Victor Haines at the Université de Montreal. The focus is on the use of information technology specifically for the HR planning process, rather than a broad range of HR activities. The properties of advanced information technologies are described. Then the use of technology to facilitate different planning activities such as skills inventories, replacement charts, and succession management is outlined. Different IT solutions to meet different HR needs are presented including HRIS, specialty products, and enterprise solutions. Prescriptions for choosing software providers are given. The implementation process is outlined, and issues such as data security are debated. The chapter concludes with descriptions of emerging HR technology solutions.

Chapter 6 explains the techniques used to forecast demand for human resources. Introduced by a new section on the importance of HR in forecasting emergencies, this chapter outlines the categories and benefits of forecasting. A description of the personnel categories used by forecasters is provided. A description of the process for estimating net HR requirements begins by determining HR demand and supply, which allows forecasters to calculate surpluses or shortages. Chapter 7 focuses on the use of methods for analyzing demand. Introduced by a new case on the Delphi technique in the health care sector, this chapter describes various approaches for assessing the demand for HR including index/trend analysis, expert forecasting, the Delphi technique, the nominal group technique, staffing tables, envelope and scenario planning, and regression analysis. Opening with the very timely analysis of the effect of the abolition of mandatory retirement on the supply of employees, Chapter 8 looks at the methods used for determining supply. These methods include skills and management inventories, replacement charts, Markov models, linear programming, movement analysis, and the vacancy model. A discussion on absenteeism and retention highlights the need for organizations to monitor these indices. Managerial succession planning and career development, discussed in Chapter 9, are important considerations for ensuring that the organization has a stock of replacements for its leaders. Succession management has evolved from replacement planning for individual executives to the development of talent pools for broad leadership roles, aligned with the organization's strategies. Development techniques such as promotions, job rotations, special assignments, and mentoring and coaching are described. The role of employees in their own career development is outlined. The chapter ends with a description of the weakness of succession management.

Part III examines the types of strategic orientations that firms may choose. Company-wide strategies, sometimes referred to as corporate strategies, are focused on overall strategy for the company and its businesses or interests. Examples of corporate strategies include decisions to merge or to establish the organization in international markets. Strategies at this level are usually also focused on long-term growth and survival goals. We discuss four major decisions facing organizations: restructuring, international operations, mergers and acquisitions, and outsourcing.

Chapter 10, written by Professor Terry Wagar of Saint Mary's University, discusses restructuring and downsizing. Starting with definitions of downsizing and restructuring, this chapter presents different strategies for reducing the workforce. The reasons for downsizing are delineated. The consequences of reducing the workforce are explained, including survivor syndrome and the impact on financial indices. New to this chapter are a debate on ethical considerations of downsizing and an introduction to other impacts of restructuring, including corporate reputation, organizational learning, and employee safety. This chapter offers suggestions for effective downsizing. The chapter concludes with a discussion on the effect of downsizing on such HR issues as the psychological contract and labour relations.

We then turn to an area of increasing importance in the strategies of organizations—growth through international initiatives. In a newly structured Chapter 11, Professor Stefan Groschl of the Faculty of Management at Le Group ESSEC in Paris, France, discusses the growth option of seeking new customers or markets by locating internationally. HR managers state that globalization of their businesses is the number-one trend affecting their organizations. Operating a business in a foreign country, particularly one that is not North American or European, poses singular problems for the Western HR manager. This chapter includes new material on how to do so effectively.

In Chapter 12, we examine another high-growth area—mergers and acquisitions. An acquisition occurs when one company acquires another, whereas a merger is typically seen as two organizations merging to achieve economies of scale. Both acquisitions and mergers lead to issues of integration of common functions, elimination of duplication or underproductive units, and a meshing of cultures and practices. This chapter outlines the benefits of M&As, and compares the alleged benefits against the real effectiveness of this strategy. HR has a significant role to play, as mergers often fail because HR issues were not managed in a timely and effective manner. Prescriptions for doing so are provided.

The hot issue of outsourcing is explored in Chapter 13, with a thorough analysis of the reasons, the risks, and the benefits of the outsourcing decision. The benefits are not always realized so the chapter offers suggestions for managing the outsourcing arrangement.

HRM issues such as HR planning, compensation, selection, training, performance evaluation, and labour relations are discussed within the overall strategies of restructuring, international initiatives, and mergers. By the end of Part III, readers will understand how specific strategic decisions can be matched with HR policies and practices.

A critical part of strategic planning is the ability to measure results and to determine if goals have been met. Chapter 14, the evaluation of HR programs and policies, ends the book with content about the importance of measuring the effectiveness of HR. Because HR is a young field, we are prone to adopt emerging trends, and so a new section describes how to distinguish a fad from an effective HR program. This chapter provides a framework for understanding how HR processes, practices, and policies can affect organizational outcomes. The chapter outlines the many ways to evaluate effectiveness, and which areas to measure. A new section on the HR scorecard captures the essence of this increasingly popular assessment tool. New to this edition is a list of the characteristics of successful measurement.

Features retained from the previous edition of this text include chapter learning objectives, extensive use of Canadian examples, use of figures and tables to convey information efficiently, margin definitions of key concepts, chapter summaries, and listings of key terms. The end-of-chapter material continues to include suggested websites to help readers access resources available through the Internet or to simply provide interesting avenues for further exploration. WWW icons in the margin (like the one shown here) indicate text for which a website URL has been provided. (However, URLs frequently change, and www.google.com is your best bet to track down a website that has gone missing or to find one that is even better!)

New features of the third edition include chapter opening vignettes, as well as "HR Planning Today" boxes to put issues in a real-life context, and "HR Planning Notebook" boxes to highlight key points that flow from the chapter. End-of-chapter material now includes discussion questions, a "using the internet" feature, exercises, and a case.

Besides these learning features, a notable new feature is a link between the textual material contained in this book and the Required Professional Capabilities (RPCs) necessary to earn a Certified Human Resources Professional (CHRP) designation. As a part of the process needed to earn this Canada-wide designation, granted by the Canadian Council of Human Resources Associations, applicants must take two exams, which cover 203 Required Professional Capabilities, organized into eight subject areas. All RPCs are listed on the Professional Assessment Resource Centre (PARC) website at www.cchra-ccarh.ca/parc/en/section_3/ss33e.asp.

The RPCs are not numbered on PARC, which makes it difficult to reference them. Therefore, the following system has been adopted. The first time an RPC is referenced in a chapter, it will be designated by the chapter number and the order in which it appears in the chapter. For example, RPC 8.2 denotes the second RPC referenced in Chapter 8, and an RPC icon (like the one shown in the margin here), will link a section of the text to a specific RPC. At the end of each chapter the specific RPCs that are referenced in that chapter will be listed. Our hope is that this linkage of our content to the RPCs will help students and practitioners preparing for the CHRP examinations.

An instructor's manual, with test questions for *Strategic HR Planning* is also available, along with PowerPoint slides, both of which can be downloaded directly from www.hrm.nelson.com. A free four-month subscription to the online version of the *Canadian HR Reporter* from Carswell will be available with the purchase of any new Nelson HR book. An access card with a PIN that students will use to activate their subscription will be packaged with the book.

We hope that the book provides an enjoyable learning experience.

Monica Belcourt
Kenneth McBey
July 2006

# Acknowledgments

The authors wish to acknowledge the contributions of three experts in HRM: Professor Terry Wagar of Saint Mary's University, Professor Victor Haines of the Université de Montreal, and Professor Stefan Groschl of the University of Guelph and the Faculty of Management at Le Groupe ESSEC, in Cedex, France. Each drew on personal research and experience to write outstanding chapters in their areas of expertise. We thank Professor Wagar for his chapter "Downsizing and Restructuring," Professor Groschl for building on the work of professors Xiayun Wang of the University of Manitoba and Sharon Leiba-O'Sullivan, of the University of Ottawa, for the chapter "Strategic International HR." We thank Professor Haines for reconceptualizing the Information Technology chapter.

The authors wish to thank the following reviewers who made helpful comments for this and past revisions: Dr. Naresh Agarwal, McMaster University; Julie Aitken Harris, University of Western Ontario; Brian Harrocks, Algonquin College; Suzanne Kavanagh, George Brown College; M.F. Mandl, British Columbia Institute of Technology; Gloria Miller, University of Regina; David Morrison, Durham College; Ash Patel, Seneca College; Sherry Price, Okanagan University College; Carol Ann Samhaber, Algonquin College; and Ted Mock, of the University of Toronto. The team at Nelson—Evelyn Veitch and Karina Hope—contributed enormously through their professionalism and dedication.

We are grateful to our students in the HR graduate program, especially those in the HRM Effectiveness class for their research projects on strategic issues, and the undergraduate course Human Resources Planning, for their thoughtful comments about the contents of the book. Above all, we wish to thank our colleagues across Canada who have supported the HRM Series by contributing their research, their experience, and their input to enable HRM students to read about the HRM landscape in this country.

Finally, we continue to owe much of our career success to the support of our families. I, Monica, thank Michael, my husband, and my sons, Marc and Brooker, who provide the affection and humour that vitalize a project like this. I, Kenneth, acknowledge the loving support of my family and the active interest and involvement of students in my Human Resources Planning courses for the evolution of this text.

Monica Belcourt
Kenneth McBey
*York University*

# PART ONE

# Introduction

CHAPTER 1   STRATEGIC MANAGEMENT

CHAPTER 2   ALIGNING HR WITH STRATEGY

CHAPTER 3   ENVIRONMENTAL INFLUENCES ON HRM

# Chapter 1

# Strategic Management

## Chapter Learning Objectives

After reading this chapter, you should be able to
- Discuss why managers need to examine the human resource implications of their organizational strategies.
- Understand the various terms used to define strategy and its processes.
- Describe organizational strategies, including restructuring, growth, and maintenance.
- Define business strategy and discuss how it differs from corporate strategy.
- Discuss the steps used in strategic planning.
- List the benefits of strategic planning.

Hudson's Bay Company (HBC) is Canada's oldest organization, established in 1670 as a fur trading company. It has survived for over 300 years by adapting its strategy to changing environmental conditions, both threats and opportunities. The following condensed history will demonstrate that it has experienced nearly all of the strategic options described in this chapter.

In 1821, HBC merged with its main rival, The North West Company. The declining demand for fur influenced the decision to change the fur trading posts to retail stores, and HBC launched its department store business in 1913. The company also had a diversification strategy and at various times throughout its history sold liquor, salmon, coffee, tobacco, and real estate. The economic downturn of the 1980s caused HBC to rethink its priorities and, like many other firms, return to its core business. Nonretail businesses were sold off and retail businesses were added. The pace of retail acquisition increased with takeovers of Zellers (1978), Simpsons (1978), Fields (1978), Robinson's (1979), Towers/Bonimart (1990), Woodwards (1994), and K-Mart Canada (1998) following in the tradition of Cairns (1921), Morgan's (1960), and Freiman's (1971). Even HBC's subsidiaries had to adopt new business-level strategies. For example, when Wal-Mart entered the Canadian retail market in 1994, competing head on with Zellers, the latter had to reposition itself from a low-cost business strategy to a differentiation strategy of selling exclusive and slightly upscale products such as Martha Stewart Everyday. Other retailers such as Eatons and Consumer Distributors were not so fortunate, and went bankrupt.

As of 2005, HBC has adopted a corporate growth strategy and a business-level strategy of differentiation coupled with low cost by opening new store concepts such as Home Outfitters and DealsOutlet.ca. But HBC faced a hostile takeover bid, and the new team plans to restructure HBC by laying off employees, closing stores, and selling valuable real estate.

The HBC example highlights the strategic decisions made by organizations in their attempts to survive and become profitable. Each strategic choice has implications for the management of human resources. We start in this chapter by establishing a common understanding of strategy, its importance, and its link to human resources management (HRM).

## A Need for Strategic HRM

Read any Canadian newspaper and you will see stories such as these:

- IBM and Apple established a joint venture to develop an object-oriented operating system to compete with Microsoft. The social-engineering challenge (to get two cultures working together) was greater than the technical-engineering challenge.

- The cities of Toronto, East York, Etobicoke, York, North York, and Scarborough merged into one megacity (called Toronto). Years later, the predicted savings of merging the cities have not been realized.
- Viasystems Canada, a manufacturer of electronic parts, adopted a low-cost strategy, which resulted in the loss of 800 jobs in Montreal, as the company transferred the work to China, with its lower labour costs.

The common theme in these stories is the adoption of a strategy that had serious HRM implications. In most cases, unless the HRM strategy is appropriately formulated and skillfully implemented, the success of the organizational strategy is at risk.

We have written this book to provide answers to those human resources (HR) professionals who have questions about the proper alignment of HR policies with organizational strategies. Managers who have implemented any kind of change within their organizations realize the importance of matching the HRM practices with organizational goals. There is a growing acknowledgment that the strategic management of people within organizations affects important organizational outcomes such as survival, profitability, customer satisfaction levels, and employee performance. Our goal is to help readers understand strategy and the HRM programs and policies that enable organizations to achieve that strategy. We discuss strategy at some length because HR professionals have been criticized for not understanding or using the language of business when discussing the value of HR programs. HR managers have to use strategy terms to show how their HR practices support organizational strategies. The next sections present a discussion of strategy and outline the types of strategies most frequently used by organizations.

## Strategy

**Strategy** is the formulation of organizational missions, goals, and objectives, as well as action plans for achievement that explicitly recognize the competition and the impact of outside environmental forces. Strategy is the plan for how the organization intends to achieve its goals. The means it will use, the courses of action it will take, and how it will generally operate and compete constitute the organization's strategy.[1]

We have presented one definition of strategy, but there are many others. A sampling is found in HR Planning Notebook 1.1.

Mintzberg has developed a useful framework for understanding strategy, incorporating many of the meanings found in the HR Planning Notebook 1.1. The five Ps of strategy he described are:

- *Plan:* an intended course of action a firm has selected to deal with a situation
- *Purpose:* a consistent stream of actions that sometimes are the result of a deliberate plan and sometimes the result of emergent actions based on reactions to environmental changes or shifting of assumptions

**strategy**
the formulation of organizational missions, goals, objectives, and action plans

### Descriptions of Strategy

Concepts of strategy can be confusing. Here is a guide to some common terms used throughout the text and in the organizations where you work:

*Strategy:* a declaration of intent

*Strategic intent:* a tangible corporate goal; a point of view about the competitive positions a company hopes to build over a decade

*Strategic planning:* the systematic determination of goals and the plans to achieve them

*Strategy formulation:* the entire process of conceptualizing the mission of an organization, identifying the strategy, and developing long-range performance goals

*Strategy implementation:* those activities that employees and managers of an organization undertake to enact the strategic plan and achieve the performance goals

*Objectives:* the end, the goals

*Plans:* the product of strategy, the means to the end

*Strategic plan:* a written statement that outlines the future goals of an organization, including long-term performance goals

*Policies:* broad guidelines to action, which establish the parameters or rules

---

- *Ploy:* a specific manoeuvre at the tactical level with a short time horizon
- *Position:* the location of an organization relative to its competitors and other environmental factors
- *Perspective:* the gestalt or personality of the organization[2]

In this text, we consider strategy as both a purpose and a plan. This perspective views strategy as a rational process in which ends are defined in measurable terms and resources are allocated to achieving those ends. In this context, organizations would set objectives such as "achieves 25% market share by 2009" or "be the best health care facility in the province." The organization then develops plans, which include HRM programs, to achieve those goals. Senior management typically sets the goals and has them approved by the board. These objectives are then negotiated and revised as they filter throughout the organization. The top management team determines these objectives through a process of environmental analysis (which is discussed in Chapter 3) and discussions.

Execution of strategy is as important as the careful crafting of strategy. Strategic planning requires thinking about the future. In a perfect world, some experts believe that the strategic planner would establish an objective for five to ten years and then formulate plans for achieving the goals. However, other experts do not perceive strategy in such a simplistic, linear fashion. They assert that the future is not that predictable. Planning for the long-term future (i.e., more than ten years) is difficult and would be more appropriately judged as a best guess. For example, the airline industry could not have predicted the catastrophic events of September 11, 2001, or the 2003 SARS crisis in Toronto and their impact on tourism and business travel. The world now awaits the impact of the avian flu on many sectors.

Because of this, many planners look at a relatively shorter period of time, a more predictable term of three to five years. Because of the uncertainty, their

FIGURE 1.1

## The Reality of the Strategic Process

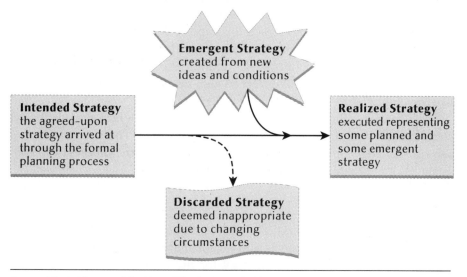

Source: Adapted from work by Henry Mintzberg. Used with permission.

plans are formulated to be somewhat flexible, so they can respond to changes in the environment. Thus, strategic planning must be viewed as a dynamic process, moving, shifting, and evolving as conditions warrant changes. The process of subtly redirecting strategy to accommodate these changes is called logical incrementalism.[3] Rather than calling for a straight path to the goal, this strategy calls for a series of actions to react to changes in competitor actions or new legislation. Another name for this reactive process is **emergent strategy**. This cumulative process can look like a dramatic revolutionary change to those on the outside, but to those on the inside, the strategy has been incrementally implemented.[4] Firms can wait passively for these changes to occur and then react, or they can anticipate these moves and adopt a proactive stance.

Writers on strategy sometimes distinguish between intended strategy and realized strategy. The **intended strategy** is the one that was formulated at the beginning of the period. The **realized strategy** is, of course, what actually happened.

Figure 1.1 illustrates these various concepts of strategy.

You may be asking why develop a strategy if the organization must continually change it to accommodate unforeseen changes? Think of strategy as a game plan or a flight plan. A pilot's flight plan appears relatively simple: fly from Toronto to Edmonton. However, before departure, the pilot is aware of the environment and the capacities (or competencies) of the plane. Based on these external and internal factors, the pilot develops a strategy for a safe flight. While on the voyage, however, environmental changes, such as strong winds or a blizzard, may require the pilot to modify the plan. Even internal factors, such as a passenger suffering a heart attack, may necessitate changes to the plan. But the plane and/or its passengers will somehow, at some time, arrive in Edmonton. This is what is meant by incremental adjustments to the

**emergent strategy**
the plan that changes incrementally due to environmental changes

**intended strategy**
the formulated plan

**realized strategy**
the implemented plan

Chapter 1: Strategic Management

strategy, adjustments that do not require changing the focus of the desired result. There is no strategy so finely crafted that adjustments aren't needed. The general rule is that, unless there is a crisis, it should not be necessary to make quantum leaps in strategies. Thus, these strategies should withstand the time test and be durable for several years.

A good strategy recognizes the complexity of these realities. To be effective, strategic management anticipates future problems, provides an alignment with external contingencies and internal competencies, recognizes multiple stakeholders, and is concerned with measurable performance[5]—just like the flight plan.

The fundamental premise of this book is that different organizational strategies demand different HR policies and practices. Therefore, before we can discuss HRM strategies, you need to understand the different types of strategies that organizations formulate and implement.

## Strategic Types

Strategies are not idiosyncratic—that is, unique to each organization that develops one. Many executives and senior managers put in an incredible number of hours forging the strategy for the firm, and they believe the strategy they developed, with much sweat and tears, is unique to their organizations. In one sense, pure, unique organizational strategies do exist, because organizations are extremely complex and no two are identical. In another sense, they do not, because it is possible to group strategies into categories or generic types. In the same way we can group our friends into personality categories of introvert and extrovert, we can group organizations by strategy. By their simplicity, these typologies, or classification schemes, aid our understanding. The more we add variables to approximate the reality of an organization, the more the typology becomes unwieldy.[6] Organizational theorists use classification schemes not only to help us understand how organizations work but also to enable us to test the concepts, leading us to better information about how to manage.

These identifiable, basic strategies can be classified into (1) corporate strategies and (2) business strategies.

### Corporate Strategies

**corporate strategy**

organizational-level decisions that focus on long-term survival

Company-wide strategies, sometimes referred to as **corporate strategies**, are focused on overall strategy for the company and its businesses or interests. Examples of corporate strategies include decisions to compete internationally or to merge with other companies. Strategies at this level are usually focused on long-term growth and survival goals and will include major decisions such as the decision to acquire another company.

Grouped within corporate strategies are three options: restructuring, growth, and maintenance.

### Restructuring Strategies

When an organization is not achieving its goals, whether these goals are business goals of profitability or social goals of helping rehabilitate prisoners, corporate strategy becomes one of trying to deal with the problem. Restructuring options include turnaround, divestiture, liquidation, and bankruptcies.

## Turnaround

A **turnaround strategy** is one in which managers try to restore money-losing businesses to healthy profitability or government agencies to viability. Turnaround methods include getting rid of unprofitable products, layoffs, making the organization more efficient, or attempting to reposition it with new products. See HR Planning Today 1.1 for a description of McDonald's turnaround efforts.

**turnaround strategy**
an attempt to increase the viability of an organization

## Divestiture

**Divestiture** refers to spinning off a business as a financially and managerially independent company or selling it outright.[7] Air Canada attempted to divest itself of its Aeroplan business and then put its maintenance division and its low-cost carrier Jazz on the market. Sometimes fit is the problem, not finances. One pharmaceutical company divested itself of a cosmetics business; the scientists in the pharmaceutical company had no respect for the cosmetic unit because they had been trained to apply their scientific knowledge to discovering miracle drugs, not making pretty faces.

**divestiture**
the sale or removal of a business

---

## HR Planning Today 1.1

### Turnaround Efforts at McDonald's

Burger chain McDonald's has, for several decades, been a success story. Each year saw increases in outlets, people served, profits, and shareholder value. In 2002, McDonald's had 30 000 outlets, served 46 million people a day in 118 countries, and generated $40 billion sales. But in 2003, restaurant sales were down nearly 5% and profits were down by 11%. McDonald's had made several attempts to revive its success. One effort focused on making its food healthier by offering salads. Related to this introduction was an alliance with Paul Newman, actor and philanthropist, to introduce Newman's Own salad dressings to McDonald's "light" menu. The company also introduced a food and nutrition website, which allowed customers to calculate the nutrients in their meal choices. But as one critic pointed out, this healthy eating effort was doomed because no one goes to fast-food restaurants for healthy food (except perhaps for the five-foot-ten, 272-pound New Yorker who sued the company because he was led to believe that the food was good for him).

Another effort attempted to tap regional food interests; grits were introduced in some southern U.S. restaurants, for example. A third attempt was to diversify; McDonald's bought interests in Donatos Pizzeria and Chipotle Mexican Grill. Finally, like other companies with declining market share, McDonald's restructured by eliminating several hundred administrative jobs and dropping a $300-million (U.S.) plan to renovate older restaurants. At the operational level, McDonald's has been introducing salads and fish in response to increasing consumer awareness of nutrition. The company's strategies have, over the long run, proven successful. In 1965, when the company went public, 100 shares could be bought for US$2250. As of the end of 2004, those 100 shares were worth US$2.4 million.

Sources: Adapted from D. Goold, "McDonald's Woes a Matter of Taste," *The Globe and Mail*, November 28, 2002, p. B9; "McDonald's Said Ready for More Restructuring," *The Globe and Mail*, March 24, 2003, p. B1; Company Fact sheet: www.mcdonalds.com, retrieved November 15, 2005.

## Liquidation

**liquidation**

the termination of a business and the sale of its assets

The least attractive alternative is **liquidation**, in which plants are closed, employees are released, and goods are auctioned off. There is little return to shareholders under this option. Nevertheless, an early liquidation may allow some resources (including human resources) to be salvaged, whereas a bankruptcy does not.

## Bankruptcy

**bankruptcy**

a formal procedure in which an appointed trustee in bankruptcy takes possession of a business's assets and disposes of them in an orderly fashion

**Bankruptcy** occurs when a company can no longer pay its creditors, and, usually, one of them calls a loan. The company ceases to exist, and its assets are divided among its creditors. Insurance company Confederation Life was a very public example of a company that went bankrupt, owing its creditors $740 million.

Restructuring strategies, like growth strategies, have profound effects on human resource issues, such as managed turnover, selective layoffs, transfers, increased demands on remaining employees, and renegotiated labour contracts. These issues are described in Chapter 10.

# Growth Strategies

Many organizations in the private sector target growth as their number-one strategy. By this they mean growth in revenues, sales, market share, customers, orders, and so on. To a large extent, the implications of a growth strategy for HR practices are profound. A firm in a growth stage is engaged in job creation, aggressive recruitment and selection, rapidly rising wages, and expanded orientation and training budgets, depending on how the organization chooses to grow.

Growth can be achieved in several ways: incrementally, internationally, or by mergers and acquisitions.

### Incremental Growth

Incremental growth can be attained by expanding the client base, increasing the products or services, changing the distribution networks, or using technology. Procter & Gamble uses all these methods:

- expanding the client base (by introducing skin-care lotion and hair conditioner for babies),
- increasing the products (by adding Pringles potato chips to a product mix of cleaning and health care products),
- changing the distribution networks (by adding drugstores to grocery stores), and
- using technology to manage just-in-time customer purchasing.

### International Growth

Seeking new customers or markets by expanding internationally is another growth option. Operating a business in a foreign country, particularly one that is not in North America or Europe, poses problems for the Western HR manager. The HR implications for an international strategy are described in Chapter 11.

## Mergers and Acquisitions

Quantum leaps in growth can be achieved through acquisitions, mergers, or joint ventures. An **acquisition** occurs when one company buys another, whereas a **merger** typically is seen as two organizations merging to achieve economies of scale. Acquisitions and mergers have an obvious impact on HR: they eliminate the duplication of functions, meld benefits and labour relations practices, and, most importantly, create a common culture. The complexity of merging two companies is outlined in Chapter 12. HR Planning Today 1.2 describes a difficult merger.

**acquisition**

the purchase of one company by another

**merger**

two organizations combine resources and become one

## Maintenance Strategies

For many reasons, some executives wish to maintain the status quo. They do not wish to see their companies grow. The executive team is content to keep market share, doing what it has always been doing (this is a neutral or even a do-nothing strategy). HRM practices remain constant, as they are assumed to be effective for current strategy. We have not included chapters on the maintenance strategy because the HRM issues would, by definition, be subsumed under another generic strategy.

Executives in other companies, recognizing that a current profitable situation will not last forever, choose to milk the investment. This *harvest* strategy can also be seen as a retrenchment strategy because no investment or efforts will be made to make the business grow; therefore, the goal will be restructuring.

Businesses can pursue several strategies over time or concurrently. Read in HR Planning Today 1.3 about the strategies implemented by Cara Operations Ltd.

## Business Strategies

Strategy, as discussed, seems to imply that only corporate-wide plans are made and these are used to manage and control the various units that exist within an

---

### HR Planning Today 1.2

#### Merger Misery

Minacs Worldwide Inc., a company that operates inbound customer contact centres (i.e., call centres), was a Canadian success story. More and more companies were using its services as they turned to outsourcing their call centres. Minacs had experienced growth rates of 50% over five years and, in 2002, employed 4500 people in 20 countries and generated sales of $250 million. The company expected to double sales and profits very quickly with the purchase of Phoenix Group, a U.S.–based call centre. But the purchase resulted in heavy losses.

Although the two cultures seemed similar, the integration proved very difficult and time consuming due to differences in accounting systems, pricing methods, and efficiency levels. The losses led to layoffs, the consolidation of offices, debt restructuring, and a severe drop in share value.

Sources: O. Bertin, "Minacs Worldwide Dials Back in After Disastrous US Purchase," *The Globe and Mail*, March 6, 2003, p. B17; www.minacs.com, retrieved June 7, 2005.

### Multiple Strategies

The mission statement of Cara Operations Ltd. declares that its aim is to be Canada's leading integrated restaurant company. Cara owns or controls such food outlets as Harvey's and Swiss Chalet. In 2005, Cara outlets served 200 million customers in 1200 restaurants; 18 million customers in the company's 98 airport-based food and concession outlets; and 30 million meals to airline passengers. Cara is an example of a company employing multiple corporate strategies—through acquisition, divestiture, and going international—to achieve increased sales and profitability.

- *Acquisitions:* Cara began an aggressive acquisition strategy in 1999 when it bought 61% of Kelsey's, a Canadian company that owned 74 restaurants

including Kelsey's, Montana's, and Outback. In 2002, Cara bought the Second Cup coffee chain and acquired a 74% stake in Milestones, a chain of upscale restaurants.

- *Divestiture:* In 2000, Cara sold its Beaver Food Catering business, and, in 2001, it sold its health care institutional food-services division.
- *International:* In 2003 Cara began to export its Second Cup concept to the Middle East, starting in Dubai.

Sources: Adapted from www.cara.com, retrieved November 7, 2005; and "Case Study: Cara Operations Ltd.," *National Post Business*, October 2002, pp. 47–50.

organization. But many large organizations operate several businesses under the same or different names, and each of these businesses might have its own strategy. For example, Alcan Aluminum Ltd. operates two "divisions" or businesses, one that focuses on primary metals and the other on fabrication. Each has a different business strategy, although the overall corporate strategy is growth.

**business strategy**

plans to build a competitive focus in one line of business

**Business strategy** focuses on one line of business (in a diversified company or public organization), while corporate strategy examines questions about which competitive strategy to choose. Corporate strategies focus on long-term survival and growth. Business-level strategy concerns itself with how to build a strong competitive position. Organizations try to become (or remain) competitive based on a core competence, which can be defined as a specialized expertise that rivals don't have and cannot easily match. As Thompson and Strickland note, business strategy is the action plan for managing a single line of business. Business strategy is concerned with competitive position.[8]

The next section introduces the concept of the business strategy and differentiates it from corporate strategies.

Corporate strategies are concerned with questions such as these: Should we be in business? What business should we be in? Business strategies are concerned with questions such as these: How should we compete? Should we compete by offering products at prices lower than those of the competition or by offering the best service? Business strategy is concerned with how to build a competitive position, and with the best way to compete in that line of business. Businesses compete for customers. Air Canada was struggling with its business strategy when it attempted to segment the market by creating a series of sub-brands—discount, high-end, and charter. The discount airline Zip was created to compete directly with WestJet. Businesses try to demonstrate to the customer that their product or service is better than their rivals' because they have lower prices or more innovative services.

Business strategy is all about means and ends. These strategies focus on the best ways to compete in a particular sector. Organizations try to become (or remain) competitive based on their core competence. Wal-Mart's core competence is inventory management, resulting in low prices. Kimberly-Clark is the best in the world at producing paper-based consumer products, choosing to specialize in category-killer brands (where the name of the product is synonymous with the name of the category—e.g., Kleenex).[9]

A business strategy is the action plan for managing a single line of business. It is possible for an organization to have one corporate strategy and many business strategies. For example, the overall corporate strategy for the Royal Bank might be growth, but the business strategy for its bank business might be to provide a unique kind of banking, and for its insurance business, to be a low-cost provider of insurance.

We will spend some time describing the process because HR professionals are expected to understand the language of business and to be able to discuss HR programs using the terminology of strategic planning. By learning the models and terms used by managers in business, HR managers will be able to propose or defend HR programs in ways that other managers will understand. The next chapter examines the functional strategies, which include compensation, training, and other HR functional areas that align with corporate and business strategies, including the development of operating strategies that facilitate execution of the corporate, business, and functional strategies. The pyramidal nature of the levels of strategy is shown in Figure 1.2.

## The Strategic Planning Process

A strategic plan describes the organization's future direction, performance targets, and approaches to achieve the targets.[10] There are many models or approaches to the development and implement of strategy. Here is a useful one:[11]

1. Establish the mission, vision, and values.
2. Develop objectives.
3. Analyze the external environment.
4. Determine the competitive position.
5. Identify the competitive advantage.
6. Determine the methods for accomplishing the objectives.
7. Evaluate the performance.

### 1. Establish the mission, vision, and values

A vision is a long-term, perhaps unrealizable goal. Take for example, the vision statement of the 3M company, "We will grow by helping our customers win—through the ingenuity and responsiveness of people who care"; or that

FIGURE 1.2

## A Company's Strategy-Making Hierarchy

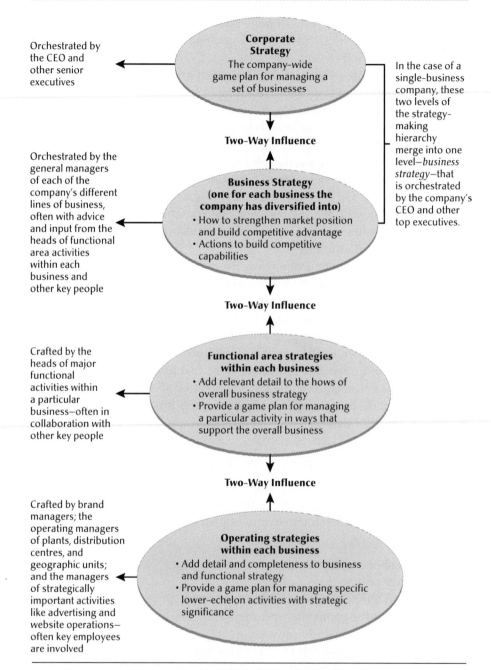

Orchestrated by the CEO and other senior executives

**Corporate Strategy**
The company-wide game plan for managing a set of businesses

In the case of a single-business company, these two levels of the strategy-making hierarchy merge into one level—*business strategy*—that is orchestrated by the company's CEO and other top executives.

**Two-Way Influence**

Orchestrated by the general managers of each of the company's different lines of business, often with advice and input from the heads of functional area activities within each business and other key people

**Business Strategy (one for each business the company has diversified into)**
• How to strengthen market position and build competitive advantage
• Actions to build competitive capabilities

**Two-Way Influence**

Crafted by the heads of major functional activities within a particular business—often in collaboration with other key people

**Functional area strategies within each business**
• Add relevant detail to the hows of overall business strategy
• Provide a game plan for managing a particular activity in ways that support the overall business

**Two-Way Influence**

Crafted by brand managers; the operating managers of plants, distribution centres, and geographic units; and the managers of strategically important activities like advertising and website operations—often key employees are involved

**Operating strategies within each business**
• Add detail and completeness to business and functional strategy
• Provide a game plan for managing specific lower-echelon activities with strategic significance

Source: Thompson, Strickland, and Gamble, *Crafting and Executing Strategy*, 14th ed. © 2005. Reprinted with the permission of The McGraw-Hill Companies.

## HR Planning Today 1.4

### The Person on the Bus Test of Mission Statements

A test of a good mission statement is its ability to pass the "person on a bus test." In other words, could an average person correctly identify the company after reading a mission statement? Can you guess which companies are attached to these mission statements?

1. Our mission is to be the best provider of entertainment options that meet consumer needs. We will accomplish this by understanding the entertainment interests of the consumer better than anyone else and by delivering unique products with high levels of customer service.

2. A computer in every home

3. We fulfill dreams through the experience of motor cycling—by providing to motor cyclists and the general public an expanding line of motor cycles, branded products and services in selected market segments.

Answers on p. 26.

of Merck, "preserving and improving human life." A **vision** is a clear and compelling goal that serves to unite an organization's efforts. It must challenge and stretch the organization.

A **mission** statement articulates a view of a realistic, credible, and attractive future for the organization. It has also been defined as the purpose for which, or reason why, an organization exists.[12] Some have said that the distinction between a vision statement and a mission statement is that the vision statement answers the question "Where are we going," whereas the mission statement answers the questions: Who are we? What do we do? Why are we here?"[13]

MacMillan Bloedel changed the company's position by articulating this mission statement "the most respected and environmentally responsible forest company in Canada, and an example for others internationally. The public has granted us a license to operate, and they have a right to expect that we will be responsible guardians of their renewable resource." Many believe that conveying a strong sense of mission is the most important role for the CEO. See HR Planning Today 1.4 for some mission statements.

**Values** are the basic beliefs that govern individual and group behavior in an organization. While vision and mission answer the questions about what must be accomplished, values answer the question: How must we behave? The mission, vision, and value statements of Cara, a leading food service and restaurant business can be found in HR Planning Today 1.5.

Sometimes values reflect the founders' ethics; sometimes they are just words on the poster on the wall. In order to develop employee buy-in to values, have them participate in the elaboration of the organization values as described in HR Planning Notebook 1.2. Then these values should be part of every orientation workshop and training course, and be modelled by all employees, especially senior management.

**vision**

a clear and compelling goal that serves to unite an organization's efforts

**mission**

an articulation of a view of a realistic, credible, and attractive future for the organization

**values**

the basic beliefs that govern individual and group behaviour in an organization

## 2. Develop objectives

At this stage, the management team develops objectives to achieve the strategy. Objectives are an expression, in measurable terms, of what an organization intends to achieve.[14] Goals can be classified as hard or soft. Hard goals

### Cara's Mission, Vision, and Value Statements

#### Vision

To be Canada's leading integrated restaurant company.

#### Mission

Enhancing stakeholder value and building leading businesses, by maximizing our resources and living our values and principles.

#### Values

Cara's strength is based on our core values or fundamental beliefs of: the importance of our people, self-responsibility, integrity, a passion for winning and quality.

**People**. Cara's success begins with and endures because of our teammates. We seek out good people, help them grow and improve their skills, appreciate their individuality and contributions, and celebrate their achievements.

**Self-responsibility**. Teammates take the initiative to do what needs to be done. We take ownership of our work and results, put forth our best effort, and challenge what needs to be challenged. We hold ourselves accountable, and blame no one.

**Integrity**. We are committed to honesty and doing the right thing. We say what we will do, do what we say, and acknowledge when we are wrong or have made a mistake.

**Passion for Winning**. Winning is much more than luck. It is dedication, desire, enthusiasm for competition, risk and hard work. We set our sights on winning, and are passionate about being first in all we do. Winners attract winners.

**Quality**. We set high standards, and expect a level of achievement that says "best-in-class," so that it becomes a state of mind and a way of life. We always give our personal best, and continually raise the bar on excellence.

Source: www.cara.com. Reprinted with permission.

### Creating Organizational Values

1. Invite all employees to offer ideas about the current and the desired values for the organization.
2. Record these without judgments, criticisms, or comments.
3. Have the group identify common themes.
4. Discuss and debate these themes, until there is consensus on a short list of core values.
5. Have subgroups take one value, and develop a definition of the value and the employee behaviours related to that value.
6. Have groups present their definitions and behaviours, which may be adopted or revised.
7. Appoint one person from each team to incorporate the revisions into a value statement, which is then combined with all the value statements. These then become the company values.

always include numbers, usually relative to performance last year, or to competition. Examples of hard goals include rank by sales in industry, return on sales, and growth in earnings per share. Soft goals usually define the targets for the social conduct of the business, and may not always be quantifiable.

Soft goals may include being ethical, environmentally responsible, and providing a working environment free of discrimination with opportunities for professional development.

## 3. Analyze the external environment

Managers must be aware of threats and opportunities in the external environment. By scanning and monitoring technology, laws and regulations, the economy, sociocultural factors, and changing demographics, managers can make reactive and proactive changes to the strategic plan. SWOT analysis is a good tool for analyzing a company's resource capabilities and deficiencies, its market opportunities, and the external threats to its future.[15] SWOT is an acronym for Strengths, Weaknesses, Opportunities, and Threats. A strength is something that a company does well or an attribute that makes it more competitive. A weakness is something that an organization does poorly or a condition, such as location, that puts it at a disadvantage relative to competitors.[16] Opportunities and threats are environmental conditions external to the firm that may be beneficial or harmful. For example, a high employment rate may mean that consumers are more willing to borrow money to purchase homes, which results in potentially higher home sales, and also increased sales of furniture, appliances, and home renovation supplies. Sometimes an external indicator, such as a rising concern with personal health, may be beneficial for one sector (health clubs) and harmful to others (tobacco companies).[17]

## 4. Determine the competitive position

A company cannot usually compete by being ready to offer any product or service at various prices through multiple channels of distribution. The senior managers must determine who are the customers, where they are located, and what products or services characteristics these customers value. Thus the organization must create a **value proposition**, which is a statement of the fundamental benefits that it has chosen to offer in the market place. The value proposition of TD Bank's Green Line Investor services was very simple—lower-cost transactions than through traditional brokerage channels.

**value proposition**
a statement of the fundamental benefits of the products or services being offered in the market place

Michael Porter made a major contribution to the field of strategic management by grouping the many ways in which organizations can compete into five generic competitive strategies:[18]

1. *Low-cost provider strategy:* The goal here is to provide a product or service at a price lower than that of competitors while appealing to a broad range of customers. Fast-food businesses use this strategy almost exclusively. A range of customers from toddlers to seniors consumes the cheap hamburger, a good, but basic product with few frills. A company competing on this basis searches continually for ways in which to reduce costs.

2. *Broad differentiation strategy:* An organization employing this strategy seeks to differentiate its products from competitors' products in ways that will appeal to a broad range of buyers. The company employing this strategy searches for features that will make its product or service

Chapter 1: Strategic Management

different from that of competitors and that will encourage customers to pay a premium for it. Thus, Burger King will introduce the Whopper with "frills," for which people will pay an extra dollar.

3. *Best-cost provider strategy:* The goal here is to give customers more value for the money by emphasizing a low-cost product or service and an upscale differentiation. The product has excellent features, including several upscale features that are offered at low cost. East Side Mario's offers hamburgers but presents them on a plate, with extras such as potato salad, served by a waiter in an attractive setting featuring focused lights and art on the walls.

4. *Focused or market niche strategy based on lower cost*: The goal here is to offer a low-cost product to a select group of customers. Red Lobster uses this approach, selling fish and seafood at reasonable prices to a narrow market segment.

5. *Focused or market niche strategy based on differentiation*: Here, the organization tries to offer a niche product or service customized to the tastes and requirements of a very narrow market segment. For example, Hy's is a very expensive restaurant that specializes in steaks and a dark wood, clubby atmosphere, thus appealing to the older, usually male, business customer.

Under Porter's schema, business strategy concerns itself with the product and market scope. What particular goods and services are to be provided? What distinguishing features or attractive attributes will characterize these products and services? Typical product characteristics include cost, quality, optional features, durability, and reliability. Market dimensions refer to the characteristics of the target market—size, diversity, buying patterns, and geographic regions. The model has been criticized for its overlapping categories. Most textbooks on strategy suggest that there are really only three competitive positions: cost, differentiation, and focus.

## 5. Identify the competitive advantage

**competitive advantage**

the characteristics of a firm that enable it to earn higher rates of profits than its competitors

What does the organization have that gives it a competitive advantage? **Competitive advantage** can be defined as those characteristics of a firm that enable it to earn higher rates of profits than its competitors.[19] These normally derive from the resources of the organization, which can be grouped in three ways:

- *Tangible assets*—These are easiest to value and the only ones to appear on a company's balance sheet; they include land, raw materials, location, and cash.
- *Intangible assets*—These assets are not consumed, and may even grow in value; they include company reputation, brands, and patents.
- *Capabilities*—These are a complex combination of people and processes that represent the firm's capacity to deploy resources that have been purposely integrated to achieve a desired end state.[20] Examples include managerial abilities, employees with specialized

skills, ability to innovate, and organizational cultures. These **capabilities**—the collective skills, abilities, and expertise of an organization—are the outcome of investments in staffing, training, and other HR areas. They are stable over time, and are not easy to measure or benchmark; therefore, competitors cannot copy them.[21]

For these resources to provide a competitive advantage, they must possess the characteristics of being valuable, rare, costly to imitate, not easy to substitute, and have the ability to create profits.[22] The culture at Southwest Airlines meets all these characteristics, as can be seen in HR Planning Today 1.6.

**capabilities**

a complex combination of people and processes that represent the firm's capacity to deploy resources that have been purposefully integrated to achieve a desired result

---

## HR Planning Today 1.6

### Culture as a Competitive Advantage

Southwest Airline's strategy is that of low cost/low price/no frills flights, a strategy that has resulted in profits every year since 1974. The organization's culture is its competitive advantage, and possesses all the key characteristics.

#### Attribute: Valuable

Does the Southwest Airlines culture offer customers something that they value? Yes, the culture results in employees who are productive, flexible, motivated and willing to accept a low base pay and work long hours. This not only keeps costs down but also improves utilization and on-time delivery performance.

#### Attribute: Rare

Is Southwest Airlines the only one with this type of culture? If not, is the level of its culture higher than that of competitors? Yes. Each airline has its own culture but only the Southwest culture has inspired employees to care so much about their company that they accept very low base salaries, yet are highly productive and flexible; work almost twice as long and are more motivated than other airline's employees; and would rather support the company than the union. The "family" at Southwest is just not found at other airlines.

#### Attribute: Imitability

Is it easy for other firms to acquire this culture? No. Duplicating this culture is likely to be difficult. Although others may think that they know what makes Southwest employees so motivated, productive, flexible, and dedicated, that may not be the case. Also, building the Southwest culture may have involved a series of events that are impossible for another firm to re-create.

#### Attribute: Substitutability

Can another capability offer customers the same value that the "Southwest culture" does? No. In an industry where utilization is critical, it is difficult for another capability to give airlines the value created by a productive, flexible, highly motivated workforce.

#### Attribute: Able to Appropriate Money

Does Southwest make money from its unique culture? Yes. Southwest's good position in relations to suppliers and customers enables it to appropriate the value from its extraordinary culture. Barring a major change that diminishes the culture or reverses the relationship, Southwest should continue to make money.

Source: Allan Afuah, *Business Models: A Strategic Management Approach* © 2004, Table 10.4, p. 207. Reproduced with the permission of The McGraw-Hill Companies.

---

NEL                    Chapter 1: Strategic Management                    **19**

**core competencies**

resources and capabilities that serve as a firm's competitive advantage

Core competencies are resources and capabilities that serve as a firm's competitive advantage. Core competencies distinguish a company competitively and reflect its personality.[23] In other words, a core competence is a competitively important activity that a company performs better than other internal activities.[24] The core competency of Southwest Airlines is culture and that of Sony is miniaturization. Core competencies can be leveraged. For example, when Amazon.com developed the competency to sell books through the Internet, it leveraged this competency to deliver other consumer products such as CDs.

## 6. Determine the methods for accomplishing the objectives

If the goal is growth, what are the techniques for achieving this goal? Should a company acquire another company or expand its distribution channels to other regions? If the goal is innovation, how can HR recruit, select, train, and create a supportive culture to accomplish this goal? The role of the HR function in enabling the execution of strategy is discussed in Chapter 2.

## 7. Evaluate the performance

Developing a strategy is easy; making it happen is not. The ability to execute strategy is becoming a more important criterion for assessing not only managers but also the whole organization. The successful implementation of a strategy is judged by the ability to meet financial targets such as profits, and the ability to meet benchmarked ratios of efficiency and effectiveness such as R&D expenses to sales, or sales to assets. As you will see in Chapter 14, companies are using the balanced scorecard approach to evaluate other important indicators of success, such as customer satisfaction or employee engagement. These measures are becoming increasingly valuable for their ability to predict financial and operational performance.

## Benefits of Strategy Formulation

Working through the strategic planning process has these benefits:

- *Clarity*: to help focus and guide decision making about resource allocations
- *Coordination*: everyone is then working toward the same goals
- *Efficiency*: daily decision making is guided toward the question "does it fit our strategy?"
- *Incentives*: employees understand the behaviours and performance that will be rewarded
- *Change*: if a major change is under consideration, then understanding the current strategy is essential
- *Career development*: a clear outline of an organization's strategy can help you decide if you want to work for the company, if there is a skills fit, and what training and development you will need in order to facilitate the achievement of the strategy.

FIGURE 1.3

## The Strategic HR Planning Model

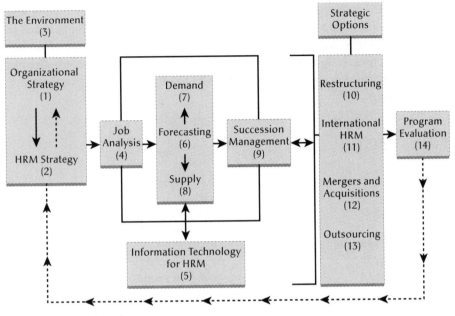

(Chapters in parentheses)

An understanding of the strategic planning process is the essential first step to creating an HR strategy that makes sense for the organization.

Our model of strategic HR planning is presented in Figure 1.3. The numbers in parentheses refer to the chapters in which each of the topics is discussed.

Our approach is different from classic approaches to HR planning but builds on the tools. Strategic HR planning complements the traditional approach to HR planning (forecasting supply and demand) but adds more strategic choices. Thus, at the most senior levels of the corporation, HR professionals move from an administrative role to the role of strategic partner. They understand strategies and business needs and create the kind of HR competencies that build competitive advantage. Our approach not only serves as a strategic planning model, but also as the structure for this text.

## Summary

It is important that HR professionals appreciate the role of strategic planning in their organizations and understand the language and terminology of strategic planning. A strategy is a planned process whereby organizations can map out a set of objectives and methods of meeting those objectives. A strategy may be intended—one that is formulated at the beginning of the process—or realized—what actually happens. The strategy may also be emergent—that is, it is reactive, changing as necessary to deal with environmental changes. Corporate or company-wide strategies are concerned with the long-term view of the organization. Business strategies focus on one line of business, building a strong competitive position. A seven-step approach to strategic planning was introduced, followed by a list of benefits of undertaking this process. By understanding strategy language and models, the HR professional can work with other executives to implement HR practices that enable strategy.

# Key Terms

acquisition 11
bankruptcy 10
business strategy 12
capabilities 19
competitive advantage 18
core competency 20
corporate strategy 8
divestiture 9
emergent strategy 7
intended strategy 7

liquidation 10
merger 11
mission 15
realized strategy 7
strategy 5
turnaround strategy 9
value proposition 17
values 15
vision 15

# Web Links

Excellent links for references on strategic planning:

**www.strategyclub.com** (p. 5)

A publication that provides articles, interviews, and case studies focused on strategic management and general business issues:

**www.strategy-business.com** (p. 7)

Articles from the Strategic Management Society:

**www.planware.org/strategy.htm#1** (p. 13)

Introduces the dynamics of university-based strategic planning as well as the history of strategic planning:

**www.des.calstate.edu/processmodel.html** (p. 20)

# RPC Icons

**RPC 1.1 Contributes to the development of the organization's vision, goals, and strategies with a focus on human capital**

**RPC 1.2 Plans for and manages the HR aspects of organizational change, e.g., mergers, acquisitions, divestitures, and downsizing, in the context of organizational strategies and legislated requirements**

# Discussion Questions

1. Using a real company as an example, describe the differences between corporate strategy and business strategy.
2. Identify companies currently operating under these corporate strategies: divestiture—turnaround, divestiture, liquidation, and bankruptcy; growth—incremental, international, and mergers and acquisitions.
3. The focus in this chapter (and in strategy literature) is on private companies. Check the websites of government departments, and identify at least ten strategies (often called plans or mission statements). Can you identify any that correspond to some of the models of business strategies? Can you create a model or typology for public-sector organizations? To start, consult J. Tomkins, "Strategic Human Resources Management in Government: Unresolved Issues," *Public Personnel Management*, vol. 31, no. 1 (2002), pp. 95–110.

# Using the Internet

1. Go to the website of HBC (or a company of your choice). Using the site and any relevant media articles, prepare a list of the tangible and intangible assets of the organization.

# Exercises

1. Identify two companies working in the same sector (hotels, restaurants, and post-secondary institutions are good choices). Compare and contrast the practices of a company using a low-cost provider strategy with one using a differentiation strategy. For example, contrast the MBA schools at the University of Athabasca or Concordia University with those of Queen's University or the Ivey School of Business at the University of Western Ontario.
2. In describing the Porter model, examples from restaurants were used to illustrate the five types. Pick another sector and identify five companies that best exemplify each of the five business strategies.
3. Conduct a SWOT analysis for a company known to you or others in your group. As a group, assess the company against the strengths,

weaknesses, threats, and opportunities contained in the SWOT matrix below:

## SWOT Analysis

### Potential Resource Strengths and Competitive Capabilities

| | |
|---|---|
| • A powerful strategy | • Superior intellectual capital relative to key rivals |
| • Core competencies in _____ | • Cost advantages over rivals |
| • A distinctive competence in _____ | • Strong advertising and promotion |
| • A product that is strongly differentiated from those of rivals | • Product innovation capabilities |
| • Competencies and capabilities that are well matched to industry key success factors | • Proven capabilities in improving production processes |
| • A strong financial condition; ample financial resources to grow the business | • Good supply chain management capabilities |
| • Strong brand-name image/company reputation | • Good customer service capabilities |
| • An attractive customer base | • Better product quality relative to rivals |
| • Economy of scale and/or learning and experience curve advantages over rivals | • Wide geographic coverage and/or strong global distribution capacity |
| • Proprietary technology/superior technological skills/important patents | • Alliances/joint ventures with other firms that provide access to valuable technology, competencies, and/or attractive geographic markets |

### Potential Market Opportunities

| | |
|---|---|
| • Openings to win market share from rivals | • Expanding the company's product line to meet a broader range of customer needs |
| • Sharply rising buyer demand for the industry's product | • Utilizing existing company skills or technological know-how to enter new product lines or new businesses |
| • Serving additional customer groups or market segments | • Online sales |
| • Expanding into new geographic markets | • Integrating forward or backward |

| | |
|---|---|
| • Falling trade barriers in attractive foreign markets | • Entering into alliances or joint ventures that can expand the firm's market coverage or boost its competitive capacity |
| • Acquiring rival firms or companies with attractive technological expertise or capabilities | • Openings to exploit emerging new technologies |

POTENTIAL RESOURCE WEAKNESSES AND COMPETITIVE DEFICIENCIES

| | |
|---|---|
| • No clear strategic direction | • Behind on product quality, R&D, and/or technological know-how |
| • Resources that are not well matched to industry key success factors | • In the wrong strategic group |
| • No well-developed or proven core competencies | • Losing market share because _____ |
| • A weak balance sheet; too much debt | • Lack of management depth |
| • Higher overall unit costs relative to key competitors | • Inferior intellectual capital relative to leading rivals |
| • Weak or unproven product innovation capabilities | • Subpar profitability because _____ |
| • A product/service with ho-hum attributes or features inferior to those of rivals | • Plagued with internal operating problems or obsolete facilities |
| • Too narrow a product line relative to rivals | • Behind rivals in e-commerce capabilities |
| • Weak brand image or reputation | • Short on financial resources to grow the business and pursue promising initiatives |
| • Weaker dealer network than key rivals and/or lack of adequate global distribution capability | • Too much underutilized plant capacity |

POTENTIAL EXTERNAL THREATS TO A COMPANY'S WELL-BEING

| | |
|---|---|
| • Increasing intensity of competition among industry rivals may squeeze profit margins | • Likely entry to potent new competitors |
| • Slowdowns in market growth | • Loss of sales to substitute products |

| | |
|---|---|
| • Growing bargaining power of customers or supplies | • Restrictive trade policies on the part of foreign governments |
| • A shift in buyer needs and tastes away from the industry's product | • Costly new regulatory requirements |
| • Vulnerability to industry driving forces | |

Source: Thompson, Strickland, and Gamble, *Crafting and Executing Strategy*, 14th ed. © 2005. Reprinted with the permission of The McGraw-Hill Companies.

# Case: Aldo Shoes Limited

The Canadian shoe market is worth $1.8 billion. The dominant shoe retailers are Wal-Mart (9.1% of market share), Payless (8.8%), Aldo (8.8%), Sears (8.0%), and the Bay (6.9%). Aldo has a variety of brands catering to the niche markets of young-spirited consumers (Aldo), sophisticated men and women (Pegabo), private labels (Simard, Calderone), comfort shoes (Feet First), and family-focused large selection (Globo). Aldo is considered a dominant player because when all its brands are included, its market share is an impressive 25%. It has achieved high growth rates since its founding in Montreal in 1972; in 2002 it had revenues of $650 million with over 600 stores. The company's growth strategies included plans to expand internationally (United States, England, and the Middle East) with future plans for Scandinavia, Australia, Singapore, and Western Europe. To date, it has built successful operations in the United States and the United Kingdom. Its business strategy was to achieve growth through the creation of private labels.

Adapted from www.aldoshoes.com; J. McCann, "Best Foot Forward," *National Post Business*, October 2002, pp. 53–61.

## Question

Aldo has grown rapidly through multibranding (differentiation) and international sales. What are the advantages and disadvantages of achieving more growth through mergers and acquisitions? Using the three business strategy models, attempt to label Aldo's business strategy.

Answers to HR Planning Today 1.4: a) Blockbuster, b) Apple, and c) Harley-Davidson

# Endnotes

1. Anthony, W.P., P.L. Perrewe, and K.M. Kacmar. 1993. *Strategic Human Resources Management*. Fort Worth, TX: Harcourt Brace Jovanovich.
2. Mintzberg, H. 1988. *In the Strategy Process*. Englewood Cliffs, NJ: Prentice Hall.
3. Quinn, J.B. 1980. *Strategies for Change: Logical Incrementalism*. Homewood, IL: Richard D. Irwin.
4. Collins, J. 2001. *Good to Great*. New York: Harper Business.

5. Lengnick-Hall, C., and M. Lengnick-Hall. 1990. *Interactive Human Resource Management and Strategic Planning*. New York: Quorum Books.
6. Duane, M.J. 1996. *Customized Human Resource Planning*. Westport, CT: Quorum Books.
7. Thompson, A.A., and A.J. Strickland III. 1995. *Crafting and Implementing Strategy*, 6th ed. Chicago: Irwin.
8. Thompson and Strickland, 1995.
9. Collins, 2001.
10. Thompson, A.A. Jr., A.J. Strickland III, and J. Gamble. 2005. *Crafting and Executing Strategy*, 14th ed. New York: McGraw-Hill.
11. Woodcock, C.P., and P.W. Beamish. 2003. *Concepts in Strategic Management*, 6th ed. Toronto: McGraw-Hill Ryerson.
12. Certo, S.C., and J.P. Peter. 1993. *Strategic Management: A Focus on Process*, 2nd ed. Boston: Irwin.
13. Thompson et al., 2005.
14. Crossan, M.M., J.N. Fry, and J.P. Killing. 2002. *Strategic Analysis and Action*, 5th ed. Toronto: Prentice Hall.
15. Thompson et al., 2005.
16. Thompson et al., 2005.
17. Dess, G.G., and G.T. Lumpkin. 2003, *Strategic Management: Creating Competitive Advantages*. Boston: McGraw-Hill.
18. Porter, M.E. 1985. *Competitive Advantage*. New York: Free Press.
19. Afuah, A. 2004. *Business Models: A Strategic Management Approach*. Boston: McGraw-Hill Irwin.
20. Hitt, M.A., R.D. Ireland, R.E. Hoskisson, W.G. Rowe, and J.P. Sheppard. 2002. *Strategic Management, Competitiveness and Globalization Concepts*. Toronto: Nelson Thompson Learning.
21. Ulrich, D., and N. Smallwood. 2004. "Capitalizing on Capabilities," *Harvard Business Review*, June, 119–127.
22. Barney, J.B. 1995. "Looking Inside for Competitive Advantage," *Academy of Management Executive*, 9, 49–61; Collis, J. and C.A. Montgomery. 1995. "Competing on Resources: Strategies for the 1990's," *Harvard Business Review* July–August, 118–218.
23. Hoskisson, R.E., M.A. Hitt, and R.D. Ireland. 2004. *Competing for Advantage*. Mason, OH: Thompson South-Western.
24. Thompson et al., 2005.

# Chapter 2

# Aligning HR with Strategy

## Chapter Learning Objectives

After reading this chapter, you should be able to

- Understand the importance of strategic HR planning.
- Identify the risks associated with not planning.
- Discuss approaches to linking strategy and HR, including the barriers to becoming a strategic partner.
- List the characteristics of an effective HR strategy.
- Delineate the steps in the strategic HR planning model.

## PEPSI VERSUS COKE IN AN HR CHALLENGE

Both the Coca-Cola Company and PepsiCo manage their employees in unique ways that match their strategies. Coke hires liberal arts graduates (and rarely MBAs) with no corporate experience and trains them extensively. Employees are committed to the company because they can count on lifetime employment, seniority-based salary increases, and promotion from within. In this family culture, decision making is centralized. The company's HRM practices produce career managers who have been thoroughly socialized into understanding and valuing the company trademark, which is the most recognized in the world.

Pepsi is not Coke. Pepsi succeeds by targeting market niches where Coke is not dominant and finding new markets through diversification. The HRM practices produce employees who are innovative. Pepsi's people-management process consists of hiring experienced employees, many with advanced degrees, and fast-tracking those employees who demonstrate early successes. In this individualistic culture, there is almost no job security and no guaranteed promotion from within. What Pepsi achieves is a continuous flow of new ideas (from experienced and intelligent employees) and the ability to change quickly (with hiring and firing policies).[1]

Those two examples neatly illustrate the concept of aligning HR practices, policies, and philosophies with organizational strategy to create strategic HR.

## Strategic HRM

Human resources management (HRM) can be viewed as an umbrella term that encompasses the following:

- Specific HR *practices*, such as recruitment, selection, and appraisal
- Formal HR *policies* that direct and partially constrain the development of specific practices
- Overarching HR *philosophies*, which specify the values that inform an organization's policies and practices

**strategic HRM**

interrelated practices, policies, and philosophies that facilitate the attainment of organizational strategy

**Strategic HRM** is a set of distinct but interrelated practices, policies, and philosophies whose goal is to enable the achievement of the organizational strategy. Ideally, these practices, policies, and philosophies form a system that attracts, develops, motivates, and trains employees who ensure the effective functioning and survival of the organization and its members.[2] There is an emerging view that the discipline of HRM should be split into two areas, much like accounting and finance or sales and marketing.[3] One area would deal with transactional activities, such as payroll, which are routine but very important, just like accounting. These operational activities are generally routine and must be done for the organization to operate on a daily basis. The second area would function like a decision science, concerned with the effective utilization of human capital, much like finance. In this model, strategic HRM would be concerned with decisions about HR practices, the composition and behaviours of employees, and the effectiveness of these decisions given various business strategies.[4] These strategic activities are comprehensive, planned, and are considered high long-term value added in terms of their contribution to organizational success.[5]

While managers recognize implicitly that marketing strategy must support the business strategy, there is not the same sense among managers that HR programs can be designed to support the organizational strategy. And yet human capital issues are at the top of the CEO agenda, with more than half of the top priorities (attraction, retention, innovation) needing HR input.[6] As Ulrich states,

> The truth is that HR has never been more necessary. The competitive forces that managers face today and will continue to confront in the future demand organizational excellence. The efforts to achieve such excellence—through a focus on learning, quality, teamwork and re-engineering—are driven by the way organizations treat their people. These are fundamental HR issues. To state it plainly: Achieving organizational excellence must be the work of HR.[7]

## Theories of the Strategic Management of Human Resources

Theory development is necessary for any field because theories are the basis on which new ideas are tested and new knowledge is created. HR is seen as atheoretical and problem driven. Practitioners themselves do not seem to value theory.[8] But the field of HR is young, and there are indeed emerging perspectives that can be seen as providing the theoretical underpinnings: the resource-based view, the behavioural perspective, and human capital theory.

### Resource-based View

Michael Porter has argued strongly that an organization's employees can provide a firm with a competitive advantage. Employees who provide superior performance because of their skills or flexibility will enable a company to beat its competitors through superior service or the development of unique products. This is a resource-based view of the organization.

The resource-based view was introduced in Chapter 1, where the culture of Southwest Airlines was described as a resource that provided a competitive advantage. Here is a simpler example. If IBM introduces a new software package in January, Microsoft can probably imitate or duplicate this package by February of the same year. However, if IBM technical support people are trained and motivated to provide "knock-your-socks-off service," Microsoft will have a difficult time imitating this service within a month. Indeed, Porter estimates that it takes approximately seven years to duplicate a competitive edge in human resources. The less a resource can be imitated, the more durable the source of competitive advantage. HRM can offer this

 2.1

kind of durable, competitive advantage. The competition can't just buy these human resources because their effectiveness is embedded in the systems and culture that allow them to work productively.[9] The HRM process that creates this human capital can't be bought or imitated. This view has led to a change in strategic thinking from an outside-in approach with its focus on external, industry-based competitive issues, to an inside-out view, in which internal resources constitute the basis for understanding organizational success. Even here, a firm's human resources are more valuable than technological and physical resources, because they are less visible, and more complex.[10]

### The Behavioural Perspective

Different strategies require different behaviours from employees, which in turn are influenced by different HR practices. For each organization, an effective HR system accurately identifies the behaviours needed to implement a strategy, provides the opportunity for employees to exhibit those behaviours, ensures that they have the knowledge and skills to engage in those behaviours, and motivates them to do so.[11] Providing expert opinion on human behaviour may be where the HR profession adds the most unique value. While most managers understand that they have little knowledge of finance and law, and will leave these areas to the experts, few feel the same way about their knowledge of people. HR's role is to tactfully challenge and refocus baseless ideas of human behaviour.[12] Take the quiz in HR Planning Notebook 2.1 to assess your understanding of the field of HR.

## HR Planning Notebook 2.1

### How Well Do You Speak HR?

1. Which of the following statements is false with respect to research on accountability:
   a) Accountability has no effect when people do not have requisite knowledge or decision rules from which to work.
   b) People often will select options or make decisions that are easiest to defend rather than those that are perceived as the best.
   c) Accountability invariably leads to a search for the most relevant facts and details of a situation.
   d) Accountability has the most pronounced effect on results when greater effort, attention, and reflection on judgment processes can make a difference.

2. In operant conditioning, a reinforcer is:
   a) An indication that something good is about to happen
   b) A consequence that increases the likelihood that a behaviour will be repeated

   c) An encouragement that precedes and motivates behaviours
   d) One behaviour that must be performed before another behaviour can be enacted

3. In management theory, Theory X essentially maintains that people are motivated by:
   a) Internal satisfactions and enjoyment
   b) Charismatic leaders
   c) Extrinsic factors such as money
   d) The need to achieve

4. People have similar reactions to stressful situations called a general adaptation syndrome. Which of the following is not a stress response:
   a) Resistance
   b) Avoidance
   c) Exhaustion
   d) Alarm reaction

5. The idea that special treatment of employees (regardless of the specific nature of that treatment) can improve performance is known as:
   a) The P.T. Barnum effect
   b) The Kohler effect
   c) The Hawthorne effect
   d) The Phi phenomenon

6. Group decisions often move in directions that are more extreme than any one individual member of the group would make on her own. This is evidence of:
   a) Group polarization
   b) Deindividuation
   c) Groupthink
   d) Group identity bias

7. A member of a group who exerts less physical or mental effort is exhibiting which social phenomenon:
   a) Developmental impairment
   b) Social loafing
   c) Group fatigue syndrome
   d) Deindividuation

8. According to equity theory, a person who feels under-rewarded and unable to be compensated further most likely will:
   a) Decrease his work effort
   b) Rationalize the lower reward as necessary
   c) Belittle others in the organization
   d) Overestimate the rewards that others are receiving

9. If there is heightened anxiety following layoffs within the surviving workforce, productivity will likely:
   a) Increase
   b) Decrease
   c) Stay about the same
   d) Increase, then decrease

10. Participatory goal setting has been found to:
    a) Enhance employee ownership
    b) Have a strong association with employee performance
    c) Increase the perceived importance of goals
    d) Be more effective than goals that are assigned without much explanation

11. One way leaders can get employees to persist on difficult tasks, particularly following failure, is to change employees' attribution for the cause of failure from [ ] causes to [ ] causes.
    a) External stable; internal stable
    b) Internal stable; internal unstable

   c) Internal unstable; external stable
   d) External unstable; internal stable

12. According to the over-justification effect, recurringly rewarding someone for activities he already enjoys tends to:
    a) Reduce satisfaction with the activity
    b) Increase the rate at which the activity is performed
    c) Have no effect on motivation
    d) Increase satisfaction with the activity

13. Muzafer Sherif's famous study on group relations shows that [ ] can evoke intergroup hostility.
    a) Name-calling
    b) Intra-group solidarity
    c) Competition
    d) Lack of structure

14. The notion of entrainment, with regard to teams, concerns:
    a) The timing or tempo of team tasks
    b) Team goals that get derailed
    c) The amount of team effort expended
    d) The means by which poor performers get removed from teams

15. Which of the following is usually not considered a component of motivation?
    a) Goal-directedness
    b) Energy
    c) Capability
    d) Ego strength

16. The job satisfaction-performance literature generally supports which of the following statements:
    a) The relationship between job satisfaction and performance is strong and robust.
    b) The relationship is modest at best, probably because other factors affect the relationship.
    c) The true relationship between job satisfaction and performance has not been adequately tested.
    d) Performance is a better predictor of satisfaction than job satisfaction is of performance.

17. According to research by Tversky and Kahneman, if you want people to choose or accept riskier options, options should be presented:
    a) In terms of potential gains
    b) In an objective, unbiased manner
    c) In terms of potential losses
    d) As ways to avoid undesirable outcomes

*(Continued)*

**18.** People who are self-efficacious:
  a) Sustain their effort despite obstacles
  b) Perform no better than people who are not self-efficacious
  c) Persist on activities even when there are no benefits to success
  d) Are dreamers, wishful thinkers

**19.** In the work–family literature, "buffering" would be evidenced by:
  a) A stay-at-home mother who is shielded from the responsibilities of the workplace
  b) A married man whose satisfying family role tempers stress at work
  c) The ability of both men and women to keep their work and family lives separate
  d) Employers' programs, such as bring-a-child-to-work day, that involve families in the workplace

**20.** An employee who doesn't complain about trivial matters, consults with others before taking action, and is willing to help peers is best described as:
  a) Altruistic
  b) Committed
  c) A good citizen
  d) A role model

### Answers

1) c; 2) b; 3) c; 4) b; 5) c; 6) a; 7) b; 8) a; 9) b; 10) d;
11) b; 12) a; 13) c; 14) a; 15) d; 16) b; 17) c; 18) a; 19) b;
20) c

Source: M.O. Malley and E. Lawler, "What Is HR Good for Anyway?" *Across the Board 2004*, pp. 33–38. Reprinted with permission from The Conference Board.

The behavioural perspective is particularly important as the HR department is asked to define the behaviours necessary to achieve organizational capabilities of innovation, speed, and accountability.[13] Capabilities are the collective skills and abilities of employees within an organization, achieved through understanding and investing in HR practices that change employee behaviour. These intangibles, the hidden value of a firm, represent a new outlook on the value that the HR profession adds—ROI (return on intangibles).[14]

## Human Capital Theory

**human capital**

the sum of employees' knowledge, skills, experience, and commitment invested in the organization

Classical economists describe three types of resources or inputs used in the production of goods and services: land, capital, and labour. Labour, or **human capital**, refers to the collective sum of the attributes, experience, knowledge, and commitment that employees choose to invest in their work. This intangible asset comprises the knowledge, education, vocational qualifications, professional certifications, work-related experience, and competence of an organization's employees.[15] As researchers have noted, "In the new economic paradigm, as the demands for continuous change make innovation, adaptability, speed and efficiency essential features of the business landscape, the strategic importance of intellectual capital and intangible assets have increased substantially. While these assets are largely invisible . . . the sources are not. They are found in the human capital of the firm's employees."[16] From the perspective of human capital, employees are viewed as a capital resource that requires investment.[17]

Employees are of value to the organization to the extent that they work toward accomplishing organizational objectives. Costs incurred in training, motivating, compensating, and monitoring employees can be viewed as investments in human capital, just as maintenance of equipment is an investment in the capital of the firm.[18] The advantages of an organization with effective HR practices may come not from having better resources but from making better use of these resources by achieving higher productivity per worker and by matching the capabilities of employees with the strategy.[19]

## Strategic HRM

HRM issues are often cited as a threat to an organization's ability to execute strategy. We hope that, by the end of this book, you will understand that HRM strategy must match the business strategy. But first, let us try to understand what we mean by HRM strategy.

A more traditional perspective of the HR planning concept implied that the organization was concerned only with possible problems of labour surpluses, and shortages. The goal was to determine the knowledge, skills, and abilities (KSAs) required within broad organizational outcomes such as growth or decline. Much emphasis was placed on the statistical techniques for analyzing resource supply and demand forecasting while ignoring managerial realities and support for the process.[20] This is now regarded as a narrow, linear approach to HR planning.

Despite the apparent link between planning and strategy, there is some concern that HR planning has been preoccupied with resource supply and demand forecasting without considering the different HR practices required by fundamentally different strategies. For example, a company that decides to grow through the development of international businesses has different personnel requirements than a company that decides to grow through mergers and acquisitions. Under traditional HR planning models, both strategies would require the acquisition and absorption of large numbers of employees, but the prescriptions for supplying labour effectively would differ radically. Under the international business growth model, labour supply would have to be managed under foreign country regulations and, in some cases, employees with minimal skills would have to be hired, and then subjected to extensive training. Growing through mergers and acquisitions implies an instant absorption of large numbers of employees, already selected and trained, but whose organizational values would have to be aligned with those of the dominant culture.

In this book, we are suggesting an approach to HR strategy that calls for tailoring HR policies and practices to the organizational needs of the future. Some writers have recognized the need to do this in specific functional areas, such as matching compensation strategies to the different phases of a business.[21] However, there is a disturbing lack of understanding of the need to align all HR functional practices with corporate strategy. The proliferation of bankruptcies, mergers, and restructuring has affected our view of employees in a profound way and highlighted the need for the input of HR professionals in formulating policy. The next section explains why HR strategy is so important to the achievement of organizational strategies.

## The Importance of Strategic HR Planning

Executives are demanding that the HR department move from articulating perceived value ("training builds employee skills") to demonstrating real value (an external client can see the economic value). As a member of the corporate team, the focus of HR must be on scoring points, not just coaching, training, or counting the number of players. The value of HR will be seen in its ability to deliver the behaviours needed to enable the organization's strategy. There are at least two reasons strategic HR planning is so important: (1) Employees help an organization achieve success because they are strategic resources and (2) the planning process itself results in improved goal attainment.

Like other resources, human resources can deteriorate. Skills and knowledge can become obsolete unless either the individual or the employer invests in further education and training. If these investments in training are not made, and the skills become obsolete, the value of that company's human resources decreases. Higher investments in training result in higher-value human capital. Thus, human capital has to be replenished.

The value of employees as a resource must be placed within a strategic framework. In other words, a strategy itself can become obsolete, making current employee skills obsolete. Suppose, for example, the current workforce is valuable because of manual skills, but the market for the company's manufactured products is declining. Environmental analyses suggest that th...

...the high-tech field, with its demand for flexible, knowledgeable workers. By changing the strategy, the "value" of the current workforce is diminished. A corollary to this is that employees can expect to face different HRM practices throughout their lifetimes, and even within a single organization. Employees may be asked to exhibit different behaviours, depending on strategic goals, and these behaviours will be motivated by different HRM practices.[22] Organizations with different business units are likely to have different HRM policies for each business unit to optimize employee performance.

To summarize, human assets offer organizations a competitive advantage. These assets must be managed and matched to the organizational strategy. An organization that manages its human resources strategically is more likely to achieve its goals, survive, and profit. HR Planning Today 2.1 describes how Sears used data from its own studies to improve the workplace for its employees.

## Improved Goal Attainment

Strategic HRM can improve an organization's performance. The goals of these HRM strategies are to shape employee behaviour so that it is consistent with the direction the organization identifies in its strategic plans. Organizations with clear strategies provide direction and meaning to employees and mitigate the need for control by substituting a consistency of purpose—in

### Sears: A Compelling Workplace

Sears was one of the first organizations in the world to document the relationship between employee behaviour and the firm's performance. The company pioneered studies that defined and empirically verified the correlation between individual sales associates' behaviours, customer satisfaction, and ultimately financial performance. Sears executives have embraced a business strategy that relies on employees as the source of competitive advantage. Sears has only three strategic imperatives: to make its stores and business

- a compelling place to work,
- a compelling place to shop, and
- a compelling place to invest.

In order to implement the first imperative, the company made sure employees received performance feedback from customers, so that they could see the direct relationship between their behaviour and profits. The executives so fully support the human capital perspective that they fund the training of over 20 000 managers (including teams of managers) every year at Sears University.

Source: Becker, B.E., and M.A. Huselid. 1999. "Overview: Strategic Human Resources Management in Five Leading Firms." *Human Resource Management*, Vol. 38, No. 4 (1999), pp. 287–301. Copyright © 1999 John Wiley & Sons, Inc. This material is used by permission of John Wiley and Sons, Inc.

other words, a mission. This articulated vision for the future may result in a more effective organization through increased motivation and performance, lowered absenteeism and turnover, and heightened stability, satisfaction, and involvement.[23]

To summarize, strategy formulation is important to the attainment of organizational goals in order to align all HR functional strategies with overall strategy and to focus employees on important missions and goals of the organization. Research and observations have demonstrated that developing HR practices that support the strategy leads to improved strategy implementation.[24]

## The Risks

Is there a downside to strategic HR planning? The strategic management of human resources seems beneficial, but some researchers point out that there are costs.[25] Research shows that these costs include the increased time and energy involved in making decisions, greater potential for information overload, impossible commitments to employees, and an over-concern with employee reactions that may be incompatible with industry conditions. In other words, the strategic management of employees is hard work. As anyone who has gone through the strategy formulation and implementation process understands, the strategy formulation phase is relatively easy. Motivating employees to commit to the strategy and implement it is far more difficult (this text offers guidelines on how to do this). A further difficulty is that any HR plan for the future may raise employees' expectations that they have jobs for life and will be trained for those jobs. The reality is that conditions change, and the plan may change, resulting in job losses.

Another problem, some would argue, is that organizations that commit to one strategy become blind to changes in the environment and lose their flexibility. However, as we have seen, incremental adjustments based on environmental scanning are part of strategy implementation. The risk of not having a strategy seems greater.

There are risks to not developing a strategy. Organizations that do not actively scan the environment (methods for doing so are discussed in Chapter 3) face the danger of being out of touch with reality. Today's operating decisions may be based on yesterday's conditions. Comfortable with past success, the managers in these organizations focus on resolving internal problems, such as making better horse carriages when automobiles are on the horizon.

An example of a company that was not in touch with reality was Consumers Distributing. Consumers Distributing did not develop a strategy to match or surpass the changing distribution networks and customer-service levels of their competitors. The company, now bankrupt, continued to require customers to come to the stores and stand in line, often for out-of-stock items. Meanwhile, their competitors were offering electronic purchasing or were providing greeters at the door of the store who helped the customers find anything they wanted, all for a competitive price. MacMillan argues that firms that develop strategies gain an advantage and control their own destinies.[26] An apt cliché is "an organization that fails to plan, plans to fail."

Therefore, strategic HR planning is important to optimize the use of the organization's human resources and to focus behaviour on the important goals of the organization.

**RPC** 2.4

WWW

## Linking HR Processes to Strategy

Strategic HRM must facilitate the formulation and implementation of corporate and business-level strategies. Senior managers must focus on issues such as: What are the HR implications of adopting a strategy? What are the internal and external constraints and opportunities? Exactly what policies, practices, and philosophies contribute to the successful implementation of the strategy?

The basic premise is that every HR policy and practice must directly support the organization's strategy and objectives.[27] This does not happen as frequently as it should. In the worst-case scenario, HR plans are developed as an afterthought and separately from organizational strategy. They are not relevant to the business and are seen as important only by the HR people; no other unit or level is committed to these plans.

While it has long been recognized that HR policies and practices must be linked to the firm's overall strategy, there has been little research that offers prescriptions on exactly how to do this. Aligning HR strategy with business strategy can be done in one of these ways:

1. Start with organizational strategy and then create HR strategy.
2. Start with HR competencies and then craft corporate strategies based on these competencies.
3. Do a combination of both in a form of reciprocal relationship.

Let us examine each approach.

## Corporate Strategy Leads to HR Strategy

**RPC** 2.5

A traditional perspective of HR planning views HRM programs as flowing from corporate strategy. In other words, personnel needs are based on corporate plans. If a firm decides to compete on the basis of offering low-cost products, HR policies and practices must align and be based on low labour costs. McDonald's is a good example of a firm that follows this strategy. This model assumes that people are more adaptable than strategy and that cause-and-effect relationships are unidirectional.[28] Square workers are forced to fit into round holes, with little consideration for their ability to adjust. If the workers can't adjust to a new strategy, they are terminated in a massive restructuring.

Given their investment in thousands of employees, larger organizations seem to prefer this approach, despite the literature showing the difficulty and time-consuming nature of organizational change. Within this approach, employees are considered means to an end, not part of the strategy formulation equation.

But another perspective reverses this view, suggesting that employee competencies determine the business strategy.

## HR Competencies Lead to Business Strategy

**RPC** 2.6

A competing view states that an organization cannot implement a strategy if it does not have the human resources necessary. In the late 1990s, companies were scrambling to find high-tech workers in order to enable them to launch web-based services and products. HR Planning Today 2.2 describes the value that "Silicon Valley" organizations place on employees.

The critical question is whether it is easier to change HR to fit the strategy or change the strategy to fit the human resource pool? Small businesses seem to choose the latter course. The owners of very small businesses are nimble and quickly recognize that, if an employee has a certain capability, it can be exploited to develop new products or services. Diversity management efforts are currently building on this theme. For example, if the number of employees who speak Mandarin reaches a sufficient number within an organization, the observant executive will start to explore Asian markets.

---

### HR Planning Today 2.2

#### Hoarding Employees

When companies face falling sales, revenues, and profits, one predictable strategy is to begin to lay off employees. However, Sun Microsystems, when faced with declining growth, refused to lay off employees. Instead, managers were summoned to the headquarters in Palo Alto, California, and urged to find other ways to cut expenses. After having faced acute labour shortages in the high–tech sector, this company was determined to keep employees who would be difficult to replace when the markets recovered. Known as labour hoarding, this strategy is an unusual one in North America and reflects an understanding that a firm's employees are its chief asset.

Source: Adapted from G. Smith, "Firm Hoards Workers Despite Pinch," *The Globe and Mail*, July 9, 2002, p. B1.

---

This "skills determine strategy" outlook relies too heavily on employee capabilities and not enough on environmental analysis; nor is consideration given to changing HR practices in training or compensation to facilitate this change in strategy.

These perspectives represent two extremes on a continuum between organizational strategy and HR practices. The reality is closer to the concept of reciprocal interdependencies.[29]

# HR Strategy and Corporate Strategy

An emerging perspective sees HR strategy as contributing to business-level strategy, and vice versa. Increasingly, in large firms, senior HR vice-presidents are asked not only to review business plans to ensure consistency with HR strategy, but also to provide input to this strategy based on HR strengths and weaknesses.

In this context, an organization chooses a business strategy, such as being a leader in innovative products, based on its in-house, highly educated, trained employees who have been socialized to value creativity. Bill Hewlett and David Packard's single founding concept for Hewlett-Packard (HP) was "who"—not "what." They wanted to build a great company together. They stumbled for months searching for what that company would be.[30] Simply phrased, an organization develops its employees and then capitalizes on their skills; the employees then learn new skills, and so it continues. In many ways, HR strategy generates the business strategy, and business strategy determines HR strategy. This concept of reciprocal interdependence is widely accepted in the HR strategy literature.[31]

An emerging view is that HR should build its strategies by starting with the issues facing the business. All HR programs should be created to solve real business problems and add value, thus becoming indistinguishable from the business.[32]

## HR Becomes a Business Partner

The key point here is the concept of *concurrent strategy formulation*. Strategy development, based on environmental analysis, is conducted at the same time that HRM issues are considered. HR issues do not solely determine strategy, nor does strategy unilaterally determine HR practices. The HR senior management team moves from outsider status to insider status. The implications are not trivial; HR managers must understand the numbers language of business or the outcome expectations of nonprofit organizations. They must be able to understand analyses presented by marketing, financial, and operational managers. Cost–benefit assessments of options within the HR domain will have to be prepared and defended. Entrepreneurial instincts will have to be sharpened, as HR managers will be expected to engage in scanning HR capabilities for business opportunities in this two-way approach to strategic HR planning. Alternative solutions to problems have to be generated. For example, if the low-cost strategy depends on hiring personnel at minimum wage, HR managers have to develop strategies to deal with rapid training and high turnover

### A Concurrent Approach to HR Strategy

Bonnie Hathcock is the chief HR officer for Siemens Rolm Communications. She claims that a revolution in approaches to HRM is needed for the challenges of the 21st century. "The 21st-century human resource imperative is to raise the company's human capital to sophisticated levels that produce competitive advantages for the enterprise," Hathcock asserts. This requires a shakedown for those in "personnel" who prefer to remain quietly on the sidelines administering employee requests.

The revolution begins with identifying the company's strategy and aligning HR work with strategic imperatives. Hathcock sees HR strategy as a planned response to corporate strategy. The HR role is to enhance the capabilities of the enterprise to execute its business strategies. Hathcock sees herself as the leader of the crusade to maximize human assets. Employees are not commodities to be treated as if they are expendable. The raison d'être for HR is to be the catalyst for human asset capability and commitment. Both dimensions are important: first, in building human commitment through culture management, and second, in building human asset capability through competency development. Hancock continues: "If the HR department is to achieve parity with other functions, then they must not just serve and support but must integrate fully with management in achieving business results."

Hathcock's efforts at Siemens won her the Optimas Award for Human Resource Excellence in managing change in 1996.

Source: Adapted from B.C. Hathcock, "The New Breed Approach to 21st Century Human Resources," *Human Resource Management*, Summer, Vol. 35, No. 2 (1996), pp. 243–250.

rates. This option will have to be compared with outsourcing, use of robots, or even increasing wages to reduce the costs of turnover. The HR manager is no longer the auditor, but a partner and problem solver. Linkages between the HR manager and other managers, both formal and informal, ensure that this partnership role is enacted. One HR manager describes her perspective on concurrent strategy formulation in HR Planning Today 2.3.

## Strategic Partnering

Human resource professionals recognize the need to play a more strategic role within the organization. Nearly nine out of ten Canadian HR executives surveyed in 2000 spoke of the need to operate more as a business partner.[33] HR managers defined their new role as one blending their HR technical skills with an in-depth understanding of the business and its goals. However, less than 25% report that they have integrated business and HR strategies and provided analytical support for business decision making.[34] But the good news is that 97% play some part in strategy.[35]

The reasons that executives give for not including HR in the strategic planning process are outlined in HR Planning Notebook 2.2.

Why do executives ignore HR's contribution to strategy? Some argue that it is because management is not satisfied with HR services in general; that "people" issues belong only to HR, and HR can take care of any problems in executing the strategy.

These attitudes are changing, however, as organizations realize the impact that HRM strategy can have on organizational effectiveness and as HR

## HR Planning Notebook 2.2

### Why Is HR Not a Strategic Partner?

- Top managers don't see a need. They don't see HR as a profession.
- HR personnel are seen as personnel experts, not experts in the business. HR is seen as economically illiterate.
- HR information is useful to HR but incompatible with business needs.
- Business managers have a short-term focus with an emphasis on current performance. Quarterly results are more important, even though some investments in training and culture development won't pay off for years.
- HR professionals are unable to think strategically because they have an incomplete understanding of the business.
- Senior managers lack appreciation for the role that HR can play in enabling the organization to achieve its goals. HR is seen as an adversary, demanding unnecessary bureaucratic work in the managers' day-to-day jobs.

- Few functional managers see themselves as HR managers. They have functional responsibilities, but do not see that the principal role of management is to manage people.
- It is difficult to quantify the benefits or outcomes of HR programs. In the competition for organizational resources, why should HR be allocated any part of the resource pie?
- HR assets are not owned by the organization, and so any resource allocation to people programs is seen as a high-risk investment.
- HR initiatives almost always mean change, which can be resisted. Any program that requires different ways of treating or managing employees upsets the status quo and means learning new behaviours.

Source: D. Ulrich 1997, *Human Resource Champions: The Next Agenda for Adding Value and Delivering Results*, Boston: Harvard Business School Press.

managers develop the internal relationships to ensure that the strategy is effective. Nevertheless, only one-third of HR managers stated that they played a major role in strategic planning. HR Planning Notebook 2.3 poses the question, Are you a strategic partner?

## HR Planning Notebook 2.3

### Are You a Strategic Partner?

Do you understand the business? What financial indicators are important to the company? Who are your customers, and what is your competitive advantage? What major technological changes will affect your work?

Do you know what the corporate plan is? Can you quickly list the major initiatives of your organization?

Do you align HR programs, policies, and practices with organizational strategies and goals? How can HR position the organization to succeed? Are the people

management processes focused and measured on deliverables and not functions? Does HR report on effectiveness (the impact that the training program had on employee behaviour) or just efficiencies (such as the number of people being trained)?

Are major organizational decisions made with your input?

*Count the number of times you answered yes. The higher the number, the greater the likelihood that you are a strategic partner or have the ability to be one.*

Formal mechanisms can ensure that HR is a partner in the planning process.

## Ways to Become Involved in the Strategic Planning Process

### Membership in the Executive Team

In order to involve HR in the strategic planning process, ensure that the person responsible for HRM is included as part of the executive team, occupying a position at the vice-presidential level. The president and CEO of Surrey Metro Savings Credit Union in British Columbia says that HR plays a critical role at the financial institution, and that is why it is important for the head of HR to be a vice-president on the senior management team. Most large organizations now position the most senior HR person at the executive vice-president level. More importantly, studies in the United Kingdom and Australia show that companies that included the HR director on the executive team experienced twice the growth in earnings per share compared to those who did not.[36]

### Review/React Linkage

Another option is a review/react linkage, proposed by Cascio.[37] In this method, HR managers have the opportunity to review strategic plans before they are implemented. They can then approve or modify them.

However, this control or veto option is too passive and reactionary for significant input about a critical resource because linkages have to be made at earlier stages. HR managers should be supplying information about employee capabilities, be part of the strategic planning committee, and be documenting implications of strategic thrusts.

### Integrative Linkage

In a truly integrative linkage, as exhibited in some companies, the interaction between the members of the executive committee and the HR director are frequent, and the HR director is involved in strategic decisions, even when the HR implications are not readily apparent.[38] In some cases, the credibility of the HR department is so high that the CEO, vice-chair, and other top officials have all held the position of HR director as part of their career development.

Organizations are more responsive to integrative linkages when the environment is turbulent (increased competition, rapid technological change, and changing labour market demographics), resulting in difficulties recruiting the right kinds of people. Organizations with multiple divisions demanding different types of strategies, and therefore different HR practices for each division, also tend to elevate the role of HR. A culture or CEO with a strong belief in the asset value of employees will also result in more attempts to link HR strategies with corporate strategies. The credibility of the HR director also influences the

### Traditional versus Strategic HR

| Factors | Traditional HR | Strategic HR |
|---|---|---|
| Responsibility for HR | Staff specialists | Line managers |
| Focus | Employee relations | Partnerships with internal and external customers |
| Role of HR | Transactional, change follower, and respondent | Transformational, change leader, and initiator |
| Initiatives | Slow reactive, fragmented | Fast, proactive, integrated |
| Time Horizon | Short term | Short, median, long (as necessary) |
| Control | Bureaucratic—roles, policies, procedures | Organic—flexible, whatever is needed to succeed |
| Job Design | Tight division of labour, independence, specialization | Broad, flexible, cross-training, teams |
| Key Investments | Capital, products | People, knowledge |
| Accountability | Cost centre | Investment centre |

Source: From *Strategic Human Resource Management*, 1st edition by MELLO. © 2002. Reprinted with permission of South-Western, a division of Thomson Learning: www.thomsonrights.com. Fax 800-730-2215.

probability of a linkage. HR managers who are able to deliver information about labour supply, or critical personnel capabilities, in a quantifiable way are likely to be deemed more credible. Historically, HR professionals were asked to deliver operational outcomes, such as administrative efficiency and employee commitment. More recently, HR professionals are now asked to deliver strategic outcomes such as customer engagement (the level of commitment of customers to the company, as evidenced by volume of sales and repeat visits) and capacity for change. In the future, HR will be asked to deliver both operational and strategic outcomes. If HR directors are responsible for bottom-line results and are measured by them, they become more focused on delivering programs that make a difference. Some organizations tie percentages of the HR manager's compensation (pay at risk) to company performance.

Many effective linkages operate in organizations, and each possesses some of the characteristics of the traditional way of doing business, as well as some from the newer strategic model (see HR Planning Notebook 2.4).

To illustrate the alignment of HR programs with business strategy, Appendix A focuses on Porter's model and discusses two strategies: the low-cost-provider strategy and the differentiation strategy. Although Porter recognized the importance of HRM, and even concedes that, in some firms, HRM holds the key to competitive advantage, he did not delineate any specific practices that can be aligned with business strategy. Appendix A attempts to fill this gap and provides one of the few "recipes" for using HR strategies to support a business strategy.

## Cost Reduction at United Parcel Service

United Parcel Service (UPS) employs 152 000 people to deliver parcels in an extremely competitive sector where "a package is a package." UPS profits by keeping costs low—a low-cost-provider strategy. How does it do this?

Its key is to manage labour costs. UPS starts by simplifying and standardizing the work to optimize efficiency. Early in the company's history, management used time and motion studies to measure the time each UPS driver spent each day on specific tasks. The engineers then changed some of these tasks to improve worker effectiveness, thus leading to work standards. For example, drivers were instructed how to place their keys on a key ring finger and step down out of the truck in standardized ways. As a result, workers were less tired at the end of each day. More than 1000 industrial engineers—experts in work efficiency—continue to monitor the work of workers engaged in repetitive tasks. The workers, who are unionized, earn about a dollar more than drivers at other companies and gain employment security if they perform at acceptable levels.

The cost-reduction strategy through work-process refinements enables UPS to gain a competitive advantage in a service sector—that of overnight delivery—that is relatively undifferentiated.

Source: ACADEMY OF MANAGEMENT EXECUTIVE: THE THINKING MANAGER'S SOURCE by SCHULLER AND JACKSON. Copyright 1987 by ACAD OF MGMT. Reproduced with permission of ACAD OF MGMT in the format Textbook via Copyright Clearance Center.

To illustrate how HR is aligned with strategies in real companies, HR Planning Today 2.4 describes how United Parcel Service aligns its HR strategy with its low-cost-provider business goal, and HR Planning Today 2.5 illustrates HR alignment with a differentiation strategy at Frost.

It seems feasible to design HR policies to match strategy, but what happens when an organization has more than one business and more than one business strategy? We attempt to answer that question in the next section.

## HR Strategy by Division

Firms with more than one business strategy are likely to have more than one approach to HR strategy. The challenge is to treat employees across divisions in an equitable fashion while motivating different behaviours that align with the divisions' strategies or functions. For example, General Electric might adopt HR practices that support innovation in the research and development branch while adopting policies that support low costs in the manufacturing branch. But, to achieve equity, employees in both branches would have the same employee benefits.

Similarly, an employee could expect to be exposed to different HR practices within his or her career, even within one firm. Flexibility in behaviour and diverse skill sets will be required from most employees. The basic prescription is to design HR programs that support the business strategy since linking HRM strategy with business strategy can result in improved organizational performance.

## Linking HR Strategy to Business Strategy at Frost

Frost, Inc. is a manufacturer of automobile parts with sales of over $20 million. The company was dependent on one product (overhead conveyor trolleys) in one sector (the automobile industry), and the president was concerned about the company's vulnerability in this cyclical industry. Attempts to design, build, and sell other products failed. The president set out to correct this problem, stating, "We had a single-purpose machine, and single-purpose people." He needed flexibility and a long-term orientation from his personnel.

To increase workers' identification with the long-term survival of the company, Frost gave each worker 10 shares of the closely held company. Employees were also able to participate in a share purchase plan and a corporate profit-sharing plan. This move accomplished the goals of increasing employee commitment to the organization and promoting a long-term focus.

Next, the president set out to restructure the rest of the compensation package to improve innovation to achieve a differentiation strategy. A balance was needed between rewards for results (productivity) and rewards for process (manufacturing). Quarterly bonuses were given for productivity, but managers also were able to tap into a "celebration fund," which rewarded employees' significant innovations. Additional soft rewards of dinner with the president or weekend holidays for the employee and his or her spouse were used to reinforce innovative processes. Executive perks were eliminated to demonstrate the egalitarian nature of the innovative climate, and all employees had access to corporate information (except payroll) through terminals placed throughout the plant.

Frost paid employees to learn new skills, both through the company training programs and from outside vendors. Only those who had developed additional skills were eligible for advancement.

Source: ACADEMY OF MANAGEMENT EXECUTIVE: THE THINKING MANAGER'S SOURCE by SCHULLER AND JACKSON. Copyright 1987 by ACAD OF MGMT. Reproduced with permission of ACAD OF MGMT in the format Textbook via Copyright Clearance Center.

Crises are often an opportunity to establish a linkage. If a company is experiencing high turnover and is unable to meet production quotas, or if a key executive departs and there is no groomed successor, many HR directors use this as an opportunity to promote the importance of HR strategic planning.

Changes in the environment overall can sometimes increase the attractiveness of HR strategy. Globalization, for example, forces managers to examine the cost–benefit of using national or international labour pools to attain desired cost and quality objectives. Either choice implicates strategic HR planning.

For all these reasons, most organizations have accepted the importance of including the HR director as part of the strategy formulation team. We offer guidelines to the development of an effective HR strategy in the next section.

**RPC 2.8**

## Characteristics of an Effective HRM Strategy

The purpose of HR strategy is to capitalize on the distinctive competencies of the organization and add value through the effective use of human resources.[39]

Effective HRM strategies include external and internal fit, and a focus on results.

# Fit

Fit is an important consideration when designing HR programs. We look at two types of important fit: fitting HR strategy to organizational strategy (external fit), and linking the various HR programs to other functional areas and to each other (internal fit).

## External Fit

HR programs must align with or fit the overall strategy of the organization. If the business strategy is to differentiate the organization from its competitors based on superior service, then selection and training programs should be developed to hire and train people in the skills and attitudes necessary to deliver superior service. Fit with other functional strategies is as important as fit with corporate strategies. HR senior management must be included in strategy discussions to be sure this happens. This is sometimes called the "best fit" approach to strategic HR, where HR strategies match organizational strategies.

## Internal Fit

We look at two types of internal fit: a fit with other functional areas, such as marketing, and a fit among all HR programs. Fit with other functional areas is important. If the marketing department is developing an advertising plan that promises 24-hour access to customer service representatives but the HR plan does not include compensation differentials for shift work, the overall marketing strategy might fail.

HR programs must also be consistent with each other. That is, training, selection, and appraisal must work together to support a strategy. If the training department decides to teach employees to use the Internet to handle customer service, the staffing department must hire people who either are computer literate or who have the kinds of intelligence that enable them to learn computer skills rapidly. This working together is commonly referred to as "bundling" HR practices. The "best practices" approach, in which bundles of HR practices are internally consistent,[40] suggests that there is a direct relationship between an internally consistent bundle of HR practices and firm performance. (In the "best practices" approach, an organization can adopt one best practice, such as structured interviewing, without adopting bundles of best practices that align with each other, and therefore increase the impact of each, in a synergistic manner.) However, there is disagreement as to what, exactly, these best practices are.[41]

Consistent cross-functional practices are critical to the achievement of an organization's goals. Imagine if the business strategy depended on exemplary customer service as its principal competitive advantage, but untrained employees were incapable of providing this level of service. It's clear, then, that the bundling of HR practices is necessary to ensure that the overall strategy is implemented consistently.

The flow of decision making can be seen in Figure 2.1.

Chapter 2: Aligning HR with Strategy

FIGURE 2.1

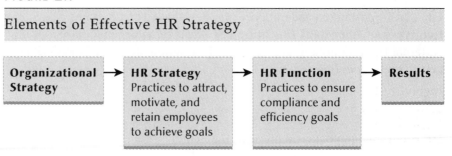

Elements of Effective HR Strategy

**RPC** 2.9

## Focus on Results

The hard work of deciding on strategy is not its formulation but its implementation and the tracking of results. Many HR managers do not have the resources or skills to measure results to see if the goals have been achieved. Unless the strategy contains performance measures—that is, is results oriented—it will be difficult to know how successfully the strategy was implemented. Chapter 14 presents various methods for evaluating programs. As James Harrington says, "Measurements are key. If you cannot measure it, you cannot control it. If you cannot control it, then you cannot manage it."[42]

We've seen that an effective HRM strategy is aligned with organizational strategy, is integrated with other departmental and HR functional area goals, and is focused on results that can be measured. We've also seen that HR strategy must explicitly recognize the dynamics of the external environment (including the competition and labour markets). The typical time period for planning HR strategy and assessing results is three to five years.

The final section in this chapter outlines the strategic HR planning model and sets the stage for the rest of the material in the book.

## The Strategic HR Planning Model

The model we use is based on generic corporate and business strategies linked with complex bundled HR policies and practices. Our perspective builds on earlier HR planning models (right numbers in the right places at the right times). Our search for a strategic HR planning model was triggered by practitioner needs for information. The model we use emphasizes monitoring and analyzing external factors (Chapter 3), assessing the strengths and weaknesses of the organizations' human resources (Chapters 4–9), determining the HR implications of such corporate strategies as restructuring (Chapter 10), going international (Chapter 11), mergers and acquisitions (Chapter 12), and assessing the effectiveness of these efforts (Chapter 13). Most of the requests we receive from CEOs and executive vice-presidents of HR are of this nature: "Our organization is developing a new strategy. How will this affect HR? What changes in our HR policies and practices do we need to make?" We have tried to provide answers to these questions.

# Summary

Strategic HRM is a set of distinct but interrelated practices, policies, and philosophies with the goal of enabling the organization to achieve its strategy. HR strategy is embedded in theories of the resource-based view of the firm, the behavioural perspective, and the human capital approach. By involving HR in discussions of strategic policies, an organization has a better chance of being effective in the implementation of these policies. There are various approaches to linking HRM strategies to organizational strategies. We can start with the corporate strategy that leads to the HR strategy, or start with the HR competencies that lead to the business strategy, or use a blend of the interrelationship of the HR strategy and the corporate strategy.

# Key Terms

human capital, 34                                  strategic HRM, 30

# Web Links

The Knowledge Centre of the Society for Human Resources Management presents articles on strategic HR:

**www.shrm.org/research/kc** (p. 34)

The *Canadian HR Reporter* website, with articles on strategic HRM:

**www.hrreporter.com/hr_strategies** (p. 38)

An example of a Human Capital Strategy by the U.S. Federal Government Human Resources Agency:

**www.opm.gov/Strategic_Management_of_Human_Capital** (p. 41)

# RPC Icons

**RPC 2.1 Develops processes to engage employees in achieving the objectives of the organization**

**RPC 2.2 Provides advice on policy, monitors activities, and, if required, initiates corrective action related to the organization's practices**

**RPC 2.3 Develops and implements a communications plan that supports strategies for employee involvement**

**RPC 2.4 Determines the best learning approaches and human capital development initiatives required for continued organizational success**

RPC 2.5 Interprets and communicates business strategies and plans

RPC 2.6 Develops an organization or unit design to fit a given set of business objectives and environmental factors

RPC 2.7 Leads in the development of HR initiatives that support the organization's strategic directions

RPC 2.8 Sets clear goals and objectives for the HR activities of the organization, maintaining evaluation measurements of all HR activities against goals and objectives of the organization

RPC 2.9 Manages the use of resources, assigns work, and gauges the effectiveness of teams and individuals in meeting specific goals.

# Discussion Questions

1. Nearly every person working in HR agrees that HR represents a body of knowledge. In Canada, about half of those belonging to a provincial HR association hold the designation CHRP (Certified Human Resource Professional). What are the advantages of this designation? People can work in HR without a CHRP, although most employers ask for this qualification for entry-level positions. Do you think that the CHRP should be mandatory (i.e., a licence to practice) in order to hold a job in HR, much like accountants, nurses, and engineers are required to have professional designations? Why or why not?
2. Visit three large companies from three different sectors. Try a hospitality sector (hotels, fast food, etc.), a high-tech sector, and a manufacturing sector. Talk with a senior HR manager, and determine how such managers work with executives on strategy formulation and development. What is the senior HR manager's role in the process?
3. The emphasis in this chapter was on private companies because much of the research in strategy has been done with for-profit organizations. But many people work for the public sector—that is, for nonprofit organizations. Does strategic HRM make sense for these companies? Explain your answer, discussing organizational strategies for public companies.

# Using the Internet

Using the Internet, find articles about the strategies of HBC and Wal-Mart. Can you identify their business strategies? Talk to someone in the HR department of these companies or to a departmental store manager. Do the HR practices of the two organizations differ in any way? Then go to a retailer that competes on a differentiation strategy, such as Harry Rosen or Holt Renfrew. Determine the differences in its HRM practices compared to HBC or Wal-Mart.

# Exercises

1. The HR function at Corning, Inc. uses a human capital approach to identify the implications of corporate strategy on HR services. Read about its approach in M.C Brush and D.H. Ruse, 2005, "Driving Strategic Success through Human Capital Planning: How Corning Links Business and HR Strategy to Improve the Value and Impact of its HR function," *Human Resource Planning*, 28, 1, pp. 49–61. In groups, discuss why Corning has chosen this approach and labelled it "HCP." Do you consider it effective? Does it share any features with the behavioural perspective, the resource-based view of the firm, or even the balanced scorecard?

2. When the employees of FCI Electronics Company heard that their plant would be closed, they did not apply for new jobs at other plants—they applied for a new company. The employees marketed themselves as a highly valuable workforce, with 26 engineers, 74 tool and die makers, 16 managers, 298 assembly-line workers, and 30 shipping workers. They figured that their hundreds of years in manufacturing, coupled with a perfect attendance record of eight years, would attract an employer to their small town of Clearfield in Pennsylvania. What type of HR strategy does this example illustrate? Do you think the group was successful? Why or why not?

# Case: A New Vision of HR

The HR department is typically organized by function. To ensure that HR policies and practices are aligned with the organization, a new vision of HR would be structured as follows.

## Corporate HR

The key officer functions as a practice director, similar to what is found in consulting companies. This person plays several roles: influencing the CEO to design and implement an HR strategy removing barriers to changes suggested by two new departments, Services Inc. and Solutions Inc.; and developing another new department, the organizational capability consultants.

## Services Inc.

The part of HR that is administrative, estimated to be 60% to 70% of HR work, is located in a separate unit called Services Inc. The administrative burden is reduced through call centres and use of the Internet and intranet. The types of HR work done in Services Inc. includes compensation and benefits administration, training and education administration, staffing administration, and records management. There are three levels of service: tier one is accessed by computer or telephone, and deals with reports of changes in addresses;

everything is processed without human intervention. Tier two directs HR requests for information not listed on tier-one sites—such as questions about retirement eligibility or finding a course on innovation—to a call centre that can provide a quick response or explanation. Tier three comprises case workers—highly skilled professionals—who provide extensive and comprehensive assistance to complex issues such as employee relations or employee assistance.

Services Inc. is driven by cost reduction—it has to be the lowest cost and most efficient provider of service, whether outsourced or provided in-house. It may be located in Information Services or wherever appropriate as part of an organization-wide effort to provide services through the centralization of technology and call centres.

## Solutions Inc.

This branch of corporate HR consists of HR subject-matter experts—all of whom possess professional credentials acquired through advanced study and extensive experience. Their role is to transform the organization through training and development, labour relations, compensation design, strategic staffing, and organizational development. They are responsible for creating solutions to organizational problems and for preparing the organization to achieve its strategic intents. These experts act like consultants to the organization and operate on a for-profit basis—that is, their efforts are measurable and must result in an increase in performance measures. The consultants are on the cutting edge of research and put innovative, state-of-the-art theories into practice.

## Organization Capability Consultants

Operating as the third branch of corporate HR, the HR professionals in this unit are dispersed throughout the organization, providing guidance and assistance to operating units, with the goal of improving the effectiveness of the organization. If asked questions about changing benefits or dealing with a potential unionization threat, they hand out cards with the contact numbers for Services Inc. or Solutions Inc. They build organizational capabilities by aligning HR strategies, processes, and practices with the needs of the business. Their HR solutions should change existing processes to create "better-faster-cheaper" approaches.

From *Strategic Human Resource Management*, 1st edition by MELLO. © 2002. Reprinted with permission of South-Western, a division of Thomson Learning: www.thomsonrights.com. Fax 800-730-2215.

## Question

What are the advantages of this structure? Would managers and employees of an organization prefer this model to the traditional functional structure? Which structure do you think HR professionals would prefer and why?

# Endnotes

1. Rollo, J.A. 2002. *Strategic Human Resources Management*. Cincinnati, OH: South-Western Thompson Learning.

2. Jackson, S.E., and R.S. Schuller. 1995. "Understanding Human Resource Management in the Context of Organizations and Their Environments," *Annual Review of Psychology*, Vol. 46: 237–264.

3. Lawler, E.E., A.R. Levenson, and J.W. Boudreau. 2004. "HR Metrics and Analytics: Use and Impact," *Human Resource Planning* 27, 4, 27-36.

4. Roos, G., L. Fernstrom, and S. Pike. 2004. "Human Resource Management and Business Performance Measurement," *Measuring Business Excellence*, 8, 1, 28–37.

5. Ruona, W.E.A., and S. K. Gibson. 2004. "The Making of Twenty-First Century HR: An Analysis of the Convergence of HRM, HRD and OD." *Human Resource Management*, 42, 1, 49–66.

6. "The New HR Executive." Corporate Leadership Council, September 2000.

7. Ulrich, D., M. Losey, and G. Lake, eds. 1997. *Tomorrow's HR Management*. New York: Wiley and Sons.

8. Ferris, G.R., A.T. Hall, M.T. Royle, and J.J. Martocchio. 2004. "Theoretical Development in the Field of Human Resources Management: Issues and Challenges for the Future," *Organizational Analysis*, 12, 3, 231-254.

9. Amit, R., and M. Belcourt. 1999. "Human Resources Processes as a Source of Competitive Advantage." *European Management Journal*, Vol. 17, No. 2 (April).

10. Paauwe, J., and P. Boselie. 2003. "Challenging Strategic HRM and the Relevance of the Institutional Setting" *Human Resource Management Journal* 13, 3, 56-70.

11. Schuller, R.S., and S.E. Jackson 2005. "A Quarter-Century Review of Human Resource Management in the U.S: The Growth in Importance of the International Perspective," *Management Review*, 16, 1, 11-35.

12. Malley, M.O., and E. Lawler 2003. "What Is HR Good for Anyway?" *Across the Board*, 40, 4, 33-38.

13. Ulrich, D., and N. Smallwood. 2004. "Capitalizing on Capabilities." *Harvard Business Review*, June, 119-127.

14. Ulrich D., and N. Smallwood. 2005. "HR's New Role: Return on Intangibles." *Human Resource Management*, 44, 2, 137-142.

15. Weatherly, L. 2003. "Human Capital: The Elusive Asset." *Research Quarterly*, Society for Human Resources Management.

16. Becker, B.E., and M.A. Huselid. 1999. "Overview: Strategic Human Resources Management in Five Leading Firms," *Human Resource Management*, Vol. 38, No. 4 (Winter): 287-301.

17. Hoskisson, R.E., M.A. Hitt, and R. D. Ireland. 2004. *Competing for Advantage*. Mason, OH: Thompson South-Western.

18. Schuller and Jackson, 2005.

19. Wright, P.M., D.L. Smart, and G.C. McMahan. 1995. "Matches between Human Resources and Strategy Among NCAA Basketball Teams," *Academy of Management Journal*, Vol. 38, No. 4: 1052-1074.

20. Zedeck, S., and W.F. Cascio. 1984. "Psychological Issues in Personnel Decisions," *Annual Review of Psychology*, Vol. 35: 461-518.

21. Milkovich, G.T., and J.M. Newman. 1987. *Compensation*, 2nd ed. Dallas, TX: BPI.

22. Schuller, R.S., and S.E. Jackson. 1989. "Determinants of Human Resources Management Priorities and Implications for Industrial Relations," *Journal of Management*, Vol. 15, No. 1: 89-99.

23. King, A.S. 1995. "Multi-Phase Progression of Organizational Ideology: Commitment," *Mid Atlantic Journal*, Vol. 31, No. 2: 143-160.

24. Lengnick-Hall, C., and M. Lengnick-Hall. 1990. *Interactive Human Resource Management and Strategic Planning*: New York: Quorum Books.

25. Lengnick-Hall and Lengnick-Hall. 1988. "Strategic Human Resources Management: A Review of the Literature and a Proposed Typology," *Academy of Management Review*, Vol. 13, No. 3: 454–470.

26. MacMillan, I.C. 1983. "Seizing Competitive Advantage," *Journal of Business Strategy*: 43–57.

27. Anderson, W. 1997. "The Future of Human Resources: Forging Ahead or Falling Behind?" *Human Resources Management*, Vol. 36, No. 1 (Spring): 17–22.

28. Lengnick-Hall and Lengnick-Hall, 1988.

29. Lengnick-Hall and Lengnick-Hall, 1988.

30. Collins, J. 2001. *Good to Great*. New York: Harper Business.

31. Bamberger, P., and A. Feigenbaum. 1996. "The Role of Strategic Reference Points in Explaining the Nature and Consequences of Human Resources Strategy," *Academy of Management Review*, Vol. 21, No. 4 (October): 926–958.

32. Wright, P.M., S.S. Snell, and P.H.H. Jacobsen. 2004. "Current Approaches to HR Strategies: Inside-out versus Outside-In," *Human Resource Planning*, 27, 4, 36–47.

33. Bratton, D. 2000. *Best Practices in HR Strategy*. Toronto: Carswell Publishers.

34. Lawler, Levenson, and Boudreau, 2004.

35. Lawler, E.E., and S.A. Mohrman. 2003. "HR as a Strategic Partner: What Does It Take to Make It Happen?" *Human Resource Planning* 26, 3, 15–28.

36. www.Accenture.com, retrieved April 5, 2006.

37. Cascio, W. 1991. *Applied Psychology in Personnel Management*, 4th ed. Englewood Cliffs, NJ: Prentice Hall.

38. Buller, P.F. 1996. "Successful Partnerships: HR and Strategic Planning at Eight Top Firms," *Organizational Dynamics*: 27–43.

39. Cooke, R., and M. Armstrong. 1990. "The Search for Strategic HR," *Personnel Management* (December): 30-33.

40. Buyens, D., and A.D. Vos. 2001. "Perception of the Value of HR." *Human Resource Management Journal*, 11, 3, 70-90.

41. Panayotopoulour, L., and N. Papalexandris. 2004. "Examining the Link between Human Resource Management and Firm Performance." *Personnel Review*, 33, 5/6, 499–520.

42. Harrington, J. 1991. *Business Process Improvement*. New York: McGraw-Hill.

# Appendix

## HR Alignment with Two Strategies

## HR Alignment with the Low-Cost-Provider Strategy

A firm competing on cost leadership attempts to be the low-cost provider of a product or service within a marketplace. The product or service must be perceived by the consumer to be comparable to that offered by the competition and to have a price advantage. McDonald's uses this approach, as do Zellers and Timex.

Buyers are price sensitive, and businesses appeal to this price consciousness by providing products or services at prices lower than those of competitors. Survival is the ultimate goal, but organizations price low to gain market share (by underpricing competitors) or earn a higher profit margin by selling at the going market rate. This strategy requires the company to balance the delivery of a product that still appeals to customers with not spending too much on gaining market share. McDonald's could deliver a cheaper hamburger, but would it have any taste? McDonald's could underprice its competitors, but it may risk its survival by going too low. The key is to manage costs every year.

The adoption of a low-cost-provider strategy by a firm has immediate implications for HR strategy. Costs are an important element of this strategy, so labour costs are carefully controlled. Efficiency and controlling costs are paramount. The implications of a low-cost-provider strategy for six key components of HR are discussed below, but first we start with the job description of a typical employee working in a company that competes as a low-cost provider.

### The Employee

To keep wages low, jobs have to be of limited scope so that the company can hire people with minimal skills at low wages. The job requires highly repetitive and predictable behaviours. There is little need for cooperative or interdependent behaviours among employees. The company directs its efforts at doing the same or more with less and capitalizing on economies of scale. For example, in 1987 Toyota produced about 3.5 million vehicles a year with 25 000 production workers, the same number of workers it employed in 1966 when it produced only 1 million vehicles. Toyota achieved what low-cost providers want—an increase in productivity and reduced output cost per employee. Doing more with fewer employees is the goal of most organizations with a low-cost-provider strategy.

Risk taking on the part of the employee is not needed, but comfort with repetitive, unskilled work is necessary. Customers like those frequenting McDonald's are "trained" not to make idiosyncratic requests (such as a "medium-rare hamburger" or "hot mustard"), and so no unique response system is required. Employees are not expected to contribute ideas.

Another way to cut costs is to eliminate as many of the support or managerial layers as possible. The impact of cutting costs in this way is that employees may have to do more with less, make more decisions, and so on, which would require a more skilled employee. Alternatively, the jobs could be so tightly designed that little supervision is required, thus saving costs. Substituting technology for labour is another way to save costs.

We now look at six HR functions that will facilitate the personnel work at a low-cost-provider organization.

### HR Planning

At the entry level, succession planning is minimal, ensuring only the feeder line to the next level. Outside labour markets are monitored to ensure that entry-level people are in adequate supply. The availability and use of fringe workers—those who are retired, temporarily unemployed, students, and so on—is part of the planning strategy, particularly if the employment market is offering better opportunities to the normal supply of low-skilled workers.

At the executive level, succession management assumes the same importance as in other organizations.

## Selection

Recruitment is primarily at the entry, or lowest, level and is from the surrounding external labour market. Recruitment is by word of mouth, and application forms are available on-site, thus saving the costs of recruiting in newspapers. Most other positions are staffed internally through promotions. Thus, career paths are narrow.

## Compensation

A low-cost-provider strategy includes lower wages and fringe benefits. Beyond the legal minimum pay requirements, firms with this strategy carefully monitor what their competitors are paying in the local labour market. These firms' strategy tends to be a lag strategy, where they attempt to pay wages slightly below industry norms.

One way of achieving these lower costs is to outsource production to sites with lower labour costs. In the United States, this means moving production from high-wage states, such as New York, to low-wage states, such as New Mexico. In Canada, wages are very similar across provinces, so firms analyze wage rates in countries such as India, which pay employees substantially less for similar productivity. Outsourcing has also meant moving the work from highly unionized plants, where workers make $20 or more an hour, to nonunionized smaller sites, where workers are paid slightly more than the minimum wage.

Cost reduction in wages can also be achieved through the use of part-time workers, who receive no fringe benefits. Canadian organizations pay around 30% in fringe benefits, so the savings gained by using part-time workers is substantial among large employers. Food franchises employ part-time workers almost exclusively to reduce labour costs.

Pay for performance, such as incentive compensation that is linked to productivity, rewards individual effort. Group rewards are based on explicit, results-oriented criteria and the meeting of short-term performance goals.

Programs designed to reduce labour costs, such as outsourcing or using part-time workers, can easily be imitated by competitors, and so may produce no long-term competitive advantage. However, an innovative compensation scheme that cannot be duplicated by rivals may provide a competitive advantage. For example, in an arrangement between the Great Atlantic and Pacific Tea Company (A&P) and the United Food and Commercial Workers (UFCW), workers took a 25% pay cut in exchange for cash bonuses. If the store's employees could keep labour costs at 10% of sales by working more efficiently or generating more store traffic, they would receive a cash bonus of 1% of store sales. This arrangement resulted in an 81% increase in operating profits. However, unions were opposed to the spread of this practice, and so A&P's rivals in the low-margin food business were unable to reduce their labour costs in the same way.[1] Any incentives for performance would reward cost savings, or improvements in efficiency, as this example shows.

## Training

Training is minimal, as few skills are required. Any training is based on increasing efficiency in the current job, or specialization for the current position. Such training is fast and inexpensive. McDonald's can train a new hamburger flipper or cashier within a few hours. There is little to no investment in the long-term development of the employee, nor in the acquisition of skills for jobs other than the current one.

The training staff is lean, with the organization relying on outside suppliers for its limited training needs. However, most training takes place on the job in the form of direct instruction from or coaching by the supervisor. The jobs are so narrow in scope, so repetitive in nature, that little need for training exists.

## Performance Evaluation

Short-term results, with explicit and standardized criteria, are used to evaluate an employee's performance. The feedback is immediate and specific. Individuals are held accountable only for their own behaviour or results, not for that of the team or the company.[2] Only the supervisor provides input for the performance evaluation. Forms are kept to a minimum, and rating is done against check marks. Feedback, if based on a performance review, tends to be one-way, with little opportunity for the employee to debate the results or receive developmental feedback. Results are used for consideration for promotion.

## Labour Relations

Low-cost providers try to prevent the formation of a union because they believe that unions drive up wages. Unions find low-cost providers, such as McDonald's, difficult to unionize. (Employees working part-time hours have little interest in unionization because they believe that this is a part-time job that they will leave in the near future, and they are unlikely to benefit from belonging to a union, to which they have to pay fees. It is also difficult to organize those working night shifts.) Furthermore, employees quit often, and many low-cost providers absorb turnover rates of 300% annually as a cost of doing business. High turnover has the primary advantage of keeping compensation levels low.

Now that we have an idea of how HR programs align with a low-cost provider strategy, let us examine what these programs would be like under a differentiation strategy.

# HR Alignment with the Differentiation Strategy

In most markets, buyer preferences are too diverse to be satisfied by one undifferentiated product. Firms providing features that appeal to a particular market segment are said to compete on a differentiation strategy. A firm competing on the basis of a differentiation strategy will offer something unique and valuable to its customers. Mercedes-Benz, Polo Ralph Lauren, Rolex, and Hewlett-Packard's scientific instruments divisions are firms that compete successfully by charging a price premium for uniqueness. The primary focus is on the new and different. Observation, experience, and market research will establish what buyers consider important, what has value, and what buyers will pay for these features. Then the firm can offer a product or service that commands a premium price, increase unit sales within this niche, and gain buyer loyalty among those who value these features. The extra price outweighs the extra costs of providing these features.

A firm can differentiate itself from its competitors in many ways:

- having quality products,
- offering superior customer service,
- having a more convenient location,
- using proprietary technology,
- offering valuable features,
- demonstrating unique styling, and
- having a brand-name reputation.

These different features can be anything. Common examples show some firms competing on service (Four Seasons Hotels), engineering design (BMW), image (Polo Ralph Lauren), reliability (Bell), a full range of products or services (Procter & Gamble), technological leadership (Corel), and quality (Honda).

Most of the time, these competitive advantages are combined, such as by linking quality products with proprietary technology and superior customer service, thus providing the buyer with more value for the money. The key in this strategy is to provide the differentiation that is perceived to be of value to customers while keeping costs down. For example, a slice of lemon in a glass of ice water delivered to the table is an obvious way to differentiate the restaurant, but at low cost. After-dinner mints are less expensive than valet parking, but may be equally appreciated by diners.

A differentiation strategy calls for innovation and creativity among employees. HRM is affected in fundamentally different ways in organizations that want to use employees' brains rather than their limited (mainly manual) skills in the low-cost-provider strategy.

The starting point for aligning HR programming with a differentiation strategy is the employee.

## The Employee

Organizations competing on a differentiation strategy require from their employees creative behaviour, a long-term focus, interdependent activity, and some risk taking, as well as an ability to work in an ambiguous and unpredictable environment. Their employees' skills need to be broad, and employees must be highly involved with the firm. Organizations encourage employees to make suggestions, through both informal and formal suggestion systems, for new and improved ways of doing their job. Employees at Corning Canada Inc., for example, submit their suggestions to their supervisors, who review them formally and give feedback directly to the employee. Contrast this with the traditional suggestion box, which many employees view as a recycling bin because of the lack of timely feedback.

To encourage innovative behaviour, 3M has an informal policy of allowing employees to "bootleg" about 15% of their time on their own projects. Job classifications are flexible.

## HR Planning

In a company that has a differentiation strategy and that recognizes people are the key to competitive advantage, HR planning is taken very seriously. For example, at Sumitomo Metals in Japan, the business planning group reports to HR because the company understands that identifying what needs to be done is less difficult than planning how to do it.

Succession management is critical as employees have to possess many attributes to move ahead in the organization. Thus, a strong emphasis on developing skills for the future is part of the promotion policy. Investments in career moves, training, and developmental experiences are substantial. Long-term job security and reciprocal loyalty are the norm.

## Selection

Companies with a differentiation strategy need employees who have a broad range of skills and the ability to learn from others. An innovative atmosphere requires employees who are self-motivated and do not require a great deal of supervision. Employees are selected for their abilities to think creatively, to be flexible in work attitudes, and to be able to work in teams. However, selection for these characteristics is more difficult and usually involves team interviews and behaviourally based evidence of innovative performance. Employees are normally recruited through reputation (word of mouth) or through graduate schools. Some testing for creative ability may be used.

## Compensation

Compensation plans affect employee behaviour more directly than most HR practices. For example, Drucker describes a compensation scheme he implemented at General Electric (GE) in which pay for performance was based only on the previous year's results.[3] As such, for ten years, GE lost its capacity for innovation because investing in innovation affects expenses and decreases profits, so everyone postponed spending on innovation.

However, compensation is carefully designed in firms that have a differentiation strategy. Pay rates may be slightly below average market rates but there are substantial opportunities to increase those base levels through incentive pay. Pay for performance is a large part of the compensation package and will be dependent on individual, group, and corporate results. These results are a combination of process and financial criteria and are set in advance, usually on a yearly basis.

There is a more varied mix of types of compensation; individuals may receive salary, bonus, or stock option incentives.

Internal equity is of greater concern than equity with the external market. Egalitarian pay structures are associated with greater product quality.[4]

Nonmonetary rewards also play a larger role in HR strategy in these types of firms. At Honda, the team that designs a unique transportation vehicle is awarded a trip to Japan.

## Training

Companies with a differentiation strategy have a strong training team. The focus of training is on both skills and attitudes. Process skills, such as decision making, the ability to work in teams, and creative thinking, are emphasized as much as skills needed for the current job.

The training itself is seen as an opportunity to generate new ideas and procedures. Indeed, customers and cross-functional teams might be included in the training program.

Developmental experiences are encouraged. The value of working in another division or another country is recognized and encouraged. Employees receive promotions or other job opportunities based, partially, on their willingness to undertake training and their track record in learning.

## Performance Evaluation

In companies with a differentiation strategy, performance appraisal is based not on short-term results but instead on the long-term implications of behaviour. Processes that are deemed to lead to better results in the long term are rewarded. Thus, companies encourage and appraise attitudes such as empowerment, diversity sensitivity, and teamwork in an effort to build future bottom-line outcomes. Working beyond the job is encouraged, not punished. Failure is tolerated, although management tries to distinguish between bad luck and bad judgment or stupidity.

Evaluation tends to be based on a mixture of individual and group (and sometimes corporate) criteria. Thus, an individual might be evaluated on his or her ability to achieve results and to work as a member of the team, the group's performance might be measured against established quotas, and the company in terms of its overall financial performance.

Appraisals that include input from employees, functional experts, peers, and so on—360° evaluations—are the norm. Organizations in the service sector are more likely to include customers as sources of input for performance appraisal.

## Labour Relations

Any structure or process that reduces the capacity to be innovative and flexible is difficult to tolerate. Traditional unions, with rigid collective agreements, are encouraged to work collectively toward a new union–management relationship. This relationship is characterized by shared information such as open books, shared decision making about best approaches, and shared responsibility for solving problems as they arise.

# Endnotes

1. Schueller, R.S., and S.E. Jackson. 1987. "Linking Competitive Strategies with Human Resource Management Practices," *Academy of Management Executive*. Vol. 1, No. 3: 207–219.

2. Ulrich, D. 1991. "Using Human Resources for Competitive Advantage." In R.H. Kilman and I. Kilman, eds., *Making Organizations Competitive*. San Francisco: Jossey-Bass.

3. Drucker, P.F. 2002. "They're Not Employees, They're People," *The Harvard Business Review*, 80, 2, 70–77.

4. Belcourt, M., and S. Thornhill. 1999. "Growing from the Inside Out: Human Resources Practices for Growth Strategies." Proceedings of the Administrative Sciences Association of Canada.

# Chapter 3

# Environmental Influences on HRM

## Chapter Learning Objectives

After reading this chapter, you should be able to

- Identify the sources that HR planners use to keep current with business and HR trends.
- List several of the methods—including trend analysis, the Delphi technique, scenario planning, and impact analysis—used to predict future trends.
- Understand how environmental scanning is practised.
- Discuss the challenges in scanning the environment.
- Delineate the environmental factors, such as the economic climate, the labour force, the political and regulatory context, and the social and cultural climate, that influence the practice of HRM.
- Describe the role of the stakeholder, and list several examples.

IBM is committed to building a workforce as broad and diversified as the customer base it serves in 165 countries. The company's key question is "Do we look like our customers, at all levels of our business?" U.S.–headquartered IBM's definition of diversity is reflective of its customer base, and includes differences such as culture, lifestyle, age, religion, economic status, sexual orientation, gender identity and expression, marital status, thought, and geography. The company has created eight executive task forces (Asian, Black, Hispanic, Native American, Gay/Lesbian, People with Disabilities, Men, and Women) to look at IBM through the lens of their group and answer four questions: What is required for your group to feel welcomed and valued here? What can IBM do, working with your group, to maximize your productivity? What can IBM do to influence the buying decisions of your group? What outside groups, which reflect the interests of your group, should IBM establish a relationship with? As a result of employee feedback, in Canada, IBM developed separate washing facilities for Muslim employees who must cleanse their feet before they pray. As the vice-president of Global Workplace Diversity states, "Workforce diversity is about effectively reaching customers and markets."[1]

To understand strategic HR planning, we must understand how HRM is affected by the environment in which it operates. Most HR managers actively scan their surroundings, looking at cultural changes or changes in laws and technologies that might affect the way that HR is practised. A good source is the daily news, where HR professionals can learn about such major legislative changes as Ontario's plan to eliminate mandatory retirement. HR planners want to track trends that influence the way in which employees can be managed. For example, the elimination of mandatory retirement affects the way performance appraisals will be conducted with long-term employees, benefit plans, pension contribution plans, health and safety accommodation—nearly everything! HR strategists need information about their environment in order to exploit the opportunities or cope with the threats.

We will look first at the sources and methods HR planners use to track these trends.

## Environmental Scanning Sources and Methods

Managers have to develop strategies and keep a keen eye on what is happening in the world outside the organization. **Environmental scanning** is the systematic monitoring of the major factors influencing the organization to identify trends that might affect the formulation and implementation of both organizational and HR strategies.

**environmental scanning**

systematic monitoring of trends affecting the organization

"Environment" is a fuzzy term. It means anything outside organizational boundaries. Even talking about an environment suggests that the environment is different, and not part of the organization. But the organization and the environment are tightly integrated. Managers are influenced by the culture in which they operate—that is, they are not independent of the environment. A manager in Vancouver will treat her employees differently than a manager in New Delhi, and the employees in each city would have expectations about how managers should supervise. Rather than attempt a definition of the word "environment," we will simply list the methods used to scan the environment and the environmental factors that seem to influence HRM strategy formulation. HR practitioners who understand the competitive environment and its implications for their organizations can then develop practices that are a source of competitive advantage.[2]

The analysis of the external environment consists of these stages:

- *Scanning:* an attempt to identify early signals of changes and trends in the environment. This information is ambiguous, incomplete, and unconnected.
- *Monitoring:* a systematic approach to following some key indicators that may affect the organization, such as absenteeism rate in the working population due to a certain type of illness.
- *Forecasting:* after monitoring a trend, an attempt to project the possible impact on the organization.
- *Assessing:* the analyst attempts to describe the impact of the monitored trend on the organization, and makes a judgment of the probability of each of several possible outcomes.[3] For example, what would be the impact of a trend in the increase in health consciousness? A food manufacturer might lower the amount of fat and cholesterol in its products.[4] An organization, eager to be seen as a best employer, might change the menu in the cafeteria, as well as introduce physical fitness activities on-site.

In the past, HR managers monitored changes that might affect their programs and policies by reading newspapers or trade publications. They kept informed of issues regarding employment laws by subscribing to particular news services, and by being a member of the provincial HR association. The scanning method was not perfect, because no one can accurately predict all the forces that will shape the future workplace and the workforce. However, some sources of information and scanning methods can help us do a better job. The next section describes the sources that HR professionals might use to monitor trends in the environment.

## Sources of Information

When developing strategies and determining their likely impact on an organization, HR professionals rely on many sources of information. These include publications, professional associations, conferences and seminars, and professional consultants.

RPC 3.1

## Publications

HR professionals actively scan Canadian newspapers, business publications, and HR magazines, journals, and newsletters. We are fortunate to have access to not only a wide range of Canadian sources of information but also the extensive publication network originating in the United States. The authors' experiences suggest that Canadian HR trends lag behind U.S. trends by a year or two. For example, workplace violence and employee retention were hot issues in the United States three years before they became important in Canada. Thus, reading U.S. publications acts as an early warning signal for Canadian HR professionals. HR practitioners subscribe to many of the publications listed in HR Planning Notebook 3.1.

---

### HR Planning Notebook 3.1

#### Publications of Interest to HR Professionals

**Canadian**

*Canadian Business*
*Canadian Compensation News*
*Canadian HR Reporter*
*Canadian Journal of Learning*
*The Globe and Mail Report on Business*
*HR Professional*
*Ivey Business Quarterly*
*The Training Report*
*Workplace today*

**U.S.**

*BusinessWeek*
*Fortune*
*HR Focus*
*HR Magazine*
*HR News*
*People Management*
*Profit*
*Training*
*Work Week*

**Research Journals**

*Academy of Management Executive*
*Academy of Management Review*

*Benefits Canada*
*Business Horizons*
*Business Quarterly*
*California Management Review*
*Canadian Journal of Administrative Studies*
*Canadian Labour Law Reporter*
*Compensation*
*Compensation and Benefits Review*
*European Management Journal*
*Harvard Business Review*
*Human Resource Management*
*HR Research Quarterly*
*Journal of Applied Psychology*
*Journal of Business Ethics*
*Journal of Labor Research*
*Journal of Management*
*Journal of Staffing and Recruitment*
*Labor Studies Journal*
*Management Review*
*Occupational Outlook Quarterly*
*Organizational Behavior and Human Performance*
*Personnel*
*Personnel Journal*
*Personnel Psychology*
*Public Personnel Management*
*Training and Development Journal*

---

## Associations of Interest to HR Professionals

| | |
|---|---|
| Administrative Sciences Association of Canada (HR division) | Conference Board of Canada |
| | Human Resource Planning Society |
| Canadian Association of Management Consultants | International Association for Human Resources Information Management Association |
| Canadian Council of Human Resource Associations– links to all provincial HR associations | North American Human Resources Management Association |
| Canadian Human Resource Planners | |
| Canadian Industrial Relations Association | Society for Human Resources Management |
| Canadian Payroll Association | Society for Industrial and Organizational Psychology |
| Canadian Public Personnel Managers Association | |
| Canadian Society for Training and Development | World at Work |

## Professional Associations

Canadian HR professionals and executives belong to a number of organizations that publish newsletters and updates on current events. Many of these organizations, such as the Human Resources Professionals Association of Ontario, have committees that actively scan the regulatory scene for upcoming changes. Some, like the Conference Board of Canada, conduct research with their members to track trends. Relevant associations are listed in HR Planning Notebook 3.2.

## Conferences and Seminars

**RPC** 3.2

Most professionals keep current and even ahead of emerging trends by attending conferences, seminars, and workshops in Canada and the United States. Most provincial HR associations hold annual conferences. The Human Resources Professionals Association of Ontario, for example, attracts over 3000 participants to its conference each February. Such events, including those sponsored by private organizations, are widely publicized in HR publications such as those listed in HR Planning Notebook 3.1.

## Professional Consultants

**RPC** 3.3

Organizations that have an active interest in understanding the influence of potential trends often hire consultants to research or interpret these trends for them. The Hudson Institute is an example of a firm that specializes in this form of consulting. Most organizations have a person on staff, often the librarian, whose job is to bring information to the consultants' attention by actively scanning multiple sources.

 **3.4**

# Methods of Forecasting

HR professionals can use several methods to generate predictions about the future or extrapolate from current events to determine their impact on HR practices. These methods include trend analysis, the Delphi technique, impact analysis, and scenario planning.

## Trend Analysis

**trend analysis**

a forecasting method that extrapolates from historical organizational indices

**Trend analysis** is a quantitative approach that attempts to forecast future personnel needs based on extrapolating information from historical changes in one or more organizational indices. A single index, such as sales, might be used. However, more complex modelling or multiple predictive techniques, used by professional planners, rely on a combination of several factors. These methods are described in Chapter 7.

## Delphi Technique

The Delphi technique is a process in which the forecasts and judgments of a selected group of experts are solicited and summarized in an attempt to determine the future of employment. This method, too, is described in Chapter 7. However, HR Planning Today 3.1 describes the Delphi technique used by the Society for Human Resources Management.

---

## HR Planning Today 3.1

### The Experts Predict the Future of HRM

In 2004–05, the Society for Human Resources Management attempted to forecast the workplace through the use of environmental scanning. They collected data from a wide variety of sources, and then used teams of individuals to filter the information, in order to target that which is truly critical. They also solicited opinions from HR expert panels and opinion leaders. They identified the top ten trends:

- rise in health care costs,
- focus on domestic safety and security,
- use of technology to communicate with employees,
- growing complexity of legal compliance,

- use of technology to perform transactional HR functions,
- focus on global security,
- preparing for the next wave of retirement and labour shortages,
- use and development of e-learning,
- exporting of manufacturing jobs to developing countries, and
- changing definition of family.

---

Source: Schramm, J. (2004, June). *SHRM 2004–2005 Workplace Forecast: A Strategic Outlook*, Alexandria, VA: Society for Human Resources Management. Reprinted with permission.

## Impact Analysis

**Impact analysis**, too, looks backward in order to look forward. Past trends are analyzed by a panel of experts who then attempt to identify future probable events and study their effects on the extrapolated trend.[5] Unlike trend analysis, which is an objective statistical technique, impact analysis relies on subjective, but expert, judgments.

## Scenario Planning

This technique consists of imaging a future radically different from an extrapolation of present trends. **Scenario planning** creates a number of plausible "futures." Royal Dutch Shell uses scenarios extensively to plan long-range (20- and 30-year) futures by understanding trends, forces, and tradeoffs. For example, the company predicts three scenarios that will shape the business environment in 2025:

- "a low-trust globalization" scenario, where the focus is on security and efficiency at the cost of social cohesion,
- an "open doors" scenario, where a pragmatic world emphasizes social cohesion and efficiency, with the market providing solutions to the crises of security and trust, and
- a "flag" scenario, where in a dogmatic world, security and community values are emphasized at the expense of efficiency.

You can read about the process Royal Dutch Shell used to arrive at these scenarios by going to its website at www.shell.com.

Other methods for assessing the future include the nominal group technique and questionnaires, and are all discussed in Chapter 7.

An excellent evaluation of all these approaches can be found in Rothwell and Kazanas.[6] Readers are invited to experience a nominal group technique as part of a group exercise at the end of this chapter.

We have described rearview-mirror ways of scanning the environment. If you examine studies or articles that are supposed to predict the future, you will see that they contain, for the most part, simple extensions of present trends. We assume that tomorrow will be much like yesterday, with minor variations. HR planners recognize that there are problems with these attempts to interpret the environment because unpredictable events such as 9/11 and SARS do happen. At the time this text was written, I predicted the trends described in HR Planning Today 3.2. It will be interesting to assess the accuracy of these guesses in a few years.

## Challenges in Environmental Scanning

There are problems in scanning the environment. These include our inability to accurately predict the future and to isolate what really is important to HR. Can we say what the world will look like in 2050? In 1900, could those working in HRM have predicted what it would look like in 2000? Not likely, because the field of HRM did not exist then. One hundred years ago,

**impact analysis**

a forecasting method in which past trends are analyzed by a panel of experts who then predict the probability of future events

**scenario planning**

a method of creating future scenarios that differ radically from those created by extrapolation of present trends

**ⓇⓅⒸ 3.5**

## Five Mega Trends

While outsourcing and diversity management occupy the headlines in today's HR news, I predict these will fade into standard practice in the short run. The future of HR, in my opinion, will be transformed over the next decade in five major areas: technology, new demands for HR expertise in measurement, branding, employee retention, and ethics.

This prediction is based on hundreds of conversations I have had in the past year, along with my own extensive experience in this ever-changing industry. Because it is my job to keep up with HR trends, I have the luxury of being able to read vast amounts of information from a variety of sources, including academic journals written by experts who have never worked in HR, e-mails from frustrated HR professionals, and essays about the future of HR written by HRM graduate students. From all these perspectives, here are my thoughts on the five mega trends coming soon to an HR department near you.

### 1. E-Everywhere

Technology is the key that opens the door to the outsourcing and offshoring of HR functions. I am hearing now that the major reason HR departments are outsourcing many of their functions is to gain access to sophisticated technology, and not necessarily to save money. Although technology is used in every organization for basic functions like payroll and benefits, the major shift emerging is the use of technology to support almost everything HR does: training, performance appraisals, recruitment, selection, etc.

I foresee technology having a dramatic effect on the structure of the HR department. There will be three levels of service:

- **Contact level one:** This will handle the vast majority of the HR work, and will be focused on efficiency, cost savings, and doing the basics right. The intranet will be used for all routine transaction work and service all employees individually. It will represent 50% of all HR work. Another 30% will be handled by call centres. Routine questions or cases (such as how to identify a relevant training course or how to terminate an employee) will be handled by a call centre employee

working from a script. IBM has adopted a model like this, and reports the reduction of costs over four years as 30%, 10%, 8%, and 5%. With 625 000 employees, the IBM service centre processes 3.4 million online transactions and 1.7 million telephone enquiries annually. IBM's customer satisfaction rating is 90%. The company's goal is to move from a ratio of one HR staff for every 100 employees (a typical ratio) to 1:1000.

- **Contact level two:** This will account for about 15% of HR work, and will be a centre of expertise focusing on effectiveness. These experts will be fully knowledgeable about best practices, benchmarks, and trends in their functional areas of compensation, labour relations, etc. HR experts will be used as consultants to improve individual and group productivity by working with managers.

- **Contact level three:** This will represent about 5% of HR work, and will operate as a centre of excellence, aligning HR practices and policies with organizational strategy. These centres will add value by designing HR systems for restructuring, mergers, rapid growth, and any strategic imperative. The ability to manage culture and organizational change will be a critical skill for the HR professional.

What does this mean? That 70% of all HR work can be handled by software or low levels of expertise, and can therefore be outsourced and devolved to line managers. The rest of the work will be high level and require expert knowledge.

### 2. Making Metrics Matter

I have sat on many boards, yet I've never heard a board member ask the right questions about the management of the organization's most important asset—human capital. For example, which HR practice would provide a better rate of return, or who is the industry leader in HR? Why does HR not report on these critical measures?

The head of the HR function is not supplying this information for many reasons. The first is that measurement of the practices of HR will add another 5%

to the cost of the program, and there is the high risk that the evaluation will not be able to demonstrate a link between the practice and the anticipated effect. This could be professional suicide. Some argue that it is difficult to measure human behaviour, or that they cannot control either the labour market or the way individual managers treat their employees. But marketing cannot control product quality and finance cannot control the interest rate, and yet these functions are held accountable.

Executives and CEOs, who have largely bought into the idea that employees are valuable assets and that the HR practices probably impact organizational results, will be demanding proof, or they will return to viewing HR as the "paper pushing, picnic planning, policy police."

We can provide this evidence and we will be expected to. Multiple studies have established that HR practices can have an impact on organizational performance in measurable ways. This research has demonstrated that sophisticated and integrated HRM practices have a positive effect on employee performance by increasing knowledge, skills, and abilities; improving organizational commitment; reducing shirking; and increasing the retention of competent employees. These best practices have a direct and economically significant effect on a firm's financial performance.

When asking for more resources, we will have to provide a cost-benefit analysis, just like every other function requesting capital funds. No longer will we simply be able to say that we will train 150 employees in this new course, because the CEO will say "So what?" We will have to demonstrate that the training course will result in a 10% improvement in customer satisfaction, which, in turn, will lead to a 1% decrease in complaints, etc. We will have to respond to the following questions when asking for resources to implement any of these programs: What impact does an empowered workforce have on the bottom line? What will the business process re-engineering accomplish? Why should we select our next generation on attributes of emotional intelligence, and where is the empirical evidence that this works? This requirement forces HR professionals to use the same language of business as the other units, and provides a rationale for making decisions. We will be able to demonstrate added value.

## 3. Employer Branding

Private-sector companies understand competition for customers. HR departments will soon adopt their language and methods in the competition for candidates. Using very sophisticated analyses, we will assess our successes and failures in recruitment and selection. We will adopt the use of focus groups so that we can learn why candidates are attracted to us, and what particular groups of potential employees want from work and their "employers of choice." We will become experts in identifying the unique attributes that define our organization and use these to build a brand.

The goal, of course, is to differentiate your organization as an employer from your main competitors. For example, Husky Injection Molding Systems Ltd. has an employer reputation as an employer that cares, investing deeply in employee health and wellness. CIBC is building a reputation as a family-friendly place to work, largely due to its funding of emergency child care facilities. 3M is known as the place to work if you are innovative.

The employer brand aligns with the customer brand. Southwest Airlines advertises the fact that employees provide humorous service, and that it is a fun place to work. I foresee a position in the HR department called the HR brand manager, responsible for the employer brand, and leading the efforts to define the brand and gain recognition for that brand. Employer of choice will cease to be a meaningful brand, replaced by a simple but sophisticated employee value proposition communicated persistently and consistently. For example, the Vancouver health region captured what employees had identified as the main appeal of this employer: "a small, friendly full service hospital." The health region then built this slogan in all their recruitment posters, newspaper advertisements, and pamphlets.

## 4. Retention of Key Employees

The Conference Board of Canada estimates that 58% of Canadian employees would consider a move to another employer. While organizations need some churn to bring in fresh talent (new ideas, new enthusiasm, new approaches), most organizations want to keep the best employees. Holding on to talented employees is important for several reasons. The first is that certain occupations

*(Continued)*

will face labour shortages. Another reason is that workers are more mobile, i.e., less attached to any organization. As employers have abandoned the concept of job security, so too have people abandoned the concept of job loyalty.

In the near future, we will regularly hire private companies to conduct anonymous exit interviews, so that we learn the real reasons (not the safe reasons of "better money" or "better jobs") employees leave the organization. We will learn, through continued monitoring of the culture within our companies, to understand what makes our particular organization a compelling place to stay. But the goal will not be to keep all employees, only those with high degrees of organizational commitment. Those employees who are unmotivated or mediocre performers will be managed out of the organization.

## 5. The HR Consultant with a Conscience

HR has traditionally been seen as the function that guards organizational integrity. From its historical role as a sounding board for employee concerns, the HR professional has retained the role of the conscience; the one person who consistently asks "Is this the right thing to do?" (Ethical values refer to doing the right thing, which is different than the compliance role, which focuses on not violating any laws or regulations). There are several evolving tasks under this "consultant with a conscience" role.

The first of these is that, in light of the scandals at Enron and Hollinger, someone in the organization has to take responsibility for ensuring that employee behaviour is ethical. The HR function is the natural choice, as it can ensure ethical behaviour in various ways.

HR is currently perceived as representing both management and employees. However, there is some evidence that HR is beginning to represent, or at least be aware of, the perspectives of other stakeholders. What is in the best long-term interests of not only shareholders but also other stakeholders, such as communities and environmentalists? Can HR evolve into a stewardship role where like a farmer, or manager of forests, the long-term sustainability interests are equal or more important than the short-term interests of shareholders and even executives, whose performance bonuses depend upon short-term results? The focus would be on developing these "human" resources, and sustaining the organization for the long term.

In this sustainability perspective, the vice-president of HR acts as consultant with a conscience to the board. As a consultant with expertise in human behaviour, the HR head can be used by the board to not only explain the compensation packages for executives, but also comment on the long-term (and even dysfunctional) implications of these pay-for-performance packages. The HR person could be the insider who can be contacted directly by board members, much like they can currently bypass the CEO to contact the audit committee or deal with external auditors. I see this as one small step toward rebuilding trust in the boards of directors and the integrity of the organization.

Source: Adapted from M. Belcourt, "Five Mega Trends," *HR Professional Magazine*, December 2005, 19–24. Reprinted with permission.

there were no payroll and benefits clerks. Even 20 years ago, it would have been difficult to forecast the flattening of organizations; downsizing; the impact of technology, outsourcing, and telecommuting; and a range of other changes we now experience. Most HR strategists limit themselves to a two- to three-year time frame and extrapolate from current trends.

## Isolating the Critical from the Insignificant

So much change is happening in so many arenas that scanners have trouble picking out the truly important events. As we enter the new millennium, we cannot determine which current issues are important enough to cause a shift in the way we practise HR. For example, which of these HR issues, taken from headlines in HR publications as this text is being written, are critical and which will prove insignificant: War for talent? Outsourcing all HR functions? Workplace privacy?

The other difficulty is that few trends exist in isolation—no issue is an island. Take the issues of the difficulty of finding employees where labour shortages exist. There is a growing concern that universities will be unable to find enough professors to replace all those expected to retire within the next ten years. If this problem is addressed in isolation, two solutions might be to (1) increase the number of spaces for doctoral students who then graduate to become professors, and/or (2) recruit professors from other countries. But other trends may influence the ability to find enough professors. The policy of mandatory retirement is being challenged through the courts. If the court challenges are successful in every province, some professors will not be forced to retire, so the shortages will not be as great as expected.

Just as there is a reaction for every action, for every trend there is a countertrend, and countertrends seem to develop in tandem with the trends. As globalization increases, so does "localization," and ethnic pride in customs and culture rises. This is not the same as thinking that the pendulum will always swing back. Trends are not cyclical in the sense that a trend appears and then disappears, returning the world to its original state. The current focus on work–life balance cannot be viewed just as a fad, with the resultant expectation that there will be another replacement fad within a few years. The concepts underlying work–life balance will be imbedded in our view of work, just as safety and labour laws are now permanently imbedded in the culture of work.

HR planners do not react only to current events; sometimes they attempt to shape the issues that will affect their practice.

## A Proactive Approach

Some HR managers do not like passively observing the game through their windows; they want to participate and influence how the game is played. Thus, we find most professional associations have a group that lobbies for legislation that will favour the association membership. Most have public relations firms that try to shape the perception of the profession and its goals (thus influencing public opinion favourably toward regulations). For example, workplace standards may be reviewed and focus groups may be held across a company with active participation of the HR professional association.

 3.6

Despite the challenges of environmental scanning, most HR strategists do monitor the environment and look for changes that may affect HR. We will now examine the major areas that these strategists typically scan.

## Environmental Factors

Nearly everything, from birth rates to pollution levels, could be said to influence organizational and HR strategies. However, there are a number of factors that HR strategists monitor more closely because these factors are more closely related to HRM. Following this tradition, we have included factors such as the economic climate, the labour force, the political and regulatory context, and issues related to technology, demographics, and social values and norms. For each factor we have provided some current examples, keeping in mind that such examples quickly lose their relevance.

## Economic Climate

The economic indices that we are so familiar with from the media are also important to HR strategists. Let us look at a few examples of how these indices influence HR managers who are

- concerned with the unemployment rate because it affects their ability to recruit;
- worried about the value of the Canadian dollar because it affects the company's ability to sell products internationally, and thus affects employment levels;
- troubled by the amount of public debt because it affects business taxes, and, therefore, a company's ability to survive and grow; and
- anxious about interest rates because they affect how much a company is willing to borrow to grow its business and invest in employees.

Interestingly, sometimes HR acts as predictor of the economy. A drop in demand for contingent, temporary, and contract employees (as reported by search and placement firms) can predict an economic slowdown before these changes are reported by firms in their financial statements.

It could be argued that anything to do with the economy touches the HR management. However, it is impossible to deal with every economic indicator and change. We will provide two examples: the economic shift from hand work (manual production) to head work (the use of mental processes), and globalization.

## From the Industrial Revolution to the Knowledge Revolution

The economy is shifting from one based on the production of goods to one in which services are delivered. One historic moment in this shift occurred when Wal-Mart became the largest corporation in America—the first service company to rise to number one among the Fortune 500 and pass General Motors (GM) and Exxon. The number of workers in the service sector increased from 40% of the workforce in 1945 to 75% in 2005.[7] These services may be "hard," such as the kinds of services a hairstylist offers, or "soft," such as the selling of information. The types of employees needed by the diminishing industrial sector are different from those needed by the service sector.

We are facing a paradox in this new century. On one hand, companies are downsizing and outsourcing. On the other, they are claiming that employees are a source of strategic advantage, and they are facing recruitment and retention problems with employees. Thus, for some types of jobs (low skilled), the economic climate consists of part-time workers, contract workers, and those working for outsourcing organizations. For jobs requiring scientific and technological competencies there is high demand, and organizations must compete on compensation, culture, and benefits. Futurists say that the times of cost containment and downsizing are over; organizations will be focusing on innovation and exploring new growth opportunities. The kind of employees they will be looking for are multiskilled, e-literate, entrepreneurial, and innovative.[8]

## Globalization

Another trend to watch is increasing globalization. Globalization is the growth in flows of trade and financial capital across borders. Globalization affects sovereignty, prosperity, jobs, wages, and social legislation. McDonald's has a great deal of experience in globalization and when the company launches a restaurant in a new country, it works closely with all disciplines to "McDonaldize" a team, so that they know the business inside out. Eighteen to 24 months before the restaurant is opened, the company starts with HR. Some of the HR challenges it faced in other countries included the fact that part-time employment and multifunctional jobs did not exist.[9] HR managers will need to develop international competencies, as discussed in Chapter 11.

## The Labour Market

A labour market is the area from which an organization recruits its employees. Such an area may be metropolitan, regional, provincial, national, or international. The number of people available for work depends on factors such as the unemployment rate, geographic migration, graduation rates from educational institutions, and so on. However, labour markets in the 21st century will become international. Ford, GM, and Nestlé already employ more people outside their countries than within. Because of India's huge population of English-speaking software engineers, companies such as Microsoft have employment centres in India. The labour market is changing, as highlighted in HR Planning Notebook 3.3.

The labour market influences an organization's ability to implement strategy. An organization may decide to enter the high-tech field, only to discover itself unable to recruit enough electrical engineers to meet its personnel requirements, and so must abandon this particular strategy. Companies wishing to grow are facing problems in recruiting and retaining qualified scientists and technologists. You are probably familiar with the phrase "war for talent," indicating that companies are launching campaigns to recruit and retain key people. There is a growing concern with the division of labour in Canada: the *shortage* of people with the right skills who can earn good money and expect benefits, and the *surplus* of people available to work in "McJobs." Human Resources Development Canada (HRDC), the government department concerned with employment issues, is addressing this concern through its National Skills agenda, which will encourage companies to increase their training budgets by one-third (to be in line with other countries), and by requiring that 65% of adult immigrants have post-secondary education.[10]

### Canadian Labour Market Facts

- Almost all labour market growth will be from immigrants.
- Visible-minority populations are growing fast and rise from the current 13.44% of the population up to 23% of the Canadian population by 2017, meaning that about one of every five Canadians will be a member of a visible-minority group.
- The number of Aboriginals in Canada grew by 22% since the last census in 1991, compared to a non-Aboriginal population growth of 2.4%. Aboriginals now make up 3.3% of the population.
- The participation rate of women grew by 13% since 1991, compared to that of men at 6%. Women now represent 46.8% of the workforce.

- The number of jobs requiring a university education grew by one-third over the last ten years; those requiring a community college diploma grew by 3.3% and those requiring a high school education decreased by 2%. Eighty percent of jobs require some postsecondary education and training. However, for every degreed professional there is a need for 15 to 20 technical support jobs.

Sources: Statistics Canada, *Census of Population 2001*, Catalogue No. 92-377-Xie; Industry Canada Small Business Research and Policy, *Small Business Financing Profiles: Visible Minority Entrepreneurs; March 2005*; Statistics Canada, *Labour Force Survey*, Catalogue no. 71-001-XIE, October 25, 2005. Salopek, J.J. 2004 "Straws in the Wind," *Training and Development*, 58, 1, 16.

**RPC 3.7**

## Political and Legislative Factors

Governments, both provincial and federal, can influence the business environment through political programs that result in changes to laws and regulations. For example, governments that wish to improve the climate for job creation emphasize tax cuts, provide tax incentives to develop jobs, increase job-training opportunities, and create balanced labour legislation. Governments can spur economic growth by reducing the public debt, balancing the budget, and cutting taxes. Such measures encourage businesses to invest in that province (or Canada) and encourage consumers to spend, resulting in more jobs.

The employer–employee relationship is governed by a legal framework that includes common law (judicial precedents that do not derive from specific laws), constitutional law (e.g., the Charter of Rights and Freedoms, acts of federal and provincial parliaments), and contract law (e.g., collective agreements). You are probably familiar with some of these laws. For example, each province has employment standards that establish the maximum number of hours to be worked each day and human rights legislation that prohibits discrimination on the basis of sex, race, and so on. Additionally, governments often enact legislation that affects HR practices directly. For example, the Government of Quebec mandates that every organization must spend 2% of its payroll on employee training.

The actions organizations take have to be legal, and the law is relatively clear on what is and is not legal. A company may be competing on a low-cost strategy and be able to find people willing to work for $3 an hour. The employment standards legislation in each province, however, governs the minimum wage, and in no province is it as low as $3 an hour. Therefore, cost savings have to be achieved elsewhere in order to implement a low-cost strategy; it is not possible to do it through wages that fall below the legal requirements.

The decisions that are not governed by law are usually governed by morals or an ethical code. The concept of ethics is not as clear as laws are. Ethical and moral decisions and practices go beyond the law, from "you must" to "you should." An employer can require an employee to work overtime and not pay him or her overtime rates (as required by the law). How? The employer gives the employee the title of "manager" (a category exempted from overtime regulations), even when the employee has no managerial responsibilities. Legal? Maybe, but not ethical.

Ethical issues are sometimes raised and resolved by employees, and sometimes organizations have official policies on ethics. For example, most organizations have explicit guidelines on the kinds of "gifts" (kickbacks) that employees may accept from suppliers. But most HRM ethical decisions are much more complicated. Should a company produce goods in a country that employs child labour? Should an organization eliminate one unit (laying off the staff in the process) only to subcontract the work to an outside supplier that employs workers at one-half the compensation rates? Obviously, these ethical decisions affect strategy formulation and implementation.

## Technological Factors

Technology is the process by which inputs from an organization's environment are transformed into outputs. Technology includes tools, machinery, equipment, and software. Technology has already had a large impact on HR and is predicted to continue to do so at an even faster pace—it took 75 years for telephones to reach an audience of 50 million people; 13 years for television and only four years for the World Wide Web to reach the same number.[11] It is estimated that IT allows companies to operate with 35% fewer HR employees.[12] HR Planning Notebook 3.4 outlines the impact of technology.

Every HR function has the potential to become managed electronically. The trend started with payroll and benefits; now software is used to manage training data and succession management information. Online counselling for managers is available, and managers can complete performance appraisals interactively. By 2005, e-learning will be the single most used application on the web.[13] As the hardware becomes smaller and the software becomes smarter, we can expect most HR functions to be managed electronically. HR professionals will need to become technology savvy and/or learn skills of managing vendors of technology solutions.

However, there continue to be concerns about identity theft of employee personal information and the vulnerability of technology to attack or disaster. According to a panel of technology experts, there will be heightened awareness of HR data privacy.[14] The line is blurring between personal and professional lives as employees answer e-mail on vacation and use the phone to telecommute. Issues of the protection of intellectual property and the safeguarding of company secrets are made more difficult because of the ease of transferring by technology.

## HR Planning Notebook 3.4

### Impact of Technology on Organizations

- Requires changes in skills and work habits of employees–employees have to be provided with constant training and skills are no longer viable for decades.
- Elimination of some lower level positions and layers of management–routine tasks, normally done by those lowest in the organization hierarchy, are automated, and the surviving employees need more advanced skills. Fewer managers and fewer layers of management are needed.
- Less hierarchy, more collaboration–the adoption of technology decreases the need for management as a supervisory control technique. Power has shifted from management to technical workers, who hold the knowledge about system processes.

- Telecommuting options–telecommuting is estimated to be growing at 20% per year, allows employees to locate farther from their offices, and allows employers to choose office facilities farther from major cities.
- Electronic monitoring and employee privacy (one study estimated that 90% of employees have used their employer-provided computer for personal business on company time)–27% of employers monitor employee e-mail. If an employee uses his break to access sites related to personal health-care issues, which the employer monitors, has this employee's right to privacy been violated?

Source: From *Strategic Human Resource Management,* 1st edition by MELLO. © 2002. Reprinted with permission of South-Western, a division of Thomson Learning: www.thomsonrights.com. Fax 800-730-2215. SHRM 2004-5 *Workplace Forecast: A Strategic Outlook,* SHRM 2004.

## Demographic Factors

**demographics**

the study of population statistics

**Demographics**, the study of population statistics, affect HR profoundly. The influence of women, the greying of the workforce, and the arrival of "Gen Xs" and "Gen Ys" all influence HR policies. The supply of baby boomers (those born between 1946 and 1964), exceeds the demand for them in middle management and senior ranks. The combination of the surge of workers in their 50s and the flattening of organizations has created a cadre of plateaued workers who are approaching retirement. If a person starts working at 21, retires at 55, and dies at 89, this person will have spent 34 years at work and 34 years in retirement. Most boomers don't think their money will last that long, and two-thirds of them expect to work during "retirement." The Income Tax Act may have to be changed to allow phased-in retirement, and HR planners will have to make work adjustments to accommodate these requests.[15]

"Baby busters" (those born between 1965 and the mid-1970s) follow the boomers, who have created a bottleneck in the organization. There are far fewer baby busters, and most are very well educated and trained, so can command significant incomes.

Gen X employees (those born between 1965 and 1980) have lived with technology all their lives. They have fewer expectations of organizations and perceive themselves as independent agents. Members of Gen Y, born after 1981, are completely comfortable with technology and have a more global and tolerant outlook than people older than they. Gen Y employees are not very interested in climbing a career ladder; indeed, they assume that they will change jobs frequently.

There is increasing diversity in the workforce. Terms such as "minority" and "majority" have lost their meaning. People may object to overly broad classifications such as "Asian," preferring "Japanese-Canadian," or "Korean-Canadian."[16]

## Social and Cultural Factors

Society can express its intent through laws and regulations and in less formal ways within organizations through discipline and terminations. One issue that is receiving increasing public attention is the right to privacy. Does the employer have a moral (and legal) right to monitor employee activities through video surveillance cameras or reading e-mail? Dow Chemical Co. terminated 50 employees and disciplined another 200 because these employees sent or distributed offensive material using the company's e-mail system. Those who downloaded, saved, or distributed the material were disciplined or terminated; those who simply opened and deleted the material were not reprimanded.[17]

Another issue is the employee's attempt to balance a personal life with an ever more encompassing work life. Research on hours worked indicates that Canadians are spending more time at work. In 2001, the province of Ontario changed its employment standards to permit 60-hour workweeks, on a voluntary basis. Critics argue that the 60-hour workweek will become an implicit part of job expectations.[18] Many employees face the challenges of trying to spend quality time with their families while vigorously pursuing a career. People are generally most active in moving ahead in their careers between the ages of 25 and 45, exactly the same stage at which most people raise their children. Both roles are demanding. Both require long hours, during the same period (6 a.m. to 10 p.m.). The demographics of the aging workforce mean that working adults will be stressed by the extra demands of caring for their elderly relatives, estimated to consume about 23 hours each month.[19] Organizations have responded to this issue by increasing workplace flexibility. Some options include flextime, part-time work, job sharing, telecommuting, elder care, and child care. The issue of employee well-being is also on the collective bargaining table, with unions asking for family support benefits such as subsidies for child and elder care, and access to wellness facilities. Although the unionized workforce is changing to include more women and older workers, many of the traditional union members, such as low-wage and hourly workers, factory and service workers, and outside workers, cannot take advantage of benefits such as flexible work hours, telecommuting, or on-site gyms.

Violence in the workplace is also attracting attention. One study estimates that 5% of female employees in Canada and 4% of male employees reported being physically assaulted on the job.[20] Certain jobs, such as health care providers and those in enforcement or inspection, are at higher risk, along with those handling money and working alone at night.

## Stakeholders

When discussing HR strategy, the natural tendency is to think only about the organization under consideration and its managers and employees. However, there is a call for an expansion of these boundaries. Many groups have an influence on the organization's strategy. These groups can be referred to as the stakeholders.

**stakeholder**

groups of people who have vested interests in an organization's decisions

**Stakeholders** are groups of people who have an interest in the projects, policies, or outcomes of an organization's decisions. Sometimes called constituent groups, they follow the actions of the organization and lobby to have their interests satisfied. These stakeholders affect strategy formulation. Employees want more wages and job security, suppliers want longer-term relationships, customers want faster service, and shareholders want more dividends and higher stock prices. Organizations will often adapt their strategies to accommodate powerful stakeholders such as unions, regulatory agencies, or customers. Let us look at some of these stakeholders.

## Shareholders

**shareholders**

those who own shares of a company

For private organizations, the primary stakeholder is the owner or those who hold shares: the **shareholders**. Public organizations are accountable to the taxpayer (the shareholder) through a complex system of departmental hierarchies and political webs. Most CEOs interviewed on television about some major change, such as a downsizing, will reply that their responsibility is not to the employees or the public but to the shareholder.

## Customers

A second stakeholder is the customer or client. Organizations have a moral duty to provide safe, hazard-free products. This appears relatively simple to do. However, if a provider knows that a product has an infinitesimal probability of being unsafe, the costs of withdrawing the product are often weighed against the costs of litigation. Car manufacturers make this kind of decision frequently. They will absorb the liability costs of an automobile that is unsafe under atypical conditions because these costs are less than the costs of redesign, remanufacture, or recall.

A powerful customer may demand changes from its suppliers, and therefore influence the skill level of the supplier's employees. Wal-Mart will train its suppliers' employees in just-in-time order processing and deal (electronically) only with those suppliers that can provide this type of service. Suppliers are forced to change to match Wal-Mart's system and to train people in the system if they want Wal-Mart's business. Some organizations include customer expectations or preferences to develop criteria to select and appraise employees.[21]

## Suppliers

Suppliers can influence the skill level of their customers' employees. Polo Ralph Lauren Canada sends its own skilled staff to the Bay to help the department store merchandise the supplier's clothing, and in doing so raises the skill level of retail clerks in this chain of department stores. Sometimes alliances are formed between supplier and customer to influence government policies.

## Governments

The federal government gives extensive assistance with implementing employment equity programs in federally regulated corporations, thus encouraging sensitivity, training, and skill development not only in equity matters but also generally in management of change programs.

## The Public

An increasingly important stakeholder is the community at large. The public expects organizations to be socially responsible, comply with laws, have ethical management practices, and be sustainable.[22] This is particularly evident when a company is the sole or largest employer in a small community. In this situation, the company would be influenced in its strategic decisions by the need to keep the community alive, the people employed, and the environment healthy in the long term. Another example occurs with the production and distribution of products such as alcohol, or with gambling casinos, which cause great hardship and upheaval to some individuals but result in programs and services that would not necessarily be affordable under normal taxation efforts.

The public expects very large organizations to be more socially responsible. Size matters, as can be seen by the research presented in HR Planning Today 3.3.

## Unions

The presence of unions in the environment will affect HRM strategy for firms entering new sectors with high unionization rates. The national unionization rate is stable at 32%, but another 21% of the workforce would join a union if given the choice.[23] (This unionization rate compares to the United States' of 12.5%—and only 7.9% in the U.S. private sector—a rate that continues to decline.[24]) Employees who are currently unionized within an organization can

---

## HR Planning Today 3.3

### Size Matters

Larger organizations adopt more sophisticated HR practices partly because acceptable economies of scale are achieved when an organization has thousands of employees. Furthermore, large organizations are more visible and subject to pressures to engage in legitimate state-of-the-art HRM practices. Compared to small organizations, larger organizations are more likely to use sophisticated staffing and training practices and are more likely to include bonuses based on profit. Job security is higher at larger companies, but smaller companies listen more to their employees.

Source: B. McConnell, "Survey: Size, Age Make a Difference in HR Strategies," *Society for HR Management*, February 2002, pp. 6 and 9.

---

influence strategy in two ways. One is a restrictive way, in which the collective agreement limits an organization's ability to make drastic changes in working methods or jobs to accommodate changes in strategic direction. A second way is that unions now play a larger role and are more cooperative than adversarial with regard to HR practices such as profit sharing, plant locations, selection procedures, and quality improvement. Savvy HR planners keep track of the policies of key unions such as the Canadian Auto Workers (CAW) because they set the benchmark for hourly workers in Canada. Any innovative benefit will filter through the economy and affect other organizations' negotiations. The key issues for unions are job security, income security, working hours, and inflation protection.[25] Unionized employees receive higher wages and have better working conditions than their nonunionized counterparts.[26] One potential trend that is worth watching is the rise in the unionization of managers. According to Statistics Canada, 9% of managers are unionized, and the number has been slowly climbing.[27] Managers are interested in becoming part of unions in order to deal with their own compensation and workload issues.

## Employees

As indicated earlier, sometimes an organization's strategy is influenced by the kinds of competencies it already possesses. If employees are motivated, committed, and flexible, an organization might be more willing to grow rapidly through numerous product introductions. If the workforce is unusually multilingual, the possibility of growing through international markets becomes more attractive. Likewise, strengths can reside in the HR department itself. If the HR department has excelled in its ability to grow rapidly by attracting, hiring, and orienting highly qualified candidates, corporate venturing or a joint venture becomes an attainable goal. If culture management is the HR department's strength, mergers and acquisitions can be considered as a strategic option.

## Top Management

Much of the research on HR planning recognizes the powerful influence of the CEO on the organization's ability to attain its goals. The concept of the rational manager is well embedded in our business psyche. We assume that the head of an organization carefully analyzes the environment—looking at competitors' actions and technological changes—and then decides the best strategy to exploit opportunities and corporate strengths. But hearts may be as influential as heads. Managers are more than rational actors: they have personal values, ethics, attitudes toward risk, and ambition.[28]

Research has shown that different types of strategies require different types of managers and executives. Studies of these managerial elites have found that managers with certain personalities—for example, those with a tolerance for ambiguity—managed firms with a growth strategy more successfully than those with a harvest strategy.[29] Let's take just one of these managerial traits—attitude toward risk. From readings on corporate strategy, we know that managers who are risk avoiders will take the conservative, cautious approach with an eye on "guaranteed," short-term profits. Risk takers will be willing to sacrifice short-term gains to "gamble" on long-term bigger payoffs. But these studies fail to recognize that the entire employee pool must have the necessary skills and attributes to carry out the strategy.

## Environment Scanning: A Case Application

Scanning must have a purpose. It must not be the collection of information just to have reports gathering dust on executive bookshelves. The information must be analyzed for its impact on the organization, and particularly for its implications for the organization's HR strategy.

In Table 3.1, we describe how this might be done by imagining how an HR planner working for a large retailer in the Canadian market would use environmental information to determine how the HR practices in a retail environment could be affected.

TABLE 3.1

### Trends and HR Implications

| TREND | HR IMPLICATIONS |
|---|---|
| **Economic** | |
| High unemployment rates | Low consumer spending, fewer staff needed |
| Global competition | Internationalization, possible domestic downsizing |
| **Labour Market** | |
| Outsourcing | Changing spending patterns to reduce labour costs |
| Aging workforce/consumers | More clients during the day, changing staff distribution |
| Flexible work arrangements | For employees, less work clothing needed, more home office leisure clothes |
| Globalization | Outsourcing to low-wage countries |
| | Need for managers with global competencies |
| **Regulatory** | |
| Pay equity | Need to review systems, allow contingency funds |
| Workforce rights | More complex terminations; privacy issues |
| Part-time benefits legislation | Increased costs of part-time employees |
| **Technological** | |
| E-commerce | Increased need for employees with technological skills |
| Computerization of work | Increased telecommuting, nontraditional offices |
| | Need for results appraisals (not face-time judgments) |

*(Continued)*

TABLE 3.1 (CONTINUED)

| TREND | HR IMPLICATIONS |
|---|---|
| **Social** | |
| Workplace violence | Development of HR policies on safety; provision of secure environment |
| Retirement trends | Retiring of bulk of boomers, fighting for jobs |
| Work–life issues | Problems recruiting nontraditional shifts |
| Diversity | Workforce reflecting customer demographic |
| **Stakeholders** | |
| Union | Increasing move to nonadversarial arrangements |
| Public | Demands for excellent customer service, therefore need to train and upgrade sales skills |
| Customers | A few large customers control type of jobs and skills |
| Suppliers | Demand for seamless connections, need for employees |
| Top management | Move to recruit global executives |

# Summary

HRM strategy is determined primarily by organizational strategy. However, there are environmental factors that shape HRM strategy, so HR managers and planners must continually monitor the environment. Typically, they scan by reading publications, retaining memberships in professional associations, attending conferences, or using professional scanners. A number of methods, such as trend and impact analyses and the Delphi technique, are used to identify future trends. The environmental factors that are monitored include the economic climate, the labour market, the political and regulatory climate, and social norms. Stakeholders such as shareholders, unions, customers, and executives contribute strongly to the formulation and implementation of strategy.

# Key Terms

demographics, 76
environmental scanning, 62
impact analysis, 67
scenario planning, 67

shareholders, 78
stakeholder, 78
trend analysis, 66

# Web Links

This website is a virtual HR consultant for small and medium-sized businesses that do not have an HR professional on staff. The information is customized by province and grouped into categories such as recruitment, pay and benefits, employment standards, and terminations:

**http://hrmanagement.ca** (p. 64)

The website of Human Resources Development Canada is a good place to look for well-researched articles on trends in collective agreements, work–life balance, and other topics of interest to students and employers:

**www.hrsdc.gc.ca** (p. 66)

A Health Canada website that offers trends in health and wellness:

**www.hc-sc.gc.ca/ewh-semt/index_e.html** (p. 71)

An excellent website of the Work Network of Canadian Policy Research Networks, which tracks trends in work issues, such as rewards, job rotation, health and safety, etc.:

**www.jobquality.ca** (p. 72)

# RPC Icons

**RPC 3.1 Identifies HR information that the organization needs to achieve its business objectives**

**RPC 3.2 Contributes to and promotes the development of the profession through active participation in the HR community**

**RPC 3.3 Contributes to an environment that fosters effective working relationships**

**RPC 3.4 Researches, analyzes, and reports on potential HR issues affecting the organization**

**RPC 3.5 Stays current in terms of professional development**

**RPC 3.6 Forecasts HR supply and demand conditions**

**RPC 3.7 Provides input on matters related to the drafting and/or application of legislation or regulations related to health, safety, security, and workers' compensation.**

# Discussion Questions

1. HR Planning Today 3.1 lists the top ten trends forecasted by experts in the United States. Develop a list of the impacts that each trend will have on an organization, and prescriptions for HR practices or policies to deal with each trend.
2. Current HR policies seem to be based on the assumption of a traditional career trajectory and a traditional life pattern of marriage, children, and retirement. What percentage of Canada's workforce fits the stereotype?

What HR policies should be changed to adapt to the reality you discover in your research?

3. Most experts are predicting labour shortages, resulting in a war for talent. Many companies will be competing for workers under 30. Various articles have described this cohort in both negative and positive terms. They are often criticized for being slackers, being bored quickly, wanting too much quality time with their bosses, impatient with their career progress, and wanting high pay, impressive titles, and fancy offices. On the other hand, many view them as flexible, techno literate, a truly green generation (i.e., concerned with environmental issues), entrepreneurial, loyal to their profession, and concerned with future marketability. In groups, develop a list of characteristics of this cohort. Then determine how an organization could change to be an "employer of choice" for this group.

Adapted from S.J. Barney, 2002, "A Changing Workforce Calls for Twenty-First Century Strategies," *Journal of Healthcare Management*, 47, 2, 81–85; J.J. Jamrog, 2002, "Current Practices: The Coming Decade of the Employee," *Human Resource Planning*, 25, 3, 5–12.

# Using the Internet

HR professionals use a variety of sources to keep current with HR and business trends; the most popular are publications, including newspapers, research journals, and HR magazines. From a list of publications in HR Planning Notebook 3.1, choose either newspapers or HR magazines and search online for their websites. Once logged on to the chosen publication website, imagine you are an HR Planner from a large organization who is in charge of scanning and looking for changes in environmental factors that might affect the HR function.

1. Search for an article relevant to an industry in which you are currently working in (or an industry of interest) that will impact HR planning.
2. Discuss the potential impact of information presented in the article to human resources and the different stakeholders in an organization.

# Exercises: The Nominal Group Technique

1. Form a group of four to six people. If you are working with a group of students, you will be discussing the future of the student role, or "job." If you are working with a group of people in the same occupation or job, your group will be discussing the future of that occupation or job. Appoint a group leader.
2. Ask everyone to individually list the trends that may change, at some likely future time, the work methods or work outcomes for the "job" under consideration. Try a time span of three, five, or ten years. (Allow 15 minutes for this step.)
3. Have each person then state the first item on his or her list and record this item on a flip chart or green board so that others can see it.

4. Have each person, in turn, continue to state items until all are listed. If an item is mentioned more than once, the group leader should ask for the number of people who listed this item. Record that number beside the item to give a rating of frequency.
5. Ask each person to discuss the relevance of his or her items to the job.
6. When all items are listed, ask each person to assign a rating from 1 to 10 to each item on the flip chart, 1 being the most important influence on the job and 10 being the least important. This is a rating of importance.
7. Analyze the results.
8. Use these results to prepare a group report on the future of the job.
9. Present this report to the class.

(Note that many of these steps can be done with group software, such as Lotus Notes.)

After the presentations, discuss the challenges of predicting the future in this manner. Should HR planners not scan the environment because of these problems? Is there a better way?

# Case: Work–Life Family Balance

Magda Hyshka, manager of HR policies for the largest telecommunications company in Canada, TelPlus, had been asked by her director of HR to develop an innovative policy to address the work–family issues facing the company. As part of her research, Magda uncovered the following facts:

- Workers spend an average of 62 minutes a day (or ten days a year) commuting to and from work.
- Forty-six percent of workers reported moderate to high levels of stress in 1999, compared to 64% in 1989; one in five workers reported high levels of stress in 1991—this changed to one in three in 1999; 10% of the workforce was depressed in 1999; two out of five disability claims were due to depression or anxiety in 1999.
- Three-quarters of female employees felt that commitment to families is a barrier to career advancement; 41% report postponing pregnancy or not having a child at all.
- Twenty-seven percent of employees report moderate to high levels of stress from balancing work and family responsibilities, an increase of 75% in a decade.
- Technology enabled employees to work seven days a week and at any time during the day or night, and many felt that they were expected to be available (online) all the time.
- Since the events of September 11, 2001, many Canadians are rethinking their commitment to work, with 81% intending to spend more time on personal matters and less on the job.

Magda also researched information from the United States, recognizing that Canada tends to lag behind the hot issues in the United States:

- The U.S. Bureau of Labor Statistics reported that work hours have been increasing steadily over the last decade. Twenty-five million Americans

Chapter 3: Environmental Influences on HRM

worked at least 49 hours per week, and 11 million Americans worked 59 hours a week.

- Forty-six percent of employees feel overworked and overwhelmed and lack the time to step back and reflect on their work; 61% say they would give up pay to spend more time with their families; 36% state that they would be willing to take a pay cut to have a shorter commute.
- Demographers predict that more than half the children born in the 1990s will be raised in a family home with both parents living with them; 62% of women with children under six are employed, and mothers with preschoolers make up the fastest-growing segment of the workforce. Forty-four percent of Americans between the ages of 45 and 55 have aging parents as well as children under 21.
- Paradoxically, the number of Americans living alone has surpassed the number of married couples with children.

Sources: Y.A. Laroche, *Fine Balance*. Ottawa: Canadian Centre for Management Development, 2000; D. Patel, *Workplace Visions*. Alexandria, Virginia: SHRM, Vol. 4, No. 2, 2002.

## Question

Continue the research started by Magda. Prepare a report summarizing your findings and recommending policies that will help your employees cope with work–family balance issues.

# Endnotes

1. Childs, J.T. 2005. "Managing Workforce Diversity at IBM: A Global HR Topic that Has Arrived," *Human Resource Management*, 44, 1, 73–77.
2. Schuler, R.S., and S.E. Jackson. 2005. "A Quarter-Century Review of Human Resource Management in the U.S: The Growth in the International Perspective," *Management Review*, 16, 1, 11–35.
3. Certo, S.C., and J. P Peter. 1993. *Strategic Management: A Focus on Process*. Boston: Irwin.
4. Hitt, M.A, R.D. Ireland, R.E Hoskisson, W.G Rowe, and J.P Sheppard. 2002. *Strategic Management: Competitiveness and Globalization*. Toronto: Nelson Thompson Learning.
5. Burack, E.H., and N.J. Mathys. 1987. *Human Resource Planning: A Pragmatic Approach to Manpower Staffing and Development*, 2nd ed. Lake Forest, IL: Brace-Park Press.
6. Rothwell, W.J., and H.C. Kazanas. 1988. *Strategic Human Resources Planning and Management*. Englewood Cliffs, NJ: Prentice Hall.
7. Lowe, G. 1998. "The Future of Work," *Industrial Relations*, Vol. 53, No. 2 (Spring): 235–257.
8. Brown, D. 2002. " Are You Prepared for the New Economy?" *Canadian HR Reporter*, Vol. 14, No. 3 (February 12): 1, 7.
9. Overman, S. 2002. "HR Is Partner in McDonaldizing Employees in New Countries," *HR News* (May): 7.
10. Brown, D. 2002. "Ottawa Unveils National Training and Development Strategy," *Canadian HR Reporter*, Vol. 15, No. 5 (March 11): 3, 6.
11. Patel, D. 2002–2003. *Workplace Forecast*. Alexandria, VA: SHRM; Schramm, J. 2005. "HR's Tech Challenges," *HR Magazine*, 50, 3, 152.
12. Chabrow, E. 2004. "World-Class Companies Use IT More Effectively for HR," *Information Week*, 10, 14, 18.

13. www.corporateleadershipcouncil.com, June 2002; retrieved April 5, 2006.

14. Schramm J. 2005. "HR's Tech Challenges," *HR Magazine* 50, 3, 152.

15. Langton, J. 2005. "Accountants Offer Two Cents on Aging Workforce," *Canadian HR Reporter*, 18, 4, 3.

16. Jamrog, J.J. 2002. "Current Practices: The Coming Decade of the Employee," *Human Resource Planning*, 25, 3, 5–12.

17. Currie, M.B., and D. Black. 2001. "E-merging Issues in the Electronic Workplace," *Ivey Business Journal*, Vol. 65, No. 3 (January/February): 18–29.

18. www.jobquality.ca; retrieved April 5, 2006; Anonymous. 2001. "Longer Work Weeks Unhealthy: Critics," *Canadian HR Reporter*, Vol. 14, No. 16 (September 24): 3.

19. Tomlinson, A. 2002. "Trickle Down Effects of Retiring Boomers," *Canadian HR Reporter*, Vol. 15, No. 11 (June 3): 1, 12.

20. Duncan, L. 2002. "An Ounce of Prevention: Ending Workplace Violence," *Canadian Employment Safety and Health Guide*, Vol. 256 (January): 3.

21. Schnieder, B., and S.S. White. 2004. *Service Quality: Research Perspectives*. Thousand Oaks, CA: Sage.

22. Schuler and Jackson, 2005.

23. Brown, D. 2001. "Following Nortel's Lead? Really?" *Canadian HR Reporter*, Vol. 15, No. 20 (November 19), A1.

24. Sweeney, J. 2005. "Labor of Politics," *Wall Street Journal*, March 4, 2005, A14.

25. Brown, D. 2002. "CAW–Big Three Negotiations Set the Mark," *Canadian HR Reporter*, Vol. 15, No. 12 (June 17): 3, 12.

26. Lawler, E.E., and S.A. Mohram. 1987. "Unions and the New Management," *Academy of Management Executives*, Vol. 26, No. 1: 293–300.

27. Statistics Canada. *Labour Force Survey 2000: Perspectives on Labour and Income*. Catalogue 70-001-XIE, October 25, 2005.

28. Guth, W.D., and R. Tagiuri. 1965. "Personal Values and Corporate Strategy," *Harvard Business Review*, Vol. 43, No. 5 (September–October): 123–132.

29. Gupta, A., and V. Govindarajan. 1984. "Business Unit Strategy Managerial Characteristics, and Business Unit Effectiveness at Strategy Implementation," *Academy of Management Journal*, Vol. 27: 25–41.

# PART TWO

# HR Planning

CHAPTER 4    JOB ANALYSIS

CHAPTER 5    INFORMATION TECHNOLOGY FOR
             HR PLANNING

CHAPTER 6    THE HR FORECASTING PROCESS

CHAPTER 7    HR DEMAND

CHAPTER 8    ASCERTAINING HR SUPPLY

CHAPTER 9    SUCCESSION MANAGEMENT

# Chapter 4

# Job Analysis

## Chapter Learning Objectives

After reading this chapter, you should be able to

- Understand the central role played by job analysis in all HR activities, and especially in the effective conduct of HR planning.
- Comprehend the two essential elements of any job: methods and time standards.
- Explain common problems associated with the job analysis process.
- Identify the five steps of the job analysis process.
- Employ criteria to select job analysis methods that are best suited to the organizational jobs being examined.
- Develop analytical questions that will permit an in-depth examination of the knowledge, skills, abilities, and other attributes required for successful evaluation of jobs.
- Analyze the advantages and disadvantages of the most common methods of job analysis.

# Competency-Based Analysis and HR Educational Training Programs

Over the past decade, the HR profession has both grown and changed dramatically in conjunction with changes in organizations and society at large. With increased globalization and complexity in organizational environments, it is critical that university- and college-based educational programs in human resources are analyzed and revised to align with the new demands and requests being placed upon HR practitioners in the marketplace.

HR practitioners have expressed concern that the HR field needs to develop educational standards and processes similar to those in areas such as accounting and law, which tightly link learning outcomes to the world of work. However to date, problems have arisen in effectively utilizing a competencies approach to determine the number of elements that should be included in the HR educational curriculum, and their relative importance. For example, one competency-based model for HR education suggests the educational process should prepare graduates to perform successfully in three work-related clusters of (1) HR practices, (2) business capabilities, and (3) managing change. Other frameworks propose (1) Interpersonal and people management, (2) goals management, and (3) analytical reasoning, or a five-factor model of (1) HR technical proficiency, (2) goal and action management, (3) influence management, (4) business knowledge, and (5) functional and organizational leadership. The reader will notice considerable variations among these competing frameworks, and this is just at the top-level analysis of identifying major competency clusters. How then are educational professionals to utilize such disparate and vague articulations to guide their analysis of program and curriculum content?

One of the most telling indictments of the competencies approach in general is the lack of agreement over what constitutes a particular competency (e.g., what is "customer service"?) and its lack of specificity in guiding and differentiating workplace behaviours and performance. Also, it's far from apparent that these various competency factors are mutually exclusive. For example, typically one associates leadership ("functional and organizational leadership:) with individuals who are able to articulate goals and ensure requisite action takes place to achieve their attainment, yet the aforementioned model separates "leadership" from "goal and action management." Furthermore, it often seems as if these competency frameworks reflect a desired future state for HR in general terms, as expressed by those holding senior HR executive appointments, rather than providing effective specific guidance as to the knowledge, skills, abilities, and other attributes (KSAs) required for entry-level HR graduates of university and college programs.

If competency-based approaches are to meaningfully inform work and job analyses for both HR practitioners and educational institutions, much more work needs to be done to fine-tune and demonstrate the real value of such an approach by avoiding buzzwords and vague generalities.[1]

# Introduction

An organization's mission statement presents the guiding rationale for the activities of all subunits and employees. As we move down the organizational hierarchy from the executive suites to the production floor, corporate and divisional strategic goals are subdivided and allocated to various units as their operational goals. To attain the strategic and operational goals, it is necessary to develop short-run production and operational budgets, as well as to specify the division of labour, commonly referred to as partitioning the work process into manageable units called jobs. A **job** can be defined as a grouping of related duties, tasks, and behaviours performed by one or more individuals, namely jobholders. Each job will have one or more **positions**— in other words, the number of individuals who are performing the duties required by that specific job. The analysis of subdivided work in the organization, both at the level of the individual job and for the entire flow of the production process, is referred to as **job analysis** and is the focus of this chapter. As HR planners, it is essential that we are knowledgeable about the nature of work and its overall contribution toward the attainment of the organization's mission.

It is important for us to see how each individual job, when aggregated with others in a process referred to as departmentalization, contributes to the performance of essential organizational tasks without unnecessary duplication or redundancy. Furthermore, as HR planners, we are responsible for determining the demand for and supply of personnel in the organization. In order to do this we must have detailed knowledge about working conditions, employee qualifications, and the educational training and skill requirements of each job, as well as the nature of the organization's work process itself. For these reasons, knowledge of the job analysis process and methods of evaluating jobs are essential components in the formulation of the successful HR planning system.[2]

**job**
a grouping of related duties, tasks, and behaviours performed by one or more individuals, namely jobholders

**position**
the number of individuals who are performing the duties, tasks, and behaviours required by a specific job

**job analysis**
the analysis of subdivided work in the organization, both at the level of the individual job and for the entire flow of the production process

®℗© 4.1

®℗© 4.2

Job analysis is not only a critical business practice utilized to ensure legal compliance, but as Cascio very aptly stated "job analysis is to the personnel specialist what the wrench is to the plumber."[3]

## Job Analysis

Job analysis can be defined as an examination of the jobs in an organization with a view to documenting the knowledge, skills, and abilities (KSAs and experience) associated with successful performance of those jobs. The written outcomes of this process are referred to either as a **job description** or a **job specification**. (See HR Planning Today 4.1.) The difference between the two documents centres on whether the emphasis is on the duties or tasks to be carried out on the job (i.e., the job description) or on the competencies or KSAs the jobholder must possess to be a successful performer in a specific job (i.e., the job specification). KSAs are defined as follows:

*Knowledge:* Knowledge is the body of information, usually of a factual or procedural nature, that allows an individual to perform a task successfully.

*Skill:* Skill is the individual's level of proficiency or competency in performing a specific task. Level of competency is typically expressed in numerical terms.

*Ability:* Ability is a more general, enduring trait or capability an individual possesses at the time when he or she first begins to perform a task.[4]

*Other attributes:* Other attributes include work experience.

HR practitioners refer to job analysis as the foundation for all HR activities, and there are extremely valid reasons for this assertion. Before we can meaningfully advertise jobs and recruit individuals to fill job vacancies identified by the HR planning process, to attract the desired applicants we must be able to specify the individual competencies that we seek. Once we have developed a pool of high-quality job applicants, the selection process will incorporate employment tests and interview questions based on the need to choose the individual who best meets the formal requirements for success identified by our job analysis process. The selection criteria that flow out of the job analysis process are also used in succession planning to appraise the organization's internal candidates for possible transfer or promotion to management or executive jobs. Once we have selected an individual to fill a job, he or she should be given a copy of the job description or specification for the job, which provides specific guidance on how to perform the job in accordance with the wishes of the organization. The performance appraisal process compares the individual's accomplishments over a predetermined period with the desired standards specified in the job description or specification. If the performance appraisal process reveals that the individual has deficiencies that can be rectified by training and development, specific programs or courses can be instigated to help the individual reach the desired

**job description (job specification)**

the written outcomes (documents) produced by the job analysis process. The job description emphasizes the duties or tasks to be carried out on the job. Job specifications emphasize identifying the competencies the jobholder must possess to be a successful performer in the specified job.

 4.3

 4.4

### Ensuring Job Descriptions Stay Relevant

Detailed written job descriptions can fail to maintain their relevance over time, as jobs change rapidly in today's dynamic global economy. Furthermore, if descriptions become outdated and do not reflect the changed realities of the contemporary job, they will be next to useless in facilitating the match between the individual's performance and career aspirations. Carla Joinson, a job analyst, recommends a minimalist approach to preparing job descriptions, reflecting a change in emphasis from detailed "skill-based" to shortened "role-based" documents. She suggests that shorter job descriptions, which are restricted to a few clearly written statements on the overall responsibilities and "roles" that will be performed by individuals holding specified jobs, are more much enduring and useful than the detailed and ponderous older descriptions. Detailed information on duties and tasks as contained in traditional job descriptions are not included in the new "minimalist job description." The advantage to this approach is that roles are more enduring than specific micro-level duties and tasks and will therefore provide better behavioural guidance over a sustained period of time, and are flexible enough to maintain their relevancy to jobholders.

Source: Adapted from C. Joinson, "Refocusing Job Descriptions, *HR Magazine*, Vol. 46, No. 1 (January 2001), 66–72.

standards. Furthermore, compensation systems in organizations typically use a classification process based on knowledge and skills, effort, responsibility, and working conditions, the four **compensable factors** of the job that are explicitly noted and formalized by the job analysis process.[5]

Finally, successful career-planning programs also draw heavily on the front-end requirement of a comprehensive job analysis. In planning future career moves, the individual and the organization note the employee's current KSAs and level of performance and compare these to the KSAs required in various target jobs for which the employee would like to apply. Once this information is provided by job analysis, the employee is informed of the explicit education and skills development that will be required prior to being considered for the target jobs. Job analysis, therefore, is not only a critical requirement for the proper implementation and operation of the HR planning process, as examined in this book, but also an essential prerequisite for the success of virtually all other HR functions.[6]

Job analysis has a long history within the HR field. Efficiency expert Fred Taylor's **scientific management** studies were key contributions to the evolution of contemporary job analysis methods.[7] Taylor's industrial engineering approach focused on reducing costs and improving the efficiency of the manufacturing worker. In particular, his analysis process concentrated on finding the "one best way" to do any job. This approach, still a central feature of present-day job analyses, examines two main aspects of each job in the organization: (1) the *methods employed* and (2) the *time measurement* for task completion.

The first aspect is concerned with how the job incumbent performs the job—that is, with the minimum requirements for success in the job. These

**compensable factors**
knowledge and skills, effort, responsibility, and working conditions

**scientific management**
examines two main aspects of each job in the organization: (1) the *methods employed* and (2) the *time measurement* for task completion

requirements include (a) the individual's knowledge of production techniques and processes (e.g., raw materials and other inputs, machinery, tools), cognitive (mental) abilities, mechanical abilities, (e.g., principles and spatial relationships), and psychomotor abilities, and (b) the working conditions in which the job is performed (e.g., whether the work is done by the individual alone or in conjunction with other members of a team).

The second aspect common to all job analyses is time measurement, or the cycle/production time required to produce the good or service to the performance standards of the organization. This time standard is completely dependent on the first aspect, which is concerned with the methods employed (or how the job is performed). Obviously, changing the process from individual to team-based production and modifying the number of raw material inputs or steps in the production process will substantially change the output or number of items that can be produced on a time basis per hour, shift, or day.

## Job Analysis and HR Planning

The information derived from job analysis is absolutely vital in conducting effective HR planning. First, the analysis of jobs and work processes ensures that effects of recent change have been incorporated into job descriptions and specifications. By utilizing the most up to date information, we can help ensure that HR demand and supply can be effectively matched by means of recruitment activities, selection methods, and HR programs being properly aligned to attracting and retaining high-quality individuals to meet the needs of today and for the future, and not the KSAs and competencies of yesteryear. Second, changes in technological processes lead to certain jobs, programs, and processes becoming redundant over time, while new jobs and work activities develop and expand (e.g., information technology personnel). Job analysis allows HR programmers to suggest the most effective and efficient ways to (a) organize work, (b) differentiate "core" work activities from those that can be outsourced and/or curtailed, and (c) structure the organization, given key strategic business goals. Third, business is becoming increasingly global in its scope and operations, and work and job analysis procedures help organizational HR planners compare and contrast the degree of similarity or difference between geographically diverse operating units and personnel around the world, thereby facilitating more effective restructuring programs (mergers, acquisitions, divestitures, etc.). Furthermore, the need for high-performing organizational management has never been so apparent in organizations, and increasingly organizations are developing their own in-house management training academies and talent schools. These programs can work effectively in helping to create continuity of effective management, by means of successful succession programs, only if they are based upon current, effective information derived from the validated personal requirements and behavioural performance standards that are outcomes of the job analysis process.

All in all, job analysis is vital to ensuring the best "fit" between workers and work requirements, and the requisite complementarities of individual and organizational needs.

HR programmers must prioritize various programming options, in order to ensure the most effective usage of scarce organizational resources.

## Problems Associated with Job Analysis

Having noted the importance of job analysis and its two constituent elements of methods and time, let's now turn to an examination of frequent problems associated with job analysis.

### 1. Job Analysis that Is Neither Updated Nor Reviewed

Consider the computer technology to recognize the impact that an extremely rapid rate of change has on how work is performed. Job analyses must be reviewed on a regular basis by incumbents, supervisors, HR staff, and so on to ensure that the written job requirements reflect the reality of contemporary job performance. Recent changes in technology, materials, and processes must be incorporated into the amended job description or specification. Obsolete job descriptions not only fail to provide job incumbents with meaningful guidance as to their required duties and tasks, but also result in an HR planning process that is attempting to match individuals to jobs based on information that is no longer valid.

### 2. Job Description or Specification that Is Too Vague

If job analysis is to provide important information to allow us to select the individual who best meets job requirements, we must be specific as to what those exact requirements are. For example, organizations often specify that applicants must have a certain number of years' experience in a certain functional area instead of specifying the exact skills or competencies the applicant should have learned over that period. Without this specific information, experience or time spent on the job has little relevance for selection. Similarly, organizations may mistakenly include elements such as "dependability" as one of their job requirements without giving specific examples of what constitutes dependable behaviour (e.g., the individual arrives on time for meetings with all preparatory work properly completed). To be an effective component of HR planning, the job analysis process must produce detailed, specific behavioural examples of successful job performance for each job in the work process.

### 3. Contamination and Deficiency

Although brevity and clarity are definite virtues with respect to job analysis (a short, clear job description is of great use to both job incumbents and the HR staff), taken to an extreme these characteristics may cause problems during job analysis efforts. If our job description or specification fails to incorporate important aspects of the job that are required for success, this error of

Chapter 4: Job Analysis

**deficiency**

an error of omission when a job description or specification fails to incorporate important aspects of the job required for success

**contamination**

an error that occurs when unimportant or invalid behaviours or attributes are incorporated into a job description or specification

omission is referred to as **deficiency**. Conversely, if we include peripheral, unimportant aspects of a job in the formal job description, we run the risk of contaminating it by diverting attention from valid, important correlates of success. **Contamination** of the job analysis process may also lead to legal consequences if we use the information to select individuals based on factors not related to the job that are discriminatory under provincial or Canadian human rights legislation. For job analysis, therefore, we should try to be as brief and clear as possible but not at the expense of excluding any important behavioural or performance element of the job.

### 4. Time and Costs of Job Analysis

Some organizations are deterred from conducting job analyses due to the significant time and start-up costs perceived to be associated with the process. Typical costs include consulting fees for job analysts (if the organization does not have in-house HR staff with relevant qualifications); licensing fees associated with usage of copyrighted job analysis methods; the costs of lost production (or overtime) involved with interviewing and surveying job incumbents, managers, and so on; and the administrative costs involved with codifying, analyzing, drafting, revising, and disseminating the information that results from the process. However, many organizations that bemoan the large time and cost expenditures associated with job analysis do so only because they have not conducted a proper cost–benefit analysis with respect to this decision. For example, organizations should also consider the time and cost savings (see HR Planning Notebook 4.1) that result from the following: (1) better matching of individual skills to organizational requirements (e.g., reduced costs, and often lower absenteeism and turnover, associated with training and development),[8] (2) incorporation of the benefits of organizational learning with respect to product and process improvements, (3) reduced job ambiguity and wastage, (4) clarification of operating procedures and job relationships,

---

### HR Planning Notebook 4.1

#### Speeding up Job Analysis

One of the oft-cited criticisms of job analysis is the time and cost associated with doing it properly. Darin Hartley's "Job Analysis at the Speed of Reality (JASR)" was designed to address these concerns by developing an abbreviated process that can create a validated task listing for most positions in approximately three hours. By utilizing approximately four to six job analysts, the group identifies six to twelve duty areas of each job, with each duty area typically containing from three to twelve "task statements" representing measurable activities.

The six steps of the JASR approach are:

1. Greet participants and conduct introductions.
2. Briefly explain the JASR process and participant roles.
3. Determine the scope of the job to be analyzed.
4. Identify the job's functional "duty areas."
5. Identify and list "task statements" for each "duty area."
6. Print the completed task list, and have it signed by the job analysts.

Source: Hartley, D., 2004, "Job Analysis at the Speed of Reality", *T + D*, 58/9, 20–23.

---

(5) explicit definition of performance expectations for individuals and teams, and (6) facilitation of other HR programs. If organizations consider the full costs and benefits associated with entering into the job analysis process, the decision to proceed is invariably very clear!

## The Process of Job Analysis

The process of job analysis involves following five steps to maximize the potential for success. We now examine each of the five steps in turn, noting the actions required at each stage.

### 1. Determine the Job or Process to Be Analyzed

Although the desired outcome of a job analysis is to have a comprehensive record of all organizational jobs and their associated duties, skill requirements, working conditions, and so on, reality dictates that organizations normally select certain well-defined jobs common throughout the industry that can be benchmarked externally—that is, the analysis commences with these well-known jobs first. Some of the factors that determine whether job analysis will be concurrent (all jobs analyzed at approximately the same time) or sequential (job analyses conducted in different stages over time) include (1) the degree to which the selected job is central or critical, (2) the availability of job analysts and other resources, and (3) the availability of external performance **benchmarks** for organizational jobs.

In the first instance, the more critical or central the job or process, the greater the tendency to analyze it and to defer examination of less central jobs or processes to a future time. The number and availability of job analysts, be they external consultants or internal HR specialists, are key factors influencing whether an organization is able to conduct concurrent job analysis or is forced to do it sequentially by stages.

Finally, the Canadian government's **National Occupational Classification (NOC)** (see HR Planning Notebook 4.2), which contains standardized job descriptions on approximately 25 000 jobs, facilitates external benchmarking for the job analyst.[9] The NOC and its U.S. counterparts, the *Dictionary of Occupational Titles* **(DOT)** and, more recently, the **Occupational Information Network (O\*NET)**, provide information on the main duties and employment requirements of each classified job, along with a listing of other job classifications that are similar to the one being analyzed.[10] This information is invaluable as it facilitates comparison to similar jobs in other organizations with respect to required applicant specifications and performance standards for key duties and tasks.

### 2. Determine Methods and Analyze the Job or Process

The second step in the job analysis process involves an appraisal of the most appropriate method(s) to use to study and record job-related behaviours. Selection criteria for job analysis methods include the following:

- *Cost*: Cost includes licence fees for such things as copyrighted questionnaires, training, and administration.

**benchmark**

external comparators for organizational jobs and performance criteria

**National Occupational Classification (NOC)**

the Canadian government database that contains standardized job descriptions on thousands of jobs

*Dictionary of Occupational Titles* (DOT)

the U.S. government's occupational database

**Occupational Information Network (O\*Net)**

The U.S. government's most recent occupational database and equivalent to the NOC; O\*Net has largely supplanted the DOT since 1998.

## Canada's National Occupational Classification (NOC)

The Canadian government's National Occupational Classification was established in 1992 in order to provide Canadians with definitive information on occupations and their associated requirements. It's easy-to-understand framework contains information on ten main occupational clusters, further divided into 520 unit groups, and over 30 000 occupational titles. For example, the ten main occupational clusters are

0. Management
1. Business, finance and administration
2. Natural and applied sciences and related occupations
3. Health
4. Social science, Education, Government service, Religion
5. Art, Culture, Recreation, and Sport
6. Sales and Service
7. Trades, Transport, Equipment operators and Related occupations
8. Primary Industry
9. Processing, Manufacturing, and Utilities.

**W W W** Let's look for information on university professors. After noting that we should examine occupational cluster #4 (see above) which contains the information on the Educational sector, we note that group #412 contains two listings, 4121: University Professors, and 4122: Post-Secondary Teaching and Research Assistants. The NOC occupational listing for *University Professors* (4121) is "University professors teach courses to undergraduate and graduate students and conduct research at universities and degree-granting colleges. University professors who are heads of departments are included in this unit group."

### Example titles

assistant professor, botany
associate professor, linguistics
chairperson, food sciences department . . .
lecturer, university
professor of computer sciences. . . .

### Main duties

University professors perform some or all of the following duties:

- Teach one or more university subjects to undergraduate and graduate students
- Prepare and deliver lectures to students and conduct laboratory sessions or discussion groups
- Prepare, administer, and grade examinations, laboratory assignments, and reports
- Advise students on course and academic matters and career decisions
- Direct research programs of graduate students and advise on research matters
- Conduct research in field of specialization and publish findings in scholarly journals or books
- May serve on faculty committees dealing with such matters as curriculum planning and degree requirements, and perform a variety of administrative duties
- May represent their universities as speakers and guest lecturers
- May provide professional consultative services to government, industry, and private individuals

University professors specialize in a particular subject matter such as biology, chemistry, anatomy, sociology, business administration or law.

### Employment requirements

- A doctoral degree in the field of specialization is required.
- Licences or professional certification may be required for professors teaching future practitioners in certain professionally regulated fields such as medicine, engineering, architecture, psychology, or law.

### Additional information

- University professors who are also practitioners in their field of specialization must have the appropriate licences or certification.

- Progression to senior positions within a department, faculty, or university is possible with experience.

**Classified elsewhere**

- Administrators—Post-Secondary Education and Vocational Training (0312)

- College and Other Vocational Instructors (4131)
- Post-Secondary Teaching and Research Assistants (4122)

Source: University Professors, Human Resources and Skills Development Canada. Reproduced with the permission of the Minister of Public Works and Government Services Canada, 2006.

- *Time*: Time includes that spent on survey and interview training and assessment, data coding and analysis, and so on.
- *Flexibility of methods*: This criterion has to do with whether the method is appropriate for the particular circumstances (e.g., clerical service jobs as opposed to those in manufacturing).
- *Validity and reliability*: These criteria relate to whether the job analysis methods have been tested and found to be accurate measures of the job's essential elements and whether the results of these methods show a consistent pattern over repeated usage.
- *Acceptance*: Some job analysis methods, such as direct observation and videotaping of work performance, may be considered intrusive by the workforce and, therefore, may be met with resistance.[11] Other methods, such as questionnaires and interviews, might be deemed more acceptable by the workers, who would then cooperate in providing information to the job analysts.[12]

The aforementioned selection criteria are used to evaluate the following common methods of job analysis.

INTERVIEWS  To gather information about a job, a job analyst may interview job incumbents, as well as coworkers, supervisors, suppliers, clients, and subordinates. This type of all-round analysis of a job is referred to as **360° evaluation**, as the job analyst has input from individuals who are in the job under evaluation and in other jobs that relate to it. Not surprisingly, self-evaluations derived from this process tend to have a positive rating bias.

**360° evaluation**
evaluation of attributes and performance dimensions of a job from "the full circle" around the job, i.e., feedback from subordinates, superiors, coworkers, clients, and the jobholder him/herself

OBSERVATION  Observation of a job can be either direct or indirect. In *direct observation*, analysts observe the production line for worker behaviours and the skills required for job success. Recording of the number and duration of individual behaviours is normally captured on a standardized recording sheet.[13] *Indirect observation* can incorporate a variety of means, such as a videotaped recording of the job being performed, for subsequent analysis by the analyst.

QUESTIONNAIRES  Numerous standardized questionnaires are used for job analysis. Some of the more frequently used instruments include (1) the Position Description Questionnaire,[14] (2) the Functional Job Analysis,[15] (3) the Job Diagnostic Survey,[16] (4) the Dimensions of Executive Positions,[17] and (5) the Position Analysis Questionnaire.[18]

These survey instruments are normally completed by jobholders, their supervisors, and people who work in other jobs that are related to the specific job being investigated.[19]

Typically, job analysis data derived from self-reports of incumbents, or current job holders, display the lowest levels of reliability, reinforcing the importance of gathering many sources of data to be used for job analysis.[20]

The questionnaires vary substantially, but common elements are questions concerning the following:

a. Education, training, and skill requirements to be successful in the job
b. Responsibility or accountability (e.g., with regard to budgets, specific duties and tasks performed, number and type of people supervised, etc.)
c. Effort—that is, the cognitive and physical demands placed on the individual
d. Working conditions—for example, whether the work is done by an individual or team, the equipment or materials used, the job context or the environmental conditions of work (e.g., telephone line repairperson), the work shifts or hours of work, the potential health hazards, and so on

**JOURNALS AND DIARIES**  This method of job analysis asks jobholders to maintain a written record of their job activities, and associated time expenditures, for a preset period that typically ranges from a complete work cycle or typical week to up to a month. Although the information can be useful in discovering actual time expenditures and activities—for example, it was a vital component of the Mintzberg (1973) research investigation into the nature of managerial work that asked managers to record their work activities and associated time expenditures—there can be the problem of selective reporting and bias as the respondent is fully aware that his or her time and activities are being monitored.

HR Planning Today 4.2 describes Bayer's revision of its job analysis and evaluation processes.

## Output and Production Analysis

Machine-generated output reports, as well as production reporting procedures, can obtain information about the job and its normal and peak levels of production. Although these techniques reveal little about the qualitative or process aspects of the job, they are useful in determining appropriate performance standards for output.

## Current Job Descriptions and Specifications

In the quest for information about the job, a useful starting point, if a previous job analysis has been performed, is an examination of the existing job descriptions and specifications. Although the information contained in these documents is already dated, it is advantageous to see how the job in question has

## Rating Jobs Against New Values

Bayer Group AG, headquartered in Leverkusen, Germany, reorganized its three U.S. companies into one entity and in so doing revised their job analysis/evaluation processes. The new system was designed to meet the vision, culture, and goals of the unified company and to identify and measure competencies required for future organizational success. The existing Hay Guide Chart–Profile Method used previously was used as a starting point for the new system, although the language describing each work-value cluster was changed. Each of the following work-value clusters is matched to a numerical scale to enable Bayer to ensure internal equity through usage of point-based evaluation. Bayer's work-value dimensions are as follows:

1. *Improvement opportunity:* "Describes the requirement for and assesses the ability to improve performance within the context of assigned roles and rate of change in the work environment."

2. *Contribution:* "Describes the requirement for and ability to achieve results that improve performance and define success."

3. *Capability:* "Describes the total of proficiencies and competencies required to support effectiveness and progress."

Each of these three work-value clusters also incorporates various subelements, such as the following components of the capability cluster:

a. *Expertise and Complexity:* "Measures the depth and breadth of specific technical and professional proficiencies and competencies required for expected individual and team performance."

b. *Leadership and Integration:* "Measures the ability to manage, coordinate, integrate, and provide leadership for diverse people, processes, and organizational resources to achieve common goals and objectives."

c. *Relationship-Building Skills:* "Measures the requirements for meeting internal and external customers' needs through effective listening, understanding, sensitivity, and analytical abilities. This capability also measures the requirements for proactive persuasiveness, organizational awareness, and collaborative influencing skills necessary to effect desired change and build effective, enduring relationships."

Source: Laabs, J. 1997. "Rating Jobs against New Values," *Workforce*, Vol. 76, No. 5 (May), pp. 38–49. Used with permission of ACC Communication/*Workforce*, Costa Mesa, CA. All rights reserved.

evolved and whether its component duties, tasks, and employee specifications, as well as the authority and status the job is accorded, have increased or diminished over time.

Despite Fred Taylor's best efforts, in fact there is no one best way to analyze a job, so most contemporary job analyses employ a combination of the aforementioned methods. This multimethod approach not only provides a more comprehensive examination of the job but also enables quantitative aspects (e.g., production reports, questionnaires, observation) as well as qualitative aspects (e.g., interviews, journals, observation) of each job to be recorded.[21]

## 3. Examine the Recorded Data on the Job or Process

Having selected the most appropriate methods to analyze the job, job analysts record the knowledge, skills, and abilities; job-related behaviours, duties, tasks, responsibilities; and working conditions of the job. The next step is to examine these data from a variety of perspectives to get a detailed profile of the current job. Some of the questions involved in the examination are as follows:

a. What is the purpose of this job? Why does it exist?
b. Where is the job physically performed? Are there compelling reasons why the job must be performed there?
c. What is the sequence of behaviours required for successful job performance? Are there ways to modify the methods and process to improve the job both qualitatively (e.g., worker and client satisfaction, worker motivation) and quantitatively (e.g., output)?
d. Who performs the job? What constitutes the employee specifications (e.g., education, training, skills, etc.) required for job success? Are these specifications optimal, or are they the minimum standards required for success on the job?
e. What are the means of performing the job? Are the materials, machines, group processes (if applicable), and operating procedures congruent with effective performance of the job?

 4.5

After addressing all these issues, the job analysts start to form a clearer picture of the present job profile. This information is used to draft the job description or specification, which should be reviewed not only by the job incumbents but also by their supervisors. Reference is also made to the NOC, which provides an external comparison for the validity of the emerging job documentation. Any inconsistencies or discrepancies in the findings are examined by all the job analysts and are taken back to the jobholders and supervisors for further feedback and elaboration.

HR Planning Notebook 4.3 provides information on downloadable job descriptions.

WWW

### 4. Define and Formalize New Methods and Performance Standards for the Job or Process

To this point in the process, the job analysts have (a) examined existing descriptions and specifications for the job (if previous analyses have been conducted), (b) analyzed data on the job as it is currently performed by the jobholder(s), and (c) compared (a) and (b) to the job classification in the NOC and

---

## HR Planning Notebook 4.3

### Job Descriptions at the Click of a Mouse

KnowledgePoint, an HR software company, has launched a fee-based website that enables downloading of thousands of job descriptions. The website (www.jobdescription.com), contains job descriptions that can be either automatically e-mailed to the user or downloaded by the client. The benefits of this service are not only speed and convenience, but also customization of the job descriptions, which are kept current by the site provider.

Source: Adapted from M. Frost, "Descriptions Now!" *HR Magazine*, Vol. 42, No. 8 (August 1997): 28.

current practices in competitive firms. At this stage, the job analysts attempt to improve on current practices by recommending new methods and performance standards for the job. To do this, analysts must present the following questions to the incumbents and managers:

a. Would you recommend any changes to materials, machinery, behavioural sequencing, training, or procedures to improve performance on the job?
b. Are there any duties or tasks that should be added to or deleted from the job?
c. Would you recommend any changes in the specifications (e.g., knowledge, skills, or abilities) for individuals selected to perform this job?
d. What changes in working conditions would you recommend to improve performance on this job?
e. What is your rationale for these recommended changes?

Having gleaned the collective wisdom of all relevant parties regarding the performance of the job under examination, the HR specialists or job analysts write the new description or specification. This will incorporate improvements in how the job is performed (i.e., methods) as well as revisions to performance and output standards (i.e., time). These changes are formalized into written documents—either a job description or a job specification.

A job description is job focused as it concentrates on the duties or tasks, responsibilities, and specific behaviours that are required to be a successful performer. These duties are listed in order of importance to the organization, with the most critical ones listed first. It is also common practice for job descriptions to indicate the amount or percentage of work time devoted to the performance of each job task. While this information is undoubtedly useful for the jobholder, it is important to remember that time-consuming tasks are not necessarily highly valuable or critical to the organization's success! Because of its emphasis on tasks, the job description is best employed for assessing individual performance.

Job specifications are person focused as they detail the profile of the individuals who are best suited to perform the job. They concentrate on the knowledge, skills, abilities, experience, and physical capabilities required for job performance (e.g., the ability to clearly express ideas in oral communication) and are used by HR planners for recruitment and selection.

Both job descriptions and specifications contain the following information: (a) the job title, (b) the job code or classification number, (c) the compensation category, (d) the department or subunit, (e) the supervising job title (the title of the person to whom one reports), (f) the date of the approved description or specification, and (g) the name of the job analyst. This information facilitates quick access to the information by HR planners.

## 5. Maintain New Methods and Performance Standards for the Job or Process

It is one thing to have formal written documents specifying the duties, tasks, and KSAs required for job success, but it is quite another to ensure that these

## HR Planning Notebook 4.4

### Why Job Descriptions Are Not Used More

Despite the fact that job descriptions have a wide variety of uses in the organizational context—one study uncovered 132 uses for them—most managers use them infrequently and only for two or three purposes. Most often they are used for recruiting staff, designing the content of jobs, and occasionally for orientation processes. Dr. Philip Grant, an organizational researcher, investigated why job descriptions were fulfilling only a small part of their potential utility for organizations. He found that the most common reason provided by managers to explain the limited usage of job descriptions was that their organization did not unify or assemble all job descriptions into a well-organized, bound volume that was linked to the organizational chart and made available to all managers.

Other reasons for their limited usage included the following:

1. Managers do not know how to use job descriptions or what to use them for.
2. Job descriptions are perceived to be lacking in sufficient detail and comprehensiveness.
3. Job descriptions are perceived to be inaccurate.
4. Managers are not motivated to use job descriptions.
5. Managers do not know what job descriptions are.
6. Job descriptions are not structured well.
7. The job is perceived to "escape definition," or it changes too often.

Source: Adapted from Grant, P. 1998. "Why Job Descriptions Are Not Used More," *Supervision*, Vol. 59, No. 4 (April), pp. 10–13. Reprinted by permission.

new methods and standards for performance are put into practice. There are four main methods to help ensure usage of the new techniques and to prevent relapses to the old, comfortable ways of performing on the job: (a) communication and training, (b) supervisory reinforcement, (c) employee feedback, and (d) reward systems.

See HR Planning Notebook 4.4 for an explanation of why job descriptions often are not fulfilling their their potential.

As soon as the job description or specification with its new methods and standards has received final approval, the affected jobholders must be given a copy of the revised job description or specification. The process of formally communicating the job changes must also provide sufficient time for questions and answers to ensure workers are clear on the new expectations for their job performance. Training and development programs may have to be instituted if there are significant changes in methods, materials, or the sequencing of behaviours required on the job.

**RPC 4.6**

After being formally notified of the changes, supervisors must spend considerable time ensuring that workers are, in fact, behaving in accordance with the new job procedures. (In a unionized environment, of course, the procedure for job reclassification will be specified under the terms of the collective agreement.) Coaching, modelling the desired behaviours, and reinforcing successful performance of the new methods are all effective techniques supervisors can employ to prevent relapses to the outdated, yet habitual, methods of performing the job.

Feedback is critical to the success of the job analysis process. We have already seen that all parties to the process must be consulted on an ongoing basis for their valuable input. Even after the written job analysis documents have been prepared, feedback is essential in ensuring the process has been successful. Employees must be given the freedom to express suggested improvements or concerns with respect to methods, performance standards, and so on if we expect them to become motivated and committed to their jobs. It is important to bear in mind that job analysis is a never-ending process of data gathering, coding, interpreting, and refining job methods and standards. Even if we "get it right" today, changes in technology, competitive practices, economic circumstances, and so on will ensure that we must change to reflect the realities of tomorrow. Besides, who is better able to provide valid feedback about the circumstances of the job than the actual jobholder?

A common downfall of work redesign and job analysis efforts is that although the job methods and standards have changed, the organizational reward system has not been altered, and it reinforces the undesirable old job behaviours.[22] Even if workers have been trained in the new methods of the job and have been provided with a written copy of their revised job description and with ample supervisory coaching, actual worker actions may be very different from formal requirements. For example, if the revised work process is team based, but the compensation system conflicts with job descriptions by being disproportionately weighted toward evaluation of individual performance, we can expect to see unplanned, dysfunctional behaviours and conduct from members of the team. In this instance, worker demeanour may be dysfunctional from the perspective of the organization or the team, but extremely functional and rewarding from the individual's point of view! The oft-repeated dictum "what gets measured gets done" comes to mind, and if workers are still rewarded for their individual actions and not for their contributions to team success, conflicting organizational systems will ensure we do not get the desired results from the job analysis process.

**(R)(P)(C) 4.7**

## Specific Job Analysis Techniques

The final section of this chapter is devoted to an examination of specific job analysis techniques that are widespread in contemporary organizational usage. We will present five well-known and widely utilized techniques.

### 1. Critical Incidents Technique

The **critical incidents technique** is a qualitative process of job analysis that produces statements of behavioural examples along a range from superior to ineffective performance for a specific job.[23] Several experts, normally trained jobholders with considerable experience in the job that is being examined, are asked to identify the key dimensions of their job. Subsequently they describe for the analyst, in writing or verbally, specific critical incidents that relate to success, as well as those that lead to job failure. Once these critical incidents have been described, they are ranked with respect to their importance to success on the job. The behavioural statements are then used to

**(R)(P)(C) 4.8**

**critical incidents technique**
a qualitative process of job analysis that produces behavioural statements along a range from superior to ineffective performance for a specific job

provide specific guidance for HR planners in refining employee specifications for the job in question.

### 2. Behaviourally Anchored Rating Scales

**Behaviourally Anchored Rating Scales (BARS)** are used by organizations for appraisal of employees' performance and for job analysis purposes. In essence, each job is examined and divided into a small number of key dimensions (e.g., customer relations). Next, behavioural statements are developed for each dimension on a continuum ranging from examples of superior performance (e.g., provides customers with required information in a prompt and friendly fashion) to examples of unsuccessful performance (e.g., fails to provide customer with the information required to resolve inquiry). In this aspect, BARS is quite similar in its approach to the critical incidents technique. The next step involves anchoring the behavioural statements by assigning numerical values to them, with perhaps a value of 7 being allocated to a behavioural example of superior performance (7: provides customers with required information in a prompt and friendly fashion ) and a value of 1 to an example of an unsuccessful behaviour (1: fails to provide customer with the information required to resolve inquiry). BARS analysis provides a qualitative and quantitative comparison of jobs based on the derived behavioural statements and numerical values generated by the process.[24]

### 3. Position Analysis Questionnaire

The **Position Analysis Questionnaire (PAQ)**[26] was developed by Earnest McCormick as a structured job analysis checklist of 194 items or job elements used to rate a job. These job elements are incorporated into the following six dimensions:

1. *Information input:* How and where the worker obtains necessary information for job functioning
2. *Mental processes:* The types of planning, reasoning, and decision-making processes required by the job
3. *Work output:* The specific items produced by the worker and the tools he or she employs to produce them
4. *Relationships with other workers:* Important interpersonal contacts for the jobholder
5. *Job context and work satisfaction:* The physical and social working environments
6. *Other job characteristics:* Elements of the job that do not fall into the other five dimensions[27]

Although the job incumbent can complete the PAQ, typically a job analyst will interview the incumbent prior to directly observing his or her actions in fulfilling the performance requirements of the job. This enables the job analyst to score each of the 194 items on several five-point scales such as frequency of usage, importance to the specific job, and so on. The resultant quantitative score enables the comparison of jobs throughout the organization and for those jobs to be grouped according to similar scores on the six different dimensions.

**Behaviourally Anchored Rating Scales (BARS)**

a job is divided into a number of key dimensions, and each dimension contains a range of statements of job behaviour "anchored" to a numerical scale

**Position Analysis Questionnaire (PAQ)[25]**

a structured job analysis checklist that includes 194 items or job elements used to rate a job

### 4. Functional Job Analysis

Sidney Fine's **functional job analysis (FJA)** was used to establish the U.S. government's DOT and had a strong formative influence on Canada's NOC.[28] The FJA employs a series of written task statements, each containing four essential elements: (1) a verb related to the task action being performed by the worker, (2) an object that refers to what is being acted on, (3) a description of equipment, tools, aids, and processes required for successful completion of the task, and (4) the outputs or results of task completion.[29] A compendium of various task statements covers all necessary tasks of the job and, although brevity and concise written statements are the norm, some analysts have devised as many as 100 statements for a job. The completed task statements are used to describe any job and contain three essential elements: (1) people (important interpersonal relationships on the job), (2) data (obtaining, using, and transforming data in aid of job performance), and (3) things (physical machinery, resources, and the environment). Each of these three dimensions is then rated on level of complexity and importance with respect to the job being analyzed. The result of the rating is a quantitative score that can be used to compare various jobs.

**functional job analysis (FJA)**

analyzes any job using three essential elements: (1) people (important interpersonal relationships on the job), (2) data (obtaining, using, and transforming data in aid of job performance), and (3) things (physical machinery, resources, and the environment). Each of these three dimensions is then rated by level of complexity and importance.

### 5. The Hay System

Edward Hay and Associates (HayGroup) has developed a system of job analysis that is used extensively for its consulting work in compensation and organizational analysis. The **Hay system** uses three key factors to analyze each job: (1) know-how (the specific knowledge and skills required to perform the job), (2) problem solving (the decisions and problems that must be successfully handled on the job), and (3) accountability (the jobholder's responsibilities for critical task completion and for organizational resources, budgets, supervision of people, etc.).[30] A fourth factor, "working conditions" was subsequently added, and may be included for analysis of jobs that have extraordinary working conditions not adequately covered by the other three factors.[31]

Points are assigned to each factor for (1) levels of knowledge (job depth) and (2) breadth of knowledge required to perform the job (job scope). The sum of the points assigned to the job locates it in an overall compensation scheme that provides higher remuneration to those jobholders whose jobs were rated higher by the job analysis.

**Hay system**

uses three key factors to analyze each job: (1) know-how (the specific knowledge and skills required to perform the job), (2) problem solving (the decisions and problems that must be successfully handled on the job), and (3) accountability (the jobholder's responsibilities for critical task completion and for organizational resources, budgets, supervision of people, etc.)

## Competency-Based Approaches

Over the past decade, concerns have been expressed that in today's business environment, characterized by increased globalization, extremely turbulent environments, and fierce competition, traditional job analysis may be unable to keep up with the rapid rate of change faced by most organizations.[32] Furthermore, a great many organizations, even those that are highly profitable entities, have reduced their complement of full-time workers by "downsizing," thereby producing flatter organizational structures with fewer workers and greater reliance on self-managed teams in achieving desired

**competency**

any knowledge, skill, trait, motive, attitude, value, or other personal characteristic that is essential to perform the job and that differentiates superior from solid performance

organizational outcomes.[33] In this context, the increased desire for flexibility and cross-training of employees has led to a trend of examining **competency** modelling in order to identify general worker requirements associated with a broad range or category of jobs.[34] Although traditional job analysis is still firmly entrenched in most organizations, it is also true that most organizations have started to examine and institute competency-based practices into their work settings. Competency-based approaches have been used to develop successful professional performance for dentists, engineers, nurses, physicians, and police officers, etc.[35] Recent surveys have shown that approximately 75% to 80% of organizations have some sort of competency-driven applications currently in place.[36] HR Planning Today 4.3 describes the use of competency modelling.

Competency advocates maintain that there are several differences in approach between more traditional job analysis methods and competency-based modelling. First, where traditional job analysis focuses on the KSAs

## HR Planning Today 4.3

### Competency Models in Practice

Innovative organizations can utilize competency modelling in order to determine the behavioural requirements for employee success now and into the future. One organization, the American Institute of Certified Public Accountants, has developed a web-based competency assessment tool that enables accounting students and CPAs to compare their current knowledge and skill levels against those competencies that have been validated for success in a variety of jobs such as "staff accountant" or "CFO: chief financial officer." The competency models incorporate four different factors: (1) leadership qualities, (2) personal attributes, (3) functional specialties, and (4) broad business perspectives. By utilizing this convenient analytical tool, current and future accountants can get invaluable feedback about their progress toward personalized career goals. This information can also assist in developing and refocusing training and development priorities for accountants to ensure they have the knowledge and skills required for success in their desired positions.

Another area that has used competency models is the leisure or recreation business. Country, golf, and family clubs require managers who are able to successfully deal with a wide variety of complex issues on a day-to-day basis. The Club Managers Association of America conducted competency assessments during the 1990s but they wanted to see how or if the demands on managers would change in the new millennium. Industry experts and club managers identified and analyzed future changes that could be expected in the environment of clubs. The key finding of this competency analysis process was that in the future managers will have to be more effective in their time-management skills in order to be able to separate and sustain their personal and professional lives. Overall, eight competencies were identified (food and beverage management; club governance; building and facility management; human and professional resources; club accounting and finance; general management; marketing, sports, and recreation management; and external and governmental interaction), which were reduced to three main categories: (1) accounting and finance, (2) human and professional resources, and (3) marketing. The findings will be used for future career planning, training and development, and performance evaluation purposes for club managers across North America.

Sources: Adapted from K. Briggs, "Competencies–The Differential!" *Journal of Accountancy*, Vol. 194, No. 3 (September 2002), 79; and J. Perdue et al., "Competencies Required for Future Club Manager's Success," *Cornell Hotel and Restaurant Administration Quarterly*, Vol. 42, No. 1, (February 2001), 60–65.

required to perform specific jobs and examines the linkages among those jobs, competency models focus on individual-level competencies that are common to a broader occupational group or an entire level of jobs (e.g., executives, production workers, supervisory management). There is a deliberate focus on a much broader set of classifying variables than is typical for traditional job analysis.[37] Competencies are typically categorized as **core competencies** (characteristics that every member of an organization, regardless of position, function, or level of responsibility with the organization, is expected to possess, e.g., is a team player) or **role or specific competencies**[38] (characteristics shared by different positions within an organization, e.g., obtains financial information from each project team leader and compiles a master budget for the entire organization).[39] Only those members of an organization in these positions are expected to possess these competencies.

Second, some job analysts maintain that competency models are worker focused, given their focus on identifying core competencies, whereas job analysis is much more focused on duties and tasks of work. In this regard, competency models include personality and value orientations (e.g., risk taking) into the mix of what is required to "fit in" and succeed in the culture of a particular organization.

Third, since much of the work in organizations is conducted by teams, it can be argued that team skills are much more relevant to today's organization than the classic approach of having each individual job finely delineated with well-defined boundaries. Management personnel recognize that workers know the limits of their jobs and could readily refuse to perform a task that fell beyond their written job description requirements. As such, managers seek to have increased flexibility and control over workers' behaviours. On the other hand, unions are justifiably concerned about management abuses of authority in the new "competencies" approach, which lack the important safeguards of written documentation and well-defined limits to arbitrary displays of managerial power as are contained in traditional job descriptions and collective agreements.[40] Widespread problems with corruption, fraud, and executive mismanagement, as displayed by the corporate crashes of Nortel, Enron, and WorldCom, among others, show that unions, as the representatives of the organization's workforce, are well advised to tread carefully with respect to innovations in this area.

On the downside, competency approaches have been subjected to widespread criticisms as to their utility, including that they are so broad and ill defined as to be of little practical use in guiding performance of job duties.[41] Second, competencies focus more on behaviours than results, and as such focus on how individuals are expected to perform and not their demonstrated achievements.[42] Third, there has been a great deal of confusion among workers, HR practitioners, and academics as to what exactly is incorporated into effective competency models. There are a very wide range of definitions as to what exactly constitutes a competency, and, as noted by Zemke, "the word 'competencies' today is a term that has no meaning apart from the particular definition agreed to by the person with whom one is speaking."[43] Fourth, it has been noted that competency modelling is far from being a novel or separate activity from job analysis, but is in fact merely an extension of job

**core competencies**

characteristics that every member of an organization, regardless of position, function, or level of responsibility with the organization, is expected to possess

**role or specific competencies**

characteristics shared by different positions within an organization. Only those members of an organization in these positions are expected to possess these competencies

### Assessing Competencies and Skills in the Workplace

Research shows that managers and workers have different perceptions about the competencies and skills associated with various jobs in organizations. The main discrepancies exist in the managers' and workers' different perceptions of "workplace autonomy" and "level of required skills." Workers report lower levels of autonomy in their jobs and higher levels of skills requirements for success than are reported by managers for the same jobs under analysis. Furthermore, it is suggested that workers do not see competency as a specific set of attributes, knowledge, skills, and abilities, but as the sum of their perceived experiences and meaning of work.

Sources: Adapted from F. Green, "Assessing Skills and Autonomy: The Job Holder versus the Line Manager," *Human Resource Management Journal*, Vol. 13, No. 1, 63–74; and J. Sandberg, "Understanding Human Competence at Work: An Interpretative Approach," *Academy of Management Journal*, Vol. 43, No. 1 (February 2000), 9–25.

analysis that focuses on what is common across jobs and occupational groups and identifies the activities and worker characteristics that are core or critical on an organization-wide basis. Fifth, by focusing only on broad general competencies, it can easily be argued that a large portion of the activities required for an individual's successful performance in a job remains largely unexplained. Furthermore, it has been noted by a number of HR specialists that unlike job analysis, which is well understood by most HR practitioners and industrial/organizational psychologists, competency modelling is so ill-defined that they see absolutely no value in its approach and they expect it to die quickly![44] See HR Planning Today 4.4 for a discussion of assessment of workplace competencies and skills.

## Summary

In this chapter, we have examined a number of important aspects of the job analysis process in preparation for the next chapter's presentation on human resources management systems (HRMS). We have noted how an organization's work process is subdivided into meaningful units of work called jobs, and how the analysis of these jobs can take many forms, such as interviews, observation, and questionnaires. The investigation of jobs focuses on two specific aspects: namely, the methods employed to perform the job and the time standards for work completion. We examined a variety of traditional methods of job analysis (e.g., interviews, observation, questionnaires, journals and diaries, output and production analysis, etc.) including the recent trend of work analysis through competency-based approaches. Once job information has been collected and analyzed, it is stored in the HRMS or database to be used in the HR planning process. This stored job analysis information will be combined with personal information on the employees to try to make the best possible match between individual needs for fulfilling and rewarding work and the organization's requirements for specific work competencies.

# Key Terms

Behaviourally Anchored Rating Scales (BARS), 108

benchmark, 99

compensable factors, 95

competency, 110

contamination, 98

core competencies, 111

critical incidents technique, 107

deficiency, 98

*Dictionary of Occupational Titles* (DOT), 99

functional job analysis, 109

Hay system, 109

job, 93

job analysis, 93

job description, 94

job specification, 94

National Occupational Classification (NOC), 99

Occupational Information Network (O*NET), 99

position, 93

Position Analysis Questionnaire (PAQ), 108

role or specific competencies, 111

scientific management, 95

360° evaluation, 101

# Web Links

Government of Canada HRSDC's National Occupational Classification (NOC):

**www23.hrdc-drhc.gc.ca/2001/e/generic/welcome.shtml** (p. 99)

The U.S. Department of Labor's *Dictionary of Occupational Titles* (DOT) is located at:

**www.oalj.dol.gov/libdot.htm** (p. 99)

Economic Research Institute's website on the *Dictionary of Occupational Titles* is:

**www.erieri.com** (p. 99)

The U.S. Occupational Information Network (O*Net) is at:

**www.doleta.gov/programs/onet/** (p. 99)

PAQ Services Inc. website is at:

**www.paq.com** (p. 102)

A useful guide to Internet resources on HR is available at:

**www.hr-guide.com** (p. 102)

Analysis from HR Next on job analysis procedures and processes can be found at:

**www.hr.blr.com** (p. 104)

Knowledgepoint's website on job descriptions is at:

**www.jobdescription.com** (p. 106)

# RPC Icons

**RPC 4.1** Contributes to an environment that fosters effective working relationships

**RPC 4.2** Contributes to improvements in the organization's structures and work processes

**RPC 4.3** Analyzes position requirements to establish selection criteria

**RPC 4.4** Implements an effective procedure for describing work-related duties, establishing their relative worth, and aligning them with the organizational structure

**RPC 4.5** Gathers and analyzes employee feedback to assist decision making

**RPC 4.6** Develops an organization or unit design to fit a given set of business objectives and environmental factors

**RPC 4.7** Manages the use of resources, assigns work, and gauges the effectiveness of teams, individuals in meeting specific goals

**RPC 4.8** Develops systems and processes that link the career plans and skill sets of employees with the requirements of the organization

# Discussion Questions

1. One of the common reasons advanced for not conducting job analyses is the substantial cost that can be associated with such an undertaking. Present a more balanced perspective by identifying both the various benefits of conducting job analyses and the incremental costs that may occur if the process is not instigated.
2. This chapter stressed that effective job analysis incorporates qualitative and quantitative aspects, as well as a multimethod approach. Why is this additional complexity an important component of an effective job analysis intervention?
3. Jobs and the nature of work itself are dramatically changing in our information-based, global economy. How will the emerging patterns of work affect the nature of organizational participation, the nature of our jobs, and the process we employ to conduct job analyses in the future?

# Using the Internet

Both the Canadian and U.S. Governments operate extensive databases of occupational information derived from job analysis, i.e., Canada's National Occupational Classification (NOC) and the U.S. Occupational Information Network (O*Net). Go to their websites at **www23.hrdc-drhc.gc.ca/2001/e/generic/welcome.shtml** and **www.doleta.gov/programs/onet,** respectively, and find the listing on each database for your current occupation (or if you are still in training, your desired future occupation), along with its associated KSAs and employment requirements. Which of these databases do you find most useful and why? What are the strengths and weaknesses of each database?

# Exercise

1. Conduct a job analysis of your current job using two of the methods described in the chapter. Identify key stakeholders with whom you interact in order to perform your job duties, and interview them to derive valid information with respect to the tasks, information, accountabilities, roles, and KSAs required to perform your job. Use this information to draft a new/updated job description for your job, and compare this document to the organization's current formal job description. Assess the similarities and differences between the two documents and attempt to identify why these differences occur.

# Case: Madness at Moosehead U

As a distinguished graduate of Moosehead University's HR program, you having been achieving considerable fortune and fame in your role as a consulting job analyst; your success is aptly reflected by your painfully fashionable clothes, the waterfront condo, the matching "his and hers" platinum Range Rovers, and of course your favourite possession, the isolated lakeside cottage in the Canadian Shield. Things are good! Well, things are good with *you* personally, but obviously there are problems that need to be addressed at your alma mater.

Just this morning you received a frantic phone call from Dr. Melinda Muckabout, the university's vice-president of Administration, seeking to engage your professional services. It seems that she has been receiving considerable pressure from her boss, Dr. Hamish Haberdashery (VP Academic) and the president, Dr. Carla Climber. They in turn have been receiving pointed directives for action from the funding arm of the Provincial Ministry for Universities. Specifically, the deputy minister has told them bluntly that if Moosehead doesn't take action within the next six months to implement "performance indicators" for university faculty members and professors, the university will be subjected to a severe funding cut. The politicians and civil servants are responding to ongoing pressure from students, parents, and other taxpayers for much greater emphasis on rewarding quality teaching, enhancing job performance, and obtaining accountability from all the provincial universities.

In your role as a job analyst, you will have your work cut out for you. Melinda let you know that for every five faculty members on campus there are probably at least six different opinions on the core elements of a faculty member's job. To quote her exact words: "It's complete madness here!" The only internal policy guide is a Senate document that specifies in very general terms that a full-time faculty member has three areas of duties and responsibility: (1) teaching, (2) research and scholarly activities, and (3) service. There are great variations within each of these three categories. Teaching workloads vary enormously among professors with respect to the number of different courses and topics taught; whether the courses are introductory or advanced, undergraduate, or graduate level; whether they are "live" or delivered by Internet; the number of students in the classes themselves; and the degree of teaching and marking support made available by the university. The second category, "research and scholarly activities" is so incredibly broad as to almost defy description. It includes not only research and publications in journals, books, and practitioner magazines, but also theatre performances; media interviews; art gallery presentations; lectures to professional groups, the public, and other bodies; and lending professional expertise to groups within and outside the university itself. There are also huge variations among faculty members with respect to the funding support they receive for research, course releases from teaching, and general computer and facility support for these "scholarly" activities. The final category, service, typically incorporates serving on various university committees and task forces at the department, faculty, or university-wide level, but it also incorporates service to community groups and outside agencies, activities that increase the prestige and visibility of the university.

Suddenly your decision to take the contract doesn't look so straightforward. Certainly this will be a much more difficult assignment than many you have taken in the private sector.

However, over and above your fond attachment to Moosehead University, you realize that the university officials are relying on you to come through for them as they will be hard pressed to sustain one more budget cut on top of the past decade of slashed budgets and decreased financial support. The finished documents you produce will be used to not only annually assess the performance of faculty members on key explicit job dimensions, but also generate quantitative scores for each faculty member on these dimensions that can be used for compensation and "merit" pay. Furthermore, the finished documents will be of a quasi-legal nature as they will guide and constrain decisions on faculty tenure and promotion, as well as the selection, training, developing, and career progression of Moosehead's faculty members. You certainly have your work cut out for you. It's time to get to it!

Source: K. M<sup>c</sup>Bey, *Madness at Moosehead U*, 2002.

## Question

As the consulting job analyst to Moosehead University, prepare an intake evaluation report that contains your recommended steps and sequencing of activities to conduct this work analysis. List the various stakeholders you will consult, and indicate specific methods and techniques you will employ in successfully completing this contractual assignment.

# Endnotes

1. Hammonds, K. 2005. "Why We Hate HR," *Fastcompany.com*, Issue 97; Wooten, K., and M. Elden, 2001. "Cogenerating a Competency-based HRM Degree: A Model and Some Lessons from Experience," *Journal of Management Education*, 25/2, 231–258; Sincoff, M., and C. Owen. 2004. "Content Guidelines for an Undergraduate Human Resources Curriculum: Recommendations from Human Resources Professionals," *Journal of Education for Business*, 80/2, 80–86; McBer and Company in Yeung, A.K. 1996. "Competencies for HR Professionals: An Interview with Richard Boyatzis," *Human Resources Management*, 35, 119–32; Ulrich, D., W. Brockbank, and A. Yeung. 1989. "HR Competencies in the 1990s," *Personnel Administration*, 34, 91–93; Lawson, T., and V. Limbrick. 1996. "Critical Competencies and Developmental Experiences for Top HR Executives," *Human Resource Management*, 35, 67–85.

2. Heneman, R. 2003. "Job and Work Evaluation: A Literature Review," *Public Personnel Management*, 32/1, 47–73; Walker, J. 1994. "Integrating the Human Resource Function with the Business." *Human Resource Planning*, Vol. 17, No. 2: 59–77; Schuler, R.S., and J.W. Walker. 1990. "Human Resources Strategy: Focusing on Issues and Actions," *Organizational Dynamics*: 5–19.

3. Cascio as quoted in Tross, S., and T. Maurer. 2000. "The Relationship between SME Job Experience and Job Analysis Ratings: Findings with and without Statistical Control," *Journal of Business and Psychology*, 15/1, 97–110.

4. Gatewood, R.D., and H.S. Field. 1990. *Human Resources Selection*, 2nd ed. New York: Dryden Press.

5. Risher, H.W. 1989. "Job Evaluation: Validity and Reliability," *Compensation and Benefits Review*, Vol. 21, No. 1 (January): 32–33.

6. Walker, J.W. 1980. *Human Resource Planning*. New York: McGraw-Hill.

7. McBey, K., and C. Hammah. 1990. "The Evolution of Managerial and Organizational Thought." In L. Allan, ed., *Introduction to Canadian Business*. Toronto: McGraw-Hill Ryerson.

8. McBey, K.J. 1996. "Exploring the Role of Individual Job Performance within a Multivariate Investigation into Part-time Turnover Processes," *Psychological Reports*, Vol. 78: 223–233.

9. Employment and Immigration Canada. 1993. *National Occupational Classification*. Cat. No. MP 53-25-1-1993E. Ottawa: Minister of Supply and Services

10. Jeanneret, R. and Strong, M. 2003. "Linking O*NET Job Analysis Information to Job Requirement Predictors: An O*NET Application," *Personnel Psychology*, 56/2, 465–480; United States Department of Labor, 1994.

11. Jenkins, G.D. 1975. "Standardized Observations: An Approach to Measuring the Nature of Jobs," *Journal of Applied Psychology* (April): 171–181.

12. Gael, S. 1988. *The Job Analysis Handbook for Business, Industry, and Government*. New York: John Wiley; Ghorpade, J.V. 1988. *Job Analysis: A Handbook for the Human Resource Director*. Englewood Cliffs, NJ: Prentice Hall; Prien, E., and W.W. Ronan. 1971. "Job Analysis: A Review of Research Findings," *Personnel Psychology*, Vol. 24: 371–396.

13. Jenkins, G.D. 1975. "Standardized Observations: An Approach to Measuring the Nature of Jobs," *Journal of Applied Psychology* (April): 171–181.

14. Denton, J.C. 1975. *The Position Description Questionnaire*. Cleveland, OH: Psychological Business Research.

15. Fine, S. 1974. "Functional Job Analysis: An Approach to a Technology for Manpower Planning," *Personnel Journal* (November): 813–818; Fine, S., and W.W. Wiley. 1971. *An Introduction to Functional Job Analysis*. Kalamazoo, MI: Upjohn Institute for Employment Research.

16. Hackman, R., and G. Oldham. 1974. *The Job Diagnostic Survey: An Instrument for the Diagnosis of Jobs and the Evaluation of Job Redesign Projects*. Springfield, IL: National Technical Information Service; Hackman, R., and G. Oldham. 1975. "Development of the Job Diagnostic Surveym" *Journal of Applied Psychology*, Vol. 60: 159–170.

17. Hemphill, J.K. 1960. *Dimensions of Executive Positions*. Columbus: Ohio State University.

18. McCormick, E.J., P.R. Jeanneret, and R.C. Meecham. 1972. "A Study of Job Characteristics and Job Dimensions as Based on the PAQ," *Journal of Applied Psychology*, Vol. 56, No. 4 (August): 347–368.

19. Jones, R., J. Sanchez et al. 2001. "Selection or Training? A Two-Fold Test of the Validity of Job Analytic Ratings of Trainability," *Journal of Business and Psychology*, 15/3, 363–389; Mueller, M. and G. Belcher. 2000. "Observed Divergence in the Attitudes of Incumbents and Supervisors as Subject Matter Experts in Job Analysis: A Study of the Fire Captain Rank." *Public Personnel Management*, 29/4, 529–558.

20. Dierdorff, E., and M. Wilson. 2003. "A Meta-Analysis of Job Analysis Reliability," *Journal of Applied Psychology*, 88/4, 635–646.

21. Chang, I., and B. Kleiner. 2002. "How to Conduct Job Analysis Effectively," *Management Research News*, 25/3, 73–82; Reynolds, R., and M. Brannick. 2001. "Is Job Analysis Doing the Job? Extending Job Analysis with Cognitive Task Analysis," *Society for Industrial and Organizational Psychology*, July; Schuler and Walker, 1990; Godet, M. 1983. "Reducing the Blunders in Forecasting," *Futures*, Vol. 15, No. 3 (June): 181–192; Mahmoud, E. 1984. "Accuracy in Forecasting: A Survey," *Journal of Forecasting*, Vol. 3, No. 2 (April): 139–159.

22. Kerr, S. 1975. "On the Folly of Rewarding A, While Hoping for B," *Academy of Management Journal* (December): 769–783.

23. Leeds, P., and R. Griffith. 2001. "Critical Incident Inter-rater Agreement among Security Subject-Matter Experts," *Journal of Security Administration*, 24/1, 31–46; Flanagan, J.C. 1954. "The Critical Incidents Technique," *Psychological Bulletin*, Vol. 51: 327–358; Ghorpade, J.V. 1988. *Job Analysis: A Handbook for the Human Resource Director*. Englewood Cliffs, NJ: Prentice Hall.

24. Campbell, J., M. Dunnette, R. Arvey, and L. Hellervik. 1973. "The Development and Evaluation of Behaviorally Based Rating Scalesm" *Journal of Applied Psychology*, Vol. 57, No. 1 (February): 15–22.; Hom, P.W., A.S. DeNisis, A.J. Kinicki, and B. Bannister. 1982. "Effectiveness of Performance Feedback from Behaviorally Anchored Rating Scales," *Journal of Applied Psychology*, Vol. 67, No. 5 (October): 568–576; Jacobs, R., D. Kafry, and S. Zedeck. 1980. "Expectations of Behaviorally Anchored Rating Scales," *Personnel Psychology*, Vol. 33, No. 3 (Autumn): 595–640; Kingstrom, P., and A. Bass. 1981. "A Critical Analysis of Studies Comparing Behaviorally Anchored Rating Scales and Other Rating Formats," *Personnel Psychology*, Vol. 34, No. 2 (Summer): 263–289.

25. McCormick, E.J., P.R. Jeanneret, and R.C. Meecham. 1972. "A Study of Job Characteristics and Job Dimensions as Based on the PAQ," *Journal of Applied Psychology*, Vol. 56, No. 4 (August): 347–368.

26. Fine, S. 1974. "Functional Job Analysis: An Approach to a Technology for Manpower Planning," *Personnel Journal* (November): 813–818; Fine, S., and W.W. Wiley. 1971. *An Introduction to Functional Job Analysis*. Kalamazoo, MI: Upjohn Institute for Employment Research

27. McCormick, E.J. 1976. "Job and Task Analysis." In M.C. Dunnette, ed., *Handbook of Industrial and Organizational Psychology*. New York: Rand McNally

28. Harvey, R. 2002. "Functional Job Analysis," *Personnel Psychology*, 55/1, 202–206; Fine, S. 1974. "Functional Job Analysis: An Approach to a Technology for Manpower Planning," *Personnel Journal* (November): 813–818; Levine, E.L. 1983. *Everything You Always Wanted to Know about Job Analysis*. Tampa, FL: Mariner Publishing.

29. Harvey, 2002; Henderson, R. 1993. *Compensation Management*, 6th ed. Reston, VA: Reston Publishing.

30. Skenes, C., and B. Kleiner. 2003. "The HAY System of Compensation," *Management Research News*, 26/2–4, 109–116; Reynolds, R., and M. Brannick. 2001. "Is Job Analysis Doing the Job? Extending Job Analysis with Cognitive Task Analysis," *Society for Industrial and Organizational Psychology*, July; Sanchez, J. 1994. "From Documentation to Innovation: Reshaping Job Analysis to Meet Emerging Business Needs," *Human Resource Management Review*, Vol. 4, No. 1: 51–74.

31. Skenes and Kleiner, 2003.

32. Buhler, P. 2002. "Tips to Improved Staffing Decisions," *Supervision,* 63/10, 20–23; Ashkenas, R., D. Ulrich, T. Jick, and S. Kerr. 1995. *The Boundaryless Organization.* San Francisco: Jossey-Bass.

33. Hayden, S. 1999. "Competency Based Management," *IHRIM Journal,* Vol. 3, No. 1: 16–18.

34. Prien, E., Prien K. and Gamble, L. 2004. "Perspectives on Nonconventional Job Analysis Methodologies," *Journal of Business and Psychology,* 18/3, 337–348; Catano, V., S. Cronshaw, W. Wiesner, R. Hackett, and L. Methot. 2001. *Recruitment and Selection in Canada,* 2nd ed. Toronto: Nelson Thomson Learning

35. Schippmann, J., R. Ash, M. Battista, et al. 2000. "The Practice of Competency Modeling," *Personnel Psychology,* Vol. 53, No. 3 (Autumn): 703–737.

36. Schippmann et al., 2000.

37. Sanchez, 1994.

38. Catano et al., 2001, 176.

39. Intagliata, J., D. Ulrich, and N. Smallwood. 2000. "Leveraging Leadership Competencies to Produce Leadership Brand: Creating Distinctiveness by Focusing on Strategy and Results," *Human Resources Planning,* Vol. 23, No. 3: 12–23.

40. Harvey, R., and M. Wilson. 2000. "Yes Virginia, There Is an Objective Reality in Job Analysis," 21/7, 829–848; Schippmann, J., R. Ash, M. Battista, et al. 2000. "The Practice of Competency Modeling." *Personnel Psychology,* Vol. 53, No. 3 (Autumn): 703–737.

41. Lievens, F., J. Sanchez, and W. De Corte. 2004. "Easing the Inferential Leap in Competency Modeling: The Effects of Task-Related Information and Subject Matter Expertise," *Personnel Psychology,* 57/4, 881–1003; Schippmann, J., R. Ash, M. Battista, et al. 2000. "The Practice of Competency Modeling." *Personnel Psychology,* Vol. 53, No. 3 (Autumn): 703–737.

42. Fine, S. 1974. "Functional Job Analysis: An Approach to a Technology for Manpower Planning," *Personnel Journal* (November): 813–818; Fine, S., and W.W. Wiley. 1971. *An Introduction to Functional Job Analysis.* Kalamazoo, MI: Upjohn Institute for Employment Research.

43. Ibid.

44. Hemphill, J.K. 1960. *Dimensions of Executive Positions.* Columbus: Ohio State University.

# Chapter 5

# Information Technology for HR Planning

This chapter was written by Victor Y. Haines III.

## Chapter Learning Objectives

After reading this chapter, you should be able to

- Demonstrate a keen awareness of the diversity of information technology (IT) solutions for human resource management (HRM).
- Explain how various IT solutions can be leveraged to improve HR planning.
- Identify specific IT applications for HR planning.
- Apply the process of IT acquisition and implementation.
- Project into the future a number of new IT applications for HR planning.

The National Film Board of Canada (NFB) has a long history of IT implementation for managing its human resources. Its mission is to produce and distribute distinctive, culturally diverse, challenging, and relevant audiovisual works that provide Canada and the world a unique Canadian perspective. In an average year, NFB produces 80 to 85 films and other original audiovisual products.

The NFB faces the challenge of managing a high percentage of temporary employments across nine sites. Of its 480 employees, 40 are long-term temporary employees. In addition, 1000 to 1300 short-term temporary employees are hired annually. The organization has embraced the Web as it distributes and sells its products on the Internet as it got involved in e-commerce activities five years ago.

The HR system at NFB is a state-of–the-art solution. Many HR applications run on the company's Intranet. Managers and employees can access and change their personal data, and access position postings, compensation data, job description, information on benefits, training provided to each employee, and a more complete directory. The Intranet also allows leave and overtime data entry and processing, and entry and approval of short-term hiring contracts. Employees can access their data directly and, for instance, view their vacation leave information. They may also enter leave time and, with paperless workflow, a message goes to their supervisors with a hyperlink for approval.

The HR system at NFB is now considered a useful management tool. But it was not always so easy. The IT initiative began a little before 1988. At that time, the NFB was using a mainframe system that did not allow additional fields to be added. The only terminals to be found in the HR department were dumb terminals (with no processing capabilities). One person, Claude Chantelois, Manager of Compensation, was chosen to head the HR technology transformation. His team reviewed various HR/payroll responsibilities (i.e., position data, employee data, payroll and salary administration, leave and overtime, training, employee benefits, pensions and pension simulation, staff relations, health and safety, workforce planning, performance appraisal, and skills management). They identified four goals for the new system:

- Meet the needs expressed by branches and interface with the new financial application.
- Ensure that the system meets the organization's HR needs.

- Ensure that the system is user friendly enough to allow data capture at source, so that the organization can eliminate duplicate data entry and reduce paperwork while remaining just as efficient.
- Restructure a payroll system for the organization's temporary employees.

These goals were achieved over time by paying attention to the potential of emerging technologies and by dealing effectively with resistance to change through extensive communication and training.

## IT and HRM

In the age of virtual or technology-driven HR, effective HR planners need to understand and leverage IT for planning purposes. IT can help project correct demand and supply levels based on realistic scenarios. Because of its powerful storage and retrieval capabilities, IT can support succession planning and career development plans.

The use of IT for HRM has increased at a steady pace over the last couple of decades. As a result, HR professionals have been able to handle a greater workload and achieve operational and strategic efficiency (see HR Planning Today 5.1). Compared to paper-based systems, IT provides better data storage, information retrieval, and tools for analysis, which reduces the burden of transactional activities. This allows more time and resources to be dedicated to more strategic roles.[1]

A recent study found that IT makes a difference to HR.[2] First, the study found that the five applications that received the highest levels of IT support were (1) storing important data such as wages, vacation, and sick time, (2) transferring employee data between HR and outside payroll systems, (3) generating organizational charts, (4) posting jobs openings within the organization, and (5) tracking labour costs. The five HR applications that received the lowest levels of IT support were (1) providing employees with self-assessment and career development guidance, (2) providing employees with ergonomics assessment assistance, (3) measuring the needs and results of diversity initiatives, (4) letting employees make changes to their own benefits records, and (5) online service delivery of employee assistance programs. More to the point, the results show that IT usage is significantly associated with HR's greater involvement in supporting the successful implementation of business strategy and delivering tangible results. IT usage is also associated with greater HR involvement in the strategic roles of business partner and change agent. Finally, IT usage is associated with more positive assessments of the technical and strategic effectiveness of the HR function. Taken together, these results suggest that IT can help HR professionals overcome the burden of administrative transactional tasks, including the processing of hundreds of résumés and benefits forms. In sum, smart use of IT allows HR professionals to dedicate themselves to being strategists and achieving results instead of being bogged down with "administrivia."

 5.1

## HR Planning Today 5.1

### IT Relief for the Headache of Performance Appraisals

Accuracy, fairness, and timeliness are the key goals that any quality newspaper strives to achieve in its news coverage. They should also be the key goals of any employee performance report.

That was the challenge facing the HR executives at Lee Enterprises (NYSE: LEE), a 114-year-old company with a passion for local newspapers. Lee's 6700 employees, working in 44 daily newsrooms and 200 weekly and specialty publications in 19 states, added up to one huge human resources headache when it was time to conduct annual performance appraisals.

Now, all full-time and regular part-time employees in Lee's workforce get regular, efficient evaluations of their work and development, using Web-based employment performance management (EPM) software. And Lee's Human Resources managers can generate relevant, high-quality performance reports faster than Britney Spears can generate headlines.

More importantly, Lee has found that its corporate values and the goals of its employees are better aligned, thanks to an integrated, efficient EPM process.

Source: Found at www.halogensoftware.com/products/case_studies/study_lee_enterprises.php. Reprinted with permission from Halogen Software.

The value of IT is in what it can do to improve functioning in various contexts. In his seminal work, George P. Huber explained that advanced information technologies share a number of properties, which are summarized in HR Planning Notebook 5.1.[3] The question of how to dedicate these properties to the improvement of human resource management and planning is the focus of this chapter.

HR professionals are now finding value in IT. They leverage IT for online recruitment and utilize résumé-processing systems to create very sophisticated databases of qualified job applicants. They are increasingly using virtual career centres and computer-based assessments. Technology-assisted training or e-learning is an area witnessing significant growth.[4] Also, some very interesting HR planning applications are being used, many of which we will explore in this chapter.

IT is also used to better manage some basic HRM requirements such as employee benefits enrollment and payroll management. One HR software provider, DLGL, offers a product that helps organizations in the areas outlined in HR Planning Notebook 5.2.

**outsourcing**

a contractual arrangement that has an outside company manage some functions that were previously handled in-house

In some of these areas, **outsourcing** is considered an appropriate option. Modern communication technologies that rely on the processing power of computers provide new outsourcing opportunities. Outsourcing providers or vendors benefit from economies of scale and, in recent years, they have developed their HR expertise beyond handling routine transactions. In its promotional material, for instance, ADP Canada claims to offer the three levels of payroll outsourcing shown in HR Planning Notebook 5.3.

HR professionals are involved in planning, selecting, and implementing IT solutions for their business. This requires information system skills as well as change management and project management skills. HR professionals need also

## HR Planning Notebook 5.1

### Properties of Advanced Information Technologies

- Basic characteristics:
  - Better data storage capacity
  - Improved transmission capacity
  - Higher levels of processing capacity
- Communication properties:
  - To communicate more easily and less expensively across time and geographic location
  - To communicate more rapidly and with greater precision to targeted groups
  - To record and index more reliably and inexpensively the content and nature of communication events
  - To more selectively control access and participation in a communication event or network

- Decision aiding ability:
  - To store and retrieve large amounts of information more quickly and inexpensively
  - To more rapidly and selectively access information created outside the organization
  - To more rapidly and accurately combine and reconfigure information as to create new information
  - To more compactly store and quickly use the judgment and decision models developed in the minds of experts, or in the mind of the decision maker, and store as expert systems or decision models
  - To more reliably and inexpensively record and retrieve information about content and nature of organizational transactions

## HR Planning Notebook 5.2

### Areas for IT Application

- Time capture and scheduling
- Payroll
- Pension administration
- Position control
- Job matching
- Career planning
- Employment equity

- Health and safety
- Applicant tracking
- Skills inventory
- Succession planning
- Recruitment
- Training

## HR Planning Notebook 5.3

### Three Levels of Payroll Outsourcing

- Best-in-class applications for on-site payroll management
- Fully hosted payroll solution with back-end processing, services, and support from ADP

- A new-breed full-service, fully outsourced solution

Chapter 5: Information Technology for HR Planning

develop constructive working relationships with consultants at different stages of the selection and implementation process. They must also become proficient at finding current, accurate, and immediate answers to business and HR questions. Their involvement is also required in ensuring the effective functioning of new organizational designs such as telecommuting and virtual teaming.[5]

To deal with the increasing complexity of technology, many HR professionals are developing their skills through networking and training. The International Association for Human Resource Management (IRHIM) provides several learning opportunities to its members. This association's annual conference, for instance, includes educational sessions, professional development seminars, and networking events. Those attending the conference may visit the technology expo and learn more about new IT solutions for HRM. Closer to home, Canadian HR professionals may find learning resources within the Human Resource Management Systems Professionals Association (HRMSP).

## IT for HR Planning

IT can be leveraged to better manage several HR activities involved in strategic HR planning. First, the data available in an employee database can be used to analyze environmental influences on HRM. For instance, available information on employees' participation in training, their competencies, and performance levels may help determine the most appropriate strategic option. Easy access to data may also help management identify areas where available talent is lacking for adequate succession. Technology may also be used to assess client satisfaction with the service levels provided by the HRM department. Electronic surveys are also increasingly used to conduct climate or engagement surveys. As such, these applications can support the evaluation stage of the strategic HR planning process.

In the next section we will further explore how IT may support HR planning with a focus on three important applications: skills inventories, replacement charts, and succession management.

## Skills Inventories

In assessing the internal supply of HR, skills inventories represent a valuable tool. They contain information on the number and the KSAs of the workforce. The IT application should thus contain a personal record or skills inventory of each member of the workforce. Included in the inventory are items such as employee name, seniority, classification, part- or full-time work status, work history and record of jobs held in the organization, education, training, skill competencies, history of performance appraisals, and future jobs desired by or recommended for the individual, as well as hobbies and interests that may be useful for organizational planning. This information can (and should) be stored on a database that allows easy search and retrieval.

Gartner's skills inventory methodology includes a Web-based tool called skillpower™, by Gartner. This tool was designed to help both develop a listing of specific skill sets and employees complete their online individual assessment. The software solution includes standard reports, and custom reports can be developed to meet specific business needs.

## Replacement Charts

Replacement planning designates the process of finding replacement employees for key managerial positions. Replacement charts are often used to support this process. These include predicted departure dates of the incumbents, along with a shortlist of possible successors. Replacement charts include employee performance appraisal data and information about how ready possible successors are to fill those key managerial positions. Some IT applications ease the process of replacement planning by providing timely and user-friendly access to replacement charts.

Replacement planning software solutions generally allow decision makers to determine which positions have sufficient "bench strength" and which positions need further planning. Authoria, provider of integrated strategic Human Capital Management (HCM) solutions, for example, offers online navigation of divisional and corporate-wide organizational charts that allows the manager to track incumbents and candidates and obtain specific information from the résumé, or historical pay or performance details. Such products are most useful for large organizations where the volume of data is sufficient to require software support for the process.

## Succession Management

Succession management is about preparing employees for future jobs within the organization and developing the next generation of leaders. The process of succession management is information intensive requiring information on competencies, talent pools, developmental plans, performance assessments from different sources, and developmental opportunities. IT solutions can help structure and manage this information (see HR Planning Today 5.2).

There are, for example, several tools available to conduct multiple source or 360° feedback performance assessments. Other succession management IT solutions, such as Nardoni Strategic Solutions, include more functionalities. The company's Succession Pulse™ allow the user to analyze comprehensive data on employees, positions, and developmental activities. It will locate and compare successors based on competency search and comparison.

One meaningful activity involved in succession management involves helping individuals realize their career plans within the organization. This may be done by advertising internal opportunities for continuous learning and growth. The Pathfinder software application implemented at Cisco Systems, for example, was an important component of its new "build" talent strategy.[6]

Another approach to helping individuals realize their career plans is to allow employees to assess their own skills as a basis for career planning and training. SkillView Technologies provides a software solution that does just that. Reporting functions allow employees to record and track their competencies and to perform comparative analysis against their job position as well as other positions in the organization. This software provider also offers a pre-populated skills dictionary containing skills data for all corporate functions and many vertical industries.

### Cisco's Pathfinder Solution

In September 2001, Cisco took a first step to implement its "build" strategy; it created the Pathfinder software application that allowed managers to post openings for jobs within high-growth areas. Pathfinder's corresponding online database, I-Profiler, allowed employees to voluntarily enter their resumes for consideration. The profiles captured employees' work and educational experience, skills, and technical qualifications and detailed their career aspirations for development discussions with their managers. Line managers had access to each of their employees' profiles to better assess existing skills on their teams. Pathfinder was the first tool designed specifically to advertise job openings internally.

Source: J. Chatman, C. O'Reilly, and V. Chang, 2005, "Cisco Systems: Developing a Human Capital Strategy," *California Management Review*, 47, 2: 153.

## Different IT Solutions for Different Needs

There is an amazing diversity of software solutions for HRM. Organizations may favour a comprehensive human resource information system (HRIS) or a specialty product focused on a single area, such as applicant tracking. Within these two broad categories, the marketplace offers a range from low-cost, to mid-market, to costly high-end systems. In this section, we review these options. We also present enterprise solutions such as those offered by SAP or PeopleSoft.

### HRIS

**human resources information system (HRIS)**

a comprehensive across-the-board software system for HRM that includes subsystems or modules

The **human resources information system (HRIS)** is often referred to as the "best of breed" solution. It involves acquiring the best available software product that will encompass a broad range of HR functions (e.g., benefits, payroll, time and attendance, training, etc.). As such, the HRIS is a comprehensive solution for HR that includes several subsystems or modules such as recruitment and selection, time and attendance management, training and development, pension administration, etc. The system collects, stores, maintains data, and retrieves information about employees and their jobs.

VIP, a product offered by DLGL, is a good example of such a system. This company offers an integrated HRM, payroll, time capture and scheduling, pension, and recruitment solution for large and very large employers. As such, the DLGL HRIS encompasses a broad range of HR functions. It covers all of the important aspects of HRM.

### Specialty Products

**specialty product**

software solutions for specific/specialized applications that may or may not interface with the main database

There are numerous **specialty products** available that address particular HRM needs. For example, time and attendance software offered by Kronos can track days, hours, overtime, and vacation balances. Meade estimates that such specialty products number between 1500 to 2000.[7] They include compensation planning solutions that allow managers to compare various salary recommendations or scenarios relative to budget. Other applications assist in managing training schedules and budgets. Faltec, Inc., for example, developed an application called Formatio to help managers, mostly in small businesses, plan and budget training and development activities to meet legislative requirements.

Such specialty products may be easily acquired off-the-shelf by smaller companies as less costly solutions to specific challenges. They are also likely to interface with a company's more comprehensive HRIS or ERP base system.

### Enterprise Solutions

**Enterprise resource planning (ERP)** solutions contrast with the "best of breed" approach. Enterprise systems are based on software that integrates data from diverse applications into a common database. An ERP can integrate HR data with other systems in the firm (i.e., finance, logistics, production, and accounting). HR then becomes one application amongst others and, as such, a subset of ERP software solutions. SAP, the world's third-largest independent software provider with more than 28 200 customers in more than 120 countries around the world, for instance, offers an ERP that includes four functional areas: financials, human capital management, operations, and corporate services. Human capital management, the HR part of SAP's ERP solution, is described in its promotional material in HR Planning Today 5.3.

Many large organizations have implemented ERP solutions in recent years. The approach promotes the use of a single, shared **relational database** for critical information across the organization. This fosters the enforcement of consistent processes and procedures throughout the organization and

**enterprise resource planning (ERP)**
commercial software systems that automate and integrate many or most of a firm's business processes

**relational database**
a database that can share information across multiple tables or files, which allows the same information to exist in multiple files simultaneously

---

## HR Planning Today 5.3

### SAP's Human Capital Management

By leveraging integrated HCM tools, you'll gain insight into—and control over—increasingly virtual workforces. With mySAP ERP HCM, you can find the best people, develop and leverage their talent, align their efforts with corporate objectives, maximize the impact of training efforts, and retain top performers. The solution provides integrated, enterprisewide functionality that:

- automates HCM processes and seamlessly integrates them across global operations,
- provides real-time information access that accelerates workforce decision making,

- allows you to assign the right people to the right projects at the right time,
- supports both employees and managers throughout the employee life cycle, and
- empowers employees to manage processes in a collaborative environment.

Designed for global business, mySAP ERP HCM supports payroll functions, regulatory requirements, and best practices for more than 50 countries. It integrates with existing business systems and can be customized to meet your requirements.

---

Chapter 5: Information Technology for HR Planning

ensures that administrative units can easily share information and communicate with each other. The ERP solution, however, is often quite costly as it involves significant organizational and contextual change.[8] Implementation time may range from 12 months to four years.[9]

For HR, the enterprise-wide solution has some benefits. It may provide a platform for a better integration of HR and finance in the management of payroll.[10] Also, as HR may not otherwise obtain budget approval for investment in a "best of breed" solution, the enterprise-wide solution offers an opportunity for automation along with other administrative functions. HR professionals may also gain credibility as a result of their effective involvement in an ERP implementation.

## Selecting Technology Solutions for HRM

Organizations rarely develop their own systems; most acquire software from a vendor. But with so many vendors and technology solutions out there, where should an HR professional start? This section presents an overview of the selection process. For a more comprehensive treatment of this topic, consult specialized books.[11]

### Conduct a Needs Analysis

Needs regarding HR technology are constantly evolving. Nevertheless, writes James G. Meade, "you are best off if you define those needs, at least in outline form, and plan for software that will meet the needs as they evolve."[12] A systematic needs analysis will include collecting information about the organization (e.g., size, industry demands), its technical environment (e.g., hardware, operating systems, network environment, database, installed software, telecommunications, possible application service providers), and the needs of its HR department. With regards to HR needs, Meade suggests exploring areas where the HR department is not accessing critical information in an accurate or timely manner. For instance, if benefits enrollment takes almost two months, it is a problem. It is also helpful to consider what information request the HR department responds to, what reports and documents it uses, what information passes through the HR unit, and what manual records are maintained.

**RPC 5.2**

### Explore the Marketplace

The marketplace offers a wide variety of software solutions. Therefore, it is important to get to know the vendors and what they have to offer by contacting software providers to ask for software literature and demo disks. Industry periodicals offer reviews of HR software, and HR professionals can participate in vendor exhibitions, meet the vendors, attend conferences, and gather documentation. By exploring the market, HR professionals can further specify needs based upon a more complete understanding of available software solutions, and come up with a shortlist of a handful of prospective vendors.

### Recommended RFP Ingredients

- An overview that describes your company
- A description of your software need and the employee population it will support
- Desired systems functionality
- Required technical environment/specifications

- A request for pricing
- A request for customer references
- Details on customer service/support available from the vendor
- A request for sample contract terms

## Request for Proposal

The next step is to issue a request for proposal (RFP) to selected vendors. This involves communicating what is sought from vendors. Interested vendors then set up sales calls where they show demos. See HR Planning Notebook 5.4 for recommendations from the Society for Human Resource Management of what to require from vendors.

## Evaluate Vendors and Products

Careful vendor selection is critical to the success of any software acquisition process. Meade suggests that **scripted demos** be used at this stage. A scripted demo is an in-person demonstration of the product that follows a clear agenda that you have prepared for the vendors. This ensures that the demo focuses on your organization's needs.

At this stage of the acquisition process it is also useful to obtain references from users of the product you are considering, both technical and functional staff. They can provide information about the product, its ease of use, levels of support offered by the vendor, and address other concerns (e.g., ease of implementation).

**scripted demo**

an in-person demonstration of the product that follows a clear agenda (in fact, a written script) that you have prepared for the vendors[13]

# Implementing and Evaluating Technology

Implementing HR technology should be considered a major organizational change that alters communication patterns and power dynamics between HR and line management.[14] This section reviews technology implementation issues. We also include some criteria for evaluating HR technology.

## Typical Implementation Process

Implementing HR technology, especially large-scale HRIS of ERP projects requires an effective change or organizational development strategy. This strategy would generally include selecting a project manager and putting together a project team. The implementation phases, from implementation planning to parallel testing, are mentioned in HR Planning Notebook 5.5. HR professionals involved in an HR technology project would be well advised to

### HR Technology Implementation

- Implementation planning
- Input of the steering committee
- Ongoing communications to all interested parties
- Policy and procedure development
- Project team training
- Installation
- Fit analysis
- Modification

- Interfaces
- Conversion
- User (and technical support) training
- Unit and integrated testing
- Parallel

Source: G.M. Rampton, I.J. Turnbull, and J.A. Doran, 1999, *Human Resources Management Systems: A Practical Approach*, 2nd ed. Scarborough, ON: Carswell.

consult a specialized textbook for a more extensive overview of these implementation phases.[15]

As for other change projects, the successful implementation of HR technology rests upon a number of factors, although top management support for the project is an essential ingredient. In addition, the plan should involve users early in the project, ideally during the design process or in the planning stage of system implementation. Face-to-face communication in a training format is more effective than written communication during system implementation.[16]

## Business Process Re-Engineering

Automation and business process re-engineering go hand in hand; it would not make sense to automate before reviewing processes. Likewise, process review needs to consider opportunities for automation. HR systems can provide unique opportunities to consolidate work and eliminate steps in otherwise complex processes. As Hammer and Champy pointed out, "Automating existing processes with IT is analogous to paving cow paths."[17] IT often plays an important enabling role in business process re-engineering projects.

The principals of **business process re-engineering** are quite straightforward. They involve rethinking organizational processes in light of enabling technologies. In some cases business process re-engineering involves going back to the drawing board and recharting processes altogether.[19] The implications for HR technology implementation are that HR professionals need to fully understand their processes and determine how new IT can be leveraged to streamline them. This can involve changing anything that gets in the way of business performance.

**business process re-engineering**

the fundamental rethinking and radical redesign of business processes to achieve dramatic improvements in critical, contemporary measures of performance, such as cost, quality, service, and speed[18]

## Ensuring Data Security

Employers have an obligation to protect employees' personal records, medical records, and employment tests. Because of the sensitive nature of HR data, it is important that the system provide robust security to protect such data, especially with more and more employees transporting data on their own personal flash drives and MP3 players. The IT solution must also comply with various legal statutes related to confidentiality and privacy concerns. The golden rule is that a company should collect and store information only for a solid business employment purpose.

Some security features include login security, row-level security (record security), and field-level security (data field).[20] Procedures to enhance security of data include the usage of PINs and passwords; the usage of encryption devices or software when sending sensitive e-mail; providing regular, ongoing education and reinforcement of clearly defined organizational policies; and turning off systems when they are not in use.

**®℗©** 5.4

## Evaluating HR Technology

User satisfaction and system usage are important indicators of HRIS success.[21] Drawing from the **technology acceptance** and user satisfaction streams, a recent study found that attitudes toward IT are influenced by behavioural beliefs about technology usefulness and ease of use.[22] These beliefs, in turn, are influenced by information satisfaction and system satisfaction, which result from information quality and system quality (see HR Planning Notebook 5.6). An audit that includes these different measures will provide useful insights into HR technology effectiveness.

**technology acceptance**
extent to which users intend or actually use technology as a regular part of their job

---

### HR Planning Notebook 5.6

#### Sample Technology Effectiveness Items

- Attitude:
  - Using this HR technology is very enjoyable.
- Usefulness:
  - Using this HR technology enhances my effectiveness on the job.
- Information Satisfaction:
  - I am very satisfied with the information I receive from this HR technology.
- System Satisfaction:
  - Overall, my interaction with this HR technology is very satisfying.
- Information Quality:
  - This HR technology produces comprehensive information (completeness).
  - The information provided by this HR technology is well laid out (format).

- There are few errors in the information I obtain from this HR technology (accuracy).
- The information provided by this HR technology is always up to date (currency).
- System Quality:
  - This HR technology operates reliably (reliability).
  - This HR technology makes information very accessible (accessibility).
  - This HR technology can be adapted to meet a variety of needs (flexibility).
  - This HR technology effectively integrates data from different areas of the company (integration).
  - This HR technology provides information in a timely fashion (timeliness).

---

A more sophisticated evaluation might include an analysis of the costs and benefits of the IT solution.[23] Similarly, a return on investment (ROI) approach would involve putting a dollar sign on the dollars saved through the HR system.[24] A company may find, for instance, that its HR system led to lower cost of hiring or reduced printing and distribution costs.

## Emerging HR Technology Solutions

Gaining access to data in a timely manner is a constant challenge. Luckily, computer capacity is increasing at a steady pace; computers have doubled in capacity every 24 months since 1970 and there is no reason to expect a slowdown in the near future. HR is leveraging this capacity to improve service delivery and, by doing so, it is transforming itself.[25] See HR Planning Today 5.4.

### Self-Service

**self-service solution**

a technology platform that enables employees and managers to access and modify their data via a Web browser from a desktop or centralized kiosk

**Self-service** is based on the principle that data is most effectively captured at source. Under this principle, for example, the employee should be the one to enter or modify changes to his or her personal information. Employees can be empowered to apply for travel reimbursement, make personal data changes, and enroll for benefits or in training classes. In some organizations employees can use self-service to view job openings within the company, create application materials, apply for a position, and check the status of pending applications. Managers may use self-service to access authorized information for employees they supervise. A manager may further use the system to compile employee absenteeism and turnover data to forecast HR demand or to manage employees from recruitment to the annual employee review and compensation planning.

### Web-Based HR

Web-based HR allows service delivery that pushes employees and managers into making transactions. Self-service is one example of Web-based service

---

## HR Planning Today 5.4

### Riverside County Internet Testing

The Riverside County Human Resources Department is quickly abandoning the traditional written test as a means of pre-screening candidates. In order to hire the best candidate in the shortest time and in the most efficient manner, Riverside County is utilizing Internet-based testing to expedite the selection process. Internet-based testing has been used to screen candidates for the county's newest career development program. Job seekers may now log onto our website 24 hours a day and test for entry level positions with our Probation Department. The Human Resources Department is currently working on expanding the use of Internet-based testing to screen candidates for other positions that require testing, further reducing the need for paper and pencil examinations.

Source: J. Mooney, 2002, "Pre-Employment Testing on the Internet: Put Candidates a Click Away and Hire at Modem Speed," *Public Personnel Management*, 31, 1, 41–52.

---

delivery. Another is Web-based HR service centres that allow employees easy access to their data (e.g., job postings, personal data, access to learning solutions, etc.) through online access to information, resulting in quicker response from experts. Hence, rather than outsource, HR may consolidate its services into an internal HR service centre and operate the centre with its own HR practitioners.

Web-based HR processes and practices are also gaining momentum. E-recruiting and e-learning are highly visible Web-based applications; in addition, some organizations are now conducting pre-employment testing on the Internet.

## Competitive Advantage

HR systems can contribute to sustained competitive advantage through facilitating the development of competencies that are firm specific, by producing complex social relationships, and generating tacit organizational knowledge.[26] How then can IT be leveraged to achieve these capabilities? Many available technology applications help firms develop internal labour markets through job posting and career pathing. **E-learning** further allows just-in-time learning on firm-specific competencies. These technology solutions may, as such, facilitate the development of competencies that are firm specific. E-recruiting can increase the probability of hiring individuals whose values and beliefs are congruent with the organization's culture, which may contribute to the development of richer social relationships within the firm. Also, implementation of employee self-service applications may reinforce a culture of employee participation and engagement.

Whatever the perspective on competitive advantage, HR professionals need to consider how IT may develop organizational resources and capabilities. This should lead to wiser technology investments based upon a clear understanding of firm-specific opportunities for improvement.

## Knowledge Management

Mapping the expertise of an organization is a common **knowledge management** activity that allows employees easy access to a map of expertise of the organization to connect people when they need guidance resulting in quicker response rates without reinvention of the wheel, increased employee satisfaction, and more.

## Enterprise Portals

**Enterprise portals** are but one of many IT tools that allow efficient access to relevant content and applications. Employees can access the portal to share information and collaborate more effectively with customers, partners, and suppliers using a secure infrastructure. See HR Planning Today 5.5 for an example.

**e-learning**
the process of learning contents distributed in digital format via computers over the Internet or other network

 5.6

**knowledge management**
a systematic and organizationally specified process for acquiring, organizing, and communicating both tacit and explicit knowledge of employees so that other employees may make use of it to be more effective and productive in their work[27]

**enterprise portals**
knowledge communities that allow employees from a single or multiple companies to access and benefit from specialized knowledge associated with tasks

## HR Planning Today 5.5

### Knowledge Portal at Singapore Technologies Ltd.

Global engineering conglomerate Singapore Technologies Ltd. knows that it just cannot compete by cutting cost only. That is why it has been busily transforming itself into a "knowledge-creating" machine, which, it says, will enable it to continuously innovate, create value, and boost customer service. To help it to move in this direction, ST Engineering last year implemented an Employee Information Management Platform (EIP), which, says CIO Teo Chin Seng, "is not just a repository of information or an IT automation system, but a platform in which streams of knowledge are continuously being fed into, and at the same time, initiated at.

This portal has enabled ST Engineering to take on a human-centric approach in increasing its productivity and value-creating capabilities," says Teo. An employee starts by simply clicking on www.stengglink.com. After typing his user name and password, the gateway to ST Engineering's knowledge repository and e-HR functions is opened to him. He is able to extract information on a diversity of topics and themes, stretching from brain-intensive readings on intellectual property to technical information, to something less tedious such as industry news, all the way to lightweights such as leisure and outdoor eating.

Source: R. Chotrain, "Intelligent Manufacturing." Retrieved March 18, 2006, from http://203.81.46.67/pcio.nsf/unidlookup/1BA3B7FF27B4619D48256CB6002F363F?OpenDocument.

## Summary

This chapter presented an overview of HR technology and described some specific applications. Much more is available, and constant progress is allowing a greater integration of IT into HRM. IT applications can also be leveraged to improve strategic HR planning. Amongst other activities, IT can support skills inventories, replacement planning, and succession management. Such applications may be made available on an HRIS, specialty product, or ERP.

Depending on the organizational context, HR professionals may call upon different IT solutions. A thorough understanding of business and HR needs is a good starting point. A keen awareness of the HR technology market will prove invaluable when acquiring new software solutions. HR professionals will need to deploy their change management skills when implementing new IT solutions. Communication and training are keys to successful HR technology implementation. HR may also find some opportunities for realigning processes and service delivery with IT. Finally, evaluating the IT solutions with various methodologies may reveal opportunities for improvement.

## Key Terms

business process re-engineering, 132
e-learning, 135
enterprise portals, 135
enterprise resource planning
    (ERP), 129
human resources information system
    (HRIS), 128

knowledge management, 135
outsourcing, 124
relational database, 129
scripted demo, 131
self-service solution, 134
specialty product, 128
technology acceptance, 133

# Web Links

National Film Board of Canada:

**www.nfb.ca** (p. 122)

ADP Canada's corporate website:

**www.adp.ca/en/index.html** (p. 124)

DLGL: Provider of integrated HR/Payroll/Time Capture & Scheduling/ Pension/Recruitment Systems for large and very large employers:

**www.dlgl.com** (pp. 124, 128)

Gartner: Provider of research and analysis about the global IT industry:

**www.gartner.com** (p. 126)

Canadian Association of Human Resource Management Systems Professionals (HRMSP):

**www.hrmsp.org** (p. 126)

International Association for Human Resource Information Management (IRHIM):

**www.ihrim.org** (p. 126)

Authoria: Integrated strategic human capital management services provider:

**www.authoria.com** (p. 127)

Nardoni Strategic Solutions: HR technology for succession planning and employee development:

**www.rennardoni.com** (p. 127)

SkillView Technologies skills management tools:

**www.skillsoft.com** (p. 127)

Kronos: A solution for time and workforce management:

**www.kronos.com** (p. 128)

A training management solution offered by Faltec Inc.:

**www.faltec.com** (p. 129)

SAP: leading provider of integrated business administrative solutions:

**www.sap.com** (p. 129)

Society for Human Resource Management:

**www.shrm.org** (p. 131)

Resource for planning knowledge management (KM) projects:

**www.kmtool.net** (p. 135)

# RPC Icons

**RPC 5.1 Contributes to the development of the organization's vision, goals, strategies with a focus on human capital**

**RPC 5.2 Evaluates the effectiveness of current HR information management within the organization**

**RPC 5.3 Contributes to development of specifications for the acquisition and/or development of HR information management systems for their implementation**

**RPC 5.4 Develops policy regarding confidentiality of HR information, including limits on the extent to which confidentiality can be assured**

**RPC 5.5 Monitors and reports on the progress of major change initiatives**

**RPC 5.6 Evaluates alternatives for providing HR information management needs, considering current and future organizational needs and capabilities, and the associated costs and benefits**

# Discussion Questions

1. Databases used for HR management and planning contain a wide variety of personal and sensitive data that require the organization to set security, privacy, and usage policies. What legislative and ethical requirements of data security need to be considered?
2. Modern communication technologies that rely on the processing power of computers provide new opportunities for service delivery. Discuss their relevance to HR and project how they may transform the HR function in the future.
3. Discuss the advantages and disadvantages of computer-mediated communication in HR service delivery, e.g., providing multisource feedback or addressing career issues through computer-mediated communication online rather than through face-to-face dialogue.

# Using the Internet

1. Using the Internet, explore alternative HR service models made possible by information technologies. Explain how, from the manager's perspective, these different service models may help improve strategic HR planning.
2. Most of the technology solutions presented in this chapter were designed to manage internal resources. As such, they may be useful for planning and managing the internal supply of human resources. What websites are available to explore the external supply of human resources?
3. Suppose you work for Bombardier Aeronautics. What Internet resources could you tap into to inform your demand forecasts?

# Exercise

1. Identify one activity involved in strategic HR planning (staffing, management development, 360° feedback, etc.). Explore the Internet to find a software solution for that activity. Provide information on the vendor, and describe the software solution in terms of its data requirements, technical and reporting capabilities, data security features, and price. Print out a couple of sample reports if available.

# Case: Building Talent at Cisco Systems

In their recent article Chatman, O'Reilly, and Chang describe the new human capital strategy at Cisco Systems, a leader in the data networking equipment market (www.cisco.com). This strategy could be described as "build" talent strategy geared at developing the next generation of leaders. It was developed in response to changes in market conditions. The company now needs people who can help their customers solve business problems rather than just technical problems. Managers need to be able to cross-functionally coordinate and mobilize the pieces of Cisco needed to solve complex customer problems.

Cisco's "build" strategy involved developing leaders who have a different skill set and who embrace a different organizational culture than the previous generation. The new Cisco would therefore focus more on motivating and developing internal talent, particularly leaders. This involved providing rich development opportunities within an environment of continuous learning and challenge. Cisco needed also to get better at moving resources and retraining.

Several new initiatives demonstrated the company's commitment to the new human capital strategy. Cisco developed a system that allowed managers to post openings for jobs within high-growth areas. Cisco University was the focal point for all career management and a cornerstone of Cisco's effort to conceptualize the development of human capital within Cisco. It was defined as more than a corporate university or a centralized training centre; rather, an initiative that involved career management and development, with linkages to feedback, job opportunities, coaching, training, and mentoring. The company also revised its performance management and development process to improve performance and support talent development. In addition, Cisco implemented a succession management process that allowed the company to identify the top 20% of its leaders, assess their progress, and evaluate future opportunities. The company also launched customized 360° feedback to provide managers with a feedback report from the people they worked with.

The significant transition from a "buy" to "build" human capital strategy was a daunting challenge. Cisco wanted nothing less than a new generation of leaders focused on the customer and who work across functions effectively. While focusing on customers and customer success, elements of the old culture needed to remain strong. All this in a large company that has been through some troubling times. There is also the challenge of maintaining this emphasis on leadership development when the market picks up and people are stretched and don't have much time for development.

Source: Adapted from J. Chatman, C. O'Reilly, and V. Chang, 2005. "Cisco Systems: Developing a Human Capital Strategy," *California Management Review, 47*, 2, 137–167.

## Question

How could IT be leveraged to support Cisco's human capital strategy and enhance decisions about its talent resources? Identify and explain three specific software applications that could help this company better manage some elements of its HR strategy.

# Endnotes

1. Ulrich, D., and Brockbank, W. 2005. *The HR Value Proposition*. Boston, MA: Harvard Business School Press.
2. Haines, V.Y., III (2005, October/November). "Want to Play a More Strategic Role? Information Technology May Make the Difference," *HR Professional*, 42.
3. Huber, G.P. 1990. "A Theory of the Effects of Advanced Information Technologies on Organizational Design, Intelligence, and Decision Making," *Academy of Management Review*, 15 (1), 47–71.
4. Saks, A.M., and R. Haccoun. 2004. *Managing Performance through Training and Development*, 3rd Canadian ed. Scarborough, ON: Thomson Nelson.
5. Jones, J.W. 1998. *Virtual HR: Human Resources Management in the Information Age*. New York: Crisp Publishing.
6. Chatman, J., C. O'Reilly, and V. Chang. 2005. "Cisco Systems: Developing a Human Capital Strategy," *California Management Review*, 47, 2, 137–167.
7. Meade, J.G. 2003. *The Human Resources Software Handbook: Evaluating Technology Solutions for your Organization*. San Francisco, CA: Wiley, p. 293.
8. Newman, M., and C. Westrup. 2005. "Making ERPs Work: Accountants and the Introduction of ERP Systems," *European Journal of Information Systems*, 14, 258–272.
9. Mabert, V.A., A. Soni, and M.A. Venkataraman. 2001. "Enterprise Resource Planning: Common Myths versus Evolving Reality," *Business Horizons*, May–June, 71–78.
10. Ashbaugh, S., and R. Miranda. 2002. "Technology for Human Resources Management: Seven Questions and Answers." *Public Personnel Management*, 31 (1), 7–20.
11. Meade, 2003.
12. Ibid., p. 84.
13. Ibid., p. 117.
14. Kossek, E.E., W. Young, D.C. Gash, and V. Nichol. 1994. "Waiting for Innovation in the Human Resources Department: Godot Implements a Human Resource Information System," *Human Resource Management, 33*, 1, 135–159.
15. Rampton, G.M., I.J. Turnbull, and J.A. Doran. 1999. "Human Resources Management Systems: A Practical Approach, 2nd ed. Scarborough, ON: Carswell.
16. Kossek et al., 1994, 135–159.
17. Hammer, M., and J. Champy. 1993. *Reengineering the Corporation*. New York: Harper Business, p. 48.
18. Ibid.
19. Obeng, E., and S. Crainer. 1994. *Making Reengineering Happen*, London: Pitman.

20. Ashbaugh and Miranda. 2002.

21. Haines, V.Y., III, and A. Petit. 1997. "Conditions for Successful Human Resource Information Systems," *Human Resource Management Journal*, 36, 2, 261–275.

22. Wixom, B.H., and P.A. Todd. 2005. "A Theoretical Integration of User Satisfaction and Technology Acceptance," *Information Systems Research*, 16, 1, 85–102.

23. Rampton, G.M., I.J. Turnbull, and J.A. Doran. 1999. *Human Resources Management Systems: A Practical Approach*, 2nd ed. Scarborough, ON: Carswell.

24. Meade, 2003.

25. Broderick, R., and J.W. Boudreau. 1991. "The Evolution of Computer Use in Human Resources Management: Interviews with Ten Leaders," *Human Resource Management*, 30, 4, 485–508.

26. Lado, A.A., and M.C. Wilson. 1994. "Human Resource Systems and Sustained Competitive Advantage: A Competency-based Perspective," *Academy of Management Review*, 19, 4, 699–727.

27. Alavi, M., and D.E. Leidner. 1999. "Knowledge Management Systems: Issues, Challenges and Benefits," *Communications of AIS*, 1, 1–37.

# Chapter 6

# The HR Forecasting Process

## Chapter Learning Objectives

After reading this chapter, you should be able to

- Identify the three different categories of HR forecasting activity and their relationship to the HR planning process.
- Understand the considerable advantages that accrue to organizations from instituting effective HR forecasting procedures.
- Discuss the rationale for giving special attention to specialist, technical, and executive personnel groups in the HR forecasting process.
- Comprehend the impact of environmental and organizational variables on the accuracy and relevant time periods for future estimates of HR demand and supply.
- Identify the various stages in the process of determining net HR requirements.
- Understand the policy and program implications of an HR deficit or an HR surplus.

# FORECASTING EMERGENCIES

Canadians frequently receive word of major emergencies occurring both at home and around the world. In Canada, over the past few years, we've experienced crippling ice and snowstorms, the Red River flood in Manitoba, devastating forest fires in British Columbia and other parts of the country, and the SARS crisis in Toronto, to name just a few. Add to that list the devastation wrought by the Asian Tsunami, earthquakes, hurricanes (e.g., Hurricane Katrina was the costliest natural disaster in U.S. history), power failures, terrorist attacks and bombings (including September 11, 2001, attacks in the United States and the London, England, transit bombings), and the threat of pandemics such as avian virus, and it should come as no surprise that governments and organizations all over the world are finally giving long overdue recognition to the importance of forecasting the requirements for specialized personnel to deal with these very disruptive and costly emergencies.

Traditionally "other people" took care of emergencies on our behalf, and these emergency responders (e.g., firefighters, police, military, medical personnel) continue to be in constant demand. However governments, and private and public organizations are now aware that the emergency responders need to be assisted and augmented by an organization unit comprising high-level emergency managers who will not only help communicate, liaise, and coordinate resources for the responders, but also act as a "one-stop shop" to educate and coordinate with citizens, businesses, and various levels of government.

As you can imagine, the demands placed upon these emergency managers are considerable and highly complex, given that they have the mandate to (1) identify and mitigate/reduce hazards (manmade, natural, and technological), (2) prepare citizens as well as public and private organizations to better deal with emergency situations, (3) coordinate the organization's response to the emergencies, and (4) spearhead post-incident recovery operations.

Although governments have taken the lead in instigating the establishment of emergency management personnel through professional training and workshops, such as those run at the Canadian federal (e.g., Public Safety and Emergency Preparedness Canada) and provincial levels (e.g., Emergency Management Ontario) there has also been considerable activity in the public and private sectors, especially with regards to business continuity personnel who will develop contingency plans to deal with emergencies (e.g., computer data backup, personnel monitoring and reporting, ability to operate "off-site" in the possibility of an emergency rendering the primary corporate headquarters inoperable, etc.).

Considerable discussion has been focused on forecasting the requisite numbers of these emergency managers and the KSAs/competencies they should possess. In some cases such as municipalities, government acts and regulations specify the minimum number of HR demand for emergency managers. For example, in Ontario, the *Emergency Management Act* requires each municipality to have a designated employee as an "emergency management coordinator." However population and geographical size differences, different sets of hazards and amounts of public and private infrastructure etc. makes a mockery of assuming the legal equivalency of a city the size of Toronto with say Aberfoyle, Ontario, as the former's far more complex environment necessitates a higher demand for emergency management personnel than does the latter small rural community's. Similarly, large widely diverse conglomerate corporations, and large Crown corporations and public agencies, have greater and more difficult hazards identification and mitigation processes than do their smaller less complex organizations.

Another key element of the HR forecasting process for emergency managers concerns their supply. Traditionally, senior ex-military or police personnel have been hired to perform coordination roles during emergencies, but with newly emerging professional competencies for "emergency managers," and the greatly increased demand for emergency management personnel since September 11, 2001, educational institutions are working with professional bodies to rapidly develop programs specifically for "emergency management" to redress the HR deficit/shortage of these personnel. Brandon University in Manitoba was the first Canadian university to develop an Emergency/Disaster Studies program, followed by York University, with other universities and colleges currently in the process of developing professional education programs to increase the supply of emergency management personnel.

HR planners have much to contribute to the ongoing development of emergency management as a profession. Recent experiences with emergency/disaster response have shown that if proper validated job analysis and forecasting processes are bypassed, the performance of key emergency management personnel can be highly dysfunctional, which leads to costs (personal, organizational, political, and societal) that far surpass those typically associated with improper HR processes with say, typical clerical positions.

The case of Michael Brown, a personal friend of President George Bush, who was appointed in 2001 as director of FEMA (the U.S. Federal Emergency Management Association) and the highest ranking U.S.

*(Continued)*

emergency manager, and then subsequently fired after his abysmal failure to provide effective emergency management during Hurricane Katrina, is a sad case study in this regard. Rather than following proper HRP planning procedures including job analysis, and forecasting requirements, it became readily apparent that the Bush administration had hired Brown to head FEMA due to cronyism rather than for his demonstrated ability to perform validated emergency management functions. The rationale for his hiring, presumably, was that because he had not been proven incompetent in his previous office management appointment he should be fine in heading the organization responsible for coordinating all U.S. emergencies and disasters. Incredibly, the director of FEMA's job requirements were presumed to differ little from the performance expected from a typical senior white-collar U.S. government office position.

Unfortunately for the citizens and organizations in Louisiana and other states in the U.S. South, Mr. Brown was director of FEMA when Hurricane Katrina made landfall in August 2005, breaking levees, flooding New Orleans and other areas, and causing billions of dollars of damage. Despite having received plenty of advance warning of the approach of this hurricane to the U.S. coastline, which would have enabled decisions to be made to pre-position relief equipment and supplies, as the hurricane made landfall, President Bush was on vacation, and Mr. Brown proved totally incompetent to lead his country's emergency management organization. When the country depended upon Michael Brown to make quick and effective decisions to deploy personnel and resources in order to safeguard citizens and property, he chose instead to remain safe in his Washington office, out of touch and communication with emergency responders on the ground in the devastated regions, thereby removing himself from being personally able to influence the situation. Bush, who was also out of touch with the situation, publicly praised Brown for "doing a heck of a job," words he would soon regret. At the same time, a FEMA official in New Orleans described the situation as "past critical" and predicted that "many will die within hours," only to receive an e-mail response from Brown reading "Thanks for the update. Anything specific I need to do or tweak?" (*Financial Times*) Brown's e-mails during the unfolding crisis, as reported to a subsequent investigation of the FEMA failure by the U.S. Congress, focused on his public image, his appearance, and his dog, rather than the disastrous failure of the relief efforts for which he was responsible. Just prior to his "resignation," the FEMA deputy director of public affairs e-mailed Brown to advise him that "in this crisis and on TV, you need to look more hard working—Roll up your sleeves" (*Washington Post* as reported by Bliss).[1] After being relieved from his appointment, command of the relief effort was turned over to a military general, LGen Russel Honore, who had only recently graduated with his Masters Degree in HR management. According to New Orleans mayor Ray Nagin, who by this time was fed up and regularly providing the media with scathing remarks about the incompetence of FEMA officials and the federal government's lack of assistance, General Honore immediately went to the disaster site and started making decisions: "He came off that doggone chopper, and he started cussing and people started moving." (Leonard)

HR forecasting, which constitutes the heart of the HR planning process, can be defined as ascertaining the net requirement for personnel by determining the demand for and supply of human resources now and in the future. After determining the demand for and supply of workers, the organization's HR staff develops specific programs to reconcile the differences between the requirement for labour in various employment categories and its availability, both internally and in the organization's environment. Programs in such areas as training and development, career planning, recruitment and selection, managerial appraisal, and so on are all stimulated by means of the HR forecasting process.

**HR forecasting**
the heart of the HR planning process, can be defined as ascertaining the net requirement for personnel by determining the demand for and supply of human resources now and in the future

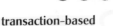

## Forecasting Activity Categories

Forecasting activity can be subdivided into three categories: (1) transaction-based forecasting, (2) event-based forecasting, and (3) process-based forecasting.[2] **Transaction-based forecasting** focuses on tracking internal change instituted by the organization's managers, while **event-based forecasting** is concerned with change in the external environment. **Process-based forecasting** is not focused on a specific internal organizational event but on the flow or sequencing of several work activities (e.g., the warehousing shipping process). All three categories are important to have a comprehensive method for ascertaining HR requirements.

Forecasting is only an approximation of possible future states and is an activity that strongly favours quantitative and easily codified techniques. As such, it is important to make an explicit effort to obtain and incorporate qualitative data into our analyses.[3] Furthermore, more successful HR forecasting processes use both qualitative and quantitative data, and a number of studies have clearly shown that accuracy of prediction improves significantly when we use a variety of forecasting techniques[4]

**transaction-based forecasting**
forecasting that focuses on tracking internal change instituted by the organization's managers

**event-based forecasting**
forecasting concerned with changes in the external environment

**process-based forecasting**
forecasting not focused on a specific internal organizational event but on the flow or sequencing of several work activities

## HR Planning Today 6.1

### HR Forecasting in a Global Economy

Organizations that operate globally face additional challenges to their effective and efficient use of human resources. For instance, differences in time zones and the vast geographic dispersion of operational units and workforces can present a problem. Technology can help companies through use of the Internet and organizational intranets, as well as e-mail and video-conferencing systems. Global HR planning managers should encourage employee collaboration through (1) maximizing use of technology such as e-mail, (2) explicitly scheduling work to take advantage of time zone differences that can be used to the company's advantage (e.g., preparation of a contract by employees in an advanced time zone, which can then be sent to a client firm that is in a time zone several hours behind that of the preparing unit), and (3) elimination of redundant costs through centralizing data in the HRMS.

Source: Adapted from C. Solomon, "Sharing Information Across Borders and Time Zones," *Workforce*, Vol. 3, No. 2 (March 1998), 12–18.

(see HR Planning Today 6.1 and 6.2). Effective forecasting also hinges on obtaining a fine balance between global and local control of the process. A study of multinational corporations operating in Ireland showed that most of the firms that analyzed adopted a local approach to forecasting, with the (global) headquarters maintaining a vigilant yet loose monitoring of financial costs and other performance criteria.[5]

## HR Planning Today 6.2

### Successful Workforce Planning

Given the plethora of organizational CEOs who state that "people are our greatest asset," it could be assumed that HR and workforce planning activities would be among the best-developed functions in organizations and regularly receive top priority with respect to funding and other resource allocations. In reality, many organizations devote insufficient time and resources to HR planning activities, which have three main factors associated with their success. Specifically, HR planning should be (1) strategic and forward looking, (2) comprehensive and encompass all employee groups and management functions, and (3) tailored to the specific culture and attributes of the organization to which it is being applied. Furthermore, by being proactive and avoiding the "feast or famine" swings in personnel numbers associated with reactive workforce staffing, HR planning can dramatically cut labour costs, increase productivity, reduce the number of "surprises," and rectify problems before they grow more complex and costly. In order to achieve these ends, workforce planning should give priority to forecasting and assessment, recruitment and selection, leadership development, and succession planning programs.

Sources: Adapted from J. Sullivan, "Workforce Planning: Why to Start Now," *Workforce*, Vol. 81, No. 12 (November 2002), 46–50; and J. Woodard, "Three Factors of Successful Work Force Planning," *The Journal of Government Financial Management*, Vol. 50, No. 3 (Fall 2001), 36–38.

## Benefits of HR Forecasting

A great number of important benefits accrue to organizations that take the time to institute effective HR forecasting processes, and the forecasting techniques employed do not have to be sophisticated to be of value to the firm.[6] A few of the more important advantages of HR forecasting are discussed below.

### 1. Reduces HR Costs

Effective HR forecasting focuses on a comparison between the organization's current stock of workforce KSAs (e.g., experience) and the numbers, skill competencies, and so on desired in the workforce of the future. This inherent comparison facilitates a proactive, sequential approach to developing internal workers and is concurrent with activities focused on obtaining the best external recruits from competitors, universities, and training programs.[7] In this manner, organizations can reduce their HR costs as they take a long-run planning approach to HR issues. This means that organizations will be less likely to have to react in a costly last-minute crisis mode to unexpected developments in the internal or external labour markets.

### 2. Increases Organizational Flexibility

An oft-cited advantage of HR forecasting is that its proactive process increases the number of viable policy options available to the organization, thereby enhancing flexibility.[8] With regard to labour supply considerations, forecasting processes develop program options that can determine whether it is more advantageous and cost effective to retrain current members of the workforce to fill anticipated job openings or fill these openings with external recruits who already possess the required competencies and skills. Given that HR forecasting is predicated on trends, assumptions, scenarios, and various planning time horizons, the process itself encourages the development of a wide range of possible policy options and programs from which the HR staff can select. Furthermore, each of the various HR programming options are ranked, subjected to cost–benefit analyses, and allocated organizational resources after being carefully examined as part of the HR forecasting process.

**RPC 6.3**

### 3. Ensures a Close Linkage to the Macro Business Forecasting Process

A serious problem develops in some organizations when the personnel planning process becomes divorced and disconnected from the overall business goals of the organization.[9] The implementation of an HR forecasting process helps to eliminate the possibility that personnel policies will veer away from the overall operating and production policies of the organization. First, HR forecasting, although an ongoing process, takes its lead from specific production, market share, profitability, and operational objectives set by the organization's top management. These objectives have been established through proactive internal and environmental scans of market and competitor strengths, weaknesses, opportunities, threats, resources, and policy actions.[10]

**RPC 6.4**

**RPC 6.5**

Once these have been established, specific HR forecasting analyses are set in motion to determine the feasibility of the proposed operational objectives with respect to time, cost, resource allocation, and other criteria of program success. The HR analyses are subsequently sent back to top management, and they either confirm the viability of the original business objectives or indicate that changes (e.g., the allocation of additional resources) need to be made to enable the objectives to be met.

The business forecasting process, therefore, establishes overall organizational objectives, which are input into the HR forecasting process.[11] The HR staff analyze whether the explicit objectives, with their associated specific performance parameters, can be met with the organization's current HR policies and programs or whether specific changes have to be instituted, with their associated costs, to achieve the objectives. These analyses and the subsequent feedback of the HR forecast summaries to senior management help to ensure that the top decision makers in the organization (1) are aware of key HR issues and constraints that might affect organizational plans for success and (2) ensure the HR objectives are closely aligned with the organization's operational business objectives.[12] See HR Planning Notebook 6.1 for reasons HR system implementation may fail.

**human resources demand**

the organization's projected requirement for human resources

**human resources supply**

the source of workers to meet demand requirements, obtained either internally (current members of the organization's workforce) or from external agencies

### 4. Ensures That Organizational Requirements Take Precedence over Issues of Resource Constraint and Scarcity

As we present each step of the HR forecasting process in sequence throughout this book, it will quickly become evident that the first step in the process is the calculation of organizational requirements, or **demand** for human resources. Determining the source of personnel—that is, the availability or **supply** of workers—is done only once the process of evaluating personnel requirements for current and future time horizons has been finalized. This sequence is not accidental, and it reinforces the fact that attainment of desired organizational goals and objectives must take priority over all issues concerning resource scarcity and other implementation issues.

---

## HR Planning Notebook 6.1

### Why HR System Implementation Efforts Fail

1. The organization's top management has not communicated the need to implement new technology or new systems.
2. People resist change efforts because they are not asked to help develop new business strategies, solutions, and plans.
3. Organizations underestimate the time, energy, budget, and planning required to successfully implement new technology.
4. Different groups within an organization either cannot agree on what a system needs to do or overburden it with too many requirements.

Source: Adapted from N. Horney and I. Ruddle, "Why HR System Implementation Efforts Fail," *Bank Marketing*, Vol. 30, No. 1 (January 1998), 24.

# Key Personnel Analyses Conducted by HR Forecasters

Although the forecasting process for personnel in an organization is conducted to determine the number of employees and the skill competencies required by subunits, as well as the entire organization, a number of personnel categories typically are given greater-than-average attention in the forecasting process. These categories are discussed below.[13]

## 1. Specialist/Technical/Professional Personnel

Workers holding trade qualifications that are in high demand or that require lengthy preparatory training for attainment of skill competency constitute a key area of focus for HR forecasting. In our increasingly global economy, these workers will be in high demand by competitive firms both in Canada and abroad, which means we will have to give special attention to programs to induce these workers to join our organization. Furthermore, we must give attention to benchmarking compensation schemes to meet or lead industry standards so as to attract and retain people who perform well in these categories. With respect to supply issues, a longer lead time is often required to recruit technicians and professionals because of the need for a more comprehensive and larger geographic search for this specialist talent pool.

## 2. Employment Equity–Designated Group Membership

Provincial and federal governments in Canada have enacted employment-equity legislation and guidelines in response to public pressure for employment practices that reflect the rapidly changing face of Canadian society. In particular, four main **designated groups** require special attention with respect to their degree of use or equitable employment in organizations: (1) people of aboriginal descent, (2) women, (3) people with disabilities, and (4) members of visible minorities. Particular attention must be paid to monitoring members of these designated groups with respect to the opportunities they receive for employment, promotion, training, and so on as compared to those received by the dominant population of the organization.[14] Furthermore, the composition of the organizational workforce should reflect the underlying characteristics of the society in which it is embedded, so the supply issue, as it relates to proportional representation of designated groups in the organization, is a key area for HR forecasting.

**designated groups**
identifiable groups deemed to need special attention; in the case of Canadian HR these are people of aboriginal descent, women, people with disabilities, and members of visible minorities

## 3. Managerial and Executive Personnel

To be successful, any organization must ensure that its executives and managers possess the skills required for success in their specific environmental niche. Executives (CEO, president, vice-presidents, etc.) interact with key environmental stakeholder groups on behalf of the organization and are responsible for setting the goals for the organization's future direction. Managers, acting as the supervisory layer of authority between executives and the operating shop-floor level, are responsible for coaching, directing, training and developing, and controlling worker behaviours to achieve the goals established by the executive group. Although there is no shortage of managers and executives who can function effectively in relatively benign, predictable, environmental situations, researchers believe that organizational leaders who are able to transform organizational culture and anticipate external change, and who possess the dynamic personal attributes necessary to unify the organization, are very rare in most public- and private-sector organizational settings.[15] For this reason, not only must greater attention be paid to identifying leadership talent within the organization, but also assessment centres or appraisals must be conducted to match the "right person to the right job at the right time."[16] The organization's survival and future success depend directly on succession and replacement planning!

### 4. Recruits

As was the case with succession and replacement planning, recruiting trainees is extremely important to the success of the organization's overall HR policies. When determining whether to obtain trainees from the internal workforce or externally, a wide variety of factors must be considered. For example, selecting current employees to attend training courses leading to promotion rewards loyalty and past performance and simultaneously diminishes the need for the organizational socialization of newcomers from outside. However, current employees may be very comfortable with the status quo and existing methods of organizational operation, and therefore may not be well suited for employment on novel, creative work processes that differ substantially from established practices. Furthermore, new entrants can bring the organization insights into how competitors structure and operate their business and may, as well, bring with them the latest trends and practices taught in universities and specialist training agencies. The relative balance of internal to external personnel to be selected for training courses is a key factor in the HR forecasting and programming operations of many organizations.

The important relationship between effective HR planning processes and the organizational bottom line has been revealed by researchers at the University of Sheffield and is described in HR Planning Today 6.3.

## HR Planning Today 6.3

### Profitable Personnel

Critics have applied the sarcastic label "big hat, no cattle" to HR managers whom they believe have little effect on the performance of the organization. The United Kingdom's University of Sheffield Effectiveness Program disputes this assertion because its research discovered that not only was "people management" critical to business performance, but it far outstripped the emphasis on quality, technology, competitive strategy, or research and development in its influence on the organization's bottom-line performance. Although research findings with respect to the relationship between individual satisfaction and job performance have been mixed, the Sheffield research found that at the macro level, satisfaction of the work group across a wide range of areas—for example, developing skills, creativity, and recognition processes—was critical to organizational productivity.

Source: Adapted from M. West and M. Patterson, "Profitable Personnel," *People Management*, Vol. 4, No. 1 (January 1998), 28–31.

The goal of HR forecasting is to obtain sufficient numbers of trained personnel who will be able to perform successfully in jobs when those jobs need to be filled. To do this, the forecasting process has five stages:[17]

1. Identify organizational goals, objectives, and plans.
2. Determine overall demand requirements for personnel.
3. Assess in-house skills and other internal supply characteristics.
4. Determine the net demand requirements that must be met from external, environmental supply sources.
5. Develop HR plans and programs to ensure that the right people are in the right place.

Before turning to aspects concerned with determining personnel demand, we will examine the effects of environmental uncertainty and of planning time horizons on HR forecasting.

## Environmental and Organizational Factors Affecting HR Forecasting

**RPC** 6.6

The HR forecasting process is extremely complex, requiring specific numerical and skill competency targets for personnel to be met despite operating in circumstances of high uncertainty.[18] This uncertainty arises from both external environmental factors and from inside the organization itself. Given this uncertainty and the natural rate of change resulting from operating in a turbulent, global economy, the key factor for HR forecasters is to incorporate flexibility into the program responses associated with demand and supply forecasts[19] (see HR Planning Notebook 6.2). When considering the following discussion of environmental and organizational factors, it is important to remember that these factors may affect the forecasting of demand, supply, or both of these key planning variables.

---

### HR Planning Notebook 6.2

#### Selected Factors Affecting the HR Forecasting Process

| Internal/Organizational | External/Environmental |
|---|---|
| Corporate mission statement, strategic goals | Economic situation |
| Operational goals, production budgets | Labour markets and unions |
| HR policies (e.g., compensation, succession) | Governmental laws and regulations |
| Organizational structure, restructuring, mergers, etc. | Industry and product life cycles |
| Worker KSAs/competencies and expectations | Technological changes |
| HRMS level of development | Competitor labour usage |
| Organizational culture, workforce climate and satisfaction, and internal communications | Global market for skilled labour |
| Job analysis: workforce coverage, current data | Demographic changes |

---

Chapter 6: The HR Forecasting Process

# HR Forecasting Time Horizons

As we have discussed earlier in the text, environmental and organizational factors increase uncertainty for HR forecasters and necessitate flexibility in the programs they devise to balance personnel demand and supply. The key point to consider from an analysis of environmental and organizational factors is that uncertainty decreases our confidence in our ability to predict the future accurately and hence reduces the HR forecasting time horizon.[20] Large organizations with substantial resources and sizable numbers of well-trained personnel who also perform well may be better able to weather the storms of future change in environmental, economic, technological, and competitive market factors. If this is the case, they will be able to extend their HR forecasting process further into the future with greater confidence in the accuracy of their predictions. Irrespective of their situation with regard to environmental and internal factors, organizational forecasters use several different time horizons for forecasting. Although there are variations among organizations with respect to how they define their specific time parameters, the typical HR forecasting time horizons are as follows:[21]

1. *Current forecast:* The current forecast is the one being used to meet the immediate operational needs of the organization. The associated time frame is up to the end of the current operating cycle, or a maximum of one year into the future.
2. *Short-run forecast:* The short-run forecast extends forward from the current forecast and states the HR requirements for the next one- to two-year period beyond the current operational requirements.
3. *Medium-run forecast:* Most organizations define the medium-run forecast as the one that identifies requirements for two to five years into the future.
4. *Long-run forecast:* Due to uncertainty and the significant number and types of changes that can affect the organization's operations, the long-run forecast is by necessity extremely flexible and is a statement of probable requirements given a set of current assumptions. The typical long-run forecast extends five or more years ahead of the current operational period.

The outcome of forecasts derived from these four time horizons leads to predictions and projections. A **prediction** is a single numerical estimate of HR requirements associated with a specific time horizon and set of assumptions, whereas a **projection** incorporates several HR estimates based on a variety of assumptions.[22] The forecasting term **envelope** is synonymous with projection, as one can easily visualize the four corners of an envelope, with each corner containing a specific prediction; for example, corner 1 contains an optimistic sales assumption (time 1), corner 2 contains a pessimistic sales assumption (time 1), corner 3 contains an optimistic sales assumption (time 2), and corner 4 contains a pessimistic sales assumption (time 2). The four corner predictions serve to anchor the envelope, which may also contain a number of other specific predictions (e.g., the most likely assumption, which may be to

**prediction**

a single numerical estimate of HR requirements associated with a specific time horizon and set of assumptions

**projection**

several HR estimates based on a variety of assumptions

**envelope**

an analogy in which one can easily visualize the corners of an envelope containing the upper and lower limits or "bounds" of the various HR projections extending into the future

maintain the current sales level). The use of a combination of predictions and projections provides the necessary forecasting flexibility required to cope with the uncertainty and change associated with the environmental and organizational factors described previously.

HR forecasters therefore devise a set of alternative **scenarios**, each with its own set of assumptions and program details associated with HR functions such as training and development, staffing (advertisement, recruiting, and selection), and succession or replacement planning.[23] Naturally, organizations must also conduct **contingency planning** to have HR policy responses ready if substantive unanticipated changes occur. Contingency plans are brought into action when such severe changes to organizational or environmental factors completely negate the usefulness of the existing HR forecasting predictions or projections (e.g., a substantial drop in consumer demand occurs due to adverse public relations, as was seen in the Classic Coke and Tylenol cases).

**scenario**

a proposed sequence of events with its own set of assumptions and associated program details

**contingency plans**

plans to be implemented when severe, unanticipated changes to organizational or environmental factors completely negate the usefulness of the existing HR forecasting predictions or projections

## Determining Net HR Requirements

Thus far we have discussed the importance of HR forecasting, key personnel groups targeted for special attention, environmental and organizational factors influencing supply and demand of personnel, and forecasting time horizons. The final part of this chapter addresses the process of determining net HR requirements. The next two chapters will be devoted to an examination of specific methods used to calculate HR demand (Chapter 7) and supply (Chapter 8), but, for now, we will lay the foundation for these chapters by examining the overall process.

### 1. Determine HR Demand

As we previously mentioned briefly, it is essential that we calculate our requirement or demand for personnel in terms of numbers and obligatory skill competencies before we consider how we will meet those requirements (i.e., what supply or source of personnel to use). In determining demand, a variety of factors must be considered. First, each organizational subunit has to submit its net personnel requirement to the corporate forecasting unit, based on future needs for labour required to meet the agreed-on corporate and subunit objectives (e.g., market share, production levels, size or expansion, etc). It is critical to note that this HR demand figure must incorporate the individuals needed to maintain or replace the current personnel who retire, die, are fired or otherwise terminated, or take long-term leave (e.g., for reasons such as disability, training courses, etc.), as well as the replacements for individuals who are promoted or transferred out of the department. All these elements must be included in the calculation of departmental or subunit HR demand. These subunit labour demands are then aggregated and used as the starting point for the HR demand forecasts. See HR Planning Today 6.4 for the federal public services' forecasting methods.

## HR Planning Today 6.4

### HR Forecasting for the Canadian Federal Public Service Workforce

The Research Directorate of the Canadian Public Service Commission uses two sophisticated forecasting models for analyzing the federal public service, specifically, ithink and PERSIM software packages. These models can be used to conduct HR forecasting with respect to overall and departmental staffing levels, gross flows (out- and in-flows) of personnel with their associated rates of movement through the organization, for developing career paths, and for conducting detailed demographic analyses of the Canadian federal public service.

#### The ithink Model

Ithink was developed by High Performance Systems Inc. in the United States in 1985. It enables the user to build dynamic models for simulation and scenario testing. Based on traditional historical rates of personnel movement (e.g., promotions, retirements, recruitments, and turnover), the model enables the different scenarios to be tested and it notes the overall aggregate effect on the system of the various assumptions and personnel movement estimates. Specifically, ithink conceives of the federal public service workforce as "stocks" (i.e., populations—e.g., all employees in a particular department or region, or all employees in a specific occupational group, an employment equity group, etc.) and "flows" (inflows into a stock include promotions, transfers, external hires, while outflows incorporate retirement and turnover [voluntary and involuntary]). The assumptions regarding rates of personnel movement are derived from outside the model, typically by historical trends or by user-developed scenarios. ithink traces movement throughout the system based on "pull" assumptions where outflow patterns (see above) are used to forecast the needed inflow personnel requirements; however, "push" models could also be readily developed.

#### The PERSIM Model

PERSIM (Personnel Simulation Model) was developed in Canada by Statistics Canada, and in many ways it operates very similarly to the ithink model, as it uses historical patterns of personnel movement, as well as user-driven scenarios, to forecast HR movement and requirements. Its strength lies in its ability to also conduct micro-simulations that can develop career paths for every individual in an organization based on its operating assumptions and historical data. This differs from the ithink model in that PERSIM is not limited to looking at aggregated groups of individuals or overall movement of personnel. PERSIM is therefore extremely useful not only for determining career paths, but also for ascertaining future staffing levels, in- and out-flows of personnel, and overall demographic composition of the Canadian federal public service.

WWW Source: Demographic Analysis of the Federal Public Service Workforce—The ithink® and PERSIM Forecasting and Succession Planning Models, URL: http://www .hrma-agrh.gc.ca/hr-rh/psds-dfps/ dafps_f_model1_e.asp, 2000. Reproduced with the permission of the Minister of Public Works and Government Services Canada, 2006.

---

Next, planned future changes in organizational design or in restructuring (e.g., expansion of certain departments, downsizing of midlevel management, planned redundancy, and elimination of specific jobs), with their associated increases or decreases in staffing levels, must be incorporated into the equation to revise the aggregated net departmental demand requirements. Furthermore, forecasters have to consider how to replace nonproductive paid time (e.g., vacation and sick days) either by increasing demand for full- or part-time personnel (i.e., slack resources[24]) or perhaps by using overtime with the existing set of current employees to prevent loss of productive capacity and required level of service to organizational clients. Finally, consideration of all these issues leads us to the *net HR demand*, broken down into the forecasting time horizons mentioned previously and containing (1) the number of employees required by each subunit and by the organization in total and (2) the employee skill sets, competencies, or specifications required for each of the positions. Finally, we conduct a cost estimate (HR budget) for the net HR demand figure as a reality check to determine whether our forecasts are realistic, given financial resource considerations. Often, at this stage, subunits are asked to rank their HR demand, identifying jobs that are most critical to the achievement of their departmental objectives.[25]

## 2. Ascertain HR Supply

Step one produced an estimate of personnel requirements or demand. Step two examines exactly how we plan to fill the anticipated future requirements for personnel. In essence, there are two supply options: (1) **internal supply**, which refers to current members of the organizational workforce who can be retrained, promoted, transferred, etc., to fill anticipated future HR requirements, and (2) **external supply**, which refers to potential employees who are currently undergoing training (e.g., university students), working for competitors, members of unions or professional associations, or in a transitional stage, between jobs, or unemployed. Typically, most organizations use a mix of both internal and external supply, rewarding loyal employees who perform well with promotion and advancement possibilities and recruiting outside individuals who possess competencies not held by the present workforce.

With respect to internal supply, the ability to meet HR demand hinges on the size of the current workforce and especially its abilities. The number and the KSAs of the workforce are analyzed using the HRMS, which contains a personal record or skills inventory of each member of the workforce. Included in the inventory are items such as employee name, seniority, classification, part- or full-time work status, work history and record of jobs held in the organization, education, training, skill competencies, history of performance appraisals, and future jobs desired by or recommended for the individual, as well as hobbies and interests that may be useful for organizational planning.[26] For example, a computer search of the HRMS database could enable us to quickly determine the numbers, names, and employment status of, and performance records for, all employees who have successfully completed a graduate degree in statistics. If the search procedure fails to find a sufficient number of employees with the necessary KSAs to meet HR demand, the policy options would be either to identify and retrain employees with related KSAs who perform well or to turn to external sources for personnel.

Although some organizations hire recruits externally only when their internal searches and job posting or bidding process fail to identify sufficient numbers of high-quality internal candidates,[27] there are several other reasons many organizations use external labour to meet their HR demand. First, and most obviously, if it is necessary to expand our operations without increasing labour efficiency or implementing labour-saving technology, we might have to increase the size of the workforce by hiring externally. Second, internal employees are socialized and may be comfortable in their *modus operandi*, whereas external applicants can introduce to the organization competitive

**internal supply**

current members of the organizational workforce who can be retrained, promoted, transferred, etc., to fill anticipated future HR requirements

**external supply**

potential employees who are currently undergoing training (e.g., university students), working for competitors, members of unions or professional associations, or are in a transitional stage, between jobs, or unemployed

insights and highly creative novel operational techniques recently learned in external institutions. Third, an internal candidate may be considerably more expensive (due to collective agreement provisions relating compensation to seniority) than an individual who is recruited from outside the organization. Fourth, the usage of "headhunters," specialist personnel placement firms that have detailed knowledge and an extensive network of industry contacts, may enable the organization to lure away from competitive firms proven high performers with distinctive profiles of competencies and experience not possessed by the organization's current executives/professionals. Finally, if organizational objectives require a shift in operating techniques, culture, and past practices, hiring external candidates is often desirable for shaking up the organization.

Irrespective of the reasons organizations seek external recruits, the key factor in determining whether the organization will be effective in meeting HR requirements from external supply sources is an analysis of how HR policies are perceived by individuals who are potential employees. By benchmarking competitor practices with respect to compensation, it is possible to examine staffing and compensation policies to make them more attractive to high-quality applicants. An organization's ability to attract the "cream of the crop" will be substantially enhanced if the organization is perceived as being the industry leader with respect to compensation, rather than just meeting or lagging behind its competitors. As well, recruiting policies must be fine-tuned to ensure communication is established with the appropriate labour markets. For example, it might be possible to fill many production jobs from local labour market sources, but specialized technicians and professionals may require external recruiting, which is national, if not international, in scope. In this case, additional resources, time, and effort may be required if we are expected to fully meet the numerical and KSA requirements specified by our HR demand process. Finally, obtaining external applicants requires not only identifying where these individuals live and work, but also ascertaining the most appropriate media to use to contact and attract them. These media may include job fairs, open houses, and career days, as well as advertising in industry and professional association journals, publications, newspapers, and websites read by potential external applicants who are trained in the skills needed.

HR Planning Notebook 6.3 refers to different ways of categorizing HR forecasting models.

### 3. Determine Net HR Requirements

The third step in the process involves the determination of net HR requirements. Personnel who can fill organizational HR demand requirements must be found from either internal or external supplies:

external supply requirements = replacement + change supply components

change supply = hiring to increase (or decrease) the overall staffing level

replacement supply = hiring to replace all normal losses

(Normal losses are those that result from retirements, terminations, voluntary turnover, promotions, transfers, and leaves, and these losses must be replaced to keep the workforce size at the current level.)

### Categorizing Forecasting Models

Forecasting models can be categorized in three ways: (1) time-series models, (2) cause–and–effect models, and (3) judgmental models. Time-series models use past data in order to extrapolate and extend trends into the future. These models are simple to use and are typically confined to short-term forecasting. An example of a time-series model is trend forecasting. Cause–and–effect models assume that an ongoing relationship exists between one or more causal or "independent" variables that produce change in the target or "dependent" variable. An example is the significant negative relationship existing between market rate of interest (cost of capital) and the demand for construction workers. Cause–and–effect models are used for short-, medium-, and long-term HR forecasting; the best-known example is regression, as discussed in Chapter 8. Finally, judgmental models are used for new ventures, situations where past data do not exist or are unreliable, or when the forecasting period extends into the distant future. They rely on the subjective judgments of experts to derive the forecasts; one widely used example is the Delphi technique.

Source: Adapted from Jain, C. 2002. "Benchmarking Forecasting Models," *The Journal of Business Forecasting Methods and Systems*, Vol. 21, No. 3 (Fall), pp. 18–20. Reprinted with permission.

Recall from our earlier discussion of HR demand that future personnel requirements must not only replace the current workforce employees (in terms of numbers and skill competencies), but also reflect desired future changes to staffing levels. Therefore, the first element in deriving our external supply calculation is to meet our *replacement needs*—that is, to maintain operations at the current level by hiring new employees to replace workers who have left due to firing, transfers, retirements, promotions, leaves, and so on. Next, if we are to increase or decrease our staffing levels, based on organizational and subunit objectives, we have to consider the *change component* that moves the overall size of the workforce to its new future level. This process can be represented by the following equation:

$$\text{external supply} = \text{current workforce size} \times (\text{replacement \% per year} + \text{change \% per year})$$

Using the example of an organization with a current workforce size of 1000 workers, an annual historical replacement/loss rate of 11%, and a desired future growth rate of 7%, the net external supply requirement is that 180 individuals be hired per year:

$$\text{external supply} = 1000\,(.11 + .07) = 110 + 70 = 180$$

Of the new hires, 110 people are allocated strictly to replacement of departing workers, and the other 70 individuals constitute the change requirement for new growth.

Another organization with a workforce of 450, which has a historical annual replacement/loss rate of 8% and a corporate downsizing policy that will reduce overall staffing levels by 9.5%, has the following supply requirement:

$$\text{external supply} = 450\,(.08 + [-.095]) = 36 - 43 = -7$$

(In the equation above, note that the figure 43 was rounded up from 42.75.) In this case, the annual replacement/loss rate is insufficient on its own to reduce the size of the organization's workforce to the desired lower staffing level. The result is a net HR surplus, and the organization must not only institute a freeze on external hiring but also further reduce the current internal workforce complement by seven positions to meet the mandated downsizing policy!

In many cases, the existence of a collective agreement between management and the union representing the employees may, due to seniority and layoff articles in the agreement, result in the organization not being able to specify which workers are to be terminated.

**⨁ⓅⒸ 6.8**

**HR deficit**

when demand for HR exceeds the current personnel resources available in the organization's workforce (HR internal supply)

**HR surplus**

when the internal workforce supply exceeds the organization's requirement or demand for personnel

**job sharing**

when two or more employees perform the duties of one full-time position, each sharing the work activities on a part-time basis

### 4. Institute HR Programs: HR Deficit and HR Surplus

When a forecast of HR demand is reconciled with the current workforce supply of personnel (i.e., HR internal supply), the result is the net HR requirement, which will be either a deficit or a surplus (unless we are exceedingly lucky and achieve parity with an exact balance of the two!).

$$\text{HR deficit} = \text{HR demand} > \text{HR internal supply}$$

Simply stated, an **HR deficit** means that forecasted HR demand requirements cannot be satisfied solely by use of the current internal workforce supply of employees. Therefore, policy options focus on external supply considerations of recruitment, selection, and compensation schemes to attract new employees. It might be possible to hire part-time employees, full-time employees, contract or freelance workers, or a combination of both in an attempt to address the deficit. Similarly, it might be possible to recall any workers (depending on their KSAs and training) who were laid off because of past lower levels of HR demand. Also, retired employees might be enticed back to work on at least a part-time basis by means of attractive, flexible work schedules. The use of temporary workers also can help the organization meet a short-run HR deficit, although in the long run, further attention to providing promotion and transfer opportunities for internal workers by means of training and development programs usually proves more advantageous.

$$\text{HR surplus} = \text{HR demand} < \text{HR internal supply}$$

An **HR surplus** occurs when the internal workforce supply exceeds the organization's requirement or demand for personnel. In this instance, a number of policy options can be considered. Employees might be laid off to reduce the excess labour supply to a level equal to the demand requirements. Alternatively, employers might terminate employees if certain jobs are considered redundant and the skill sets associated with these jobs will not be required in the future. **Job sharing** occurs when two or more employees perform the duties of one full-time position, each sharing the work activities on a part-time basis. This policy option is gaining strength in Canadian industry as it allows the company to retain valued employees, albeit with reduced hours and lower income levels, with the intention of reinstating them to full-time status once HR demand levels increase at some time in the future, usually when the economy rebounds.

Other programs for addressing an HR surplus include reducing the number of hours, shifts, or days worked by each worker so that all workers can be retained, while reducing overall work hours to the level required by operational demand imperatives. Secondments or leaves occur when the organization lends some of its excess workforce to community groups or permits those surplus workers to take educational leave or training away from the operational workplace. **Attrition** is the process of reducing an HR surplus by allowing the size of the workforce to decline naturally due to the normal pattern of losses associated with retirements, deaths, voluntary turnover, and so on. This decrease of internal supply over time can be accentuated by a **hiring freeze**, which is a prohibition on all external recruiting activities. Early-retirement packages attempt to induce surplus workers to leave the organization when granted severance benefits and outplacement assistance. Finally, if internal supply exceeds HR demand for specific positions, organizational retraining and development, assistance with the expenses associated with moving to a better labour market (geographic mobility), and transfer and demotion can also be considered as possible policy options for the organization's affected personnel.[28]

**attrition**
the process of reducing an HR surplus by allowing the size of the workforce to decline naturally because of the normal pattern of losses associated with retirements, deaths, voluntary turnover, etc.

**hiring freeze**
a prohibition on all external recruiting activities

## Summary

This chapter has examined a wide variety of aspects associated with HR forecasting. The advantages of instituting effective forecasting procedures include reducing the costs of HR, increasing the flexibility of the organization, ensuring a close link to the process of business forecasting, and ensuring that the requirements of the organization take precedence over other specific issues. Some groups—executives or specialist/technical personnel, for example—attract special attention in the HR demand and supply reconciliation process. Both environmental and organizational factors have a tremendous impact on various forecasting procedures, and many of these factors have to be addressed explicitly in HR forecasting procedures. The various stages associated with the HR forecasting process are determining the demand, ascertaining the supply, determining net HR requirements (formulae were supplied), and instituting the program. Finally, we discussed the policy implications of reconciling HR demand and supply, ending up with either an HR deficit or surplus, and the various programs that may have to be instituted by organizations to address these varying situations; these programs include job sharing, attrition, and a hiring freeze.

The next two chapters are devoted to an examination of specific techniques used by organizations to calculate HR demand and supply. Chapter 7 presents specific techniques employed by organizations to derive HR demand forecasts.

## Key Terms

attrition, 161
contingency plans, 155
designated groups, 151
envelope, 154
external supply, 157
event-based forecasting, 147

hiring freeze, 161
HR deficit, 160
HR forecasting, 147
HR surplus, 160
human resources demand, 150
human resources supply, 150

internal supply, 157
job sharing, 160
prediction, 154
process-based forecasting, 147

projection, 154
scenario, 155
transaction-based forecasting, 147

# Web Links

Public Safety and Emergency Preparedness Canada is at:

**www.psepc.gc.ca** (p. 144)

Emergency Management Ontario's website is:

**www.mpss.jus.gov.on.ca/english/pub_security/emo/about_emo.html** (p. 144)

The U.S. Federal Emergency Management website is at:

**www.fema.gov** (p. 145)

The Canadian government's Human Resources and Social Development website is at:

**www.hrsdc.gc.ca/en/home.shtml** (p. 147)

The report on HR planning in the Canadian government, and an Integrated HR and Business Planning Tool is located at:

**www.hrma-agrh.gc.ca/hr-rh/hrp-prh/toolkit/chr-crh_e.asp** (pp. 148, 155)

The Canadian government's advisory website on HR planning for employers is located at:

**http://hrmanagement.gc.ca/gol/hrmanagement/site.nsf/en/hr10777.html** (p. 149)

Guidance on preparing a HR plan from the Canadian Government's Public Service Commission is at:

**www.psc-cfp.gc.ca/staf_dot/staf_strat/section_1_e.htm** (p. 149)

HR forecasting information, hotspots, sectors, and salary information on Australia and New Zealand can be found at Hays Specialist HR Forecast:

**www.hays.com.au/forecast/hr.aspx** (p. 151)

Guidelines from the Government of Saskatchewan on HR planning are located at:

**http://www.gov.sk.ca/psc/hrmanagement/hrplanning/moreinfo.htm** (p. 154)

The Canadian Public Service ithink and PERSIM Forecasting and Succession planning models are at:

**www.hrma-agrh.gc.ca/hr-rh/psds-dfps/dafps_f_model1_e.asp** (p. 156)

Statistics Canada website is at:

**www.statcan.ca** (p. 157)

The U.S. Government's Bureau of Labour Statistics website is at:

**www.bls.gov** (p. 157)

The U.K. Government's HR & Training website is located at:

**www.dh.gov.uk/PolicyAndGuidance/HumanResourcesAndTraining/fs/en**
(p. 159)

Guidance for human resource planning from the New Zealand Government can be found at:

**www.ssc.govt.nz/display/document.asp?NavID=235** (p. 160)

Information on workplace trends and forecasting is available from the U.S. Society for Human Resource Management at:

**www.shrm.org/research/about.asp** (p. 161)

# RPC Icons

**RPC 6.1  Identifies the organization's HR needs**

**RPC 6.2  Identifies the data required to support HR planning**

**RPC 6.3 Interprets and communicates business strategies and plans**

**RPC 6.4 Gathers, analyzes, and reports relevant business and industry information including global trends**

**RPC 6.5 Leads in the development of HR initiatives that support the organization's strategic directions**

**RPC 6.6 Encourages interaction between the organization and external stakeholders (e.g., public, government, educational institutions, community groups) that supports the development and implementation of the HR plan**

**RPC 6.7  Forecasts HR supply and demand conditions**

**RPC 6.8  Using available data, develops HR plans that support the organization's strategic directions**

# Discussion Questions

1. Over the past decade, there have been dramatic employment shifts in many industries because of product life cycles and technological change, as well as general changes in demand for workers with specific KSAs—for example, in computer and systems engineering. Select a particular industry and conduct a literature review and Internet search for business and labour employment statistics related to its operations (access the websites for industry associations and Statistics Canada). Based on this historical review and your knowledge of current business trends, forecast possible employment shifts for the specific industry you selected. How would you use this information as an HR planner?

2. A wide range of HR programming options is available to address either an HR deficit or an HR surplus. However, these programs have widely

divergent consequences for the workforce, service to clients, and the local labour market, as well as for the organization's financial bottom line. Identify specific criteria to evaluate and differentiate the effectiveness of the various HR program options.

# Using the Internet

1. The Government of Canada's Public Service has developed the ithink and PERSIM Models of HR Forecasting and Succession.

Go to **www.hrma-agrh.gc.ca/hr-rh/psds-dfps/dafps_f_model1_e.asp** to review these models and conduct an assessment of their effectiveness for usage in other private- and public-sector contexts. Assess the benefits and strengths of these models, as well as limitations and deficiencies associated with their assumptions and process steps.

# Exercise

1. Conduct a comprehensive analysis of the various stakeholders involved in an organization with which you are familiar. From this analysis, ascertain the key uncertainties that would be associated with the HR forecasting process for this organization. Based on the material in this chapter and your own knowledge, how would you address these environmental and organizational uncertainties in your modifications to the HR forecasting process?

# Case: Sun Microsystems

Sun Microsystems has experienced extremely rapid growth as the company has evolved from an entrepreneurial operation to a major player in the computer systems industry. As a result, there is a strong need to forecast and identify managerial and executive talent both within and outside the corporation. Ken Alvares, vice-president of human resources, is well aware of the need to "grow" high-potential employees into these key managerial appointments.

Sun has 600 directors, which is the entry-level executive job, and these individuals report to 110 vice-presidents, who in turn report to the president and the 11 executives who sit on Sun's senior management team. Alvares pays close attention to the profile and performance of each of these individuals: "We watch the directors closely, but give more attention to the VPs. We look at each person's particular profile and tailor individual coaching to their needs." Because of this policy, the forecasting and developing of senior managerial and executive talent at Sun takes on a very personalized approach, one that seems to be working, at least to date.

Alvares says he has a good idea who would fill a job if something happened to a specific person, but he is still unsatisfied with Sun's system. "When you look at our bench strength, I don't get the feeling that we've got ourselves covered. I worry about developing people to step up to the next level. In some cases, I have one guy who can fill 10 jobs. If I have to use him, then I'll have to do some scrambling."

Source: "Heirs Unapparent: Sun Microsystems," *HR Magazine* (1999), Society for Human Resource Management. Reprinted with the permission of *HR Magazine*, published by the Society for Human Resource Management (www.shrm.org), Alexandria, VA.

## Question

Prepare a report analyzing Sun Microsystem's forecasting program for managerial and executive talent. What additions, modifications, or changes would you make to this program?

# Endnotes

1. Johnson, R. 2005. "Controversy over FEMA Chief Puts Cronyism in the Spotlight," *Workforce Management*, 84/11, 14–15; Tumulty, K., M. Thompson, and M. Allen. 2005. "How Many More Mike Browns Are Out There?" *Time*, 166/14, 49–55; Leonard, B. 2005. "Hurricane Katrina Recovery Commander Puts Advanced HR Degree to Good Use," *HR Magazine*, 50/11, 34; Bliss, J. 2005. "E-mails Nail ex-FEMA Boss," *The Vancouver Sun*, November 4, 2005, A9; *Financial Times*, "Brownie's Image," London UK, November 4, 2005, 14; Sullivan, L. 2005. "FEMA's Foul-Up," *InformationWeek*, Issue 1058, 24; Ripley, A. 2005. "How the Coast Guard Gets It Right," *Time*, 166/18, 150–153.

2. Atwater, D.M. 1995. "Workforce Forecasting," *Human Resource Planning*, Vol. 18, No. 4: 50–53.

3. Godet, M. 1983. "Reducing the Blunders in Forecasting," *Futures*, Vol. 15, No. 3 (June): 181–192.

4. Patterson, B. 2003. "Weighing Resources," *HR Magazine*, 48/10, 103–108; Hogan, A. 1987. "Combining Forecasts: Some Managerial Experiences with Extrapolation," *Socio-Economic Planning Sciences*, Vol. 2, No. 3: 205–211; Mahmoud, E. 1984. "Accuracy in Forecasting: A Survey," *Journal of Forecasting*, Vol. 3, No. 2 (April): 139–159.

5. Bechet, T. 2000. "Developing Staffing Strategies that Work: Implementing Pragmatic, Nontraditional Approaches," *Public Personnel Management*, 29/4. 465–478; Wagner, R., S. Hlavacka, and L. Bacharova. 2000. "Slovakia's Health System: Hospital Human Resource Planning in Slovakia," *Journal of Management in Medicine*, 14/5-6, 383–407; Monks, K. 1996. "Global or Local? HRM in the Multinational Company: The Irish Experience," *International Journal of Human Resource Management*, Vol. 7, No. 3 (September): 721–735.

6. Pynes, J. 2004. "The Implementation of Workforce and Succession Planning in the Public Sector," *Public Personnel Management*, 33/4, 389–404; Stone, T., and J. Fiorito. 1986. "A Perceived Uncertainty Model of Human Resource Forecasting Technique Use," *Academy of Management Review*, Vol. 11, No. 3: 635–642; Meehan, R., and B.S. Ahmed. 1990. "Forecasting Human Resources Requirements: A Demand Model," *Human Resource Planning*, Vol. 13, No. 4: 297–307.

7. Schramm, J. 2005. "Planning Ahead," *HR Magazine*, 50/10, 152–153; Bechet, T. 2000. "Developing Staffing Strategies That Work: Implementing Pragmatic, Nontraditional Approaches," *Public Personnel Management*, 29/4. 465–478; Walker, J.W. 1980. *Human Resource Planning*. New York: McGraw-Hill.

8. Wagner, R., S. Hlavacka, and L. Bacharova. 2000. "Slovakia's Health System: Hospital Human Resource Planning in Slovakia," *Journal of Management in Medicine*, 14/5-6, 383–407; Beck, B.M. 1991. "Forecasting Environmental Change," *Journal of Forecasting*, Vol. 10, No. 1: 3–19; Schuler, R.S. 1989. "Scanning the Environment: Planning for Human Resource Management and Organizational Change," *Human Resource Planning*, Vol. 12, No. 4.

9. Bechet, T. 2000. "Developing Staffing Strategies That Work: Implementing Pragmatic, Nontraditional Approaches," *Public Personnel Management*, 29/4. 465–478; Fulmer, W. 1990.

"Human Resource Management: The Right Hand of Strategy Implementation," *Human Resource Planning*, Vol. 12, No. 4: 1–11.

10. Helton, K., and J. Soubik. 2004. "Case Study: Pennsylvania's Changing Workforce: Planning Today with Tomorrow's Vision," *Public Personnel Management*, 33/4, 459–474; McEnery, J., and M. Lifter. 1987. "Demands for Change: Interfacing Environmental Pressures and the Personnel Process," *Public Personnel Management*, Vol. 16, No. 1 (Spring): 61–87.

11. Fulmer, W. 1990. "Human Resource Management: The Right Hand of Strategy Implementation," *Human Resource Planning*, Vol. 12, No. 4: 1–11.

12. Schuler, R.S., and J.W. Walker. 1990. "Human Resources Strategy: Focusing on Issues and Actions," *Organizational Dynamics* (Summer): 4–19.

13. Adapted from Burack, E.J., and N.J. Mathys. 1996. *Human Resource Planning: A Pragmatic Approach to Manpower Staffing and Development*, 3rd ed. Northbrook, IL: Brace Park.

14. Grabosky, P., and D. Rosenbloom. 1975. "Racial and Ethnic Integration in the Federal Service," *Social Science Quarterly*, Vol. 56, No. 1 (June): 71–84.

15. Zaleznik, A. 1977. "Managers and Leaders: Are They Different?" *Harvard Business Review*, Vol. 55, No. 3 (May): 67–78.

16. Bucalo, J. 1974. "The Assessment Center: A More Specified Approach," *Human Resource Management* (Fall): 2–12.

17. Adapted from Schuler, R.S., and J.W. Walker. 1990. "Human Resources Strategy: Focusing on Issues and Actions," *Organizational Dynamics* (Summer): 4–19.

18. Helton, K., and J. Soubik. 2004. "Case Study: Pennsylvania's Changing Workforce: Planning Today with Tomorrow's Vision," *Public Personnel Management*, 33/4, 459–474; Beck, B.M. 1991. "Forecasting Environmental Change," *Journal of Forecasting*, Vol. 10, No. 1: 3–19.

19. McEnery, J., and M. Lifter. 1987. "Demands for Change: Interfacing Environmental Pressures and the Personnel Process," *Public Personnel Management*, Vol. 16, No. 1 (Spring): 61–87; Schuler, R.S. 1989. "Scanning the Environment: Planning for Human Resource Management and Organizational Change," *Human Resource Planning*, Vol. 12, No. 4.

20. Beck, B.M. 1991. "Forecasting Environmental Change," *Journal of Forecasting*, Vol. 10, No. 1: 3–19; Butinsky, C.F., and O. Harari. 1983. "Models vs. Reality: An Analysis of 12 Human Resource Planning Systems," *Human Resource Planning*, Vol. 6, No. 1: 11–20.

21. Adapted from Bechet, T.P., and J.W. Walker. 1993. "Aligning Staffing with Business Strategy," *Human Resource Planning*, Vol. 16, No. 2: 1–16; Walker, J.W. 1980. *Human Resource Planning*. New York: McGraw-Hill.

22. Burack, E.J., and N.J. Mathys. 1996. *Human Resource Planning: A Pragmatic Approach to Manpower Staffing and Development*, 3rd ed. Northbrook, IL: Brace Park.

23. Fink, A., B. Marr, A. Siebe, and J. Kuhle. 2005. "The Future Scorecard: Combining External and Internal Scenarios to Create Strategic Foresight," *Management Decision*, 43/3, 360–381; Millett, S., and Zelman, S. 2005. "Scenario Analysis and a Logic Model of Public Education in Ohio," *Strategy & Leadership*, 33/2, 33–41; Van Der Heihden, K. 2000. "Scenarios and Forecasting: Two Perspectives," *Technological Forecasting and Social Change*, 65, 31–36; Mason, D.H. 1994. "Scenario-Based Planning: Decision Model for the Learning Organization," *Planning Review*: 6–11.

24. Thompson, J. 1967. *Organizations in Action*. New York: McGraw-Hill.

25. Burack, E. 1995. *Creative Human Resource Planning and Applications: A Strategic Approach*. Englewood Cliffs, NJ: Prentice Hall.

26. Greengard, S. 2001. "Make Smarter Business Decisions: Know What Employees Can Do," *Workforce*, 80/11, 42–46; Martin, R. 1967. "Skills Inventories," *Personnel Journal* (January): 28–83; Kaumeyer, R.H. 1982. *Planning and Using a Total Personnel System*. New York: Van Nostrand Reinhold; Seamans, L. 1978. "What's Lacking in Most Skills Inventories," *Personnel Journal* (March): 101–106.

27. Connolly, S. 1975. "Job Posting," *Personnel Journal* (May): 295–299.

28. McLaughlin, G. 1975. "A Professional Supply and Demand Analysis," *Educational Record*, Vol. 56, No. 3 (Summer): 196–200.

# Chapter 7

HR Demand

## Chapter Learning Objectives

After reading this chapter, you should be able to

- Understand the importance of demand forecasting in the HR planning process.
- Recognize the linkages between the HR plan, labour demand forecasting techniques, and the subsequent supply stage.
- Compare and contrast the advantages and disadvantages of various demand forecasting techniques: index/trend analysis, expert forecasts, the Delphi technique, the nominal group technique, HR budgets (or staffing tables), envelope/scenario forecasting, and regression analysis.

# UTILIZING DELPHI TECHNIQUE IN THE CANADIAN HEALTH CARE SECTOR

The Delphi technique, as discussed in this chapter, is a sequential process whereby experts are polled for their forecasts of HR demand. This technique can also be effectively employed to help improve the matching of HR demand and supply by means of identifying, and eliminating, underlying factors of stressful and dissatisfying work, which may cause employees to quit or be absent unnecessarily.

The Delphi technique is a commonly used expert forecasting technique for the health care sector in Canada and worldwide. Over the past decade, dramatic changes in public and private health care have occurred, including massive operational restructuring, and downsizing, with obvious attendant effects upon nurses' perceived stressors, role conflict, ambiguity, and overload, as well as the changed nature of their work experiences. The effects of these changes on the health care sector, and in particular on nurses and nurse-managers are still in dire need of research attention. Forty-one Canadian nurse-managers took part in a two-round Delphi process. Round one tasked the experts with identifying present and future roles and challenges for nurse-managers, while round two asked them to rank-order the stressors, as well as their training and development recommendations.

The findings of the Delphi process highlighted the increasing importance of managerial roles for nurse-managers above and beyond their normal clinical role performance requirements. Key stressors were identified as being insufficient resources, work intensification, and faster pace of work, as well as job enlargement. Studies have also highlighted the importance of nurses feeling empowered through participative management style and involvement in key decision-making processes. A lack of professional respect from physicians has also been noted as a key stressor. As the changed role of nurse-manager has incorporated a downloading of significant managerial responsibility, without having provided the requisite training to meet these responsibilities, the Delphi process recommendations focused upon providing skill-based training for nurse-managers and nurses in interpersonal communication and feedback, conflict resolution, budgeting, etc. The development and reinforcement of mentoring relationships were also deemed to be desirable in the aim of reducing stress and enhancing the effectiveness of nurses and nurse-managers.[1]

Successful organizations combine statistically driven quantitative forecasts with more qualitative expert processes to achieve the most comprehensive demand forecasts possible.[2] As well, organizations must consider demand for personnel not only for the current operational period, but also well into the future to ensure the right numbers of workers with the requisite skills and competencies are ready and available to work when the organization requires them.

**RPC** 7.1

## Index/Trend Analysis

Examining the relationship over time between an operational index, such as level of sales, and the demand for labour (as reflected by the number of employees in the workforce) is a relatively straightforward quantitative demand forecasting technique commonly used by many organizations (see Table 7.1 on p. 177).[3] This technique, also known as trend analysis, reveals the historical relationship between the operational index and the number of employees required by the organization (demand for labour).[4] Although sales level is probably the most common index used by organizations, other operational indices include (1) the number of units produced, (2) the number of clients serviced, and (3) the production (i.e., direct labour) hours. Similarly, although the relationship between the operational index and workforce size (number of employees) can be calculated for the entire organization, as well as for the department or operational subunit, some organizations use trend analysis to ascertain demand requirements for (1) direct labour and (2) indirect labour (e.g., HR staff).

HR Planning Notebook 7.1 shows an example of index/trend analysis.

---

### HR Planning Notebook 7.1

#### Index/Trend Analysis

**Puslinch Pottery**

| Year | Sales ($ Thousands) | Number of Employees | Ratio (Sales [$ Thousands] per Employee) |
|------|---------------------|---------------------|-------------------------------------------|
| 2004 | $2800 | 155 | 18.06 |
| 2005 | 3050 | 171 | 17.83 |
| 2006 | 3195 | 166 | 19.25 |
| **2007** | **3300** | **177** | **18.64** |
| 2008 | 3500[a] | 188[b] | 18.64[c] |
| 2009 | 3600[a] | 193[b] | 18.64[c] |
| 2010 | 3850[a] | 207[b] | 18.64[c] |

[a] Time now is the year 2007. We are forecasting labour demand for 2008, 2009, and 2010, and therefore sales figures for those years are future estimates.

[b] Employee numbers are historical, except for the figures for 2008, 2009, and 2010, which are our future HR demand forecasts.

[c] The index used to calculate future demand (number of employees) can be the most recent figure, or an average of the up-to-date period (e.g., the past four years, for which the average is 18.44). In this trend analysis, the most recent ratio (18.64) for the year 2007 was used for forecasting.

---

Chapter 7: HR Demand

There are five steps to conducting an effective index/trend analysis.

### 1. Select the Appropriate Business/Operational Index

The HR forecaster must select a readily available business index, such as sales level, that is (a) known to have a direct influence on the organizational demand for labour, and (b) subjected to future forecasting as a result of the normal business planning process.

### 2. Track the Business Index over Time

Once the index has been selected, it is necessary to go back in time for at least the four or five most recent years, but preferably for a decade or more, to record the quantitative or numerical levels of the index over time.

### 3. Track the Workforce Size over Time

Record the historical figures of the total number of employees, or, alternatively, the amount of direct and indirect labour (see above) for exactly the same period used for the business index in Step 2.

### 4. Calculate the Average Ratio of the Business Index to the Workforce Size

**employee requirement ratio**

the relationship between the operational index and the demand for labour

Obtain a ratio by dividing the level of sales for each year of historical data by the number of employees required to produce that year's level of sales. This **employee requirement ratio** is calculated for each year over the period of analysis so an average ratio describing the relationship between the two variables over time can be determined.

### 5. Calculate the Forecasted Demand for Labour

Divide the annual forecast for the business index by the average employee requirement ratio for each future year to arrive at forecasted annual demand for labour. For example, obtain future sales forecast figures for the next five years. For each of the years, divide the level of sales by the average employee requirement ratio to obtain the forecasted numerical demand for labour for each future year.

Although index/trend analysis is widespread due to its ease of use, remember that the analysis incorporates only the relationship between a single business variable and demand for labour (workforce size). By design, any single-variable relationship provides a simplistic forecast for demand. For more comprehensive analyses that reflect a variety of factors affecting business operations, such as interest rates, level of unemployment, consumer disposable income, and so on, the quantitative techniques normally employed are multivariate regression or other similar modelling/programming models.[5] Although these sophisticated, multiple-predictor techniques require detailed knowledge of statistics and systems programming, we will present an example of simple regression later in the chapter.

## Expert Forecasts

Direct managerial input is the most commonly used method for determining workforce requirements.[6] Using experts to arrive at a numerical estimate of future labour demand is considered to be a qualitative process for determining future labour requirements because it is a detailed process of stating assumptions, considering potential organizational and environmental changes, and deriving a rationale to support the numerical estimate.

A wide variety of individuals may be considered experts for their knowledge of organizational operations, competitive HR practices, international trends in the labour markets, etc.[7] First and foremost, the organization's own line managers, who each have detailed knowledge of workload, responsibilities, and overall task responsibilities for a department, possess important insights into how future demand for labour should or might change in the manager's own areas of responsibility. Second, the organization's HR and business planning staffs certainly have critical information to provide wise guidance in forecasting future levels of labour demand. For example, the planning staff may use econometric and strategic models to predict the future level of sales of or demand for the organization's goods and services, as well as provide important insights into future economic indicators affecting labour demand such as interest rates, change in gross national product, level of consumer disposable income, savings, and so on. The HR staff, whether they are HR generalists or a team of HR planning specialists, are able to draw up a detailed set of assumptions with respect to industry, local, and international labour market trends that affect how the organization organizes and employs its own workforce. Third, business consultants, financial analysts, university researchers, union staff members, industry spokespersons, and others possess detailed knowledge of specific industries or types of organizational activity and are able to give rich, detailed, and largely impartial judgments on future labour demand because of their external perspective relative to the organization. Finally, but not exclusively, federal, provincial, and local governmental staff and officials are important individuals to consult because they possess knowledge of future environmental changes in labour and business legislation that can dramatically change labour demand not only for a specific organization, but also for the industry in general. For example, pending legislation to ban the use of certain materials in product manufacturing might cause a substantial drop in demand for these products and hence an associated reduction in demand for employees who are involved in their manufacture.

Governmental ministries and departments, most specifically those devoted to labour, HR, and economic development, and, of course, the highly regarded Statistics Canada, can all provide expert information for our labour demand forecasting process. Irrespective of which experts we select, a number of options are available for obtaining labour demand estimates and assumptions from those concerned. Interviews, questionnaires (conducted in person or by mail or e-mail), and telephone conference calls are some of these options, but other techniques can be employed to maximize the benefit of each expert's contributions in specific circumstances. We now turn our attention to two of these methods of facilitating high-quality labour demand forecasts—namely, the Delphi technique and the nominal group technique.

 7.2

## Delphi Technique

**Delphi technique**

"a carefully designed program of sequential, individual interrogations (usually conducted through questionnaires) interspersed with information feedback on the opinions expressed by the other participants in previous rounds"[9]

The **Delphi technique**, which was named after the Greek oracle at Delphi, was developed by N.C. Dalkey and his associates at the Rand Corporation in 1950 and is an especially useful qualitative method for deriving detailed assumptions of long-run HR demand.[8] This forecasting technique is "a carefully designed program of sequential, individual interrogations (usually conducted through questionnaires) interspersed with information feedback on the opinions expressed by the other participants in previous rounds."[9] A key feature of this demand forecasting technique is that once a group of experts is selected, the experts do not meet face to face.[10] Instead, a project coordinator canvasses them individually for their input and forecasts by means of a progressively more focused series of questionnaires. The advantage of the Delphi technique is that it avoids many of the problems associated with face-to-face groups, namely, reluctance by individual experts to participate due to (1) shyness, (2) perceived lower status or authority, (3) perceived communication deficiencies, (4) issues of individual dominance and groupthink (i.e., group conformity pressures), and so on.[11] Because the Delphi technique does not employ face-to-face meetings, it can serve as a great equalizer and can elicit valid feedback from all expert members. It is also advantageous that the Delphi technique can effectively use experts who are drawn from widely dispersed geographical areas.[12] See HR Planning Today 7.1 for more details on the Delphi technique.

---

## HR Planning Today 7.1

### The Delphi Technique in Action

The Delphi technique is used in a wide variety of applications for HR forecasting. For example, an agricultural research organization started by deriving nine organizational core competencies from interviews and internal organizational documentation. The experts were identified by the organization, which asked them to respond to set of questionnaires based on the Delphi technique. The questionnaires investigated (1) the importance of human competencies in the future, (2) the capacity of the organization's current human resources, and (3) ranking the nine organizational core competencies in order of priority. HR policy interventions were developed from the resulting information.

A three-round Delphi procedure was used to identify the basic competencies of research chefs, who develop new products, create new recipes, and conduct food testing. Thirty-three expert chefs were involved in the Delphi undertaking, and they were asked questions concerning (1) factors differentiating successful from less successful research chefs, (2) knowledge and skills required by successful

research chefs, and (3) how tasks differ for a research chef from ordinary chefs. The experts identified 19 basic competencies that a successful research chef should possess.

Finally, subsequent to the September 11, 2001, terrorist attacks on the United States, the Delphi technique was used by the government and insurance and risk managers to estimate the possibility of future losses due to terrorism, and the likely types of terrorist acts various organizations might experience. Experts used the Delphi technique to analyze databases on landmarks, tourist attractions, "vital points," and property assessment data to come up with their forecasts.

Sources: Adapted from T. Guimaraes et al., "Forecasting Core Competencies in an R&D Environment," *R&D Management*, Vol. 31, No. 3 (July 2001),. 249–255; K. Birdir and T. Pearson, "Research Chefs' Competencies: A Delphi Approach," *International Journal of Contemporary Hospitality Management*, Vol. 12, No. 3 (2000), 205–209; and B. Coffin, "Forecasting Terrorism Losses," *Risk Management*, Vol. 49, No. 11 (November 2000), 8–9.

There are disadvantages associated with the Delphi technique, as indeed there are with all forecasting techniques. In particular, because of the series of questionnaires administered to derive a forecast, the time and costs incurred when using the Delphi technique can be higher than those incurred when using alternative forecasting methods. Another deficiency is that since the results cannot be validated statistically, the process is greatly dependent on the individual knowledge and commitment of each of the contributing experts.[13] Furthermore, if the experts are drawn from one specific field, it may be that their common professional training will guide them along a single line of inquiry rather than pursuing more innovative and creative courses of action. Finally, if insufficient attention has been paid to developing criteria for the identification and selection of experts, the personnel selected to derive the demand forecasts may lack sufficient expertise or information to contribute meaningfully to the process.[14]

There are six steps associated with using the Delphi technique for HR demand forecasting.

### 1. Define and Refine the Issue or Question

During this stage, a project coordinator is assigned, and he or she works with the HR staff to determine the specific personnel category or activity that will be the focus of the Delphi technique. It is essential that the group targeted for HR forecasting be well defined so that relevant, focused, and detailed feedback based on a minimum of assumptions (redundant assumptions are associated with loss of the experts' time) can be derived.

### 2. Identify the Experts, Terms, and Time Horizon

The project coordinator, normally in conjunction with the HR staff, identifies and selects a team of individuals who are deemed to be experts with respect to the specific personnel grouping that requires a forecast. Next, given that in many cases the group of experts will include individuals who are not members of the organization, it is important for both parties to reach agreement on the terms and conditions for participation in the forecasting process, as well as setting the context and explicitly defining the nature of the work. For example, the team of experts must be absolutely clear as to which jobs constitute "production workers" if those experts are being asked to derive a demand forecast for this category. Similarly, the exact time horizon(s) must be specified for the personnel category being analyzed.

### 3. Orient the Experts

In addition to identifying the relevant time horizon(s) and clarifying which personnel groups are of interest, the orientation process for experts includes an overview of the demand forecasting decision process (which is very similar to the structural framework in which you are now engaged!). The experts are told either that there will be a predetermined number of questionnaire iterations or that the sequence will continue until a majority opinion exists among the experts.

### 4. Issue the First-Round Questionnaire

The project coordinator sends each expert the questionnaire by courier, fax, mail, or e-mail and includes a time frame for completing and returning it. Typically, this first questionnaire focuses on defining both the explicit assumptions made by each of the experts and the background rationale supporting his or her own particular demand estimate.

### 5. Issue the First-Round Questionnaire Summary and the Second Round of Questionnaires

Following the completion of the first questionnaire, the project coordinator sends the second and subsequent rounds of questionnaires to the experts with a written summary of the findings from the previous round. The aim of the subsequent questionnaires is to focus the experts' initial assumptions and estimates by providing summarized feedback from all members of the group. Points of commonality and conflict are identified in the summary, as is the need to clarify specific assumptions identified by the responses to the previous round.

### 6. Continue Issuing Questionnaires

The project coordinator continues to issue questionnaires until either all the predetermined questionnaire stages have been completed and summarized or the group reaches a clear majority decision. In either case, the majority or nth-round summary summarizes the experts' future demand estimate for the HR category under analysis.

## Nominal Group Technique

**nominal group technique (NGT)**

long-run forecasting technique utilizing expert assessments

Although the **nominal group technique (NGT)** is also a long-run, qualitative demand forecasting method, it differs from the Delphi technique in several important respects. First, unlike in the Delphi technique, the group does, in fact, meet face to face and interact, but only after individual written, preparatory work has been done and all the demand estimates (idea generation) have been publicly tabled, or written on a flip chart, without discussion.[15] Second, each demand estimate is considered to be the property of the entire group and to be impersonal in nature, which minimizes the potential for dominance, personal attacks, and defensive behaviour in support of estimates presented in the group forum.[16] Finally, the expert forecast is determined by a secret vote of all group members on their choice of the tabled demand forecasts. The estimate receiving the highest ranking or rating during the voting process is deemed to be the group's forecast.[17] See HR Planning Today 7.2 for more information on the NGT.

## Assessing the Utility of the Nominal Group Technique

Studies have shown that nominal group technique (NGT) is especially effective for brainstorming sessions to ensure all participants have an equal voice in the sessions, and when a problem or issue stems from several widely diverse causes. Furthermore, studies have shown that NGT provides highly reliable and valid qualitative data that is ranked by importance and is superior to that derived from focus group sessions. Nominal group sessions investigating teaching performance competencies on 13 dimensions (technical knowledge, planning and organizing, managing interaction, commitment to teaching objectives, proactive orientation, student development orientation, class presentation ability, impact on the class, adaptability and flexibility, personal motivation, listening skills, oral communication skills, and presentation skills) were dramatically superior to information obtained from focus groups. The study predicted that nominal group technique will replace focus groups as the qualitative research method of choice and will reduce the need for the administration of surveys.

Sources: Adapted from B. Andersen and T. Fagerhaug, "The Nominal Group Technique," *Quality Progress*, Vol. 22, No. 2 (February 2000), 144–145; and B. Langford et al., "Nominal Grouping Sessions vs. Focus Groups," *Qualitative Market Research*, Vol. 5, No. 1 (2002), 58–70.

There are seven steps associated with implementing the NGT.

### 1. Define and Refine the Issue or Question and the Relevant Time Horizon

This step is similar to the first step of the Delphi technique. The HR forecasting staff or coordinator is responsible for identifying the specific personnel category or activity that will be the focus for the NGT. The more refined the problem definition, the more likely it is that relevant, focused, detailed feedback will be derived with a minimum of redundant assumptions. Second, it is essential that the time horizon(s) of interest for the demand estimate be clearly specified. Overall, the issue is often phrased as a question: "What will ABC Corporation's demand for production workers be in the year 2008 (or in five years from the present)? Please provide your demand estimate and the explicit assumptions and rationale supporting your forecast."

### 2. Select the Experts

In the second step, the coordinator or HR forecasting staff selects the individuals who have expert knowledge of the specific personnel group being analyzed. Experts are then contacted to confirm their participation in the process and to schedule the time for the face-to-face meeting.

### 3. Issue the HR Demand Statement to the Experts

Next, the coordinator sends each of the experts a concise statement of the HR demand he or she is being asked to address. As stated in the first step, the issue is normally framed as a question that the experts are being asked to answer, and an accompanying sheet of terms, definitions, and assumptions may accompany the question or issue statement.

### 4. Apply Expert Knowledge, State Assumptions, and Prepare an Estimate

Having received the issue or question posed by the coordinator on behalf of the organization, each expert now considers his or her specific knowledge of the particular personnel group that is the subject of the demand estimate. In particular, experts will undoubtedly have personal insights or insider information not available to other members of the group and should explicitly state the various assumptions that arise from this information, as well as their numerical estimate of demand. In this way, once the nominal group meets face to face, the supporting rationale for what may be widely divergent demand estimates quickly becomes apparent to the group as a whole.

### 5. Meet Face to Face

Having prepared their individual assumptions and a numerical estimate of demand, the experts then meet face to face. The first item of business will be a brief presentation of each expert's demand estimate with the associated supporting assumptions. Individual interaction and discussion are strictly forbidden so as not to stifle creativity. The coordinator will arrange for individual introductions and ice-breakers to facilitate group interaction only after all estimates have been tabled either prior to or at the beginning of the meeting. He or she will also specify the process for the nominal group's subsequent actions.

### 6. Discuss the Demand Estimates and Assumptions

After each expert has presented his or her demand estimate, the process shifts to detailed analyses and group discussion of the estimates and their assumptions. To minimize individual defensiveness and personal ownership of estimates, group members are asked to focus on ascertaining supportive information for estimate assumptions and to avoid attacks on the soundness of any specific estimate. The question, answer, and discussion session continues until all pertinent information affecting the HR demand estimates has been presented to the satisfaction of the experts in attendance, or at least to the point where all positions and assumptions are clear to group members.

### 7. Vote Secretly to Determine the Expert Demand Assessment

A secret vote is taken, and the estimate drawing the highest ranking or number of votes from the experts is selected to be the group's HR demand estimate solution to the question posed in the first step.

## HR Budgets: Staffing Table

**HR budgets** are quantitative, operational, or short-run, demand estimates that contain the number and types of personnel (i.e., personnel classes, such as bank clerks, loans officers, and branch managers) required by the organization as a whole and for each subunit, division, or department (see Table 7.1).[18]

**HR budgets**

quantitative, operational, or short-run demand estimates that contain the number and types of personnel (i.e., personnel classes, such as bank clerks, loans officers, and branch managers) required by the organization as a whole and for each subunit, division, or department

## TABLE 7.1

### Staffing Table and HR Budget

**Ennotville Eateries**

| STAFF DEMAND REQUIREMENTS | SALES ($ MILLIONS) | | | |
|---|---|---|---|---|
| Administrative Positions | $1–10 | >$10–25 | >$25–50 | >$50–75 |
| President | 1 | 1 | 1 | 1 |
| Vice-presidents | 1 | 1 | 2 | 3 |
| Marketing managers | 1 | 1 | 2 | 2 |
| Sales staff | 4 | 7 | 10 | 18 |
| HR staff | 2 | 4 | 5 | 7 |
| Treasurer | 1 | 1 | 1 | 2 |
| Financial staff | 3 | 5 | 7 | 9 |
| Clerical and general staff | 5 | 8 | 12 | 14 |
| **Production Positions** | | | | |
| Executive chef | 1 | 1 | 1 | 1 |
| Chef | 2 | 4 | 5 | 6 |
| Cook | 8 | 15 | 25 | 35 |
| Haggis helper | 10 | 20 | 30 | 40 |
| Saucier | 1 | 3 | 5 | 6 |

These HR budgets are prepared by the HR staff in conjunction with line managers and take into consideration information from historical company staffing trends, competitor staffing practices, industry and professional associations, and Statistics Canada.

 **RPC** 7.3

The HR budget process produces a **staffing table**, which contains information related to a specific set of operational assumptions or levels of activity (e.g., maintain the current organization structure, increase the sales level by 5% over last year's level). The staffing table presents the total HR demand requirement, as well as the number of personnel required, by level (e.g., vice-presidents) and function (e.g., marketing personnel).

**staffing table**

total HR demand requirement for operational or short-run time periods

In this way, HR planners can determine short-run future demand requirements for subunits and the organization as a whole. This enables budgeting processes to incorporate changes in compensation costs linked to the level of future personnel demand.

## Envelope/Scenario Forecasting

Previously, we noted that an HR budget is focused on deriving short-run operational HR demand and a staffing table for each organizational department, as well as for the entire organization, assuming a specific future outcome (e.g., a constant level of sales). This constitutes a prediction or single

**envelope/scenario forecasts**

projections, or multiple-predictor estimates, of future demand for personnel based on a variety of differing assumptions about how future organizational events will unfold

estimate of future HR demand. If, however, we wish to conduct much more comprehensive future planning of operational and short-run HR demand, we should instigate **envelope/scenario forecasting**. Simply put, envelope/scenario forecasts are projections, or multiple-predictor estimates, of future demand for personnel based on a variety of differing assumptions about how future organizational events will unfold.[19]

Scenario forecasting is based on the premise that since we have no certain knowledge of the future course of events, we would be well served by developing several plausible sets of outcomes. Based on certain assumptions, experts search for causality by linking cause-and-effect events together. Scenarios are developed by having brainstorming sessions with line managers and HR managers, who formulate the group's combined expert view of the workforce five years or more in the future, and then work back in time to identify key change points. The group members then try to make sense of the various future states by further developing and discussing the linkages and courses of action that will lead from the present to the proposed future scenarios.[20] Figure 7.1 illustrates envelope/scenario forecasting.

This flexible demand forecasting process is much more useful for incorporating the effects of uncertainty and change into our strategic HR planning process than is consideration of the single assumption of an HR budget. Each of the scenarios or predicted future states contains its own set of assumptions, resulting in an entirely different estimate presented in *a single staffing table for each specific course of action*. In this way, an organization's HR staff are able to develop, with the associated staffing tables, future scenarios that are optimistic (e.g., sales levels will increase by 10% to 15%), realistic or most

## Figure 7.1

### Envelope/Scenario Forecasting

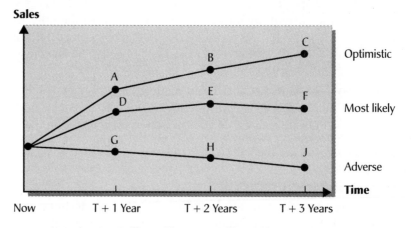

Note that A = Staffing table A; B = Staffing table B, etc.

likely (e.g., sales levels will increase by 5% to 10%), or pessimistic (e.g., sales levels will remain constant or increase by less than 5%). Furthermore, as we consider the optimistic, realistic or most likely, and pessimistic scenarios extended into the future, the impact of the time horizon (e.g., year 1, year 2, year 3, year 4, and year 5) forms the shape of a letter envelope. The optimistic and pessimistic scenarios, and their associated staffing tables, constitute the four corners of the envelope from the initial time period to the final time period being forecasted. Other scenarios are plotted as midpoints on the envelope. By means of this comprehensive, explicit set of staffing tables, which reflect a wide variety of future organizational circumstances, the scenario/envelope technique allows us to have ready access to flexible, preplanned demand estimates when circumstances rapidly change.

HR Planning Today 7.3 provides information on e-recruiting and how it can be used to help meet HR demand.

HR Planning Notebook 7.2 provides information on Saskatchewan's HR planning process.

## HR Planning Today 7.3

### Meeting HR Demand Requirements through E-Recruiting

Utilizing information systems technology to meet HR demand requirements is not only cost and time efficient compared to placing ads in journals or hiring recruiting firms, but also allows applicants to submit résumés from the comfort of their own homes. Organizations such as Hewlett-Packard, Dell Computer, and Cisco Systems conduct e-recruiting by placing job postings online (company or third-party Internet career websites), and use tracking systems that sort résumés and candidates by conducting content-based analyses of the applicants' résumés. However, e-recruiting should not be regarded as a stand-alone tool; it should be incorporated into an integrated HR system that also uses behavioural and skills assessments, job analysis, performance management, and training tools to enhance individual and team productivity and satisfaction. These integrated systems increase the demand for effective decision-making and communication skills, and highlight the fact that fast and efficient data collection is insufficient without fast and efficient decisions resulting from the process.

With online recruiting sites often being the first point of contact between the potential applicant and the organ-ization, it is critical that the technological processes associated with e-recruiting do not frustrate and deter applicants, especially the "best and brightest" who are well versed in leading-edge technology. Cumbersome application forms with poor instructions, accompanied by lengthy and marginally relevant online test and assessment instruments, can discourage applicants, as can the fact that having completed the online process, many people do not even receive a thank-you message acknowledging the receipt of their application. This can leave applicants feeling that the company is cold, impersonal, untrustworthy, and perhaps even manipulative in its relations with employees, perceptions that can prove extremely detrimental to any firm.

Sources: Adapted from E. Goodridge, "Online Recruiters Feel the Pinch," *InformationWeek*, No. 837 (May 14, 2001), 83–84; B. Cullen, "E-Recruiting Is Driving HR Systems Integration," *Strategic Finance*, Vol. 83, No. 1 (July 2001), 22–26; and I. Kotlyar and L. Karakowsky, "If Recruitment Means Building Trust, Where Does Technology Fit In?" *Canadian HR Reporter* (October 7, 2002), 21.

### The Province of Saskatchewan's HR Planning Process

 The Saskatchewan Government has a comprehensive, well-thought-through process of determining its demand for human resources. Listed on their website are the government's HR planning guidelines and a checklist that details the process for ensuring business planning priorities are intimately linked to the HR planning process. The checklist lists five main stages:

1. Link human resources planning to strategic and operational business goals
2. Workforce analysis and internal and external environmental scans
3. "Gap analysis" of issues arising from steps one and two
4. Priority setting and HR work plans (including HR demand and supply); and
5. Measure, monitor, and report on progress

This process not only helps ensure that HR plans are aligned to business goals, but also explicitly incorporates priority setting and flexibility for change into the HR demand and supply plans that result from the forecasting process.

Source: Adapted from the Government of Saskatchewan Human Resources Planning Checklist, August 17, 2004. Retrieved April 17, 2006, from www.gov.sk.ca/psc/hrmanagement/hrplanning/default.htm.

## Regression Analysis

**regression analysis**

presupposes that a linear relationship exists between one or more independent (causal) variables, which are predicted to affect the dependent (target) variable—in our instance, future HR demand for personnel (i.e., the number of personnel)

The final demand forecasting technique to be discussed in this chapter is **regression analysis**.[21] Regression analysis is a very effective quantitative forecasting technique for short-, medium- and long-range time horizons and can be easily updated and changed.[22] This section presupposes that readers possess a basic knowledge of statistical techniques as instruction in statistics is not the focus of this book. The section will enable HR practitioners to understand the essence of what regression can do for them[23] but will not explain the mathematical derivation of the regression equation from first principles. Readers who would like more information about such statistical methods should refer to any one of a number of high-quality statistical textbooks. Regression is such a powerful technique for forecasting demand, however, that we will present a brief and simple explanation of the underlying rationale and basic principles behind its use in HR planning.

Simply put, regression analysis presupposes that a *linear relationship* exists between one or more *independent (causal) variables*, which are predicted to affect the *dependent (target) variable*—in our instance, future HR demand for personnel (i.e., the number of personnel required). Based on logic similar to that used in trend analysis, regression projects into the future based on the past historical relationship between the independent and dependent variables. *Linearity* refers to the observed relationship between the independent and dependent variables. For example, if a per-unit increase or decrease in the level of sales and the market rate of interest result in a concurrent associated change in HR demand (the dependent variable), then the assumption of linearity might be met and regression analysis could be used for our demand forecasting. If, however, the relationship between the independent and dependent variables was random or nonlinear (e.g. curvilinear "U-shaped" relationships, which exist between individual performance and turnover, or stress and motivation), the use of normal regression procedures would not be valid, and/or specialized regression adjustment would have to be used. If there are several causal or independent variables, such as the market interest rate (i.e., the cost of capital), the unemployment rate, the organization's sales level, and so on, then the analysis is referred to as a *multivariate regression analysis*. Because of the complexity of the calculations, such multiple regressions are inevitably carried out by statistical software programs such as SPSS (Statistical Program for the Social Sciences) or the SAS Programming Language. For our purposes, we will present an example of what is referred to as *simple regression*: a prediction model based on the impact on HR demand (the dependent variable) of a single causal independent variable.

## Simple Regression Prediction Model

The simple regression prediction model is as follows:

$$Y = A + BX$$

Y = the *dependent variable* (HR demand/number of personnel required)

A = constant (intercept)

B = the slope of the linear relationship between X and Y

X = the *independent/causal variable* (e.g., level of sales, production output)

Where

$$B = \frac{\sum XY - N(\bar{X})(\bar{Y})}{\sum(X^2) - N(\bar{X})^2}$$

$$A = -Y - B\bar{X}$$

In other words, the predicted value for HR demand (Y) will be a function of a constant starting point (A) (i.e., the value of Y when X = 0) plus the interaction between the value of the causal/independent variable (X) multiplied by a slope factor (B). Let's turn to a specific example to make sense of it all!

## Regression Exercise

As HR planning manager for Keele Kontainers Ltd., a dynamic, fast-growing company located in Wawanesa, Manitoba, you have an important task to fulfill. To continue the company's history of successful growth, you need to forecast the number of marketing personnel required for $8 million and $10 million of sales activity. You have the following historical information available to guide your regression analysis and HR demand forecast:

| X<br>Sales Level<br>($ Millions) | Y<br>Number of<br>Marketing Personnel |
|---|---|
| 2.0 | 20 |
| 3.5 | 32 |
| 4.5 | 42 |
| 6.0 | 55 |
| 7.0 | 66 |

Note that the above information represents five sets of observations for both the independent (X) and dependent (Y) variables: set 1 (2.0; 20), set 2 (3.5; 32), set 3 (4.5; 42), and so on. Record that N = *the number of sets of observations,* in this instance, five.

There are five steps to conducting the regression analysis:

1. *Calculate XY, $X^2$, average $X(\bar{X})$, and average $Y(\bar{Y})$:* We can do this by extending the two columns shown above to a four-column set. XY is simply the result of multiplying each observation set's X level by the associated Y level, and $X^2$ is determined by multiplying the X value by itself:

| X<br>Sales Level<br>($ Millions) | Y<br>Number of<br>Marketing Personnel | XY | $X^2$ |
|---|---|---|---|
| 2.0 | 20 | 40 | 4.00 |
| 3.5 | 32 | 112 | 12.25 |
| 4.5 | 42 | 189 | 20.25 |
| 6.0 | 55 | 330 | 36.00 |
| 7.0 | 66 | 462 | 49.00 |
| 23.0 | 215 | 1133 | 121.50 |

Average X or $\bar{X}$ = 23/5 = 4.6
Average Y or $\bar{Y}$ = 215/5 = 43.0
Recall N = 5, and Y = A + BX

2. *Calculate the value of B (slope of the linear relationship between X and Y):*

$$B = \frac{\Sigma XY - N(\bar{X})(\bar{Y})}{\Sigma(X^2) - N(\bar{X})^2}$$

Plug in the values calculated in step 1; therefore

$$B = \frac{1133 - (5)(4.6)(43)}{121.5 - (5)(4.6)^2}$$

$$B = \frac{1133 - 989}{121.5 - 105.8} = 9.17$$

3. *Calculate A (constant or intercept):* Recall that

$$Y = A + BX$$

Then

$$A = \bar{Y} - B\bar{X}$$

Plug in the values calculated in step 1; therefore

$$A = 43 - (9.17)(4.6) = 0.82$$

4. *Determine the regression prediction equation:* We know that the general prediction model for regression is

$$Y = A + BX$$

For our specific problem, we have calculated A and B, so we insert these values into the equation, which will be used to calculate our HR demand (Y) as follows:

$$Y = 0.82 + (9.17)(X)$$

What does this mean? For our comparison between the level of sales (the independent/causal variable represented by X) and the predicted HR demand for marketing personnel (the dependent variable represented by Y), even when level of sales is at a zero level (i.e., less than $1 million of sales), the A value (the constant/intercept) shows that we have one marketing person (0.82 of a person rounds to 1.0). Furthermore, the prediction model shows that for every one unit ($1 million) increase in the level of sales (the independent variable X), there is a predicted increase of 9.17 marketing staff (Y) associated with that change.

5. *Calculate predicted HR demand (Y) by inserting values for X:* To predict our HR demand for marketing personnel at $8 million and $10 million of sales, as has been asked of us, we simply plug these levels into the values of X as follows:

For $8 million of sales (X = 8)

$$Y = A + BX = 0.82 + (9.17)(8) = 74.18$$

or 74 marketing staff are required.

For $10 million of sales (X = 10)

$$Y = A + BX = 0.82 + (9.17)(10) = 92.52$$

or 93 marketing staff are required.

As we can see, regression models can be extremely valuable tools for the HR planner. In our calculation of the simple regression problem above, we used five years or sets of observed historical data for our organization with respect to matching levels of sales and their relationship to levels of marketing personnel (HR demand). Most recent sales levels of $7 million of sales were associated with a marketing staff size of 66 personnel. We wish to predict into the future what our personnel requirements for $8 million and $10 million of sales will be. Our calculations of the regression equation noted that for every $1-million increase in sales, our marketing staff increased by approximately 9 (9.17) personnel, indicating the linear relationship between the two variables. Furthermore, we now know that for $8 million and $10 million of sales, we require 74 and 93 marketing staff respectively. This valuable forecasting technique enables us to plan and execute recruitment, selection, training, and development programs in a planned, proactive fashion to ensure the trained marketing staff are on hand exactly when required by the organization.

## Summary

In this chapter we examined various techniques organizations use to forecast future requirements for HR demand. We noted that index/trend analysis examines the historical relationship between workforce size and a measure of operational efficiency, such as sales, to determine the ratio between the two measures for forecasting purposes. Expert forecasts revealed that there are a number of individuals, not necessarily just those who are HR staff, who have valid information on organizational policies, procedures, and planned future changes. This information can have a dramatic impact on deriving accurate forecasts of numbers and types of employees required for the organization's workforce of the future.

With respect to experts, we saw that the Delphi technique and the nominal group technique can be used effectively to obtain demand estimates from individuals while minimizing the time wastage and interpersonal dominance that often occurs in group settings. The HR budget process produces staffing tables that are concerned with short-run operational time horizons in planning HR demand. Specifically, the staffing table presents a prediction of the number of personnel required by authority or functional level, given a specific set of assumptions regarding the future organizational activity. Plotting a wide variety of possible future scenarios produces what is referred to as envelope forecasting of HR demand, in which each corner of the envelope has its own specific staffing table.

Finally, we demonstrated the tremendous usefulness of the regression analysis technique in determining future workforce requirements. Our example of simple regression revealed how this statistical technique can enable us to be proactive with respect to determining future HR requirements and planning and programming to fulfill those requirements.

We have examined specific techniques associated with the first element of HR forecasting—that is, the calculation of demand or requirement for personnel. In Chapter 8, we look at specific methods used to ascertain personnel supply. The sources of labour supply derive from either the current organization (internal workforce) or from the external environment.

# Key Terms

Delphi technique, 172
employee requirement ratio, 170
envelope/scenario forecasts, 178
HR budgets, 176

nominal group technique, 174
regression analysis, 180
staffing table, 177

# Web Links

Information on the Canadian Government's demand for health personnel and resources can be found at:

**www.hc-sc.gc.ca/sr-sr/alt_formats/iacb-dgiac/pdf/pubs/hpr-rps/bull/
2004-8-hhr-rhs/2004-8-hhr-rhs_e.pdf** (p. 168)

The Government of Prince Edward Island's document on meeting HR demand in health can be found at:

**www.gov.pe.ca/photos/original/hss_humres.pdf** (p. 168)

Information on Canadian HR demand, work, and labour trends can be found at:

**www.jobsetc.ca/jobs** (p. 170)

Statistics on trends in HR demand in the United Kingdom for various skills including human resources, can be found at:

**www.jobstats.co.uk/jobstats.d/Details.d/Trends.d/SKILL/HUMAN-RESOURCES.d/** (p. 170)

U.S. government standardized industrial classification job codes are found at:

**www.osha.gov** (p. 171)

HRM Guide to Labour Participation and Demand (for the United Kingdom) can be found at:

**www.hrmguide.co.uk/hrm/chap3/ch3-links4.htm** (p. 171)

The Government of Canada's HR resources for business are listed at:

**www.hrmanagement.gc.ca** (p. 177)

Information on the Government of Saskatchewan's human resource planning is at:

**www.gov.sk.ca/psc/hrmanagement/hrplanning/default.htm** (p. 177)

The Government of Manitoba's Advanced Education and Training agency publishes a document on "High Demand Occupations in Manitoba," which is located at:

**www.edu.gov.mb.ca/aet/lmi/hdo/hdo.htm** (p. 186)


# RPC Icons

**RPC 7.1 Identifies the organization's HR needs**

**RPC 7.2 Forecasts HR supply and demand conditions**

**RPC 7.3 Develops and administers a departmental or project budget**


# Discussion Questions

1. The Delphi technique and the nominal group technique are often used to facilitate creative and innovative solutions to HR demand issues. List the conditions associated with successful employment of each of these two demand forecasting techniques.
2. Index or trend analysis can be a very effective method for determining HR demand. Identify a wide variety of relevant indices that can be used for this demand forecasting technique in different organizational contexts, including public nonprofit organizations, as well as in diverse industrial settings in the private sector.

# Using the Internet

1. Manitoba is renowned for many things, including its beautiful summer weather, abundance of lakes, relatively low cost of living, very friendly population, and the birthplace of both authors. You are thinking of relocating to friendly Manitoba, but wish to consider whether or not there is a demand for someone in your occupational field. Go to **www.edu.gov.mb.ca/aet/lmi/hdo/hdo.htm**, which is the Government of Manitoba's listing of occupations that are in high demand throughout the province. Search to determine the demand for your occupation (listed and sorted by National Occupational Classification [NOC] category), as well as for information on starting and average salaries, sectors for which occupational demand is most pronounced, and the regions of Manitoba where the demand is most highly concentrated.

# Exercise

1. As HR forecasting manager for the Downsview University Dating Service, you have been faced with a tremendous increase in customer demand over the company's five years of operations. As a result, you are using regression analysis to ascertain future requirements for staff to handle customer inquiries. In particular, you need to forecast the number of customer service representatives required for 5000 and for 7000 dating contracts. The following information will help guide your regression analysis:

| X<br>DATING CONTRACTS<br>(THOUSANDS) | Y<br>CUSTOMER SERVICE<br>REPRESENTATIVES | XY | X² |
|---|---|---|---|
| 1.5 | 9 | | |
| 2.0 | 14 | | |
| 3.0 | 21 | | |
| 3.8 | 25 | | |
| 4.2 | 27 | | |

# Case: Recruiting with Bells and Whistles

Alcatel, a telecommunications corporation, launched The Talent Network, which utilized its 3000 employees as recruiters by offering cash rewards as high as $8000 for individual employees who delivered top-notch new recruits. Over the first six months the program netted 160 employee referrals, accounting for approximately 35% to 40% of the personnel hired during that time, and the percentage of employee referrals continued to rise steadily. The company also tracks and contacts its "alumni"—former employees who have left for positions in other companies—in an attempt to let them know about the positive events and opportunities that exist in Alcatel. They don't hide their attempts to lure their ex-employees back to the company. Alcatel employs a "holistic" approach to recruiting, using all available tools including newspaper ads, on-site career fairs, and Web-based career sites, in an attempt to attract scarce skilled labour.

High-tech firms such as Nortel and Lumenon use stock options, signing bonuses, profit sharing, free trips, and finder's fees, among a wide variety of other incentives, and such media as mobile billboards, club advertising, and recruiting booths at conferences and rock concerts, to attract new recruits. Retention is encouraged by rewarding staff with barbecues, "time-outs" at the go-cart track, cruises, white-water rafting adventures, golf outings, beer festivals, and treats ranging from jackets and T-shirts to hockey tickets and $10,000 cash incentives.

"Quite frankly, I couldn't care less if they come in wearing their pyjamas," said an organizational recruiter. "Those days are gone forever where people coming in had to wear a navy blue suit, white shirt, and red striped tie. They can come in with a paper bag over their heads and the eyeholes cut out. If they have the skills we're looking for, that's what we're interested in."

Source: Adapted from *The Ottawa Citizen Online*. 2000. High Tech Supplement: "The HR Crisis," October 17. Reprinted with permission.

---

## Question

Prepare a report discussing the benefits and limitations of using the techniques described to meet organization demand for labour. Consider the impact of environmental factors such as competitor response to such actions.

# Endnotes

1. Loo, R., and K. Thorpe. 2004. "Making Female First-Line Nurse Managers More Effective: A Delphi Study of Occupational Stress, *Women in Management Review*, Bradford, 19/1–2; and Chan, C., and K. M^cBey, et al. 2004. "Nursing Crisis: Retention Strategies for Hospital Administrators," *Research and Practice in Human Resource Management*, 12/2, 31–56.

2. Schuler, R.S., and J.W. Walker. 1990. "Human Resources Strategy: Focusing on Issues and Actions," *Organizational Dynamics* (Summer): 5–19.

3. Elbo, R. November 15, 2000. "In the Workplace: Competing with Poaching Employers," *BusinessWorld*: 1–3; Cascio, W.F. 1991. *Applied Psychology in Personnel Management*, 4th ed. Englewood Cliffs, NJ: Prentice Hall; Ward, D. 1996. "Workforce Demand Forecasting Techniques," *Human Resource Planning* Vol. 19, No. 1: 54–55.

4. Al-Harbi, K. 2000. "Optimization of Staff Numbers in the Process Industries: An Application of DEA," *International Journal of Manpower*, 21/1; McLaughlin, G. 1975. "A Professional Supply and Demand Analysism" *Educational Record* Vol. 56, No. 3 (Summer): 196–200. Example adapted from Hughes, C. 1995. "Four Steps for Accurate Call-Center Staffing," *HR Magazine* (April): 87–89 and Cascio, W.F. 1991. *Applied Psychology in Personnel Management*, 4th ed. Englewood Cliffs, NJ: Prentice Hall.

5. Al-Harbi, K. 2000. "Optimization of Staff Numbers in the Process Industries: An Application of DEA," *International Journal of Manpower*, 21/1; Meehan, R., and B.S. Ahmed. 1990. "Forecasting Human Resources Requirements: A Demand Model," *Human Resource Planning*, Vol. 13, No. 4: 297–307.

6. Ward, D. 1996. "Workforce Demand Forecasting Techniques," *Human Resource Planning*, Vol. 19, No. 1: 54–55.

7. Anonymous. 2005. "Tool Forecasts Labour Needs," *On-Site*, 49/6, 10–11; Gatewood, R.D., and E.J. Gatewood. 1983. "The Use of Expert Data in Human Resource Planning: Guidelines from Strategic Forecasting," *Human Resource Planning*, Vol. 6, No. 2 (June): 83–94.

8. Passmore, D., E. Cebeci, and R. Baker. 2005. "Market-based Information for Decision Support in Human Resource Development," *Human Resource Development Review*, 4/1, 33–49; Luthans, F. 1992. *Organizational Behavior*, 6th ed. New York: McGraw-Hill.

9. Helmer cited in Bramwell, L., and E. Hykawy. 1999. "The Delphi Technique: A Possible Tool for Predicting Future Events in Nursing Education," *Canadian Journal of Nursing Research*, Vol. 30, No. 4: 47–58.

10. Passmore, D., E. Cebeci, and R. Baker. 2005. "Market-based Information for Decision Support in Human Resource Development," *Human Resource Development Review*, 4/1, 33–49; Fusgeld, A.R., and R.N. Foster. June 1971. "The Delphi Technique: Survey and Comment," *Business Horizons*.

11. Loo, R., and K. Thorpe. 2003. "A Delphi Study Forecasting Management Training and Development for First-Line Nurse Managers," *The Journal of Management Development*, 22/9–10, 824–825; Hampton, D.R., C.E. Summer, and R.A. Webber. 1987. *Organizational Behavior and the Practice of Management*, 5th ed. Glenview, IL: Scott Foresman. Milkovich, G., A. Annoni, and T. Mahoney. 1972. "The Use of Delphi Procedures in Manpower Forecasting," *Management Science*, Vol. 19, No. 4 (December): 381–388; Milkovich, G.T., and T.A. Mahoney. 1978. "Human Resource Planning Models: A Perspective," *Human Resource Planning*, Vol. 1, No. 1.

12. Bramwell, L., and E. Hykawy. 1999. "The Delphi Technique: A Possible Tool for Predicting Future Events in Nursing Education," *Canadian Journal of Nursing Research*, Vol. 30, No. 4: 47–58.

13. Loo, R., and K. Thorpe. 2004. "Making Female First-Line Nurse Managers More Effective: A Delphi Study of Occupational Stress, *Women in Management Review*, 19/1–2; Meehan, R., and B.S. Ahmed. 1990. "Forecasting Human Resources Requirements: A Demand Model," *Human Resource Planning*, Vol. 13, No. 4: 297–307.

14. Bramwell, L., and E. Hykawy. 1999. "The Delphi Technique: A Possible Tool for Predicting Future Events in Nursing Education," *Canadian Journal of Nursing Research*, Vol. 30, No. 4: 47–58.

15. Fraser, C., and A. Fraser. 2000. "Measuring the Performance of Retail Managers in Australia and Singapore," *International Journal of Retail & Distribution Management*, 28/6; Van de Ven, A.H. 1974. *Group Decision-Making Effectiveness*. Kent, OH: Kent State University Center for Business and Economic Research Press.

16. Rohrbaugh, J. 1981. "Improving the Quality of Group Judgement: Social Judgement Analysis and the Nominal Group Technique," *Organizational Behavior and Human Performance* (October): 272–288.

17. Fraser, C. 2000. "The Influence of Personal Characteristics on Effectiveness of Construction Site Managers," *Construction Management & Economics*, 18/1, 29–36; Delbecq, A.L., A.H. Van de Ven, and D.H. Gustafson. 1975. *Group Techniques for Program Planning*. Glenview, IL: Scott Foresman; Green, T.B. 1975. "An Empirical Analysis of Nominal and Interacting Groups," *Academy of Management Journal* (March): 63–73.

18. McBeath, G. 1992. *The Handbook of Human Resource Planning: Practical Manpower Analysis Techniques for HR Professionals*. Oxford: Blackwell.

19. Van der Heijden, K. 2000. "Scenarios and Forecasting: Two Perspectives," *Technological Forecasting and Social Change*, Vol. 65: 31–36; Mason, D.H. 1994. "Scenario-Based Planning: Decision Model for the Learning Organization," *Planning Review*: 6–11. Bechet, T.P., and J.W. Walker. 1993. "Aligning Staffing with Business Strategy," *Human Resource Planning*, Vol. 16,

No. 2: 1–16. Burack, E.H., and N.J. Mathys. 1996. *Human Resource Planning: A Pragmatic Approach to Manpower Staffing and Development*, 3rd ed. Northbrook, IL: Brace Park.

20. Van der Heijden, K. 2000. "Scenarios and Forecasting: Two Perspectives," *Technological Forecasting and Social Change*, Vol. 65: 31–36. Ward, D. 1996. "Workforce Demand Forecasting Techniques," *Human Resource Planning* Vol. 19, No. 1: 54–55.

21. Drui, A.B. 1963. "The Use of Regression Equations to Predict Manpower Requirements," *Management Science* Vol. 9, No. 4 (July): 669–677.

22. McDermott, R. 2001. "Using Simple Multiple Regression to Establish Labour Rates," *Healthcare Financial Management*, 55/9, 50–57; Georgoff, D.M., and R.G. Murdick. 1986. "Manager's Guide to Forecasting," *Harvard Business Review*, Vol. 64, No. 1. Meehan, R., and B.S. Ahmed. 1990. "Forecasting Human Resources Requirements: A Demand Model," *Human Resource Planning*, Vol. 13, No. 4: 297–307.

23. McDermott, R. 2001. "Using Simple Multiple Regression to Establish Labour Rates," *Healthcare Financial Management*, 55/9, 50–57; Tullar, W. 1991. "Theory Development in Human Resource Management," *Human Resource Management Review*, Vol. 1, No. 4 (Winter): 317–323.

# Chapter 8

# Ascertaining HR Supply

## Chapter Learning Objectives

After reading this chapter, you should be able to

- Understand the relationship between demand and supply forecasting techniques in the HR planning process.
- Recognize the importance of the HRMS (human resources management system) in implementing effective supply forecasting procedures.
- Comprehend the critical relationship between supply forecasting and succession planning.
- Discuss and evaluate the advantages and disadvantages of the following specific methods of determining external and internal supply of an organization's personnel:
  a. Skills and management inventories
  b. Succession/replacement analysis
  c. Markov models
  d. Linear programming
  e. Movement analysis
  f. Vacancy/renewal models

Ensuring the continuation of an adequate supply of HR not only necessitates the implementation of effective HR planning, job analysis and selection processes, but also requires that attention be given to the retention of personnel already employed by the organization (i.e., HR internal supply).

Mandatory retirement has already been abolished in many countries and jurisdictions around the world (such as New Zealand, the United States, and most Canadian provinces), and the time is fast approaching when the once-common retirement age of 65 will be a thing of the past. Why has this occurred and what are the implications for HR planners?

Several important factors have led to the move toward abolishing a fixed age for retirement. From the *individual's perspective*, with higher levels of education, literacy, and improved health care, life expectancies for both men and women have increased, even though the average age for individual's choosing to retire from work has been decreasing steadily to its present level of 61 years of age (Canada). Although many individuals are retiring from full-time employment at an earlier age to pursue hobbies or other personal interests, at the same time there are many other Canadians who simply cannot afford to retire given their state of finances due to employment in low-wage jobs, exacerbated by decades of adversarial corporate cost-cutting initiatives with respect to employee wages, pensions, and health benefits. Furthermore, businesses have often failed to address quality of work–life issues, which would have made work more interesting and fulfilling for their employees, and the resultant outcome is that people are "voting with their feet." Senior long-service employees, who may otherwise have chosen to keep working full-time, are deciding instead to work only on a part-time basis, or to retire completely from paid employment.

*Organizationally*, the situation is quite complex. On the one hand, lack of attention to validated HR planning processes meant that many organizations dramatically downsized their supply of trained workers in order to achieve short-run cost savings, but at much greater long-run cost. Cynics have noted how few executive personnel were downsized in conjunction with workers drawn from the operational core. Now, just a few years later, organizational HR planning staffs are about to hit a "demographic wall," with the reality of decreased Canadian birth rates, the retirement of baby-boom personnel, and reduced labour-force participation. As a result, organizations are now scrambling to attract and retain workers who just a few years ago were incorrectly categorized as being "surplus to requirement" and then downsized with impunity. Fast-food restaurants, unable to attract sufficient labour in the 16–24 years of age segment are increasingly targeting homemakers and retired personnel to fill their labour supply shortages.

In Canadian universities, long-standing questionable HRP (human resource planning) practices resulted in retiring full-time faculty members who were not being replaced by new full-time hires, but with part-time instructors. Although these HRP decisions led to short-run cost savings, the implications are now costing universities dearly. Instead of having taken a long-run HR planning perspective to meet their supply requirements by replacing full-time retirements on an ongoing basis, augmented by expanding postgraduate program enrollments, the HRP decisions of Canadian universities have considerably worsened the already dire effects of governmental funding cuts, and the looming retirements of their baby-boom faculty. This has resulted in the present-day crisis-hiring situation to rectify a huge HR faculty supply deficit/shortage to enable continuation of their academic programs. Their now essential high-cost global hiring war, in competition with universities all over the world, is increasingly difficult as there is an insufficient supply of global faculty talent. After many years of having few if any prospects of being hired for a full-time appointment in academia, many bright and qualified graduates of Doctoral programs were forced to started their own businesses or seek employment in the private and public sectors.

Having taken actions that reduced external HR supply of appropriately qualified graduates, universities are increasingly being forced to solve their HR supply issues by lowering their hiring standards to consider Doctoral students early in their training, instead of hiring fully trained graduates of Doctoral programs. Even for these partially trained students, market demand is leading to ever-increasing starting salaries and much more costly hiring for the universities.

In 2005 the University of Toronto took the lead in abolishing mandatory retirement for its professors. University officials noted that not only is it increasingly difficult to find and attract new talented faculty, but also that positive steps had to be taken to retain the supply of proven, accomplished scholars in order to continue the delivery of high-quality academic programs.

*(Continued)*

Other universities are currently scrambling to revise their retirement policies, and to weigh the associated salary and benefits costs of having senior academics continue working past what was considered normal retirement age.

The end to mandatory retirement is being demanded not only by individuals who quite naturally wish the flexibility to determine when to cease employment, or by organizations seeking continuity of operations and retention of qualified proven workers, but also by governments.

Research by the Organisation for Economic Co-operation and Development (OECD) has advised the Canadian government that the abolition of mandatory retirement will be necessary to sustain continued economic growth and health of the Canadian economy (Berman). Furthermore, even with the end to mandatory retirement, the increased competition for high-quality labour supply (commonly referred to as the "war for talent") has led several HR experts to predict that retention programs/turnover reduction will very soon prove to be the top priority for HR practitioners.

With proper HR planning, and the necessary safeguards to ensure requisite job performance criteria and KSAs continue to be demonstrated by all workers irrespective of age, the abolition of mandatory retirement is a situation in which flexibility in being able to extend work beyond the age of 65 years will lead to benefits for individuals, organizations, and Canadian society as a whole.[1]

In the preceding chapter, we examined a variety of methods used to forecast HR demand. Many of these procedures (e.g., the Delphi technique, the nominal group technique, index/trend analysis) can also be used to determine personnel supply.

When considering the issue of supplying personnel to meet organizational demand, one aspect of the analysis is quite simple. Our personnel must be obtained from a source that is either *internal* (current employees) or *external* (individuals currently not employed by the organization) or, more commonly, some combination of these. Many organizations give preference to internal supply because selecting these individuals for training and development, and subsequent promotion, enables the organization to reinforce employee loyalty and performance. Other reasons for giving preferential consideration to your own workforce to fill job openings include the following: (1) your employees are already socialized to the norms, rules, and procedures of your organization, and (2) you possess detailed knowledge (as listed on their human resources management system skill inventories) of their performance and KSAs over time (e.g., work history and experience). We now turn our attention to this latter point concerning organizational databases on current workforce members—namely, skills and management inventories.

## Skills and Management Inventories

The first step in supply analysis is an examination of the number and capabilities of current employees. Individual records on the HRMS database are called inventories, of which there are two types, skills inventories and management inventories.[2] A **skills inventory** is an individualized personnel record held on each employee except those currently in management or professional positions. Typically, a skills inventory contains information for each individual on the following areas: (1) personal information (e.g., name, employee number, job classification and compensation band, emergency notification, and telephone number); (2) education, training, and skill competencies (e.g., certificates, licences, and diplomas or degrees completed, including the area of specialization, dates of attendance, and names of the institutions attended); (3) work history (e.g., date of hire, seniority, current job and supervisor, and previous jobs held in the organization and the dates associated with them); (4) performance appraisals (i.e., a numerical score of the employee's history of performance in jobs in the organization); (5) career information (e.g., future jobs desired by employee and those recommended by supervisors); and (6) hobbies and interests (including community and volunteer associations).[3] This skills inventory record is entered into the HRMS database and can be searched when looking for people with the skills and competencies required by a specific job. For this reason, skills inventories must be kept current, and employees should be given frequent opportunities to update or correct their personal entries; otherwise, an employee may not be considered for a job that he or she could fill successfully.

Management inventories can be considered to be enhanced skills inventories because they contain all the above information and the following: (1) a history of management or professional jobs held, (2) a record of management or professional training courses and their dates of completion, (3) key accountabilities for the current job (i.e., organizational resources, including the size of the budget controlled, the number of subordinates, important organizational outcomes for which the incumbent is primarily responsible), (4) assessment centre and appraisal data, and (5) professional and industry association memberships. Only when an organization has a properly functioning HRMS, complete with the skills and management inventories described above, is it really able to assess correctly the numbers and competency levels of its current workforce. In this way, HR planners can determine the organization's workforce strengths and weaknesses and plan training and development courses accordingly, while noting which job openings must be filled from external sources because current employees lack the skill competencies required.

**RPC 8.2**

**RPC 8.3**

**skills inventory**

an individualized personnel record held on each employee except those currently in management or professional positions

**management inventory**

an individualized personnel record for managerial, professional, or technical personnel that includes all elements in the skills inventory with the addition of information on specialized duties, responsibilities, and accountabilities

Chapter 8: Ascertaining HR Supply

## Succession/Replacement Analysis

*Succession planning* is critical to effective organizational functioning.[4] With demographic trends predicting even greater shortages in the market supply of skilled labour, organizational succession planning is now assuming much greater importance. It is absolutely essential that organizations create systems that meaningfully reward managers for developing and retaining their employees or it is very likely that these critical tasks will not be performed.[5] Furthermore, the highly dynamic and changing global business environment is forcing HR managers to expand their succession planning beyond the traditional identification of a shortlist of replacements for specific jobs. Increasingly, the focus is on identifying and developing the broad skills and behaviours (i.e., competencies) that will be required by the organization to accomplish its competitive strategy.[6]

There are two aspects to succession planning: (1) *long-term succession,* which is a process of training and work experience to enable individuals to assume higher-level job appointments in the future; and (2) *short-term emergency replacement* of individuals who have quit, been terminated because of performance problems, have died, and so on. Succession planning can help the organization be more effective in filling vacant positions.

There are several reasons succession planning is critical for effective HR planning:[7]

1. Succession planning enables an organization to respond appropriately and stay on track when inevitable and unpredictable changes occur. It provides for continuity and future direction even in the turmoil of change.
2. It helps develop people as they prepare for new experiences and jobs, and this development can also help improve their performance in current positions.
3. When succession planning takes into account employees' performance and promotes them for it, employees are positively motivated.
4. It supports new organizational structures and flexibility by explicitly providing backups to various positions, thereby reducing organizational dependency on any one employee.
5. It saves time and money by having plans already in place to enable smooth internal employee movement and continuity; therefore, external hiring is an exception to the process.

It should come as no great surprise that the skills and management inventories described in the previous section are extremely useful information for succession and replacement planning. Furthermore, they are important for matching an individual's qualifications to the requirements of a specific job in the organization (e.g., it is easy to derive shortlists of potential successors, such as employees with a degree in marketing, performance evaluations of "above average" or better over the past three years, and fluently bilingual in English and French) and for identifying possible successors for specific positions. The key requirement for succession and replacement planning to

FIGURE 8.1

## Succession/Replacement Chart

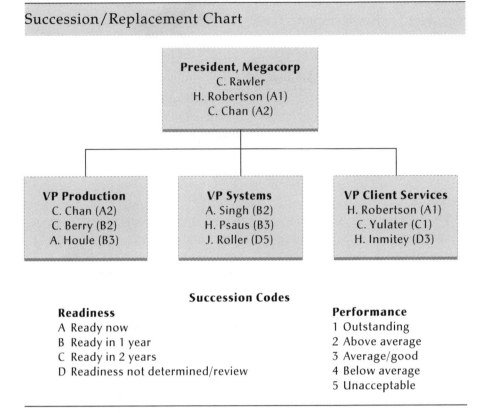

**President, Megacorp**
C. Rawler
H. Robertson (A1)
C. Chan (A2)

**VP Production**
C. Chan (A2)
C. Berry (B2)
A. Houle (B3)

**VP Systems**
A. Singh (B2)
H. Psaus (B3)
J. Roller (D5)

**VP Client Services**
H. Robertson (A1)
C. Yulater (C1)
H. Inmitey (D3)

### Succession Codes

| **Readiness** | **Performance** |
|---|---|
| A Ready now | 1 Outstanding |
| B Ready in 1 year | 2 Above average |
| C Ready in 2 years | 3 Average/good |
| D Readiness not determined/review | 4 Below average |
| | 5 Unacceptable |

function effectively is that supervisors, in conjunction with the HR staff, must develop *succession/replacement charts and tables* for key executive, managerial, and professional jobs in the organization (see Figure 8.1 and Table 8.1). The information that fuels this process is derived not only from current managerial assessments of subordinates, but also from information contained in the inventories concerning education, training, and skills, as well as historical records of each potential successor's performance appraisals. Obviously, given the large amount of personal information used and the sensitive nature of the information, succession planning documents are highly confidential. Access to the succession/replacement charts and tables, and to their supporting documentation, must be strictly controlled and limited on a "need-to-know" basis to such people as the CEO, vice-president of HR, HR planning staff, and divisional executives. Access by the latter should be restricted solely to their own area of responsibility.[8] Although a manager should naturally consider his or her current subordinates in the process of developing succession plans, the skills and management inventories are important to ensure that other employees who have been transferred, seconded to other divisions, or are working in areas different from those for which they received functional training will not be overlooked. In fact, such employees will be identified by the search capabilities of the HRMS.

## TABLE 8.1

### Succession/Replacement Table

KEITH KILTMAKERS
CHIEF EXECUTIVE OFFICER (POSITION A01)

| Incumbent | Employee Number | Current Appointment and Tenure[a] | Expected Date of Movement |
|---|---|---|---|
| Robert James | 060422 | CEO | 06 April 2010 |
| **Potential Successors** | **Succession** | **Codes** | |
| June Catharine | 070121 | VP Operations (A21)/61 | H, F |
| Roderick Alexander | 010753 | VP Legal (B24)/52 | S, D |
| Kenneth James | 010956 | VP HR (D19)/48 | B, F, D |
| Donald Martin | 290959 | VP Systems (C24)/16 | Y, D |

[a] The tenure of the current appointment is listed in number of months' duration.

HR supply and succession aren't important for just corporations. HR Planning Today 8.1 discusses the importance of planning for succession in family businesses.

The first type of document used in succession planning is referred to as a succession/replacement chart. As you will notice from Figure 8.1, it closely resembles a typical organizational chart in that it represents the organizational hierarchy and the key jobs with their inherent reporting relationships. However, on closer inspection, the succession/replacement chart provides more detailed information on each job, specifically, the name of the current job incumbent and a shortlist (determined by managers in conjunction with the

## HR Planning Today 8.1

### Take Steps to Keep Business All in the Family

A study by Deloitte & Touche states that the majority of Canada's family businesses are facing a leadership crisis due to a lack of succession planning. John Bowey, a Deloitte & Touche partner, says that family businesses in Canada account for 4.7 million full-time jobs, 1.3 million part-time jobs, and $1.3 trillion in annual sales. Furthermore, customers often prefer these businesses because of the personal contact and perceived high standards of credibility and quality. However, a full 75% of family business owners believe that the future success of their business depends wholly on them, reflecting a failure to develop future leaders and a neglect of the succession and replacement planning process. Almost half (44%) of these same business owners doubt their businesses will survive once they bow out of the operations. To cast a further dire light on the situation, 27% of the family business owners plan to retire within five years, a further 29% in six to ten years, and 22% in eleven to fifteen years.

Source: Adapted from Ian Harvey, "Be Careful to Keep Biz All in the Family," *Toronto Sun*, January, 19, 1999. Reprinted with permission.

HR staff) of the top internal candidates who might replace the incumbent if he or she left the job.

An important aspect of the succession/replacement chart is the **succession readiness code**, which is listed next to the names of all employees. This code contains two elements of information essential for succession planning: (1) the employee's level of performance in the current job (e.g., represented by a value on a five-point scale ranging from 1 to 5, where 1 = outstanding and 5 = unacceptable) and (2) the employee's readiness for movement or promotion (e.g., A = ready now, B = probably ready within one year, C = needs development [i.e., probably ready in two years], D = not suitable for this job). By including the two elements of the succession coding next to the name of each employee on the succession chart, we are able to get an accurate, although admittedly incomplete, picture of the state of succession readiness for each department and for the entire organization. Because no chart can capture all the information required for succession decisions, tables are used for supplementation.

Although we will have to refer back to specific inventories, performance appraisal records, and assessment centre reports (which summarize the potential of employees after they complete a series of tests) to get further information on potential successors, the key benefit of a succession/replacement chart is that it allows us to identify what are referred to as **ripple** or **chain effects**: one promotion in the organization can cause several movements in the organization as a series of subordinates are promoted to fill the sequential openings.[9] The succession/replacement chart, with its graphic illustration of ripple or chain effects, allows us to determine HR blockages or problem areas.[10] For example, the organization may not be able to immediately promote a top-performing potential successor to a particular jobholder because no subordinates to the potential successor are trained and ready to replace him or her. The successor who was rated second but who has ensured that his or her departmental subordinates have been properly trained by being exposed to increasingly more challenging job assignments and thereby are ready to be promoted themselves may be chosen by the organization to replace the jobholder who is leaving.

The second document that is produced for succession/replacement planning is referred to as a succession/replacement table (see Table 8.1 on p. 198). We have seen how the succession/replacement chart gives an important yet incomplete pictorial representation of the state of succession readiness throughout a department or the entire organization. The succession/replacement table complements the succession/replacement chart in that it provides additional information on each specific job, the incumbent jobholder, and all potential internal successors.

Being consumed by day-to-day sales operations can spell disaster for organizations that don't consider their HR supply in a the long-term context. HR Planning Today 8.2 presents information on the looming succession crisis among Canada's car dealerships.

A succession/replacement table is prepared for each key job in the organization. In considering a replacement for the HR planning manager, for example, although the succession/replacement chart provides us with the top

**succession readiness codes**

codes listed next to the names of all potential successors; contain two elements of information essential for succession planning: (1) the employee's level of performance in the current job and (2) the employee's readiness for movement or promotion

**ripple or chain effects**

the effect caused when one promotion or transfer in the organization causes several other personnel movements in the organization as a series of subordinates are promoted to fill the sequential openings

### Car Dealers Steer Clear of Succession

According to a survey by Coopers & Lybrand and DesRosiers Automotive Consultants Inc., many of Canada's more than 3400 new car retailers and dealerships have a looming succession problem. The study found that more than 80% of dealers plan to retire or be semi-retired within ten years. Yet almost half of the dealers who responded to the survey did not have a succession plan, including a full third of those older than 55 years of age. Approximately 70% of dealers would like to keep their dealerships within their families, but fewer than half (44%) think that will actually happen. Dealers are facing this succession problem because of their short-run orientation on selling cars today, without considering the costs and implications of not planning for the future.

Source: Adapted from Keenan, G. 1998. "Car Dealers Steer Clear of Succession," *The Globe and Mail* (June 16), p. B14. Reprinted with permission from *The Globe and Mail*.

two or three candidates and their succession codes, all it may indicate is that promoting any of these individuals could be problematic for a variety of reasons (e.g., because of their performance or lack of training). By turning to the succession/replacement table, we get a list of *all* potential internal successors, not just the shortlist or top three individuals, as well as a very detailed information code for each candidate. Typically, a series of alphanumerical code combinations will provide us with important information not presented on the succession/replacement chart because of space limitations (e.g., using the coding from Table 8.1 A21/61, "A" might signify a manufacturing operations position (#21), with 61 being the number of months in the current position. Succession/replacement table codes summarize information on personal career and training preferences, long-run historical data on performance appraisal, family, geographical posting preferences, and so on, all of which may affect movement or promotion and are not included on the succession/replacement chart.

The succession/replacement tables and charts are very useful tools for HR planners who are analyzing the state of the current workforce. Once we have used these two instruments of succession/replacement analysis, other details concerning specific job blockages or problems with our current internal workforce and the resultant requirement to process new hires from external sources become much clearer.[11] We may find that a perceived shortage of labour is the result of specific personnel policies concerning how we use our workforce and is not due to any shortage in the actual number of workers.[12] Chapter 9 contains further detailed information on succession planning.

## Markov Models

Markov models are the most popular technique used for contemporary supply-side HR planning applications.[13] These models are widely used in both educational and personnel planning processes.[14] Furthermore, they have been found to be more accurate than regression models when used in HR planning systems.[15] **Markov models**, also referred to as *probabilistic* (using probabilities of various movement options) or *stochastic models*,[16] determine the pattern of employee movement throughout an organization's system of jobs.[17] Markov analysis produces a series of matrices that detail the various patterns of movement to and from the wide variety of jobs in the organization. When considering employee movement patterns in the organization, an employee has five possible options: (1) remaining in the current job, (2) promotion to a higher classified job, (3) a lateral transfer to a job with a similar classification level, (4) exit from the job (e.g., termination, layoff, voluntary leaving by the employee), and (5) demotion (which is relatively rare).[18] Probabilistic or Markov models do not examine individual employees but instead examine overall rates of movement between various job levels, and this movement between jobs is based on historical movement patterns.[19] It is normally assumed, for calculation purposes, that the pattern of employee movement is relatively stable over time. If this is not the case, then adjustments have to be made to the historical data to allow them to be used for HR planning in the present day. Markov Model data should be based upon movement during "typical" business operations. However, if environmental conditions change dramatically, the information should be adjusted, using the HR planners' best judgment. However, it is important to note that Markov techniques depend on stable transition probabilities, so dynamic and unstable environmental scenarios may preclude the effective usage of Markov models.[20] See HR Planning Today 8.3 for an example of a Markov model.

There are three main steps to using a Markov model for HR planning purposes.[21] First, we collect historical data on mobility rates between jobs in the organization. Second, based on this data we develop matrices to forecast future personnel movement between jobs. Third, we use the forecasts of the model to analyze our HR policies and programs, and instigate the necessary adaptive measures.[22]

By using employee movement data from the past five years or so, we are able to calculate *transitional probabilities,* or the likelihood that an individual in a specific job will exhibit one of the five aforementioned movement behaviours, normally one year into the future. By multiplying the total number of employees or positions in a particular job (e.g., 18 managers) by the associated probabilities for each of the five possible movement scenarios, the HR planner derives numerical data on employee flow patterns throughout the organization, and between various job levels (see Table 8.2 on p. 203).

The sequences of movements between various job states are referred to as *Markov chains.*[23] (Markov chains are derived from the model and can be considered a subset of the model as they refer to movement sequences between specified job states, not the overall matrix.) Detailed examination of the Markov model enables us to determine the number of external recruits required at various levels of the organizational hierarchy to fill openings caused by turnover, termination, promotion, and so on. Furthermore, we earlier referred to blockages or problems in succession planning, and these problems become readily apparent when we use this supply model based on

**Markov model**

a model that produces a series of matrices that detail the various patterns of movement to and from the various jobs in the organization

## HR Planning Today 8.3

### Using Markov Models to Forecast Ocean Deck Officers

An interesting application of Markov models concerns its usage by the Taiwanese Ministry of Communications to develop a five-year moving average of the "transitional probabilities" that the supply of ocean deck officers available to be employed on ships based in Taiwan would be able to meet forecast demand. The key forecasting issue was that the demand for deck officers was rising annually and exceeded supply, due to expansion in the local economy that resulted in an increased number of ships operating from Taiwan. The forecasting issue was of critical importance for several reasons. First, Taiwan is a significant maritime power as two local carriers—the Evergreen and Yang Ming shipping companies—rank among the 20 biggest shipping companies in the world. Second, since Taiwan is a maritime nation, the shipping industry is a key contributor to the success of the local economy.

The Markov model was derived from historical information about the current number of shipping officers in the four hierarchical levels (masters, chief officers, ship officers, and deck officers), the seniority time at each level, as well as the supply of new shipping officers who have obtained their certificates of proficiency. Demand information was obtained from the five-year plot of the grand total of ships that operated domestically as well as ships that used Taiwan as their flag of convenience.

The resulting findings, which reconciled demand with supply, came up with a number of important conclusions. Not only did the study confirm that demand exceeded supply for shipping officers, the forecasts predicted this situation would worsen in the future, leading to a 64% shortage in positions just three years into the future. Second, the worst imbalance in supply was for the lower-ranking positions, specifically deck officers and shipping officers. Concurrent research determined that graduates from the marine university in Taiwan perceived military service in the navy as offering the most prestigious and desirable jobs following graduation and that they would prefer not to work on a commercial vessel. Policy recommendations that derived from the study included (1) having the government establish ocean internships to support the shipping industry; (2) encouraging increased support for maritime colleges and universities to expand training programs for their ships' officers; (3) aggressively encouraging crew members to seek opportunities to train for their officer certificates; and (4) helping alleviate supply shortages by conducting overseas recruiting.

Source: Adapted from Lin, C., S. Wang, and C. Chiang. 2001. "Manpower Supply and Demand of Ocean Deck Officers in Taiwan," *Maritime Policy & Management*, Vol. 28, No. 1, pp. 91–102. Reprinted with permission of Taylor and Francis, Ltd. http://www.tandf.co.uk.

historical trends of movement probability. The Markov model enables us to determine the specific number of replacements or successors required for any job family annually, as well as for specified future planning periods (based on normal attrition assumptions), which can help us to be more proactive in our external recruitment programs. Additionally, we can calculate the chain of movement from an entry-level job all the way to the CEO appointment, along with forecast times of arrival, stay, and departure, in conjunction with breaks in career progression along the way. In fact, White refers to the length of a vacancy chain (the number of personnel who will move as a result of having to replace one individual) as its *multiplier effect*, and his study of U.S. churches showed that for any one retiring minister, a chain of movement for five subsequent ministers was created.[24] The

TABLE 8.2

## Markov Model

OTTERMERE OUTBOUND ADVENTURES

| | | Year 2009[b] | | | |
| --- | --- | --- | --- | --- | --- |
| | | Chief Outfitter | Outfitter | Guide | Exit |
| Year 2008[a] | Chief Outfitter (n = 4) | 3 (.75) | 9 (.75)[a] | – | 1 (.25) |
| | Outfitter (n = 2) | 1 (.08)[c] | 9 (.75)[a] | – | 2 (.17)[c] |
| | Guide (n = 16) | – | 3 (.19) | 9 (.56) | 4 (.25) |
| | Supply = 32 | 4 | 12 | 9 | 7 |

[a]The future year is shown in each row.
[b]The current year is shown in each column.
[c]The probabilities of movement (percentages) are expressed horizontally and sum to 1 (100%).

length of an average chain is approximately three.[25] Apart from its obvious appeal for the career planning of individuals who have upward aspirations in the organization,[26] HR planners can use the derived information to plan when training and development courses, job rotations, and so on should be conducted for a specific group of employees, based on predicted time to move from their current jobs to target jobs several levels higher in the organization's hierarchy.[27] Therefore, a Markov model has great value for determining (1) the number of personnel who move annually, and over specified time periods, between various job levels; (2) the number of external hires that are required by the organization, and where the specific jobs are needed; (3) the movement patterns and expected duration in specified jobs associated with patterns of career progression for employees in the organization (i.e., career paths);[28] and (4) the number and percentage of all starters at a particular job level who will successfully attain a future target job level by a specified time period.[29] All this information provides us with important insights in calculating the most appropriate balance between training and promoting internal employees on the one hand, and external recruiting on the other. All in all, the Markov model is a very useful tool for analyzing HR supply.

HR professors can provide valuable information to companies on how best to utilize their internal labour markets, as explained in HR Planning Notebook 8.1.

## Linear Programming

**Linear programming** is a mathematical procedure commonly used for project analysis in engineering and business applications. It has utility for HR planners because it allows us to determine the future supply of personnel based on achieving the best staffing outcome while minimizing constraints

**linear programming**
a complex mathematical procedure commonly used for project analysis in engineering and business applications; it can determine an optimum or best-supply mix solution to minimize costs or other constraints

## Managing the Firm's Internal Labour Market: Lessons from the Field

Professors at Simon Fraser University's Faculty of Business Administration have uncovered four lessons in properly using internal labour markets to supply the organization's staffing requirements based on their study of a large manufacturing firm:

1. Managers should recognize that there are often *multiple internal labour markets* typically operating in one firm.

2. Managers should conceptualize their staffing task as managing a system of human resource *flows*.

3. Managers need to develop an appreciation for the *temporal* and *situational contexts* within which staffing decisions are made.

4. Staffing decisions themselves can be appropriately viewed as garbage-can models (a classic model of decision making) in which *multiple issues* and *multiple criteria* are typically invoked in matching individuals and jobs.

Source: Adapted from L. Pinfield and V. Bushe, "Managing the Firm's Internal Labour Market: Lessons from the Field," Burnaby, BC: Faculty of Business Administration, Simon Fraser University. Paper presented at the Western Academy of Management Annual Meeting, Spokane (April 1992).

such as labour costs.[30] Furthermore, conditions such as desired staffing ratios (e.g., the internal/external mix of employees) can be programmed into the equation for determining HR supply. The optimum or best supply-mix solution is provided by the model, and the best conditions obviously vary among organizations.[31] Some companies may seek to minimize turnover or total labour costs, while others may seek to achieve an optimum level of staffing with respect to designated groups (e.g., visible minorities, women, Aboriginal people, people with disabilities) in all job levels throughout the organization.[32] By providing the level of personnel supply that is best with respect to explicitly defined constraints or criteria, linear programming enables us to calculate "what if" scenarios by changing or relaxing various model assumptions in order to determine the impact these changes will have on final numerical requirements for supply, both internal and external. To use linear programming, our assumptions must be similar to those used in regression analysis (discussed in Chapter 7), namely, that the mathematical model must contain variables that have *linear relationships* among the various constituent elements. If this situation does not hold, we have to employ nonlinear or quadratic programming techniques to determine supply requirements. As linear programming is a relatively complex mathematical procedure normally performed on a computer, a detailed presentation on this technique is beyond the scope of this book.

**RPC 8.4**

**movement analysis**
a technique used to analyze personnel supply, specifically the chain or ripple effect that promotions or job losses have on the movements of other personnel in an organization

## Movement Analysis

**Movement analysis** is a technique used to analyze personnel supply, specifically the chain or ripple effect that promotions or job losses have on the movements of other personnel in an organization.[33] Specifically, we are able to identify the total number of vacant or open positions in the organization or department, as well as the total number of personnel movements that are caused by replacing and filling these vacant positions. The total number of personnel movements is always greater than or equal to the number of vacant positions to be filled. If we rely solely on external personnel, the number of vacant positions to be filled is exactly equal to the number of new hires obtained by the organization, as there are no internal promotions of current employees to replace the losses. Conversely, if we rely heavily on current employees (i.e., internal supply) to fill position openings, the total number of personnel movements will be greatly in excess of the number of open positions because any one opening (e.g., due to a promotion or termination) will result in a whole chain of subordinates sequentially moving up one authority level to fill the gaps.[34] Movement analysis enables the HR planner to select the desired mix or percentage of internal and external supply for those positions requiring replacements, ranging from a promote-from-within policy to the other extreme of replacing losses entirely through hiring personnel from outside the organization.

Movement analysis can be performed for the organization as a whole, although analysts normally find it more useful to conduct separate analyses for each department, division, or functional area.[35] The normal planning time horizon is one year, and we start by identifying the number of personnel in each authority or compensation band level at the start of the forecasting period. Next, we consider changes in the level of staffing for the department—that is, whether we are going to increase the number of jobs in some or all authority levels or downsize to reduce the total number of employees in the department. Having increased or decreased the personnel requirement from that which was forecast at the start of the period, we now turn to calculating the losses requiring replacement for each authority level of the department. We are interested only in losses (e.g., because of promotions, transfers out of the department, voluntary turnover, termination) that need to be *replaced*; therefore, it is important that we not "double-count" positions that have already been incorporated into the staffing changes column! We add changes in staffing level to personnel losses requiring replacement to give us the total number of positions requiring replacement. At this stage, having determined the total number of positions to be filled, the actual number of personnel movements, as briefly described previously, can vary widely, depending on our organization or department's desired policy concerning the supply mix of internal and external replacements. To demonstrate, we now turn to a practical example of a movement analysis.

## Movement Analysis Exercise

As HR forecasting manager of Keele Kontainers Ltd., your focus of interest is the organization's finance department. You wish to determine (1) the total number of positions requiring replacements over the next one-year period, and, equally important, (2) the impact these openings will have on the current employees' movements throughout the department. Keele Kontainers has a policy of "promote from within" for all authority levels above the basic entry level (level 9), which obviously must be filled externally with new recruits. The

Chapter 8: Ascertaining HR Supply

finance department does not have any personnel in authority levels 1 to 3 inclusive (i.e., president, senior vice-president, vice-president); the senior appointment is a level 4 (senior manager) position. Based on historical trends and information provided by the strategic planning cell, you know the following:

1. A 5% staffing (position) increase for each of authority levels 6 to 9 inclusive will be required to meet additional financial processing activity in the department; one additional senior manager (level 4) will be required, as management wants one senior manager to handle financial forecasting while one senior manager is responsible for financial claims (i.e., current operations); six additional managers (level 5) will be required to supervise the financial analysts and clerks (i.e., the increases in levels 6 to 9 mentioned above) added over the course of the year.

2. Historical annual loss rates include the following:

   a. Retirements (requiring replacements): two positions for level 5, 15% of current positions for levels 6 to 9 inclusive

   b. Turnover = resignations (voluntary) + terminations (involuntary):

   Levels 5 and 6 = 10% of positions at start of period
   Level 7 = 15% of positions at start of period
   Level 8 = 20% of positions at start of period
   Level 9 = 25% of positions at start of period

   Note: The loss rates can be grouped into one column or broken into individual components (e.g., terminations, retirements).

3. The number of personnel/positions at the start of the year are as follows:

   Level 4 (senior manager) = 1
   Level 5 (manager) = 6
   Level 6 (senior analyst) = 20
   Level 7 (analyst) = 32
   Level 8 (clerk) = 40
   Level 9 (clerical assistant) = 50

In calculating our movement analysis, we construct two separate tables: the first determines the total number of positions to be filled, while the second identifies the internal and external personnel movements required to fill the open positions identified. When conducting a movement analysis, there are two rules to follow:

1. Work from the top down: Start at the highest authority or hierarchy level in the organization, since normal personnel movement in organizations is upward as people are promoted to replace higher-level losses.
2. Calculate the movement figures for one authority or compensation level at a time.

Let's construct a movement analysis table, shown in Table 8.3, and use historical information to calculate position replacement requirements or positions to be filled.

TABLE 8.3

## Number of Positions to Be Filled

| Authority Level | Number of Positions at Start of Period | Staffing Changes | Personnel Losses | Positions to Be Filled |
|---|---|---|---|---|
| 4 | 1 | 1 | 0 | 1 |
| 5 | 6 | 6 | 3 | 9 |
| 6 | 20 | 1 | 5 | 6 |
| 7 | 32 | 2 | 10 | 12 |
| 8 | 40 | 2 | 14 | 16 |
| 9 | 50 | 3 | 21 | 24 |
| | 149 | 15 | 53 | 68 |

Sources: Adapted from E.H. Burack and N.J. Mathys, *Human Resource Planning: A Pragmatic Approach to Manpower Staffing and Development*, 3rd ed. Northbrook, IL.: Brace Park, 1996; D. Bartholomew, *Stochastic Models for the Social Sciences*, New York: Wiley, 1982; E. Burack and J. Walker, *Manpower Planning and Programming*, Boston: Allyn & Bacon, 1972; R. Grinold and K. Marshall, *Manpower Planning Models*, New York: Elsevor North-Holland, 1977; R. Niehaus, "Models for Human Resource Decisions," *Human Resources Planning*, Vol. 11, No. 2 (1988), 95–107; J. Walker, *Human Resources Planning*, New York: McGraw-Hill, 1980; and H. White, *Chains of Opportunity: System Models of Mobility in Organizations*, Cambridge, MA: Harvard University Press, 1970.

By using historical information, we are able to determine that the finance department, with 149 positions at the start of the year, requires 68 positions to be filled over the year. These positions are needed because of a planned staffing increase of 15 positions and because 53 individuals are required to replace personnel losses (i.e., losses due to retirements, resignations, and terminations). The calculations to arrive at these numbers are straightforward. For example, the increased staffing requirement for level 7 is determined by multiplying the original number of positions at that level by the percentage increase (i.e., $32 \times 0.05 = 1.6$ positions), and since we don't normally hire fractions of people, the requirement is for two new positions! Similarly, total personnel losses for level 8 consist of 14 positions, which is the sum of six retirements (i.e., 40 starting positions $\times$ 15%) plus eight turnover losses (i.e., 40 starting positions $\times$ 20%).

Starting with the "Positions to Be Filled" column from Table 8.3, we construct a second table, Table 8.4, that reveals the employee movement at all levels of the finance department caused by promotions to fill the identified vacancies.

What does this all mean? Overall, to fill the 68 positions that require replacements over the next year, a total of 167 movements will occur in the finance department due to the ripple or chain effect on promotions. In Table 8.3, note that for level 5, although we start off with having to find replacements for nine open positions, we also have to promote one individual from level 5 to fill the requirement for an additional senior manager at level 4. Therefore, the total number of individual movements at level 5 is ten, although only nine

Chapter 8: Ascertaining HR Supply

# TABLE 8.4

## Personnel Movement

| POSITIONS TO BE FILLED | | TOTAL RIPPLE OR CHAIN MOVEMENT | | | | | PERSONNEL MOVEMENT |
|---|---|---|---|---|---|---|---|
| 1 | – | – | – | – | | | 1 |
| 9 | + 1 | – | – | – | | = | 10 |
| 6 | + 1 | + 9 | – | – | | = | 16 |
| 12 | + 1 | + 9 | + 6 | – | | = | 28 |
| 16 | + 1 | + 9 | + 6 | + 12 | | = | 44 |
| 24 | + 1 | + 9 | + 6 | + 12 | + 16 | = | 68 |
| 68 | 5 | 36 | 18 | 24 | 16 | = | 167 |

Sources: Adapted from E.H. Burack and N.J. Mathys, *Human Resource Planning: A Pragmatic Approach to Manpower Staffing and Development*, 3rd ed. Northbrook, IL: Brace Park, 1966; D. Bartholomew, *Stochastic Models for the Social Sciences*, New York: Wiley, 1982; E. Burack and J. Walker, *Manpower Planning and Programming*, Boston: Allyn & Bacon, 1972; R. Grinold and K. Marshall, *Manpower Planning Models*, New York: Elsevor North-Holland, 1977; R. Niehaus, "Models for Human Resource Decisions," *Human Resources Planning*, Vol. 11, No. 2 (1988), pp. 95–107; J. Walker, *Human Resources Planning*, New York: McGraw-Hill, 1980; and H. White, *Chains of Opportunity: System Models of Mobility in Organizations*, Cambridge, MA: Harvard University Press, 1970.

open positions had to be filled at that level. Similarly, at level 6, in addition to having to fill six open positions, we also have to promote nine individuals to fill the openings one level higher at level 5, and one individual must be promoted to replace the level 5 individual who was promoted to level 4. Although there were only six open positions at level 6, the ripple or chain effect of sequential movement means that 16 individuals had to move to fill the organizational job openings. Furthermore, our assumption that we promote from within means that all 68 new hires originate from outside (i.e., from an external supply) at the entry level of clerical assistant (level 9). All other vacancies are filled by upward movement of current employees. Additionally, 99 promotions occur for current employees (i.e., internal supply) as is reflected in the ripple or chain effect matrix (i.e., 99 promotions = 5 + 36 + 18 + 24 + 16). In other words, movement analysis has allowed us to identify that for this year's need to fill 68 position vacancies, a total of 167 individual moves will be required because of extensive promotion from within. If we were to balance external and internal supply, the only adjustment would be that fewer individuals would be promoted from within the organization. This would lead to a decrease in the individual moves to a number closer to the number of open positions to be filled.

**vacancy, renewal, or sequencing model**

analyzes flows of personnel throughout the organization by examining inputs and outputs at each hierarchical or compensation level

## Vacancy Model

The **vacancy model**, sometimes referred to as a **renewal** or **sequencing model**, analyzes flows of personnel throughout the organization by examining inputs and outputs at each hierarchical or compensation level.[36]

Vacancy models have been found to have more predictive capacity than Markov models over short- and long-term periods (of three, five, and ten years),[37] although the common time frame for this model is one year into the future. It is important that we always calculate our personnel supply requirements one level at a time in a "top-down" fashion, beginning at the highest relevant authority level, because the normal direction of personnel movement in an organization is from the bottom to the top. The underlying rationale behind the vacancy model is simple; the supply needs of each salary level are determined by staffing changes—the number of personnel who are promoted away from the level—and personnel losses (e.g., retirements, departures, terminations).

Organizational policy will determine the extent to which these openings will be filled by internal and external supply. Personnel losses are normally based on historical trends with respect to the percentage of personnel at each level who normally exit from that level annually, while growth estimates are based on the normal business forecasting process. Overall, vacancies in the organization lead to a sequence of internal promotions from lower levels as the open positions are filled by the replacement personnel. The vacancy model identifies the specific number of external and internal personnel required at each level and for the organization as a whole. We now turn to an illustrative example of the vacancy model.

## Vacancy Model Exercise

Hamish's Hamburgers and Eats offers high-quality, low-cost snacks and meals to budget-conscious students at Moosehead University. Based on the following information, calculate the company's vacancy model for next year's HR supply forecast.

1. Staffing changes: None (i.e., stable size)
2. Personnel losses during the year:

   | Level 1 (president) | = 100% (compulsory retirement) |
   Level 2 (vice-presidents) = 15%
   Level 3 (managers) = 17%
   Level 4 (team leaders) = 20%
   Level 5 (associates) = 25%
   Level 6 (trainees) = 50%

3. Personnel replacement policy (% external supply : % internal supply)

| | % external hiring | % internal promotion |
| --- | --- | --- |
| Level 1 | 0 | 100 |
| Level 2 | 10 | 90 |
| Level 3 | 20 | 80 |
| Level 4 | 30 | 70 |
| Level 5 | 55 | 45 |
| Level 6 | 100 | 0 |

Remember that the key to successful completion of the model is to start your calculations at the top of the organization and work down one level at a time. So let's start our analysis at level 1, the position of the president:

| Level | No. of personnel at start of year | Annual losses | Promotions to level | Level outflows | External hiring |
|---|---|---|---|---|---|
| 1 | 1 | 1 | 1 | 1 | 0 |

The president of Hamish's will be retiring this year, so there will be an annual loss of one person. The company's personnel replacement policy states that for the president's job (level 1), all (100% of) loss replacements will come from internal promotions, in this case, from level 2 below. Therefore, there is one promotion to level 1 (from level 2) with no external hires, and annual losses are exactly equal to outflow at that level. Now consider the situation for level 2:

| Level | No. of personnel at start of year | Annual losses | Promotions to level | Level outflows | External hiring |
|---|---|---|---|---|---|
| 1 | 1 | 1 | 1 | 1 | 0 |
| 2 | 6 | 1 | 2 | 2 | 0 |

Having completed level 1, we now calculate the personnel flows one level lower in the organization's authority or compensation system. For level 2, the annual losses are one, consisting of the number of personnel at that level at the start of the year multiplied by the historical loss rate (i.e., $6 \times 0.15 = 0.9$, rounded to one person). Next, it is crucial to note that the outflows from level 2 are not the same as losses because we must take losses due to termination, retirement, and so on of one person and add to that the one individual who was promoted to level 1 to replace the retiring president. Therefore, our total personnel outflows from level 2 are two people. Total outflows from any organizational level are equal to losses at that level plus promotions to higher levels.

HR supply isn't just a matter of finding new workers; as HR Planning Today 8.4 points out, retention planning is a vital component of effective HR supply.

Now we refer to the company's personnel replacement policy, which dictates that we are required to replace the two personnel who left level 2 by 10% external hires and 90% internal promotions. Naturally, we do not deal in fractions of people, so $2 - 0.9 = 1.8$, which is rounded to two persons. Both replacements are promoted from level 3, and we do not hire any individuals externally for the level 2 losses. The analysis continues in a like manner until all organizational levels have been completed. The finished vacancy model is as follows:

| Level | No. of personnel at start of year | Annual losses | Promotions to level | Level outflows | External hiring |
|---|---|---|---|---|---|
| 1 | 1 | 1 | 1 | 1 | 0 |
| 2 | 6 | 1 | 2 | 2 | 0 |
| 3 | 18 | 3 | 4 | 5 | 1 |
| 4 | 45 | 9 | 9 | 13 | 4 |
| 5 | 88 | 22 | 14 | 31 | 17 |
| 6 | 156 | 78 | 0 | 92 | 92 |
| | 314 | 114 | 30 | 144 | 114 |

In this instance, our vacancy model meets the specified requirement of a stable workforce size (i.e., no growth) as annual personnel losses of 114 are exactly replaced by 114 new hires from outside the organization.

## HR Planning Today 8.4

### Developing Effective Employee Retention Policies

Although most organizations tend to devote considerable time and resources to the process of *attracting* new workers, a great many fall short by not placing enough emphasis on *retaining* the high-quality personnel they currently employ. In order to rectify this situation, studies note the importance of making retention policies a top corporate priority. Several studies have clearly shown that managers at all levels should be held responsible for the retention of their personnel, and managerial performance evaluation should incorporate specific measurable goals in this matter. Greater importance should be placed on identifying high-performing and high-potential employees, as well as their associated values, interests, needs, etc., before they leave to work for competitors. Organizations should conduct a demographic analysis and compensation reviews by using their HRMS. These analyses will enable HR planners to identify potential gaps in the personnel ranks and develop policies to ensure

sufficient well-trained, high-quality employees are on hand over the medium and long term. Other retention policy recommendations include (1) forming a "retention task force" to include HR personnel, line unit managers, and senior executives; (2) reinforcing employee loyalty and performance by "promoting from within" wherever possible; (3) measuring turnover on an ongoing basis at corporate, division, and local levels, utilizing multiple measures; (4) holding line managers responsible for retention; and (5) reviewing and addressing compensation and working condition issues before they become issues for dissatisfaction that prompt employees to leave the organization.

Sources: Adapted from M. Young, "The Case of the Missing CEO," *Canadian HR Reporter*, February 14, 2000: 117–120; and M. Abrams, "Employee Retention and Turnover: Holding Managers Accountable," *Trustee*, Vol. 55, No. 3 (March 2002), T1–T4.

Furthermore, we know that in addition to the 114 annual losses (from a stable organizational workforce of 314), there are 144 total personnel movements, consisting of 114 new hires from external supply sources and 30 internal promotions across all levels. If instead of a no-growth scenario we predict a staffing increase or decrease, the above table is merely revised with the growth percentages (e.g., 5% at level 3, 8% at level 5) multiplied by the original number of personnel in each level to arrive at a column containing the revised (increased or decreased) number of personnel. This adjusted number of personnel is then used as the base point for calculating losses, promotions, and other flows from and to each authority level in the organization. Given the vacancy model information, it is possible to calculate the promotion rate (sometimes called the "upward mobility rate") for each authority level in the organization. For example, the promotion rate for level 4 is 8.8%, which is obtained by dividing 4 (the four people who were promoted to level 3) by 45 (the total number of personnel who are in level 4). As we can see, the vacancy model is a very useful tool for ascertaining specific personnel supply requirements for internal promotions of current employees, as well as for specifying the exact number of external new hires required at each level of the organization.

HR Planning Notebook 8.2 lists steps being taken to address Canada's skill shortages.

## HR Planning Notebook 8.2

### Taking Proactive Steps to Address Canada's Skills Shortage

Widespread attention has been given to the growing shortage of skilled workers in Canada's economy. Apart from insufficient numbers of qualified personnel graduating from Canada's training infrastructure, an ever-increasing global economic reach has led to strong recruiting drives from organizations based in the United States, Europe, and elsewhere to "poach" skilled Canadian workers, further exacerbating an already significant skills shortage. The Canadian Human Resources Technology Board, comprising government personnel and practitioners, has drafted an action plan to address this problem based on several main strategies: (1) enact a Canada-wide coordinated approach to skills training; (2) market careers to students emphasizing skilled trades facing extreme personnel shortages; (3) enhance career awareness by working with educational institutions to promote the benefits of skilled trades occupations; and (4) reduce barriers to recognizing prior learning and foreign skilled-trade qualifications, thereby better utilizing the potential of Canada's current labour force.

Sources: Adapted from D. Brown, "Give Us Your Poor, Your Hungry—Your High-tech Workers," *Canadian HR Reporter*, September 25, 2002; and *Canadian HR Reporter*, "HR Technology Board Tackles Skills Shortage," February 20, 2003.

---

**RPC** 8.5

# HR Supply and Retention Programs

Any presentation on HR supply would be incomplete without a discussion of the need for organizations to monitor and control levels of absenteeism and employee turnover ("labour wastage," in British parlance). It may be helpful to think metaphorically of the organization's supply of employees as the level of water in a bathtub. Even with the water taps fully open and water pouring into the tub, if the drain plug is not in place, inevitably we will soon be looking at an empty tub! Organizationally, even if we are highly successful in *recruiting* a large number of high-quality applicants (a situation that is increasingly rare for most organizations, given demographic and competitive factors), if we are unable to *retain* experienced, high-performing employees, we face dire consequences, not only in the short run in failing to achieve desired organizational goals, but also, perhaps even more critically, in an inadequate HR supply and lost opportunities for future succession. Apart from normal levels of retirement and voluntary turnover, high levels of involuntary turnover normally signify a mismatch between the individual and the organization.[38] Attention should be paid to selection procedures to ensure that proper skills and competencies are possessed by the individual, as well as to orientation and training and development in ensuring that personnel are provided with clear guidance with regard to their employment and desired performance levels.

With labour shortages projected for the next decade, and unemployment rates remaining at low levels, retention programs are no longer an option for most North American companies; they are fast turning into a key requirement for organizational survival.[39] The costs of replacing workers can be staggering. Apart from "hard" costs (e.g., advertisements, headhunter and recruiting fees, interview training and travel costs, administration expenses, cost of lost production, bonuses or increased salaries to act as inducements to join, etc.), there are also the "softer" elements (such as lost business and customer contacts, decreased quantity or quality of work due to training and "learning curve" gaps, orientation and training time, decline in team morale and productivity, and increased turnover due to the "follow-me" effect) to consider. It is estimated that the cost of replacing a trained worker ranges from 70% to 200% of the departing person's annual salary![40] Successful retention programs not only consider the organization's desire to "fill the job slots," but also explicitly attempt to address the needs of its workforce. Organizations that demonstrate flexibility and a genuine effort to assist their employees are perceived to be more attractive places to work (see HR Planning Today 8.5). Retention can be greatly facilitated by offering effective communication programs, facilitating an enjoyable and collegial work atmosphere, designing *meaningful jobs*, formulating and administering performance and compensation systems that identify and differentially reward better performers—based on clearly communicated criteria—and offering more flexible and attractive work arrangements (e.g., flextime, telecommuting, cafeteria-style benefits plans). Mentoring programs have also been found to be highly effective for retention through positively influencing individual commitment and potential for career success, and thereby reducing turnover intentions.[41] The need is clear as is the fact that our employees—or "human capital"—are our key competitive advantage, self-renewing resources that clearly differentiate between organizational success or failure.[42] After years of shortsighted "downsizing" and "restructuring" initiatives, a great many of which have severely crippled organizations' development of intellectual capital and customer service delivery, many organizational managers still don't seem to get it. Until they take action to become "preferred employers" to their employees, by working hard to rebuild trust and mutual commitment, organizations will continue to have HR supply and retention problems, which will prove increasingly costly given looming demographic shortages in the labour force.[43] (See HR Planning Notebook 8.3.) The onus is on organizational and HR managers to deliver!

## Summary

This chapter presented six models or techniques used by organizations to determine future HR supply requirements. Skills and management inventories contain information that allows a detailed analysis of the current workforce to determine whether we can meet the demand for personnel replacement from current employees in the organization. Succession/replacement analysis expands on the inventories approach by using succession/replacement charts and tables to identify specific replacements for key organizational jobs and to examine whether problem areas or blockages would occur if specified individuals were to be promoted or transferred. The Markov model uses historical patterns of individual movement between jobs in the organization and attaches transitional probabilities for promotion, transfer, and remaining in the particular job for an annual or specified future period. In this way, we are able to derive exact numbers of open positions throughout the organization and can track career progression and the time required for individuals to reach specified target jobs. Linear programming uses mathematical equations to determine the optimal or best mix of

### Want to Solve Your HR Supply Problems? Try Some R-E-S-P-E-C-T in the Workplace!

Given the widespread greed, fraud, and corruption scandals involving corporate executives and the propensity of many senior managers to terminate large numbers of employees' jobs even when their business units are operating in a highly profitable fashion, it should come as no surprise that worker loyalty and trust in organizations and executives are at an all-time low. The layoffs, plant closings, mergers and acquisitions, and downsizings of the 1990s, all conducted for the benefit of executives and shareholders and to the detriment of the organization's employees, have largely destroyed the bonds of trust and loyalty workers may have felt previously for their senior managers or toward the organization itself. However, in an era when many other organizations are having tremendous problems attracting high-quality applicants, SaskTel, Saskatchewan's Crown-owned telephone company, with a history of unwavering consideration and respect toward its employees, is still viewed as "the employer of choice" for workers in the Canadian prairie province. Since its formation in 1908, SaskTel has never laid off an employee, and the company is swamped with job applications from university and college HR graduates, allowing it to pick and choose only "the best and brightest." Furthermore, the company's employees have rewarded their employer with high levels of performance that have enabled the firm to outperform and fend off several out-of-province competitors in the long-distance market, in which SaskTel holds a 90% market share, the top performance level in Canada.

Too many executives just don't seem to get it: employees have learned to mistrust them because of lack of congruence between their espoused statements and subsequent self-serving actions. Faced with this organizational mismanagement, workers remain in their companies only for as long as unfavourable market or external family or personal conditions prevent them from leaving. Many of today's executives have a long way to go to try to re-establish relationships based on trust and respect, and to close the gap between them and the workers in the organization. Studies show that, in order to achieve this end, there is an overwhelming need for multidirectional open communications, and for transparency and equity in workplace policies and compensation matters through clearly written, well-disseminated policies that minimize executive favouritism and subjectivity in the assignment of rewards and work assignments. Furthermore, simply "throwing money at employees," however well intentioned, rarely solves the problem as workers leave companies for many reasons apart from compensation, most notably a lack of trust, respect, and challenge in the workplace. Recommended actions to heal the wounded relationships executives have created with their workers include (1) clearly linking professional development training with career planning and compensation; (2) ensuring a direct connection between demonstrated individual performance and compensation received; (3) implementing HR policies that enhance the personal and family lives of employees (e.g., flextime, telecommuting, employee wellness programs, promotion of employee volunteer activities in the community, etc.); (4) enhancing upward as well as downward communication in the firm, by means of e-mail bulletins, meetings with management to discuss proposed changes and to respond to questions and concerns from the employees, and confidential suggestion boxes; and (5) employee recognition, incentive, and retention programs that reinforce and celebrate the successes of all members of the workforce.

Sources: Adapted from S. McGovern, "Earning the Trust of Employees Is a Major Factor in Staff Retention," *Montreal Gazette*, February 26, 2001; "No Layoffs, Plenty of Loyalty," *Maclean's*, November 5, 2001, 51; and T. Sothern, "Retaining Employee Talent," *CA Magazine*, Vol. 135, No. 3 (April 2002), 39–44.

## HR Planning Notebook 8.3

### Winning the War for Talent

Organizations cannot afford to lose experienced, talented employees. Given that highly qualified, high-performing staff will always have alternative employment options, what are some of the steps organizations can take to help attract and retain talented employees? The following recommendations are drawn from the research literature:

1. Train managers in strategies for the retention of employees, and hold them accountable for retention.
2. Pay is not the main reason for losing talent. Pay attention to "toxic" bosses and coworkers, bad management practices, and a lack of autonomy and respect at work.
3. Implement flexible working arrangements to facilitate work–life balance (e.g., flexible work hours, compressed workweek, telecommuting, job sharing, day care centres, etc.).
4. Reward fairly, consistently, and differentially based upon performance and results. Give recognition to employee preferences for different types of work benefits (time off, nonmonetary rewards such as travel or goods, tuition assistance, pension plans, life insurance, etc.).
5. Hold regular feedback and career development discussions with your employees.
6. Recognize that talented, highly motivated employees do not view training as a discretionary item that should get cut during the first round of annual budget reviews!
7. Deal with "slackers" and underperformers! Talented employees resent being burdened with additional stress and workload.
8. Reward organizational seniority in addition to rewarding performance.
9. Identify "high (turnover) risk'" occupations, classifications, and personnel, and develop appropriate talent retention strategies.
10. Develop a managerial academy to teach talented employees the technical and interpersonal skills necessary to assume higher managerial positions in the future.
11. Review and pare to the minimum the following potential "dissatisfiers": rules, regulations, micromanagement, policy manuals, meetings, etc.
12. Take action on talent management; don't just meet, discuss, or prepare a report.
13. Employee retention will soon become the number one priority for HR professionals (Frank & Taylor).

Sources: Adapted from F. Frank and C. Taylor, 2004.,"Talent Management: Trends That Will Shape the Future," *Human Resource Planning*, 27/1, 33–42; J. Greenwald, 2004, "Benefits Programs Aim to Keep More Moms in the (Work) Family, *Business Insurance*, 38/5; Anonymous, 2004, "The Return of Work/Life Plans, *HR Focus*, 81/4; K. Hilton and J. Soubik, 2004, "Case Study: Pennsylvania's Changing Workforce: Planning Today with Tomorrow's Vision," 33/4, 459–474; C. Trank, S. Rynes, and R. Bretz, 2002, "Attracting Applicants in the War for Talent: Differences in Work preferences among High Achievers," *Journal of Business and Psychology*, 16/3, 331–345; M. Hay, 2002, "Strategies for Survival in the War of Talent, *Career Development International*, 7/1, 52–56; S. Langan, 2000, "Finding the Needle in the Haystack: The Challenge of Recruiting and Retaining Sharp Employees," *Public Personnel Management*, 49/4, 461–478.

personnel supply given specified constraints, such as minimizing labour cost or achieving a desired mix of diverse employee group memberships. Movement analysis enables us to identify not only the location and number of open positions that must be filled by the organization, but also the total number of individuals who will be moved to fill these openings. The vacancy model provides specific information on total personnel flows into and out of each authority or compensation level, as well as for the organization as a whole. Accordingly, we are able to calculate the exact numbers of internal promotions and external recruits that will be required by the organization.

Finally, we concluded our discussion of HR supply by pointing out the need for organizations to develop retention programs to control absenteeism and turnover.

# Key Terms

linear programming, 203

management inventory, 195

Markov model, 201

movement analysis, 204

ripple or chain effects, 199

skills inventory, 195

succession readiness codes, 199

vacancy, renewal, or sequencing model, 208

# Web Links

The Government of British Columbia's Labour Force Statistics on HR Supply and other indices can be found at:

**www.aved.gov.bc.ca/labourmarketinfo** (p. 194)

*Canadian HR Reporter* is at:

**www.hrreporter.com** (p. 194)

The supply of available jobs in the U.S. Government can be found at the official job site of the U.S. Federal Government (USAJOBS) at:

**http://jobsearch.usajobs.opm.gov/jobsearch.asp?jbf563=1&vw=d&brd=3876&FedPub=Y&FedEmp=Y** (p. 195)

Useful information on HR supply, jobs, etc. can be found at:

**www.hr.com** (p. 196)

The U.K.'s HR professional association, the Chartered Institute of Personnel and Development, has a website at:

**www.cipd.co.uk** (p. 204)

The Canadian Government's report on balancing HR supply and demand in health resources is located at:

**www.hc-sc.gc.ca/sr-sr/alt_formats/iacb-dgiac/pdf/pubs/hpr-rps/bull/2004-8-hhr-rhs/2004-8-hhr-rhs_e.pdf** (p. 212)

Information on the Supply and Demand of the British Labour Force can be found at HRM Guide UK's website at:

**www.hrmguide.co.uk/hrm/chap3/ch3-links4.htm** (p. 212)

# RPC Icons

**RPC 8.1 Forecasts HR supply and demand conditions**

**RPC 8.2 Maintains an inventory of HR talent for the use of the organization**

**RPC 8.3 Identifies potential source of qualified candidates**

**RPC 8.4 Identifies potential sources and the markets in which the organization competes for qualified candidates**

**RPC 8.5 Performs a cost-benefit analysis of developing existing staff versus acquiring new staff, or outsourcing**

# Discussion Questions

1. A Markov model provides important information to the HR supply analyst with respect to movement or flows of personnel through various jobs in the organization. Discuss how this supply-forecasting technique could also provide useful information to rank-and-file members (i.e., non-HR staff) of the organization's workforce.

2. Movement analysis analyzes the ripple effects or workforce movements resulting from various supply policy options selected by the organization. Discuss the varying implications of using internal sources of labour (i.e., the current workforce) rather than external sources of labour (i.e., recruits) for the supply needs of an organization. What are the advantages, disadvantages, costs, and benefits associated with the different options?

# Using the Internet

1. There is a global shortage of health care professionals, and many Canadian jurisdictions find themselves facing an inadequate supply of nurses and physicians. Governments at various levels are continuing their efforts to rectify the HR deficit/shortage, by not only encouraging increased enrollment in professional training programs, but also providing various financial and other incentives to encourage health workers to move to, and practise in, underserviced areas. The federal government, and the Government of Prince Edward Island have developed their own HR programs to address this issue. Go to their websites at

   **www.hc-sc.gc.ca/sr-sr/alt_formats/iacb-dgiac/pdf/pubs/hpr-rps/bull/2004-8-hhr-rhs/2004-8-hhr-rhs_e.pdf**

   and

   **www.gov.pe.ca/photos/original/hss_humres.pdf**

   Analyze the similarities and differences in their approaches to this HR supply issue, and develop recommendations concerning how their programs might be improved.

# Exercise

1. Dave's Dumpsters offers a low-cost disposal system for the high-quality campus food served at Moosehead University, as well as for many other institutions of higher learning. The company has retained your services

on a lucrative contract to calculate the vacancy model for next year's HR forecast, based on the following assumptions:

a. Workforce complement at beginning of period (i.e., before staffing changes):

Salary level 1 = 1

Salary level 2 = 4

Salary level 3 = 18

Salary level 4 = 40

Salary level 5 = 75

Salary level 6 = 136

b. Organizational growth: 5% increase in each salary level with the exception of salary level 1 (CEO), which remains at one position.

c. HR losses during year:

Salary level 1 = 100%

Salary level 2 = 20%

Salary level 3 = 22%

Salary level 4 = 25%

Salary level 5 = 30%

Salary level 6 = 50%

d. HR supply policy:

| | Outside % | Inside % |
|---|---|---|
| Salary level 1 | 0 | 100 |
| Salary level 2 | 10 | 90 |
| Salary level 3 | 20 | 80 |
| Salary level 4 | 30 | 70 |
| Salary level 5 | 50 | 50 |
| Salary level 6 | 100 | 0 |

Source: K. M<sup>c</sup>Bey, 2002.

# Case: Ontario's Faculty Shortage Crisis

According to Dr. Deborah Flynn, the former president of the Ontario Confederation of University Faculty Associations (OCUFA), Ontario universities were facing a dire shortage in the supply of professorial talent and needed to hire 15 300 new faculty by the year 2010 in order to keep pace with enrollment growth and retiring faculty members, and to reduce Ontario's student-to-faculty ratio to the Canadian national average. Citing a variety of studies, including one conducted by PricewaterhouseCoopers, she noted that there were already 2000 fewer professors in the Ontario university system than there were just ten years previously, a figure representing over 15% of the total faculty complement.

This shortage will increase substantially when the baby-boomer faculty retire in just a few years' time. More than one-third of all Ontario faculty members were currently between 55 and 64 years of age, and they will be retiring over the next few years just as universities are facing a substantial increase in enrollments because of the demographic increase in the "echo" generation students (18 to 24 years of age) entering university. In total, this represents 5500 additional professors who have to be hired.

Further adding to the problem was the impact of secondary school reform ("the double cohort"), which saw as many as 33 500 additional students seeking access to universities over the next two years. As well, changing workforce requirements and the need for "lifelong learning" to secure and retain meaningful employment in a knowledge-based economy had led students to demand university courses that could be taken over an extended period of time (i.e., they never really leave university) in order to keep their knowledge and skills relevant in an extremely dynamic environment.

Compounding the problem was the fact that university administrators had been addressing their budgetary problems (and associated reductions in provincial government funding) by reducing the number of full-time faculty members and relying on part-time course directors. These individuals often had part-time jobs at several educational institutions or alternatively work full-time in other jobs and lectured on the side, but they were not full-time employees of the universities. Furthermore, the relatively low pay scales offered to university faculty, as compared to people with equivalent qualifications in private industry or in other public institutions, further diminished the available pool of potential faculty members. Readers may be surprised to note that fewer than 40% of all people holding earned doctorates in Canada are employed in universities (Council of Ontario Universities, 2000). Furthermore, OCUFA commissioned the HayGroup to conduct a compensation analysis of skills, qualifications, and jobs that were equivalent to university professors in the public and private sectors. They found that salaries favoured employment outside universities, as the average salary of university professors was $78,001, whereas comparable jobs in the public sector paid $84,100, and salaries were a full one-third higher in the private sector at $103,900 (all figures 1998–99). The competition for available faculty was not just from the local public and private sectors. All provinces across Canada were also facing faculty shortages, as was the case worldwide, with the situations being especially acute in the United States and the United Kingdom.

The consequences of this situation were that university students, who had seen their average tuition fees rise by 60% over the previous five years, were now facing a reduced number of course options, crowded classrooms, reductions in services and contacts with professors, and a decreased quality of education. For the faculty members, the time and quality of their research and teaching was affected as faculty workloads skyrocketed to handle the increased number of students and the decreased number of faculty colleagues to deal with these issues. The result was often a migration of faculty member to other institutions and employment opportunities in Canada or abroad, further exacerbating an already bad situation.

Source: Ontario Confederation of University Faculty Associations (OCUFA), 2001. "Less Isn't More: Ontario's Faculty Shortage Crisis," *OCUFA Research Reports*, Vol. 1, No. 4 (January), pp. 1–18. Reprinted with permission. The report cites numerous other reports by the Association of Universities and Colleges of Canada (AUCC), Statistics Canada, Council of Ontario Universities, and PriceWaterhouseCoopers (1999).

## Question

Conduct a detailed analysis of causes of the supply deficit among Ontario's university faculty. What were the causal factors? How could this situation have been prevented? Finally, specify the steps that should be taken by the various stakeholder groups to rectify this supply crisis.

# Endnotes

1. Sinnema, J. November 11, 2005. "Celebrated Prof Leaving over Policy, *Edmonton Journal*, B7; Kirk, J. November 12, 2005. "Reaping the Rewards of Experience," *Toronto Star*, D10; Vu, U. 2005. "End of Mandatory Retirement the Start of Work for HR," *Canadian HR Reporter*, 18/13; Berman, D. September 21, 2005. "Keep Older Canadians Working OECD Says," *National Post*, FP5; Klie, S. 2005. "Ending Mandatory Retirement Not a Benefit Worry Experts Say," *Canadian HR Reporter*, 18/18; Greenberg, L. June 7, 2005. "Ontario to End Mandatory Retirement," *National Post*, A5; Lowe, G. 2004. "Revamp HR Policies to Retain Older Workers," *Canadian HR Reporter*, 17/19, 17; Munro, J. 2004. "The Debate about Mandatory Retirement in Ontario Universities," *Ontario Confederation of University Faculty Association Forum*, Fall, 21–24; Kalinowski, T. March 12, 2003. "Universities Scrambling for Professors," *Toronto Star*, A24; Wellner, A. 2002. "Tapping a Silver Mine," *HR Magazine*, 47/3, 26–32.
2. Buhler, P. 2004. "Managing in the New Millennium," *SuperVision*, 65/2, 20–23; Martin, R. 1967. "Skills Inventories," *Personnel Journal* (January): 28–83; Kaumeyer, R.H. 1979. *Planning and Using Skills Inventory Systems*. New York: Van Nostrand Reinhold.
3. Schwarzkopf, A., R. Mejias et al. 2004. "Effective Practices for IT Skills Staffing," *Communications of the ACM*, 47/1, 83–88; Martin, R. 1967. "Skills Inventories," *Personnel Journal* (January): 28–83. Seamans, L. 1978. "What's Lacking in Most Skills Inventories," *Personnel Journal* (March): 101–106.
4. Pynes, J. 2004. "The Implementation of Workforce and Succession Planning in the Public Sector," *Public Personnel Management*, 33/4, 389–405; Cooke, R. 1995. "Succession Planning," *Credit Union Management* (October): 27–28.
5. Rothwell, W. 2002. "Putting Success into Your Succession Planning," *Journal of Business Strategy*, Vol. 23, No. 3: 32–37.
6. Guinn, S. 2000. "Succession Planning Without Job Titlesm" *Career Development International*, Vol. 5, No. 7: 390–394.
7. Pynes, J. 2004. "The Implementation of Workforce and Succession Planning in the Public Sector," *Public Personnel Management*, 33/4, 389–405; Cooke, R. 1995. "Succession Planning," *Credit Union Management* (October): 27–28.
8. Cooke, 1995.

9. White, H. 1970b. "Matching Vacancies and Mobility," *Journal of Political Economy*, Vol. 78, No. 1 (January): 97–105.

10. Foot, D., and R. Venne. 1990. "Population, Pyramids, and Promotional Prospects," *Canadian Public Policy*, Vol. 16, No. 4 (December): 387–398.

11. Foot, D., and R. Venne. 1990. "Population, Pyramids, and Promotional Prospects," *Canadian Public Policy*, Vol. 16, No. 4 (December): 387–398.

12. Hammonds, K. 2005. "Why We Hate HR," http://pf.fastcompany.com, Issue 97, August, p. 1–8; Lewin, D., and J. Keith. 1976. "Managerial Responses to Perceived Labor Shortages: The Case of Police," *Criminology*, Vol. 14, No. 1 (May): 65–92.

13. Bechet, T.P., and W.R. Maki. 1987. "Modeling and Forecasting: Focusing on People as a Strategic Resource," *Human Resource Planning*, Vol. 10, No. 4: 209–217; Konda, S., and S. Stewman. 1980. "An Opportunity Labor Demand Model and Markovian Labor Supply Models: Comparative Tests in an Organization," *American Sociological Review*, Vol. 45, No. 2 (April): 276–301; Weigel, H., and S. Wilcox. 1993. "The Army's Personnel Decision Support System," *Decision Support Systems*, Vol. 9, No. 3 (April): 281–306.

14. Bartholomew, D.J. 1973. *Stochastic Models for the Social Sciences*. London: Wiley; Law, H. 1977. "A Projection Model and a Rational Policy for the Supply and Demand of Human Resources from an Educational Institution," *Applied Mathematical Modeling*, Vol. 1, No. 5 (June): 269–275.

15. Venezia, I., and Z. Shapira. 1978. "The Effects of Type of Forecasting Model and Aggregation Procedure on the Accuracy of Managerial Manpower Predictions," *Behavioral Science*, Vol. 23, No. 3 (May): 187–194.

16. Meehan, R., and B.S. Ahmed. 1990. "Forecasting Human Resources Requirements: A Demand Model," *Human Resource Planning*, Vol. 13, No. 4: 297–307.

17. Heneman, H.G., and M.G. Sandiver. 1977. "Markov Analysis in Human Resource Administration: Applications and Limitations," *Academy of Management Review* (October): 535–542; Vassiliou, P.C. 1976. "A Markov Chain Model for Wastage in Manpower Systems," *Operational Research Quarterly*, Vol. 27, No. 1: 57–70.

18. Gans, N., and Y. Zhou. 2002. "Managing Learning and Turnover in Employee Staffing," *Operations Research*, 50/6, 991–1007; Bechet, T.P., and W.R. Maki. 1987. "Modeling and Forecasting: Focusing on People as a Strategic Resource," *Human Resource Planning*, Vol. 10, No. 4: 209–217.

19. Blakely, R. 1970. "Markov Models and Manpower Planning," *Industrial Management Review* (Winter): 39–46.

20. Stone, T., and J. Fiorito. 1986. "A Perceived Uncertainty Model of Human Resource Forecasting Technique Use," *Academy of Management Review*, Vol. 11, No. 3: 635–642.

21. Zeffane, R., and G. Mayo. 1995. "Human Resource Planning for Rightsizing: A Suggested Operational Model," *American Business Review*, Vol. 13, No. 2 (June): 6–17.

22. Zeffane, R., and G. Mayo. 1995. "Human Resource Planning for Rightsizing: A Suggested Operational Model," *American Business Review*, Vol. 13, No. 2 (June): 6–17.

23. Gans, N., and Y. Zhou. 2002. "Managing Learning and Turnover in Employee Staffing," *Operations Research*, 50/6, 991–1007; Nielsen, G.L., and A.R. Young. 1973. "Manpower Planning: A Markov Chain Applicationm" *Public Personnel Management* (March): 133–143.

24. White, H. 1970a. *Chains of Opportunity: System Models of Mobility in Organizations*. Cambridge, MA: Harvard University Press.

25. Stone, T., and J. Fiorito. 1986. "A Perceived Uncertainty Model of Human Resource Forecasting Technique Use," *Academy of Management Review*, Vol. 11, No. 3: 635–642.

26. Gridley, J. 1986. "Who Will Be Where When? Forecast the Easy Way," *Personnel Journal*, Vol. 65, No. 5 (May): 50–58.

27. Sandefur, G. 1981. "Organizational Boundaries and Upward Job Shifts," *Social Science Research*, Vol. 10, No. 1 (March): 67–82; Bartholomew, D. 1996. *Mobility Measurement Revisited in the Statistical Approach to Social Measurement*. San Diego: Academic Press.

28. Tuma, N. 1976. "Rewards, Resources, and the Rate of Mobility: A Nonstationary Multivariate Stochastic Model," *American Sociological Review*, Vol. 41, No. 2 (April): 338–360.

29. Rowland, K., and M. Sovereign. 1969. "Markov Chain Analysis of Internal Manpower Supply," *Industrial Relations* (October): 88–99; Glen, J.J. 1977. "Length of Service Distributions in Markov Manpower Models," *Operational Research Quarterly*, Vol. 28, No. 4: 975–982.

30. Al-Harbi, K. 2000. "Optimization of Staff Numbers in the Process Industries: An Application of DEA," *International Journal of Manpower*, 21/1, 47–55; Gans, N., and Y. Zhou. 2002. "Managing Learning and Turnover in Employee Staffing," *Operations Research*, 50/6, 991–1007; Weigel, H., and S. Wilcox. 1993. "The Army's Personnel Decision Support System," *Decision Support Systems*, Vol. 9, No. 3 (April): 281–306.

31. Patz, A.L. 1970. "Linear Programming Applied to Manpower Management," *Industrial Management Review*, Vol. 11, No. 2 (Winter): 131–138.

32. Gans, N., and Y. Zhou. 2002. "Managing Learning and Turnover in Employee Staffing," *Operations Research*, 50/6, 991–1007; Walker, J.W. 1980. *Human Resource Planning*. New York: McGraw-Hill.

33. Bartholomew, D. 1982. *Stochastic Models for the Social Sciences*, 3rd ed. New York: John Wiley; Bartholomew, D. 1996. *Mobility Measurement Revisited in the Statistical Approach to Social Measurement*. San Diego: Academic Press; Burack, E.H., and N.J. Mathys. 1996. *Human Resource Planning: A Pragmatic Approach to Manpower Staffing and Development*, 3rd ed. Northbrook, IL: Brace Park; White, H. 1970a. *Chains of Opportunity: System Models of Mobility in Organizations*. Cambridge, MA: Harvard University Press; White, H. 1970b. "Matching Vacancies and Mobility," *Journal of Political Economy*, Vol. 78, No. 1 (January): 97–105.

34. Geerlings, W. and Van Veen, K. 2001. "Simulating Patterns of Organizational Careers," *Computational and Mathematical Organization Theory*, 7/4, 287–310; White, H. 1970a. *Chains of Opportunity: System Models of Mobility in Organizations*. Cambridge, MA: Harvard University Press; White, H. 1970b. "Matching Vacancies and Mobility," *Journal of Political Economy*, Vol. 78, No. 1 (January): 97–105.

35. Monks, K. 1996. "Global or Local? HRM in the Multinational Company: The Irish Experience," *International Journal of Human Resource Management*, Vol. 7, No. 3 (September): 721–735.

36. Geerlings, W., and K. Van Veen. 2001. "Simulating Patterns of Organizational Careers," *Computational and Mathematical Organization Theory*, 7/4, 287–310; White, H. 1970a. *Chains of Opportunity: System Models of Mobility in Organizations*. Cambridge, MA: Harvard University Press; White, H. 1970b. "Matching Vacancies and Mobility," *Journal of Political Economy*, Vol. 78, No. 1 (January): 97–105; Bartholomew, D. 1982. *Stochastic Models for the Social Sciences*, 3rd ed. New York: John Wiley; Bartholomew, D. 1996. *Mobility Measurement Revisited in the Statistical Approach to Social Measurement*. San Diego: Academic Press.

37. Konda, S., and S. Stewman. 1980. "An Opportunity Labor Demand Model and Markovian Labor Supply Models: Comparative Tests in an Organization," *American Sociological Review*, Vol. 45, No. 2 (April): 276–301.

38. M<sup>c</sup>Bey, K., and L. Karakowsky. 2000. "Examining Sources of Influence on Employee Turnover in the Part-time Work Context," *Leadership and Organization Development Journal*, Vol. 21, No. 3: 136–144.

39. Kohl, N. 2000. "HR Managers Losing the Retention Game," *Pro2Net*, November 7: 2.

40. North, N., E. Rasmussen et al. 2005. "Turnover amongst Nurses in New Zealand's District Health Boards: A National Survey of Nursing Turnover and Turnover Costs," *New Zealand Journal of Employment Relations*, 30/1, 49–63; Kohl, N. 2000. "HR Managers Losing the Retention Game," *Pro2Net*, November 7: 2.

41. Gram, J. 2004. "New Approaches to Human Resource Forecasting in the Public Sector," *Public Manager*, 32/4; Joiner, T., T. Bartram, and T. Garreffa. 2004. "The Effects of Mentoring on Perceived Career Success, Commitment and Turnover Intentions," *Journal of American Academy of Business*, 5/1–2, 164–171.

42. Lofgren, E., S. Nyce, et al. 2002. "Will You Be Stranded by a Worker Shortage?" *Electric Perspectives*, Vol. 27, No. 3: 22–29.

43. Walker, J. 2003. "Perspectives: Where Are We Going?" *Human Resource Planning*, 26/1, 14–16.

# Chapter 9

# Succession Management

## Chapter Learning Objectives

After reading this chapter, you should be able to

- Understand why succession management is important.
- Trace the evolution of succession management from its roots in replacement planning, comparing the two models with respect to focus, time, and talent pools.
- List the steps in the succession management process.
- Compare and contrast the job-based and competency-based approaches to aligning future needs with strategic objectives.
- Discuss the four approaches to the identification of managerial talent.
- Describe several ways to identify high-potential employees.
- Evaluate the advantages and disadvantages of the five management development methods: promotions, job rotations, special assignments, formal training, and mentoring and coaching.
- Recognize the difficulties in measuring the success of a management succession plan.
- Outline the employee's role in the succession management process.
- Describe the limitations of succession management, and propose some possible solutions to these limitations.

## LEADERSHIP PLANNING AT SUN LIFE FINANCIAL

Sun Life Financial is a Canadian organization that has recognized the importance of grooming employees for senior executive positions. This represents a change; prior to 2000, many companies searched outside their organizations for top talent. However, now, due to restructuring, many of those holding middle management positions have lost their jobs, thus reducing the supply of talent for upper-level positions. Half the senior leaders within Canadian organizations will retire in the next ten years. So the focus has shifted to the next generation of potential leaders, and leadership development has become a top priority for Canadian companies. The program at Sun Life is one of the most structured, with a dedicated executive in charge of the program. Each year, Sun Life, with an employee population of 12 000, asks its managers to nominate high-potential employees, and a committee reviews this top tier of 100 employees and a second tier of another 100 employees. Goals are set for each person in the pool. Progress is monitored through regular informal meetings with senior executives in their divisions. Those candidates making the most progress are invited to attend an eight-week customized leadership program managed by the Harvard Business School.[1]

Executives of any organization must develop the next generation of leaders, just as sports teams need to develop the next generation of players.

**9.1**

**succession management**
the process of ensuring that pools of skilled employees are trained and available to meet the strategic objectives of the organization

## Importance of Succession Management

**Succession management** refers to the process of ensuring that pools of skilled employees are trained and available to meet the strategic objectives of the organization. Succession management consists of a process of identifying employees who have the potential to assume key positions in the organization and preparing them for these positions. The identification of talent is always paired with ongoing programs to develop that talent. Succession management ensures continuity in leadership and, like any rookie program, develops the next generation of players.

As Peter Drucker says, the ultimate test of good management is succession management, ensuring that there is a replacement for the CEO.[2] Organizations must prepare for expected and unexpected turnover, for key players do die, retire, or quit. Unexpected events sometimes have dramatic consequences. The New York Fire Department lost 350 employees as a result of September 11, 2001, but its leadership succession plan helped it to replace many of its top leaders within days. Fiery young entrepreneurs who build hugely successful businesses often see them fail in the hands of their

## Family Firms Fail

Family-owned businesses represent a significant part of the economy in Canada, generating $1.3 *trillion* in revenues, and employing 4.7 million full-time employees and 1.3 million part-time employees. Yet only 40% of these family firms have a business plan, and less than 25% have a long-term strategic plan. Four out of five owners will retire in the next 15 years; 70% say that they have not selected a successor; and 66% indicate that they have no process for succession management. Nearly half of these owners believe that the business will not survive without them, which could result in an economic disaster for Canada. They are right. Research has established that hereditary owners have a poor track record: businesses handed to sons and daughters fail 50% of the time. There is no such thing as the "lucky sperm club"—the factors that drive entrepreneurs to succeed cannot be passed down. As A. Mac Cuddy, the bitter founder of Cuddy International, a multimillion-dollar poultry producer whose company was torn apart in a family feud among his five sons, said, "You can hire better than you can sire."

One of Canada's largest family-owned businesses, Thomson Corporation and Magna International, is handling succession management well. Ken Thomson's family owns 70% of Thomson Corp., a $30-billion giant founded by Roy Thomson, father of Ken. David Thomson, Ken's son, has been groomed since birth to take over the company and did so in 2002. Investors have not reacted negatively because Thomson Corp. has always used independent professional management that remains intact.

Sources: "Leadership Crisis," *CMA Management*, Vol. 73, No. 5 (June 1999), 25–27; M. McClearn, "A New Era," *Canadian Business*, Vol. 75, No. 5 (March 18, 2002), 24; T. Watson, "The Rich 100– Succession: Family Circus," *Canadian Business*, Vol. 74, No. 24 (December 31, 2000), 104–110.

untrained children. Succession management is the great failing of entrepreneurs. Many Canadian dynasties (Eaton's, Woodward's, McCain's) have failed because their heirs were incapable of managing the business. See HR Planning Today 9.1 for a discussion of the problems facing family firms.

Goldman Sachs Group Inc. is an extremely successful investment bank because its president spends much of his day not doing deals as might be expected but addressing issues of succession, staffing, and compensation. Getting the right people in place was the key element in ensuring that the company passed successfully to a new generation of partners. The founding partners of Goldman Sachs realized profits of US$75 million when they sold the company because the president got the people part right. Contrast the Goldman Sachs case to that of Gordon Capital, a company that has been humbled significantly because it suffered from "founder's mentality," never nurturing the next generation of leaders. Its executives were working 16-hour days because there were no skilled replacements to relieve them. The firm never realized its potential due to low profits and employee exodus.

Succession management is needed even when retirements and company sellouts are predictable. The baby boomers who currently hold most of the leadership positions are retiring (see HR Planning Today 9.2). Twenty percent of top management positions and 25% of middle management positions will become vacant in 2005 and retirements will accelerate beyond that.[3] An organization that can weather this type of management change will survive.

RPC 9.2

## HR Planning Today 9.2

### Early Retirement and the Impending Labour Shortage

One in three Canadians is 50 or older. While retirement has been welcomed by both unions and workers as the start of a new life, data from Statistics Canada suggest that one impact will be a shortage of experienced workers. Organizations predict that one-third to one-half of their management and professional employees will be eligible to retire in the next few years. Workers are retiring earlier, from an average of 65 in the late 1970s to 61 in the late 1990s. Over the same period, the employment rate for those 55 to 64 has declined.

Early retirement produces many benefits, including creating job opportunities for those entering the labour force. Younger workers are often less expensive than those they replace, because they are employed at the low end of scales, including vacation entitlements and pay levels. However, because of the impending labour shortages, there have been over 60 federally sponsored pilot projects to test ideas about how to keep these older workers in the labour force, including phased retirement.

Sources: D. Brown, "Impending Labour Shortages Put Focus on Older Workers," *Canadian HR Reporter* (August 12, 2002), 1 and 11; R. Stuart and C. Graham, "Early Retirement on the Bargaining Table," *Canadian HR Reporter* (January 27, 2003), 12–13.

At a minimum, firms need to plan for replacements, and personnel planning was the first step in the march toward sophisticated models of succession management. Some reasons for succession management are listed in HR Planning Notebook 9.1. The next section traces this evolution.

## Evolution of Succession Management

**replacement planning**

the process of finding replacement employees for key managerial positions

**Replacement planning** can be defined as the process of finding replacement employees for key managerial positions: if the CEO dies, who will be prepared to take over that position? Is there a replacement for the vice-president

## HR Planning Notebook 9.1

### Reasons for Succession Management

1. Provide increased opportunities for high-potential workers.
2. Identify replacement needs as a means of targeting necessary training, employee education, and employee development.
3. Increase the talent pool of promotable employees.
4. Contribute to implementing the organization's strategic business plans.
5. Help individuals realize their career plans within the organization.
6. Tap the potential for intellectual capital in the organization.
7. Encourage the advancement of diverse groups.
8. Improve employees' ability to respond to changing environmental demands.
9. Improve employee morale.
10. Cope with the effects of voluntary separation programs.
11. Decide which workers can be terminated without damage to the organization.
12. Cope with the effects of downsizing.
13. Reduce headcount to essential workers only.

Source: Portions of this material originally appeared in Effective Succession Planning Copyright© 2001 AMACOM, a division of American Management Association, New York, NY. Used by permission of the publisher. All rights reserved. http://www.amanet.org

of marketing if she suddenly quits to take another job? The events of September 11, 2001, tragically presented a worst-case scenario. Bond trading firm Cantor Fitzgerald lost 700 of its 1000 World Trade Center staff, including most of its executives.

® ℗ © 9.3

Formal and methodical replacement planning has existed for over 30 years. This section examines how replacement planning has evolved into succession management by

- broadening the focus,
- expanding the time horizon,
- creating a talent pool of replacements, and
- improving the evaluation system.

## Broader Focus

The focus of replacement planning was the job, and having a replacement ready to fill that job if the incumbent died or quit. This concept referred mainly to the succession and replacement charts for the high-level or key positions in the organization. Each key position was represented by a box on the chart, with the name and possible retirement or departure date of the incumbent in the box. Below the box were the names of two or three potential successors, with codes next to their names. These would be, for example, codes such as "PN" for "promotable now" or "RD" for "ready with development."

In short, replacement planning consisted of a periodically updated table of employees who might be nominated if a need arose. This type of planning focused on the high-potential candidates (replacement track stars), all ready to step into vacant positions, and in doing so set off a chain effect throughout the organization. This model assumed that people have single careers within one organization. Thus, replacements were replicas of the current jobholders.

This planning depended on a stable future, where the KSAs of future managers looked pretty much like those of the current managers. Jobs of the next five to ten years were assumed to be identical to the existing jobs. Organizational structures (i.e., how the organization was set up along divisional lines, product lines, or functional lines) were unchanging, and few new competitors were seen on the horizon. Obviously, this type of scenario just doesn't exist for most companies.

In replacement planning, the starting point was the job, whereas in succession management, the starting point is the strategy of the organization. Employees are selected based on long-term goals, and the developmental plans for employees are aligned with strategic plans, not position replacements.

A case might best illustrate how succession management aligns with strategy. Traditionally, the goal of a large utility like Ontario Hydro was to provide safe, reliable energy. Its core competencies were reliability of distribution, measurement of consumption, and the maintenance of its power plants. However, deregulation and a more competitive environment forced Ontario Hydro to compete on price and services. Sales and marketing were the new

Chapter 9: Succession Management

competencies needed. The strategy changed from providing energy to marketing energy. Thus, in the long run, Ontario Hydro must identify or develop managers who have not only sales and marketing abilities, but also the ability to change a production culture to one of marketing.[4]

## Time Horizon

The traditional planning approach was concerned with immediate and short-term replacements. Who is our backup for the vice-president we are planning to promote in six to twelve months? A strategic focus of under one year is a "business as usual" perception, which, if repeated, will not be true over a ten-year period. This short time perspective does not allow for the intake or career management of those with different skills in growth areas.

Succession management looks at a longer term (after ensuring that immediate replacements are in place) and focuses on a future of two years or more. Obviously, this is harder to do, and so, rather than identify one replacement, succession managers identify talent pools.

## Talent Pools

Traditional models of HR planning looked at succession as the passing of the baton to the next capable runner. Managers would identify their top performers and groom them for success. Sometimes two or three successors would be identified, and they would be in a race to the finish line of executive promotion. This practice may have worked when organizations consisted of dozens of levels, each manager having many assistant managers. Currently, organizations have found that their designated backup personnel fill only 30% of the open positions for which they were slotted.[5] Flatter organizations with fewer "apprentices" can no longer rely on this approach. The key is not to develop a specific successor to fill any position (done by about one-third of organizations) but to develop several multiple successors (about two-thirds of organizations do this) for every position.[6] The place to start is with positions that are difficult to fill because of talent shortages.

As employees cannot trust organizations to provide lifetime job security, so too, organizations cannot rely on single individuals or a small group of employees for their succession plans. Organizations are trying to identify and develop as many employees as possible to not only ensure employee departures and changing needs will not leave them harmed, but also to avoid the "crown prince" syndrome (see "Elitism" below).

Any organization needs a pool of talent and must develop many employees with flexible job skills and competencies. A "pool" is a good description of the next generation of talented leadership because the term implies fluidity and responsiveness to the impact of forces. The talent pool is considered a corporate resource and is not the property of individual organizational units. This evolution from personnel planning to succession management has led to a model of generating pools of leadership talent within an organizational context of global competition, environmental turbulence, delayered organizations, and new technologies.

Talent segmentation, the identification of employees who are critical to the success of the organization, is expected to become as important as customer segmentation.[7]

Furthermore, a succession management approach should not depend only on internal candidates, but should also track external candidates. Rather than rely on inbred internal managers, the new generation of succession managers tracks high performers in the external market, thus ensuring that new skills and ideas flow into the organization. Large companies such as IBM and AT&T have recruited over half their executives from outside the organization to obtain the skills that these megacompanies were unable to predict they would need or to develop internally. HR Planning Notebook 9.2 compares the advantages and disadvantages of internal and external candidates. However, it appears that when a company is doing well, internal candidates are favoured to sustain high performance because they possess valuable firm-specific knowledge.[8]

## Rating System

Traditional planning relied on the identification of the replacement people by a single rater. Previously, only the boss of the high-potential employee supplied information about that employee, and the information on which succession plans were based could be both out of date and unreliable. The gathering

---

### HR Planning Notebook 9.2

#### Internal versus External

**Advantages of Internal Candidates**

- Organizations have more and better information about internal candidates.
- Organizations that offer career development and opportunities to internal candidates increase commitment and retention among their employees.
- Internally developed leaders preserve corporate culture.
- Internal candidates can hit the road running, because they know the organization, its people, and its processes. Other employees know the internal candidate, and there is less internal disruption waiting to see who the new executive is and what changes he or she will make. Internally chosen executives do not replace those who

report to them as often as external candidates do; externally chosen candidates often get rid of the "old guard."
- Recruitment and selection costs are lower. For example, the replacement cost of a CEO is estimated to be $750,000, including the use of a search firm and lost opportunities getting the external candidate up to speed.

**Advantages of External Candidates**

- The external candidate may have better skills to lead the organization through a major transformation or change in strategy.
- The external candidate brings new knowledge and skills to the organization and prevents the organization from becoming inbred and stale.

## Comparison of Replacement Planning with Succession Management

| Factors | Planning | Management |
|---|---|---|
| Environment | Stable | Dynamic |
| Focus | Jobs | Strategy |
| Time frame | 6–12 months | 2+ years |
| Selection criteria | Job experience | Competencies |
| Appraiser | Immediate manager | 360° feedback |
| Selection pool | Internal | Internal and external |
| Successors | Slated individuals | Talent pools |
| Development | Limited | Flexible, multiple |

and recording of these judgments may have been seen as a personnel function, which incorporated little understanding of the real needs of the organization. Thus, managers may not have bought into the process.

In a succession management approach, several raters give current evaluations on an employee's performance. The increasing use of 360° degree feedback mechanisms sheds light on various aspects of any candidate's style and performance. HR Planning Notebook 9.3 compares replacement planning and succession management.

## Succession Management Process

The succession management process links replacement planning and management development. Until recently, in some organizations, succession planners worked with one database, management trainers with another. Now, both databases are integrated, with succession managers working in strategic planning committees, performance management groups, and organizational learning and training functions.

The succession management process is simple to understand but difficult to implement. The process involves five steps, each of which we will now consider in some detail.

### 1. Align Succession Management Plans with Strategy

Management development must be linked to business plans and strategies. If the business plan focuses on global markets, then managers have to be trained to manage global businesses. How does this translate into everyday skills? To build global talent, an organization could start by asking these questions: What are the specialized skills and perspectives necessary to compete globally? How many managers possess these skills? What percentage of employees could represent the firm to the world? How many could have an extended dinner with key international customers?[9]

The strategic connection is important, so organizations must start with the business plan. Coupled with environmental scanning, managers try to predict where the organization will be in three to five to ten years.

## 2. Identify the Skills and Competencies Needed to Meet Strategic Objectives

🅡🅟🅒 9.5

🅡🅟🅒 9.6

From the strategic plan, managers can then develop a list of the employee skills and competencies needed. There are at least two approaches to identifying the characteristics of successful managers: the job-based and the competency-based approaches.

**JOB-BASED APPROACH** The first impulse is to start with the job. We know that employees have jobs with duties and responsibilities (discussed in Chapter 4, Job Analysis). The job-based approach suggests that employees who have significant experience as managers and have acquired job skills such as motivating, delegating, marketing, or managing finances, will make successful managers. Additionally, organizations such as Procter & Gamble insist that their leaders understand the marketing of brand names.

Others suggest that this job-based approach to successors is not inadequate because jobs change rapidly. Furthermore, the increase in knowledge work has led many organizations to search for a different approach to employee development, particularly for those employees at the managerial level. Therefore, many organizations are turning to a competency-based approach in which the capabilities of individuals are the primary focus.[10]

**COMPETENCY-BASED APPROACH** Competencies are groups of related behaviours that are needed for successful performance.[11] They are measurable attributes that differentiate successful employees from those who are not. These competencies are a collection of observable behaviours and can be "hard" or "soft." Hard competencies might be the ability to build new technologies. Soft competencies might be the ability to retain top talent. Given an uncertain future in which skill needs change rapidly, succession management should focus on the development of competencies.

Consulting firms are the perfect example of companies in which the skills and capabilities of individuals drive the business, and business opportunities drive the development of new capabilities. Thus a list of skills (rather than jobs or positions) forms the basis for succession management. Rather than moving *up* a career ladder, individuals move *through* a certification process, developing increasingly complex capabilities along the way. There may be several skill acquisition paths, rather than one sure path to the top.

### Managerial Competencies

*General mobility skills and knowledge:* These competencies facilitate re-employment and include effectiveness in group process, communication skills, and flexibility and adaptation.

*General managerial core competencies:* These competencies were identified by studying successful managers and include "being able to build a cohesive team" and "being able to persuade employees to accept much needed organizational changes."

*Detailed, job-specific competencies:* Job-specific competencies vary by function, but in HR would include "the ability to implement a change program" and to "identify the best selection tool to identify high-potential candidates." These abilities would vary by level, with a junior manager mastering the ability to identify performance gaps in a subordinate and a senior manager being able to initiate change programs to improve performance.

Source: Adapted from E.H. Burach, W. Hochwarter, and N.J. Mathys, "The New Management Development Paradigm," *Human Resource Planning*, Vol. 20, No. 1 (2000), 14–21.

A good place to start preparing a list of competencies is to look at what experts have said about the competencies of successful managers. Many lists are available that outline the kinds of generic skills and competencies managers should possess. HR Planning Notebook 9.4 presents a list of these characteristics.

The skills managers need to possess are endless, and each "expert" develops a preferred list. These lists could be used as a starting point and then be customized to identify and develop managers in any organization. By emphasizing competencies rather than job skills, individuals will be more flexible in adapting to changing organizational needs. ("Skills" and "competencies" are terms that are often used interchangeably. However, skills are narrower and refer more specifically to skills for one job; competencies are broader and can be applied to many jobs at many levels. For example, proficiency in PowerPoint and installing Windows are skills; the ability to think creatively and work in teams are competencies.) Catano and his colleagues provide a full discussion of competencies; they distinguish between several types:

- *Core competencies*—characteristics, such as thinking skills, that every member of the organization is expected to possess.
- *Role or specific competencies*—characteristics, such as business knowledge, shared by different positions within an organization.
- *Unique or distinctive competencies*—characteristics, such as expertise in media relations, that apply only to specific positions within an organization.[12]

**RPC 9.7**

**RPC 9.8**

### 3. Identify High-Potential Employees

Once we know what competencies are needed, we can turn to the identification of employees who might ultimately acquire these sets. Regularly scheduled discussions about succession force the leaders of the organization to think about the future of the business and the kinds of employee skills needed to facilitate the chosen strategy. By concerning themselves with the future directions of the organization, executives focus on the managers who will guide that future. The performance appraisal process becomes meaningful and not just another personnel form to complete. Executives come to "own" the succession and development plans because they are integral to the success of the organization.

In HR, we often state that the best predictor of future performance is past performance. Executives must be able to move beyond descriptions of high-potential employees that use descriptions such as "She is very bright and very strategic" and "He has the support of his team" to listing specific achievements.[13]

Organizations use several approaches to identify managerial talent, including the following:[14]

1. *Temporary replacements:* At the most primitive level, most individual managers will have identified a designated backup and potential successor. This is done in case the manager is away from the office for extended periods (e.g., vacations, training). A manager who fails to pick a successor may never be promoted as no replacements would be ready to succeed him or her.

2. *Replacement charts:* At the next level, some organizations prepare replacement charts with predicted departure dates of the incumbents, along with a shortlist of possible successors. This is usually done around performance appraisal time, using the performance evaluation data. Typically, a handful of senior executives targets a diverse list of employees for growth and creates annual development plans. These executives stay in touch with each individual assigned to them and become responsible for the development of the leadership competencies of those individuals. The list identifies those candidates who are ready now, those who will be ready in three to five years, and the long shots. These approaches tend to replicate current strengths (and weaknesses) and are not necessarily future oriented, nor are they strategically aligned with the needs of the business. This stair-step approach is too rigid during times when organizational structures are changing rapidly and employee loyalty is weak.

3. *Strategic replacement:* A more advanced succession management program exists in an organization that is less inclined simply to replicate existing incumbents but instead identifies the leadership competencies it needs, based on organizational plans. The organization then tries to support and train these managers from within. The identification of high-potential people moves beyond the evaluations conducted by one or two managers. The Public Service Commission of Canada, for example, uses a formal assessment centre to identify those public servants who will become the future executives in the federal public service. Wary of evaluations done by only one individual with one perspective on employee performance, many organizations are moving to a 360° evaluation. For many employees, such an evaluation is the first time they have received feedback on how others perceive them. Some employees likened the experience to holding up a mirror,

others to a breath of fresh air.[15] Employees who had undergone 360°
feedback reported that they felt their peers often knew better than
their managers how to improve the employees' performance.

All these systems favour the selection of internal candidates. As
such, these systems have a motivating impact on employee performance. However, they are limited in their ability to introduce new ways
of thinking and working, and may not suit the strategic direction of
the organization. In the next approach, the managers more actively
scan the environment to identify and retain top talent.

4. *Talent management culture:* Many organizations, whose CEOs lie awake
   at nights worrying about their ability to find and keep top talent, have
   adopted a talent management culture.[16] The winners in the war for
   talent have developed a talent mindset—that is, they believe that
   talent matters and it must be developed not only at the top level, but
   also at all levels. Managers are committed to define and model an
   employee value proposition that answers the question "Why would a
   talented person want to work here?" The employee "brand" is managed as much as the company brand. See HR Planning Today 9.3 for
   a discussion of brand positioning to attract and retain employees.
   Managers actively scan the environment (e.g., for the actions of their
   competitors or the actions of the world's best industry leaders in other
   areas with overlapping functions, such as finance or logistics) looking
   for external talent. They have developed both internal and external
   lists of high-potential candidates.

   Recruitment is opportunistic—that is, when a top candidate is found, that
person is hired regardless of whether there is a vacancy. For example, MDS, a
medical supply company, is so interested in securing talent that it will hire

---

### HR Planning Today 9.3

#### Building the Brand: An Employee Value Proposition

Some companies develop an employee value proposition
(EVP) that will help attract and retain employees. They
base this EVP on concepts that they have learned in customer attraction and retention. An EVP is a brand positioning aimed at employees so that the company will be
seen as an employer worth working for, and all company
messages sent to the labour market are compelling and
consistent. The external brand of Southwest Airlines is
"Freedom to Fly," and their employee brand is "Freedom
begins with me"—freedom to learn, to be financially

secure. Key candidates seem to be attracted to companies that pose one of four brand positions:

- a "winning" company, which is characterized by
  growth and development
- a "big risk, big reward" company, which offers great
  potential for advancement and compensation
- a "save the world" organization, which is attractive
  to those wanting a mission
- a "lifestyle" company, where employees want flexibility and a good relationship with the boss

Source: S. Cliffe, "Winning the War for Talent," *Harvard Business Review*, Vol. 76, No. 5 (September/October, 1998), 18–19; S. Hood, "The PR
of HR," *HR Professional* (February/March 2001), 17–21.

---

even when there is not a position open, and make that person an "executive-in-residence" and give him or her a special project to manage until a vacancy arises.[17] As David Guptil, vice-president of HR Lafarge Canada, a large supplier of construction materials, states,

> What keeps me awake at night is my very thin bench strength. . . . We are resisting that temptation to scale back on strategic recruiting. And when I say strategic recruiting, what I mean is that you don't wait for a vacancy and the predicted retirees. I and our senior managers are always on the lookout for talent that may be available. If I find a very talented person . . . my freedom is to go out and hire that person whether we have a vacancy or not.[18]

The process of continually searching for talent is correlated with success. A McKinsey study found that nearly one-third of HR directors at top-performing companies constantly search for talented executives, compared to less than 10% at average-performing companies.[19] These talent management companies analyze turnover statistics and always include in their reports the reasons for the voluntary turnover. Managers, not HR, have the responsibility for identifying and cultivating talent.

Finally, some companies operate with all four approaches, using replacement planning for highly predictable jobs such as accounting, and talent management to deal with rapid changes in strategic needs.

Assessing employees to identify high-potential candidates must be done both fairly and accurately: fairly so that employees buy into the process and feel that the search for talent is an equitable procedure, and accurately so that the selection process is both reliable and valid. Organizations typically use the direct supervisor's informal judgments and formal evaluations such as performance appraisals and assessment centres. (More information can be found in the performance evaluation chapter of any introductory HRM text.) HR Planning Notebook 9.5 contains a brief description of common assessment methods. Usually about 10% of employees are identified as high potential. Syncrude Canada Ltd., an oil producer, with headquarters in Fort McMurray, Alberta, has identified about 8% of its 3600 employees as high potential.[20]

However, the use of annual reviews of talent can result in a mechanical approach leading to the goal of completing the forms provided by HR, rather than quality dialogues about leaders. Some managers simply update forms to meet a deadline. A better process would be to commit to quarterly reviews and the allocation of one full day to choose the top candidates by ranking them against all other candidates. Even these discussions can become politicized when

- Executives rate their own candidates too positively.
- People fear to criticize the choices of others.
- Members distrust the motivation of others' recommendations ("passing the trash").
- Running conflicts between executives result in cheap shots about candidates.
- Information about the best players is withheld as executives want to own this talent.

## Techniques for Assessing Employee Potential

*Performance appraisals:* Managers identify high-potential employees through performance appraisal systems. Raters, who may include the supervisor, colleagues, customers, and subordinates of an employee, evaluate the employee against some predeveloped standards. The goal is to identify and communicate the employee's performance strengths and weaknesses. The information is then used for developmental purposes, so that gaps in performance can be closed. High-potential employees are tracked in this way using a standardized organizational assessment tool. Managers are forced to identify high-potential employees through performance appraisal systems and may be rewarded for developing employees.

*Assessment centres:* Assessment centres involve a process by which candidates are evaluated as they participate in a series of exercises that closely resemble the situations faced on the job. Simulations include negotiating a merger, handling the press, managing interdepartmental conflicts, or making a decision without all the facts. Trained and experienced managers observe the candidates' behaviour during this process and

provide an evaluation of their competence and potential. The newest form of assessment centres is the Acceleration Centre, in which the first stop is a website where candidates can learn everything about the fictitious company they will manage for a day. All testing, correspondence, and decisions are completed online, enabling the assessors to compare candidates more objectively.

*HRMS:* Large amounts of information about employees' KSAs can be stored in databanks and used to identify employees with needed skills. Employee files can document their experiences, skills, abilities, and performance evaluations. Employees' interests and career objectives may also be recorded. Basic matching to identify high-potential candidates is simplified with an effective HRMS. A useful feature of an HRMS is its ability to construct scenarios. Planners can create "what-if?" models to determine the effect of employee movements.

The assessment of all employees may result in the segmentation of employees by their current performance and their potential performance, as show in Table 9.1.

TABLE 9.1

## Performance Potential Matrix

|  | LOWER POTENTIAL | HIGHER POTENTIAL |
| --- | --- | --- |
| Higher Performance | Sustain development in current roles | Continually provide challenges |
| Lower Performance | Improve performance or remove | Improve performance or change assignments |

Source: Reprinted with permission from HUMAN RESOURCE PLANNING, Vol. 25, Issue 3, 2002 by The Human Resource Planning Society, 317 Madison Avenue, Suite 1509 New York, NY 10017, Phone: (212) 490-6387, Fax: (212) 682-6851.

To minimize the politics involved in identifying talent, management should develop a set of principles such as "Talent is managed in the larger interests of the company. Managers are simply stewards of this talent, and company-wide interests prevail."[21]

## 4. Provide Developmental Opportunities and Experiences

**RPC** 9.10

Before we discuss the methods used to develop managers, we should first consider two issues:

- Are leaders born or made?
- Should organizations produce their own managerial talent or buy it on the open market?

**RPC** 9.11

*Born or made?* Many great leaders have had no formal management training. Shouldn't we just select leaders with the inherent qualities of leaders and not try to teach leadership skills?

**RPC** 9.12

**RPC** 9.13

Peter Drucker, considered by many to be the founder of management as a discipline, is credited with saying, "Most managers are made, not born. There has to be systematic work on the supply, the development, and the skills of tomorrow's management. It cannot be left to chance."[22]

*Buy or make?* Organizations invest many dollars and other resources to develop managers, but perhaps experienced, trained managers could simply be hired from other organizations.

Some organizations do prefer to pick up their needed executive talent by buying it on the open market. For example, Elliot Whale, president and CEO of Dylex Ltd., had been president of Toys R Us (Canada) Ltd. and director of player personnel for the Toronto Blue Jays baseball club before he moved to Dylex. Selecting outsiders allows companies to bring in fresh perspectives, people who can lead the organization through a transformation. By bringing in an outsider, the board of directors sends a strong message to employees and shareholders that the old way of doing things is going to change.[23] Other organizations feel strongly that they want to indoctrinate and train their own leaders, who then have a deep commitment to the organizational vision.

There are no easy answers to these questions. Organizations may find outstanding leaders by chance, or they may commit to the development process. Some may choose to hire from the outside to obtain fresh approaches; others will commit significant time and money to train their own managers. However, most large organizations have a policy of promotion from within. There are many advantages to this: the organization has accurate records of employees' past performance, and employees understand and are committed to organizational objectives, know the ropes, and know how to get things done. Another reason to recruit internally is that CEOs recruited from the outside delivered annual returns 3.7% lower than insiders.[24] Most large organizations have formal management development programs to ensure a ready supply of "promotables." Let us look at some of the methods such organizations use.

MANAGEMENT DEVELOPMENT METHODS In the succession management process, the focus in management development is on the development of competencies, not just on job preparation. Because the goal is to develop many skills that may be needed in an uncertain future (in contrast to simply

**RPC** 9.14

**RPC** 9.15

replicating the skills of the present incumbents), management is much more open to various approaches to develop the talent pool. More traditional approaches might have relied on a senior leadership course and one developmental assignment, perhaps mimicking exactly what the current CEO did. The key point is that the approach has changed from one of providing training to fill jobs to one of providing experiences to realize leadership potential. The most common development methods are promotions, job rotations, special assignments and action learning, formal training and development, and coaching and mentoring.

**promotion**

an employee's upward advancement in the hierarchy of an organization

*Promotions*  **Promotion** refers to an employee's upward advancement in the hierarchy of an organization and usually involves increased responsibilities and compensation. Traditional models of management development saw managers moving up a pyramid, managing larger and larger units until they reached their appointments at the top. Each organization had its favourite route to the top, some through sales, others through operations. These paths became worn over time, and few succeeded by using other paths, such as an HR track. However, this all changed in the mid-1970s, when the oil crisis made unlimited growth of the pyramid more difficult: the baby boomers were bunching up at the bottom; rough economic times delayered the pyramid, making it flatter; and the development of generalists became more popular, reducing the use of the few footpaths to the top.[25] One organization used a system of temporary rotations, resulting in a win-win combination. Senior executives nearing retirement were given the option of a week's vacation in every month, which they welcomed, and were replaced by high-potential employees who could try new leadership skills in a safe setting. In flat organizations, where promotions are rare, a preferred developmental method is job rotations—developing managers horizontally rather than vertically.

**job rotations**

a process whereby an employee's upward advancement in the hierarchy of an organization is achieved by lateral as well as vertical moves

*Job Rotations*  **Job rotations** are lateral transfers of employees between jobs in an organization. Rotations involve a change in job assignments but not necessarily more responsibility or money. For example, one way of orienting a new employee quickly is to place him or her in a new department every few weeks, thus providing the employee an overview of the organization. The CEO of Maritime Life Insurance believes that rotation is the best indicator of whether an employee is ready for a top position. To avoid costly placement decisions, staff with potential are placed in a variety of roles across the organization. Succeeding at rotation is a prerequisite for a top-level position.[26]

Rotations have several motivational benefits for employees, including the reduction of boredom and fatigue. Trying out new jobs also benefits employees who have reached a career plateau. The development of additional skills may increase an employee's job and career prospects. Almost all the research suggests that job rotation makes employees more satisfied, motivated, involved, and committed.[27]

From the organization's standpoint, rotations are useful for orientation and career development. Rotations allow an employee to increase his or her experience. A common use of job rotation is to take a functional specialist, such as an accountant, and rotate this specialist through both HR and operations in preparation for management positions. An information technology specialist, before a rotation in sales, might try to sell his idea to management by saying, "We have to invest in a multiprotocal router," and might be met with complete incomprehension. After a rotation through the sales department, the same specialist might sell the same program by explaining, "We're building an infrastructure so salespeople can get access to product or inventory information from anywhere." The technician has learned a business skill.[28] Jet Form, an Ottawa-based business with about 650 employees, uses cross-functional mobility as a key part of its strategic planning.[29] The results are encouraging, and employees are regularly rotated between functions to increase their knowledge and skills.

Besides the additional knowledge of the functional areas, such as sales, and management areas, such as business knowledge, the rotated employee is making contacts and establishing a network that might prove useful in the future. Learning new ways of doing things, with different co-workers and bosses, also might make employees more adaptable in their managerial jobs. The research shows that rotation improves an employee's knowledge of the organization (e.g., of business, strategy, and contacts) and improves his or her ability to cope with uncertainty. Furthermore, employees who have tried out several jobs gain a better insight into their own strengths and weaknesses. However, job rotation produces generalists and should be supplemented by training for any specific skills needed.

Of course, the downside of employee rotations includes the increased time needed to learn the new jobs, the cost of errors while learning, and the loss of efficiency that otherwise is gained through repetition and specialization.[30] In other words, workload may increase for the employee while productivity decreases and additional work and stress for other employees in efforts to socialize, orient, and train the newcomer.

At the managerial level, employers should be concerned about producing a short-term orientation in the organization's leadership ranks. Employees in six-month jobs may put their efforts into creating fast results, which might hurt the unit in the long term. For example, employees with a short-run focus may neglect plant safety in a rush to exceed production quotas. Furthermore, the rotation of managers places new expectations on performance, creates new goals, and results in reassignment of work, producing stress on the unit managed by rotation.[31]

One approach is to give an employee a number of assignments within the company or a related sector. For example, the president of Zellers (now merged with Kmart) has been president of Kmart, and worked at Zellers, Hudson's Bay Company (the parent company), and Woodward's.

Ultimately, managers may be better formed by developing skills horizontally, throughout an organization, rather than by developing specialized skills vertically, up a career ladder.

*Special Assignments* On-the-job learning is still a favoured path to the development of managerial skills. Most organizations test high-potential employees by giving them an assignment in addition to their regular duties.

Chapter 9: Succession Management

For example, the manager of corporate banking might be placed on a task force that is considering the acquisition of another bank. A manager who needs international experience might be sent to work in China with a vendor to the company. In another case, a team of managers might be given a special assignment, such as developing an equity plan for the organization or developing an e-commerce plan for the company. These types of special projects enable candidates for future executive positions to network and test their skills in new environments. Mistakes must be tolerated, as candidates may quickly assume that these special assignments are synonymous with failure, fostering a culture of fear where no employee dare be innovative or take bold measures, and finally, derailment from the fast track. Remember the story about the executive who is called into his boss's office expecting to be fired, because of a business decision that cost the company a million dollars. The CEO instead gives him another special assignment, reasoning, "Why should we fire you? We just invested $1 million in your development." Interviewers for executive positions routinely ask candidates about a difficult challenge or unsuccessful project. If the candidates indicate no failures, then the executive search firm concludes that the candidate is not open about these experiences, or he or she may not have the skills to handle an unsuccessful project in the next assignment. The best assignments are those that entail a high degree of risk and accountability, such as launching a new business, or turning around a struggling project. If these are coupled with decision-making authority and the opportunity to manage a large group of people, this is the recipe for producing effective executives.

*Formal Training and Development*   Management training and education is big business. Hundreds of thousands of dollars may be spent preparing one executive to become the CEO of the organization. This cost appears relatively minor when it is estimated that the total career investment in an individual employee is 160 times the initial starting salary.[32] In this book, we use the term "management development," but others label a similar process "executive education" or "leadership training" or a combination of any of these words.

**RPC 9.17**

According to a study of U.S. organizations, 87% offer management development programs that were designed, developed, and delivered in-house.[33] Only a small number use external vendors. The majority of companies use traditional and passive instructional techniques and rate them least effective, but they are fast and easy to use. Most use lectures, seminars, and discussion groups more often than behaviour modelling and experiential learning. (For a fuller discussion of these methods, see Saks and Haccoun, 2007, *Performance Management through Training and Development*, Toronto: Nelson Thomson.) Senior managers need the soft skills of delegation and motivation, rather than hard technical skills such as website development or benefits management. Thus we would recommend that role-playing, case studies, behaviour modelling, and action learning, which are effective techniques, be used as training methods for management development. In most cases, the effectiveness of the training method is evaluated by the "smile sheets"—course evaluation sheets in which participants rate the course and instructors—at the end of the program rather than the application of the learned skills on the job. Techniques for increasing the extent to which training is then applied to and endures in the performance of the job have been described by Belcourt and Saks.[34] Critics believe that these training programs teach very specific skills that might not be robust enough to stand the test of time and successfully prepare managers for rapidly changing environments.

Many companies prefer an educational approach that broadens intellectual skills such as the ability to analyze. These companies turn to universities to teach their executives conceptual skills, which would be useful in many situations. Others create their own training centres, which they label corporate universities.

U.S. organizations, more than 1000 of them, have begun opening corporate universities—available only to the employees—because these organizations view training as a lifelong process, rather than as discrete courses taken occasionally. Most of these universities focus on building competencies and skills that are aligned strategically to meet both employee and corporate needs. Individual corporate universities offer a wide range of courses, which together constitute something resembling a mini-MBA. Through case studies and action learning, the courses offer managers a chance to practise and receive feedback. Unlike professional athletes or musicians, managers seldom get a chance to practise their skills and try out new ideas and methods. Sometimes these corporate universities have mentors on staff, often with more than 20 years in the business, who coach and assist in the transfer of knowledge.

**RPC** 9.18

**RPC** 9.19

*Mentoring and Coaching*   Many very successful managers will explain that their success resulted directly from having been mentored; a senior executive took an interest in them and their careers at a critical time in their lives. **Mentors** are executives who coach, advise, and encourage junior employees. The mentor takes an active interest in the career advancement and the psychosocial development of the protégé. Career development aspects include examining approaches to assignments and learning how tasks should be handled, which conferences or networks have high career value, and which senior managers to emulate. Psychosocial considerations include building the self-confidence of the protégé, as well as offering counselling and friendship to make him or her aware of the political open doors and open pits of the organization. One company offers coaching to help high-potential candidates understand the executive derailers—those personality traits that might cause an otherwise effective executive to fail (such as arrogance, micromanagement, risk aversion, volatility, and low tolerance for ambiguity).[35]

**mentors**

executives who coach, advise, and encourage junior employees

Mentoring used to happen informally, but organizations have recognized the value of having a senior manager take a career interest in a junior employee and so have started formal mentoring programs. One survey showed that 70% of highly productive organizations have mentoring programs, and employees in these programs report greater career satisfaction and experience faster career growth.[36] These programs link executives who have the motivation and time to nurture managerial talent with employees who are motivated to advance quickly. Two-thirds of the top-performing companies provide high-potential employees with frequent access to the CEO, and

## HR Planning Notebook 9.6

### Benefits of External Coaches

**For the organization**

- Retain high performers with incentives other than financial rewards.
- Develop key employees for succession planning.
- Guide individuals and organizations through transition.
- Change skills and attitudes for long-term sustainable results.
- Give new perspectives on business experience and practices.

**For the individual**

- Reconnect the individual with personal values or missions.
- Provide clarity and focus to accelerate the achievement of goals.
- Compress learning time to optimize skills by building competencies faster through one-on-one coaching.
- Translate leadership theories and concepts into "useful insights" to affect communication, decision making, and overall strategies.

Sources: Adapted from L. Hyatt, "Best Practices for Developing Great Leaders," *Workplace Today* (January 2003), 14–17; G. Voisin, "When to Use an Internal or External Coach," *HR Professional* (June/July 2001), 30–33.

opportunities to interact on projects with senior managers.[37] Mentors are almost always more senior people who volunteer within an organization, while coaches tend to be paid counsellors from outside the organization. The advantages of external coaches are described in HR Planning Notebook 9.6.

While it is necessary for discussion purposes to separate management development methods, all companies will use a combination of methods. Some focus on formal programs, such as a three-week leadership course followed by an assignment in a foreign country. Other companies, such as 3M, allow their employees to choose assignments and to work on ad hoc committees to manage new projects, as well as giving them free time to tinker and play with ideas. Cisco, a leader in hardware and software technology, uses the 3E Model: 70% of development occurs through Experience (assignments, rotations, special projects); 20% through Exposure (feedback, mentoring, and shadowing) and 10% through Education (readings, e-learning, and courses).[38] The choice of a method depends on the employee's learning style and the goals to be achieved. Learning about foreign cultures is best done by spending time in a foreign office or with representatives from overseas, not from a book; nor is shadowing an IT employee the best way to learn about IT.

Some companies following these processes but press the fast-forward button for candidates to intentionally accelerate their development. These candidates are part of an acceleration pool and

- obtain assignments that offer the most intense learning and high visibility,
- spend less time in assignments,
- are given stretch assignments,

- receive more training,
- are given developmental activities designed especially for them,
- are assigned a mentor, but
- are not guaranteed promotion.[39]

Companies that do this well are called "academy companies"—a kind of executive-finishing school—known for breeding the best leaders. In Canada, these incubators are PepsiCo, IBM Corp, General Electric, Maple Leaf Foods, EnCana Corp, Petro Canada, and Manulife Financial Corp.[40] Headhunters go to these companies to poach new leadership blood. Does this mean that companies risk losing leaders if they invest in them? Not necessarily, according to research by Canadian professors Jack Ito and Celeste Brotheridge, who concluded that supervisory support for career development strengthens employee's intentions to stay.[41] Generally, providing opportunities to grow and develop new skills are seen as a good retention tool.

Another reason for using different methods is that the development of a senior executive may take 25 years. It is unusual to see a vice-president of a large company who is younger than 40 years old. So some companies, such as Wal-Mart, start early, grooming the store managers under a mentoring system to take on more and more responsibility.

## 5. Monitor Succession Management

**RPC 9.20**

Some succession plans are placed on an executive's top shelf, ready to be dusted off to prepare for the annual discussion. In no way do they form part of a strategic plan, nor are they used to guide employee development. To measure the effectiveness of succession management, succession planners used to count the number of predicted "high-potential replacements" with the actual number of those placed in the position. However, If the needs of the business change dramatically, this may be a poor way of measuring.

Nevertheless, there are internal ways to judge if a succession management program is successful, and include HR metrics such as

- average number of candidates for key positions,
- average number of positions having no identified successors,
- percentage of managers with replacement plans,
- percentage of key positions filled according to plans,
- ratio of internal hires to external hires in key positions,
- retention rates of key talent,
- percentage of positive job evaluations after promotion,
- assessment of the quality of preparedness for new roles, and
- assessment of bosses as talent developers.[42]

However, one study found that the single most important driver of an effective plan was that the executive team modelled the behaviour, believed in it, and held managers accountable (in performance reviews and bonuses) for developing employees. Top-performing companies allocate 20% of executive incentives to leadership development and assess them on the ability to retain this talent.[43]

One expert asked, "If this process worked perfectly and everything happened the way it was supposed to happen, what would the results look like?"[44] The answer? Employees would receive regular feedback based on the assessment process and would participate in development plans. The best result would be an organization with skilled employees prepared to contribute to the goals of the organization under changing conditions. Organizations measure their success not only by the percentage of positions filled by designated high-potential employees, but also by attitude surveys of these employees, and exit interviews if these "hi-pots" leave the organization. The word "success" in succession is illuminating, in that studies are starting to show that corporations with strong succession management programs are higher performers measured by revenue growth, profitability, and market share.[45]

Another international study surveyed thousands of leaders, employees, and HR staff from 117 organizations in 14 countries and identified the following characteristics as critical to perceptions of succession management effectiveness:

- a timeframe for achieving planned action,
- flexible adjustments to changes in strategic plans,
- the sharing of information about the nomination process performance and rankings with identified candidates,
- visible support from top management, and
- the involvement of line management in the identification and development of candidates.[46]

Until this point, we have examined succession management from the organizational perspective. No consideration has been given to the employee's perspective.

 **9.21**

**EMPLOYEE ROLE IN SUCCESSION MANAGEMENT**   A top-down, organization-directed approach to succession management assumes that employees are ready and willing to be prepared for the next generation of leadership. A top-down approach treats employees as pieces in a chess game. But employees are not pawns; their voices need to be heard.

The first consideration is that an employee's relationship with any organization is not permanent. The employee can quit, or the employer can terminate him or her. Today's new employment contract does not guarantee jobs to anyone, even to those performing competently. The former contract was built on an implied promise of a long-term, mutually satisfying relationship. However, market forces create turbulence that sometimes causes companies to restructure or fail. These changes have resulted in a change in the psychological contract that an employee has with the employer. The traditional employment contract with the organization was built on an implicit understanding that the employee would work hard, develop additional skills provided mainly by the employer, and, in return, would be promoted on a regular basis. At a minimum, the employer would reward the loyalty and

### Comparing Traditional and Emerging Career Management Concepts

| Characteristics | Traditional | Emerging |
| --- | --- | --- |
| Employment contract | Implicit | Explicit |
| Duration | Long term | Useful term |
| Career responsibility | Employer | Self-directed |
| Career identity | Organization | Profession/occupation |
| Benefits | Focus on security | Focus on experience |
| Loyalty | To the organization | Profession, friends, family |
| Mindset | Inward, political | Outward, entrepreneurial |
| Development | Formal training | Work experiences |
| Career progression | Vertical | Horizontal |
| Employment stability | Job security | Employability |
| Role of manager | Control/coordination | Coach |
| Career goal | Corporate success | Meaningful contributions |

Source: Adapted from D. Hall and J.E. Moss, "The New Protean Career Contract: Helping Organizations and Employees Adapt," *Organization Dynamics* (Winter 1988), 22–37. Craig, E.F and D.T. Hall, "The New Organizational Career: Too Important to Be Left to HR?" *Reinventing HRM: Challenges and New Directions,* R.J. Burke and C.L. Cooper, eds. Routledge, New York, 2005.

efforts of employees with job security. This contract is dead. Today's career model may be perceived as a transactional one in which benefits and contributions are exchanged for a short period.[47]

The new contract, transactional in nature, lists the responsibilities and rights of each party in the employer–employee relationship, and employees want this contract stated explicitly in writing. If loyalty to any organization still exists, it is to the professional organization, to a network of peers and to certifiable credibility that confers collegiality and respect. HR Planning Notebook 9.7 contains a comparison of the two concepts of career management.

This transactional view of employer–employee relationships suggests that, as organizations develop employees, they must take into consideration employee aspirations and goals. Employees will participate in management development programs more eagerly if their goals match the succession plans of the company. Employees will enthusiastically engage in self-development if they are aware of the strategic goals of a company, thus enhancing their own job security or marketability. If, for example, employees of *The Globe and Mail* knew that the company was changing from a newspaper publishing business to an international information marketing business, employees would likely undertake, on their own time and at their own expense, to study languages or marketing. Managerial preferences cannot be the sole determinant in employee development. Career counselling and discussions at performance appraisal time will help ensure that the employee's voice is heard. While organizations cannot promise lifetime employment, competition for leadership talent is so intense that high-potential employees must be given a reason to stay with an organization.

An added benefit of listening to employees is the opportunity to customize the development plan. Employees are very aware of their strengths and weaknesses and their preferred learning styles. One employee might suggest that she could learn decision making by being given a leadership role; another might prefer a seminar on decision making. Some organizations, such as Ford Financial, which has 20 000 employees around the world, provide information to employees that enables them to make their own career plans. Ford Financial has a sophisticated skill- and competency-based learning program with direct links to the company's three core businesses and job requirements. Employees can determine the skills and competencies needed for any job within the organization, then undertake a self-development plan to master any of the 15 knowledge domains, 80 functional areas, and 800 separate skills.[48]

By creating a process that invites employee participation, succession managers are more likely to gain employee commitment to and ownership of the plans. We turn now to a discussion of the limitations of succession management.

## 🅡🅟🅒 9.22     Succession Management's Soft Spots

So far, we have discussed the many benefits of succession management and introduced a way to manage succession effectively. However, there are challenges to the implementation of a succession management program; these include the creation of an elite corps of employees, the managerial risk encountered in spotlighting the best employees, the perennial problem of selection bias, and, finally, the very human inability to predict the future.

### Elitism

Management development programs, particularly if they support the training of selected employees for specific senior positions, may lead to the perception that there is an elite group on the one hand and the "unwashed masses" on the other. There are several advantages to preparing a limited number—a select group of the elite—including the reduced costs of training. However, many managers fear that by publicly identifying those who will be promoted, a cadre of "crown princes" will be created. Those who are on the list (and expect to be the next vice-president) may coast in their careers, as they know that their contribution has already been recognized and the reward is in the near future. The organization, too, may relax and not invest sufficiently in the further development of these promotable employees, thus increasing the risk that their competencies and motivation will decline. A bigger problem will occur (and it happens frequently) when the star on the chart is not chosen to be the successor. At that point, the person who expected to be the "winner" feels publicly humiliated and will either leave the organization or not fully support the new candidate. Sometimes, things do not happen as quickly as first expected. As Prince Charles, another crown prince, will testify, sometimes the head never dies or departs, leaving the heir apparent to wait forever.

Employees can be "demotivated" by succession planning in several ways. The attitudes of the elite may create discontent among other employees with uncertain futures. Suppose the successors were identified on organizational charts and these charts were made public. Those not on the successors' list may consider leaving the organization for another where their career prospects are brighter. Managers may ignore the development of other employees who, with some training and assignments, would become likely contenders.

These disadvantages—the demotivating effects on those not chosen, and the disappointment and withdrawal if the employee's succession plans are not realized—have resulted in about one-third of companies not telling employees that they are on a fast track.[49]

At MDS, many of the high-potential employees are not aware of being tracked, because "we do not want to create a culture in which some people feel they are special and others feel their potential is not being recognized."[50]

By not telling employees this, companies risk having employees leave the organization for one that offers better opportunities, and they also risk having to groom someone who may not want the job. (However, most employees realize their special status through the frequency of their promotions, assignments, and training.) Employers must avoid promises such as "you will become CEO in five years"; such promises are an implicit contract that may be judged to be binding.

Does identifying many successors solve these problems? Surely competition between successors will ensure that the best candidate wins by trying harder and demanding better training. Furthermore, if one successor does not develop to the potential that was anticipated or quits the organization, then others are willing and ready. But this approach has problems too. One is that candidates might sabotage each other by not sharing important information or by raiding key employees to improve their own track records. As well, many might engage in managing impressions and performing for short-term results in order to be evaluated more highly. This strategy does not encourage team playing, which is a force in organizational culture.

There is no easy solution to these problems. At NCR, the management development plan is labelled Project 64K because it is meant for all 64 000 employees, not an elite group. At Johnson & Johnson, the focus is on the top 700 managers.[51]

The key is to communicate to these star employees that they are valued, and that they have leadership potential, without ever promising anything.

## Risk of the Spotlight

Another problem with succession management is that executives may be reluctant to shine the spotlight on their most talented employees. Such executives may fear that if they identify their top performers, other units will grab

**RPC** 9.23

these talented employees, necessitating the onerous task of finding and developing other talented employees. On the other hand, managers may fear that by developing their own replacements they will be replaced sooner than desired. However, managers have to know that this talent represents an organizational resource, not a departmental hidden asset. An effective succession program would force managers to identify backfill candidates (workers who can act as replacements, or those in the succession line). Ask these managers, "Who can do your job?" If they are unable to provide names, then ask, "What can I expect to be different next year?" This question leads to a developmental action plan.[52] A manager who does not identify and develop talent is like a high school coach who plays the most senior players to win this year's game with no thought of winning games in the years that follow.

Highly developed professionals and managers make good recruitment targets for competitors, suppliers, and even customer organizations. Increased attrition is a risk, especially if the job offers are attractive. Should companies not develop employees and thereby avoid this risk? The riskier proposition might be to not develop managers and then be unable to find them on the open labour market when the company badly needs their skills.

## Selection Bias

Asking senior executives to determine the high potentials ("hi pos") poses three problems: (1) the criteria for selection is not clear; (2) evaluation strategies may vary by department; and (3) rating errors, such as those of recency, contrast, and leniency or strictness, can occur. Leaving the identification and development of the next generation of managers in the hands of the current one often leads to a "similar-to-me" selection bias. Unfortunately, managers have a tendency to select as their successors those who seem similar to themselves and who work in styles that are comfortable: the heirs apparent fit in; they look like the rest of the family members. Despite decades of employment equity, most key executives-in-waiting are white males.

## Unpredictable Futures

Organizational careers are no longer guaranteed, if indeed they ever were. However, there seems to be a greater state of uncertainty and chaos today, and even those who have given exemplary service are subject to layoffs and job loss.

Organizational executives are not psychic; they cannot predict the future accurately. There is a tendency to clone the incumbent executives and to plan the future as a continuation of the present. But as Wayne Gretzky says, "Pass the puck not to where the player is, but to where he is going to be."[53] This is the challenge for organizations—determining where the play is going to be. High potential is very different from high performance, and just as executives cannot predict the future, they cannot predict accurately the future performance of the high-potential employees under changing conditions.

These kinds of problems may be the reason that only 40% of companies surveyed had a formal succession plan.[54] After a decade of restructuring, many organizations saw no point in planning for the future when survival and downsizing occupied all their thoughts. Now that growth is a primary objective for many companies, succession management is increasingly on the agenda.

## Summary

In this chapter, we defined succession management and contrasted it with personnel planning. The five-step model of effective succession management includes these steps: (1) align succession management plans with strategy; (2) identify the skills and competencies needed to meet strategic objectives; (3) identify high-potential employees; (4) provide developmental opportunities and experiences through promotions, job rotations, special assignments, formal training and development, and mentoring and coaching; and (5) monitor succession management. The employee's role in the process must be considered. The limitations of the succession management process include the creation of an elite corps of employees, the managerial risk incurred by spotlighting the best employees, the possibility of selection bias, and the difficulty of predicting the future.

## Key Terms

job rotations, 238

mentors, 241

promotion, 238

replacement planning, 226

succession management, 224

## Web Links

A succession management process guide by the province of Nova Scotia:

**www.gov.ns.ca/psc/pdf/InnovationGrowth/SuccessionManagement.pdf**
(p. 230)

Insights on job rotation and job rotations trends in Canada:

**www.jobquality.ca/indicator_e/des001.stm** (p. 238)

Alberta Government Succession Management Framework:

**www.pao.gov.ab.ca/learning/framework/framework.html** (p. 244)

## RPC Icons

**RPC 9.1 Assesses the contribution of OD [organizational development] initiatives to the performance of the unit or organization**

**RPC 9.2 Forecasts HR supply and demand conditions**

**RPC 9.3 Contributes to improvements in the organization's structures and work processes**

**RPC 9.4 Leads in the development of HR initiatives that support the organization's strategic directions**

RPC 9.5 Sets clear goals and objectives for the HR activities of the organization; maintains evaluation measurements of all HR activities against goals and objectives of the organization

RPC 9.6 Identifies the data required to support HR planning

RPC 9.7 Collects data, analyzes and reviews the organization's existing HR programs to ensure they are consistent with business activities

RPC 9.8 Identifies potential source of qualified candidates

RPC 9.9 Evaluates the total compensation strategy to ensure it is consistent with the objectives of attracting, motivating, and retaining the qualified people required to meet organizational goals

RPC 9.10 Coordinates the implementation of HR and succession plans

RPC 9.11 Develops processes to engage employees in achieving the objectives of the organization

RPC 9.12 Ensures performance feedback is an integral part of the organization's HR information system

RPC 9.13 Interprets HR information to meet the needs of the organization (e.g., labour costing, succession planning, legislated reporting requirements, reorganization planning, and training priorities)

RPC 9.14 Determines the best learning approaches and human capital development initiatives required for continued organizational success

RPC 9.15 Provides development information, support activities and procedures for learners, supervisors, and managers to assist in achieving performance improvement (e.g., training, coaching, feedback, and techniques for setting objectives)

RPC 9.16 Applies business fundamentals of production, operations management, finance, information technology, marketing, and strategic planning to people management issue

RPC 9.17 Evaluates the effectiveness of HR strategies using various measurement, assessment, and accountability approaches

RPC 9.18 Provides performance feedback, coaching, and career development to teams and individuals to maximize their probability of success

RPC 9.19 Develops, implements, and monitors the success of performance feedback and coaching

RPC 9.20 Applies measurement, evaluation, and assessment processes to business situations

RPC 9.21 Defines and establishes appropriate terms and conditions of employment to meet organizational goals

RPC 9.22 Promotes a productive culture in the organization that values diversity, trust, and respect for individuals and their contributions

# Discussion Questions

1. Well Point Health Networks meets the health care needs of more than 50 million members through subsidiaries such as Blue Cross and Healthlink. Its Human Resources Planning System (HRPS) won the Optimas Award in 2002 for its succession plan. Read why WellPoint was so successful in the article by P.J. Kiger, "Succession Planning Keeps WellPoint Competitive," *Workforce*, Vol. 81, No. 4, April 2002, pages 50–54. Compare WellPoint's system to the model presented in this chapter.
2. Do you plan to align your career goals and developmental experiences with your employer's goals and needs? If so, how will you do this? If not, why not?
3. This chapter has focused only on managers, implying that they are the key talent that needs to be managed. However, there are people who believe that the organization's most critical employees are not those who make the highest salary, but those who have the most impact on the customer: the couriers at FedEx, and the street sweepers at Disney World. Describe why these people should be considered key talent, and what succession management plans could be used for them.

# Using the Internet

The governments of Alberta and Nova Scotia have website lists that outline their succession management programs. See

**www.pao.gov.ab.ca/learning/framework/framework.html**

and

**www.gov.ns.ca/psc/pdf/innovationgrowth/successionmanagement.pdf**

Compare these programs against the principles outlined in this chapter. What differences are there? As a consultant, what would you advise the program managers to do differently?

# Exercise

Consider the following three scenarios:

1. Lee Ki Chung managed all the operating systems for 8 Star Manufacturing Company. Always reliable and never absent, Lee was indispensable. One day, Lee phoned to say that he had been diagnosed with cancer, had to enter treatment immediately, and did not know when he would return to the office.

2. The president of Overseas Banking Corporation, the second largest bank in the country, had chosen as his successor the vice-president of Finance. However, as the president's retirement date approached, he began to worry that this star employee could no longer handle the stress and long hours of banking. The VP was absent for extended periods as he tried to deal with his son, who was a drug addict, which in turn caused problems in his marriage.
3. Hi Tech Corp is a company created by the next generation of Bill Gates clones. They had succeeded in attracting the best and the brightest to help them build a billion-dollar company to develop the ultimate software applications. On Tuesday, October 10, the entire design team announced they were quitting to start a rival company and recapture that entrepreneurial culture of the early years.

Could succession management have mitigated the impact on the organization of any of these situations? How could succession management mitigate the seriousness of the consequences?

# Case: Acceleration Pools at PepsiCo

PepsiCo is a world leader in convenient foods and beverages, with revenues of about $27 billion and over 143 000 employees. The company consists of the snack businesses of Frito-Lay North America and Frito-Lay International; the beverage businesses of Pepsi-Cola North America, Gatorade/Tropicana North America, and PepsiCo Beverages International; and Quaker Foods North America, manufacturer and marketer of ready-to-eat cereals and other food products. PepsiCo brands are available in nearly 200 countries and territories.

PepsiCo replaced its traditional personnel planning model with a system to groom high-potential employees for organizational levels, not jobs. PepsiCo found that 25 000 hours a year were spent discussing replacement plans and filling out forms. There was little return on this investment of executive time, so changes were needed. Under the new system, employees were no longer handpicked as replacements for specific positions. Talent pools by both level and business unit have been created. For example, there might be a supervisory/professional level pool and a plant management pool. Once pool members are targeted, their development needs are diagnosed in a number of ways: through use of an acceleration centre, 360°-feedback instruments, and interviews. Their skills are assessed in four areas:

- organization knowledge (what the employee knows about functions, processes, products, etc.);
- job challenges (what the employee has done, such as preparing a budget);
- competencies (what the employee is capable of based on his or her knowledge, behaviour, technical skills, and motivations important to senior management such as change leadership); and
- executive derailers (the personality traits that might cause failure, such as arrogance or low tolerance for ambiguity).

Those in the talent pool are given difficult assignments and are assigned to task forces, two methods that offer the best opportunities for intensive learning and the highest visibility. Each candidate is assigned a mentor and receives training, coaching, and developmental opportunities such as university executive education programs.

The Executive Resource Board (made up of the CEO/COO and senior line managers) is responsible for the pool and meets twice a year to review talent development; they then meet with the candidate, the manager, and the mentor. Discussions might focus on how to gain a new skill or effectively deal with a derailer. The focus is on measurable results, not just the process. Thus, a candidate who attended a training program is not given credit for taking the course, until there is proof of changes made as a result of the program. Each candidate creates and maintains a Career Development Portfolio, which includes a current CV, completed appraisal forms, and a development plan with progress reports. This portfolio is accessible by the Executive Resource Board.

Sources: "A New Look at Succession Management," by William C. Byham, Reprint #9B02TC03, *Ivey Business Journal*, May/June 2002, Vol. 66, No. 5, pp. 10–12. Copyright© 2002 Ivey Management Services Inc.; www.pepsico.com.

## Question

Analyze the effectiveness of PepsiCo's succession management program. Include in your report the strengths and weaknesses of the model and suggestions for increasing its effectiveness.

# Endnotes

1. Immen, W. 2005. "Rising Stars Get a Chance to Shine," *The Globe and Mail* (November 16), C1, C3.
2. Drucker, P. 1998. "Management's New Paradigms," *Forbes* (October 5): 152–177.
3. Willins, R., and W. Byham. 2001. "The Leadership Gap," *Training*, Vol. 38, No. 3 (March): 98–106.
4. Leibman, M., R. Bruer, and B.R. Maki. 1996. "Succession Management: The Next Generation of Succession Planning," *Human Resources Planning*, Vol. 19, No. 3: 16–29.
5. Byham, W.C. 2002. "A New Look at Succession Management," *Ivey Business Journal*, Vol. 66, No. 5 (May/June): 10–12.
6. Corporate Leadership Council, 2003. *Hallmarks of Leadership Success: Strategies for Improving Leadership Quality and Executive Readiness*, Corporate Executive Board, New York.
7. Boudreau, J.W., and P.M. Ramstead 2005. "Talentship, Talent Segmentation, and Sustainability: A New HR Decision-Science Paradigm for a New Strategy Definition," *Human Resource Management*, Summer, Vol. 44, No. 2, pp. 129–136.
8. Hoskisson, R.E., M.A. Hitt, and R.D Ireland, 2004. *Competing for Advantage*. Mason, OH: Thomson South-Western.
9. Eichlinger, B., and D. Ulrich. 1996. "Are You Future Agile?" *Human Resource Planning*, Vol. 11, No. 2: 30–41.
10. Lawler, E.E. III. 1994. "From Job-Based to Competency-Based Organizations," *Journal of Organizational Behaviour*, Vol. 15: 3–15.
11. Catano, V. M., S.F. Cronshaw, W.H. Wiesner, R.D. Hackett, and L.L. Methot. 2005. *Recruitment and Selection in Canada*, 3rd ed. Toronto: ITP Nelson.
12. Catano et al., 2005.

13. Kessler, G.C. 2002. "Why the Leadership Bench Never Gets Deeper: Ten Insights About Executive Talent Development," *Human Resources Planning*, Vol. 25, Iss. 1, 32–45.

14. Joinson, C. 1998. "Developing a Strong Bench," *HRM Magazine* (January): 92–96.

15. Lenz, S.S., and S. Wacker. 1997. "Career Development in an Uncertain World," Unpublished paper presented at the Human Resource Planning Society Symposium, Ithaca, New York.

16. Gore, N. 2000. "Managing Talent Replaces Static Charts in a New Era of Succession Planning," *Canadian HR Reporter*, Vol. 13, No. 15 (September 11): 12.

17. Immen, 2005.

18. Guptil, D. 2003. "HR Leaders Talk," *Canadian HR Reporter* (February 10): 16.

19. Yancey, G.B. 2001. "Succession Planning Creates Quality Leadership," *Credit Union Executive Journal*, Vol. 41, No. 6 (November/December): 24–27.

20. Newell, E. 2001. "CEO's Talk," *Canadian HR Reporter*, Vol. 14, No. 17 (October 8).

21. Kessler, 2002, 34.

22. Walter, G. 1996. "Corporate Practices in Management Development," *Conference Board*, Report No. 1158-96-RR. New York: Conference Board Inc., 89.

23. Church, E. 1998. "New-Style CEOs Follow Zig-Zag Path," *The Globe and Mail* (February 20), B23.

24. Gagne, C. 2004. "Get Good Help," *Canadian Business*, Vol. 77, Iss. 14/15, 71–72.

25. Pieperl, M., and Y. Baruch. 1997. "Back to Zero: The Post-Corporate Career," *Organizational Dynamics* (Spring): 7–22.

26. Black, B. 2002. "CEO's Talk." *Canadian HR Reporter* (October 7): 17.

27. Campion, M.A., L. Cheraskin, and M.J. Stevens. 1994. "Career-Related Antecedents and Outcomes of Job Rotation," *Academy of Management Journal*, Vol. 37, No. 6 (December): 1518–1525.

28. Horwitt, L. 1997. "It's Your Career: Manage It," *Network World* (March 17): 39–43.

29. Francis, K. 2001. "CEO's Talk," *Canadian HR Reporter*, Vol. 14, No. 11 (June 4): 17.

30. Horwitt, 1997.

31. Chereskin, L., and M.A. Campion. 1996. "Study Clarifies Job Rotation Benefits," *Personnel Journal* (November): 31–38.

32. Dahl, H.L. 1997. "Human Resource Cost and Benefit Analysis: New Power for Human Resource Approaches," *Human Resource Planning*, Vol. 11, No. 2: 69–78.

33. Walter, 1996.

34. Belcourt, M., and A.M. Saks. 1998. "Benchmarking Best Training Practices," *Human Resource Professional* (December 1997/January 1998): 33–41.

35. Byham, 2002.

36. Butyn, S. 2003. "Mentoring Your Way to Improved Retention," *Canadian HR Reporter* (January 27): 13.

37. Hewitt Associates Inc. 2005. "How the Top 20 Companies Grow Great Leaders," *Research Highlights*, Hewitt Associates, Toronto, Ontario.

38. Chatman, J. O'Reilly, C. and V. Chang. 2005. "Cisco Systems: Developing a Human Capital Strategy," *California Management Review* Vol. 47. No. 2, Winter 2005, 137–167.

39. Busine, M., and B. Watt. 2005. "Succession Management: Trends and Practices," *Asia Pacific Journal of Human Resources*, 43, 2, 225–237.

40. Pitts, G. 2005. "Need a Leader: Just Look for a GE Graduate," *The Globe and Mail* (July 11), B11.

41. Ito, J., and C.M. Brotheridge. 2005 "Does Supporting Employees' Career Adaptability Lead to Commitment, Turnover or Both?" *Human Resource Management* (Spring), Vol. 44. No. 1. pp. 5–19.

42. Corporate Leadership Council, 2003; Fulmer, R.M. 2005. "Keys to Best Practice Succession Management," Human Resources, October 14, 2005, 17–18.

43. Hewitt, 2005.

44. Borwick, C. 1993. "Eight Ways to Assess Succession Plans," *HRM Magazine*, Vol. 38, No. 4: 109–114.

45. Willins and Byham, 2001.

46. Bernthal, A., and R.S. Wellins. 2003. *The Leadership Forecast: A Benchmarking Study* Pittsbury, PA, Developmental Dimensions International.

47. Hall, D., and J.E. Moss. 1988. "The New Protean Career Contract: Helping Organizations and Employees Adapt," *Organization Dynamics* (Winter): 22–37.

48. Greengard, S. 2001. "Make Smarter Business Decisions: Know What Employees Can Do," *Workforce*, Vol. 80, No. 11 (November): 42–46.

49. Hewitt, 2005.

50. Immen, 2005, C1.

51. Fulmer, R.M. 1997. "The Evolving Paradigm of Leadership Development," *Organizational Dynamics* (Spring): 59–72.

52. Beeson, J. 1998. "The CEO's Checklist," *Across the Board* (June): 41–42.

53. Lear, R. 1998. "Making Succession Succeed," *Chief Executive* (March): 14.

54. Rothwell, W.J. 2001. *Effective Succession Planning*. New York: Amacom.

# Strategic Options and HR Decisions

CHAPTER 10   DOWNSIZING AND RESTRUCTURING

CHAPTER 11   STRATEGIC INTERNATIONAL HRM

CHAPTER 12   MERGERS AND ACQUISITIONS

CHAPTER 13   OUTSOURCING

CHAPTER 14   EVALUATION OF HR PROGRAMS
AND POLICIES

# Chapter 10

# Downsizing and Restructuring

This chapter was written by Professor Terry H. Wagar, Department of Management, Sobey School of Business, Saint Mary's University, Halifax, Nova Scotia.

## Chapter Learning Objectives

After reading this chapter you should be able to

- Appreciate the importance of defining "downsizing."
- Be familiar with the complexity of the downsizing decision.
- Recognize the need to address concerns of both the victims and survivors of downsizing.
- Be aware of the ethical issues and consequences of downsizing.
- Understand what downsizing strategies are effective in enhancing organizational performance.
- Comprehend the concept of the "psychological contract."
- Develop an awareness of the importance of HRM in managing the downsizing process.

**downsizing**

activities undertaken to improve organizational efficiency, productivity and/or competitiveness that affect the size of the firm's workforce, its costs, and its work processes

## DOWNSIZING: A THING OF THE PAST?

"GM to Shut Star Oshawa Plant." "Trenton Car Works Lays Off 400; U.S., Mexican Plants to Gain." "Plant Shutdown (Cascades Inc.) Deals Thunder Bay a Blow."[1] No, these are not old headlines from the downsizing era of the 1990s. Rather, they are a sample of employee cutbacks announced during a one-week period in late November 2005. While some observers argue that downsizing is a thing of the past, there is growing evidence that this is not the case.

Consider a couple of high-profile downsizings. General Motors recently announced plans to eliminate almost 30 000 jobs and close nine plants over the next three years, with 3600 jobs being lost in Canada. Buzz Hargrove, president of the Canadian Auto Workers Union, reported that the cuts represent almost 20% of General Motors' workforce in Canada and "are a shocking addition to the 2000 to 2500 productivity-improvement reductions negotiated during recent contract talks."[2]

Approximately two months after the General Motors announcement, Ford Motor Company released plans to close 14 plants and slash between 25 000 and 30 000 jobs worldwide, with about 1200 of the job cuts occurring in Canada. Company Chairman Bill Ford stated that "you can't cut your way to success. We need to change the business model that has existed for many decades at Ford. We must reduce capacity in North America. From now on, our products will be designed and built to satisfy customers, not just fill a factory."[3]

## The Downsizing Phenomenon

**survivor**

an employee remaining with an organization after a downsizing

**downsizing strategies**

strategies to improve an organization's efficiency by reducing the workforce, redesigning the work, or changing the systems of the organization

In the 1990s, organizations became obsessed with reducing the workforce and operating in a "lean and mean" fashion. However, there is growing evidence that a number of firms became too "lean," and downsizing cut into the muscle of the organization. Furthermore, a number of the reductions have been characterized as "mean"—destroying the lives of victims of cutbacks and leaving a demoralized and frightened group of "**survivors**." In today's environment, downsizing and restructuring are critical components of HR planning.

Until the 1990s, the focus of many organizations was on growth or the "bigger is better" syndrome. As a result, managers responsible for developing a **downsizing strategy** often had little experience in effectively managing the HR planning process and very little guidance from the management literature. Although the past 15 years have seen a considerable volume of articles on downsizing and restructuring, the suggestions they contain often are based on a single experience, are not supported by research, and frequently are in conflict. For instance, should cuts be targeted or across the board? Will the firm's stock price increase or decrease when the firm announces a major layoff or restructuring? Should an employer carry out all of the cuts at once or stage them over a period of time?

Downsizing is not simply a Canadian phenomenon. Organizations around the world are striving to improve their competitive position and respond to the challenges of a global economy. It has been observed that "downsizing has turned into one of the inevitable outcomes of living in a global economy where continual adjustments to products, services and the price of labour are needed to remain competitive."[4]

Furthermore, downsizing is not restricted to the private sector; governments intent on trimming deficits and managing costs reduced public service employment in dramatic ways, and cutbacks in traditionally secure industries such as education, health care, and government became very common during the 1990s.[5]

## Defining Downsizing and Restructuring

It is important to clarify what is meant by the word "downsizing." Managers and academics use it to mean a number of different activities: some examples of words used as synonyms for downsizing include building-down, dehiring, derecruitment, reduction in force, resizing, and rightsizing (for a summary of words used to describe downsizing, see HR Planning Notebook 10.1). Obviously, it is difficult to understand the effect of downsizing if we do not understand clearly what it means.

Kim Cameron, a leading scholar in the area of organizational change, has defined downsizing in the following way:

> Downsizing is a set of activities undertaken on the part of management and designed to improve organizational efficiency, productivity, and/or competitiveness. It represents a strategy implemented by managers that affects the size of the firm's workforce, the costs, and the work processes.[6]

## HR Planning Notebook 10.1

### Examples of Words Used to Describe Downsizing

| | | | |
|---|---|---|---|
| Axed | Disemployed | Reallocated | Restructured |
| Building-down | Dismantled | Rebalanced | Retrenched |
| Chopped | Displaced | Redeployed | RIF'd |
| Compressed | Downshifted | Redesigned | Rightsized |
| Consolidated | Downsized | Reduction-in-force | Slimmed |
| Declining | Fired | Redundancy elimination | Slivered |
| Degrown | Involuntarily separated | Re-engineered | Streamlined |
| Dehired | Personnel surplus | Reorganized | Workforce imbalance |
| Demassed | reduction | Reshaped | correction |
| Derecruitment | Ratcheted down | Resized | |
| Destaffed | Rationalized | Resource allocation | |

Sources: These examples are taken from various sources including K. Cameron, "Strategies for Successful Organizational Downsizing," *Human Resource Management*, Vol. 33 (1994), 189–211; M. Moore, *Downsize This*, New York: Harper Perennial, 1996; and L. Ryan and K. Macky, "Downsizing Organizations: Uses, Outcomes and Strategies," *Asia Pacific Journal of Human Resources*, Vol. 36 (1998), 29–45.

**workforce reduction**

a short-term strategy to cut the number of employees through attrition, early retirement or voluntary severance packages, and layoffs or terminations

**work redesign**

a medium-term strategy in which organizations focus on work processes and assess whether specific functions, products and/or services should be eliminated

Cameron identifies three types of downsizing strategies:

- **Workforce reduction:** Typically a short-term strategy aimed at cutting the number of employees through such programs as attrition, early retirement or voluntary severance packages, and layoffs or terminations. While a number of these approaches allow for a relatively quick reduction of the workforce, the problem is that their impact is often short term, and, in many instances, the organization loses valuable human resources.

- **Work redesign:** Often a medium-term strategy in which organizations focus on work processes and assess whether specific functions, products, and/or services should be changed or eliminated. This strategy, which is frequently combined with workforce reduction, includes such things as the elimination of functions, groups, or divisions; the reduction of bureaucracy; and the redesign of the tasks that employees perform. Since some planning is required, this strategy takes somewhat longer to implement and gets away from the problem of the organization simply doing what it always has done but with fewer people.

- It is possible to prioritize the work of the organization based on its business strategy. In carrying out this task, it is important to examine more carefully the work activities within the business. Work can be classified into four categories: (1) competitive advantage work—core work processes; (2) strategic support work, which assists in completing competitive advantage work; (3) essential support work, which is not a source of competitive advantage but must be completed if the firm is to continue to operate (e.g., completing tax or zoning forms); and (4) nonessential work, which does not add value and is not required for the firm to operate but continues to be done because of past organizational practices.[7] The elimination of nonessential work often produces significant benefits for the organization.

*3 Types Downsizing:*
*1. Workforce reduction*
*2. Work redesign*
*3. Systematic change*

**systematic change**

a long-term strategy that changes the organization's culture and attitudes, and employees' values, with the goals of reducing costs and enhancing quality

- **Systematic change:** A long-term strategy characterized by changing the organization's culture and the attitudes and values of employees with the ongoing goal of reducing costs and enhancing quality. By its very nature, this strategy takes considerable time to implement. The thrust of the strategy is to consider downsizing as an evolutionary part of an organization's life with the goal of continuous improvement: employees assume responsibility for cutting costs and searching for improved methods and practices. Because of the human and financial commitment to this strategy, the impact on the organization's bottom line is rarely immediate and, consequently, the approach is less than appealing to firms that focus on short-term profits or budget goals.

Although some downsizing efforts were limited to reducing the size of the workforce, many employers discovered that merely cutting back the number of people in the organization was insufficient to achieve organizational goals. Consequently, some firms began placing more attention on "right-sizing" or "restructuring" the workplace.

**RPC 10.1**

There are three types of "restructuring": (1) portfolio restructuring, which involves changes to the organization's business portfolio (changes in the mix and/or percentage makeup of the organization's businesses, including divestures and acquisitions), (2) financial restructuring, which may include such financial changes as reducing cash flow or increasing levels of debt, and (3) organizational restructuring, which is "any major reconfiguration of internal administrative structure that is associated with an intentional management change program."[8] While portfolio and financial restructuring are important, the emphasis in this chapter will be on organizational restructuring. It is important, when considering downsizing, to distinguish an approach involving a reduction in the number of employees with one based on a strategically oriented organizational redesign or restructuring.[9]

*[handwritten margin note: 3 Types Restructuring: 1. Portfolio 2. Financial 3. Organizational]*

## How Common Is Workforce Reduction and Restructuring?

One issue that comes up regularly involves how common workforce reduction is in Canada. In three studies conducted in 2001 and 2002,[10] I found that between 40% and 45% of participants reported that their organization permanently reduced the workforce over a two-year period. Moreover, when we consider the size of the workforce reduction, we are not referring to a small percentage of employees losing their jobs; among organizations reducing the workforce, the average reduction was around 15% of the workforce. Similarly, when investigating how the workforce reductions were carried out, combining the results from the studies revealed that about 35% of the reductions were by attrition, 25% by voluntary severance or early retirement, and 40% by layoffs. Compared with the 1990s, these results suggest that organizations are relying less on layoffs and more on voluntary severance or early retirement programs as a means of reducing the number of employees.

In order to provide more information on the extent to which employers are restructuring the workplace and introducing organizational change, I merged the results of three surveys conducted in 2001–2002 and present the findings in Figure 10.1. Overall, about 15% of Canadian organizations are involved in an extensive restructuring program. The most common activities include eliminating unnecessary tasks, redesigning jobs, increasing collaboration among functional areas, and increasing the use of cross-functional teams. However, there is considerable variation across organizations with respect to restructuring and change efforts.

## Why Do Organizations Downsize?

There are several reasons organizations decide to downsize the workforce. Some of the factors most commonly mentioned include the following:

- declining profits,
- business downturn or increased pressure from competitors,
- merging with another organization, resulting in duplication of efforts,

FIGURE 10.1

## Restructuring and Organizational Change

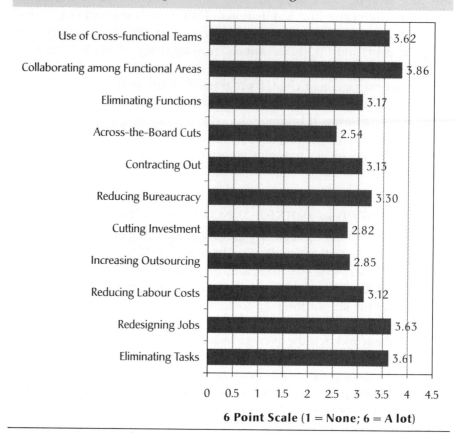

6 Point Scale (1 = None; 6 = A lot)

- introduction of new technology,
- the need to reduce operating costs,
- the desire to decrease levels of management, and
- getting rid of employee "deadwood."

Simply put, many organizations engage in downsizing because managers perceive that cutting people will result in reduced costs (with costs being more predictable than future revenues) and improved financial performance. In addition, labour costs are often seen as easier to adjust relative to other expenditures (such as capital investment).

Figure 10.2 provides empirical evidence of why organizations downsize using data from the Workplace and Employee Survey conducted annually by Statistics Canada. Clearly, the major objective of downsizing for many organizations is to reduce costs, followed by a desire to increase productivity and improve product/service quality.

Although executives often believe that reducing the number of people in the organization will lead to lower overhead costs, reduced bureaucracy, better communications and improved decision making, increased innovative

FIGURE 10.2

## Objectives of Downsizing

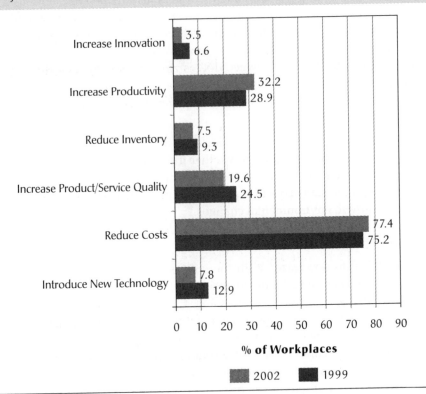

**% of Workplaces**

2002 ■ 1999

activity, and higher productivity, there is considerable evidence that workforce reduction programs often fail to meet their objectives, as has been observed by Cascio.[11]

> Study after study shows that following a downsizing, surviving employees become narrow-minded, self-absorbed, and risk averse. Morale sinks, productivity drops, and survivors distrust management.

There are some organizations that drastically reduce the workforce and employ a severe reduction strategy despite increasing demand and a favourable competitive environment.[12] This development, which has been mentioned by HR managers in personal interviews, may be due to a variety of reasons including a decision to follow the lead of other firms engaging in cutback management and an increasing desire to operate in a lean and mean fashion.

## The Downsizing Decision

For many organizations, going through a downsizing is a very painful and difficult experience. However, some senior executives believe that reducing the workforce is just part of the job. In a 1996 *Newsweek* story on downsizing, a banner headline was titled "Corporate Killers," and featured the names and

Proactively design strategy of downsizing whether it ever used or not

pictures of CEOs and the number of layoffs their firms had engaged in.[13] One executive, when discussing his role in a cost-cutting plan at a previous company, stated, "I don't get frustrated any more. I just fire people."[14]

Too often, organizations embark on a downsizing program without careful consideration of whether there are feasible alternatives to downsizing. Study after study reveals that many downsizings are not well planned, frequently ignore the linkage between downsizing and the strategic direction of the organization, and underestimate the impact of downsizing on the organization and its human resources. Proactive organizatiions plan for downsizing by careful planning:

> A downsizing plan should be included in the strategic plan of all organizations, regardless of whether they plan to downsize or not. By including such a plan, the organization will be better prepared to begin the staff-reduction process should it be forced to do so in response to environmental changes.[15]

## Some Ethical Considerations

Is it unethical to downsize? With the increase in popularity of downsizing, this question has received more attention.

Downsizing is, in most circumstances, perfectly legal. Of course, there may be contractual provisions (such as terms of a collective agreement) and legal restrictions (such as human rights legislation, labour or employment standards, or the common law of wrongful dismissal) that restrict how an employer may engage in downsizing. For example, labour standards codes often require that an employer provide a specified period of notice before engaging in a mass layoff.

**RPC 10.2**

Assuming that a downsizing is legal, can it still be unethical? There is evidence that downsizing may have negative impacts on laid-off employees, survivor employees, and the downsizers. A number of downsizings may infringe on principles of distributive, procedural, and interactional justice (see "Perceptions of Justice" later in this chapter). Moreover, communication during a downsizing may be mismanaged, and managers may use and abuse information as a source of power. For instance, organizations may choose to conceal information from employees (such as failing to inform employees about impending job loss) or distort information concerning the financial status of the business.[16]

Downsizing may be considered a breach of the psychological contract that exists between an employer and employee (that is, an individual worker's perception of the agreement he or she has with the employer). In addition, downsizing may also involve the violation of social contracts; an organization is a member of different local communities, and a failure to adhere to certain values and mores (an ethical floor or basic standards of ethics) would result in the organization being considered a "poor" corporate citizen.

It is possible to evaluate both the decision to downsize (Is downsizing justified?) and how the downsizing was carried out (Did the employer treat its employees in a fair manner?) from an ethical perspective. Morever, it is possible to consider the employment relationship as having both private and public or social components.[17] In other words, while downsizing is a legitimate business practice, it raises several ethical issues.

## Alternatives to Downsizing

Downsizing can be a costly strategy for organizations to pursue, and, as a result, it is desirable to investigate whether alternatives to downsizing exist. In a number of instances, organizations discover that pursuing different alternatives to downsizing may eliminate the need to reduce the workforce or allow for a less severe downsizing strategy.

Some of the alternatives include (1) cutting nonpersonnel costs (e.g., through energy conservation, planned capital expenditures, leasing of capital equipment, reductions in travel or club memberships), (2) cutting personnel costs (e.g., through a hiring freeze, job sharing, a reduction in work hours, reduced benefits, wage concessions), and (3) providing incentives for voluntary resignation or early retirement.[18] While this list is not complete, it emphasizes the need to consider other ways to manage costs within an organization.

High Road Communications Inc. asked each member of its staff to take one week of unpaid leave during the summer months. According to Senior Partner Mia Wedgbury, "it let us keep our core team together while reducing costs. And it went over well with the staff because it precluded layoffs."[19] Another organization, Acxion Corporation, cut the pay of each employee earning more than $25 000 by 5% but also gave each employee the option to buy company stock that was matched one-for-one by the firm.[20]

**RPC 10.3**

## Inplacement and Outplacement Issues

In examining the downsizing decision, it is necessary to consider both inplacement and outplacement issues.[21] **Inplacement** refers to a career management approach aimed at reabsorbing excess or inappropriately placed workers into a restructured organization, while **outplacement** focuses on the provision of a program of counselling and job search assistance for workers who have been terminated. In making career management decisions, organizational decision makers may opt for an inplacement program or termination with outplacement.

In a survey of Canadian manufacturing firms completed in 2000, I asked organizations that had gone through downsizing to report on the benefits they provided to displaced workers. These results are provided in Figure 10.3. The most common benefits were severance pay, continuation of employee benefits, outplacement counselling, and an extended notice period. A minority of firms provided retraining assistance or family counselling.

**inplacement**
reabsorbing excess or inappropriately placed workers into a restructured organization

**outplacement**
providing a program of counselling and job-search assistance for workers who have been terminated

**RPC 10.4**

## Planning for Downsizing

Assuming the organization has decided to embark on a downsizing strategy, planning is essential. Some key issues include the following:

- Determining how many people will lose their jobs.
- Determining who will be let go. For example, will the decision be made on the basis of seniority, performance, or potential?

## FIGURE 10.3

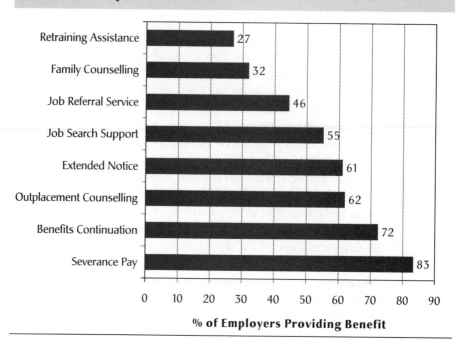

Benefits to Displaced Workers

Retraining Assistance — 27
Family Counselling — 32
Job Referral Service — 46
Job Search Support — 55
Extended Notice — 61
Outplacement Counselling — 62
Benefits Continuation — 72
Severance Pay — 83

**% of Employers Providing Benefit**

- Determining how the reduction will be carried out. For example, to what extent will the organization use attrition, early retirement or voluntary severance programs, and layoffs or termination? It is possible to consider the approach to workforce reduction from the perspective of the employee. As indicated in Figure 10.4, the approaches to workforce reduction vary in terms of the degree of protection to employees and the implementation time.

- Determining the legal consequences. For example, organizations often ignore or are unaware of legal requirements when downsizing the workforce. Some areas of law to consider include the law of wrongful dismissal, employment standards legislation, trade union law, existing collective agreement provisions, and human rights legislation. For instance, there is a very narrow line between voluntary and involuntary termination, and with the termination of older workers, there exists a possibility of an age discrimination claim.[22]

- Designing current and future work plans. This issue represents a key challenge for the organization and is frequently neglected.

- Implementing the decision. Implementation includes such elements as the communication of the termination decision, the timing of the decision, security issues, severance payments, outplacement counselling, and communications with remaining employees.

- Performing follow-up evaluation and assessment of the downsizing efforts. Although this step is critical, it is often ignored in many organizations.[23]

 10.5

FIGURE 10.4

## Approaches to Workforce Reduction

| Workforce Reduction Approach | Examples | Degree of Protection to Employee | Implementation Time |
|---|---|---|---|
| Attrition | Hiring freeze | High | Slow |
| Voluntary Redeployment | Early retirement<br>Voluntary buyout<br>Work sharing | | |
| Involuntary Redeployment | Transfer<br>Demotion<br>Imposed job sharing | | |
| Layoff with Assistance | Retraining<br>Job counselling<br>Advance notice | | |
| Layoff without Assistance | Termination<br>No advance notice<br>No severance | Low | Fast |

Source: ACADEMY OF MANAGEMENT REVIEW by GREENHALGH, LAWRENCE AND SUTTON. Copyright 1988 by ACAD OF MGMT. Reproduced with permission of ACAD OF MGMT in the format Textbook via Copyright Clearance Center.

## Adjusting to Job Loss

Workers who have lost their job frequently experience tremendous pain. As well, job loss can be very difficult for family members (see HR Planning Today 10.1). Furthermore, many downsized employees are very bitter and angry with their former employer. A U.S. study of downsized workers revealed that 67% would never work for their former company again, 54% would not recommend that others purchase the organization's products or services, and 11% considered going to the media and talking about their layoff experiences.[24]

---

## HR Planning Today 10.1

### Parents' Job Insecurity and Children's Work Beliefs

Does the job insecurity of parents influence the work beliefs and attitudes of their children? Three researchers at Queen's University collected data from undergraduate students, their mothers, and their fathers in seeking to answer this question.

The results of the study indicated that children who observed their parents experiencing layoffs and job insecurity were able to perceive that insecurity and develop negative work beliefs that in turn predict their work-related attitudes. In other words, family stressors result in negative consequences for children.

Source: Adapted from J. Barling, K. Dupre, and C. Hepburn, "Effects of Parents' Job Insecurity on Children's Work Beliefs and Attitudes," *Journal of Applied Psychology*, Vol. 83 (1998), 112–118.

An angry mill worker expressed frustration with the Newfoundland Minister of Natural Resources upon hearing of the closure of the paper mill in Stephenville, Newfoundland:

> During the last election, your boss (Premier Danny Williams) stood outside those gates and met every person at the gate and told them that the mill would not go down on his watch. People went on with their lives. They invested in real estate, they bought cars, they had families . . . and here we are today. What are we supposed to do?[25]

A number of organizational interventions and practices have been identified as helping previously employed workers adjust to job loss and secure new employment.[26] They include

- advance notification of layoffs, which gives employees time to deal with the reality of job loss and seek future employment;
- severance pay and extended benefits, which provide an economic safety net;
- education and retraining programs, which give individuals time to acquire marketable skills;
- outplacement assistance to inform employees of new job opportunities and to improve their ability to "market" themselves;
- clear, direct, and empathetic announcement of layoff decisions; and
- consideration of HR planning practices that represent alternatives to large-scale layoffs.

However, organizations don't always manage the process properly. As one employee observed:

> You know, they [former employees] were told that their positions were being eliminated, they were given counselling—financial and counselling about their package . . . but then they were actually ushered right out the door and I think that is despicable. People that had been with the company for 20 years that had been very good employees are made to think that they've done something wrong . . . very, very demeaning.[27]

## The "Survivors" of Downsizing

While we see media accounts of people rebounding from downsizing and starting a new life for themselves, the reality is that for many individuals, the pain of being downsized is very severe. The impact on family life, career plans, and personal esteem are devastating and the social costs can be enormous.

What about the survivors of a downsizing? How do employees who remain with an organization react? Here is a description of a typical response, also known as survivor syndrome:[28]

> The initial anger and pain are often followed by fear and cynicism. Stress, bred of uncertainty and the necessity of doing more with less, skyrockets. Trust in the company and its management plummets. Employees who remain spend their days juggling more work and avoiding anything that approaches risk taking or innovation.

Although surviving a downsizing can be traumatic, there is growing evidence that perceptions of job insecurity (even in the absence of a downsizing) may be associated with negative consequences for employees and employers. Job insecurity has been defined as "an individual's expectations about continuity in a job situation" or "overall concern about the future existence of a job."[29] In other words, even employees in organizations that have not downsized the workforce may have perceptions of job insecurity, which has been related to impaired well-being, increased stress, mental distress, and lower job satisfaction.[30]

## Perceptions of Justice

Perceptions of fairness and equity play a key role in understanding how survivors of a downsizing react to the experience. In examining the survivors of downsizing, three types of justice warrant consideration:[31]

- **Procedural justice:** This focuses on the procedures (or "decision rules") used to determine which employees will leave or remain with the organization.
- **Interactional justice:** This addresses the type of interpersonal treatment employees receive during the implementation of the downsizing decision.
- **Distributive justice:** This deals with the fairness of the downsizing decision. For example, responses from employees may include feelings of guilt after seeing coworkers lose their jobs, support for the downsizing decision as necessary for the firm, or feelings of unfairness and concern that further layoffs may place their own job in jeopardy.

## Survivor Reactions

There is considerable evidence that downsizing may produce a number of dysfunctional behaviours among the employees who remain with the organization. Some of these impacts are discussed below:[32]

- *Negative attitudes and behaviours:* In a number of downsizings, employees who retain their jobs report increased job insecurity, fear, stress, and burnout. They may also experience lower self-confidence and self-esteem, reduced job satisfaction, and lower commitment to the organization. Not surprisingly, these factors may lead to increased turnover, absenteeism, and lateness.
- *Reduced performance capabilities:* There is growing evidence that it is not necessarily the poor performers who leave the downsized organization. Of particular concern to organizations is the fear that the best employees will leave, since quality workers are more attractive to other firms. This result undermines the HR activities of the organization.
- *Lower organizational productivity:* Negative employee attitudes and behaviour, in conjunction with lower performance capabilities, may destroy or markedly harm team activities and result in lower productivity. See HR Planning Today 10.2.

**procedural justice**

procedures or rules used to determine which employees will be downsized

**interactional justice**

the interpersonal treatment employees receive during the implementation of the downsizing decision

**distributive justice**

the fairness of the downsizing decision

**RPC** 10.6

## HR Planning Today 10.2

### White-Collar Reactions to Job Insecurity

Are insecure white-collar employees less committed to their organizations and more concerned about their own careers? A recent study of more than 400 white-collar workers examined the relationship between job insecurity and a variety of employee- and employer-oriented outcomes.

The results of the study indicated that a higher level of job insecurity was associated with the following:

- less effort to ensure that the quality of the individual's work was higher than his or her peers,
- a lower score on "organizational citizenship behaviour" (which involves engaging in activities

such as volunteering for things not required by the organization or helping out new employees),
- lower organizational loyalty (commitment to the organization),
- higher levels of career loyalty (a focus on the individual's career), and
- more job-search behaviour (seeking alternative employment).

Source: Adapted from J. King, "White-Collar Reactions to Job Insecurity and the Role of the Psychological Contract: Implications for Human Resource Management," *Human Resource Management*, Vol. 39 (2000), 79–92.

Few studies have focused specifically on managers' reactions to downsizing. One exception is a study by O'Neill and Lenn, entitled "Voices of Survivors: Words That Downsizing CEOs Should Hear."[33] The authors conducted interviews with middle managers who had survived a downsizing in their organization (a large financial services firm). The managers were trying to come to grips with what happened, attempting to determine their new roles as change agents and mentors in the new organization, and struggling to make sense of what had happened. Among the emotions that emerged were the following:

- *Anger:* For instance, one manager stated, "Stop telling us to work smarter. Show us how . . . Stop blaming us! We've been loyal to the company. We've worked hard and did everything we were told."
- *Anxiety:* Comments included "We don't know who we are anymore." "We talk about empowerment, but we've still got shackles on people. We have to go to senior managers for permission."
- *Cynicism:* There is often very little trust in upper management.
- *Resentment:* Managers frequently compare their rewards with those of others, and even small symbols of inequity trigger emotional responses.
- *Retribution:* There is a need to redress past problems and then move on with the business of improving the new organization.
- *Hope:* While negative feelings often dominate in a downsizing environment, there are occasional voices of hope and expressions of a desire to enhance quality and productivity, and rebuild the organization.

## Impact on the "Downsizers"

Although there has been a fair bit of research on the survivors of downsizing, what about the individuals who are responsible for carrying out the downsizing and actually terminating members of the workforce? In one study, detailed interviews were conducted with ten managers responsible for implementing the downsizing. The results showed that participating in the downsizing process was very difficult for a number of the managers. Of particular note was the experience of social and organizational isolation, a decline in personal health and well-being, and an increase in family-related problems.[34]

Downsizers may begin speaking in less personal terms to describe their job—for instance, a workforce reduction may be described as a realignment or "revectoring." One human resource manager involved in a downsizing described his reaction like this:

> When the rumblings started, I brought the family together, and I said, "There's some big changes in the works and if you see me coming home unhappy or whatever or worried or concerned, it's nothing you've done. . . . I said to my three boys that I'm going to try not to bring my problems home, but if you see me kind of down or whatever, let's just do something fun.[35]

# Financial Performance and Downsizing

Do organizations that have reduced their workforces perform better than other firms? This is an important question; one would anticipate that organizations engaging in downsizing expect that their financial performance will improve.

How does the stock market react to downsizing announcements? While some analysts suggest that downsizing will improve the value of a firm's stock, investors generally respond negatively to the announcement of a layoff, particularly if the reduction is due to financial factors or involves a large-scale permanent cutback of employees.

A recent study indicated that downsizing had a negative impact on stock market returns, and this was even more pronounced for larger downsizings. However, the negative effects associated with downsizing were reduced or eliminated when the firm adopted a relocation strategy in which specific units and functions were targeted for layoffs; targeted cuts allow the firm to retain the most valuable human resources whereas across-the-board cutbacks result in the loss of quality employees. If engaging in a large downsizing is inevitable, firms with disengagement incentives/strategies are viewed more favourably by the stock market relative to firms without such incentives/ strategies.[36] Disengagement incentives/strategies are incentives offered to employees to entice them to voluntarily leave the organization; they may include extraordinary cash payments or continuation of benefits for a stated period of time after employment ceases.

When we look at financial performance outcomes, academic research does not paint a very clear picture; some studies suggest that downsizing is linked with increased profitability while other studies indicate that downsizing is

Chapter 10: Downsizing and Restructuring

associated with poorer financial performance. Why the conflicting results? In examining the various studies, it is difficult to make comparisons because authors don't use similar measures of performance and each defines downsizing somewhat differently. In addition, the research tends to look at workforce reduction behaviour without considering the overall downsizing strategy.

However, there is some U.S. evidence supporting the position that improved return on assets and common stock may be related, at least in part, to the downsizing strategy employed by the organization.[37] Firms following a "pure employment" downsizing (a workforce cutback of at least 5% but little change in plant and equipment expenditure) did not outperform other firms in their industry. However, "asset downsizers" (firms that cut at least 5% of the workforce accompanied by a decline of at least 5% in expenditures on plant and equipment) generated higher returns relative to other industry competitors.

In addition, a recent study of Fortune 500 companies revealed that firms that had downsized their workforce had substantially poorer financial results up to two years later. However, these results began to dissipate by the third year. The findings were particularly negative for employers reducing 10% or more of the workforce. In addition, there was modest evidence that the use of more frequent (ongoing) layoffs was associated with poorer performance.[38]

## Consequences of Downsizing

There is growing evidence that many downsizing efforts fall well short of meeting organizational objectives. Moreover, many workforce reductions are carried out with little strategic planning or consideration of the costs to the individuals and the employer.[39] More often, job cuts represent a short-term reaction to a much more complex problem. While senior executives often focus on financial issues during a reorganization, the benefits of restructuring frequently fail to transpire if HR issues are not carefully thought out and resolved appropriately.

Despite the guilt associated with permanently reducing the workforce, a growing number of firms are willing to downsize and are discovering that workforce reduction can lead to many unwanted consequences.[40] Some of these consequences include the high human costs, psychological trauma experienced both by those let go and the survivors, reduced employee commitment, lower performance among employees due to job insecurity, greater attention by management to the downsizing process while ignoring customer and client needs, loss of valuable employees, a shift from innovation to protection of one's turf, lower morale, and potential litigation by employees who believe that they are victims of discrimination.

One issue that has received little attention is the effect of downsizing on the organization's reputation for corporate social performance (RCSP). Reputation for corporate social performance can be defined as "the firm's reputation for principles, processes and outcomes related to the social impact of the firm's operations."[41] An organization's RCSP is one of the most important intangible assets of a business and an important source of competive advantage. In addition, it may be critical to attracting and retaining quality employees. Although downsizing is considered an acceptable business practice, there is evidence that downsizing has a negative impact on an organization's RCSP. Moreover, this negative effect of downsizing on a firm's RCSP is even more pronounced for organizations that had high financial performance prior to the downsizing.[42]

There is evidence that organizational learning is fundamental if an employer is to outperform the competion; the ability of a firm to learn quicker than the competition may be a critical source of competitive advantage. Although one would assume that downsizing is associated with lower levels of organizational learning, the relationship is not that simple. When considering employers who had downsized, it appears that organizational learning (as measured by commitment to learning, open-mindedness, and a shared vision) is higher when organizations employ a "reorientation strategy" (characterized by redesign of jobs and tasks and developing a philosophy of continuous improvement) and lower if they follow a "convergent strategy" (which focuses on reducing the number of employees).[43]

Another issue that is beginning to attract attention is the relationship between downsizing and employee safety. The research evidence suggests that downsizing creates job insecurity which is strongly associated with low levels of job satisfaction. Low job satisfaction, in turn, is related to safety motivation (the motivation to perform a job in a safe manner) and safety knowledge (an understanding of safe operating procedures). When safety motivation is low, employees are less likely to comply with safety procedures and carry out their work in a safe manner (what is known as safety compliance). Finally, lower levels of safety compliance are associated with more workplace accidents. It is suggested that during a downsizing, employees concerned with keeping their jobs view productivity as more important than safety. However, in downsizings in which employees perceived that the safety climate was positive and the organization viewed safety as very important, the negative outcomes associated with job insecurity were not seen.[44]

RPC 10.7

## Some Canadian Evidence

One study of almost 2000 Canadian workplaces indicated that establishments reporting employee cutbacks also had lower overall employee satisfaction and less favourable employer–employee relations.[45] A second study examined "serial downsizers" (that is, firms that had downsized the workforce both when the study began and five years later). The serial downsizers had the poorest scores when considering changes in employee satisfaction (for instance, poorer morale, quality of work life, commitment to the organization). While the "late downsizers" (those organizations that had downsized only recently) also had negative scores on the employee satisfaction measures, the "early downsizers" did not significantly differ from those employers that did not downsize throughout the period of the study. In other words, it appears that the negative people consequences associated with the early downsizing had dissipated over the five-year period.[46] These consequences include lower morale and job satisfaction, and reduced commitment to the organization.

Workforce reduction has a more immediate impact on the people in the organization; the announcement of job cutbacks affects both those losing their jobs and the survivors, resulting in lower morale, job satisfaction, and commitment to the employer. The degree to which this poses a problem is open to question. If a single organization acting alone decided to engage in workforce cutbacks, the employees would have the option of seeking alternative employment; however, in an economy in which several firms are downsizing, frustrated employees have few alternative employment opportunities and survivors may be unwilling to engage in negative behaviour for fear that they would lose the jobs they currently hold.[47] Still, firms that have not treated employees well may encounter difficulties in attracting and keeping quality employees when the demand for workers is high.

## Effective Downsizing Strategies

Some organizations are not lean and mean, and downsizing may be an appropriate strategic response. However, cutting the number of people in an organization is not a "quick fix" remedy; prior to embarking on any workforce reduction effort, firms should carefully consider the consequences (see HR Planning Today 10.3). Considerable care and planning must go into the decision, and the reasons for the reduction must be effectively communicated to employees. Organizations tend to focus on workforce reduction while ignoring the critical aspects of redesigning the organization and the implementation of cultural change. In addition, managers frequently have little experience or training with regard to downsizing and restructuring.

**RPC 10.8**

From a strategic perspective, an important decision involves answering such questions as these: Should we downsize? When should we do it? How should we do it? The focus should be on *rightsizing*, which involves establishing a shared vision of the organization and a clearly stated strategy supported by management, understood by employees, and involving a sense of "ownership" by members of the firm.[48]

---

## HR Planning Today 10.3

### Who Stays (and Who Goes) During a Downsizing?

When an organization engages in downsizing, one very important issue concerns who remains with the company and who leaves. From the employer's perspective, it is preferable to retain those employees most critical to organizational success. A recent study of a successful downsizing revealed important differences between stayers and leavers.

The results indicated that those accepting a severance package from the employer had lower levels of job satisfaction and commitment to the organization and higher rates of absenteeism. In terms of management implications, the findings suggest that successful downsizing is associated with encouraging the least valuable employees to leave and retaining those workers who are most valuable to the firm.

Source: Adapted from B. Cross and A. Travaglione. 2004. "The Times They Are A-Changing: Who Will Stay and Who Will Go in a Downsizing Organization?" *Personnel Review* 33: 275–290.

---

It is critical that the HR department play a very active role in the early stages of formulating a downsizing strategy. There is evidence that negative outcomes associated with downsizing could be mitigated by increased communication and employee participation and systematic analysis (in advance) of tasks and personnel requirements.[49] In addition, senior management must take an aggressive, visible, and interactive role in formulating the downsizing strategy. However, the identification, development, and implementation procedures should involve the employees. In many instances, the identification of inefficiencies and areas where improvements are possible is best left to employees, who typically are in a better position to make such judgments.

## Strategic Downsizing

Why do so many workforce reduction programs fail to meet expectations? More than half of the organizations engaging in downsizing had no policies or programs to address problems associated with cutting human resources, and several organizations failed to anticipate the dramatic impacts workforce reduction has on the work environment, employees, customers, and clients. Furthermore, a number of downsizing efforts were not carefully thought out or integrated as part of the organization's overall strategic plan.[50]

Organizations embarking on a downsizing strategy may also be going through considerable organizational change. As indicated in HR Planning Notebook 10.2, there are several change issues to be considered by organizations seeking to remain competitive in today's economy.

An effective downsizing depends on comprehensive planning for change; proper communication of the plan; credibility of the organization with employees, customers, suppliers, and other stakeholders; and consideration

---

### HR Planning Notebook 10.2

#### Organizational Change and Downsizing

| Characteristic | Old Approach | New Approach |
|---|---|---|
| Organizational structure | Functional specialization | Matrix/cross-functional teams |
| Operational focus | Internal (production) | External (customer/client) |
| Decision making | Top down | Bottom up |
| Response to change | Centralized | Decentralized |
| Communication | Slow | Fast |
| Career paths | Downward | Multidirectional |
| Recognition | Hierarchical | Lateral/diagonal |
| | Individual | Teamwork |

Source: Reprinted with permission from HUMAN RESOURCE PLANNING, Vol. 16, Issue 1, 1993 by The Human Resource Planning Society, 317 Madison Avenue, Suite 1509 New York, NY 10017, Phone: (212) 490-6387, Fax: (212) 682-6851.

---

and compassion for both employees who are terminated and those remaining with the organization.[51] Moreover, firms engaging in downsizing typically focus only on workforce reduction aspects of the strategy and ignore the more time-consuming but critical strategies of redesigning the organization and developing a systematic strategy predicated on massive cultural change within the firm. Research in both Canada and the United States indicates that while almost all organizations engaging in downsizing focus on the first component (workforce reduction), only about one-half make some attempt at work redesign and less than one-third implement a systematic change strategy.

One study compared the effect of the three downsizing strategies (workforce reduction, organizational redesign, and systematic change) on two performance outcome measures (cost reduction and quality improvement).[52] It found that the workforce reduction strategy was negatively related to organizational performance while the organizational redesign and systematic change strategies were associated with improved performance. In other words, firms that simply focus on reducing the number of employees typically will find the results fail to meet organizational objectives. Moreover, mutual trust between employees and senior management plays an important role in the success of organizational redesign and systematic change strategies. The creation of a culture of trust is essential prior to embarking on a downsizing strategy.

It has been noted that an effective downsizing strategy requires a consideration of the tactics used to reduce the workforce (for instance, the time over which downsizing will take place, the use of harsh tactics such as layoff, and the provision of outplacement assistance), the implementation processes used during downsizing and the redesign of work (e.g., employee participation in the change process, communication issues, and the degree to which the organization engages in a systematic analysis of structure, work, and HR needs), and the changes to or impacts on structures and processes within the organization.[53]

Of particular relevance is whether the organization follows a strategy in which downsizing drives redesign (that is, getting the work done with fewer people) or whether redesign drives downsizing (in other words, what is key is changing the way the work is done). While either of the approaches can be used, the redesign-drives-downsizing strategy will see much greater changes within the organization and a dominant focus on restructuring.

## Effective and Ineffective Downsizing Strategies

A number of studies have pointed out downsizing strategies and practices that do not work. For instance, one study identified nine ineffective downsizing practices (most of which have been identified in other studies):

1. offering voluntary early retirement programs,
2. instituting across-the-board layoffs,
3. eliminating training programs,

4. making personnel cutbacks that are too deep,
5. placing survivors in jobs for which they lack the necessary skills and hoping that they will learn by experience,
6. emphasizing employee accountability instead of employee involvement,
7. expecting survivors to "row harder,"
8. implementing layoffs slowly in phases over time, and
9. promising high monetary rewards rather than careers.[54]

The role of communications in the downsizing decision cannot be overemphasized. Consider the experience of one receptionist in a dot.com firm: "They called us down for a meeting and told us the dream was over. They laid everyone off. The company is gone."[55]

It is important to (1) attend to rumours, (2) provide survivors with available information on the downsizing, (3) ensure that survivors are aware of the new organizational goals, (4) make expectations clear, (5) tell survivors that they are valued, and (6) allow time for grieving.[56] HR Planning Notebook 10.3 contains a summary of some key points of effective downsizing.

Although the importance of communication is widely acknowledged, it appears that communication during downsizing is particularly difficult because of the negative effect on the informal communication networks in an

---

## HR Planning Notebook 10.3

### Some Key Issues in Effective Downsizing

**Approach**

Envision downsizing as a long-term strategy.
Treat the organization's human resources as assets.
Develop early warning signals to identify HR needs.
Establish HR planning systems that focus on redeployment of the organization's human assets.
Prepare in advance for downsizing.

**Downsizing Strategy**

Formulate strategy based on the future mission of the organization and its core competencies.
Communicate in a direct, honest, and empathetic manner with employees.
Involve employees in the design and implementation of worker assistance programs.
Carefully consider the impact of downsizing on employees, the organization, customers, and the community.

Cooperate with relevant organizations, agencies, and institutions (such as labour unions, government agencies, community groups, and educational institutions).
Ensure that organizational leaders are visible, accessible, and interacting with the individuals affected by downsizing.
Smooth the transition for employees losing their jobs by providing safety nets (such as advance notice of layoff, severance pay, outplacement counselling, and job skills training).
Don't neglect to evaluate the impact of the downsizing strategy.

Sources: Adapted from K. Cameron, S. Freeman, and A. Mishra, "Best Practices in White Collar Downsizing: Managing Contradictions," *Academy of Management Executive*, Vol. 5 (1991), 57–73; D. Feldman and C. Leana, "Better Practices in Managing Layoffs," *Human Resource Management*, Vol. 33 (1994), 239–260; B. Kane, Downsizing, TQM, Re-engineering, Learning Organizations and HRM Strategy," *Asia Pacific Journal of Human Resources*, Vol. 38 (2000), 26–49.

organization. As a result, downsizing may impair or disrupt the ability of an employer to adapt to a changing environment.[57]

To summarize, one might expect that organizations today would be able to effectively manage the downsizing process. However, many downsizings are poorly managed.[58] The majority of organizations embarking on a downsizing use very few "best practices" when carrying out the downsizing or do not effectively utilize such practices. Employees reported major levels of dissatisfaction with a number of practices including the lack of opportunity to be involved in the downsizing decision-making process, the low level of trust between employees and managers, the inability to correct information used in the downsizing decision, and the failure to obtain feedback from survivors on how the downsizing was carried out. When comparing survivors and victims, both groups were dissatisfied with how the employer managed the process but victims had even lower levels of satisfaction.[59]

## Summary of Best Practices

Cameron, Freeman, and Mishra developed a list of six best practices in downsizing firms:

1. Downsizing should be initiated from the top but requires hands-on involvement from all employees.
2. Workforce reduction must be selective in application and long term in emphasis.
3. Special attention should be paid both to those who lose their jobs and to the survivors who remain with the organization.
4. Decision makers should identify precisely where redundancies, excess costs, and inefficiencies exist and attack those specific areas.
5. Downsizing should result in the formation of small, semi-autonomous organizations within the broader organization.
6. Downsizing must be a proactive strategy focused on increasing performance.[60]

# HRM Issues

A critical issue revolves around the impact of downsizing on an organization's HRM initiatives. In light of the growing evidence that HRM practices do matter and are related to organizational performance, it is essential that any downsizing decision be made with consideration of the impact on HRM initiatives.[61]

**R P C 10.10**

**psychological contract**

an unwritten commitment between employers and their employees that historically guaranteed job security and rewards for loyal service

## Managing the Changing Psychological Contract

An important part of the employment relationship is the **psychological contract** (those unwritten commitments between employers and employees). Over the past two and a half decades, the psychological contract between employers and employees has changed dramatically. Historical notions of job security and rewards for loyal and long service to the organization have, in many instances, been replaced by ongoing change, uncertainty, and considerable shedding of employees. Associated with such developments are the considerable pain, stress, and hardship inflicted on employees, including both workers who have lost jobs and those survivors who remain with an organization.

A number of organizations try, as part of their HR planning and development activities, to hire from within the firm (where possible). Such organizations develop internal labour markets in which new employees are hired at specific "ports of entry," and other positions are filled through internal transfers and promotions. Historically, employers and employees often had an implicit contract that was based on the notion that there was a mutual commitment by both employers and workers to long-term employment, and job hirings were viewed as "implicit contracts" in which employees are given certain assurances regarding security of wages and employment. However, such contracts have been radically altered or have ceased to exist in many organizations.

## The "New Deal" in Employment

In recent years, many organizations have been unwilling to promise job security and continued employment to loyal, senior employees. Rather, a new employment arrangement between employees and a number of employers is emerging. This "new deal" has been described in the following way:

> You're expendable. We don't want to fire you but we will if we have to. Competition is brutal, so we must redesign the way we work to do more with less. Sorry, that's just the way it is. And one more thing—you're invaluable . . . We're depending on you to be innovative, risk-taking, and committed to our goals.[62]

What does this mean for employees? In many organizations, we have moved away from the expectation of lifetime employment.[63] Rather, workers should prepare for a "multiorganizational career" and recognize that it is highly unlikely that they will remain with the same organization throughout their working lives.

While nonmanagerial employees have been the victims of downsizing for years, the trend toward cutting huge numbers of managers is a recent phenomenon. However, the massive cutbacks of management personnel are more than simply a response to competitive pressure or to the introduction of new technology. They demonstrate that we are experiencing a dramatic change in the employment relationship characterized by a movement away from paternalism and a community of loyalty to the new order of "community of purpose," which focuses on completion of the task or mission rather than on loyalty to the organization.[64]

## Altering the Psychological Contract

How does an organization go about changing the psychological contract with its employees? There are two different approaches that may be taken:

- *Accommodation:* This approach involves working with the existing contract and changing parts of the agreement over time. For example,

Chapter 10: Downsizing and Restructuring

there may be a change in hours of work, job duties, or benefits. While this approach is preferable in a number of instances since workers do not experience dramatic changes, it requires a positive relationship between the employer and employees.

- *Transformation:* This approach involves establishing a new employee mindset and requires workers to *radically* change the old way of doing things. Examples include moving from individual to team-based work or learning to operate new technology. There are four steps in implementing transformational contract change:

  1. *Challenge the old contract:* An organization that wants to introduce major changes to the employment contract and yet still retain valued employees needs to provide solid reasons for the changes. Without effective communication and trust, workers simply will not buy into the changes.
  2. *Prepare for change:* This involves creating credible signs of change (that is, that the organization is committed to change and will follow through), reducing losses associated with change (such as loss of authority, emotional distress, and increased uncertainty), and establishing transition structures (such as phased-in change or the setting up of task forces to help employees adjust to change).
  3. *Generate the new contract terms:* It is critical that managers communicate the new expectations and secure employee acceptance of the terms.
  4. *Live the new contract:* Organizations must make it clear that the old contract is over and there is no going back. Too often, managers send mixed messages to employees who then may try to cling to the old agreement. Training for all organization members is critical.[65]

Can flexible employment contracts be the source of product and process innovation? Despite the growth in contingent work arrangements, most organizations make relatively little use of short-term contracts. Among those employers using such contracts, it was rare that the primary focus was as a strategic lever to increase innovation. Rather, the major reasons for using short-term contracts were to cut labour costs, and address fluctuations in product or service demand. Contracting out key functions may negatively affect the innovation potential of an employer.[66]

Does it really matter if the psychological contract is breached (that is, the perception that one party failed to live up to its obligations)? Employees who perceived that their employer breached the psychological contract were more likely to report lower levels of trust in the employer, reduced performance, increased use of sick leave, and a greater intention of leaving the organization. When asked to assess the perceived breach of a psychological contract associated with downsizing, individuals with a strong belief in the ideologies of market competition or shareholder interest were significantly less likely to indicate a breach of the psychological contract compared with individuals who believed in the ideology of employee worth (that is, an obligation on the part of organizations to focus on employee interests).[67]

# Downsizing and "High Involvement" HRM

Over the past decade, some employers have been placing increasing attention on what has become known as **high involvement human resource management**.

Although it has taken some time, a growing number of organizations are introducing programs such as total quality management or continuous quality improvement, self-managed work teams, selective hiring, extensive training, joint labour–management committees, and incentive compensation. However, a number of these same firms have also undertaken (or are planning to undertake) large-scale restructurings. From the perspective of the employee, these strategies appear to be in competition—if human resources are so valuable and worthy of development, why is the organization getting rid of its assets? Management credibility is destroyed since employees view the notion of progressive HRM practices as diametrically opposed to the shedding of workers—employee involvement and empowerment programs require employee attachment and commitment while downsizing programs focus on organizational detachment.

Although downsizing can be a quick way to lower labour costs, proponents of strategic human resource management (SHRM) believe that downsizing may undermine competitive advantage over the long term. It is asserted that HRM practices coming after a downsizing should help the organization retain valued employees and promote discretionary efforts by workers.

Can high-performance work practices exist in an environment of layoffs and restructuring? It has been argued that downsizing may be incompatible with the introduction of high-performance work practices because team-based work requires relatively stable membership of team members and high-performance work practices are based on the notion of substantial employee commitment to the organization.

A recent study investigated downsizing in hospitals and the relationship between HRM and performance. Consideration for employee well-being (attention to the job insecurity of survivors, respectful treatment of those laid off, and extensive communication) during downsizing was associated with higher performance.[68]

HR experts have a considerable role to play in downsizing and restructuring. Some considerations are as follows:

- advising on restructuring the organization (including work groups, teams, departments, and so on) to maximize productivity and retain quality performers, and
- developing skill inventories and planning charts to evaluate the impact of a downsizing on HR needs and projected capabilities.
- communicating the downsizing decision effectively.
- evaluating the downsizing program after completion. This includes an assessment of who left the organization and who remains. Some key issues include job design and redesign, worker adjustment to change, the need for employee counselling, organizational communication, and a review of the appropriateness of HRM policies and programs (such as training, compensation and benefits, orientation of employees into the "new" organization, etc.).[69]

**high involvement human resource management**

a commitment to human resource management practices that treat people as assets

Ⓡ Ⓟ Ⓒ 10.11

Ⓡ Ⓟ Ⓒ 10.12

Ⓡ Ⓟ Ⓒ 10.13

## Labour Relations Issues

Consider the comments by local union president Howard Sim in discussing the recent downsizing at Trenton Car Works (referred to at the start of this chapter),

> The first we heard about it (the layoff of 400 employees) was 9 o'clock this morning. We thought everything was going smooth. The workers can only do so much. The company wanted so many railcars; they got them. It's up to management to manage. All we can see is Christmas coming.[70]

Practitioners in unionized organizations often face additional challenges when participating in the restructuring process. In any downsizing involving a union, it is critical that management representatives *read* the collective agreement—while this should go without saying, in many instances practitioners do not follow this advice. The collective agreement often outlines the procedures to be followed in the event of a reduction of bargaining unit employees. Of particular relevance are clauses addressing notice-period requirements in the event of a layoff and provisions dealing with seniority.

**RPC 10.14**

There has been a movement in labour relations toward greater cooperation between labour and management and the emergence of new employment relationships. However, changes in managerial attitudes and behaviours are necessary if cooperation between labour and management will succeed; unfortunately, many downsizing programs have destroyed positive labour relations programs.

When General Motors announced that it would shut down a star Oshawa plant that is a leader in auto-industry quality rankings and one of the most productive facilities in North America, CAW leader Buzz Hargrove stated:

> These are tough times for General Motors, but we've got to fight to save them from themselves. Not putting in a new product in your best plant is not the greatest strategy to revive North America.[71]

Securing commitment to joint labour–management initiatives is, not surprisingly, very difficult when an organization is also cutting the number of employees. One study of workforce reduction in the unionized environment revealed that labour–management climate was lower (the quality of the labour–management relationship was more adversarial) for those bargaining units that experienced a reduction of the workforce. Of note was that this result was consistent when considering *both* employer respondents and union officials.[72]

Should unions participate in management-initiated restructuring efforts? A recent case study documented the experiences of three union locals involved in the process of restructuring. Each union local negotiated with the employer over the issue of workplace restructuring but the substance of the bargaining as well as the level of involvement by the union and its members varied noticeably. However, it is possible to identify two distinct union responses. The *interventionist* response was characterized by early involvement in the restructuring process and the involvement of a broad cross-section of the union membership in the development and implementation of

## HR Planning Today 10.4

### Unionized Employees' Perceptions of Role Stress and Fairness During Downsizing

Do union members who survive a downsizing have lower job satisfaction and less favourable attitudes toward the union? Very little research has examined the effects of downsizing on union members' attitudes and perceptions. A recent study of unionized workers in a Swedish hospital sheds some light on the consequences of downsizing in a unionized environment.

Downsizing was associated with reduced levels of job satisfaction and perceptions of poorer health but was not related to union members' satisfaction with their union. However, union members who perceived that their union treated employees fairly during the downsizing reported higher levels of job satisfaction and well-being.

Source: Adapted from J. Hellgren and M. Sverke, "Unionized Employees' Perceptions of Role Stress and Fairness During Organizational Downsizing: Consequences for Job Satisfaction, Union Satisfaction and Well-Being," *Economic and Industrial Democracy*, Vol. 22 (2001), 543–568.

the new form of work organization. On the other hand, the *pragmatic* response was one in which the union relied on the employer to make workplace changes and then negotiated with management over the impact of such changes. While this response is not surprising, the study results indicate that it may not be the optimal response—in redesigning the work, management has limited information about the work itself and workplace norms, the change does not proceed through a series of steps in which union input is sought, and the lack of involvement in the process leads to lower commitment to change on the part of the union and its members.[73]

It remains to be seen how true cooperation can exist when the job security of employees is threatened. By way of example, union leaders frequently report that joint committees and employee involvement programs are designed to get workers to make suggestions that increase productivity at the cost of job security. Although a positive labour climate is often associated with favourable organizational outcomes, achieving such a climate is very difficult, and several good relationships have been destroyed when firms embark on a program of cutting jobs. Furthermore, there is evidence that downsizing may be harmful to the health of employees (see HR Planning Today 10.4).

## Summary

HR planning plays an important role in the development and implementation of an effective downsizing strategy. The "job for life" approach has been radically changed in the past decade, resulting in a number of new challenges for both employees and employers. It does not appear that the downsizing phenomenon is over, and, consequently, HR professionals must have a solid understanding of how to manage the downsizing process.

There is considerable evidence that many downsizings fell far short of achieving the goals that senior management expected. In a number of organizations, downsizing was followed by lower morale, greater conflict, reduced employee commitment, and poorer financial performance. Moreover, many downsizings were carried out without considering the strategic objectives of the organization, and many employers failed to assess how downsizing would affect its victims, surviving employees, the organization, customers, or society. Managing human resources in a time of cutback management presents several unique challenges to the HRM professional.

## Key Terms

distributive justice, 271
downsizing, 260
downsizing strategies, 260
high involvement human resource management, 283
inplacement, 267
interactional justice, 271

outplacement, 267
procedural justice, 271
psychological contract, 280
survivor (of downsizing), 260
systematic change, 262
work redesign, 262
workforce reduction, 262

## Web Links

An introductory paper on downsizing and links to 15 other downsizing papers that were part of a special issue of the journal *M@n@gement:*

**www.dmsp.dauphine.fr/MANAGEMENT/PapersMgmt/23Rabin.html** (p. 260)

Guidelines on how to downsize with dignity:

**http://humanresources.about.com/od/layoffsdownsizing/a/downsizing.htm** (p. 268)

A case study on the effects of downsizing/restructuring on employees:

**http://faculty-gsb.stanford.edu/oyer/wp/whostays.htm** (p. 270)

Describes the effect of restructuring and job insecurity on the job satisfaction of nurses:

**www.isma.org.uk/stressnw/hospnurse1.htm** (p. 272)

A longitudinal study of the effects of downsizing on the health of employees:

**http://bmj.bmjjournals.com/cgi/content/full/320/7240/971** (p. 274)

Examines the relationship between how an organization downsizes and its culture:

**www.clg.com/download/How%20You%20Let%20Go.pdf** (p. 275)

A practical article discussing how an employee newsletter can be used to communicate during downsizing:

**www.companynewsletters.com/downsize.htm** (p. 279)

# RPC Icons

**RPC 10.1** Plans for and manages the HR aspects of organizational change (e.g., mergers, acquisitions, divestitures, and downsizing, in the context of organizational strategies and legislated requirements)

**RPC 10.2** Directs the organization in ethical HR practices, and application of conflict of interest guidelines

**RPC 10.3** Advises clients on alternatives to terminations

**RPC 10.4** Assists employees in identifying career paths, and establishing learning plans and activities required for achieving personal success

**RPC 10.5** Researches, analyzes, and reports on potential HR issues affecting the organization

**RPC 10.6** Ensures compliance with legally required programs

**RPC 10.7** Develops and delivers learning strategies to close the gap between current human resource capital capabilities and the future needs of the organization

**RPC 10.8** Contributes to the development of the organization's vision, goals, and strategies with a focus on human capital

**RPC 10.9** Communicates information to serve current and future needs of the organization

**RPC 10.10** Identifies HR information that the organization needs to achieve its business objectives

**RPC 10.11** Leads in the development of HR initiatives that support the organization's strategic directions

**RPC 10.12** Acts as an agent for major initiatives

**RPC 10.13** Maintains an inventory of HR talent for the use of the organization

**RPC 10.14** Collects and develops information required for good decision making throughout the bargaining process

# Discussion Questions

1. What can managers embarking on an organizational downsizing do to minimize the impact of the process on the "survivors" of downsizing?
2. In light of the negative consequences often associated with downsizing, why do organizations downsize? Why do so many downsizings fail to meet organizational objectives?
3. What are the challenges facing an organization deciding to pursue Cameron's three downsizing strategies?

4. What is the "psychological contract"? Why has it changed over the past 25 years? When considering the next ten years, what changes to the psychological contract do you envision?
5. Can a high-involvement human resource management strategy succeed in an organization that is also going through a downsizing?

## Using the Internet

1. Use the Internet to identify at least one successful and one unsuccessful downsizing/restructuring.
2. Outline the factors that distinguished the successful and unsuccessful downsizing/restructuring.
3. Discuss the impact of the downsizing/restructuring on the people within each organization.

## Exercises

1. Discuss the following statement: "Restructuring is unavoidable. Firms that want to survive and prosper in the global economy need to engage in restructuring strategies."
2. Interview three classmates, friends, or family members who are currently working. Ask them to describe their perception of the psychological contract that exists between the organization and its members.
3. Meet with an HRM professional or a senior management official whose organization has gone through a downsizing. Ask the individual to describe the downsizing strategy employed by his or her organization. Consider Cameron's three downsizing strategies of workforce reduction, work redesign, and systematic change. To what extent did the organization use any or all of these strategies?

## Case: A Downsizing Decision at the Department of Public Works

Kathleen Pool is a human resource officer with a municipal government in a town of just over 25 000 people. A well-known consulting firm, in cooperation with senior government officials, recently completed a detailed audit of government operations. As a result of the audit, selected government departments (including the Department of Public Works) were targeted for restructuring. The consultants made it clear in their report that they believed that the budget allocation for the Department of Public Works was "adequate" and recommended that the department not expect any increase in funding for the next two years. Note that operating costs for the department are projected to increase at a rate of about 3.0% annually.

Kathleen has been given the responsibility of managing the restructuring at the Department of Public Works. Rather than directing the department to cut a specific number of jobs, Kathleen has been asked to develop a restructuring strategy that will meet the town's mission of "providing quality service to its residents in a cost-effective manner." She is currently reviewing the operating policies at the Department of Public Works.

The Department of Public Works is responsible for such tasks as garbage collection, basic sidewalk and road maintenance, city parks and arenas, installation of street signs and parking meters, and snow removal. At the present time, employees work in one of three subunits—garbage collection, parks and recreation, or city maintenance. Each of the subunits is housed in a separate building, and has its own equipment and supplies, and its own operating budget. As well, while employees can formally apply to transfer to a different subunit, the managers of the subunits involved and the Director of Public Works (who is responsible for the overall operation of the Department) must all agree. Unless a vacancy at one of the subunits arises, it is rare that any employee transfer will be approved.

In 1999, the Department of Public Works underwent a considerable downsizing and 5% of its permanent positions were cut. In addition, the department stopped its practice of hiring summer students from local high schools and universities in an effort to cut costs. Prior to this, students were employed over the summer to help with special projects and to cover vacation periods for full-time employees. In 2000, a smaller cutback of 2% of the workforce took place.

In 2005, the municipality brought back the practice of hiring summer students. This decision was welcomed by the full-time employees at the Department of Public Works, in particular because it allows the employees much more flexibility in selecting their vacation time. From 1999 to 2004, management placed considerable restrictions on when employees could go on vacation; employees with ten or more years of service could have a maximum of one week's vacation in July or August while employees with less than ten years of service were not permitted to go on vacation during these two months. Under the collective agreement, management has the right to determine the vacation schedule of unionized employees.

In reviewing turnover data for the Department of Public Works, Kathleen found that very few full-time employees quit their jobs to pursue other employment opportunities. In addition, dismissals for cause were rare; over the past ten years, only two employees were terminated for cause. In both cases, the union lost the discharge grievance at an arbitration hearing.

Since the mid-1990s, the municipality has had a local consulting firm conduct surveys of both municipal employees and the users of government services. A summary of the findings from the employee survey (for Department of Public Works employees only) is contained in Table 10.1. Note that each of the items (such as employee morale) is measured using a five-point scale (1 = very low; 5 = very high). Similarly, Table 10.2 contains summary information from the survey of municipal residents concerning the performance of the Department of Public Works. Again, respondents were asked to reply using a five-point scale (1 = very low and 5 = very high). Note that on both the employee

TABLE 10.1

## Summary Results from a Survey of Public Works Employees

| Year | Employee Morale | Employee Commitment to Department | Overall Employee Job Satisfaction | Intention to Stay with the Municipality |
|------|-----------------|-----------------------------------|-----------------------------------|------------------------------------------|
| 1999 | 3.89 | 3.72 | 4.02 | 4.77 |
| 2000 | 2.21 | 1.99 | 2.34 | 4.11 |
| 2001 | 2.36 | 2.22 | 2.87 | 3.77 |
| 2002 | 2.65 | 2.62 | 3.22 | 3.99 |
| 2003 | 2.38 | 2.33 | 2.66 | 4.44 |
| 2004 | 2.88 | 3.01 | 2.99 | 4.50 |
| 2005 | 3.54 | 3.52 | 3.88 | 4.72 |

TABLE 10.2

## Summary Results from a Survey of Municipal Residents

| Year | Level of Satisfaction with the Board of Public Works | Quality of Service Provided by the Board of Public Works |
|------|------------------------------------------------------|----------------------------------------------------------|
| 1999 | 3.95 | 3.88 |
| 2000 | 3.22 | 3.01 |
| 2001 | 3.34 | 3.24 |
| 2002 | 3.65 | 3.66 |
| 2003 | 3.56 | 3.49 |
| 2004 | 3.78 | 3.72 |
| 2005 | 4.01 | 3.98 |

survey and users of government services survey, there were only minor differences in the results when the data were broken down by subunit (garbage collection, parks and recreation, or city maintenance).

1. Outline the issues that Kathleen should consider prior to designing a restructuring strategy.
2. Design a strategy to restructure the Department of Public Works. Be sure to provide support for the decisions/recommendations you propose.
3. A recent newspaper editorial suggested that the town contract out the collection of garbage. What are the advantages/disadvantages of contracting out services that had been provided by government?

# Endnotes

1. The sources of these headlines are G. Keenen, "GM to Shut Star Oshawa Plant," *The Globe and Mail*, November 22, 2005, A1; M. Graham, "Trenton Car Works Lays Off 400; U.S., Mexican Plants to Gain," *The ChronicleHerald (Halifax)*, November 25, 2005, 1; and K. Howlett, "Plant Shutdown Deals Thunder Bay a Blow," *The Globe and Mail*, November 23, 2005, A10.

2. Norris, G. "GM Cutting 3,600 Jobs at Canadian Plants," *The ChronicleHerald (Halifax)*, November 22, 2005, E12.

3. Keenen, G. "Massive Ford Restructuring to Cut 1,200 More Canadian Jobs," *The Globe and Mail*, January 24, 2006, p. B1, B15.

4. Kets de Vries, M., and K. Balazs, 1997. "The Downside of Downsizing," *Human Relations* 50: 11–40.

5. Swimmer, G. 2000. *Public Sector Labour Relations in an Era of Restraint and Restructuring*, Toronto: Oxford University Press.

6. Cameron, K. 1994. "Strategies for Successful Organizational Downsizing," *Human Resource Management* 33: 189–211.

7. Dalton, G., L. Perry, J. Younger, and W. Smallwood. 1996. "Strategic Restructuring," *Human Resource Management* 35: 433–452.

8. McKinley, W., and A. Scherer. 2000. "Some Unanticipated Consequences of Organizational Restructuring," *Academy of Management Review* 25: 735–752.

9. Kane, B. 2000. "Downsizing, TQM, Re-engineering, Learning Organizations and HRM Strategy," *Asia Pacific Journal of Human Resources* 38: 26–49.

10. See Wagar, T. 2002. *Human Resource Management, Strategy and Organization Change: Evidence from Canadian Employers*. Report to study participants, July 2002.

11. Cascio, W. 1993. "Downsizing? What Do We Know? What Have We Learned?" *Academy of Management Executive* 7: 95–104.

12. Tomasko, R. 1990. *Downsizing: Reshaping the Corporation of the Future*, 2nd ed. New York: AMACON.

13. Van Buren, H. 2000. "The Bindingness of Social and Psychological Contracts: Toward a Theory of Social Responsibility in Downsizing," *Journal of Business Ethics* 25: 205–219.

14. *Financial Post*, June 30, 2001, p. C2.

15. Davis, J. 2003. "Organizational Downsizing: A Review of Literature for Planning and Research," *Journal of Healthcare Management* 48: 181–199.

16. See Rosenblatt, Z., and Z. Schaeffer. 2000. "Ethical Problems in Downsizing" in R. Burke and C. Cooper (eds.) *The Organization in Crisis: Downsizing, Restructuring and Privatization*. Malden, MA: Blackwell.

17. Van Buren, 2000.

18. Adamson, B., and M. Axmith. 1983. "Managing Large Scale Staff Reductions," *Business Quarterly* 48: 40–52.

19. "Better Than Downsizing," *National Post Business*, December 2001, p. 29.

20. LaReau, J. 2001. "Firm Picks Pay Cuts Over Pink Slips." *The Globe and Mail*, April 11, B13.

21. Latack, J. 1990. "Organizational Restructuring and Career Management: From Outplacement and Survival to Inplacement." In G. Ferris and K. Rowland, eds., *Research in Personnel and Human Resources Management*. Greenwich, CT: JAI Press.

22. Tomlinson, A. 2002. "Did They Really Want to Retire?" *Canadian HR Reporter*, February 11, 1,16.

23. This material is adapted from Adamson, B., and M. Axmith. 1983. "Managing Large Scale Staff Reductions," *Business Quarterly* 48: 40–52.

24. "If You Must Lay Off," *Canadian HR Reporter*, April 22, 2002, 4.

25. Moore, D. "Nfld. Asks Residents Not to Despair over Abitibi," *The ChronicleHerald (Halifax)*, August 4, 2005, p. A8.

26. Feldman, D., and C. Leana. 1994. "Better Practices in Managing Layoffs," *Human Resource Management* 33: 239–260.

27. Amundson, N., W. Borgen, S. Jordan, and A. Erlebach. 2004. "Survivors of Downsizing: Helpful and Hindering Experiences," *The Career Development Quarterly* 52: 256–271, 260.

28. Lee, C. 1992. "After the Cuts," *Training* 29: 17–23.

29. See Davy, J., A. Kinicki, and C. Scheck. 1997. "A Test of Job Security's Direct and Mediated Effects on Withdrawal Cognitions," *Journal of Organizational Behavior* 18: 323–349 and Rosenblatt, Z., and A. Ruvio. 1996. "A Test of a Multidimensional Model of Job Insecurity: The Case of Israeli Teachers," *Journal of Organizational Behavior*, 17: 587–605.

30. Sverke, M., and J. Hellgren. 2002. "The Nature of Job Insecurity: Understanding Employment Uncertainty on the Brink of a New Millennium," *Applied Psychology: An International Review* 51: 23–42.

31. Armstrong-Stassen, M. 1993. "Survivors' Reactions to a Workforce Reduction: A Comparison of Blue-Collar Workers and Their Supervisors," *Canadian Journal of Administrative Sciences* 10: 334–343.

32. Mone, M. 1994. "Relationships between Self-Concepts, Aspirations, Emotional Responses, and Intent to Leave a Downsizing Organization," *Human Resource Management* 33: 281–298.

33. O'Neill, H., and J. Lenn. 1995. "Voices of Survivors: Words That Downsizing CEOs Should Hear," *Academy of Management Executive* 9: 23–34.

34. Wright, B., and J. Barling. 1998. "The Executioner's Song: Listening to Downsizers Reflect on their Experiences," *Canadian Journal of Administrative Sciences* 15: 339–355.

35. Adamson, B., and M. Axmith. 1983. "Managing Large Scale Staff Reductions," *Business Quarterly* 48: 40–52.

36. Nixon, R., M. Hitt, H. Lee, and E. Jeong, 2004. "Market Reactions to Announcements of Corporate Downsizing Actions and Implementation Strategies," *Strategic Management Journal* 25: 1121–1129.

37. Cascio, W., C. Young, and J. Morris. 1997. "Financial Consequences of Employment-Change Decisions in Major U.S. Corporations," *Academy of Management Journal* 40: 1175–1189.

38. DeMeuse, K., T. Bergmann, P. Vanderheiden, and C. Roraff, 2004. "New Evidence Regarding Organizational Downsizing and a Firm's Financial Analysis," *Journal of Management Inquiry* 16: 155–177.

39. Cascio, W. 2002. *Responsible Restructuring: Creative and Responsible Alternatives to Layoffs.* San Francisco: Berrett-Koehler.

40. Tomasko, R. 1990. *Downsizing: Reshaping the Corporation of the Future,* 2nd ed. New York: AMACON.

41. Zyglidopoulos, S. 2004. "The Impact of Downsizing on the Corporate Reputation for Social Performance," *Journal of Public Affairs* 4: 11–25, 13.

42. Ibid., 11–25.

43. Farrell, M., and F. Mavondo. 2004. "The Effect of Downsizing Strategy and Reorientation Strategy on a Learning Organization," *Personnel Review* 33: 383–402.

44. For an interesting review of the safety–job insecurity issue, see Probst, T. 2004. "Job Insecurity: Exploring a New Threat to Employee Safety" in J. Barling and M. Frone (eds.) *The Psychology of Workplace Safety.* Washingon: APA: 63–80.

45. Wagar, T., 1998. "Exploring the Consequences of Workforce Reduction," *Canadian Journal of Administrative Sciences* 15: 300–309.

46. Wagar, T., and K. Rondeau. 2002. "Repeated Downsizing, Organizational Restructuring and Performance: Evidence from a Longitudinal Study," *Proceedings of the Administrative Sciences Association of Canada (HRM Division)*, Winnipeg. For a study with similar results based on data from New Zealand see Gilson, C., F. Hurd, and T. Wagar. 2004. "Creating a Concession Climate: The Case of the Serial Downsizers," *International Journal of Human Resource Management* 15: 1056–1068.

47. Cappelli, P. 1995. "Rethinking Employment," *British Journal of Industrial Relations* 33: 563–602.

48. Hitt, M., B. Keats, H. Harback, and R. Nixon. 1994. "Rightsizing: Building and Maintaining Strategic Leadership and Long-term Competitiveness," *Organizational Dynamics* 23: 18–32.

49. Cameron, K. 1994. "Strategies for Successful Organizational Downsizing," *Human Resource Management* 33: 189–211. Also see Chadwick, C., L. Hunter, and S. Walston. 2004. "Effects of Downsizing Practices on the Performance of Hospitals," *Strategic Management Journal* 25: 405–427.

50. Cascio, W. 2002. *Responsible Restructuring: Creative and Responsible Alternatives to Layoffs.* San Francisco: Berrett-Koehler.

51. Kammeyer-Mueller, J., H. Liao, and R. Arvey. 2001. "Downsizing and Organizational Performance: A Review of the Literature from a Stakeholder Perspective," in G. Ferris (ed.) *Research in Personnel and Human Resource Management.* Amsterdam: JAI Press, 269–329.

52. Mishra, A., and K. Mishra. 1994. "The Role of Mutual Trust in Effective Downsizing Strategies," *Human Resource Management* 33: 261–279.

53. Freeman, S. 1999. "The Gestalt of Organizational Downsizing: Downsizing Strategies as Packages of Change," *Human Relations* 52: 1505–1541.

54. Hitt, M., B. Keats, H. Harback, and R. Nixon. 1994. "Rightsizing: Building and Maintaining Strategic Leadership and Long-term Competitiveness," *Organizational Dynamics* 23: 18–32.

55. Mason, M. 2001. "The Other Dot-com Workers," *The Globe and Mail,* (April 17), B15.

56. Dunlap, J. 1994. "Surviving Layoffs: A Qualitative Study of Factors Affecting Retained Employees After Downsizing," *Performance Improvement Quarterly* 7: 89–113.

57. Fisher, S., and M. Write. 2000. "Downsizing in a Learning Organization: Are There Hidden Costs," *Academy of Management Review* 25: 244–251.

58. Cascio, W. 2002. *Responsible Restructuring: Creative and Responsible Alternatives to Layoffs.* San Francisco: Berrett-Koehler.

59. Macky, K. 2004. "Organisational Downsizing and Redundancies: The New Zealand Workers' Experience," *New Zealand Journal of Employment Relations* 29: 63–87.

60. Cameron, K., S. Freeman, and A. Mishra. 1991. "Best Practices in White Collar Downsizing: Managing Contradictions," *Academy of Management Executive* 5: 57–73.

61. See Wood, S. 1999. "Human Resource Management and Performance," *International Journal of Management Reviews* 1: 367–413. For an excellent critical review, see Godard, J. 2004. "A Critical Assessment of the High Performance Paradigm," *British Journal of Industrial Relations* 42: 349–378.

62. O'Reilly, B. 1994. "The New Deal: What Companies and Employees Owe One Another," *Fortune* (June 13): 44–52, at p. 44.

63. Cappelli, P. 1995. "Rethinking Employment," *British Journal of Industrial Relations* 33: 563–602.

64. Heckscher, C. 1995. *White Collar Blues: Management Loyalties in an Age of Corporate Restructuring.* New York: Basic Books.

65. Rousseau, D. 1996. "Changing the Deal While Keeping the People," *Academy of Management Executive* 10: 50–59.

66. Storey, J., P. Quintas, P. Taylor, and W. Fowle. 2002. "Flexible Employment Contracts and their Implications for Product and Process Innovation," *International Journal of Human Resources Management* 13: 1–18.

67. Rust, K., W. McKinley, G. Moon-Kyungpook, and J. Edwards. 2005. "Ideological Foundations of Perceived Contract Breach Associated with Downsizing: An Empirical Investigation," *Journal of Leadership and Organizational Studies* 12: 37–52.

68. Chadwick, C., L. Hunter, and S. Walston. 2004. "Effects of Downsizing Practices on the Performance of Hospitals," *Strategic Management Journal* 25: 405–427.

69. Mone, M. 1994. "Relationships between Self-Concepts, Aspirations, Emotional Responses, and Intent to Leave a Downsizing Organization," *Human Resource Management* 33: 281–298.

70. "Trenton Car Works Lays Off 400; U.S., Mexican Plants to Gain," *The ChronicleHerald (Halifax)*, November 25, 2005, pp. 1–2.

71. Keenen. G. "GM to Shut Star Oshawa Plant," *The Globe and Mail*, November 22, 2005, p. A1.

72. Wagar, T. 2001. "Consequences of Work Force Reduction: Some Employer and Union Evidence," *Journal of Labor Research* 22: 851–862.

73. Frost, A. 2001. "Reconceptualizing Local Union Responses to Workplace Restructuring in North America," *British Journal of Industrial Relations* 39: 539–564.

# 11

# Strategic International HRM

This chapter was written by Dr. Stefan Gröschl and is based on the previous edition's chapter by Dr. Xiaoyun Wang, I.H. Asper School of Business, University of Manitoba, Winnipeg, Manitoba; and Dr. Sharon Leiba-O'Sullivan, Department of Management, Faculty of Commerce and Administration, University of Ottawa, Ottawa, Ontario.

## Chapter Learning Objectives

After reading this chapter, you should be able to

- Identify key challenges influencing HR practices and processes within an international context.
- Identify key characteristics of strategic international HRM (IHRM).
- Understand the relationship between different approaches of IHRM and corporate business strategy options.
- Understand the impact of globalization and internationalization on key HR practices and processes

## DUAL-CAREER COUPLES: TRAILING SPOUSE'S JOB NEEDS START TO GET MORE COMPANY TIME

Ruth Whitby loves her husband, Ben—and she also loves her job. When he was transferred to Japan, Whitby, a British medical doctor, struggled for a year to get a license to practise in Japan. She eventually succeeded and built a thriving medical practice in Tokyo, only to see her diplomat husband transferred again. This time all attempts at practising medicine in their new home of Vienna failed. Dr. Whitby, 39, now leaves her two small children, Joe, 8, and Isobel, 6, every third week to practise at a clinic in London.

Thirty years ago, a diplomat's wife like Whitby might have busied herself planning luncheons and ironing her husband's shirts. Times have changed. Almost half of spouses of overseas employees have their own jobs and their unwillingness to give these up is an increasing impediment to mobility, according to corporate surveys. In a time of cost cuts and economic downturns, overseas employers are loath to spend money finding a job for an accompanying spouse. . . .

The issue of dual-career partners is quietly becoming a crisis in multinational human resources circles, but still one that many employers would rather not address. . . . A 1999/2000 survey by the accountants PricewaterhouseCoopers of 270 European employers found that almost two thirds listed the spouse or partner's career as a barrier to mobility. The authors of the study also noted that "factors rated least highly by companies when selecting people for assignments such as partner adaptability and dual career management are the most likely to be the cause of failed assignments."

"We are seeing this problem more and more," said Pam Braun, a spokeswoman for Royal Dutch Shell Group. "The dual career issue is hot. Now every partner, and more and more are men, wants to have a career." Despite these findings, and numerous other surveys showing the same trends, companies are slow to address this issue. Only 19% of companies participating in the Windham survey helped spouses to find jobs, 20% helped with career planning, and 11% paid a job-finding fee. A third offered no assistance at all.

"A lot of human resources managers know this dual career issue exists," said Britain-based lecturer and career counselor Joanna Parfitt. "But they still have their heads in the sand."[1]

The challenge of accommodating the particular needs of dual-career couples is one of many HR aspects in the internationalization of organizations and their managers. Based on worldwide economic, political, and technological development and changes such as the opening of China's market, the Eastern expansion of the European Union, and improved and faster communication systems, many organizations are now expanding beyond their national borders. This trend toward internationalization and globalization requires organizations to operate in increasingly complex business environments, and to consider the appropriateness and effectiveness of organizational processes and managerial practices in cultural settings other than their own.[2] Comparative international and cross-cultural management research projects[3] and multinational teams[4] concluded that, in particular, the planning and managing of human resources play a key role in the successful expansion of organizations across national borders.

# Key Challenges Influencing HR Practices and Processes within an International Context

When entering new markets organizations confront a wide range of challenges mostly related to socioeconomical, political, and technological aspects. Following is a brief discussion of some of the key issues HR managers faced when their organizations expand across national borders.

## Workforce Diversity

**RPC 11.1**

Many articles in academic journals and the popular press have documented Canada's growing workforce diversity. While the different dimensions of diversity provide Canadian organizations with many opportunities, Canada's workforce diversity also produces a wide range of HR-related challenges including the integration and accommodation of an increased number of older workers and employees with disabilities, gender issues, and aspects related to ethnic and cultural differences amongst employees. The complexity of the current workforce diversity will grow with each foreign market Canadian organizations decide to enter, multiplying the workforce diversity–related challenges HR managers currently face. International Human Resource Management (IHRM) systems must consider and accommodate the needs of such an increasingly diverse labour force and tailor international HR policies and practices accordingly.

## Employment Legislation

HR managers of organizations operating across Canadian provinces are faced with a complex employment legislation framework consisting of different provincial Employment Standard acts and Human Right codes, and a federal Labour Code and Human Rights Act. Adding to this complexity are the Health and Safety legislation, Labor Relations legislation, the Employment Equity Act, and many other provincial and federal employment-related laws and regulations. When crossing national borders, Canadian HR managers encounter additional, host-country employment legislation—and in the case of a European Union (EU) member state being the host country, employment laws and regulations of the host country and the EU. This wide range of home and host-country employment legislations represent a key challenge to HR managers and the development and implementation of employment policies, processes, and practices in Canadian organizations operating internationally.

## The Role of the HR Function

HR departments are often understaffed, underfunded, and limited to a supporting role with little key decision-making power. Yet, employment legislation, socioeconomic, and technological differences in local markets demand sophisticated IHRM systems. The creation of such systems requires sufficient financial and human resources and support. It is crucial that HR managers responsible for the development and implementation of such systems are equipped with the necessary staff, and are integrated in the organizational strategic decision-making process and the development of organizational goals and objectives. Previous chapters have shown the importance and the challenge of matching HRM practices with organizational goals. Within an international context, this matching process becomes even more challenging and, at the same time, even more imperative for the successful expansion beyond national borders. The increased complexity of the HR function requires HR managers to redefine their role and outsource some of their responsibilities to specialists and consultants (e.g., international employment lawyers).

### Flexibility

**flexibility**
the ability to respond to various demands from a dynamic competitive environment

In an international context, the changes are dramatic and fast paced, though they are different from country to country. In such a dynamic global competitive environment, IHRM systems need to be flexible to quickly adjust their policies and practices to respond to the changes. **Flexibility** is defined as a firm's ability to respond to various demands from a dynamic competitive environment."[5] Yet, no matter how capable the HR manager is, it is impossible to expect him or her to know or follow all the changes in the international competitive environment. Advanced IHRM systems, however, can obtain a high level of fit and flexibility by developing a strategic approach toward the management of international workforces.

## Strategic International Human Resource Management

**strategic international HR planning**
projecting global competence supply, forecasting global competence needs, and developing a blueprint to establish global competence pools within companies

Due to the complex and challenging nature of the global business environment, the methodical and careful planning of a strategic international HR approach is imperative. **Strategic international HR planning** typically involves projecting global competence supply, forecasting global competence needs, and developing a blueprint to establish global competence pools within companies, so that the supply of global managers worldwide will be sufficient to meet with the multinational company's (MNC) global strategies. Attracting and retaining managers who are competent to represent the company in a global arena have been rated as the most critical goals of international HRM by multinational corporations (MNCs).[6]

Moreover, international HR planning needs to fit with both the internal factors, such as a firm's strategies, competencies, and existing HR system; and the external factors including local economic, political, social, cultural, legal, and HR systems. A fit and, as mentioned earlier, flexible IHRM system is critical for firms to successfully implement their international strategies and to gain competitive advantage. Studies found that MNCs implement their home HR practices in their subsidiaries abroad on some issues, such as pay systems, management development, or employee communications. However, with other issues, such as wage determination, hours of work, forms of job contract, and redundancy procedures that are subject to local laws and convention, MNCs tend to follow the local practices, although the extent to which IHRM practices fit with the local environment or with home headquarters varies from company to company and from country to country.[7] Strategic thinking is needed for IHRM to project HR supply and to forecast HR needs for the foreign subsidiaries. Therefore, **strategic international HRM** is defined as "human resource management issues, functions, and policies and practices that result from the strategic activities of multinational enterprises and that impact the international concerns and goals of those enterprises."[8]

**strategic international HRM**
human resource management issues, functions, policies, and practices that result from the strategic activities of multinational enterprises and that affect the international concerns and goals of those enterprises

## Strategic IHRM Fits with Corporate International Business Strategies

As mentioned in previous chapters, HR planning should fit with the overall business strategies of the firm. This principle should apply to IHRM as well. **Fit** is defined as "the degree to which the needs, demands, goals, objectives and/or structure of one component are consistent with the need, demands, goals, objectives and/or structure of another component."[9] Based on this principle, IHRM approaches and policies will be influenced by the overall corporate international strategies, the type of product or service, and the organizational structure and culture (*internal fit*). At the same time, it is important to consider the local legal, political, economic, and cultural factors (*external fit*). The internal and external fits of IHRM are vital to the effective implementation of a corporate strategy.

**fit**
the degree to which the needs, demands, goals, objectives, and/or structure of one component are consistent with the need, demands, goals, objectives, and/or structure of another component

## The Domestic Stage

Organizations applying a **domestic strategy** become international by exporting goods abroad as a means of seeking new markets, focusing on domestic markets and exporting their products without altering the products for foreign markets. Since this is an initial step of going international and there is no subsidiary in foreign countries, there is very little demand on the HR department to conduct its practices any differently than domestic HR practices. Usually, an export manager is appointed by headquarters to take charge in the exporting business.

**domestic strategy**
internationalizing by exporting goods abroad as a means of seeking new markets

## The Multidomestic Stage

As the firm develops expertise in the international market and as the foreign market grows in importance for the success of the organization, a subsidiary is typically set up reflecting a **multidomestic strategy**.[10] Management at

**multidomestic strategy**
a strategy that concentrates on the development of foreign markets by selling to foreign nationals

this stage realizes that there are "many good ways" to do business and that cultural sensitivity is important to be successful in the local market. A polycentric perspective is a trademark of this stage, and firms use the multidomestic strategy to develop culturally appropriate products for local markets.

In line with this polycentric business strategy, the company's IHRM system will apply an **adaptive IHRM approach**, adopting local HR practices in their host country's subsidiaries. For example, French lodging giant ACCOR is taking this approach and has adopted many local HRM practices in its U.S. subsidiaries in order to attract and retain local employees. Following an adaptive IHRM approach, a local executive is usually hired to take charge of the subsidiaries' HR management. The advantage of this method is that the local HR manager for the subsidiaries is familiar with local issues, and there is no language barrier between the HR manager, local partners, and employees. Hiring a local HR manager can also guarantee the consistency of the HR practices with the local legal system and environment. One disadvantage of this approach is if the local HR manager does not know the corporate culture well enough to reflect the overall corporate strategies and the corporate principles in the subsidiary HR system. Nevertheless, because HRM is very sensitive to local legal and economic systems, compared to other business functions, such as finance and manufacturing, HRM has mostly adhered to local practices in many multinational corporations.[11]

**adaptive IHRM approach**
HRM systems for foreign subsidiaries that will be consistent with the local economic, political, and legal environment

## The Multinational Stage

When more and more MNCs enter the same market, the competition from other multinationals forces management to shift its strategy, resulting in the standardization of its products and services around the world to gain efficiency. Such a **multinational strategy** promotes a price-sensitive perspective with limited emphasis on cultural differences.[12]

Following the company's multinational business strategy, HR systems will be standardized across its subsidiaries all over the world. Numerous MNCs, such as Ernst & Young have adopted such an **exportive IHRM approach** to reduce transaction costs, ensure the consistency of their corporate policies all over the world, and gain control over their subsidiaries.[13] The advantage of this approach is that the HR managers at headquarters have a "tried and true" HR system and can readily implement it efficiently in subsidiaries in other countries. The disadvantage of this approach is that the local environment will not have been considered in the HR system, and the fit with the local system will be missing, which may cause some problems for the subsidiaries' management.

**multinational strategy**
standardizing the products and services around the world to gain efficiency

**exportive IHRM approach**
transferring home HRM systems to foreign subsidiaries without modifying or adapting to the local environment

## The Global Stage

Companies adopting a **global strategy** are striving to introduce culturally sensitive products, with the least amount of cost. To accomplish this, resources and materials within regional branches are reallocated globally to make quality products at the lowest cost. A geocentric perspective is taken by the company management at this stage.

**global strategy**
introducing culturally sensitive products in chosen countries with the least amount of cost

Fitting this global business strategy is an **integrative IHRM approach** combining home HR practices with local practices. The best HR policies and practices will be chosen for the foreign subsidiaries. For example, some Japanese companies have transferred some of their HR practices, such as job flexibility, intensive on-the-job training, teamwork, and cooperative relations between management and employees, to North America, but abandoned other practices, such as the use of uniforms.[14] With this approach, not only can the best context-free HR practices be transferred to subsidiaries, but also sound foreign practices can be learned and transferred to headquarters. The decision making regarding HR policies and practices will be jointly in the hands of headquarters and foreign subsidiaries. Therefore, this approach usually goes along with the global strategy and is recommended for the purpose of mutual learning between headquarters and subsidiaries. The challenge of using this approach is that the HR managers at headquarters need to have a geocentric or global perspective, be culturally sensitive, and be able to strategically move HR resources around the subsidiaries and headquarters.

The above four corporate strategies are usually adopted by MNCs. Companies may not practise one strategy exclusively at any one time; they might simultaneously implement the four strategies for different products at the same time. Of the different IHRM approaches, it is not difficult to see that the adaptive approach has the highest external fit, the exportive approach has the highest internal fit, and the integrative approach has the maximum fit both internally and externally. The integrative approach is highly recommended since, as mentioned above, both internal factors and external factors are important to successfully implement corporate international strategies.

## Key HR Practices and Processes within an International Context

As previously mentioned, the global expansion of organizations particularly influences the management of their human resources. Organizations operating internationally are challenged by issues such as managing an increasingly culturally diverse workforce with different work values, attitudes, and behaviour. The implications are reflected, for example, in the adaptation process of expatriates in host countries, when conflicts or tensions between expatriates and host-country nationals are often the result of cultural differences.[15] The author selected a number of key HR areas demonstrating how HR processes and practices are influenced by the internationalization of organizations.

### Recruitment

In the domestic context, one of the key strategic decisions in recruitment is the internal recruitment versus external recruitment. This two-option decision has a three-option parallel in the international domain and includes recruitment opportunities such as **home-country nationals (HCNs), parent-country nationals (PCNs)**, and **third-country nationals (TCNs)**. HCNs are individuals from the subsidiary country who know the foreign cultural environment well. PCNs are individuals from headquarters who are

**integrative IHRM approach**

combining home HR practices with local practices and selecting the most qualified people for the appropriate positions no matter where these candidates come from

**home-country nationals (HCNs)**

individuals from the subsidiary country who know the foreign cultural environment well

**parent-country nationals (PCNs)**

individuals from headquarters who are highly familiar with the firm's products and services, as well as with its corporate culture

**third-country nationals (TCNs)**

individuals from a third country who have intensive international experience and know the corporate culture from previous working experience with corporate branches in a third country highly familiar with the firm's products and services, as well as with its corporate culture. TCNs are individuals from a third country who have intensive international experience and know the corporate culture from previous working experience with the corporate branches in the third country.

While each recruitment option has its strategic advantages and disadvantages (see HR Planning Notebook 11.1) it is crucial that any staffing decisions be based on the MNC's short- and long-term strategies and follow best

## HR Planning Notebook 11.1

### Strategic Advantages and Disadvantages of Key Recruitment Options

| | Advantages | Disadvantages | SIHRM |
|---|---|---|---|
| **PCNs** | • well versed in company's needs and norms | • potential unfamiliarity with the cultural norms of the host country (including norms of supervision)<br>• potential blocking of HCNs' career progression within the firm<br>• considerable costs of relocating abroad | Strong exportive SIHRM approach |
| **HCNs** | • familiarity with the host-country culture | • limited familiarity with firm's own operations<br>• PCNs at headquarters may lack sufficient understanding of the subsidiary's needs, and corporate strategy for the subsidiary may suffer as a result | Strong adoptive SIHRM approach |
| **TCNs** | • greater familiarity with the host-country culture than PCNs (if, that is, the TCNs come from a proximal nation) but loyalty will be to the firm (rather than to the host country per se)<br>• relocation costs lower than for PCNs<br>• enhanced career development opportunities by allowing employees from the various subsidiaries to move to other subsidiaries<br>• improved understanding of the subsidiaries' needs by the corporation and vice versa through greater interaction between TCNs positioned in regional or corporate headquarters and PCNs | • some cross-cultural preparation may still be required<br>• potentially suffering from a lack of knowledge of the corporate culture<br>• use of TCNs is often part of a strategy that entails the use of employees from many nationalities (including HCNs and PCNs) increasing the overhead for expatriate relocation across the entire firm considerably<br>• using TCNs to the exclusion of HCNs may create the same problem of blocked career advancement that occurs when PCNs are used in this manner | Mixture of exportive and adoptive SIHRM approach |

## HR Planning Today 11.1

### The Eight Developmental Goals of Global Competence

| Category | Proposed Developmental Goal |
| --- | --- |
| Ability | Increase an individual's ability to transact business in another country. |
| | Increase an individual's ability to change leadership style based on the situation. |
| Knowledge | Increase an individual's knowledge of the company's worldwide business structure. |
| | Increase an individual's knowledge of international business issues. |
| | Increase an individual's network of professional contacts worldwide. |
| | Increase an individual's openness. |
| | Increase an individual's flexibility. |
| | Reduce an individual's ethnocentrism. |

Source: Reprinted with permission from HUMAN RESOURCE PLANNING, Vol. 24, Issue 3, 2001 by The Human Resource Planning Society, 317 Madison Avenue, Suite 1509 New York, NY 10017, Phone: (212) 490–6387, Fax: (212) 682–6851

recruitment practices. The latter include the development of a job analysis identifying job specifications and providing the basis for job descriptions.

Each specific assignment might have different job descriptions and require different knowledge, skills, and abilities (KSAs), which is similar to domestic assignments. However, general KSAs are also required to carry out these assignments in a foreign context. Caligiuri and Di Santo's[16] empirical study identified a list of abilities, knowledge, and personality characteristics that are essential for global managers with different positions in diverse cultures (see HR Planning Today 11.1).

**RPC 11.2**

Once the international assignment needs have been identified and the appropriate recruitment pool has been chosen, the right candidates must be selected.

## Selection

Selecting the right candidates for global assignments is crucial for the long-term success of both the MNC and the individual managers. Increasing numbers of firms have realized the importance of this issue and started to initiate programs with better selection and preparation to improve their return on investment (ROI) (see HR Planning Today 11.2).

**RPC 11.3**

### Personality as a Selection Criterion

The five-factor personality model (FFM)[17] has been demonstrated crucial to expatriate adjustment.[18] These five factors are emotional stability, extraversion, openness, agreeableness, and conscientiousness (see HR Planning Today 11.3 for a detailed explanation). Expatriates who scored high on these five dimensions were found to be better adjusted in overseas assignments.[19] This personality model should be used for selecting the potential global managers.

### International Selection

The 2001 Global Relocation Trends Survey was conducted by Windham International GMAC GRS, the National Foreign Trade Council (NFTC), and the SHRM Global Forum. It revealed that among organizations that planned major expatriate and family-support initiatives for 2002 to improve their expatriate ROI, 32% planned to have better candidate assessment and selection, 26% used career path planning and cross-border skills upon the expatriates' return, 24% wanted to be more effective in communicating assignment objectives, 20% would do better assignment preparation, 17% were instituting a company-sponsored monitoring program, 10% were introducing mandatory cross-cultural preparation, 7% were going to develop or expand the company's intranet for expatriates, 6% would become more communicative and provide more recognition during an assignment, 5% were using Web-based cross-cultural training, and 4% installed mandatory destination-support services. The large number of verbatim comments from organization respondents indicates a high level of interest in this topic.

#### Verbatim Comments: Programs to Improve ROI

The following are some of the comments companies repeatedly gave when discussing what they planned to do to improve initiatives to support expatriate employees and their families:

- We are improving the planning of the assignments.
- There are no support initiatives. It's only been a recent initiative to even standardize our approach to an international program. The global human resources department that created the program probably will not review the process for some time. They are dealing more with downsizing issues and outsourcing.
- Our company made significant progress in clearly identifying goals upfront and finding suitable candidates to fill specific roles overseas. The number of "failed" assignments has been significantly reduced over the last three years due to better expatriate preparation and selection.
- For most expatriates, assignments are part of a budgeted project execution plan with clear objectives.

Source: Global Relocation Trends 2001 Survey, February 2002.

The instrument for measuring these dimensions of personality can be found at www.parinc.com.

### Trainability as a Selection Criterion

Research so far appears to have presumed that cross-cultural training (CCT) is the panacea for most expatriate ills.[20] Yet it is quite possible that some individuals are simply more cross-culturally adaptable than others, and that, accordingly, CCT will have a more positive effect on them. Other researchers have also observed that there is a synergistic relationship between selection and training.[21] If you select someone who is "ready to hit the ground running," you are less likely to need to invest costly training dollars in that person. Therefore, the question of selecting for trainability is an important one. **Trainability** refers to an individual's ability to acquire certain skills to a desired level of performance.[22] Preliminary conceptual research on expatriate trainability has observed that the various cross-cultural KSAs may be classified according to their stable properties (e.g., personality) versus their

**trainability**

an individual's ability to acquire certain skills to a desired level of performance

Part III: Strategic Options and HR Decisions

## Five-Factor Model of Personality

*Emotional stability:* Individuals who score high on emotional stability are usually calm, even-tempered, and relaxed, and they are able to face stressful situations without becoming upset or rattled.

*Extraversion:* Individuals who score high on extraversion are sociable, like people, and prefer large groups and gatherings; they are also assertive, active, and talkative. They like excitement and stimulation and tend to be cheerful in disposition. They are upbeat, energetic, and optimistic.

*Openness to experience:* Individuals who score high on openness are curious about both inner and outer worlds, and their lives are experientially rich. They are

willing to entertain novel ideas and unconventional values, and they experience both positive and negative emotions more keenly than do closed individuals.

*Agreeableness:* Individuals who score high on agreeableness are fundamentally altruistic. They are sympathetic to others and eager to help them and believe that others will be equally helpful in return.

*Conscientiousness:* Individuals who score high on conscientiousness are purposeful, strong-willed, and determined.

Source: P.T. Costa, Jr., and R.R. McCrae, *Revised Neo Personality Inventory*. Lutz, FL: Psychological Assessment Resources, Inc., 1992. Reprinted with permission.

dynamic properties (e.g., knowledge, skills).[23] Put simply, we may be able to gain incremental success in our selection efforts if we select expatriates who possess a minimum level of the stable characteristics (e.g., extraversion) because such individuals may be better able to acquire the interpersonal skills (e.g., developing and maintaining relationships with culturally different others) that contribute to that success.

## Other Personal Characteristics

Many other different antecedent factors of cross-cultural adjustment have been identified in the literature. These include cultural knowledge, stress-management skills, conflict resolution skills, communication skills, and cognitive flexibility.[24] Several authors have simplified the above lengthy list into the following three dimensions of cross-cultural competencies:[25]

- self-maintenance competencies, which refer to the capability to substitute sources of reinforcement when necessary and deal with alienation and isolation;
- relationship competencies, which refer to the capability to develop and maintain relationships with home-country nationals (HCNs); and
- perceptual competencies, which refer to the capacity to understand why foreigners behave the way they do, to make correct attributions about the reasons or causes of HCNs' behaviour, and to correct those attributions when they prove to be incorrect.

Selecting candidates based on their true potential, using the above criteria, means choosing global managers for their personality, trainability, interpersonal skills, and attitudes, regardless of whether they are PCNs, HCNs, or TCNs. A capable global manager should be able to work in different countries to successfully implement his or her headquarters' strategies. This is usually the integrative approach, which seeks, for the most part, to place the best-qualified person in the position, regardless of the nationality of that person. In order to select the best person at the right time for the right place, managers should start by identifying the best potential global managers, then putting them through training and helping them develop their global careers. With this resultant group of managers available around the world, the firm will be able to recruit one of them for any global position that comes along.

## Pre-Assignment Training

The well-being of these expatriates and their families in the local country depends largely on how well they were prepared for the global assignment. Cross-cultural training for global managers and their accompanying relatives plays a crucial role in this pre-assignment process. Studies have consistently found that cross-cultural training positively influences expatriate self-development, interpersonal skills, and cross-cultural perception. Training was also found as having a major impact on the adjustment and effectiveness of expatriate managers.[26] Researchers have been calling for firms to conduct more formalized CCT for years. However, in reality, many firms still fail to heed this call, even though the situation has been improved (see HR Planning Today 11.4).[27] Part of

---

### HR Planning Today 11.4

#### Cross-Cultural Training

##### Cross-Cultural Program Availability

Most companies (69%) provide cross-cultural preparation of at least one day's duration—up from 57% in 2000 and compared to a historical average of 62%. Forty-four percent provide training for the entire family, 21% for expatriate and spouse, and 4% for expatriates alone. In addition, 50% of these cross-cultural programs extend to two days, and they are most commonly offered as a pre-departure service.

##### Effectiveness of Cross-Cultural Programs

When cross-cultural preparation is available, 67% of expatriates participate. When asked if cross-cultural preparation is mandated for all employees going on international assignments, only 30% responded yes, compared to 41% in 2000. When asked to rate the value of cross-cultural preparation with regard to expatriate success, 80% of companies report that it has great or high value, compared to a historical average of 84%. Only 2% indicate that it has little or no value.

##### CD-Based and Web-Based Cross-Cultural Programs

When asked if their formal cross-cultural programs include CD-based or Web-based alternatives, only 22% of respondents make these alternatives available. Of those who provide CD-based and Web-based alternatives, 58% use them as additional pre-move and post-move support to reinforce in-person cross-cultural programs, 33% use them as standalone alternatives to in-person programs, and 20% rely on CD-based or Web-based alternatives as the only type of cross-cultural preparation offered.

Source: Adapted from Global Relocation Trends 2001 Survey Report, February 2002, www.gmacglobalrelocation.com. The fall 2002 Global Relocation Trends Survey report and reports from previous years can be accessed from www.gmacglobalrelocation.com.

the problem could be a lack of coordination with HR planning activities; many firms find that expatriates are often selected too quickly, which precludes a lengthy training process.[28] Because of the improper usage of expatriate training, many companies have not benefited from the training.[29]

Strategic HR planning is needed for training in order to meet the goals of the career development for global managers and to focus on the development of global competencies as defined previously. Ptak et al.[30] interviewed professionals who were experienced in expatriate training. These professionals were asked to suggest some useful guidelines for overseas training. The researchers found that effective training should emphasize five points: (1) assess and evaluate the needs of training for expatriates; (2) clarify the purpose and goals of training that are relevant and applicable to participants' daily activities; (3) plan and design the training programs to meet training goals; (4) implement the training plan; and (5) use several techniques to increase the effectiveness of training programs. Based on the work of Ptak et al., the following four steps are provided for guiding the effective training:

- *Training planning:* Assess and evaluate the needs of training for every selected potential global manager. Clarify the purpose and goals of training that are relevant and applicable to global managers' daily activities. Plan and design the training programs to meet training goals.
- *Training contents:* Training can cover many areas depending on the needs of individual managers, ranging from technical training and managerial training to interpersonal skills training and cultural training. Typically, cultural training involves the following aspects:[31] (1) area studies programs that include environmental briefings and cultural orientations; (2) culture assimilators—essentially multiple-choice questions about cultural characteristics (each answer choice has a paragraph associated with it, describing why that answer was correct or incorrect; until the right answer is picked, the reader is asked to read the paragraph and then return to the question for another guess); (3) language training; (4) sensitivity training (which could include role-playing exercises and behavioural modelling videos designed to raise awareness of cultural differences in behaviour); and (5) field experiences, such as visits to the restaurants of the target nationality or actual visits to the host country itself. These cultural training activities are not only useful for the global managers, but also helpful for their spouses and children.
- *Training approaches:* Several training approaches have been used in reality, ranging from (1) an information-giving approach (such as lecture-based area briefings), to (2) behavioral modelling videos or case studies that offer vicarious learning, and (3) the most experiential forms (e.g., training based on role-playing and immersion in the form of field experiences).[32] These three methods should be encompassed in the training plan based on the training needs. An information-giving approach will increase the knowledge competency of the global managers; the other two approaches will increase

the trainees' other skills, such as interpersonal and analytical skills. All methods will be effective if they are planned properly to meet the training needs of the global managers, but the experiential methods are usually considered more "rigorous" (i.e., as having a greater degree of trainee involvement).[33]

- *Treating the international assignment as on-the-job training:* Global experience has been found to be the best way to help employees gain global competence. For example, Warner-Lambert has its Global Leadership Associates Program (GLAP), which is designed to rotate potential global mangers through various foreign Warner-Lambert businesses. By gaining experience in different cultures and functions, these managers will gain skills, ability, and knowledge to lead anywhere in the world.[34] To treat the international assignment as merely one step in an overall career development plan, one must consider the issues and principles involved in job rotation in general.[35] More specifically, the employee should remain on the rotation long enough to attain a level of proficiency that enhances context-specific knowledge and self-efficacy. The rationale for this is as follows: if one of the objectives of the expatriate's assignment is to acquire cross-cultural interpersonal skills that are available only in the subsidiary, then ample time should be allowed for the expatriate to develop these skills; similarly, if an objective of the assignment is to learn, from headquarters, how the organization works, ample time should be allowed for this to happen. The point is that removing the employee from the assignment prior to some degree of mastery being achieved may be detrimental to his or her self-efficacy (and, hence, to the actual expertise the firm sought to cultivate in the first place because self-efficacy is closely related to performance outcomes of various kinds).[36] In addition, on-the-job training and mentoring at the host-country site should also be arranged.[37] This could be provided by other expatriates at the host-country site or by HCNs. Moreover, to fully regard the international assignment as part of a long-term career development process, a plan must be in place for the expatriate's return to the home country (presuming, that is, that the PCN is to remain a PCN or to become a TCN). This, unfortunately, is where a lot of organizations fall short, and it has led to what has become known as the "repatriation issue."

**repatriation**

the process of PCNs, TCNs, or even HCNs returning to their home headquarters or home subsidiaries

## Post-Assignment Activities

### Repatriation

**Repatriation** usually means that the PCNs, TCNs, or even HCNs (working in headquarters as part of a career development plan) finish their overseas assignment and come back to their home headquarter or home subsidiaries. It is somehow expected that one will encounter "culture shock" when moving to another country. That one might experience culture shock upon return from abroad is usually not a concern. Yet research[38] suggests that the "big picture"

## HR Planning Today 11.5

### Once Abroad, Always Abroad?

A study by CIGNA International Expatriate Benefits, the National Foreign Trade Council (NFTC), and WorldatWork suggests that employers and employees hold significantly different opinions on the success of expatriate assignments. Forty-four percent of employees who had returned from an assignment reported leaving their employers within two years of their expatriate experience. A major problem of repatriation was the employees' status upon return. Twenty-one percent of employers implied that there was a commitment to have a job for the employee upon their return, according to the survey. More often, there was

no commitment and employees found a troubling situation upon their return. Sometimes, expatriates like the overseas experience so much that they seek another assignment. Seventy-seven percent of those surveyed reported they are more likely to accept an international position with another employer than a domestic position with their current employer. Eighty-seven percent would accept another overseas assignment with their current employer.

Source: Jeremy Handel, "Out of Sight, Out of Mind," *Workspan* (June 2001), 54–58.

of the cross-cultural adjustment process is that it is not just a U-curve process (i.e., the high of the post-arrival honeymoon, the low of the cultural shock experience, and the eventual regained high of adjustment and mastery), but rather a W-curve process, with the last "V" of the "W" happening in the form of "reverse culture shock" on return to the home country.[39]

It has been argued that reverse culture shock upon repatriation leads to several serious consequences for the employee and the organization, for example:

- Prior to the return home, the employee may become anxious at the thought of having no appropriate position to return to; this anxiety can affect productivity abroad and work adjustment shortly after repatriation.[40]
- The employee may become dissatisfied with his or her standard of living upon return, having become accustomed to the special status that accompanied the expatriate position.[41]
- Coworkers may not be interested in hearing about the repatriate's experiences; lots of things have gone on in their own lives over the last few years, and they've had their own preoccupations and focus.[42]
- The repatriate's job may not make as much use of internationally acquired KSAs as it could.[43] In this case, "out of sight, out of mind" is the operative phrase.[44] HR Planning Today 11.5 illustrates how this attitude can create "perpetual expatriates" and deprive a firm's headquarters of badly needed international competencies.
- There is a high rate of turnover among repatriates, ranging from 20% to 25% for U.S. repatriates[45]; comparable figures are not available for Canadian repatriates.

Clearly, a career development plan for global managers will minimize these negative consequences; the MNC can also make the most of the repatriate's internationally developed KSAs by treating them as candidates for global managers. The career planning for repatriates will also let the soon-to-be-repatriated individual have a clearer idea of what's in store, which will go a long way toward minimizing these negative consequences.

## Career Development

Two issues are of great importance for the long-term career development of global managers. The first is to regard the international assignment as merely one step in an overall career development plan. The second is to ensure that the next step (i.e., the candidate's subsequent assignment) makes good use of the KSAs developed internationally, as these will serve as a source of competitive advantage to the firm. There are a number of ways to incorporate KSAs acquired internationally into the repatriates' subsequent career development. The repatriate could serve as a mentor or formal trainer to future expatriates or provide input into the CCT process by recounting critical incidents experienced abroad. (This could have the benefit of giving the repatriate an appropriate forum in which to discuss his or her experiences.) Alternatively (or as well), the repatriate can apply his or her understanding of the subordinate's needs by eventually serving as a long-distance supervisor to other expatriates. Another option is for the expatriate not to be repatriated but instead to join the pool of global managers and remain an international employee for the duration of his or her career, rotating from subsidiary to subsidiary. HR Planning Today 11.6 provides anecdotal evidence of how consideration of the repatriation issue proved to be effective for Colgate-Palmolive.

## Performance Appraisal

Two broad categories of global assignments exist: technical/staff specialist and managerial.[46] The managerial expatriate may perform technical/staff specialist roles as well (usually at a low- or mid-level managerial position) or may hold a higher level managerial position, such as being the general

---

### HR Planning Today 11.6

#### An Effective Repatriation Policy

Colgate-Palmolive Co. recognized the wealth of information it already had on expatriate skills—in a system not originally designed for that purpose. Coleen Smith, New York-based vice-president for global people development, says that the company began putting together a global succession-planning database almost 10 years ago. "It has taken a variety of forms over the years," she says. While Colgate-Palmolive's database is primarily for succession planning, it also contains data on each manager's experience with or awareness of particular cultures. The information is made available throughout the company's worldwide network. "Senior leaders," Smith says, "have come to expect a certain level of information, which we really manage through our global succession-planning database."

Source: Robert O'Connor, "Plug the Expat Knowledge Drain," *HR Magazine* (October 2002), 101–107

manager of the entire subsidiary itself. Performance criteria should be developed ahead of time, and the criteria will vary according to the particular international assignment under consideration.

This may sound straightforward—after all, the job has objectives, and the objectives become criteria for evaluation. But, in the international realm, several additional environmental factors combine to make the choice of criteria significantly more complex than they would first appear.

- One such factor is the extent of interaction that the position requires.[47] A technical position in one context may demand greater interaction with HCNs than would a similar position in another context. For example, a computer specialist charged with the task of resolving a computer database problem may have relatively greater isolation when performing the task than would, say, a marketing manager charged with establishing a local distribution network. The greater the amount of interaction demanded, the greater the extent to which performance is contingent on the expatriate's cross-cultural skills. Expatriates hired in operational element positions may face a different kind of challenge. Such individuals, particularly those with managerial responsibilities, will often be faced with tasks that may both be novel and require considerable interaction with the environment. Such cross-cultural contextual factors will need to be incorporated into the performance targets set (either as criteria, or as a moderator of the level at which other targets are set). Otherwise, the set of criteria used may not be truly valid in content.

- Expatriates sent abroad to serve as upper-level managers, such as the general manager of a subsidiary, are often evaluated on the basis of the subsidiary's bottom-line results. But how comparable are these results internationally? Differences in accounting systems and financial reporting across countries can often lead to misinterpretation of results.[48] For example, Peruvian accounting rules count sales on consignment as firm sales.[49] Can this measure of sales performance be reliably and fairly used as an indicator of successful performance if none of the firm's other subsidiaries count their sales figures in this way?

- Another complicating factor is the volatility of the foreign labour market. If labour costs are high in a particular host country (e.g., Hong Kong) but not in any of the other countries in which the firm's subsidiaries operate, is it fair to penalize the general manager operating in the country with high labour costs for lower returns because of costs that are beyond his or her control? Or, if the skill level of HCNs is fairly low, but the host-country government requires the firm to employ a minimum percentage of locals in their operations, can the resultant lackluster productivity levels (as compared to other subsidiaries of the firm) be justly blamed on the general manager?

- In addition, telecommunication and transportation infrastructures are severely lacking in many host countries, which adds to the time inefficiencies (and hence, costs) of doing business in these places.[50] Sometimes the infrastructure may exist, but it may operate in a way that is thoroughly foreign to the expatriate. Performance may be fairly slow until the expatriate has reached a more advanced level in his or her learning curve regarding "the way things are done around here" (i.e., in the host country). All of the above must be taken into consideration when setting target levels for performance.

Therefore, the international performance appraisal should be conducted within the contextual considerations mentioned above. Everything we know about performance appraisals says that measuring observable behaviour (e.g., using behaviourally anchored rating scales, or BARS) is the most valid and reliable means of assessing performance. When using this standardized instrument (BARS) for an international assignment, it is recommended to have both host-country supervisors and subordinates and home-country supervisors and subordinates perform the appraisal.[51] When taking the bottom-line financial results as appraisal criterion, the targets should be set in accordance with the environmental considerations mentioned above.

## Compensation

Expatriates and their families will usually incur the following categories of cash outlays:[52] (1) goods and services (food, personal care, clothing, household furnishings, recreation, transportation, and medical care); (2) housing (major costs associated with the employees' principal residence); (3) income taxes (payments to federal and local governments for personal income taxes); (4) reserve (contribution to savings, benefits, investments, education expenses, social security taxes, etc.); and (5) shipment and storage (major costs associated with shipping and storing personal and household effects). Employees working in any particular subsidiary may come from a multitude of countries; consequently, the first three of these outlay categories are where the greatest discrepancies can arise if the firm does not take careful action.

The multinational firm has several choices to make regarding how to cover these expenses. For example, salary can be paid at the home rate rather than the local rate or in the home currency rather than local currency. Ceilings can be established for payment of certain expenses (or certain expenses can be completely prohibited if excessive). The expatriate candidate should be informed of these ceilings in advance. The firm can also alter the combination of the package according to its direct and indirect compensation components to alleviate the effects of tax discrepancies across borders.[53] Finally, benefits such as home leave allowances (trips home) are commonly offered.[54]

By having a policy for the firm's strategic approach to international compensation, the firm will increase the likelihood that the above choices will be made in a fairly consistent manner and that there exists some incentive to be posted abroad. Three common policy options typically are considered: (1) a home-based policy, (2) a host-based policy, and (3) a region-based policy:[55]

- The home-based policy approach links the expatriate's and TCN's base salary to the salary structure of the relevant home country. For example, a Canadian executive transferred to Mexico would have his or her compensation package based on the Canadian base salary level rather than that of the host country, Mexico. The advantage is that this policy (1) creates equity with home-country colleagues and (2) can be cheaper when some home countries have lower wages than the host country (e.g., if a Mexican employee was stationed in a Canadian subsidiary for a while). The key disadvantage is that international staff performing the same function in a given subsidiary may be paid at different base salaries merely due to an accident of birth location. This option can become a problem when the expatriate has been bouncing around from subsidiary to subsidiary over many years and no longer identifies himself or herself as a birth-country national.
- The host-based policy approach links the base salary to the salary structure in the host country but retains the home-country salary structure for other international supplements (e.g., cost-of-living adjustment, housing, schooling, and other premiums). The one advantage of this approach is that it attracts PCNs or TCNs to a higher-paying location. Disadvantages are that it does not eliminate inequities between PCNs and TCNs unless the home-country supplements are phased out over time (something that would apply primarily to expatriates who are unlikely to be repatriated to their country of origin).
- Finally, the region-based policy compensates expatriates working in their home regions (e.g., Canadians working in North America) at somewhat lower levels than those who are working in regions far from home. This approach has the advantages of (1) providing incentives for distant foreign relocation and (2) allowing significant cost savings, since those stationed in neighbouring countries will not receive the same premiums as those travelling farther away, and so it remains a promising option.[56]

## Labour Relations

Knowledge of the types of unions that exist in a country (i.e., the union structure) and the rate of unionization in that country can be critical to international HR managers. This is because union activities can influence the HR practices that may be implemented and how implementation may proceed. In short, such knowledge can influence international HR strategy.

At least four types of unions can be identified:[57] industrial, craft, conglomerate, and general. Industrial unions represent all grades of employees in an industry; craft unions are based on skilled occupations across industries; conglomerate unions represent members in more than one industry; and general unions are open to all employees in the country. This diversity of types of unions can be found to varying extents in different countries.[58] For example, Canada's union structure is industrial, craft, and conglomerate. In Australia, the United Kingdom, and the United States, all four types of union structures exist, although the United States has white-collar unions as well. Germany's union structure is primarily industrial and white collar, and Norway's is both industrial and craft. Japan's union structure consists of enterprise unions, which operate within the enterprise and have the employees of this enterprise as its members.

In addition to the diversity in types of unions, nations vary in their rates of unionization:[59] The United States has the lowest unionization rate, at 17%. Japan's rate is slightly higher, at 29%. Canada's unionization rate is tied with Germany's, at 38%. Australia's rate is 46%, while the United Kingdom's is 52%. One of the highest rates of unionization exists in Norway, where it is 65%.

Awareness of practical differences in labour relations, while laudable, is by itself insufficient. International HR managers need to translate this awareness into practice. Labour relations activities can constrain MNCs' abilities to influence wage levels (perhaps even to the extent that labour costs become noncompetitive).[60] Such activities may also limit the ability of MNCs to vary employment levels at will and may hinder or prevent global integration of the operations of the MNC.[61]

Accordingly, international HR managers must devise strategies to improve the fit between their labour relations activities and the external environment. Strategic compensation might be limited in countries with strong governmental or union wage interference. Firms operating in such countries may need to find other ways of maintaining low costs. Staffing may be affected in countries that limit the firm's ability to implement redundancy programs.[62] In such countries, worker retraining may be important because of the economic necessity to cross-train and retain workers to adapt to environmental and technological changes affecting the firm rather than lay off workers.[63] In short, the presence of unions need not be disastrous for the international firm; rather, the wise international HR manager will simply learn the constraints posed by the local union conditions and devise an effective strategy to plan accordingly.

## Summary

This chapter has addressed many of the strategic issues and decisions that must be taken into consideration in the context of managing employees internationally. Organizations seeking to expand their businesses globally would do well to do the following: first, recognize the strategic decision issues inherent in managing the HR function in an international context; second, strive to make these decisions in ways that take into account their firm's strategic objectives and recognize the added complexity that the international context brings; and third, the continuous career development of global managers should be arranged starting from the point of expatriate selection, followed by ongoing training and career arrangement after repatriation. Overall, all IHRM practices and issues should be implemented strategically and a global competence pool should also be developed strategically.

# Key Terms

adaptive IHRM approach, 300
domestic strategy, 299
exportive IHRM approach, 300
fit, 299
flexibility, 298
global strategy, 300
home-country nationals (HCNs), 301
integrative IHRM approach, 301

multidomestic strategy, 299
multinational strategy, 300
parent-country nationals (PCNs), 301
repatriation, 308
strategic international HRM, 299
strategic international HR planning, 298
third-country nationals (TCNs), 301
trainability, 304

# Web Links

A well-designed site that caters to the Canadian expatriate; it provides information and resources—including a forum—that are equally useful to Americans and other expatriates or those wishing to become so:

**www.canuckabroad.com** (p. 304)

The Canadian employee relocation council provides information about workforce mobility and employee relocation at its site:

**www.cerc.ca** (p. 305)

To view a listing of global expatriate sites, regional and country expatriate websites, and expatriate forums, discussion groups, and blogs visit:

**www.transitionsabroad.com/listings/living/resources/expatriatewebsites. shtml** (p. 308)

For embassy contacts and information about consulates around the world visit:

**www.globescope.com/portfolio.html** (p. 308)

For listings for and links to online newspapers from around the world go to:

**www.onlinenewspapers.com** (p. 308)

# RPC Icons

**RPC 11.1 Gathers, analyzes, and reports relevant business and industry information including global trends**

**RPC 11.2 Maintains an inventory of HR talent for the use of the organization**

**RPC 11.3 Identifies potential source of qualified candidates**

# Discussion Questions

1. This chapter has highlighted a number of internal and external challenges organizations currently face. Discuss how these challenges influence HR managers and their approaches to and development of

Chapter 11: Strategic International HRM

HR-related aspects and practices such as recruitment and selection, training and development, and reward systems when expanding across national borders.

2. What are global competencies, and how can they be established in multinational organizations?

3. This chapter introduced three international HRM approaches. Discuss the ways in which these different approaches will (or should) influence the selection, training, and compensation of global managers.

# Using the Internet

1. Use sites such as **www.canuckabroad.com/femaletravel/intro.shtml** to discuss whether there are challenges and barriers that are (or should be) of particular concern to a HR manager when sending female expatriate managers on international assignments.

2. Use sites such as **www.voyage.gc.ca/consular_home-en.asp** as a starting point for conducting an environmental scan to identify aspects in a country of your choice that could greatly influence your HR strategy of and approach to opening a unit or subsidiary in that country.

# Exercises

1. Go to the library and collect current articles about five companies in one functional area of international HRM. Articles can be found in journals such as *International Executive, Personnel, Human Resource Management*, and other practitioner journals in HRM. Summarize these articles. Then compare and contrast the practices used by these companies with the kinds of principles and issues raised in this chapter. Do the companies appear to be successful at what they are trying to do? Do they appear to be adhering to the prescribed theoretical approaches for managing these international HR functions? Comment on the similarity and differences between practice and theory. If real-life companies are not managing in the ways that are recommended by theory, which deviations from the text theory appear to be having the greatest impact, and what is it about the firm and its particular circumstances that appears to be causing certain deviations to be more significant than others?

2. Pick a well-known multinational and identify the countries in which it has subsidiaries. Next, compile a short (ten-page) CCT module that will prepare PCNs from the multinational to successfully adjust to the host-country culture of one of the firm's subsidiary countries. Using both pre- and post-tests, have your classmates evaluate the module based on its impact on their self-efficacy for interacting with HCNs from that culture.

# Case: An International Career Move

John Markham is a biochemist who now works as a manager with Drugs from Bugs (DFB), an innovative international pharmaceutical firm. John has been with DFB for the past ten years. He is married and has two children (a daughter in high school and a son in kindergarten). His wife, Anya, is a certified general accountant who works for a major accounting firm in the Toronto area. Their combined household income is $150,000. The president of DFB has asked John to become the managing director of DFB's operations in Israel. The government there has just offered a number of incentives to international pharmaceutical firms that make Israel a highly desirable location in which to operate.

John is keen on increasing the business in Israel, but he has concerns about his future with the company. He has heard that life in Israel can be fascinating but also quite difficult for someone who has never lived outside Canada.

John has received a memo from Anne Monty, DFB's vice-president of HR: "John, I hear there are quite a few good websites about Israel. You might want to check them out. Meanwhile, I have asked the Israeli Tourist Board to forward some material to you. Are you free for lunch next week? I look forward to hearing your thoughts. Cheers, Anne."

---

## Questions

1. Discuss the various issues that John should be concerned about regarding the transfer.
2. What additional information should John seek from the HR department?
3. Suggest the types of financial and nonfinancial incentives that DFB might offer John to induce him to accept the transfer.
4. Using the material discussed in this chapter, what issues should DFB consider when setting John's performance objectives for the international assignment?

# Endnotes

1. Lang, G. "Dual Career Couples: Trailing Spouse's Job Needs Start to Get More Company Time," *International Herald Tribune*, March 27, 2004. © 2004 I.H.T / iht.com. Reprinted by permission.
2. Schneider, S., and J. Barsoux. 1997. *Managing Across Cultures*. Hemel Hempstead, U.K.: Prentice Hall Europe.
3. For example, "The Price Waterhouse Cranfield Project" in Hegewisch, A., and C. Brewster. 1993. *European Developments in Human Resource Management*. London: Kogan Page.
4. For example, Brodbeck, F., Frese, M., Akerblom, S., Audia, G., Bakacsi, G., Bendova, H., Bodega, D., Bodur, M., Booth, S., Brenk, K., Castel, P., Den Hartog, D., Donnelly-Cox, G., Gratchev, M., Holmberg, I., Jarmuz, S., Correia Jesuino, J., Jorbenadse, R., Kabasakal, H., Keating, M., Kipiani, G., Konrad, E., Koopman, P., Kurc, A., Leeds, C., Lindell, M., Maczynski, J., Martin, L., O'Connell, J., Papalexandris, A., Papalexandris, N., Prieto, J., Rakitski, B., Reber, G., Sabadin, A., Schramm-Nielsen, J., Schultz, M., Sigfrids, C., Szabo, E., Thierry, H., Vondrysova, M., Weibler, J., Wilderom,

C., Witkowski, S., and Wunderer, R. 2000. "Cultural Variation of Leadership Prototypes across 22 European Countries," *Journal of Occupational and Organizational Psychology*, 73(1): 1–30.

5.  Sanchez, R. 1995. "Strategic Flexibility in Product Competition," *Strategic Management Journal*, Vol. 16, Special Issue: 135–159.

6.  Cuthill, S. 2000. "Managing HR Across International Borders," *Compensation and Benefits Management*, Vol. 16, No. 3: 43–45.

7.  Ferner, A. 1997. "Country of Origin Effects and HRM in Multinational Companies," *Human Resource Management Journal*, Vol. 7, No. 1: 19–37; Rosenzweig, P.M., and N. Nohria. 1994. "Influences on Human Resource Management Practices in Multinational Corporations," *Journal of International Business Studies*, Vol. 25: 229–251.

8.  Taylor, S., S. Beechler, and N. Napier. 1996. "Toward an Integrative Model of Strategic International Human Resource Management," *Academy of Management Journals*, Vol. 21, No. 4: 959–985.

9.  Nadler, D., and M. Tushman. 1980. "A Model for Diagnosing Organizational Behavior," *Organizational Dynamics*, Vol. 9, No. 2: 35–51.

10. Dowling, P.J., R.S. Schuler, and D.E. Welch. 1994. *International Dimensions of Human Resource Management*, 2nd ed. Belmont, CA: Wadsworth Publishing Company.

11. Rosenzweig, P.M., and N. Nohria. 1994. "Influences on Human Resource Management Practices in Multinational Corporations," *Journal of International Business Studies*, Vol. 25: 229–251.

12. Adler, N.J., and F. Ghadar. 1990. "Strategic Human Resource Management: A Global Perspective." In R. Pieper, ed., *Human Resource Management in International Comparison*. Berlin: de Gruyter: 235–260.

13. Bonache, J. 2000. "The International Transfer of an Idea Suggestion System," *International Studies of Management and Organization*, Vol. 29, No. 4: 24–44.

14. Beechler, S., and J. Yang. 1994. "The Transfer of Japanese-Style Management to American Subsidiaries: Contingencies, Constraints, and Competencies," *Journal of International Business Studies*, Vol. 25: 467–491; Bonache, 2000.

15. Mayrhofer, W., and C. Brewster. 1996. "In Praise of Ethnocentricity: Expatriate Policies in European Multinationals," *The International Executive*. 38(6): 749–778.

16. Caligiuri, P., and V. Di Santo. 2001. "Global Competence: What Is It, and Can It Be Developed Through Global Assignments?" *Human Resource Planning*, Vol. 24, No. 3: 27–35.

17. Costa, P.T., and R.M. McCrae. 1992. *Revised NEO Personality Inventory* [NEO-PI-R] *and NEO Five-Factor Inventory* [NEO-FFI] *Professional Manual*. Odessa, FL: Psychological Assessment Resources, Inc.

18. Deller, J. 1997. "Expatriate Selection: Possibilities and Limitations of Using Personality Scales." In Z. Aycan, ed., *Expatriate Management: Theory and Research,* Greenwich, CT: Jai Press: 93–116; Ones, D.S., and C. Viswesvaran. 1997. "Personality Determinants in the Prediction of Aspects of Expatriate Job Success." In Z. Aycan, ed., *Expatriate Management: Theory and Research*. Greenwich, CT: Jai Press, pp. 63–92.

19. Ones and Viswesyaran, 1997.

20. Leiba-O'Sullivan, S. 1999. "The Distinction between Stable and Dynamic Cross-cultural Competencies: Implications for Expatriate Trainability," *Journal of International Business Studies*, Vol. 30, No. 4: 709–725.

21. Wexley, K.N., and G.P. Latham. 1991. *Developing and Training Human Resources in Organizations*, 2nd ed. New York: Harper-Collins.

22. Tannenbaum, S.I., and G. Yukl. 1992. "Training and Development in Work Organizations," *Annual Review of Psychology*, Vol. 43: 399–441.

23. For example, Leiba-O'Sullivan, 1999.

24. Mendenhall, M., and G. Oddou. 1985. "The Dimensions of Expatriate Acculturation," *Academy of Management Review*, Vol. 10: 39–47; Walton, S.J. 1990. "Stress Management Training for Overseas Effectiveness," *International Journal of Intercultural Relations*, Vol. 14: 507–527; Black, J.S., and M. Mendenhall. 1990. "Cross-cultural Training Effectiveness: A Review and a

Theoretical Framework for Future Research," *Academy of Management Review*, Vol. 15, No. 1: 113–136; Abe, H., and R.L. Wiseman. 1983. "A Cross-cultural Confirmation of the Dimensions of Intercultural Effectiveness," *International Journal of Intercultural Relations*, Vol. 7: 53–67; Parker, B., and G.M. McEvoy. 1993. "Initial Examination of a Model of Intercultural Adjustment," *International Journal of Intercultural Relations*, Vol. 17: 355–379.

25. For example, Black and Mendenhall, 1990; Mendenhall and Oddou, 1985.

26. Phatak, A.V. 1989. *International Dimensions of Management*, 2nd ed. Boston: PWS–Kent Publishing Co.

27. Belcourt, M., and P.C. Wright. 1996. *Managing Performance through Training and Development.* Toronto: Nelson Canada; Feldman, D. 1989. "Relocation Practices," *Personnel*, Vol. 66, No. 11: 22–25; McEnery, J., and G. Des Harnais. 1990. "Culture Shock," *Training and Development Journal*, Vol. 44, No. 4: 43–47.

28. Mendenhall, M., E. Dunbar, and G. Oddou. 1987. "Expatriate Selection, Training, and 'Career-Pathing': A Review and Critique," *Human Resource Management*, Vol. 26: 331–345.

29. Black, S., and H.B. Gregersen. 1991. "When Yankee Comes Home: Factors Related to Expatriate and Spouse Repatriation Adjustment," *Journal of International Business Studies*, Vol. 22, No. 4: 671–694; Thomas, D.C. 1998. "The Expatriate Experience: A Critical Review and Synthesis," *Advances in International Comparative Management*, Vol. 12: 237–273; Tung, R.L. 1981. "Selecting and Training of Personnel for Overseas Assignments," *Columbia Journal of World Business*, Vol. 16: 68–78.

30. Ptak, C.L., J. Cooper, and R. Brislin. 1995. "Cross Cultural Training Programs: Advice and Insights from Experienced Trainers," *International Journal of Intercultural Relations*, Vol. 19, No. 3: 425–453.

31. Tung, 1981.

32. Black and Mendenhall, 1990.

33. Tung, R. L. 1982. "Selection and Training Procedures of U.S., European, and Japanese Multinationals," *California Management Review*, Vol. 25, No. 1: 57–71.

34. Caligiuri and Di Santo, 2001.

35. Nicholson, N. 1984. "A Theory of Work Role Transitions," *Administrative Science Quarterly*, Vol. 29: 172–191; Pinder, C.C., and K.G. Schroeder. 1987. "Time to Proficiency Following Job Transfers," *Academy of Management Journal*, Vol. 30, No. 2: 336–353.

36. Gist, M.E., C. Schwoerer, and B. Rosen. 1989. "Effects of Alternative Training Methods on Self-Efficacy and Performance in Computer Software Training," *Journal of Applied Psychology*, Vol. 74: 884–891; Gist, M.E., C.K. Stevens, and A.G. Bavetta. 1991. "Effects of Self-Efficacy and Post-Training Intervention on the Acquisition and Maintenance of Complex Interpersonal Skillsm" *Personnel Psychology*, Vol. 44: 837–861.

37. Katz, J.P., and D.M. Seifer. 1996. "It's a Different World Out There. Planning for Expatriate Success through Selection, Pre-Departure Training, and On-site Socialization," *Human Resources Planning*, Vol. 19, No. 2: 32–47.

38. Welch, D., T. Adams, B. Betchley, and M. Howard. 1992. "The View from the Other Side: The Handling of Repatriation and Other Expatriation Activities by the Royal Australian Airforce." In O. Yau and B. Stening, eds., *Proceedings of the AIB Southeast Asia Conference.* Brisbane, Australia.

39. Black, J.S., and M. Mendenhall. 1991. "The U-Curve Hypothesis Revisited: A Review and a Theoretical Framework," *Journal of International Business Studies*, Vol. 22, No. 2: 225–247.

40. Black and Gregersen, 1991.

41. Ibid.

42. Harvey, M.G. 1982. "The Other Side of Foreign Assignments: Dealing with the Repatriation Dilemma," *Columbia Journal of World Business*, Vol. 17, No. 1: 52–59.

43. Beck, J.E. 1988. "Expatriate Management Development: Realizing the Learning Potential of the Overseas Assignment." In F. Hoy, ed., *Best Papers Proceedings, Academy of Management 48th Annual Meeting* (August 1988). Anaheim, CA: 112–116; Tung, 1988.

44. Dowling et al., 1994; Handel, J. 2001. "Out of Sight, Out of Mind," *Workspan* (June): 54–58.

45. Adler, N.J. 1997. *International Dimensions of Organizational Behavior*, 3rd ed. Cincinnati, OH: South-Western College Publishing.

46. Dowling et al., 1994.

47. Ibid.

48. Ibid.

49. Garland, J., R.N. Farmer, and M. Taylor. 1990. *International Dimensions of Business Policy and Strategy*, 2nd ed. Boston: PWS-Kent.

50. Dowling et al., 1994.

51. Ibid.

52. Ibid.

53. Bishko, M.J. 1990. "Compensating Your Overseas Executives, Part I: Strategies for the 1990s," *Compensation and Benefits Review* (May/June): 33–34.

54. "Trends in Expatriate Compensation," *Bulletin to Management* (October 18, 1990): 336.

55. Anderson, J.B. 1990. "Compensating Your Overseas Executives, Part 2: Europe in 1992," *Compensation and Benefits Review* (July/August).

56. Dowling et al., 1994.

57. Katz, J.P., and S.W. Elsea. 1997. "A Framework for Assessing International Labor Relations: What Every HR Manager Needs to Know," *Human Resource Planning*, Vol. 20, No. 4: 16–25.

58. Ibid.

59. Ibid.

60. Ibid.

61. Ibid.

62. Ibid.

63. Ibid.

# Chapter 12

# Mergers and Acquisitions

## Chapter Learning Objectives

After reading this chapter, you should be able to

- Understand the various types of mergers and acquisitions.
- Explain why organizations merge and the methods used to achieve a merger.
- Identify the financial and human impacts of mergers.
- Describe the issues involved in blending cultures.
- Discuss how a merger affects HR planning, selection, compensation, performance appraisal, training and development, and labour relations.

## BIG IS BEAUTIFUL

The biggest IT merger in Canadian history occurred in 2001 when Hewlett-Packard and Compaq merged. In 2002, the merged organization placed third in the *Report on Business*'s ranking of Canada's top employers. Much of the credit for this successful merger can be given to the HR team, which managed the integration of systems and people coming from two different cultures. Another example of a successful merger occurred when Beatrice Foods and Alt Foods merged to become Parmalat, a multinational food company with 10 000 employees in over 30 facilities in North America. Key to the success was the development of vision, mission, and guiding principles, which were introduced throughout the organization via a two-day training program for groups of 20 employees over six weeks.[1]

Mergers and acquisitions (M&As) play a critical part in a corporation's survival, growth, and profit strategies. Many great companies were built on a track record of mergers and acquisition; they include GE, Thomson Corp., Alcan, and Power Financial. Power Financial bought London Life in 1997, McKenzie in 2001, and Canada Life in 2003, choosing only companies that reflect its core business and conducting professional due diligence. Merger activity in Canada increased by 71% in 2004[2]; therefore, HR professionals should add the ability to manage a merger as part of their skill set.[3]

In the world of mergers and acquisitions, Canadian companies are more often the prey, not the hunters. Foreign companies are launching bids to acquire Canadian companies, such as HBC, Canada's oldest organization, and our natural resource companies, such as steel companies. Henry Mintzberg, Canada's management guru, suggests that Canadians are less aggressive, being seen more as northern mice, rather than northern tigers. The result of this takeover activity is that we end up with shells, which means less work for head office specialists such as advertising, law, financial services, and human resources.[4]

Before we embark on a discussion of the motives for mergers, readers are encouraged to become familiar with the terms used to describe them.

## Definitions

A merger is a consolidation of two organizations into a single organization.[5] Within mergers, there are three categories:

**horizontal merger**
the merging of two competitors

- A **horizontal merger** is the merging of two competitors. The competitors combine to increase market power. These mergers typically are subject to review by regulators who fear monopoly power in the marketplace. The merging of Coles Books and SmithBooks to form

### A Rough Ride

One of the mergers that attracted a great deal of attention was the multi-billion-dollar merger of Chrysler and Daimler-Benz. There are always problems merging two cultures, but this merger posed additional problems because the rivals were also from two different countries. Behaviours based in national differences are very difficult to identify and describe. For example, the Daimler-Benz German culture is strong on formality, which the Americans judged as brutal and harsh, whereas to the Germans it meant respect. Likewise, the Germans saw the American informal or casual way of doing business as "goofy" and "acting like a game show host." Added to this mix were the two fiercely competitive organization cultures with each "rival" trying to establish who was best at what.

Source: D. Brown, "Everything's Fine, and Then...." *Canadian HR Reporter* (October 22, 2001), 1.

Chapters (which was then acquired by Indigo), is an example of competitors uniting to achieve economies of scale and to withstand the attack from American mega-bookstores. HR Planning Today 12.1 describes a merger of two big competitors.

- A **vertical merger** occurs when a buyer and a seller (or supplier) merge to achieve the synergies of controlling all factors affecting a company's success, from the production of raw goods to manufacturing to distribution and retail sales. A real estate agency might merge with a real estate developer, for example.

**vertical merger**
the merger of a buyer and seller or supplier

- A **conglomerate merger** occurs when one company merges with another but the two companies have no competitive or buyer-seller relationship. In other words, they are in different businesses competing in different markets. For example, IBI Income Fund, a land development specialist, merged with Daniel Arbour and Associates, specialists in the long-term management of recreational properties. Together they provide a wide range of services for land development and management.

**conglomerate merger**
the merger of two organizations competing in different markets

An acquisition is the purchase of an entire company or a controlling interest in a company. The purchase of Federated Department Stores by Robert Campeau is a public example. By purchasing Federated Department Stores for $6.6 billion, Campeau, a Canadian, became the fourth-largest retailer in the United States.

A **consolidation** occurs when two or more companies join together and form an entirely new company. In this case, the assets and liabilities of both companies are taken on by the third company, usually after the original companies are dissolved. Burroughs and Sperry, two computer manufacturers, consolidated to form UNISYS. Three hospitals in Toronto—York Finch, Humber Memorial, and Northwestern General—merged in response to budget cutbacks.

**consolidation**
the joining of two or more organizations to form a new organization

**takeover**

one company acquiring another company

A **takeover** occurs when one company seeks to acquire another company. Usually, a takeover refers to a hostile transaction, but it can mean a friendly merger as well. A hostile takeover refers to the acquisition of a company against the wishes of its management. ClubLink, known for operating 18-hole golf courses, received a hostile takeover bid from Tri-White Corp. The ClubLink management team campaigned successfully to win the support and votes of more than 50% of the outstanding shareholders.

For the purposes of this chapter, M&As will be treated as one category, that of two or more companies joining together. The next section examines three motives for merging.

## The Urge to Merge

Companies merge for three reasons: strategic benefits, financial benefits, and/or the needs of the CEO or managing team.

### Strategic Benefits

Companies that have growth as a strategic objective can expand in many ways: leveraging current customers, opening new markets internationally, corporate venturing, and M&As. The first three are slower methods. Acquisitions of companies in different regions or serving different markets are much quicker than internal expansion. Compaq and HP both sell computers but target two different markets: home offices and home entertainment customers. Their merger created more sales than two single brands.

Another strategic rationale that can be achieved through mergers and acquisitions is the strengthening of competitive position. Pfizer, a pharmaceutical company, took over its competitor, Warner-Lambert, in order to obtain the powerful cholesterol drug Lipitor. Companies may want to acquire competencies that make their core competence less imitatable.[6]

**operating synergy**

the cost reductions achieved by economies of scales produced by a merger or acquisition

Companies may acquire or merge with others to achieve complementarities. Different types of synergies can be achieved through M&As. (*Synergy* is a term taken from the physical sciences and refers to the type of reactions that occur when two substances or factors combine to produce a greater effect together than would result from the sum of the two operating independently. More simply stated, synergy can be described as two plus two equals five.) **Operating synergy**, which usually is referred to as economies of scale (decreases in per-unit costs), is the cost reduction produced by a corporate combination. Compaq and HP can renegotiate contracts with suppliers for memory chips and hard drives to save a total of $3 billion annually.[7] The merger of Inco and Falconbridge will result in a savings of $350 million achieved through synergies.[8] These gains are achieved by the spreading of overhead, the increased specialization of labour and management, and the more efficient use of capital equipment. Closely related to the economies-of-scale benefit is the economy-of-scope advantage. This is the ability of a firm to use one set of inputs to produce a wider range of products and services.[9] Banks, for example, like to use their bank tellers (now called financial consultants) to do not only banking, but also mortgage financing, insurance selling, and so on. Another type of synergy may occur when the acquiring firm believes that it can manage the target firm better and could increase its value. For example, a small firm may benefit significantly by using the larger firm's distribution networks and experienced management.

Companies may merge to gain access to new markets. For example, Air Canada was facing a domestic market that was mature, with little likelihood of growth. Therefore, Air Canada joined with several other carriers, including Thai Airways, Lufthansa, SAS, and United Airlines, under the Star Alliance banner, to pool costs, revenues, and destinations. More importantly, the merger allowed Air Canada, Canada's largest airline, to serve foreign markets such as Asia and northern Europe, which it was forbidden to access under bilateral agreements.

Diversification may be another strategic motive. A company may wish to reduce its dependency on a market that is cyclical in nature to capitalize on excess plant or employee capacity. For example, a ski resort may acquire a golf course in order to fill its hotel rooms and restaurants during the stagnant summer months. General Electric pursued this diversification strategy; not wanting to depend entirely on electronics, the company became a diversified conglomerate by acquiring insurance businesses, television stations, plastics manufacturing businesses, credit card businesses, and so on over a ten-year period.

Companies may even wish to redefine their businesses through acquisitions. Nortel Networks made a series of acquisitions in the 1990s to move from being a supplier of switches for traditional voice networks to a supplier of technology for the Internet. Of course, this strategy is not always successful.

Companies may also wish to achieve the benefits associated with vertical integration and horizontal integration. **Vertical integration** refers to the mergers or acquisitions of companies that have a buyer–seller relationship. Such a move may ensure either a dependable source of supply or control over quality of the service or product. PepsiCo acquired KFC, Taco Bell, and Pizza Hut and thus ensured the distribution of its products in these restaurant outlets. (However, Coke then convinced Wendy's and other fast-food chains that selling Pepsi in their outlets would indirectly benefit their competitors.[10])

**vertical integration**
the merger or acquisition of two organizations that have a buyer–seller relationship

**Horizontal integration** refers to the increase in market share and market power that results from M&As of rivals. Metro Inc. of Montreal purchased A&P Canada to gain access to a network of 579 food stores, mainly in Ontario. As the CEO of Metro Inc. stated, "We are very pleased to be acquiring the second largest food retailer in Ontario . . . which will enhance Metro's strategic position in Canada's two largest markets."[11] Western Canada's BC Telecom and Telus merged to become a stronger regional telephone company that was better able to compete against Bell Canada's launch of a new national company.

**horizontal integration**
the merger or acquisition of rivals

## Financial Benefits

Organizations look to M&As to achieve some financial advantages. Among these are the following:

- Organizations expect to reduce the variability of the cash flow of their own business. An organization lowers its risk by putting its "eggs in different baskets." However, a counterargument suggests that executives cannot manage unrelated businesses and must focus on and protect the core business from competitive and environmental pressures. The suggested wisdom is to put eggs in similar baskets.[12]

- Organizations expect to use funds generated by their own mature (or cash cow) businesses to fund growing businesses. However, some experts argue that the advantages of using one division to fund another division may be risky in the long run. Labelling one business in the portfolio a "cash cow" and another a "star" results in negative effects. Employees in the "mature" business may feel neglected, as resources are poured into the star, and may reduce their commitment to production and innovation. Management may misjudge which businesses have potential for market share increases and which do not. For example, most industry observers viewed the piano market as having slow or no growth. However, Yamaha saw the industry quite differently: the company looked worldwide for market share, saying, "Anyway, we are not in the piano business, we are in the keyboard business."[13] Sometimes slow-growth, highly competitive industries offer stable (not risky) returns.

- There may be tax advantages to the takeover, which vary by country. Considerable tax losses in the acquired firm may offset the income of a parent company.

- It is expensive to enter new markets and to develop new products. Compared to internal innovation and product development, acquisitions result in more rapid market entries. Acquisitions provide speedy access to new markets and to new capabilities, as exemplified by pharmaceutical companies that purchase biotechnology companies for their scientists and patents.[14]

- Astute corporations may analyze the financial statements of a company and decide that the company is undervalued. By acquiring the company, and sometimes by merging it with the administration already in place, a company can achieve financial gains.

The overriding goal is to increase the shareholders' wealth.

## Management Needs

Some argue that corporate life is a game, and managers love to play it. The theory here is that managers seek to acquire firms for their own personal motives, and economic gains are not the primary consideration.[15] This hypothesis may help explain why some firms pay questionably high premiums for their takeover targets.

One theory examines the "incentives" or payoffs to the CEOs if they engage in acquisition behaviour. Managers may pursue their personal interests at the expense of stockholders. For example, there is a positive correlation between the size of the firm and management compensation, and so CEOs can expect higher salaries for managing larger firms.[16] Other indirect incentives may include the prestige or status of owning larger firms or companies in fashionable sectors, such as the entertainment or sports sectors.

Another perspective examines the unconscious motives of CEOs. Robert Campeau's takeover of Allied Stores and Federated Department Stores has been subject to "armchair" analysis because he overpaid for his acquisitions and ultimately went bankrupt servicing the debt. Speculation on his motives ranges from the simple need to prove himself to complex theories espoused by psychoanalysts. But does the research support the theory that managers make decisions based on Freudian or unconscious motivators?

Most of the work in this area analyzes the role that a manager's unconscious desires or neuroses play in formulating corporate strategy or decision making.[17] Some research is based on the intensive analyses used by therapists to explore motives. A few studies attempt to link personality characteristics, such as the need for power, with growth strategies.[18] One study found that the greater the ego of the acquiring company's CEO—as reflected in the CEO's relative compensation and the amount of media attention given to that CEO—the higher the premium the company is likely to pay.[19] However, few studies arrived at helpful conclusions that would explain the behaviour of executives.

## Merger Methods

How do companies merge? The process, in a friendly environment, is relatively simple. The management of one company contacts the management of the target company. Sometimes an intermediary is used, such as an investment banker or, in smaller firms, a colleague who makes an introduction. During the first tentative talks, the boards of directors are kept informed of the procedures, and, ultimately, they approve the merger. Friendly deals can be completed quickly. Hostile takeovers become dramatic, with management pushing for "poison pills" and seeking "white knights" to protect themselves. (The term "poison pills" refers to the right of key players to purchase shares in the company at a discount—around 50%—that makes the takeover extremely expensive. "White knights" are buyers who will be more acceptable to the targeted company.) There is even a "Pac-Man" defensive manoeuvre, by which the targeted company makes a counteroffer for the bidding firm.

## The Success Rate of Mergers

Many studies have established that about 50% to 80% of M&As ultimately fail.[20] Some studies estimate that companies may lose up to 10% of their market value during the first year after a deal.[21] Acquisitions of related businesses fare better than acquisitions of businesses unrelated to the parent business.[22] The novice M&A management team does as poorly as the experienced team. Why? Perhaps because each merger is different, with different synergies and cultures.

Not only is the merged firm at risk, but the subsidiaries are also. There is some indication that a merger occupies so much management time, attention, and other resources that the original businesses are neglected. Executives of HP and Compaq spent more than one million person-hours planning for the integration.[23] There are enormous challenges in joining two companies. The problems include integrating computer systems, eliminating duplication, re-evaluating supplier relationships, reassuring clients, advising employees, and reconfiguring work routines.

The success rate may also vary by sector and by size. The manufacturing sector, for example, differs from the service sector. In the manufacturing sector, much more is fixed, with capital investments already made, with technology controlling process, and with lower job skills. The service sector, in contrast, relies on social-control mechanisms, which are highly subject to culture management. As such, the risk is greater with acquisitions in the service sector.

Size appears to influence success rates. A large firm can absorb a small firm in a relatively inconsequential fashion. The merger of two large firms generates more problems.

## Financial Impact

For many reasons, the financial returns are rarely those that were envisioned. Sometimes, a premium price was paid, and the company is unable to service the debt or recover the investment. At other times, the forecasted economies of scale or complementarities are not achieved. The market may have changed, resulting in revised forecasts.

During the merger of two health care facilities in the United States, chaos was created in the resulting company by the collapsing of 525 branches into 350, the attempt to standardize the two facilities' computer systems, the termination of a tenth of the workforce, an attempt at a second acquisition, and the defence of the company against a barrage of lawsuits.[24] The result was that outstanding bills jumped 30% in one year, payment times increased from 109 days to 131 days, earnings were down substantially, revenues were less than those of previous years, and the stock price dropped.

Overall, studies by consulting company McKinsey & Co. report that only 23% of mergers end up recovering the costs incurred in the deal, and about half of those analyzed by the American Management Association resulted in profit reductions.[25] Four out of five fail to produce any shareholder value.[26] Most devastating of all for merger maniacs was the analysis that demonstrated that nonacquiring companies (i.e., those that made no acquisitions) outperformed acquiring companies on Standard & Poor's industry indices.

Many mergers fail because the buyer overextends itself financially.[27] The buyer borrows heavily and then must engage in cost cutting to service the debt. Assets are spun off, employee numbers are reduced, and the new company is left in a financial shambles.

Even if the overall financial picture of the merged company appears rosy, there are indications that different functional areas suffer. For example, a firm that has to use cash to pay for the debt incurred in acquiring another business now has less to spend on certain projects that can be postponed, such as research and development.

The specialists in post-integration mergers at PricewaterhouseCoopers have conducted research that compares the goals of mergers to their success rates (see HR Planning Notebook 12.1). As you will note, most of the studies of mergers have examined U.S. mergers. One of the few studies to examine the mergers of Canadian companies shows a different trend. From an analysis of all mergers between 1994 and 2000, two Canadian academics concluded that there are

## Goals of Mergers and Achievement Rates

| Goals | Rationale for deal (%) | Rate of achievement (%) |
|---|---|---|
| Access to new markets | 76 | 74 |
| Growth in market share | 74 | 60 |
| Access to new products | 54 | 72 |
| Access to management/tech talent | 47 | 51 |
| Enhanced reputation | 46 | 48 |
| Reduction in operating expenses | 46 | 39 |
| Access to distribution channels | 38 | 60 |
| Access to new technologies | 26 | 63 |
| Reduction in number of competitors | 26 | 80 |
| Access to new brands | 25 | 92 |

Source: K. Frers and A. Chaday. 2000. "Why You Can't Create a Purple-Footed Booby." *Canadian HR Reporter* (November 20), p. 16. Adapted by permission of Carswell, a division of Thomson Canada Ltd.

positive and significant returns to shareholders, in contrast to American studies, which show negative or nonsignificant returns. Why? One explanation is that Canadian capital markets, industries, and companies are much smaller.[28]

However, there are some winners, namely the merger advisers. The Campeau–Federated Department Stores deal alone generated approximately US$500 million in fees for M&A advisory firms.[29]

## Impact on Human Resources

The real costs of a merger may be hidden—that is, not evident when analyzing financial records. Takeovers result in human displacement, and the cost of losing the best sales rep, who either is anxious about her job or does not wish to work for the acquired company, cannot be measured in accounting terms. The time involved in replacing this employee with a new one represents a cost to the employer.

Another study showed that nearly half of the senior executives in large acquisitions leave within a year of the takeover, and 75% leave within three years.[30] Add to this the thousands of jobs that are lost in the restructuring or downsizing of the merged companies. That is a national effect. The organizational effects are that it takes from 6 to 18 months for an organization to assimilate the results of an M&A, and the productivity loss is estimated to be 15%.[31] The loss of employee productivity stems from many sources:

- Employees go underground, afraid to make themselves visible or do anything that may put their jobs at risk.
- Overt sabotage occurs when employees deeply resent the turmoil the merger is causing in their lives.

- Self-interested survival tactics emerge, including hiding information from team members to accumulate a degree of power (the employee feels that he or she is "the only one who really knows how things work around here").
- A resigned attitude appears, stemming from the belief that no amount of work will prevent one from being fired.[32]
- Employees spend at least one hour a day dealing with rumours, misinformation, and job-search activities.[33]

But the real cost is to the thousands of employees who lose their jobs. Those who survive are affected in different ways. Most experience stress and anxiety, with a resultant loss of productivity.

To summarize, the feeling among those experienced in M&As is that, while mergers are forged for strategic and financial reasons, they succeed or fail for human reasons. Experts estimate that employee issues are responsible for the failure of one third to one half of mergers.[34] These people problems include the difficulty in blending cultures, reduction in service levels, poor motivation, loss of key people and clients, and the loss of focus on longer-term objectives.[35] The next section examines what many consider to be the greatest challenge of M&As—the blending of corporate cultures.

## ⒭⒫⒞ 12.2    Cultural Issues in Mergers

In an effort to increase the probability that the merger will work, many managers are turning to the principal reason that they fail: the meshing of cultures. The friendly merger of TransCanada Pipelines Ltd. and Nova Corp. was described as GI Joe meets the Care Bears.[36] The nearly US$10 billion merger of Nortel and Bay Networks was greeted with skepticism about its possible success, principally because of a predicted clash between the cultures[37] of a traditional telephone equipment manufacturer with a brash upstart newcomer. **Culture** is the set of important beliefs that members of an organization share. These beliefs are often unspoken and are shaped by a group's shared history and experience. Culture can be thought of as the "social glue" that binds individuals together and creates organizational cohesiveness.[38] Cultures, growing slowly over time, are not easy to describe, and employees are often aware of their corporate culture only when they try to integrate with people from another organization that has a different culture.

It is estimated that mismanagement of the culture is responsible for as high as 85% of all merger failures.[39] The longevity of an organization's culture cannot be underestimated. Canadian Airlines International was formed by merging about half a dozen different airlines. A decade after the merger, employees still referred to themselves as veterans of Wardair or Canadian Pacific Airlines—that is, they retained their original cultures. Integrating two cultures is a difficult process. Early on, the merger executives have to decide if one company's culture will be grafted onto the other company's, or if the two cultures will merge to create a third culture.

In some cases, firms that are aware of the difficulties of merging cultures attempt to negotiate, in the form of a contract, many aspects in advance.

**culture**

the set of important beliefs that members of an organization share

The assignment of positions or the acceptance of a culture, such as one of empowerment, seems like good advance planning. But those who have been through this process liken it to a marriage. The couple may agree, in writing, on who will do the dishes and how many children they want, but the day-to-day living may be quite different, and the assumptions change over time. Recognizing this, some employees may choose to leave the corporation rather than endure the pain of culture mergers.

Anthropologists have something to say about the blending of cultures. According to researchers, there are four options open to those involved in M&As:[40]

- *Assimilation:* Assimilation occurs when one organization willingly gives up its culture and is absorbed by the culture of the acquirer or the dominant partner.
- *Integration:* Integration refers to the fusion of two cultures, resulting in the evolvement of a new culture representing (one hopes) the best of both cultures. This form rarely occurs because the marriage is rarely one of two equals, and one partner usually dominates.
- *Deculturation:* Sometimes the acquired organization does not value the culture of the dominant partner and is left in a confused, alienated, marginalized state known as deculturation. This is a temporary state, existing until some integration or separation occurs.
- *Separation:* In some instances, the two cultures resist merging, and either the merged company operates as two separate companies or a divorce occurs.

Merging two cultures is difficult. How can a rule-bound, bureaucratic organization such as the Bank of Montreal merge with the "cowboys" of the brokerage firm Nesbitt Burns? To complicate this issue, the acquiring company typically wants to retain the entrepreneurial spirit of the target company and to infuse this spirit into its own troops. Instead, the entrepreneur is squashed by the rules and rigid decision making of the parent company. For example, Novell purchased WordPerfect (currently owned by Corel) and managed to stifle the innovative talent it had bought.

The level of difficulty in merging two cultures is increased when the merger is one between companies from two different countries—i.e., an international M&A. For example, Canadians tend to look to employee task forces and committees to provide input on decisions; people from other countries expect their managers to provide direction. Mexicans want more structure and definition of roles and responsibilities than do Canadians. In one case, a merger was stalled because Mexicans needed this information but would not ask for it as it was seen as questioning management's authority.[41] Similarly, basic concepts of time can make international mergers more difficult. "Long term" in Canada means three years; in Japan, "long term" is 30 years.

The blending of cultures can take years. As in all organizational change programs, a process must be undertaken. The first step is to identify the differences, to ensure that employees are aware of the differences and can verbalize or label them. Is one company entrepreneurial and the other risk

**RPC** 12.3

Chapter 12: Mergers and Acquisitions

averse? Does one have programs of team building while the other rewards individual achievements? Our recommendation is to appoint a sprinter to deal with urgent matters. Likewise, we suggest that a team of "long-distance runners" be appointed to address broad issues of mission statements, the creation of culture to achieve the strategic goals, and similar matters. Part of their mandate would be to measure current attitudes, solicit opinions, and give the employees a voice in the process.

Here is an example of how this is done. Two hospitals that merged had very different cultures, which did not blend. One had a culture of controlling employees; the other, a culture of encouraging employees.[42] The hospitals began the culture-blending process by conducting a comprehensive audit, using a paper-and-pencil diagnostic tool. The results were terrible, and the only positive finding was that *everyone* wanted a change. Two teams were appointed, one to change the culture of both hospitals to a culture of employee development and the other to help form this new culture.

Sometimes, cultural characteristics that are common to both merging companies can be identified. For example, two very different firms found out that they both placed top priority on customer service, and this common focal point became the link for their merger. Sometimes a superordinate goal can be created.

**RPC 12.4**

The formation of task forces or one-off projects has integration as a sub-goal. As is the case when warring nations are forced to fight together against an alien force, the ways in which two corporate cultures are more similar than different are apparent when a superimposed goal becomes the catalyst. American Express uses this technique regularly. Managers from merging firms work together on projects to develop new products or services, for which the merged firms can claim ownership. Besides integration, such projects have other benefits: they develop in-house talent, provide an opportunity to solicit broad perspectives, and facilitate transfers as the project ends.[43] General Mills used an integration team as part of a successful strategy in its acquisition of Pillsbury (See HR Planning Today 12.2). While all of this seems time consuming, it may, in fact, save time in the longer term. Organizational change experts realize that time spent ensuring employee buy-in will speed implementation. If time is not spent ensuring that employees are committed to the changes, employees will resist the changes.

Another approach is to "seed" the company with experienced managers who "walk the talk" and can facilitate the adoption of the new culture. However, just transferring personnel from one company to another may only increase the differences between them and promote subcultures or cliques. "Living together" before the marriage may also help ease merger shock. Japanese companies usually have worked on a joint venture or a collaborative project, designed to assess cultural fit, before they acquire another company. Turf battles are a problem unless companies establish the new structure, including the reporting relationships, early in the merger process.

**RPC 12.5**

Consultants specializing in post-merger integration practices at PriceWaterhouseCoopers believe that two cultures cannot be merged by just

### HR Systems Effective in Acquisition

In 2001, General Mills acquired Pillsbury. The goal of General Mills was to double revenues, be a market leader in 14 food categories and be in a position for international growth in every country in the world, through the dough business. Both companies were the best in their class, not only having brand icons like the Pillsbury Dough Boy, but also having won many awards for being best employers. Conscious of the research that demonstrated that most acquisitions fail, the vice-president of HR set out to manage the process of integrating 10 500 GM employees with 16 000 Pillsbury employees.

The integration strategy started with a transition team who anticipated the fundamental concerns of employees: (1) *Will I have a job in the new organization?* (2) *How do I win?* (i.e., how can I do my best and reap rewards?) and (3) *Do I have a future here?*

The transition team paid attention to three areas:

1. Develop the systems that mattered most to employees: rewards, performance management, and individual development.
2. Sequence the implementation of these systems, at a pace that employees could absorb.
3. Use the climate survey to monitor employee feedback and concerns.

The acquisition was a success. During the first 12 months of the integration, turnover dropped to 5.4% from 9.9% (GM) and 17.8% (Pillsbury). They were able to retain 98% of the top value creators. Although business results were disappointing in the first fiscal year, the following year sales increased by 32%, and net earnings doubled. These results are attributed directly to the integration strategy, and prove that HR systems can be key drivers of success in a merger or acquisition.

Source: Adapted from K.D. Wilde, "HR Systems Drive Successful Post-Acquisition Integration at General Mills," *Journal of Organizational Excellence*, 2004. John Wiley and Sons. Reprinted with permission.

---

waving the common-vision banner above the employees. They suggest these specific steps be undertaken:

- *Deploy role models:* those in highly visible positions of authority should exemplify the new and desired behaviours.
- *Provide meaningful incentives:* shower the role models and employees who replicate the desired behaviours with quick and visible rewards.[44]

More radical measures may be necessary. Some companies force employees who are opposed to the merger or cannot adapt to the new culture into early retirement or some other exit option.

A more positive story is that of the merger of Lotus and IBM, discussed in HR Planning Today 12.3. The steps necessary to do a cultural audit or due diligence are outlined in HR Planning Notebook 12.2.

## HR Issues in M&As

Experts in HRM have much to say about increasing the success rate of mergers. Indeed, when HR is involved early in the process, the merger is more likely to be successful.[45] The impact of a merger on HRM is discussed below, using the familiar functional areas of HR.

### The Blending of Cultures

IBM and Lotus had agreed to merge, but many Lotus employees were worried about the impact of the IBM culture on the Lotus culture. Lotus employees were used to a culture known for its quality-of-life programs. Lotus had won awards for its willingness to accommodate the needs of its employees through spousal benefits programs, job sharing, allowing employees to work from home or at remote sites, on-site child care, summer camp programs, a lunch-and-learn wellness series, tuition reimbursements, and so on. Lotus employees were understandably worried that IBM would challenge these programs. But IBM was intrigued by the Lotus culture and chose to adopt Lotus's innovative approach to quality of working life. The result was that the Lotus employees who left before the merger phoned a year later asking to be rehired.

Successful mergers may result from an analysis of the cultures. Each firm could identify its strengths, such as empowered employees, and the merged firm could attempt to retain this aspect and build on it. For example,

in the Lotus–IBM merger, the senior manager of HR reports:

> What's been unique to Lotus is that IBM, in the past, has absorbed companies it has bought and found that total absorption can actually put people at risk. With us, it has tried to figure out what we do well that it could do better; it has tried to figure out in what ways to leave Lotus alone so that it retains its unique culture, and it has also tried to figure out how to leverage us so that the merged company can become stronger in the market.

These culture audits provide an objective means to identify differences, provide a basis for discussion, and track merger progress.

Source: Adapted from V. Frazee, "Winning Ideas Prove Timeless," *Workforce Magazine* (November 1996), pp. 48–57. Reprinted with permission.

### The Cultural Due Diligence Checklist

Research tells us that those companies that actively manage their cultures attain higher revenues and profits than those that do not. This is particularly important during a merger, but indeed less than 10% of companies actively spend time on cultural fit issues during integration. Here are the steps:

1. Conduct a cultural audit of each organization, through qualitative research (interviews, focus groups) or through quantitative surveys.
2. Identify similarities and differences, and discuss these. Create a new employee value proposition from the strengths of each culture.
3. Use acculturation strategies such as cross-functional seminars and graduation ceremonies (to let go of the

"old"), and provide cultural mentors to strengthen integration.
4. To overcome cultural challenges, celebrate small wins, acknowledge value in past practices, and measure progress at regular intervals.

Source: Anonymous 2004, "HR Issues Are Bottom of M&A Checklists," *Personnel Today*, 3, S.H. Applebaum and J. Gandlel, 2003, "A Cross Method Analysis of the Impact of Culture and Communications upon a Health Care Merger: Prescriptions for Human Resources Management," *Journal of Management Development*, 78, 6, 108–116, M. Johne, 2000, "The Human Factor: Integrating People and Culture after a Merger," *CMA Management*, 74, 3, 30–37, R. Miller, 2000, "How Culture Affects Mergers and Acquisitions," *Industrial Management* 42, 5, 22–27; K Walker, 1998, "Meshing Cultures in a Consolidation," *Training and Development* 52, 5, 83–88.

# HR Planning

In a merger, planning moves beyond the traditional concepts of HR planning for several reasons. HR planning in an M&A situation has several dimensions that are not part of the normal planning process.

## 1. The Contingency Plan

Strategic planners must be aware of the board of directors' interest in M&As. Based on this expressed interest, a contingency plan that can be implemented when a deal is in play should be prepared. The plan should identify the contact person and the merger coordinator, who should have received training in effective merger management. The contact person should develop a plan, similar to emergency plans developed for fires or gas leaks. The plan should outline the chain of command, methods for communicating, procedures to follow during a takeover, and negotiation skills training and media response training for the senior team, and should identify a transition team.[46] Some companies even keep lists of compatible white knights (in cases of being targeted for acquisition) and prepare lists of consultants who are experts in negotiation techniques or productivity enhancement methods.

## 2. HR Due Diligence

The second element of HR planning in an M&A situation is the need to conduct a due diligence review.[47] Due diligence is a process through which a potential acquirer evaluates a target firm for acquisition.[48] Hundreds of questions are asked in areas from tax implications to differences in culture to ensure that the right price is paid, and that the chances of success are measured. The first question to be asked is how the transaction is structured as this affects the treatment of employees, as described in HR Planning Notebook 12.3.

**RPC 12.6**

---

## HR Planning Notebook 12.3

### Share or Asset Purchase

*Share purchase:* The purchaser acquires the shares of a company. The corporate entity continues to exist, and employees are retained.

*Asset purchase:* The purchaser acquires all or some of the company's shares, but there is a different corporate entity that continues the management of the business. Employees of the company are transferred to the purchaser (i.e., no longer work for the seller) and a new employment relationship must be worked out with the purchaser. In general, the purchaser has no legal obligation to hire all or some of the employees or provide them with the same working conditions and terms. But in practice, most purchasers do so in order to carry on with business and to limit liability for terminations.

Source: D. Corbett, "HR Issues in M&A," *HR Professional* (August/September 2002), pp. 18–21.

---

Chapter 12: Mergers and Acquisitions

From an HR perspective, the due diligence would include a review of the following:

- collective agreements,
- employment contracts,
- executive compensation contracts (particularly golden parachutes, which are lump-sum payments made to executives who lose their jobs as a result of an M&A),
- benefit plans and policies,
- incentive, commission, and bonus plans,
- pension plans and retirement policies,
- Workers' Safety and Insurance Board (WSIB) statements, claims, assessments, and experience rating data,
- employment policies, and
- complaints about employment equity, health and safety, wrongful dismissal, unfair labour practices, and applications for certification and grievances.

Sometimes these liabilities (e.g., an enriched retirement plan) or obligations (e.g., an incentive plan) may kill the deal. Once the legal obligations have been thoroughly assessed, the level of employees' KSAs must be evaluated. The HR planning team then addresses the suitability of current management talent and cultural fit. A deal may be aborted if talent shortfalls are extreme or if the cultures are seriously incompatible. Despite the obvious benefits of involving the HR team in due diligence, only four out of ten companies do so.[49]

### 3. Transition Team

A third element of HR planning is the need to appoint a transition team. This team is necessary because of the urgency of the M&A situation and the information gaps and employee stress that characterize it:

- *Urgency:* Staffing decisions, such as terminating, hiring, evaluating, and training, become urgent. Planners don't have the luxury of planning in three-year periods, during which orderly succession proceeds as predicted. Job analyses must be conducted immediately to identify duplicate positions and new work processes. Soon after the merger is announced, decisions about the retention of employees and the reassignment of others have to be made and executed humanely. At the same time, marketable employees are finding jobs elsewhere and customers are re-examining their business relationships. The uncertainty impedes productivity and new business development.
- *Information gaps:* While both companies may have excellent plans for employees and reams of documentation, these plans have to be adjusted to the merged needs. For example, the targeted company may have prepared succession plans for its finance department, but

**RPC** 12.7

now most of these positions (and people) are redundant because the bidder may have its own finance department. Furthermore, the merged company may use its combined resources to seek businesses in new countries (with different financial reporting or tax laws), and neither of the merged companies has that expertise. Thus, the information accumulated to date may have to be updated rapidly and revised in light of the new needs. The loss of capable employees, those who are marketable and can easily find other jobs, also results in the need to update plans continuously during a merger. Upon the announcement of its merger, AOL Time Warner immediately created an online tutorial that explained the reasons for the merger, how it affected employees, and career opportunities under the new regime.[50]

- *Stress:* The moment that the companies go "into play," employees are stressed because they are aware of the traditional fate of employees in merged companies. Most employees realize that most positions are duplicated. A transition team, whose sole concern is HR issues in the merger, must be appointed. The transition team may be the most important determinant of merger success. The role and responsibilities of the transition team are outlined in HR Planning Notebook 12.4.

**RPC** 12.8

**RPC** 12.9

**RPC** 12.10

The goals of the transition team are to retain talent, maintain the productivity (both quantity and quality) of employee performance, select individuals for the new organization, integrate HR programs (e.g., benefits, incentive plans), and take the first steps toward the integration of cultures. Some have adopted a 100-day strategy. The anxiety felt by employees and other stakeholders is lessened when the merger team announces that within 100 days of closing, all job decisions will have been made.

**RPC** 12.11

As the transition team is handling the urgent matters, the HR planners can undertake the revisions necessary to prepare HR plans. Employee skills inventories must be updated and succession plans revised. If the business enters new sectors and they require new labour pools, these labour pools have to be identified and the need for them assessed. Employment equity data have to be revised and, perhaps, resubmitted to the relevant agencies. Based on the revised strategic plans, the HR department must revise and align its plans and produce a new forecast for HR requirements.

A review of the HR policies will likely reveal three types of situations:

- *Complementary:* one company may focus on career development, while the other focuses on benefits,
- *Duplicated:* both companies have identical Human Resource Information Systems (HRIS),
- *Contradictory:* one organization uses the performance management system for career development while the other uses its system to support incentive pay programs,[51] by measuring employee productivity to determine bonuses or merit pay.

### The Transition Team

Senior vice-presidents of HR who have had a lot of experience in mergers recommend that a transition team be appointed to deal with the concerns of employees in mergers. These vice-presidents cite the need to deal with employee stress before the stress renders employees incapable of working. In addition, it is known that employees who have access to information about their future are less likely to begin a job search and leave the organization. Communication is critical, and employees should be the central focus of communication efforts. The transition team should comprise employees from both companies and union representatives (if there is a union in either company).

Here are some elements of a good merger management process:

- *A formal announcement*: When a merger or acquisition is announced, the CEO should issue a statement containing the following items of information:
  - the rationale for the merger—that is, its intended benefits
  - general information about both companies
  - information about changes in the corporate name and structure, particularly changes in key management positions

- plans for employee reductions
- plans for recognizing and working with the union
- plans for changes in products or services
- detailed information about changes in benefits, or the date for decisions about such changes

- *A merger hotline*: When Inland Gas purchased Mainland Gas, creating BC Gas, the company immediately set up a hotline so that employees could call the vice-president of HR and ask direct questions. Another company created a video where the CEO talked about the changes.

- *A managerial tool kit*: This toolkit had identifiable support resources who could address employee concerns and fears.[52]

- *A newsletter or web page*: Experts agree that the formation of communication channels must be swift and consistent, and all communication must be honest. One company created a fictional employee (called Frank) who, on behalf of the workforce, asked questions about the merger and reported back to the employees, from their perspective.[53]

---

**RPC 12.12**

**RPC 12.13**

**RPC 12.14**

## Selection

Retention and reduction, paradoxically, are two critical areas that must be addressed immediately. Duplicate positions and redundant employees must be terminated while highly qualified employees in critical positions must be motivated to stay. The first critical question is, How many employees does the merged company need? The answer is not to eliminate the most jobs possible in an attempt to operate a lean and mean corporation; the result would be work overload and stress. The answer may lie in benchmarking statistics. Increasingly, HR professionals are developing benchmark data, by sector. For example, one merged hospital, which employed six full-time workers per occupied bed, reduced the number of employees to match the benchmark of four full-time workers per occupied bed.[54]

Of course, it is not just the numbers of employees that are subject to analysis but the types of employees. One company classified workers in these ways: critical to ongoing operations; critical to retain through to the close of the deal; highly marketable; and potential redundant.[55] Key workers must be identified and offered retention bonuses and employment agreements. Employees are offered incentives to stay at least until the deal closes and, often, for periods after the closure. The superstar financial brokers at Merrill Lynch were offered a one-time retention bonus of 110% of their take-home pay (more than $1 million a year) by CIBC in order to retain them. The retention bonus was structured as a five-year loan, so that each year 20% of the loan was forgiven.[56]

Reductions might be necessary. The dismissal process can be heart-breaking, as is described in one merger case.[57] In the rush to terminate quickly, some employees were notified by voicemail or e-mail or in hurried and short meetings with strangers. A supervisor was forced to fire three of his employees before being fired himself. His termination was particularly diffi-cult to understand, as his performance reviews were excellent. As wave after wave of salespeople were laid off, customers became confused about their contacts. Departing employees took advantage of this and went to the compe-tition, taking the business relationships with them.

Chapter 10 covered this aspect of restructuring in detail. A number of decisions must be made immediately. Employees will want to know if they will be offered employment in the merged company; if not, they will want to know what the severance packages contain. If jobs are offered, can employees choose not to accept them? For those wary of the new owner or who fear being dumped once the sale closes, will there be a safety net? For those who are terminated, will assistance such as financial planning, job relo-cation, and career planning be offered? Will benefits continue for a short adjustment period? One organization, which could not promise job security to its employees, did promise to position them for work in the new organiza-tion or outside it.[58] This pledge was kept; employees were trained, at organi-zational expense, for other positions. Part of the training included seminars in which employees were taught to be responsible for their own develop-ment and were given assistance to develop a survival kit called Making Me Marketable. Jobs were reanalyzed to focus on basic skills. For example, the job specifications for a patient-care technician stated that a high school diploma was required, but a review showed that certain skills, and not a high school diploma, were needed to do the job. Managers used their contacts and networks to assist departing employees. Employees were encouraged to work on cross-functional teams to expand their horizons and skills. The result was that productivity did not diminish dramatically, as occurs in most mergers. Furthermore, the downsizing and exodus were orderly, lessening the stress on remaining employees. The culture was changed, and employees were rewarded.

Those who stay with the newly acquired or merged company face sev-eral fates:

- *Demotion:* Under the new organizational structure, some employees are given less responsibility, less territory, or fewer lines due to amalgamation.

Chapter 12: Mergers and Acquisitions

- *Competition for the same job:* Some companies force employees to compete for their old jobs by having to apply as new candidates for a position.
- *Termination*: If not successful in the competition, employees are then let go. Sometimes, the acquiring firm waits until it can obtain its own appraisal of employee capabilities and has a chance to determine fit.

**RPC 12.15**

The survivors have adjustments to make, and these were detailed in Chapter 10. Like employees involved in a restructuring, the survivors of a merger are dealing with their loss of identity as the company changes, a lack of information and the resultant anxiety, a lack of protection from adverse effects over which they have no control, the loss of colleagues, and a change in their jobs.[59] Those remaining with the corporation will need to know about compensation plans.

## Compensation

Two companies with two different compensation systems have to merge their systems, adopt one, or create a new one. AOL Time Warner replaced the straight salary system of Time Warner with the AOL system of salary plus stock options.[60] Incentive plans have to be aligned to support the merger strategy. But consideration can be given to incentives to make the merger work. BC Gas gave each employee 50 free shares and introduced an attractive stock purchase plan to promote commitment to the new company.[61]

In a merger, a major issue for the HR department is the integration of benefit plans. Which company's plan should be adopted? Employees obviously wish for the most favourable benefits, but organizations are concerned with cost. If the buyer's benefit packages are significantly lower than the seller's programs, any attempt to match this would result in staggering additional costs.[62] However, when benefits are removed or reduced in the integration of companies, employees may experience loss of morale. Thus, for employees in the process of considering their futures with the organization, the resolution of the benefits package may affect their decision.

**RPC 12.16**

The best resolution of this problem would be to conduct a cost–benefit analysis of the benefits, package by package. For example, child-care centres or health and wellness centres may seem to be costly benefits. But if the number of sick days and mental health days taken is reduced or employee turnover is diminished, then the benefits may outweigh the costs. Pension concerns will be high. Although there are regulations governing certain pension credits, different approaches to pension plan transfers must be analyzed, as variances can run into the millions of dollars.

For employees who are being terminated, retaining certain benefits during the months or years after the merger may be a humane way to soften the adverse effects of the merger. Companies may wish to offer extended medical and dental coverage, modified retirement plans, and some counselling to deal with unemployment and with career plans.

## Performance Appraisal

RPC 12.17

During a merger, employees undergo stress, and productivity can be expected to drop. Focusing on long-term goals may be difficult and so short-term goals should be substituted. Business is not as usual. The role of the manager may change from one of supervisor to one of coach. Employees may play it safe and may require constant positive reinforcement for the work they do accomplish under the new house rules.

One model constructs employee behaviour during a merger as falling into one of three categories: not knowing (remedied by more communication), not able (the solution is training), or not willing (a strong case for performance management through feedback and incentives).[63]

Performance appraisals for development purposes may have to be redone. The merged company may be larger or engaged in different businesses, allowing for more or different promotion paths and developmental experiences. Employee intentions and aspirations under the new regime will have to be redocumented.

Stress levels may necessitate a relaxation of the rules and more counselling and coaching. Personal problems (such as financial or marital difficulties), rather than performance problems, may surface as the stress begins to affect employees.

## Training and Development

Once the strategic plan has been developed, an inventory of the KSAs needed to align with the strategy should be undertaken. Information based on previous needs analyses may have to be revised in light of the new strategy, which may create new jobs.

RPC 12.18

Managers and peers may need some additional training in the role of coach and counsellor. Every employee might benefit from stress reduction or relaxation programs. Developmental programs, such as overseas assignments or executive exchanges, or long-term educational opportunities, may be put on hold while the new organization establishes long-term plans.

RPC 12.19

## Labour Relations

Unionized employees are covered by a collective agreement, which is a legally binding document. Typically, these agreements set out the conditions under which job changes must occur. Various issues will need to be considered. For example, will unionized employees continue with the same working conditions and benefits, as negotiated, or will the contracts be renegotiated? At a minimum, the collective agreements must be read to determine what provisions exist for job security and what the notification periods are for layoffs and terminations. Merger experts say that unions should be informed and involved from the outset of the merger so that they can make valuable contributions. Unions are perceived as independent from management and can help to obtain the trust and confidence of the workforce to participate in a change program. Those companies that involved unions had reduced labour disruptions and grievances.[64]

### HR Making a Difference in Mergers

- Encana was created out of the acquisition of Alberta Energy Co. by PanCanadian Energy in 2002. The transaction has been called a stunning success, and the share price has risen 14% since its initial listing. Officials attribute this success to speed, saying, "The quicker you remove uncertainty the better off you are. We all know mergers that have dragged on for a year or two, and that would be extremely counterproductive." One week after shareholders gave their approval, layoffs were announced internally. Within four weeks, employees were given the names of their new supervisors, their compensation packages, and a high-performance contract, which outlined career objectives and goals for the year.

- TD Bank acquired Canada Trust in 1999, and had to integrate 1500 branches, 44 000 employees, ten million customers, and $265 billion in assets. Senior executives immediately notified employees about how their jobs would be affected. Realizing that if a glitch occurred in its bank machine network, which handles 700 transactions per second, customers, as well as employees and shareholders would resist the merger, branches were converted in waves, starting on the East Coast.

Source: J. Kirby, 2004, "The Trouble with Mergers," *Canadian Business, 77,* 4, 65–75.

As you can see, HR plays a pivotal role in the success of M&As. Today, fully two-thirds of all deals now involve HR professionals in due diligence.[65] Read about HR practices in two very successful deals in HR Planning Today 12.4.

## Summary

The focus of this chapter was the HRM implications of M&As. Mergers are undertaken to provide a strategic benefit or a financial benefit, or to fulfill the psychological needs of the managers. The financial and other results of mergers are not always as positive as expected, and the effect on staff can be devastating, whether they stay with the merged company or not. The culture of the previously separate companies and the new merged company is the area that experts say is the most important predictor of merger success. The merger has an impact on each of the functional areas—HR planning, selection, compensation, performance appraisal, training and development, and labour relations.

## Key Terms

conglomerate merger, 323
consolidation, 323
culture, 330
horizontal integration, 325
horizontal merger, 322

operating synergy, 324
takeover, 324
vertical integration, 325
vertical merger, 323

# Web Links

The annual directory of mergers and acquisitions in Canada:

**www.crosbieco.com/M&A.html** (p. 322)

Provides policies and reports about the issue of mergers between Canadian banks:

**www.canadaonline.about.com/cs/bankmergers** (p. 342)

# RPC Icons

**RPC 12.1** Plans for and manages the HR aspects of organizational change (e.g., mergers, acquisitions, divestitures, and downsizing, in the context of organizational strategies and legislated requirements)

**RPC 12.2** Guides and facilitates change in organizational culture and/or values consistent with business strategies

**RPC 12.3** Contributes to the development of the organization's vision, goals, and strategies with a focus on human capital

**RPC 12.4** Assembles and leads teams to achieve established goals

**RPC 12.5** Develops and implements necessary organizational development model.

**RPC 12.6** Collects data, analyzes, and reviews the organization's existing HR programs to ensure they are consistent with business activities

**RPC 12.7** Develops and delivers learning strategies to close the gap between current human capital capabilities and the future needs of the organization

**RPC 12.8** Interprets and communicates business strategies and plans

**RPC 12.9** Communicates information to serve current and future needs of the organization

**RPC 12.10** Develops and implements a communications plan that supports strategies for employee involvement

**RPC 12.11** Using available data, develops HR plans that support the organization's strategic directions

**RPC 12.12** Identifies the organization's HR needs

**RPC 12.13** Selects candidates and negotiates terms and conditions of employment

**RPC 12.14** Develops procedures for the defensible termination of employees in circumstances where termination is determined to be the only course of action

RPC 12.15 Evaluates the total compensation strategy to ensure it is consistent with the objectives of attracting, motivating, and retaining the qualified people required to meet organizational goals

RPC 12.16 Develops systems and processes that link the career plans and skill sets of employees with the requirements of the organization

RPC 12.17 Provides performance feedback, coaching, and career development to teams and individuals to maximize their probability of success

RPC 12.18 Provides support and expertise to managers and supervisors with respect to managing people

RPC 12.19 Defines and establishes appropriate terms and conditions of employment to meet organizational goals

# Discussion Questions

1. Prepare a list of all the reasons an organization would want to acquire a competitor.
2. Describe the effects that a merger may have on employees. What can management do to lessen the more negative effects of a merger? What can employees do to protect themselves when they start to hear rumours of a merger?
3. One of the urgent issues facing executives immediately after the merger is announced is the retention of key employees. How would you define or describe a key employee? What methods would you use to identify key employees? Describe some programs that you could use to retain your key employees during and after the merger.

# Using the Internet

1. Many mergers and acquisition occur each year. Many fail because of mismanagement of employee issues. Search for an example of a failed merger or acquisition, and another one that observers believe was successful.
   a. Summarize the chosen articles and explain in each case why the mergers and acquisition succeeded or failed.
   b. What was the role of Human Resources? Did the management of employees issues make a difference in the success of the M&A activity?

# Exercise

1. The treatment of employees during a merger is critical; employees will be asking lots of questions. If you are currently working, imagine that your company is merging with a competitor. In groups, prepare a list of questions that you would like management to answer. If you are not working, imagine the merger of your university or community college with another, and prepare a list of questions that you would like answered regarding your status in your program.

# Case: The City of Toronto—Courage in the Face of Chaos

On January 1, 1998, the new unified city of Toronto was created from the cities of Etobicoke, North York, Toronto, York, and Scarborough; the borough of East York; and the municipality of Metropolitan Toronto. Few mergers have attempted to integrate seven organizations. The goal was to integrate the policies, practices, and systems of municipalities as large as Toronto (with a staff of 11 000) and as small as East York (with a staff of 430) and to achieve savings from the overlapping of administrative and staffing costs of the seven municipalities. Toronto is now the fifth-largest city in North America, with 2.5 million residents. Its budget of $6 billion and staff of 26 000 are larger than those of several Canadian provinces. More than 800 municipal staff from all seven jurisdictions worked on the integration project, developing a vision, a mission, and a governance structure. About 70% to 95% of departmental budgets cover staffing costs.

An important position, particularly in the merger process, was that of the executive director of Human Resources and Amalgamation, a position that was filled through an internal and external search. Brenda Glover, formerly the HR commissioner of the city of Etobicoke, was chosen for the position of executive director. Ms Glover had the critical task of designing an HR strategy that would accomplish the integration in a seamless fashion by building a new vision and culture. She noted, "If HR was not organized, then the rest of the city is in chaos. The first goal is to have all people in place."

Glover discussed the staffing, labour relations, compensation, benefits, and culture issues in this very large public-sector merger:

*Staffing:* An HR transition team focused first on staffing. On January 1, 1998, only six new employees were working for the merged city. The goals, which were met, were to have separation programs ready by February 1, all HR directors in place by March 1, and all managers in place by April 1. Every municipal employee had the opportunity to compete for the "new" jobs, his or her former job, and jobs two levels down. Within one year, from March 1998 to March 1999, the HR department had posted 900 jobs, and an average of 12 candidates competed for each job. The priority was to hire internally, but the HR staff also looked at 16 000 résumés from external candidates during this period.

About 10% of the total number of jobs (or 2500) were to be eliminated. Attrition and voluntary exit packages were the primary basis for workforce reduction. Those facing termination were given counselling, retraining opportunities, incentive programs for early retirement, and assistance in the job search process.

*Labour relations:* The seven cities operated with 56 collective agreements. The unions were given time to work through their members to determine who would be the bargaining agent. It might have been faster to force the Labour Relations Board to make this decision, but urgency was subordinated to longer-term issues of trust and collaboration.

Chapter 12: Mergers and Acquisitions

*Compensation:* Working with the seven municipalities, the transition team developed an interim salary schedule. It had problems and, in hindsight, a compensation consultant should have been hired to design a completely new salary schedule. There were significant integration problems, such as the case of two people who were doing the same job for which one employee was earning $20 000 more than the other.

*Benefits/payroll:* The goal was to harmonize the benefits and move from seven systems to one benefits policy. This was not easy, as the new city wanted to achieve savings and rationalize benefits whereas employees rarely want to give up their "rights" to achieved benefits. So the decision made was to go neither to the lowest nor the highest standard but to benchmark, creating a new standard.

*Culture:* When mergers occur between just two partners, cultural issues are a challenge. Imagine a merger between seven partners. Here are some of the cultures, without naming names, that had to be harmonized:

City A: Cheap, fiscally prudent; has meagre compensation and resources; has a history of downsizing and little job security
City B: Politically correct; an advocate for change
City C: Bureaucratic, process oriented
City D: Quick, entrepreneurial, rich; does little research or analysis; has good job security

As could be predicted, early encounters were filled with comments such as "I am from Etobicoke, and we think . . ." or "The way we do things . . ." The goal was to create new values and a new mentality that was not wedded to old ways of doing things.

## Lessons Learned

When asked what she would have done differently, Glover mentioned several lessons learned:

1. *Communication:* "We had websites, brochures, hotlines, everything to inform employees about emerging policies. But we found that unless and until a policy impacts an employee personally, it is not heard or absorbed. So we found we were answering the same questions over and over again. We learned that timing, frequency, and repetition are very important."
2. *Training:* "It became obvious very early that the transition team needed skills, and employees needed unique skills, to integrate the seven municipalities. For example, the move to City Hall required new skills, such as enhanced project management. We should have realized this earlier."
3. *Profile:* Mergers in the public sector are particularly difficult because they tend to be high profile, and many of the merger decisions are made public. For example, the separation packages, which had to be approved by Council, were leaked to the press before there was time to inform employees.

4. *Services:* The integration was accomplished in such a way that the public saw no disruption in services. Ms. Glover states, "Not one heartbeat was missed in service, even when management was in chaos, with some managers leaving and others coping with loss [of employees] and organizational memory. The frontline employees deserve a lot of credit."

What was done right? Ms. Glover reports, "No merger works without a sense of urgency. We met deadlines. We balanced urgency against fairness. We had to create teams, which is a slow process, while balancing the need to deal with immediate issues. We communicated, with lots of meetings, updates, answering questions personally. But a merger presents incredible opportunities to create a culture, handpick staff . . . basically a blank sheet to do things right."

## Questions

1. Compare the process used by the city of Toronto with the prescriptions for an effective merger as outlined in this chapter.
2. What do you see as the differences?
3. Would you have handled the merger of the cities any differently?

# Endnotes

1. Slain, L. 2003. "Strategic Emphasis," *HR Professional* (February/March): 42–45. Hood, S.B. 2003. "Do You Know What Your CEO Really Wants?" *HR Professional* (February/March): 38–40.
2. Corbett, A., and C. Lemire, 2005. "Smart Deal-making," *Canadian Business*, 78, 9, 57–61.
3. Wells, S.J. 2004. "Merging Compensation Strategies," *HR Magazine*, 49, 5, 66–74. Bryson, J. 2003, "Managing HRM Risk in a Merger," *Employee Relations* 25, 2, 14–31.
4. Pitts, G. 2005. "Timid Canada Falls Prey to a Global M&A Boom," *The Globe and Mail*, October 12, B9.
5. Schraeder, M. and D.R. Self, 2003. "Enhancing the Success of Mergers and Acquisitions: An Organizational Cultural Perspective," *Management Decision* 41, 5, 511–523.
6. McIntyre, T.L. 2004. "A Model of Levels of Involvement and Strategic Roles of Human Resource Development (HRD) Professionals as Facilitators of Due Diligence and the Integration Process," *Human Resource Development Review* June 2004, 3, 2, 173–183.
7. Edwards, C., and A. Park. 2002. "HP and Compaq: It's Showtime," *BusinessWeek*, June 17, 2002: 76–77.
8. Gilbert, C., K. Louiseeize, and A. Larmour 2005. "Exploring the Inco Merger," *Northern Ontario Business*, 26, 1, 1–2.
9. Master, L.J. 1987. "Efficient Product of Financial Services: Scale and Scope Economies," *Federal Reserve Bank of Philadelphia* (January/February): 15–25.
10. Anand, J. 2000. "A Match Made in Heaven," *Ivey Business Journal*, Vol. 64, No. 6 (July/August): 68–73.
11. Tutunjian, J. 2005. "Metro Inc's Purchase of A&P Canada the Biggest Canadian Grocery Acquisition in Six Years," *Canadian Grocer*, 119, 6, 8.
12. Lubatkin, M.H., and P.J. Lane. 1996. "Post—The Merger Mavens Still Have It Wrong." *Academy of Management Executive*, Vol. 10, No. 1 (February): 21–39.
13. Hamel, G., and C. Prahalad. 1989. "Strategic Intent," *Harvard Business Review*, Vol. 3: 73.
14. Hosskisson, R.E., M.A. Hitt and R.D. Ireland. 2004. *Competing for Advantage Thompson South-Western, Mason OH.*

15. Roll, R. 1986. "The Hubris Hypothesis of Corporate Takeover," *Journal of Business*, Vol. 59, No. 2 (April): 197–216.

16. Kroll, M., P. Wright, L. Toombs, and H. Leavell. 1997. "Form of Control: Determinant of Acquisition Performance and CEO Rewards," *Strategic Management Journal*, Vol. 18, No. 2 (February): 85–96.

17. Kets de Vries, M.F.R. 1991. "Introduction: Exploding the Myth That Organizations and Executives Are Rational." In M.F.R. Kets de Vries and Associates, *Organizations on the Couch: Clinical Perspectives on Organizational Behavior and Change*. San Francisco, CA: Jossey-Bass.

18. Rovenpor, J.L. 1993. "The Relationship between Four Personal Characteristics of Chief Executive Officers and Company Merger and Acquisition Activity," *Journal of Business and Psychology*, Vol. 8, No. 1 (Fall): 27–55.

19. Zwieg, P.L. 1995. "The Case against Mergers," *BusinessWeek* (October 30): 122–130.

20. Bryson, 2003; Nalbantian, H.R., R.A.Guzzo, D. Kieffer, and J. Doherty. 2005. "Making Acquisitions Work," *Journal of Organizational Excellence* (online) www.interscience.wiley.com. Spring 2005. Retrieved October 13, 2005.

21. De Voge, S., and J. Shirake, 2000. "People Factors: The Missing Link in Merger Success," *Compensations and Benefits Management* 16, 1, 68–74.

22. Gaughan, P.A. 1996. *Mergers, Acquisitions, and Corporate Restructuring*. New York: John Wiley & Sons.

23. Edwards and Park, 2002.

24. Schonfeld, E. 1997. "Have the Urge to Merge? You'd Better Think Twice," *Fortune* (March 31): 114–116.

25. Fisher, A. 1994. "How to Make a Merger Work," *Fortune*, Vol. 129, No. 2 (June 24): 64–66.

26. Laroche, L., G. Gitelson, and J. Bing. 2001. "Culture Shock," *CMA Management*, Vol. 75, No. 1: 40–44.

27. Kadlec, R.E. 1990. "Managing a Successful Merger," *Business Quarterly* (Autumn).

28. Yuce, A., and A. Ng. 2005. "Effects of Private and Public Canadian Mergers," *Canadian Journal of Administrative Sciences*, 22, 2, 111–125.

29. Harshbarger, D. 1990. "Mergers, Acquisitions, and the Reformatting of American Businesses." In D.B. Fishman and C. Cherniss, eds., *The Human Side of Corporate Competitiveness*. Newbury Park, CA: Sage Publications.

30. Galin, T.J., and M. Herndon. 2000. *The Complete Guide to Mergers and Acquisitions*. San Francisco, CA: Joss-Bassey.

31. Laroche et al., 2001.

32. Hollister, M. 1996. "Competing Corporate Cultures Can Doom Acquisition," *Human Resource Professional* (January/February): 7–10.

33. Laroche et al., 2001.

34. Dackert, I., Jackson, P.R, Brenner, S. and C.R. Johansson, 2003. "Eliciting and Analyzing Employees' Expectations of a Merger," *Human Relations* 56, 6, 26–32.

35. Bryson 2003.

36. Howes, C. 2001. "There Is More to a Merger than Making a Buck: Making Cultures Fit," *Financial Post*, February 2: C5.

37. Bernhut, S. 2000. "Bridging Cultures Adding Value in a Merger," *Ivey Business Journal*, Vol. 64, No. 3: 53–58.

38. Cartwright, S., and C.L. Cooper. 1993. "The Role of Culture Compatibility in Successful Organizational Marriage," *Academy of Management Journal*, Vol. 7, No. 2: 57–70.

39. Pekala, N. 2001, "Merger They Wrote: Avoiding a Corporate Culture Collision," *Journal of Property Management* 66, 3, 32–37; Miller, R. 2000, "How Culture Affects Mergers and Acquisitions," *Industrial Management* 42, 5, 22–27.

40. Berry, J.W. 1990. "Social and Cultural Change." In H.C. Triandis and R.W. Brislin, eds., *Handbook of Cross-cultural Psychology*, 5th ed. Boston: Allyn & Bacon.

41. Laroche et al., 2001.

42. Riddel, A., and F. Lipson. 1996. "Bankrupt Hospital Lands on Its Feet," *Personnel Journal* (August): 83–86.

43. Koeth, B. 1985. "Expressly American: Management's Task Is Internal Development," *Management Review* (February): 24–29.

44. Frers, K., and A. Chada. 2000. "Why You Can't Create a Purple-Footed Booby," *Canadian HR Reporter*, Vol. 13, No. 20: 16.

45. Anonymous, 2005. "HR's Growing Role in M&A Due Diligence," *HR Focus*, August 2005, 82, 8, 1–5.

46. Stuart, P. 1993. "HR Actions Offer Protection during Takeovers," *Personnel Journal* (June): 84–95.

47. Walker, J. 1992. *Human Resource Management*. New York: McGraw-Hill.

48. Hoskisson, 2004.

49. Galpin and Herndon, 2000.

50. Adams, M. 2002. "Making a Merger Work," *HR Magazine*, Vol. 47, No. 3: 52–57.

51. Kemp, A., and P. Lytwyn. 2002. "Merging HR Departments: How to Make It Work," *HR Professional* (August/September): 29–30.

52. Parks, N. 2004. "Managing the HR Challenges of a Major Global Merger," *Strategic HR Review* 4, 1, 24–27.

53. Galpin and Herndon, 2000.

54. Riddel and Lipson, 1996.

55. Wade, M., and B. Zimmerman, 2003. "Please Don't Go: Retaining Key People during the Ups and Downs of M & A's," *Workspan* 46, 11, 50–56.

56. Alphonso, C. 2002. "Top Staff Gain Clout in Mergers," *The Globe and Mail* (May 29), C1.

57. Schonfield, 1997.

58. Riddel and Lipson, 1996.

59. Walker, 1992.

60. Buchanan, R., and M. Daniell. 2002. "The Leadership Testing Ground," *Journal of Business Strategy*, Vol. 23, No. 2: 12–17.

61. Kadlec, 1990.

62. O'Rourke, R.W., and B.R. Berg, 2005. "Avoiding Costly Benefits Bloopers in Mergers and Acquisitions," *Employee Benefit Plan Review*, 60, 1, 11–14.

63. Galpin and Herndon, 2000.

64. Bryson, 2003.

65. Brown, D. 2005. "More HR Input Leads to More Merger Success: Study," *Canadian HR Reporter*, 18, 1, 1–2.

# Chapter 13

# Outsourcing

## Chapter Learning Objectives

After reading this chapter, you should be able to

- Define outsourcing.
- List the reasons organizations outsource functions and programs.
- Identify the advantages of outsourcing.
- Cite the risks and limitations of outsourcing.
- Develop the criteria necessary for managing the outsourcing relationship.

## OUTSOURCING HR AT BRITISH PETROLEUM

BP (British Petroleum) outsourced HR to Exult for several reasons. The first was to reduce costs, the second to provide quality support for its employees and the third was to focus on its core HR strategies, and offload the time-consuming administrative work. As the VP for HR stated, "Our cost of delivering HR activities was uncompetitive, and the quality of the delivery was uncertain. Further, the burden of administration on the HR departments in the business units was preventing the function from performing more effectively in the more strategic HR services." At US$600 million, this was the largest outsourcing contract on record. Through rapid growth, BP had acquired 10 000 new employees and dozens of incompatible systems in compensation and appraisal. The BP–Exult agreement specified that the outsourcer would handle the administrative elements of compensation, benefits, payroll, organizational development, performance management, employee development, training, recruitment and relocation for 56 000 U.S. and U.K. employees. BP retained everything that required judgment and policy.

The deal achieved the following results: a 40% reduction in HR staff, a reduction in operating costs of $15 million a year, and the avoidance of funding $30 million in capital costs for technology. The outsourcing allowed HR professionals the time to support the business lines.[1]

Outsourcing refers to a contractual relationship for the provision of business services by an external provider. In other words, a company pays another company to do some work for it. Currently, outsourcing is being promoted as one of the most powerful trends reshaping management. However, organizations have always outsourced some functions. For decades, most organizations hired firms to operate their cleaning or restaurant functions. What is different now is the scale. Firms are outsourcing everything from information technology management to entire functions such as human resources.

## Outsourcing

Outsourcing occurs when an organization contracts with another organization to provide services or products of a major function or activity.

Work that is traditionally done internally is shifted to an external provider, and the employees of the original organization are often transferred to the service provider. Outsourcing differs from alliances, partnerships, and

## HR Outsourcing Examples

Many organizations outsource their HR functions. Gow Corp., a 90-employee Alberta organization that processes livestock for institutional and restaurant clients, teamed with its vertical partners (a distributor and a supplier) to outsource and share two HR professionals who would handle payroll, training, health and safety, etc. The United Church of Canada outsourced job evaluation, recruitment, and compensation, in order to tap a wealth of experience that was not available in-house. Pratt & Whitney Canada outsourced its training function to

DDI (Development Dimensions International). Pratt & Whitney executives wanted a partner that could handle not only the tactical level in managing administrative tasks, but also the strategic level in matching learning solutions to business needs.

Sources: Adapted from A. Patel, "Vertical HR: Will the Experiment Work," 14; L. McKibbin-Brown, "Who Is Outsourcing What?" 32; P.J. Labrie and J. Bedard, "Outsourcing Training at Pratt & Whitney Canada," 42—all from *HR Professional*, Vol. 10, No. 3 (June/July 2002).

joint ventures in that the flow of resources is one-way, from the provider to the user. Typically, there is no profit sharing or mutual contribution.

## Outsourcing HR Functions

Surveys continue to show that nearly all organizations have outsourced parts of their HR functions.[2] Over half of these organizations plan to outsource even more functions. IBM outsourced its entire HR department, which was called Workforce Solutions, a profit centre that produced gains in flexibility, accountability, competitiveness, and profitability. HR Planning Today 13.1 provides examples of other companies that outsourced parts of their HR functions.

In HR, the functions most likely to be outsourced are temporary staffing, payroll, training, recruiting, and benefits administration. HR Planning Notebook 13.1 lists the functions within HR that are likely to be outsourced.

**RPC 13.1**

HR departments are under increasing pressure to produce deliverables, not just do-ables, and so are searching to determine which activities add value and who can best do these. Outsourcing is also a response to the demand from executives that HR reduce costs for its services. Outsourcing to service providers with international expertise also allows HR departments to harmonize employee packages for a global workforce, while complying with local laws.

**RPC 13.2**

While smaller firms might outsource all HR functions, most large firms retain the critical components. HR Planning Notebook 13.2 describes the reasons that small businesses outsource HR. Larger organizations rarely engage in 100% outsourcing for three reasons. First, as has been argued throughout this text, the HR function is so critical to the culture and strategic objectives of an organization that it must be closely managed by the organization itself. Second, situations arise that are impossible to predict, such as industrial relations disputes, and this unpredictability makes it difficult to develop a contractual arrangement with a vendor; timeliness of response is crucial.

## HR Planning Notebook 13.1

### HR Functions That May Be Outsourced

**Compensation**

- Payroll
- Benefits
- Compensation administration
- Pension

**Training**

- Program delivery
- Program design and development
- Training consulting to line departments
- Training needs analysis
- Program evaluation
- Strategic planning for T&D
- Administration
- Developing training policy

**Recruitment and Selection**

- Advertisements
- Screening of applications
- Testing
- Reference checking
- Preliminary interviews
- Salary negotiations—at the executive level
- Exit interviews

**Health and Safety**

- Employee assistance programs
- Wellness programs

## HR Planning Notebook 13.2

### Small Business and HR Outsourcing

Most businesses do not hire an HR professional until the employee numbers reach about 100, or even 400. But legislated HR functions, such as payroll and benefits, are necessary for every organization, regardless of size, so small businesses turn to other small businesses specializing in HR. The advantages are the following:

- lessens the handling of routine, transactional HR work (payroll) by in-house staff,
- offers access to experts who may provide advice in atypical situations (employee fraud),
- provides the management of one-off services (such as computer training), and
- ensures that the company is complying with current legislation.

Outsourcing is not the same as using consultants who may provide assistance on a project-by-project basis. Small businesses are looking for a long-term relationship with a provider that understands small business in general and their business in particular.

Third is the lack of providers of total HRM services. The field of outsourcing is replete with hundreds of small companies specializing in market niches. One company might do an excellent job of benefits counselling, and another might specialize in employee assistance, but few can do everything from training to managerial succession to payroll. These competencies have to reside within the firm.

### Outsourcing at CIBC

One of Canada's largest companies outsources major portions of its HR functions. CIBC employs about 44 000 people, about 450 in HR. In 2001, CIBC outsourced payroll processing, benefits administration, a call centre for employment enquiries, occupational health and safety services, and HR technology to a company specializing in HR services, EDS, in a seven-year, $227 million deal. Two hundred CIBC HR employees have been transferred to EDS, cutting the bank's HR department nearly by half. CIBC's vice-president of HR commented, "I don't think that in today's world, power is about the number of employees you have working for you. HR should get its power from how much it helps the business units meet their goals."

The reasons for outsourcing included the desire to improve service, to increase automation, and to have the HR department focus on the strategic issues of making a contribution to the company. CIBC does not add value by administering pension plans; EDS does. The HR department is freed from routine transactions and can focus on

policy, providing advice and programs to move the business forward.

The CIBC–EDS deal was unique as an outsourcing arrangement for several reasons. CIBC arranged with EDS to introduce best practices back into its organization and to update the bank on industry trends on a regular basis. CIBC searched for a vendor that would be a cultural fit with its organization. The main attribute the bank was looking for was "adapting to client needs." As the CIBC vice-president of Strategic Alliance Management said, "You can't put everything in a contract, so it is important to choose a company you can work with. You should be as clear as possible in terms of defining roles and responsibilities, but you cannot possibly think of all eventualities upfront. . . . It is important to have a process built into the contract to manage these issues."

Sources: D. Brown, "CIBC HR Department Halved as Non-strategic Roles Outsourced," *Canadian HR Reporter*, Vol. 14, No. 11 (2001), 1 and 6; S. Geary and G. Coffey-Lewis, "Are You Ready to Outsource HR?" *HR Professional* (June/July 2002), 26–29.

## The Rationale for Outsourcing

Almost all organizations outsource, and the trend is growing. In a study conducted by Hewitt Associates, 94% said of those surveyed said that they had outsourced one or more HR functions.[3] CIBC's decision to outsource is explained in HR Planning Today 13.2.

If the organization needs experts and cannot afford to hire or train them, outsourcing may be a solution. Most organizations want to achieve cost savings or improved services, or access to experts or technology, as the basis for their decision to outsource. However, many managers approach outsourcing as a solution without first defining the problem.[4]

There are at least six major reasons that organizations outsource: financial savings, strategic focus, access to advanced technology, improved service levels, access to specialized expertise, and organizational politics.

## Financial Savings

**RPC** 13.3

The first reason cited for the outsourcing decision is to save money. Organizations believe that costs can be reduced by outsourcing a function such as payroll. Economies of scale can be achieved when the provider, such as Ceridien, which specializes in providing benefits administration, concentrates on one area and provides this service to many corporations. Specialized vendors are more efficient because they can spread the costs of training personnel and undertaking research and development across more users. Studies of outsourcing arrangements of at least two years' duration showed that outsourcing resulted in cost savings ranging from 10% to 20%, with an average of 15%.[5] About 50% of the firms believed that their cost savings objectives had been met, and labour productivity had improved.

Related to the issue of saving money is cost control. Company users of a service may be more cautious when the contractor charges them for each service, as opposed to the "free" in-house service. Training is a good example. If in-house training is free and training provided by an external vendor costs $1,000 per day, then managers are more stringent about requiring employees to prove that the training is needed and that there would be measurable benefits. Sometimes, when an organization is just starting to offer a service, such as fitness training for employees, it is cheaper to contract this out than to make the capital investments in a gym and specialized staff. This capital can then be redirected to other initiatives that have a higher rate of return. Outsourcing also makes sense when usage of a service is variable or unpredictable. An organization may recruit on an irregular basis for IT staff; in this case, retaining an in-house IT recruiter is not economically viable.

## Strategic Focus

Employers recognize that they cannot pursue excellence in all areas. Therefore, they decide to focus on their core competence, such as customer service or innovation, and move secondary functions, such as benefits administration, to firms in which these functions are a core competence.

How is core defined? There are four meanings:[6]

- Activities traditionally performed internally.
- Activities critical to business success. Core work contributes directly to the bottom line; noncore work doesn't.
- Activities creating current or potential competitive advantage.
- Activities that will influence future growth or rejuvenation.

The notion of core competencies was created by Prahalad and Hamel, who argued that the real sources of competitive advantage were not products but management's ability to consolidate skills and technologies into competencies to adapt to changing circumstances.[7] A competence is a combination of technology, management, and collective learning. For Nike, that core competence is product design, and the company outsources nearly everything else.[8]

Executives will decide to concentrate on what the organization does best, and contract everything else out to vendors. Core functions that should not be outsourced are orientation, leadership development, employee relations, final selection, performance management, succession management, and organizational change as these depend on an understanding of organizational culture, a long-term orientation, consistency, trust, and confidential information.

By outsourcing noncore activities, managers hope to be able to focus on value-added roles. For example, CIBC outsourced the design of training programs and development and delivery, allowing the company to focus on planning, needs analyses, and coaching after program completion.[9] Companies that did outsource reported that they reduced administrative tasks by more than half and increased their strategic focus by 40%.[10] Avenor Inc. of Montreal outsourced all pensions, benefits, and payroll administration. As James Merchant, vice-president of Human Resources at Avenor, explained,

> Outsourcing allowed us to get out of low value-added administrative work and become more strategic. We now focus on health and safety, leadership development, total compensation, and employee and labour relations. Our department at head office has 12 staff today compared to 40 in 1994. But, with our change in focus, our performance within the organization has taken a quantum leap.[11]

## Advanced Technology

Another driver of this trend has been technology. Many functions are outsourced because organizations want to improve technical service, they cannot find technical talent, or they need quick and reliable access to new technologies.[12] Much of traditional HR service has involved answering employee inquiries about benefits or making changes to employee files. These kinds of tasks can be handled easily by interactive voice responses and managed by companies that specialize in this service. Technology also enables a company to reduce transaction time (the time it takes to handle a request).

## Improved Service

Quality improvement is cited as another benefit of outsourcing. Performance standards can be written into the contract more tightly than may be possible with current and long-tenured employees. Managers can choose the "best-of-breed" vendors that have outstanding track records and more flexibility in hiring and rewarding their employees.

HR departments are often criticized for being overly bureaucratic. When using a service provider whose focus is service, clients of HR see a marked improvement in flexibility, response, and performance. Most firms gain control of their service levels, because their outsourcing agreement can quantify deliverables in the contract.[13]

Confidentiality is also a good reason to outsource. An employee with a drinking problem, for example, is more likely to seek assistance from an external counsellor than an in-house employee assistance officer.

## Specialized Expertise

Another reason cited by some companies for outsourcing is that they find the laws and regulations governing HR so complex that they decide to outsource to firms that have the specific expertise required. The motto is "Outsource when somebody can do it better than you."

Employees who are outsourced to the service provider may see opportunities for career development in their disciplines. In an organization specializing in training, for example, employees would have greater access to expert colleagues to use them as sounding boards, and to career paths and opportunities to upgrade their knowledge and skills.

The use of experts also reduces the risks and liabilities for organizations. Specialists know the legislation better than anyone and can assure the user organization that all their practices comply with legislation.

Access to leading practices is another motivator to outsource.

## Organizational Politics

An outsourced function is not as visible as an in-house department performing the same tasks. Some organizations make the decision to outsource to get rid of a troublesome department, such as one where employees are underperforming. Outsourcing a function also reduces the head count. Head counts are important in the public sector; the fewer civil servants on payroll, the happier the tax-paying public. Organizations that outsource achieve a ratio of 1:231 (one HR person to 231 employees) compared to the tradition 1:100.[14] The contractor is often able to justify and negotiate technology improvements and other investments more easily than in-house managers.

## Risks and Limitations

As with any major decision, there are positives and negatives to outsourcing. The decision to outsource carries risks and has limitations. Are the anticipated benefits realized? What are the risks to service levels? What is the effect on employee morale? Does outsourcing reduce the value of the organization? These four questions are discussed below.

**🅡🅟🅒 13.4**

## Projected Benefits vs. Actual Benefits

For organizations with experience in outsourcing functions, there are hints that the process is not as cost effective and problem-free as expected. Surveys have indicated that about half of the respondents found that it was more expensive to manage the outsourced activity than originally expected and that service levels were not as good as expected.[15] About 40% reported problems with higher costs than forecasted. The reasons for the cost overrides include system incompatibilities and client demands outside the standard vendor package. Interestingly, one study found that about one-quarter of HR staff time was still spent on benefits administration, which had been outsourced (e.g., addressing problems that the outsourcing company could not handle or mishandled with employees). Worse, half of this routine work was being done by the wrong people: senior specialists and managers.[16] Outsourcing compares poorly to other processes designed to save costs. For example, re-engineering can generate cost savings over 50%; outsourcing savings seem to be, on average, 10% to 15%.[17] Over 30% of outsourcing arrangements were not renewed because the cost savings were not achieved.[18]

## Service Risks

The vendor will provide services as specified in the contract. If the needs of the user organization change, contracts will have to change. The flexibility of adding new features or enhancing or reducing service is reduced. Furthermore, it is possible that the vendor may enter the market and become a competitor. For example, Schwinn, a U.S. manufacturer of bicycles, outsourced the manufacture of its bicycle frame to a Taiwanese organization, Giant Manufacturing. A few years later, Giant entered the bicycle market and damaged Schwinn's business. Companies can lessen this risk by erecting strategic blocks—terms in the contract that limit the replication of certain competitive advantages, such as propriety technology—or spreading the outsourcing among many vendors.

A SHRM survey found that about 25% of respondents reported a decrease in customer service from the in-house service and a less personal relationship with its own employees.[19]

## Employee Morale

One of the primary risks in outsourcing is the effect on employee morale and performance.[20] Outsourcing is a form of restructuring that always results in displaced employees. Organizations provide employees with a sense of identification and feelings of security and belonging. When these are disrupted, employees, as stakeholders, may feel resentful and retaliatory. About one-third of HR professionals resist outsourcing because they risk losing their jobs, may be forced to work for a vendor, and fear that management believes that outsiders are more competent.[21]

In an outsourcing arrangement, employees are transferred to the outsourcing firm, transferred internally to other functions, outplaced, and/or offered voluntary retirements. Despite all these options, redundancies and layoffs of staff do occur. In certain cases, the service provider employs the entire displaced workforce but may negotiate higher fees to accommodate what is perceived to be surplus or inefficient labour. Employees are resentful of these arrangements, with their connotations of "serfdom" in which the "serfs" are sold as capital equipment.[22]

Outsourcing can lead to the disintegration of an organization's culture. Instead of empowering and valuing employees, an outsourcing decision alienates and "deskills" employees. The transferred employees will experience emotional loss and a change in culture. The outsourced function may have served as a developmental site for managers and this is now lost, unless arrangements can be made with the vendor.

In most cases, negotiated arrangements of pay and job security are not transferrable. The vendor is able to offer cost savings because of reduced wages and increased work intensity.[23]

Organizations that attempt to outsource face a backlash. The City of Toronto endured a three-week strike by garbage workers over the issue of outsourcing. Citizens lived with rotting garbage on the streets during a heat wave while the strike was under way. Members of CUPE were demanding job security ("lifelong employment") for employees, but the city won a public relations battle by saying that the demands were unreasonable because no working and tax-paying citizen enjoyed this right.

Once rumours of outsourcing arrangements are started, HR managers can expect talented employees to start job searches and all employees to suffer anxiety resulting in lost production. Managers will have to deal with the reactions of displaced employees and survivors and allow for a period of mourning.

### Reduced Value

Extreme levels of outsourcing hollow out a company, leaving it a shell. There may be unintended consequences of outsourcing the organization's knowledge and skills to outsiders. The vendor may even sell the acquired know-how and company secrets to a competitor. Organizations can find that outsourcing employees' skills limits these organizations' ability to learn and exploit changes.

The organization experiences a reduced capacity to generate profits or innovate. Even a noncore activity, such as IT, may be tightly linked to other functions such as HR, so outsourcing IT reduces the firm's capability for cross-functional synergies and creativity. The vendor cannot know your organization's special needs, nor can it distinguish your high-profile customer (the president of the company that outsourced the function) from any other customer. When HR functions are outsourced, the internal image of HR may deteriorate as there is less interaction with internal customers and less and less HR work is performed by the HR department.[24]

However, even with these risks and limitations, it is estimated that between 1% and 20% of outsourced HR functions have been brought back in-house.[25]

 13.5

## Management of Outsourcing

Managing the outsourcing well is critical. First, outsourcing must be subjected to a cost–benefit analysis. Can the contractor do a better job, faster, while maintaining service levels and meeting legislative requirements? How will this be measured? The following sections describe ways of selecting vendors, negotiating the contract, and monitoring the arrangement.

### Selecting the Vendor

Once a decision is made to explore outsourcing a function, the organization should

**request for proposal (RFP)**

describes the responsibilities to be outsourced and invites potential providers to present their proposal for carrying out the job

- inform the staff of the affected function,
- prepare an **RFP (request for proposal),**
- invite internal and external bids, and
- establish a team to evaluate these bids.

See HR Planning Notebook 13.3 for a summary of the key information that should be contained in a response to an RFP.

**HR Planning Notebook 13.3**

### Response Requirements to a Request for Proposal for Outsourcing

In a response to a request for proposal, the potential provider should do the following:

- Explain how the provider is uniquely qualified to accomplish the measurable objectives that are described in the request.
- Describe actual situations in which the provider is currently providing the services that are proposed for this operation.
- Identify the challenges that the provider expects to encounter while improving the operation.

- Explain how these challenges will be met and present a proposed timetable for meeting them.
- Describe the economic model that is proposed for the operation.
- Specify the fee that the provider believes to be reasonable compensation for its services.

Source: Moneta, L., and W.L. Dillion. 2001. "Strategies for Effective Outsourcing." In *New Directions for Student Services*, No. 96 (Winter), John Wiley & Sons, p. 42. Copyright ©2002. Reprinted with permission of John Wiley & Sons, Inc.

The point at which the staff should be informed about the potential outsourcing is hotly debated. If informed early in the process, the most talented and marketable employees may leave, and the stress and anxiety among those remaining affects productivity. However, employees will find out sooner than management might like, and it is far better to keep them in the loop of communication; they may even play a vital role in the development of the RFP.

The items to be included in an RFP vary by the service to be outsourced. Typical details include activity levels, errors, response rates, deliverables, and goals.[26] Costs are never included.

Companies that have had successful outsourcing arrangements always started by comparing vendor bids against bids newly submitted by in-house functional experts.[27] The internal group may have had ideas to reduce costs or improve services, but were thwarted for many reasons. Once it is clear that outsourcing is the preferred route because the same service cannot be provided in-house, the organization can proceed with its outsourcing plans, secure that every avenue has been explored.

The evaluation team should include the technical experts, including a manager who will not be affected by the outcome, procurement officers who can qualify suppliers, and even customers who can check out the suppliers' track records and personnel.[28] This team sets the evaluation criteria, analyzes bids against the criteria, and chooses the vendor. The process should be as obsessive and detailed as the due diligence undertaken with mergers and acquisitions. Examples of evaluation criteria can be found in HR Planning Today 13.3.

## Negotiating the Contract

**RPC** 13.6

Experts advise organizations looking to outsource to not work with the contract the vendor will offer because these contracts typically do not include performance standards or penalty clauses if the vendor does not meet requirements.[29] Payment provisions in these standardized contracts also tend to

## HR Planning Today 13.3

### Outsourcing at Autoglass

Autoglass, a company in the business of repairing and replacing automobile windows, uses and weights ten criteria in choosing a vendor:

| | |
|---|---|
| 1. Commitment to implement urgently needed system | 10 |
| 2. Software competency | 10 |
| 3. Cultural fit | 9 |
| 4. Contract conditions | 9 |
| 5. Hardware competency | 8 |
| 6. Knowledge of user requirements | 7 |
| 7. International capability | 7 |
| 8. Cost | 7 |
| 9. Client references | 6 |
| 10. Contract length | 5 |

Other companies look at
- HR process expertise (95%)
- Prior experience and track records (93%)
- Service-level agreements in the contracts (65%)
- Leading-edge technology (65%)

Sources: Gurchiak, K. 2005. "Record Growth in Outsourcing of HR Functions," *HR Magazine*, 50, 6, 35–36., M. Milgate, *Alliances, Outsourcing, and the Lean Organization*. Copyright © 2001 Michael Milgate. Reproduced with permission of Greenwood Publishing Group Inc., Westport, CT.

favour the vendor. The vendor also has a tendency to want to start the service before the contract is signed and "take care of the details later." Anything not provided at the beginning is then subject to excess fees.

An essential first step that the user organization must undertake is the establishment of benchmark levels with current services. The goal is to document baseline services currently being provided, using criteria such as response time, response cost, and customer satisfaction ratings. Thus, a performance standard might read that "90% of benefits enquiries must be answered within 24 hours." Of course, everyone forgets about the other 10%, so that too must be specified (e.g., "The remaining 10% must be answered within three working days"). Quality measures have to be included; for example, "Clients rate the service satisfactory or excellent 98% of the time." The most common service-level agreements are transaction accuracy, data delivery, service availability, issue resolution, and client satisfaction.[30] Failure to meet these levels must result in penalties, such as reduction in the costs or payments to the user. On the other hand, if service is superior, incentives should be built into the contract. It may be necessary to include clauses for severe fluctuations in demand. Finally, any contract should include a termination clause.

The negotiations tend to be imbalanced, with the vendor having employed many technical and legal experts in order to prepare the agreement. The user organizations should do likewise and hire an expert to protect their interests. A technical expert can help develop performance standards, and a legal expert ensures that the customer's wishes are expressed in the contract.

## Monitor the Arrangement

The work is managed by results—in other words, there are targets or objectives such as "All calls answered within 90 seconds"—not necessarily by time expended to generate the results. A person will need to be assigned to monitor that the results are as expected; in complex arrangements, it may take a team to do this monitoring. The outsourced project or function must be clearly defined. If the terms are fuzzy, however, the contractor might be invited to brainstorm and help generate the guidelines and standards.[31] A relationship with the firm must be established to ensure that the outsourcer acts in the firm's best interests and has knowledge of its unique needs. References must be checked, just as they are when hiring any employee. Demand frequent and accurate reporting. Conduct internal and external client satisfaction surveys.

When managed according to these guidelines, organizations can maximize the benefits of outsourcing while mitigating the risks.

## Summary

Outsourcing refers to the contractual arrangement wherein one organization provides services or products to another. There is a growing trend to outsource HR functions. The advantages of outsourcing include the reduction of costs; the increased energy and time to focus on an organization's core competencies; access to technology and specialized expertise, which both result in increased levels of service; and the political advantages of removing a troublesome function or reducing headcount. But there are disadvantages: the anticipated benefits may not be realized; service levels may decrease; and employee morale and commitment, as well as the value of the organization, may be reduced. Managing the contractual arrangement with the service provider is the key to optimizing the benefits and minimizing the risks.

## Key Term

request for proposal (RFP), 360

## Web Links

An outsourcing problem analysis by Canadian Technology Human Resources Board:

**www.cthrb.ca/ArticleResources/outsourcing-problem-analysis.shtml** (p. 355)

Provides highlights, analysis, and research findings on outsourcing:

**www.gartner.com/it/products/research/asset_129505_2395.jsp** (p. 360)

An example of a detailed outsourcing policy by the University of Alberta:

**www.conman.ualberta.ca/stellent/groups/public/@finance/documents/ procedure/pp_cmp_054400.hcsp** (p. 362)

# RPC Icons

**RPC 13.1**  Contributes to improvements in the organization's structures and work processes

**RPC 13.2**  Collects data, analyzes, and reviews the organization's existing HR programs to ensure they are consistent with business activities

**RPC 13.3**  Applies measurement, evaluation, and assessment processes to business situations

**RPC 13.4**  Evaluates the effectiveness of HR strategies using various measurement, assessment, and accountability approaches

**RPC 13.5**  Develops business cases for HR activities, e.g., return on investment (ROI) evaluations, data collection, and assessment

**RPC 13.6**  Establishes goals, deliverables, timelines, and budgets

**RPC 13.7**  Provides advice on policy, monitors activities, and, if required, initiates corrective action related to the organization's practices

# Discussion Questions

1. Experts suggest that core functions should never be outsourced. Make a list of all the services and products that a large HR department in a large organization would provide. Prepare a definition of core functions. On a scale of 1 to 10, assign a weight to each HR service or product to assess if it is core or noncore.
2. Canadians have experienced several strikes over outsourcing. Identify these, and focus on the most recent strike. Analyze the media reports, and consult the employer and union websites to determine the perspectives of each on the issue of outsourcing. Have one team prepare the arguments against outsourcing from the union perspective; have another group prepare the arguments for outsourcing from the employer's perspective. Have each group write a two-page message to be given to the media.
3. Using a search engine, determine which public companies have made major outsourcing decisions. List the value of their shares one year before the announcement, one day before, one day after, and one year later to calculate the impact of an outsourcing decision on shareholder value.

# Using the Internet

Log on to the website

**www.conman.ualberta.ca/stellent/groups/public/@finance/documents/ procedure/pp_cmp_054400.hcsp**

The web link describes a detailed outsourcing policy, which includes procedures and definitions of outsourcing used at University of Alberta. Compare and contrast the outsourcing policy on the website with the specific HR outsourcing procedures mentioned in this chapter.

1. What are the similarities and differences? Can you identify ways in which the outsourcing policy from the website can be applied specifically to HR outsourcing?
2. Search for the Business Case Template link located at the bottom of the home page. Study the elements of a business plan, which is an essential outline to follow when building a business case to outsource the function.

## Exercise

1. Most of you reading this text are students at a community college or university. Using your educational institute's directory, make a list of all organizational functions. In groups, determine which functions are possible candidates for outsourcing. Choose one and establish a business case for the president to outsource the function. Identify one or two service providers, and consult with them about the benefits of outsourcing. Choose another function and establish a case for retaining the function internally.

## Case: Calgary Health Region

In November 2001, the Calgary Health Region issued an RFI (Request for Information) to suppliers interested in forming a partnership to finance and deliver an HRIS and provide certain human resources functions. A steering committee, composed of the vice-president, Human Resources; executive director, Human Resources; vice-president, Finance; executive director, Finance; director of Compensation, Benefits, and HR Systems; and executive director, Information Technology, was formed to steer the project and screen the responses to the RFIs. The steering committee selected three of the responses and issued an RFP (Request for Proposal). Each supplier was given six weeks to provide a systems solution and shared-service outsourcing arrangement reflecting best HR practices, expertise, and financial arrangements. They were given detailed specifications and asked to bid on identified HR and payroll functions (e.g., payroll, benefit administration, pension) as a core service and bid on options such as recruitment services and occupational health and safety services.

The Evaluation and Selection team reviewed the submissions, and all met most of the requirements. Each consortium of suppliers was invited to present their proposals and respond to questions during a one-day presentation.

All consortiums included a change management consultant and an information systems consultant. A detailed scoring system was developed that included an emphasis on service delivery and the impact on the current HR staff. The Evaluation and Selection team conducted site visits and reference checks on organizations in Boston, Vancouver, Edmonton, Toronto, and Calgary. The consortium chosen comprised Telus (providing the lead with an investment in the software application PeopleSoft 8.8), PricewaterhouseCoopers (for change management and implementation support), together with additional individual advisers. Due diligence was conducted in the fall of 2002. The negotiations continued for weeks in an attempt to craft a detailed proposal and a shared service contract that would result in the creation of a new organization and service provider.

The advantages of this potential partnership to the Calgary Health Region would be that its HRIS needs would be met by a state-of-the-art HRMS with no capital outlay. The region's current cost of "business as usual" for the staff and associated expenses transferring to the new organization would be paid to the provider throughout the term of the contract. In turn, the new organization would benefit from efficiencies generated by new systems and processes as well as revenue generated by building the client base. Additionally, the Calgary Health Region would potentially benefit from any new business generated. Each current HR employee would be guaranteed a job for at least one year, with the same or better compensation, benefits, and performance bonus plan as well as additional perquisites such as stock options. Some employees seemed to be excited by the possibility of working in an organization whose core business is HR and not always competing for funds with the dominant health care divisions.

The consortium saw a benefit from a long-term contract and the possibility of generating revenues from increasing the business and client base. Indeed, the major expectation was that this service could be provided to other organizations, particularly in the health care and educational sectors, where there is limited capital available for investment in human resources services and associated systems.

However there were some risks. The service delivery may not have met expectations despite standards such as "99.9% accuracy in payroll," and financial penalties would occur for failure to meet these standards. There may have been some loss of control related to the direct supervision of the service, although there would be contract managers in both organizations. The separation of groups of employees who normally worked together, such as the recruitment consultants and the recruitment assistants, may have posed problems (i.e., what is the impact of splitting strategic and transactional functions?). Finally, several groups of employees might have had to relocate to the new company; some were unionized, others exempt. There might have been a fight for successorship rights and the possibility of labour board challenges.

Source: Personal interview, Spring 2003, with Duncan Truscott, Acting Vice-President, HR; and Diane Pollo, Director, Compensation, Benefits, and HR Systems, Calgary Health Region. Courtesy of Calgary Health Region.

## Questions

1. If you had been a member of the Calgary Health Region, what conditions would you have insisted be included in the contract with the vendor?
2. Prepare a report for management on the advantages of outsourcing, and the risks of this decision and your recommendations for managing each risk.

# Endnotes

1. Adler, P. S. 2003. "Making the HR Outsourcing Decision," *MIT Sloan Management Review*, 45, 1, 53–60; Oshima M., T. Kao, and J. Tower. 2005. "Achieving Post-Outsourcing Success," *Human Resources Planning*, 28, 2, 7–12.
2. Gurchiek, K. 2005. "Record Growth in Outsourcing of HR Functions," *HR Magazine*, 50, 6, 35–36.
3. Gurchiek, 2005.
4. McCauley, A. 2000. "Know the Benefits and Costs of Outsourcing Services," *Canadian HR Reporter*, Vol. 13, No. 17 (October 9): 18–19.
5. Adler, 2003; Henneman, T. 2005. "Measuring the True Benefit of Human Resources Outsourcing," *Workforce Management*, 84, 7, 76–77; Oshima et al, 2005.
6. Alexander, M., and D. Young. 1996. "Strategic Outsourcing," *Long Range Planning*, Vol. 29, No. 1: 116–119.
7. Prahalad, C.K., and G. Hamel. 1990. "The Core Competence of the Corporation," *Harvard Business Review*, Vol. 68, No. 3: 79–91.
8. Leavy, B. 2005 "Nike, Ikea and IBM's Outsourcing and Business Strategies," *Human Resources Management International Digest*, 13, 3, 15–17.
9. Burn, D. 1998. "To Outsource Training or Not to Outsource Training: That Is the Question," *Human Resources Professional*, Vol. 15, No. 1(February/March): 18–23.
10. Oshima et al, 2005.
11. Burn, D. 1997. "Outsourcing: Transforming the Role of Human Resource Professionals," *HR Professional*, (February/March): 26–33.
12. LaCity, M.C., and R. Hirschheim. 1995. *Beyond the Information Systems Outsourcing Bandwagon*. Toronto: John Wiley & Sons.
13. Cooke, B. 2004 "HR/Benefits Outsourcing: Updating the Conventional Thinking," *Employee Benefit Plan Review*, 58, 8, 18–22.
14. Oshima et al, 2005.
15. Albertson, D. 2000. "Outsourcing Shows Limited Impact for Strategic HR," *Employee Benefit News*, Vol. 14, No. 10: 70.
16. Rison, R. P., and J. Tower. 2005. "How to Reduce the Cost of HR and Continue to Provide Value," *Human Resource Planning*, 28, 1, 14–18.
17. Bryce, D.J., and M. Useem. 1998. "The Impact of Corporate Outsourcing on Company Value," *European Management Journal*, Vol. 16, No. 6: 635–643.
18. Geary, S., and G. Coffey-Lewis. 2002. "Are You Ready to Outsource HR?" *HR Professional*, Vol. 19, No. 3 (June/July): 26–29.
19. Lilly, J.D., D.A. Gray, M. Virick. 2005. "Outsourcing the Human Resources Function: Environmental and Organizational Characteristics that Affect HR Performance," *Journal of Business Strategies*, 22, 1, 55–74.

20. Elmuti, D., and Y. Kathawala. 2000. "The Effects of Global Outsourcing Strategies on Participants' Attitudes and Organizational Effectiveness," *International Journal of Manpower*, Vol. 21, No. 2: 112–128.

21. Babcock, P. 2004 "Slicing off Pieces of HR," *HR Magazine*, 49, 7, 70–76.; Sullivan, J. 2004. "The Case against Outsourcing," *Canadian HR Reporter*, 17, 3, 15.

22. "Outsourcing and the Implications for Human Resource Development," *Journal of Management Development*, Vol. 19, No. 8 (2000): 694–699.

23. Bryce and Useem, 1998.

24. Sullivan, J. 2002. "The Case Against Outsourcing," *IHRIM Journal* (July): 38–41.

25. Gurchiek, 2005; Pollitt, D. 2004. "Outsourcing HR: The Contrasting Experiences of Amex and DuPont," *Human Resource Management*, 12, 6, 8–10.

26. The Economist Intelligence Unit. 1995. *New Directions in Finance: Strategic Outsourcing*. New York: The Economist Intelligence Unit.

27. LaCity and Hirschheim, 1995.

28. Laabs, J. 2000. "Are You Ready to Outsource Staffing?" *Workforce*, Vol. 70, No. 4: 56–60.

29. LaCity and Hirschheim, 1995.

30. Gurchiek, 2005.

31. Petrick, A.E. 1996. "The Fine Art of Outsourcing," *Association Management* (December): 42–48.

# Chapter 14

# Evaluation of HR Programs and Policies

## Chapter Learning Objectives

After reading this chapter, you should be able to

- Understand the importance of measuring the effectiveness of HRM activities.
- Outline five aspects of HRM that can be evaluated using the 5C model for measuring effectiveness: compliance with laws and regulations, client satisfaction, culture management to influence employee attitudes, cost control of the labour component of the budget, and the contribution of HR programs.
- Discuss methods of measurement, such as cost–benefit analysis, utility analysis, and auditing techniques.
- Identify the challenges in measuring HR activities.

Jane Haberbusch, VP of HR for Enbridge Gas Distribution, is a keen supporter of the HR scorecard. "The scorecard works like this: Motivated employees provide great customer service, which results in overall customer satisfaction, which is then correlated with reduced operating costs and increased net profit margins.

"Our customer satisfaction ratings are the highest in our sector. We know that motivated and engaged employees provide the best levels of customer service. If you had a workforce that was highly motivated and actively engaged, what types of evidence would you see?

- low levels of employee turnover, especially of the "critical keepers,"
- high levels of employee engagement and employee satisfaction (usually measured through employee feedback instruments),
- low levels of absenteeism and "presenteeism," [showing up for work but not necessarily being productive]
- high levels of alignment to company goals and objectives,
- effective development of succession candidates to ensure leadership continuity, and
- enhanced levels of innovation and creativity in response to business challenges.

Using these types of outcomes as measures and assigning stretch targets ensures focus and alignment of all HR-related initiatives. So, for example, before we introduce an HR practice such as a mentoring program for high potentials, we need to establish the connection or the "line of sight" to the company's overall goals." The company's mission and goals can be found at www.egd.enbridge.com.[1]

Aligning HRM programs and policies with organizational goals is the beginning of the strategic HR planning process. Assessing whether these policies and practices were effective is the end of one cycle in the planning process because HR professionals need to know how their programs and policies are performing.

## Keeping Score

Corporate scorekeeping allows organizations to make the adjustments necessary to reach their goals. The scorecard, with its measures of key indicators, focuses managers' and employees' attention on what is important to the organization. Focusing on desired results increases the ability to attain the results. Scorecard measures allow us to make judgments about the relative effectiveness of various policies and practices, just as baseball scores and records allow fans to track the success of sports teams.

The model of strategic HRM planning outlined in Chapter 1 called for the measurement of the success of the plan. The tracking of customer satisfaction or absenteeism rates not only measures progress, but also pinpoints weaknesses and identifies gaps. Just as organizations keep scorecards on their financial effectiveness, so too must the HR department track the effectiveness of its programs.

## The Importance of Evaluating HRM

An article in *Fortune* magazine called for the abolition of the HR function, arguing that HR managers are unable to describe their contribution to value except in trendy, unquantifiable, and "wanna-be" terms.[2] The author also proposed that efficiencies could be increased by outsourcing legislated activities (such as payroll and equity) and returning "people" responsibilities to line managers. His exact words were "Blow up the HR department." Senior executives who read *Fortune* asked themselves, "Does HR make a difference?" Does it add value?" Nearly a decade later, another journalist wrote an article called "Why We Hate HR," and said that HR practitioners did not have a seat at the table; they didn't even have a key to the boardroom.[3] Clearly, until HR managers can talk about the contribution and value of HR activities in the numbers language of business, the HR department and the HR profession will be vulnerable to destructive proposals such as those listed above.

Increasingly, the HR department is being treated like other operational units—that is, it is subject to questions about its contribution to organizational performance. In the simplest terms, HRM must make a difference; if it doesn't, it will be abolished. Decision makers within organizations view HR activities, such as training courses, as expenses. They view results as value. The deliverables, not the do-ables such as training, are what make a difference to the organization. Measurement of the HR function is critical for improving both the credibility and the effectiveness of HR. If you cannot measure contribution, you cannot manage it or improve it. What gets measured gets managed and improved.

Business is a numbers game. Some surveys have shown that HR practitioners, while familiar with some numbers (such as the number of people employed in the organization), can't always recite other key numbers (such as the sales volumes, market share, profit levels, and rates of return for their organization). When asked to assess their contribution, most HR professionals describe it in such terms as "number of training courses" or "new hires." They do not provide numbers for outcomes. They say things such as "One hundred and twenty people attended the training course," and rarely "The training courses resulted in a 15% improvement in customer satisfaction."

### Resistance

Some HR managers resist measuring their work. They argue that HR activities cannot be measured, since outcomes such as employee attitudes or managerial productivity are impossible to calibrate meaningfully or precisely.

They assert that they cannot control the labour market. But the finance department cannot control the inflation rate, and the marketing department has little control over product quality, and yet each of these departments measures its activities and is accountable for results. Measuring is expensive, but not as expensive as continuing an ineffective program. The main reason that HR is not measured is that there is no standard way of measuring. Think of finance and accounting with their widely accepting principles of measurement.[4] As the field of HR evolves, the analytic and data-based decision-making capability will develop.[5] There may evolve two types of HR, with one branch similar to sales and accounting transactions, and the other more like the marketing and finance strategic decision making.[6]

Very few organizations measure the impact of HRM; about two-thirds of HR professionals in Fortune 500 companies measure HR productivity.[7] However, those that do measure are more likely to be treated as a strategic partner.[8] Interest in measuring HR is growing slowly, fuelled by

- business improvement efforts across organizations,
- attempts to position HR as a strategic partner, and
- the need for objective indicators of success to accompany the analysis of HR activities.

There are other pressures that make measurement a hot topic in HR. The Sarbanes-Oxley requirements force HR to provide information about executive compensation, pension plans, and whistleblower protection. More HR professionals are now trained in the field of measurement and capable of developing HR scorecards, and measuring human capital. There is an increased awareness among leaders that investments in HR can impact customers and then the bottom line.[9]

Deutsche Bank is a leader in the measurement—or metrics—of HR, because it reports human capital metrics in its annual report, as reported in HR Planning Today 14.1. When introducing a new compensation scheme or training program, the proposer must be prepared to justify costs with predicted results, expressed in the numbers language of business. We will show you how to do this later in the chapter.

## Rationale

Determining the quantitative impact of HR programs is so important that the Society for Human Resources Management, the largest HR association in the United States, has designated HRM impact as a top research priority and is funding research in this area.

There are seven compelling reasons for measuring HRM effectiveness:

1. Labour costs are most often a firm's largest controllable cost.
2. Managers recognize that employees make the difference between the success and failure of projects and organizations. Good performance can be rewarded objectively.
3. Organizations have legal responsibilities to ensure that they are in compliance with laws governing the employer–employee relationship.

### Human Captial Metrics

Deutsche Bank publishes indicators as part of its strategy to remain an attractive employer and maintain a balance of interest among employees, shareholders, customers, and society. In addition to numbers such as head counts, which are normally published in annual reports, Deutsche Bank provides the following information.

|  | 2000 | 1999 | 1998 |
|---|---|---|---|
| Employee commitment index | 72 | 66 | n/a |
| Absentee rate | 2.3% | 2.4% | 2.7% |
| Employees leaving bank for a new job | 7.8% | 6.8% | 5.7% |
| Expenses for training (in euros) | 237.2 | 222.4 | 201.7 |
| Employees purchasing shares | 65% | 65% | 62% |
| Managers in Global Equity Plan | 77% | 79% | 83% |

Sources: www.db.com; and S. Gates, "How to Improve Human Capital Measurement," *IHRIM Journal*, Vol. 6, No. 6 (November 2002), 18–25.

4. Evaluations are needed to determine which HR practices are effective because, at this point, managers and HR professionals cannot distinguish between a fad and a valid change program.[10] Professor Terry Wagar, of St. Mary's University, in Halifax, Nova Scotia, has studied fads and determined that many of the practices are not integrated with other HR systems, and that they are fragile and do not survive.[11] For example, take a current fad: emotional intelligence. There is little, if any, empirical evidence that emotional intelligence is correlated with either individual performance or organizational performance, according to Professor Victor Catano of St. Mary's University.[12] Professor Simon Taggar of Wilfrid Laurier University teaches students about validity by having them complete the emotional intelligence survey and feeding them randomly generated responses that are identical for every student. He then asks students to assess how valid their individual feedback is and how accurately the survey describes their personalities. Most feel that the feedback, with one or two exceptions, describes them well (although people who read horoscopes are left with the same impressions). He then asks the critical question: "Would you recommend this survey to your employer as a valid selection?" Most would, and then he reveals the procedure he has used to teach about validity. The characteristics of fads are outlined in HR Planning Notebook 14.1.

5. Measuring and benchmarking HR activities will result in continuous improvements. Performance gaps can be identified and eliminated.

6. Audits will bring HR closer to the line functions of the organization. The practices must demonstrate that they enhance competitive advantage, not just that they are efficient or "best-in-class.[13]

7. Data will be available to support resource allocations.[14]

## HR Planning Notebook 14.1

### Characteristics of a Fad

1. It is simple and claims to solve complex problems.
2. It claims to apply to and help anyone.
3. It is not anchored or related to any known and generally accepted theory.
4. Proponents hesitate to present it in academic settings or write about it in referred journals.
5. Proponents cannot tell you exactly how it works.
6. It is a "track" topic at 75% of the conferences that you have attended.

7. Its proponents claim that it has changed their lives and that it can change yours too.
8. Its greatest proponents are those with the least experience in the field.
9. It is just too good to be true.

Source: D. Ulrich, 1997, *Human Resource Champions*, Boston, MA, Harvard Business School Press, 63.

The next section describes the areas in which HRM departments can be evaluated.

**RPC 14.1**

**RPC 14.2**

## The 5C Model of HRM Impact

Executives, investors, customers, and HR professionals themselves make judgments in many ways about the effectiveness of the HR function. The numerous areas that are judged can be grouped into five clusters—the 5 Cs of evaluating HRM: compliance, client satisfaction, culture management, cost control, and contribution.[15]

## Compliance

Senior management depends on HR expertise to ensure that organizational practices comply with the law, and many HR departments were started because of the need to record compliance with employment standards, such as hours worked and overtime payments. Legislation dealing with the employer–employee relationship is increasing, and the areas of safety, health, employment equity, and industrial relations are all highly regulated. Indeed, some people estimate that 20% to 30% of the increase in the salaries of HR professionals is due to the need to trust someone with the responsibility for compliance.

Highly publicized cases of safety violations in which board members of industrial organizations have been fined hundreds of thousands of dollars or threatened with jail time serve as another wake-up call. Other public cases that have cost organizations not only the expense of fines but also loss in business have occurred because managers have been held responsible for the sexual harassment of their subordinates. HR can make a difference by ensuring that managers and employees comply with the law, thus saving the company legal costs, fines, and damaging publicity.

## Client Satisfaction

**RPC** 14.3

Across Canada, many organizations are tracking their success by measuring customer satisfaction or soliciting input on client complaints and attitudes. These measures have been found to predict financial performance, on a lagged basis. This means that if employee morale drops, management can expect to see customer satisfaction levels drop in about six months.

Stakeholders, who include external and internal clients, are those people who can influence or must interact with the HR department. External clients of HR comprise candidates for positions, suppliers of HR services such as technology, and government regulators. Internal clients include employees grouped by occupation, union leaders, and managers.

Managers are turning to client or stakeholder perceptions of the HR department for input about the effectiveness of HR performance. This approach stems from earlier efforts in total quality management and tries to reconcile the gaps between client expectations and levels of satisfaction. The bigger the gap, the less effective the HR department. This qualitative approach surveys stakeholders about their perceptions of the effectiveness of the HR function. However, recent surveys have indicated that only one-half of managers and employees rate HR's overall performance as good.[16] "Keeping the clients happy" has important political reverberations for the HRM department, as "clients" such as the CEO control the purse strings and have the authority to approve HR policies and programs.

## Advantages of Measuring Client Satisfaction

The advantages of measuring client satisfaction with the HR department include the following:[17]

- Measuring client satisfaction reminds the HR department that it is indeed a "service" that must deal with the expectations of its clients. The clients, in turn, use assessment criteria that are important to them, such as response time and helping them to meet their goals.
- Surveying clients about their unmet needs increases the credibility of the HR function.
- Initiating and managing change by surveying stakeholders before, during, and after a change program increase the possibility that the HR department will understand the clients' perceptions; identify resistance to change, and overcome such resistance; and prove that the change program meets its goals.

## Methods of Measuring Client Satisfaction

Information can be gathered from clients in several ways.

### Informal Feedback

**RPC** 14.4

Stakeholder perceptions can be obtained informally, as part of the feedback process, whenever the HR professional is undertaking an assignment or completing a routine task such as filling a position. People can simply be asked if they are satisfied with the service.

Chapter 14: Evaluation of HR Programs and Policies

Informal feedback is of limited use, however, for several reasons. Line managers may be reluctant to give honest feedback face to face; an individual HR officer may not be able to see patterns in the feedback as there is no method for measuring the frequency of problems; and HR professionals have little incentive to report negative feedback to superiors in the organizational hierarchy. For these reasons, a more systematic method must be developed to identify gaps in the performance of the HR department.

### Surveys

Surveys can be used to solicit feedback confidentially, anonymously, and from a larger number of stakeholders. One approach is to list the HR activities, such as selection, and ask specific questions about them, such as questions about satisfaction with the time it takes to fill a vacant position and the satisfaction with a new employee's performance. Some questions that might be included in such a survey are

- To what degree do you find the HR department cooperative?
- How would you rate the quality of service given?
- To what degree are HR employees available to deal with problems?
- Do you have confidence in HR advice?
- How would you rate the effectiveness of HR solutions?
- What is your opinion on processing time?
- To what extent does HR understand the needs of your department?
- Overall, how satisfied are you with the HR department?

Another survey, developed by Ulrich asks managers to rate the quality of the various roles that HR plays in strategy formulation.[18] HR Planning Notebook 14.2 contains a sample of the questions used in this survey.

Managers could be asked to list the chief strengths and principal weakness of the HR department. Line managers could be asked questions about what the HR department has been doing particularly well or particularly poorly, what it should not be doing, how it could contribute more effectively, and so on.[19]

---

## HR Planning Notebook 14.2

### HR Role Assessment Survey

The following is a sample of the type of survey clients can expect.

Please rate your satisfaction with the HR department on the following items* (1 = low; 5 = high):

HR helps the organization accomplish business goals.
HR participates in the process of defining business strategies.

HR makes sure that HR strategies are aligned with business strategies.
HR is effective because it can measure how it helps make strategy happen.
HR is a business partner.

*The selected items measure the strategic role of HR.

Source: D. Ulrich, *Human Resource Champions.* Boston: Harvard Business School Press, 1996, p. 49.

---

## Critical Incident Method

In the critical incident method, clients are asked to describe a situation in which the HR department provided assistance that was particularly useful, the consequences of this help, and why it was seen as helpful. Similarly, they are asked to describe a situation in which the assistance was not at all useful, and why. Clients' responses help the HR department identify issues and services that affect unit effectiveness.

## Problems with Measuring Client Satisfaction

Measuring client satisfaction is not without its weaknesses.

### High Expectations of Clients

The goal of surveying clients is to identify gaps between their expectations and their satisfaction. If the clients in one business unit have extremely high expectations, their dissatisfaction scores will also be high, even though the level of HR service is constant across units. The temptation on the part of the HR department might be to promise or commit to less with regard to programs so as to appear to have performed better.

### Conflicting Expectations

Another problem occurs when different stakeholders have competing or conflicting expectations. The employee group may desire extensive counselling (a nurturing role) from the HR department, while senior managers may be concerned about maximizing productivity per employee (an efficiency goal). One group will be dissatisfied because it is difficult for the HR department to be both nurturing and efficient.

### Professional Affiliations

Furthermore, gaps between expectations and performance may occur because HR professionals are more closely tied to the norms and values of their profession than to the norms of managers or line operators.[20] For example, line managers may value how fast a job is filled, while the HR professional may value the creation of a valid selection test. In other words, the HR professional may be trying to do what is right in the profession ("validate the selection test"), rather than what managers consider important ("just hire someone quickly").

Whatever the problems with the client satisfaction approach, the important message is that the viability of the HR function depends to a large extent on stakeholder perceptions of value and effectiveness. These must be measured and managed.

### Culture Management

**RPC 14.5**

Highly effective organizations seek to influence employee attitudes through the development of an appropriate culture that will support optimum performance. (Remember that culture can be defined as the set of important beliefs that members of a community share—"the way we do things around here.") Executives carefully monitor cultural programs (such as that of empowerment) through attitude surveys of employees. The results of these surveys can then be linked to the objective results of the department.

The assumption underlying the culture management model is that HR practices can have a positive influence on employee attitudes, which in turn influence employee performance.

**attitudes**

perceptions or opinions about organizational characteristics

**Attitudes**, in an organizational context, can be defined as perceptions or opinions about organizational characteristics. Some examples include the attitudes expressed in these statements: "I think that management expects too much for the resources it gives me," or "I feel that I can talk to management about any problems I am experiencing." The most frequently measured attitudes in the organization are job satisfaction and commitment. Surveys of satisfaction and commitment measure attitudes toward supervisors, colleagues, pay, promotions, and the work itself. The research supports the proposition that attitude affects behaviour. Highly committed employees will make personal sacrifices for the job, perform beyond normal expectations, work selflessly, endure difficult times, and will not leave the organization for personal gain.[21] A landmark study of 800 Sears stores demonstrated that for every 5% improvement in employee attitudes, customer satisfaction increased by 1.3% and corporate revenue rose by 0.5%.[22]

Organizations should pay attention to employee attitudes and should attempt to manage the culture to improve individual and organizational performance.

### Cost Control

Traditional organizations continue to see personnel as an expense. The labour component of the production process in service organizations, such as universities and government departments, is an organization's single largest expense. This cost represents up to 85% of the expenses in white-collar organizations. The cost of employees consists of pay and benefits, the cost of absenteeism, and the cost of turnover. HR practices can reduce labour costs by reducing the workforce while attempting to get the same volume of work done with fewer employees. One of the most frequently used ways to cut labour costs is to increase the use of technology. Technology to process benefits claims and pursue e-learning has replaced HR staff, resulting in cost savings of about 30%.[23] Firms are also outsourcing major activities in order to manage the costs of labour. However, there are detrimental effects of cutting costs in this way. Core talent may be lost and the capacity for innovation diminished.[24] See Chapter 13 for a more detailed discussion of outsourcing.

Often, companies try to reduce the headcount in the HR department, as part of a strategy to save costs. But the savings may be deceptive. For example, a financial services company cut its HR headcount by 30% (around 300 people). But then the line managers hired their own staff to handle the HR issues and the shadow organization of HR specialists now numbers 150.[25]

HR departments can reduce expenses associated with employees in at least two other ways. The first is to increase the efficiencies of those working (i.e., achieve the same results at lower costs or faster speeds), and the second is to reduce the costs associated with behaviours such as absences or accidents that are, to some extent, under the control of the employee.

## Increasing Efficiency

**Efficiency** is expressed in terms of the results achieved (outputs) in comparison to the resource inputs. Measures of efficiency include the following:

**efficiency**

results achieved compared to resource inputs

- time (e.g., average time to fill an opening, process a benefits claim);
- volume (e.g., the number of people interviewed to fill a job, the number of requests processed per employee); and
- cost (e.g., cost per training hour or per test).

HR managers should measure these resource inputs and then attempt to improve the measurements over time or across units. The use of benchmarks is critical in comparing one organization's efficiency ratios against the best in the field. Data revealing a cost per hire of $500 or turnover rates of 15% are meaningless without relevant comparison points. For example, a turnover rate of 15% among senior executives indicates a problem; a turnover rate of 15% in a fast-food restaurant is very low. HR Planning Notebooks 14.3 and 14.4 describe cost benefit and analysis.

The ratios generated must be interpreted and analyzed by comparisons made over time, across departments, and against the benchmarks of best practices. These benchmarks allow the HR manager to make the following kinds of statements: "The cost per hire is $500, which is $50 less than last year and $60 less than another company. That shows we are doing a better job than we did last year and than other HR departments."

## HR Planning Notebook 14.3

### Examples of Efficiency Measures

**Cost**

Ratio of compensation expense to total operating expense

Benefit cost per employee covered

Ratio of benefits expense to total operating expense

Processing costs per benefit claim

Administration costs per benefit claim

Cost per training day

Cost per trainee per program

**Volume**

Number of training days

Number of interviews per selection

Ratio of filled positions to authorized positions

Percentage of employees with formal performance evaluations

Percentage of designated employees

**Response Time**

Time between requisition and filling of position

Time to process benefits

Time from identifying a training need to program implementation

Time to respond to requests by category

### Measuring the Contribution of HRM Practices

A wholesale produce company hired, and then fired, seven ineffective sales representatives over a two-year period. The company calculated the costs of these actions.

**Costs**

| | |
|---|---|
| Training | $493,738 |
| Recruiting | $30,100 |
| Management time to train and terminate | $25,830 |
| Lower profits and higher waste due to poor performance | $1,612,000 |
| Total costs | $2,161,668 |

The HR department interviewed line managers to develop a profile of the ideal sales representative and identified 12 critical success factors. Then the company's HR department developed a solution involving three types of training:

- behaviour-based interview training for managers,
- a training program for newly hired sales representatives to accelerate performance readiness or weed out those who didn't meet the standards, and
- performance counselling training for managers so that they could learn to discuss performance problems and ensure that trainees accepted responsibility for their own learning and performance.

The cost to implement these three programs was $15,400 (development and attendance costs).

The savings that resulted from this solution were then calculated.

**Savings**

| | |
|---|---|
| Cost of the problem | $2,161,668 |
| Cost of the solution | − $15,400 |
| Total savings | $2,146,268 |

The cost–benefit ratio is as follows:

$$\$2,146,268 \div \$15,400 = 139:1$$

Source: Adapted from D.M. Burrows, "Increase HR's Contributions to Profits," *HR Magazine*, September 1996, pp. 103–110. Reprinted with the permission of *HR Magazine*, published by the Society for Human Resource Management (www.shrm.org), Alexandra, VA.

These efficiency measures must be managed with effectiveness in mind. Conceptually, it is possible to reduce training costs to zero, but the performance of employees would suffer in the long run. Therefore, most companies add a qualifier to the ratio when judging efficiency. For example, lowering the cost per trainee would be acceptable only if job performance remained the same or improved.

## Cost of Employee Behaviour

The costs of absenteeism, turnover, and occupational injuries and illnesses can all be measured, benchmarked, and managed. Any introductory textbook in HRM will describe how to measure these factors and will provide prescriptions for reducing the costs related to them. To control the expenses associated with employees, organizations should carefully track and compare the rates of absenteeism, turnover, and occupational injuries and illnesses. Here are some figures to think about: the number of short-term absences has doubled from 2% of payroll in 1997 to 4.2% in 2000, with a direct cost of $3,440 per employee.[26] The costs of turnover, which include termination, replacement, loss of revenue when the position is vacant, and the learning time for new employees to become productive, are estimated at between six and 18 months

### The Costs of Smoking

Decades of research have established that smoking is addictive, and that it is a health hazard. The costs to society of smoking include those associated with health care and income loss. The costs to organizations include those associated with absenteeism, medical care, morbidity and premature mortality, insurance, property damage and depreciation, maintenance, and passive smoking effects. It is estimated that about 35 minutes a day are lost to smoking, resulting in 18.2 lost days per year per employee. Smokers are absent three more days per year than nonsmokers. Furthermore, each smoker increases by about one-fifth the expenses incurred by nonsmokers (through involuntary smoke inhalation). The price tag is Cdn$4,113 for each employee who smokes: $2,140 in lost productivity and $1,973 in excess medical expenses. However, it may be illegal to prohibit smoking on company property. In a case involving Cominco Ltd. and the United Steelworkers of America, Locals 9705 and 480, the arbitrator ruled nicotine addiction is a disability similar to alcoholism or drug addiction and that Cominco's policy of no smoking on company property discriminates against heavily addicted smokers. Under section 13(1)(b) of British Columbia's Human Rights Code, discrimination in employment on the basis of physical or mental disability is prohibited. However, in a recent case (2001) the court found that smoking and addiction to cigarettes is not a disability.

Sources: Adapted from W.F. Cascio, *Costing Human Resources: The Financial Impact of Behaviour in Organizations*, 3rd ed., Kent Series in Human Resource Management. Boston: PWS Kent, 1991; T. Humber, 2005, "Snuffing out Smoking" *Canadian HR Reporter*, April 11, 19.

of the employee's annual compensation. At Taco Bell, the stores with the lowest turnover yielded double the sales and 55% higher profits than stores with the highest turnover rates.[27] HR Planning Today 14.2 provides an example of how a smoking cessation program for employees can result in cost savings.

In keeping with the trend to view employees as investments, and not just as expenses, the next section examines how organizations measure the return on this investment.

## Contribution

Unless HR can demonstrate its impact on the bottom line, it will continue to be seen as "overhead," as a department that grabs resources while contributing nothing. Many executives feel that it is time for the HR department to identify and evaluate its contribution, as other departments are expected to do.

 14.6

The thesis underlying the contribution model is that HRM practices shape the behaviour of employees within an organization, and thus help the organization achieve its goals. In other words, the effective management of people makes a difference to how well an organization functions. Research has shown that HR practices can affect organizational performance in measurable ways. Studies have established that sophisticated and integrated HRM practices have a positive effect on employee performance: they increase knowledge, skills, and abilities; improve motivation; reduce shirking; and increase retention of competent employees. These best practices have a direct and economically significant effect on a firm's financial performance.

# How HR Contributes to Organizational Performance

Empirical studies have established some important findings:

- Organizations that used employee involvement practices (information sharing, rewards, skills training, etc.) reported a 66% higher return on sales, a 20% higher return on assets and investments, and a 13% higher return on equity.[28]
- Specific HR practices have been found to positively and significantly affect the financial performance of a company, as high as a 30% increase in shareholder value.[29] For example, flexible work arrangements are associated with a 3.5% gain in market value, while 360° feedback systems negatively affect market value by 5%.[30]
- Fifteen percent of a firm's relative profit can be attributed to HR strategy.[31]
- HR systems can affect a firm's market valued by $15,000 to $45,000 per employee.[32]
- HR can affect the probability of survival of a new venture by as much as 22%.[33]
- HR can improve the knowledge, skills, and abilities of a firm's current and potential employees, increase their motivation, reduce shirking, and enhance retention of quality employees while encouraging nonperformers to leave the firm.[34]
- An increase in sophisticated HR practices of one standard deviation raises sales per employee by an average of US$27,000 for one year, increases profits by US$3,814 per employee, and decreases turnover by 7%.[35] The advantages to employees of these high-performance firms may be higher wages and benefits and greater job security.
- Managing people by using high-performance management systems can result in gains of 40% or more, in most of the studies reviewed.[36]
- Investments in HRM do pay off: proactive firms that plan for future labour needs and make investments in recruitment and selection for the job at the outset are rewarded with higher labour productivity. Firms that systematically develop their employees receive a productivity payoff.[37]

The majority of published studies find an association between HR practices and firm performance.[38] HR matters. The basic causal model shows that HR practices impact collective commitment, operational performance, expenses, and profts.[39] We will look now at two ways of measuring contribution: financial measures and measures of managerial perceptions of effectiveness.

## Financial Measures

### Survival

Private or for-profit organizations can measure a dramatic indicator of success: survival. This can be considered a zero-sum index. If the company survives—that is, does not go bankrupt or cease business—the organization is a success. Survival is the first measure of effectiveness, and the contributions of HRM practices should be judged against this life-or-death index. When researchers tracked the survival rates over five years of new organizations listed on the stock exchange, they found that HR practices were associated with this ultimate measure of a firm's performance.[40] This crude measure is not satisfying for most businesspeople, however, because it doesn't give relative measures of success. (Teachers who give a pass or fail, rather than an A, B, C, D, or F grade, leave the same sense of dissatisfaction among students.) Most employees desire a relative measure and will even ask, "How am I doing compared to the others?" at performance evaluation interviews. The most common measures of business success provide these points of comparison, which allow judgments to be made across divisions, companies, and even sectors. They are the bottom-line measures such as profits.

### Profits or Return on Investments

All companies track sales, or revenues, return on investments **(ROI)**, return on equity **(ROE)**, expenses relative to sales, and other financial ratios. These indices measure the relative success of an organization in meeting its goals. Any HRM practice that contributes to these measurements likely would be endorsed by senior management. Measuring the impact of HRM investments in training or performance appraisal allows HR professionals to use the same language (e.g., basic costs, ROI) as other corporate units and provides a rational way of making decisions. HR Planning Today 14.3 illustrates how this might work.

There are some limitations to financial analyses, however; they capture certain immediate aspects of performance, but they do not capture managerial perceptions of effectiveness.

**RPC** 14.9

**ROI**
return on investments

**ROE**
return on equity

## Measures of Managerial Perceptions of Effectiveness

Sometimes financial measures are not available to researchers who are studying privately owned organizations, and sometimes financial measures are not appropriate for public-sector organizations. It is meaningless to talk about government departments in relation to profits, for example. Therefore, other measures have been sought. One method is to ask managers to assess their organization's performance relative to the performance of sector competitors.[41] Despite the biases that could be introduced into such a measure, these perceptions have been found to correlate positively with objective measures of a firm's performance.[42] The principal advantage of using a perceptual measure such as this one is the ability to compare profit-seeking firms with public organizations.

Templer and Cattaneo argue that organizational effectiveness is not easily defined.[43] Measures beyond survival and those discussed above may include the following: the achievement of one group's political objectives at the expense of a competing interest group, and the adaptation of an organization to its environment (which obviously contains an element of the survival measure).

The measure that supersedes all of these may be one of goal optimization. Templer and Cattaneo combined these various perspectives to conclude that "an effective organization is one in which the behaviour of employees

## Return on Investment Example

### Safety Incentive Program: National Steel

National Steel was concerned about its safety record and was experiencing unacceptable accident frequency rates, accident severity rates, and total accident costs. A performance analysis indicated that the employees knew and understood safety guidelines and practices, so training was not the issue. The central safety committee felt that incentives were needed to motivate safe behaviour. The incentive plan was to offer each employee $75 cash (after taxes) for every six months without a medical treatment case. The committee established goals of reducing accident frequency from 60 to 20, and the disabling frequency rate from 18 to 0. The committee tracked the number of medical treatment cases, lost-time accidents, lost-time days, accident costs, hours worked, and incentive costs.

The costs over four years were as follows:

### ROI Calculation

The cost of the annual incentive payout (two-year average) plus annual administrative plan cost was $72,172. The benefits were calculated as an annual improvement of **$431,372** (accident costs for year 1 and 2 totalled $1,046,488 for an average of $523,244 annually; accident costs for years 3 and 4 averaged $90,872, for an annual improvement of $432,372).

An interesting twist in this case is that managers were asked what contributed to these improvements, and they estimated that 80% was due to the incentive program and 20% to their renewed managerial attention. So the calculations of benefits were revised to indicate that 80% of the annual improvement ($345,898) was due to the incentive program.

ROI of the safety incentive program

= Net benefits ÷ Costs

= $345,898 − $72,172/$72,172

= 3.79 × 100 = 379%

| | Year 1 Before plan | Year 2 Before plan | Year 3 After plan | Year 4 After plan |
|---|---|---|---|---|
| Needs assessment costs | $1,200 | $1,200 | n/a | n/a |
| Plan administration/evaluation | $1,600 | $1,600 | n/a | n/a |
| Safety incentive pay-outs | $58,013 | $80,730 | n/a | n/a |
| Cost of accidents | $468,360 | $578,128 | $18,058 | $19,343 |
| Total costs accidents + prevention | $468,360 | $578,128 | $78,871 | $102,873 |

Source: Adapted from *Human Resources Scorecard* by Phillips J., S. Stone, and P.P. Phillips, pp. 439–448, copyright © 2001, with permission of Elsevier Science.

contributes towards the attainment of organizational goals and enables the long-term adaptation of the organization to its environment"—that is, survival and effectiveness.[44]

Which is the best measure of HRM performance? Managers will choose whichever of the 5C measures meets their needs for information. Some will require measurement of all the five Cs; others will focus on one important indicator, such as cost control. Some companies are moving toward a balanced approach.

We have examined five areas in which HR practices and policies should be tracked. However, there is an emerging area for which the organization seems to hold the HR function responsible: the ethical behaviour

**RPC** 14.10

of employees. See HR Planning Today 3.2, Five Mega Trends (pp. 68–70), which describes the role of HR in facilitating ethical behaviour in organizations.

Now we turn to an examination of the various approaches to measuring the effectiveness of HR policies, practices, and programs.

# Approaches to Measuring HRM Practices

This section outlines a number of quantitative and qualitative approaches to measuring the impact of HRM policies and practices. Typical ways of measuring HR activities include the following:

- activity-based measures—the number of employees completing training; the number of employees hired;
- costing measures—the cost of the training program, the cost per hire; and
- client satisfaction—the manager has a problem solved; the HR department changed an employee's benefits information quickly

Most of these methods use numbers, which can measure the impact of HRM in the language of business: costs, days lost, complaints, and so on. But the question has to be asked: Where is the added value? What do we mean by added value? The following examples help explain this concept:

- An *activity* measure for an HR professional would be the number of people trained.
- A *performance* measure for an HR professional would be the number of trainees who passed the training test or rated the training courses as above average.
- An *added-value* measure for an HR professional would be the increase in profits, sales, customer satisfaction, or decrease in complaints, errors, defects, as a result of the skills learned in the training course.

The next three approaches—cost–benefit analysis, utility analysis, and benchmarking—attempt to prove value.

## Cost–Benefit Analysis

HRM activities, such as the process of selecting employees, cost money. Most organizations absorb the costs of these activities without conducting analyses to determine benefits. **Cost–benefit** analysis examines the relationship between the costs of a program and its benefits.

Costs included in these calculations are classified in several ways. **Direct costs** are those that are used to implement the program, such as the cost of selection tests or training materials. **Indirect costs** are those that an organization absorbs, such as the trainee's time away from work. Indirect costs are often unrecognized, and sometimes are not included in cost–benefit analyses. HR Planning Notebook 14.4 (on p. 380) contains an example of a cost–benefit analysis.

**14.11**

W W W

---

**14.12**

**cost–benefit analysis**

the relationship between the costs of a program and its benefits

**direct costs**

the hard costs that can be measured by expenditures

**indirect costs**

the soft costs whose value can be estimated but not measured easily by financial expenditures

Most programs can be subjected to a cost–benefit analysis if hard data are available, or the value of a program can be estimated from soft measures such as supervisors' estimates of productivity.

## Utility Analysis

Senior managers are often faced with decisions about the most effective programs. For example, to motivate employees, should HR managers implement a leadership training program or a pay-for-performance program for new supervisors? To hire the best candidate, should HR managers use peer interviews or the new selection test? HR managers would have much to gain if they were able to estimate if program A provided a greater return than program B. The training director, for example, could argue that grouping 100 managers in a classroom for training is more expensive and less effective than e-learning.

A tool that calculates, in dollar terms, the costs and probable outcomes of decisions would assist HR managers in making choices between programs. **Utility analysis** is such a tool. It is a method of determining the gain or loss to the organization that results from different courses of action. Faced with a decision, managers use utility analysis to help them choose the strategy that produces the outcomes the organization is seeking.[45] This method measures the utilities (gains and losses) by using human resource accounting. Human resource accounting uses standard accounting practices to calculate and report an organization's human assets (or employees) in economic turns. The costs of recruiting, selecting, training, and retaining employers is calculated and then these costs are amortized over the employee's working lives. Human resource (or asset accounting) is described in the Appendix to this chapter. It seeks to quantify, in dollars, the value of improvements in HR activities, particularly selection. In utility analysis, which is an extension of cost–benefit analysis, the costs and benefits of alternative solutions to a problem are calculated and compared. The decision maker then can use the quantitative data that result from utility analysis to choose the alternative with the highest net value. HR Planning Notebook 14.5 provides an example of how utility analysis can be used to reach a decision.

Utility analyses have been used in various studies. Selection using assessment centres within the company instead of first-level management assessment was found to have a utility, over four years, of about US$12,000 in improved job performance per manager.[46] However, the computations involved are beyond the competencies of most managers. See Alan Saks, 2000, *Research, Measurement and Evaluation of Human Resources*, Toronto: Thomson Nelson, for a detailed treatment of decision making using utility analysis.

## Auditing and Benchmarking

A plan needs an audit. An **audit** measures progress against goals. If the goal of the HR function is to train 100 managers, at some point data need to be gathered to determine if that goal was achieved. Audits keep the HR department on track and are the primary tool to assess current performance to develop action plans and future goals.[47] Audits can be done annually or

**ⓡⓟⓒ 14.13**

**utility analysis**
a method of determining the gain or loss that results from different approaches

**ⓡⓟⓒ 14.14**

**audit**
a measurement method that assesses progress against plan

### An Example of Utility Analysis

Utility analysis is statistically complex but can be illustrated by the following simple example.

An organization has a choice between two types of selection procedures (or can use neither). The utility of a selection procedure is the degree to which it results in a better quality of candidate than would have been selected if the selection procedure had not been implemented. Quality can be measured by tenure (Did the employee selected using the selection procedure remain with the organization at least one year?) or performance (Did the new employee rate above average in performance after one year?) or other objective outcomes (Did the employee sell more accounts or process more files?). The costs of using procedure one (an ability test), procedure two (peer interviews), or the usual selection method (or base rate) of managerial interviews are calculated. Then the benefits of the candidates chosen under each of the three methods are determined. If tests resulted in higher-performing candidates but cost more than the performance increase is worth, the tests have little utility. If peer reviews result in greater performance at no greater cost, peer reviews have great utility.

Source: M. L. Blum and J.C. Naylor, *Industrial Psychology: Its Theoretical and Social Foundations*, rev. ed. New York: Harper-Row, 1968.

quarterly, but a consistent checking against the plan ensures no year-end surprises and allows managers to take corrective action. For example, if the goal is to achieve four out of five on an employee satisfaction scale, and an audit shows pockets of low satisfaction, the HR department can target those areas for remedial action before year-end. Nevertheless, the audit is not the last step in the cycle of plan, execute, and measure. The numbers used in auditing (number of dollars invested in training per employee) make sense only when compared to sector norms.

**Benchmarking** is concerned with enhancing organizational performance by establishing standards against which processes, products, and performance can be compared and subsequently improved.[48] It is a tool that can be used to accomplish the following:

- Stimulate an objective review of processes, practices, and systems.
- Motivate employees to perform to a higher standard, by providing a common target for improvement.
- Provide objective comparative data with best-in-class organizations.
- Raise questions and stimulate discussions about better ways of operating.[49]

The process starts by targeting an area for improvement, such as university recruitment in the staffing function. Key measures are identified for comparison. In recruitment these might be cost per hire, quality of hire, processing times, and number of acceptances or rejections. The next step is to identify the best-practice organizations through publications, associations, experts, and awards ceremonies. There are four sources of benchmarking partners:

- Internal (e.g., compare university recruitment with high-tech recruitment),
- Competitive (compare exact functions),

**benchmarking**

a tool that can enhance organizational performance by establishing standards against which processes, products, and performance can be compared and improved

**RPC** 14.15

- Sector (some conditions may differ for your organization), and
- Best-in-breed organizations (whose products, culture, etc. may not be comparable). Except for competitors, many organizations are willing to share this information if there is an incentive for them, such as a copy of the report, access to your metrics, etc.

Benchmarking can be done by internal personnel or external consultants. Internal consultants have the advantage of knowing more about the organization and being trusted by the staff supplying the information. However, external auditors may be more objective, have greater numbers of outside references or benchmarks, and are more likely to convey bad news to management. Sometimes an independent body, such as the Conference Board of Canada, will act as the project manager for the benchmarking study so that confidentiality is not an issue in data collection. This third-party intervention helps with the obvious question: Why would competitors want to reveal best practices: And if they do so, is it because they have developed even more powerful processes that they do not share?[50] Obviously, the results obtained from audits can be compared with benchmarks obtained from previous years, with other organizational units, or with other companies.

**RPC 14.16**

After the data have been collected and compared, the differences will be obvious. The best organization might have metrics such as a six-week processing time, while your organization processes in 12 weeks. Interviews during or after the data collection might reveal the reasons for the speed—perhaps the entire processing is done on the Internet. The goal then becomes to match the best target for each of the indices.

For instance, the training function can be examined as a percentage of payroll spent on training, training dollars spent per employee, profits per employee, training costs per hour, and so on. The results of these examinations can be compared to comparable figures for other organizations. As an example, in Canada, organizations spend about $800 per employee on training, and each employee receives about seven hours of training a year.[51] These benchmark statistics can be used as guidelines. If statistics are available on the best-performing companies, organizations can attempt to match those figures. Read about how benchmarking helped the Bank of Montreal achieve its diversity objectives in HR Planning Today 14.4.

Benchmarking is popular because the measures are easy to collect and the numbers have a superficial credibility, but there is no published research that supports a relationship between HR benchmarks and ultimate firm performance.[52] We all like to know benchmarks such as there is on average one HR person for every 100 employees, or that the profit per employee is about US$24,000.[53] But these numbers are relatively meaningless. For example, an organization can have one HR professional per 1000 employees because it has outsourced most of the HR work. Knowing that your organization's cost per employee is higher than the sector benchmark does not provide you with anything of value, anything that would lead you to a cause and a solution. Finally, you cannot build competitive advantage by copying it, because the best capabilities (like the culture at Southwestern Airlines) are complex and difficult to imitate. An organization must create its own capabilities.[54]

## HR Planning Today 14.4

### Metrics Drive Diversity

BMO Financial Group, which has 34 000 employees, included in its 1990 corporate strategic plan the goal of creating an equitable workforce. At that time, only 9% of female employees were executives, and 13% were in senior management, from a workforce that was 75% female. BMO has achieved remarkable success through the formation of its National Advisory Council on the Equitable Workplace, chaired by the CEO of BMO, and through other measures such as employee assistance programs, a comprehensive diversity index in the annual employee survey, goal setting, and monitoring. Here are the comparison rates of the percentages of women at senior levels:

PricewaterhouseCoopers also uses metrics to measure the accomplishment of diversity goals. Three categories of metrics (communication, recruitment, and retention) assess progress toward goals. Within each category are subcategories such as "conversion of interns into hires" and "percentage increase of women partners." Meeting diversity targets is a component of executive bonuses.

| Category | 1990 | 2002 |
|----------|------|------|
| Vice-presidents | 0% | 30.8% |
| Executives | 9 | 35 |
| Senior management | 13 | 42 |

Sources: Adapted from S. Black, "What Gets Measured Gets Done: Using Metrics to Support Diversity"; and S. Patten, "In 12 Years, BMO Women Execs Rise from 9 to 35%." Both in *Canadian HR Reporter*, December 16, 2002, pp. 13 and 17.

**RPC** 14.17

## The HR Scorecard

Although the most popular way of measuring HR is benchmarking, the HR balanced scorecard is gaining momentum, with about one-third of companies using this method.[55] The **balanced scorecard** rests on the assumption that any successful business satisfies the requirements of investors (financial performance measures), customers (market share, customer commitment, and retention), and employees (employee satisfaction and organization commitment).[56] The original idea of a balanced scorecard arose from the idea that financial measures alone do not capture the true performance of an organization, and that these measures tend to reflect past performance and are not necessarily predictive. Other measures deemed of value to the analysis of a company included not only financial performance, but also customer satisfaction and employee engagement. The balanced scorecard provides answers to these four basic questions:

**balanced scorecard**
a balanced set of measures to show contribution to organizational performance

1. How do customers see us? (the customer perspective)
2. What must we excel at? (the internal business perspective)
3. Can we continue to improve and create value? (innovation and learning perspective)
4. How do we look to shareholders? (the financial perspective)[57]

The opening vignette with Enbridge Gas describes these relationships and the impact on HR practices.

The process starts with the organizations' strategy and then HR looks for ways that the HR processes and practices can support that strategy. What can HR do to support the organization's goals, and how can this be measured? For example, the goal at a pipeline company was to increase revenues; one way to accomplish this was to reduce downtime for repairs. The HR goal in this case was to increase the amount of time devoted to preventive maintenance, by increasing employee skills sets in repairs, and to change the compensation system to include incentives to perform preventative maintenance.[58] This set of linkages is more fully described in Figure 14.1.

## Measuring the Worth of Employees

Many company presidents say, "Employees are our greatest assets," or, as the president of Dofasco said, "Our product is steel; our strength is people." What do they mean? Human capital can refer to factors such as the employees' knowledge, skills, capability, and attitudes that impact performance.[59] Remember that it is not just the sum total of employee competencies, but the application of these competences in a way that has value to the organization which provides the true measure of human capital.[60] There have been attempts to measure the worth of employees by counting them and then attempting to put a number value on their knowledge. Trying to assess the worth of intellectual capital or human capital in an organization is incredibly

FIGURE 14.1

### HR Deliverables Linked to Strategy

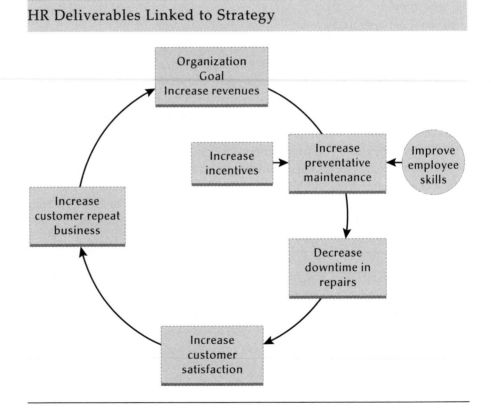

complex; however, some methods are discussed in the Appendix to this chapter. Our focus here is not on measuring the worth of employees but on measuring the effect of organizational practices and policies.

Readers interested in a fuller description of measuring HR effectiveness should consult *Research, Measurement and Evaluation of Human Resources*.[61]The choice of measurement tool depends to a large extent on the organization's strategy and the stage of sophistication of its HR department. For example, an HR department that continues to focus on administration in a support role to employees and managers will measure efficiencies. Reports from HR will include statements such as "Processed 1250 benefits questions; trained 10% more employees than last year." An HR department that is a business partner with line management will measure culture and employee productivity, and will establish direct links with organizational performance.

The measurement options available to HR professionals are summarized in Table 14.1. The first approach examines the efficiency of the HR operations. The second is an effectiveness measure, looking at the link between individual HR practices and a specific financial outcome. The third approach is the HR scorecard approach tying HR activities to business activities. The last approach is the cause–and–effect analysis, which focuses on measuring the links between HR programs, the links to employee links, and business outcomes. The final two columns in the table list the advantages of each approach, and then expose the limitations by asking tough questions.

The measurement of HR effectiveness is not easy. The next section outlines some of the difficulties faced by those attempting to track HR effectiveness.

# Challenges in Measuring the Impact of HRM

Measuring the effectiveness of HRM practices has been widely viewed as a progressive step in the development of HRM as a profession and the positioning of HR as a strategic partner at the boardroom table. But, in fact, most organizations do not undertake this evaluation because the measurement of HRM activities is not easy (i.e., advanced skills are required) and the problems in measurement are difficult to resolve. Let us look at some of the problems that arise when we attempt to measure the impact of HRM practices.

## Universality of Best Practices

No single best practice works in every situation. Some companies, such as banks, consist of many different companies, all with unique characteristics; in the case of banks these companies include insurance companies, discount brokerages, and venture capital firms. The HRM policies and practices that benefit performance in the bank may hinder performance in the venture capital arm. The environment and culture of the parts of the larger company are very different. For example, the routine transaction work of the bank lends itself to compensation systems based largely on base salaries, while the entrepreneurial, risk-taking nature of the venture capital firm cries out for incentive-based pay.

TABLE 14.1

## Summary of HR Measurement Alternatives

| MEASUREMENT APPROACH | EXAMPLES MEASURES | PRIMARY APPEAL | TOUGH QUESTIONS |
| --- | --- | --- | --- |
| Efficiency of HRM operations. | Cost-per-hire, time-to-fill, training costs, ratio of HR staff to total employees. | Explicit currency-value calculations.<br><br>Logic of cost savings is easy to relate to accounting.<br><br>Standardization makes benchmarking comparisons easier. | "Wouldn't outsourcing cut costs even more?"<br><br>"Do these cost savings come at the price of workforce value?"<br><br>"Why should our costs be the same as the industry" |
| HR activity, "best practice" indexes. | Human capital benchmarks, human capital index. | HR practices are associated with familiar financial outcomes.<br><br>Data from many organizations lends credibility.<br><br>Suggests there may be practices or combinations that generally raise profits or sales, and so on. | "What is the logic connecting these activities with such huge financial effects?"<br><br>"Will the practices that worked in other organizations necessarily work in ours?"<br><br>"Does having these practices mean they are implemented well?" |
| HR dashboard or HR scorecard. | How the organization or HR function meets goals of "customers, financial markets, operational excellence, and learning." | Vast array of HR measures can be categorized.<br><br>"Balanced Scorecard" concept is known to business leaders.<br><br>Software allows users to customize analysis. | "Can this scorecard prove a connection between people and strategic outcomes?"<br><br>"Which numbers and drill-downs are most critical to our success?" |
| Causal chain. | Models link employee attitudes to service behaviour to customer responses to profit. | Useful logic linking employee variables to financial outcomes.<br><br>Valuable for organizing and analyzing diverse data elements. | "Is this the best path from talent to profits?"<br><br>"How do our HR practices work together?"<br><br>"What logic can we use to find more connections like this?" |

Source: From M. Effron, R. Gandossy, M. Goldsmith, *HR Measurement Alternatives*, p. 85, (John Wiley, 2003). Reprinted with permission.

Furthermore, organizations and businesses may have different strategic goals. The goal of the financial sector is to maximize ROE, while the goal of the Department of Immigration may be to implement the government's immigration policy, which could include increasing the number of immigrants with certain skills. Within a single organization, the goals of one business unit may be to maximize market share (at the expense of profit), while another unit is attempting to maximize profit. These differences lead to the conclusion that the impact of HRM must be measured against unit goals, not against some generality such as growth or profits.

## Separation of Cause and Effect

The perennial problem in measuring the impact of HRM practices is separating cause and effect. For example, if a profitable company shares its profits with employees through bonuses, does the possibility of earning such a bonus make employees more productive and their companies more profitable? Research suggests that businesses that do well invest in HR practices and that this investment pays off in improved financial performance.[62]

Associated with the lack of confidence in the explanation of causal links between specific HRM practices and organizational performance is the observation that the culture of an organization may explain more than a specific HRM practice. The day-to-day norms of an organization may influence employee behaviour more than any specific practice. For example, if an organization is deeply committed to valuing employees, the day-to-day actions of all managers have more powerful effects than a stand-alone program such as 360° feedback.

## Successful Measurement

As you have just read, there are many ways to measure the contributions of the HR function. Organizations seem to focus on background, functional, and efficiency measure. According to a study of Canadian leaders, the most frequent measures are headcount and hires and terminations.[63] Other popular operational measures can be found in HR Planning Today 14.5. According to one study, HR professionals preferred to report, in descending order, on performance against HR strategy objectives, training and development return, HR function effectiveness, leadership team capability, employee competency and motivation, and effectiveness of change programs.[64] Whatever measure you decide to use should have the following characteristics:

- *Alignment:* The measure and the potential results must offer some value to the strategy or goals of the organization. Measuring the ratio of HR professionals to the number of employees does not. Measuring the impact of the performance management system on customer satisfaction does. If your organization does not have clear goals, then choose metrics that are meaningful. Why measure cost per hire if you don't know if this number should be increased or decreased? Decreasing it might result in less qualified candidates who are easier to find, but ultimately result in poor quality work or increased

## Popular HR Measures

According to a Canadian survey, the most frequently reported measures are

| | |
|---|---|
| Headcount change | 80% |
| Hires and terminations | 80% |
| Total compensation | 66% |
| Performance against HR strategy and objectives | 59% |
| Training and development return | 52% |
| HR function effectiveness | 48% |

| | |
|---|---|
| Leadership team capability | 45% |
| Frequency of performance reviews | 41% |
| Customer feedback | 34% |
| Corporate social responsibility activities | 34% |
| Discipline and grievance cases | 32% |
| Agency/Consultancy costs | 31% |

Source: D.S. Weiss and R. Finn, 2005, "HR Metrics that Count: Aligning Human Capital Management to Business," *Human Resource Planning*, 28, 1, 33–39.

turnover, thus increasing costs. In other words, the full cost of reducing or increasing these measures must be calculated.

- *Actionable:* As Albert Einstein said, "Not everything that can be counted counts, and not everything that counts can be counted." Choose only those measures that you can control. Why choose to measure work–life balance issues if your organization is not prepared to make substantial investments in changing working hours or options? Obtain metrics on things like employee commitment or turnover, items for which you can develop action plans.
- *Trackability:* A good metric must be trackable over time so that improvements, as a result of the introduction of solutions, can be assessed. Some measures, such as time to hire, should be tracked weekly for all positions; others like employee engagement may be tracked semiannually with a stratified sample.[65]
- *Comparability:* Try to choose measures that can be compared across units and even with best-in-world organizations. To obtain an employee engagement number of 4.5 is not helpful, unless you know that this is lower than in other departments, and much lower than, for example, the best employers.
- *Report and communicate a limited number of measures:* The availability of databases allows us to accumulate mountains of data, but very little meaningful information. Information overload is a more serious problem than not measuring at all. Decide on five to ten key measures, and report on these in the same way over time. This should be both historical (lag) and predictive (lead) measures. These key metrics almost always included indices of employee engagement, retention rates by occupational group and unit, absenteeism by occupational group and unit, productivity measures, and cost-benefit analyses for the introduction of any new program.

The HR department can increase its credibility and power to help managers, and change the perception of the function from a cost centre to one that contributes to profits. HR professionals should continually identify instances of contribution such as "That executive search would have cost the organization $50,000, and we did it for $10,000"; "we have worked with the union and reduced grievances by 20%, saving 1500 hours of managerial time," and "We changed our benefits provider and saved the company 10%."[66]

At this time, metrics seem to inform, rather than drive strategy. Measurement is the key to the management of human capital, and the art of managing people is turning into the science of HRM. This trend will continue as more HR practitioners will be well educated in their discipline, certified and regulated, and adept at validating their profession through the measurement of its activities.

## Summary

This chapter attempts to close the loop in the strategic HR planning process by examining evaluation; when managers implement a plan, they need to know if the plan was successful. In addition, it is important to measure the impact of HRM so as to prove the value of HR and to improve its performance. The 5C model for measuring HR effectiveness has five areas: compliance with laws and regulations, client satisfaction, culture management, cost control, and contribution. Methods to measure the impact of HRM include cost–benefit analysis, utility analysis, and audits. Benchmarking is a valuable tool that provides comparative data on key ideas and stimulates discussion about better ways to operate. There are challenges in measuring HR effectiveness, however; overall organization goals may not be applicable to all branches or subsidiary companies; it is difficult to relate cause and effect; and some HR professionals do not see the benefit in such measuring.

## Key Terms

attitudes, 378
audit, 386
balanced scorecard, 389
benchmarking, 387
cost–benefit analysis, 385
direct costs, 385

efficiency, 379
indirect costs, 385
ROE, 383
ROI, 383
utility analysis, 386

## Web Links

The International Alliance for Human Resources Research posts articles on HR effectiveness, based on studies by Canadian university professors:

**www.atkinson.yorku.ca/~hrresall** (p. 371)

Templates of different types of surveys available for review. Numerous HR surveys include employee evaluation, job satisfaction, and training evaluation:

**www.surveyconsole.com/console/showLibrary.do** (p. 376)

Tools to measure and improve the value of human resources. Information on using metrics and performance measures to assess the effectiveness of government HR activities:

**www.spb.ca.gov/METRD/metricsconference.htm** (p. 385)

# RPC Icons

**RPC 14.1** Provides input into the development of employee feedback systems that support the organizational directions and culture

**RPC 14.2** Applies measurement, evaluation, and assessment processes to business situations

**RPC 14.3** Encourages interaction between the organization and external stakeholders (e.g., public, government, educational institutions, community groups), which supports the development and implementation of the HR plan

**RPC 14.4** Gathers and analyzes employee feedback to assist decision making

**RPC 14.5** Guides and facilitates change in organizational culture and/or values consistent with business strategies

**RPC 14.6** Provides performance feedback, coaching, and career development to teams and individuals to maximize their probability of success

**RPC 14.7** Contributes to improvements in the organization's structures and work processes

**RPC 14.8** Monitors and reports on the results of HR development activities in terms of their effect on organizational performance

**RPC 14.9** Develops business cases for HR activities, e.g., return on investment (ROI) evaluations, data collection, and assessment.

**RPC 14.10** Evaluates the effectiveness of HR strategies using various measurement, assessment, and accountability approaches

**RPC 14.11** Assesses the contribution of organizational development to the performance of the unit or organization

**RPC 14.12** Performs a cost–benefit analysis of developing existing staff versus acquiring new staff, or outsourcing

**RPC 14.13** Collects data, analyzes, and reviews the organization's existing HR programs to ensure they are consistent with business activities

**RPC 14.14** Monitors HR activities of the organization; identifies problem areas, initiates responses, and resolves issues that stand in the way of business success

**RPC 14.15** Evaluates progress on deliverables

**RPC 14.16** Monitors and evaluates HR effectiveness as it relates to business success and identifies areas that need improvement and development

**RPC 14.17** Develops and delivers learning strategies to close the gap between current human capital capabilities and the future needs of the organization

# Discussion Questions

1. Refer back to the information in HR Planning Today 14.1. Why did Deutsche Bank choose these performance indicators?
2. The president of your company has said, "I see no value in having an HR department. Let's get rid of it. We can outsource payroll and benefits. Anything else, like training, can be arranged by each manager." You, as the vice-president of HR, want to save the department (and your job!). Prepare a report, describing areas in which the HR department does (or can) make a difference to the company.
3. We all know that being able to prove that a program is effective is a good way to ensure continued funding. List the ways you might prove that a training program for supervisors is good for the organization. List some reasons HR managers would not want to measure the effectiveness of a training program.
4. A company wishes to increase the sales performance of its staff. It has been determined that for each $15 product sold, the company makes $5 in profit. Currently, employees, who are paid $20 an hour, sell an average of four products an hour. A consultant is persuading the company to purchase a four-hour training course. The consultant guarantees that sales capacity will increase by 25% and that the effect will last one year (50 weeks of selling time, assuming an eight-hour day). The cost of the course is $400 per employee. Should the company buy the training course for its ten sales representatives? Conduct a cost–benefit analysis to determine the answer.

# Using the Internet

1. One of the 5Cs of evaluating HRM is client satisfaction. It is important to measure internal and external client satisfaction to gain feedback and track client perceptions. Conducting surveys is one of the more popular methods of measuring client satisfaction.

a. Log on to **www.surveyconsole.com/console/showLibrary. do?mode=1&categoryID52** and browse through the different employee satisfaction and evaluation survey templates.

b. After exploring the content and layout of different survey templates, choose one that would work for your organization. Why did you choose this one? Discuss the characteristics of an effective employee survey.

# Exercises

1. The Workforce Optimas Award for Vision is given to an HR department that has proactively dealt with an issue. GTE was the winner of this prestigious award in 2000 because it found a credible way to measure HR's contribution to the business. HR strategy at GTE had five targets to measure: managing talent, developing world-class leadership, customer service, customer integration, and HR capability. In groups, determine how you would measure the success of these targets. To start designing your research, ask these two questions: What are you trying to measure? How will the information be used?

   Source: C.M. Solomon, "Putting HR on the Scorecard," *Workforce*, Vol. 70, No. 3, March 2000, 94–98.

2. The president of George Brown College, based in Toronto, uses a number of measures to determine if the HR department is doing a good job. Examples of such measures include student satisfaction, number of grievances, and participation in training and development activities. In groups, develop five key measures of student satisfaction (similar to the client satisfaction surveys done by private organizations) that will help assess the effectiveness of the HR department in the management of faculty.

   Source: A. Macaulay, J. Grant, and U. Vu, 2005, "Gauging HR's Contribution," *Canadian HR Reporter*, 18, 10, 5–8.

# Case: Measuring HR Impact at Wells Fargo

The CEO of Wells Fargo declared, "The way I see it, when you take care of your employees, they take care of your customers, and your shareholders wind up winning." But could he prove it? Wells Fargo implemented an integrated group of HR practices and policies known as PACA (People As a Competitive Advantage). These practices included leadership training, 360° degree feedback and development process, competency-based interviewing, and communicating business plans and goals. Managers were held responsible for business planning and HR planning, selection, performance management, employee development, and communications. PACA was to affect three metrics: employee commitment, customer loyalty, and financial performance.

One hundred and twenty branches were chosen to be part of the research and were evenly divided between those with PACA and those without (the control group). Data would be collected over two blocked time intervals—one year prior to the implementation of PACA and one year after. The results were both expected and surprising. There were strong links between PACA usage and measures of employee commitment, satisfaction, and productivity. Strong correlations were also found between PACA usage and financial performance. For example, the use of PACA tools and practices increased revenue per FTE (full-time equivalent—i.e., number of full-time employees) by 5.1% or $10,511. Turnover was reduced by nearly 60% through the use of PACA. Overall, PACA improved ROE, ROA, and ER (the bank's efficiency ratio, which measures how much it costs the bank to generate one dollar of revenue). The surprising result was that there seemed to be no effect on various measures of customer satisfaction and loyalty. This finding contradicts earlier studies, which found a flow-through from employee measures to customer measures to financial measures.

Source: T.E. Lawson and R.L. Hepp, "Measure the Performance Impact of Human Resource Initiatives," *Human Resource Planning*, Vol. 24, No. 2, 2001, 36–44; A. Kover, "Dick Kovacevich Does It His Way," *Fortune*, May 15, 2000, 299–306.

## Question

As the CEO, would you accept these results (i.e., was it a well-designed study)? As the CEO, would you increase the HR budget to implement PACA (the entire package) in other branches? Defend your decision.

# Endnotes

1. Courtesy of Haberbusch, J.
2. Stewart, J. 1996. "Blow Up the HR Department." *Fortune* (January 15).
3. Hammonds, K.H. 2005. "Why We Hate HR." *Fast Company* August, 97, 41–47.
4. Toulson, P.K., and P. Dewe. 2004. "HR Accounting as a Measurement Tool" *Human Resource Management Journal*, 14, 2, 75–91.
5. Lawler, E.E., A.R. Levenson, and J.W. Boudreau. 2004. "HR Metrics and Analytics: Use and Impact," *Human Resource Planning*, 27, 4, 27–36.
6. Boudreau, J.W., and P.M. Ramstad. 2005. "Talentship and the New Paradigm for Human Resource Management: from Professional Practices to Strategic Talent Decision Science," *Human Resource Planning*, 28, 2, 17–27.
7. Corporate Leadership Council. 2001. *The Evolution of HR Metrics*. May, Cat. No. CLC13LNPC.
8. Lawler, Levenson, and Boudreau, 2004.
9. Anonymous, 2005. "Getting Real and Specific—With Measurements," *HR Focus*, 82, 1, 11–12.
10. Dolan, S.L., and A. Belout. 1997. "Assessing Human Resource Effectiveness: The Emergence of the Stakeholder Approach," *HRM Research Quarterly*, Vol. 1, No. 1 (Spring).
11. Wagar, T. 2002. "Seemed Like a Good Idea, but ... The Survival (and Death) of High Involvement Work Practices," *HRM Research Quarterly*, Vol. 6, No. 1 (Spring).
12. Catano, V.M. 2001. "Empirically Supported Interventions and HR Practice." *HRM Research Quarterly*, Vol. 5, No. 1 (Spring).
13. Huselid, M.A. 1994. "Documenting HR's Effect on Company Performance." *HR Magazine*, Vol. 39, No. 1: 79–85.; Boudreau, J.W. and P.M. Ramstad, 2003 "Strategic HRM Measurement in

the 21st century: From Justifying HR to Strategic Talent Leadership" in Goldsmith, M, Gandossy, R.P and Effron M.S. 2003, *HRM in the 21st Century*, New York: John Wiley, 79–90.

14. Fitz-enz, J. 2000. *The ROI of Human Capital*. New York: AMACOM.

15. Belcourt, M. 2001. "Measuring and Managing the HR Function: A Guide for Boards." *Ivey Business Journal* (January/February 2001): 35–39.

16. Pfau, B.N. *"The State of HR,"* a presentation at the Human Resources Planning Society Conference, April 27, 2004.

17. Tsui, A.S. 1987. "Defining the Activities and Effectiveness of the Human Resource Department: A Multiple Constituent Approach." *Human Resource Management* (Spring): 35–70.; Dolan and Belout, 1997.

18. Ulrich, D. 1996. *Human Resource Champions.* Boston: Harvard Business School Press.

19. Rothwell, W.J., and H.C. Kazanas. 1988. *Strategic Human Resources Planning and Management.* Englewood Cliffs, NJ: Prentice Hall.

20. King, A.S., and T.R. Bishop. 1991. "Functional Requisites of Human Resources: Personnel Professionals' and Line Managers' Criteria for Effectiveness." *Public Personnel Management,* Vol. 20, No. 3 (Fall): 285–298.

21. Meyer, J.P, N.J. Allen, and C.A. Smith. 1993. "Commitment to Organizations and Occupations: Extent and Test of a Three Component Conceptualization." *Journal of Applied Psychology,* Vol. 78: 538–551.

22. Kiger, P.J. 2002. "Why Customer Satisfaction Starts with HR." *Workforce,* Vol. 81, No. 5: 26–32.

23. Caudron, S. 2001. "How HR Drives Profits." *Workforce,* Vol. 80, No. 12: 26–31.

24. Wright, P.M., and S. A. Snell. 2005. "Partner or Guardian? HR Challenges in Balancing Value and Values," *Human Resource Management* 44, 2, 177–182.

25. Rison, R.P., and J. Tower. 2005. "How to Reduce the Cost of HR and Continue to Provide Value," *Human Resource Planning,* 28, 1, 14–18.

26. Brown, D. 2001. "Short Term Absences Double in Three Years." *Canadian HR Reporter,* Vol. 13, No. 18 (October 15): 1.

27. Fitz-ens, 2000.

28. Caudron, 2001.

29. Gerhart, B. 2005 "Human Resources and Business Performance: Findings, Unanswered Questions and an Alternate Approach," *Management Review,* 16, 2, 174–185.

30. www.watsonwyatt.com; retrieved April 5, 2006.

31. Huselid, M.A. 1995. "The Impact of Human Resource Management Practices on Turnover, Productivity, and Corporate Financial Performance." *Academy of Management Journal,* Vol. 38: 635–672.

32. Davidson, W.N. III, D.L. Worrell, and J.B. Fox. 1996. "Early Retirement Programs and Firm Performances." *Academy of Management Journal,* Vol. 39, No. 4 (August): 970–984; Huselid, M.A., and B.E. Becker. 1995. "High Performance Work Systems and Organizational Performance." Academy of Management meeting, Vancouver; Huselid, M.A., and B.E. Becker. 1996. "Methodological Issues in Cross-Sectional and Panel Estimates of the HR–Firm Performance Link." *Industrial Relations,* Vol. 20: 245–259.

33. Welbourne, T.M., and A.O. Andrews. 1996. "Predicting the Performance of Initial Public Offerings: Should Human Resource Management Be an Equation?" *Academy of Management Journal,* Vol. 39, No. 4 (August): 891–919.

34. Jones, G.R., and P.M. Wright. 1992. "An Economic Approach to Conceptualizing the Utility of Human Resource Management Practices." In K. Rowland and G. Ferris, eds., *Research in Personnel and Human Resources Management,* Vol. 10. Greenwich, CT JAI Press.

35. Huselid, 1995.

36. Pfeffer, J. 1998. *The Human Equation: Building Profits by Putting People First.* Boston, MA: Harvard University Press.

37. Koch, M.J., and R. Gunther-McGrath. 1996. "Improving Labour Productivity: Human Resource Management Policies Do Matter." *Strategic Management Journal,* Vol. 17, No. 5 (May): 335–354.

38. Guest, D., J. Michie, M. Sheenan, and N. Conway. 2003. "A UK Study of the Relationship between Human Resources Management and Corporate Performance." *British Journal of Industrial Relations*, 41, 291–314.

39. Wright, P.M., T.M. Gardner, L.M. Moynihan, and M.R. Allen. 2005. "The Relationship between HR Practices and Firm Performance: Examining Causal Order." *Personnel Psychology*, 58, 2, 409–447.

40. Welbourne and Andrews, 1996.

41. Delaney, J.T., and M.A. Huselid. 1996. "The Impact of Human Resource Management Practices on the Perceptions of Organizational Performance." *Academy of Management Journal*, Vol. 39, No. 4: 949–969.

42. Powell, T.C. 1992. "Organizational Alignment as Competitive Advantage." *Strategic Management Journal*, Vol. 13: 119–134.

43. Templer, A., and R.J. Cattaneo. 1995. "A Model of Human Resource Management Effectiveness." *Canadian Journal of Administrative Studies*, Vol. 12, No. 1: 77–88.

44. Ibid, 79.

45. Brealey, R., and S. Meyers. 1991. *Principles of Corporate Finance*, 3rd ed. New York: McGraw-Hill.

46. Cascio, W.F., and R.A. Ramos. 1986. "Development and Application of a New Method for Assessing Job Performance in Behavioural/ Economic Terms." *Journal of Applied Psychology*, 71: 20–28.

47. Tyler, K. 2001. "Evaluate Your Next Move." *HR Magazine*, Vol. 46, No. 11: 66–71.

48. Pemberton, J.D., G.H Stonehous and D.J. Yarrow 2001 "Benchmarking and the Role of Organizational Learning in Developing Competitive Advantage." *Knowledge and Process Management*, 8, 2, 123–135.

49. Fitz-enz, 2000.

50. Maire, J.L, V. Bronet, and M. Pillet. 2005. "A Typology of Best Practices for a Benchmarking Process." *Benchmarking: An International Journal*, 12, 1, 45–60.

51. Thomlinson, A. 2002. "T & D Spending up in US as Canada Lags Behind," *Canadian HR Reporter* 15, No. 6, (March 25).

52. Becker, B. and M. Huselid. 2003. "Measuring HR?" *HR Magazine*, 48, 12, 56–66.

53. Davison, B. 2003. "Reviewing Corporate Financials Shows How HR Measures Up," *Employment Relations Today*, 30, 1, 7–17.

54. Woodcock C.P., and P.W. Beamish. 2003. *Concepts in Strategic Management* 6th edition, McGraw Hill Ryerson, Toronto.

55. Anonymous, 2005, *Strategic HR Review*.

56. Ulrich, D. 1997. "Measuring Human Resources: An Overview of Practice and a Prescription for Results." *Human Resource Management*, Vol. 36, No. 3 (Fall): 303–320.

57. Kaplan, R.S. and Norton, D.R. 2005. "The Balanced Scorecard:Measures that Drive Performance," reprinted in *Harvard Business Review*, 83, 7, 1–10.

58. Becker, B., M.A. Huselid, and D. Ulrich. 2001. *The HR Scorecard: Linking People, Strategy and Performance"* Boston, MA: Harvard Business School Press.

59. Chen, J., Z. Zhu, and H.Y. Xie. 2004. "Measuring Intellectual Capital: A New Model and Empirical Study" *Journal of Intellectual Capital*, 5, 1, 195–212.

60. Elias, J. 2004. "Evaluating Human Capital: An Exploratory Study of Management Practice" *Human Resource Management Journal*, 14, 4, 21–40.

61. Saks, A.M. 1999. *Research, Measurement and Evaluation of Human Resources.* Toronto: ITP Nelson.

62. Wright et al, 2005.

63. Uyen, V. 2003. "Finding the Right Numbers to Measure HR," *Canadian HR Reporter* 16, 15, 1.

64. Weiss, D.S., and R. Finn. 2005. "HR Metrics that Count: Aligning Human Capital Management to Business," *HR Planning*, 28, 1, 33–39.

65. Anonymous, 2005 *Strategic HR Review*.

66. Cascio, W.F. 2000. *Costing Human Resources* 4th edition, Cincinnati, OH: South-Western College Printing.

# Appendix

## HR Accounting Methods

## The Human Asset Accounting Approach

The *human asset accounting approach* attempts to use accounting principles, such as those used to calculate the historical costs or replacement costs of assets, to put a value on the worth of an organization's human assets. The models used in this approach measure the investment made in employees, treating them as capitalized resources, in economic terms.

- *Historical costs model:* The historical costs model of accounting measures the investment in employees.[1] The investment consists of the costs of acquisition, training, orientation, informal coaching, and experience and development. These costs are amortized over the expected working lives of individuals. Those expenses incurred on behalf of employees who left the company (the unamortized costs) are written off. This approach has the advantage of being relatively objective and consistent with the accounting treatment of other assets, thus allowing comparisons. Critics of this approach complain that this method is seriously flawed because the assets are not saleable, and, therefore, there is no independent check of valuation. They say that estimating costs of informal training and experience is too subjective. In addition, allowances must be made for the changing value of the dollar. The main problem is that the process measures only costs and cannot distinguish between two employees: both may have cost the organization the same dollar amount in acquisition and training, but one may be an outstanding performer and the other a minimally effective worker.
- *Replacement costs model:* This model measures the cost of replacing an employee as an esti-

mate of market value. The cost includes recruitment, selection, compensation, training, and orientation.[2] This model is unsatisfactory for several reasons. Although substituting replacement cost for historical cost provides an updated valuation, the actual opportunities to do these calculations are limited. Most organizations have limited turnover, particularly at senior levels, and so building a complex human asset formula into the accounting system would not be worthwhile. Furthermore, a badly managed HR department that incurred abnormal expenses in recruiting or selection might overestimate the cost of replacing an employee.[3] A highly sophisticated system of staffing, orientation, and training would also generate high replacement costs, but the measure of the value added by exceptional employees would not be part of the accounting process.
- *Present value of future earnings model:* This model measures contributions, not costs. The organization tries to determine what an employee's future contribution is worth today by calculating future earnings, adjusted for the probability of an employee's death.[4] Contribution is calculated by the compensation paid to an employee. Probability of death is estimated using mortality tables. The problem with this model is that it assigns a value to the average worker, rather than to an individual. No investment in individual employees—for example, in training—is taken into account, and yet this training investment should have a payoff in future contributions.

These three models of human asset accounting value employee service at gross book value (the original investment expenses), net book value (the original investment minus depreciation), and economic value (the anticipated financial return on the investment).[5] These models, however, have not been accepted by HR professionals or by researchers for many reasons.

## Limitations of Human Asset Accounting Models

As can be seen, the main problem with human asset accounting models is their failure to take into account employee effectiveness. They tend to measure only inputs, such as costs incurred in acquiring and training employees, and not outputs, such as employee productivity. Secondly, who is the best judge of employee worth—the employee, the manager, or the HR department? Another major problem is the cost and difficulty of obtaining these data. The focus seems to be on an industrialized economy rather than one that depends on knowledge management.[6] The most recent trend is to measure the intellectual capital—the brainpower—of employees in the hope of measuring actual and potential contributions.

## Intellectual Capital Approach

The productivity of most organizations entering the 21st century is highly dependent on the intellectual capabilities of their employees. The software, communications, educational, and medical sectors, which provide 79% of all jobs, owe their success to the knowledge of their employees.[7] For example, the value of Microsoft was greater than that of General Motors, Ford, Boeing, Lockheed Martin, Deere, Caterpillar, Weyerhauser, Union Pacific, Kodak, Sears, Marriott, Safeway, and Kellogg combined![8] Yet a real source of Microsoft's value is the knowledge of its employees. What is intellect and how is it measured?

*Intellectual capital* can be thought of as intellectual material (knowledge) that can be formalized, captured, and leveraged to produce a higher-valued asset.[9] Intellectual capital can be seen as employee brainpower, some of which is described in skills inventories and patent lists.

Quinn and his colleagues described and ranked the importance of this intellectual capital:[10]

1. Cognitive knowledge (know what)
2. Advanced skills (know how)
3. System understanding and trained intuition (know why)
4. Self-motivated creativity (care why)

Employers pay premiums for smart workers. In the United States, men with postgraduate degrees earn incomes 130% higher than men who never finished high school.[11] The pay gap between men with these different levels of education has doubled since 1980. Companies like Scandia and Dow Chemical are struggling to identify, describe, and measure these intellectual assets in order to manage them. The chief financial officer for Northern Telecom states, "As a technology company, much of our ability to differentiate ourselves from our competitors depends on being able to market new product solutions more quickly than anyone else. For this, we rely on our intellectual capital".[12]

Intellectual assets have characteristics highly distinct from other assets. First, intellectual assets grow with use. Anyone who has gone back to school or completed a training course realizes that the learning of new knowledge, and its application, leads to even greater knowledge and a motivation to acquire more. Intellectual capital can be shared and cannot be depleted. Sharing it results in increased feedback, acquisition of new knowledge, and modifications and adjustments to current knowledge. Accenture links via e-mail 82 000 employees in 360 offices in 76 countries, allowing the posting of problems on bulletin boards. Company management believes that this taps dormant capabilities of employees and expands energy and solutions to problems. However, there are also disadvantages to investing in intellectual assets. One is exclusivity. If you own a capital asset such as a building, you can prevent competitors from using it. However, a highly knowledgeable employee can moonlight, freelance, or subcontract for other companies or leave to work for a competitor.

## Issues in Measuring Intellectual Capital

Experts in this nascent field estimate that the intellectual assets of an organization are worth three to four times the tangible book value. A common approach is to claim that the intellectual capital of a firm is equal to the difference between a firm's capitalized stock value and its book value. It is still very difficult to put a dollar value on the brain resources of employees. CIBC tries to do so by counting employee skills (e.g., the ability to manage a portfolio of clients), which can be used to build a competency inventory. But as skills change, the dynamics of measuring them become difficult. Furthermore, most of this asset is left idle: observers and employees alike guess that only 20% of the knowledge available in their companies is used.[13] You can see when a factory is producing at a reduced capacity; you cannot always determine if your knowledge workers are working at capacity.

Educational and medical institutions have measured intellectual capital for decades, relying on peer reviews (and publication records) for decisions about the worth of the faculty or professionals. Thus, first measures of intellectual capital include peer review, although in some cases, it may be done by colleagues working together on projects. Some organizations add another review level, that of customer or client evaluations of outputs.[14] Customers are asked to rank team participants on professional knowledge and specific project contributions, and on overall satisfaction with results. To supplement these human evaluations, some organizations add measures of efficiency and effectiveness, which normally are measured in business terms (e.g., costs, fulfillment time and accuracy, delivery times). Finally, some organizations track the intellectual assets created. CIBC charts the growth of intellectual capital by tracking the flow of knowledge among employees. The company counts, as indicators of intellectual capital, the number of new ideas generated, the number of new products created, and the percentage of income from new revenue streams.

The competitive advantage of intellectual capital is enormous. This asset cannot be traded or expropriated. Competitors fall farther behind because the top talent goes to organizations such as Microsoft to be part of a leading-edge organization.

Many researchers have tried and failed to come up with a single, limited criterion to measure the worth of an organization's human resources. Accountants cannot value intellectual capital because there is no market for it—it cannot be bought and sold, and so valued. After reviewing the literature, researchers concluded that the search should be abandoned, despite its attraction for managers making internal management and external investment decisions.[15] But the start of the new century has seen a revival in attempts to measure human capital, driven by consulting companies and academics. The rationale for the search for the holy grail of human capital assessment is fuelled by the belief that these measures give a clearer indication of a firm's potential and future profitability than backward-looking accounting techniques.[16] The other explanation is that a larger number of organizations depend entirely on their employees (and not technology or machinery) for survival.

# Endnotes

1. Cascio, W.F. 1991. *Costing Human Resources: The Financial Impact of Behavior in Organizations*, 3rd ed. Kent Series in Human Resource Management. Boston: PWS Kent.
2. Flamholtz, F.L.K., D.G. Searfoss, and R. Cof. 1988. "Developing Human Resource Accounting as a Decision Support System," *Accounting Horizon*, Vol. 2: 1–9.
3. Steffy, B.D., and S.D. Maurer. 1988. "Conceptualizing and Measuring the Economic Effectiveness of Human Resource Activities," *Academy of Management Review*, Vol. 13: 265–280.
4. Lev, B., and A. Schwartz. 1971. "On the Use of the Economic Concept of Human Capital in Financial Statements," *Accounting Review*, Vol. 46: 103–112.
5. Cascio, 1991.
6. Chen, J., Z. Zhu, and H. Y. Xie. 2004. "Measuring Intellectual Capital: A New Model and Empirical Study," *Journal of Intellectual Capital*, 5, 1, 195–212.
7. Quinn, J.B., P. Anderson, and S. Finkelstein. 1996. "Leveraging Intellect." *Academy of Management Executive*, Vol. 10, No. 3, 7–28.
8. Lermusiaux, Y. 2002. "Managing Human Capital in a Downturn," *Ivey Business Journal*, Vol. 66, No. 4 (March/April): 14–16.
9. Stewart, T.A. 1994. "Intellectual Capital." *Fortune* (October 3): 68–74.
10. Quinn et al., 1996.
11. Quinn et al., 1996.
12. Edwards, S. 1997. "The Brain Gain," *CA Magazine* (April): 21–25.
13. Edwards, 1997.
14. Quinn et al., 1996.
15. Scarpello, V., and H.A. Theeke. 1989. "Human Resource Accounting: A Measured Critique." *Journal of Accounting Literature*, Vol. 8: 265–280.
16. Toulson, P.K., and P. Dewe 2004 "HR Accounting as a Measurement Tool," *Human Resources Management Journal* 14, 2: 75–91.

# Index

## A

absenteeism, 212, 276, 380–381
academy companies, 243
accommodation, 281–282
ACCOR, 300
acquisitions, 11
    see also mergers
actionable, 394
activity-based measures, 385
Acxion Corporation, 267
adaptive IHRM approach, 300
added-value measure, 385
adjustment to job loss, 269–270
advanced information technologies, 125
agreeableness, 305
Air Canada, 9, 12–13, 325
Alcan Aluminum Ltd., 12, 322
Alcatel, 186–187
Aldo Shoes Limited, 26
alignment, 393–394
alignment of HR strategy
    basic premise, 38
    concurrent strategy formulation, 40–41
    corporate strategy leads to HR strategy, 39
    differentiation strategy, 57–59
    executive team membership, 43
    HR competencies lead to business strategy, 39–40
    HR strategy and corporate strategy, 40
    illustration of, 44–45
    integrative linkage, 43–45
    with low-cost-provider strategy, 55–57
    review/react linkage, 43
    strategic partnering, 43
    strategic planning process, involvement in, 43–45
Allied Stores, 327
Alt Foods, 322
Alvares, Ken, 164
Amazon.com, 20
American Express, 332
American Institute of Certified Public Accountants, 110
American Management Association, 328
analysis of external environment, 63
AOL Time Warner, 340

A&P. See Great Atlantic and Pacific Tea Company (A&P)
A&P Canada, 325
Apple Computer, 4
assessment, 63
assessment centres, 236
asset purchase, 335
assimilation, 331
AT&T, 229
attitudes, 378
attrition, 161
audit, 386–387
Authoria, 127
Autoglass, 362
autonomy, 112
Avenor Inc., 357

## B

baby boomers, 76, 225
baby busters, 76
balanced scorecard, 370–371, 389–390
Bank of Montreal, 331
bankruptcy, 10
BARS analysis, 108, 312
the Bay, 78
Bay Networks, 330
Bayer Group AG, 103
BC Gas, 340
BC Telecom, 325
Beatrice Foods, 322
behavioural perspective, 32–34
Behaviourally Anchored Rating Scales (BARS), 108, 312
Bell Canada, 57, 325
benchmarking, 387–388
benchmarks, 99
benefits, 340
best-cost provider strategy, 18
best practices, 391–393
"best practices" approach, 47
BMO Financial Group, 389
BMW, 57
Bowey, John, 198
BP (British Petroleum), 352
Brandon University, 145
Braun, Pam, 296
broad differentiation strategy, 17–18
Brotheridge, Celeste, 243
Brown, Michael, 145–146
bundling HR practices, 47
Burger King, 18
Burroughs, 323

business process re-engineering, 132
business strategy
    see also corporate strategies
    defined, 12
    described, 11–13
    HR competencies lead to, 39–40
    international strategies, and strategic international HRM, 299–301
    linking HR processes to, 38–43

## C

Cairns, 4
Calgary Health Region, 365–366
Cameron, Kim, 261
Campeau, Robert, 323, 327, 329
Canada, 331
Canada Life, 322
Canadian Airlines International, 330
Canadian Auto Workers (CAW), 80, 260
Canadian labour market facts, 74
Canadian Pacific Airlines, 330
Canadian Public Service Commission, 156
Cantor Fitzgerald, 227
capabilities, 18–19
Cara Operations Ltd., 12, 15, 16
career development, 20, 310
career management concepts, 245
cases
    Acceleration Pools at PepsiCo, 252–253
    Aldo Shoes Limited, 26
    Building Talent at Cisco Systems, 139–140
    Calgary Health Region, 365–366
    The City of Toronto—Courage in the Face of Chaos, 345–347
    A Downsizing Decision at the Department of Public Works, 288–290
    An International Career Move, 317
    Madness at Moosehead U, 115–116
    Measuring HR Impact at Wells Fargo, 398–399
    A New Vision of HR, 51–52
    Ontario's Faculty Shortage Crisis, 218–220
    Recruiting with Bells and Whistles, 186–187

cases (*continued*)
Sun Microsystems, 164–165
Work-Life Family Balance, 85–86
cash cows, 326
causal links, 393
cause-and-effect models, 159
Ceridien, 355
chain effects, 199
change component, 159
Chantelois, Claude, 122
Chapters, 323
children's work beliefs, 269
China, 297
Chrysler, 323
CIBC, 355, 357
CIGNA International Expatriate
Benefits, 309
Cisco Systems, 127, 128, 139–140,
179, 242
City of Toronto. *See* Toronto
client satisfaction
advantages of measurement, 375
conflicting expectations, 377
critical incident method, 377
described, 375
high expectations of clients, 377
informal feedback, 375–376
measurement problems, 377
measures, 385
methods of measurement, 375–377
professional affiliations, 377
surveys, 376
clients, 78
ClubLink, 324
coaching, 241–243
Coca-Cola Company, 30, 325
Coles Books, 322
Colgate-Palmolive Co., 310
company culture. *See* culture
Compaq, 322, 324, 327
comparability, 394
compensable factors, 95
compensation
differentiation strategy, 58
home-based policy, 313
host-based policy, 313
in international context, 312–313
low-cost-provider strategy, 56
mergers, 340
region-based policy, 313
competency
core competencies, 20, 111
defined, 110
managerial competencies, 232
role competencies, 111
specific competencies, 111

competency-based approaches,
92–93, 109–112, 231–232
competition for same job, 340
competitive advantage
culture as, 19
defined, 18
and downsizing, 283
identification of, 18–20
and information
technology (IT), 135
competitive position, 17–18
complementary situations, 337
compliance, 374
concurrent strategy
formulation, 40–41
Confederation Life, 10
Conference Board of
Canada, 65, 69, 388
conferences, 65
confidentiality, 357
conflicting expectations, 377
conglomerate merger, 323
conscience, 70
conscientiousness, 305
consolidation, 323
"consultant with a conscience," 70
Consumers Distributing, 4, 38
contamination, 97–98
contingency planning, 155, 335
contract negotiation, 361–362
contradictory situations, 337
contribution of HRM practices, 380,
381–385
Coopers & Lybrand, 200
core competencies, 20, 111, 356
Corel, 57, 331
Corning Canada Inc., 58
corporate strategies
*see also* business strategy
defined, 8
domestic strategy, 299
global strategy, 300–301
international strategies, and
strategic international HRM,
299–301
leading to HR strategy, 39
linking HR processes to, 38–43
multidomestic strategy, 299–300
multinational strategy, 300
cost-benefit analysis, 385–386
costing measures, 385
costs
control of, 378–381
direct costs, 385
of employee behaviour, 380–381
and HR forecasting, 149

indirect costs, 385
of job analysis, 98–99
of mergers, 329–330
of smoking, 381
countertrends, 71
crises, 46
critical incident method, 377
critical incidents technique, 107–108
critical trends, 70–71
cross-cultural training
(CTT), 304, 306, 310
cross-functional practices, 47
Cuddy, A. Mac, 225
Cuddy International, 225
cultural due diligence
checklist, 334
cultural factors, 77
culture
blending of, 334
as competitive advantage, 19
defined, 330
management of, 377–378
and mergers, 330–333
culture shock, 308–309
current forecast, 154
customers, 78

**D**
Daimler-Benz, 323
Dalkey, N.C., 172
Daniel Arbour and Associates, 323
data security, 132–133
DealsOutlet.ca, 4
deculturation, 331
deficiency, 97–98
Dell Computer, 179
Deloitte & Touche, 198
Delphi technique, 66, 168, 172–174
demand forecasting
Delphi technique, 172–174
e-recruiting, 179
employee requirement ratio, 170
envelope/scenario forecasts,
177–179, 178f
expert forecasts, 170–171
forecasted demand,
calculation of, 170
HR budgets, 176–177
index/trend analysis, 169–170
net HR demand, 156–157
nominal group technique, 174–176
regression analysis, 180–183
staffing table, 177
demographics, 76–77
demotion, 339
designated groups, 151

DesRosiers Automotive Consultants Inc., 200
Deutsche Bank, 372
developmental goals of global competence, 303
developmental opportunities and experiences, 237–243
diaries, 102
*Dictionary of Occupational Titles* (DOT), 99
differentiation strategy, 57–59
Dimensions of Executive Positions, 101
direct costs, 385
direct observation, 101
disengagement incentives/strategies, 273
displaced workers, benefits to, 268f
distributive justice, 271
diversification, 325
diversity in workforce, 77
diversity management, 39
divestiture, 9
division, 45–46
DLGL, 124, 128
Dofasco, 390
domestic strategy, 299
Dow Chemical Co., 77
downsizers, 273
downsizing
   adjustment to job loss, 269–270
   altering the psychological contract, 281–282
   alternatives to, 267
   benefits to displaced workers, 268f
   best practices, 280
   Canadian evidence, 275–276
   communication, role of, 279
   and competitive advantage, 283
   consequences of, 274–275
   decision to downsize, 265–266
   defined, 260, 261–263
   effective downsizing strategies, 276–277
   ethical considerations, 266–267
   and financial performance, 273–274
   frequency of, 263
   and high involvement human resource management, 283
   HRM issues, 280–285
   impact on the "downsizers," 273
   ineffective downsizing strategies, 278–280
   inplacement issues, 267
   key issues, 279

labour relations issues, 284–285
   managers' reactions to, 272
   "new deal" in employment, 281
   objectives of, 265f
   organizational change, 264f
   outplacement issues, 267
   perceptions of justice, 271
   phenomenon of, 260–261
   planning for, 267–268
   psychological contract, 280–281
   reasons for, 263–265
   reorientation strategy, 275
   reputation for corporate social performance (RCSP), 274–275
   restructuring, 262–263, 264f
   strategic downsizing, 277–278
   survivor reactions, 271–272
   survivors, 270–271
   systematic change, 262
   words used to describe downsizing, 261
   work redesign, 262, 278
   workforce reduction, 262, 263, 269f, 276
downsizing strategies, 260, 262, 276–280
   *see also* downsizing
Drucker, Peter, 224, 237
dual-career couples, 296, 297
due diligence, 335–336
duplicated situations, 337
Dylex Ltd., 237

**E**
e-learning, 135
e-recruiting, 179
early downsizers, 275
early retirement, 226
East Side Mario's, 18
Eaton's, 4, 225
economic climate, 72
economies of scale, 324, 355–356
Edward Hay and Associates, 109
effective HRM strategy
   characteristics of, 46–48
   elements of, 48f
   external fit, 47
   focus on results, 48
   internal fit, 47
efficiency, 379–380
efficiency measures, 379–380
electronic surveys, 126
elitism, 246–247
emergencies, 144–147
*Emergency Management Act* (Ont.), 145

emergency management personnel, 144–145
emergent strategy, 7
emerging HR technology solutions, 134–135
emotional stability, 305
employee branding, 69, 234
employee productivity, and mergers, 329–330
employee requirement ratio, 170
employee retention policies, 211
employee retention programs, 212–213
employee value proposition, 234
employees
   adjustment to job loss, 269–270
   assessment of potential, 236
   attitudes, 378
   career management, 245–246
   costs of behaviour, 380–381
   demotivation, 247
   and differentiation strategy, 58
   displaced workers, benefits to, 268f
   diverse skill sets, 45
   flexibility, 45
   high-potential employees, 232–236
   and low-cost-provider strategy, 55
   measurement of worth, 390–391
   multiorganizational career, 281
   outsourcing, and morale, 359–360
   psychological contract. *See* psychological contract
   retention of key employees, 69–70
   as stakeholders, 80
   succession management, role in, 244–246
   survivor, 260, 270–271, 271–272, 340
   value of, 35, 36
employer-employee relationship, 74
employment equity–designated group membership, 151
employment legislation, 297–298
Enbridge Gas Distribution, 370, 389–390
EnCana Corp., 243
Enron, 70
enterprise portals, 135
enterprise resource planning (ERP), 129–130
envelope, 154
envelope/scenario forecasts, 177–179, 178f
environment, 63

environmental factors
  affecting HR forecasting, 153
  cultural factors, 77
  demographic factors, 76–77
  described, 71–72
  economic climate, 72
  knowledge revolution, 72–73
  labour market, 73
  legislative factors, 74–75
  political factors, 74–75
  social factors, 77
  stakeholders, 78–81
  technological factors, 75
  top management, 80–81
environmental scanning
  case application, 81–82
  challenges, 67–71
  conferences and seminars, 65
  defined, 62
  forecasting methods, 66–67
  information sources, 63
  isolation of the critical, 70–71
  proactive approach, 71
  professional associations, 65
  professional consultants, 65
  publications, 64
  rearview-mirror methods, 67
ERP, 129–130
ethical issues, 75, 266–267
European Union, 297
evaluation
  *see also* evaluation of HRM
  corporate scorecard, 370–371
  of downsizing efforts, 269
  of HR technology, 133–134
  KSAs, 336
  outsourcing, 361
  performance. *See* performance evaluation
evaluation of HRM
  activity-based measures, 385
  audit, 386–387
  balanced scorecard, 370–371, 389–390
  benchmarking, 387–388
  challenges in measurement of impact, 391–395
  client satisfaction, 375–377
  client satisfaction measures, 385
  compliance, 374
  contribution of HRM practices, 380, 381–385
  cost-benefit analysis, 385–386
  cost control, 378–381
  costing measures, 385
  culture management, 377–378

efficiency, 379–380
employee worth, 390–391
financial measures, 382–383
5C model of HRM impact, 374–383
HR scorecard, 370–371, 389–390
importance of, 371–374
managerial perceptions of effectiveness, 383–385
measurement approaches, 385–391
popular measures, 394
rationale, 372–374
resistance to, 371–372
ROE (return on equity), 383
ROI (return on investments), 383, 384
separation of cause and effect, 393
successful measurement, 393–395
summary of measurement alternatives, 392*t*
and universality of best practices, 391–393
utility analysis, 386
event-based forecasting, 147
executive personnel, 151–152
executive team membership, 43
expatriates. *See* strategic international HRM
expert forecasts, 170–171
experts, 357–358
exportive IHRM approach, 300
external candidates, 229
external coaches, 242
external environment, 17
  *see also* environmental factors
external fit, 47, 299
external supply, 157
extraversion, 305
Exult, 352
Exxon, 72

**F**
fads, 374
Faltec Inc., 129
family businesses, 198, 225
Federated Department Stores, 323, 327, 329
feedback
  informal feedback, 375–376
  and job analysis process, 106–107
  in low-cost-provider strategy, 57
  360° evaluation, 101
FEMA, 145–147
Fields, 4
financial measures, 382–383

Fine, Sidney, 109
fit, 47
five-factor personality model (FFM), 303–304, 305
five Ps of strategy, 5–6
5C model of HRM impact
  client satisfaction, 375–377
  compliance, 374
  contribution of HRM practices, 380, 381–385
  cost control, 378–381
  culture management, 377–378
flat organizations, 228
flexibility, 298
flexible employment contracts, 282
Flynn, Deborah, 218
focused niche strategy, 18
Ford, Bill, 260
Ford Motor Company, 73, 260
forecasting. *See* HR forecasting
formal training and development, 240–241
Four Seasons Hotels, 57
Frieman's, 4
Frost, Inc., 46
functional job analysis (FJA), 101, 109

**G**
Gartner's skills inventory methodology, 126
Gen Xs, 76
Gen Ys, 76–77
General Electric (GE), 45, 58, 243, 322, 325
General Mills, 332, 333
General Motors (GM), 72, 73, 260, 284
Giant Manufacturing, 359
global competence developmental goals, 303
Global Relocation Trends Survey (2001), 304
global strategy, 300–301
globalization
  cost-benefit planning, 46
  as environmental factor, 73
  and HR forecasting, 148
Glover, Brenda, 345–347
goal optimization, 383–384
goals, 15–17
Goldman Sachs Group Inc., 225
Gordon Capital, 225
governments, 79
Gow Corp., 353
Grant, Philip, 106

Great Atlantic and Pacific Tea Company (A&P), 56
Gretzky, Wayne, 248
Gröschl, Stefan, 295
growth strategies
acquisitions, 11
described, 10
incremental growth, 10
international growth, 10
mergers, 11
Guptil, David, 235

# H

Haberbusch, Jane, 370
hard goals, 15–16
Hargrove, Buzz, 260, 284
Harrington, James, 48
Hartley, Darin, 98
harvest strategy, 11
Harvey's, 12
Hathcock, Bonnie, 41
Hay Guide Chart–Profile Method, 103
Hay system, 109
HayGroup, 109, 219
health care sector, 168
Hewitt Associates, 355
Hewlett, Bill, 40
Hewlett-Packard (HP), 40, 57, 179, 322, 324, 327
high expectations of clients, 377
high involvement human resource management, 283
High Performance Systems Inc., 156
high-potential employees, 232–236
High Road Communications Inc., 267
hiring freeze, 161
Hollinger, 70
home-country nationals (HCNs), 301
see also strategic international HRM
Home Outfitters, 4
Honda Motor Co., 57, 58
Honore, Russel, 147
horizontal integration, 325
horizontal mergers, 322–323
hospital mergers, 323
hostile takeover, 324
HP. See Hewlett-Packard (HP)
HR budgets, 176–177
HR deficit, 160
HR demand. See human resources demand

HR educational training programs, 92–93
HR forecasting
activity categories, 147–148
benefits of, 149–150
categorizing forecasting models, 159
cause-and-effect models, 159
contingency planning, 155
current forecast, 154
defined, 147
Delphi technique, 66, 172–174
demand forecasting. See demand forecasting; human resources demand
described, 63
for emergency managers, 144–147
envelope, 154
envelope/scenario forecasts, 177–179, 178f
environmental factors, 153
event-based forecasting, 147
expert forecasts, 170–171
in global economy, 148
goal of, 153
and HR costs, 149
human resources demand, 150, 155–157
human resources supply, 150, 157–158
impact analysis, 67
institution of HR programs, 160–161
judgmental models, 159
key personnel analyses, 151–153
long-run forecast, 154
and macro business forecasting process, 149–150
medium-run forecast, 154
methods of, 66–67
net HR requirements, determination of, 155–161
nominal group technique, 174–176
organizational factors, 153
and organizational flexibility, 149
organizational requirements, precedence of, 150
prediction, 154
process-based forecasting, 147
projection, 154
scenario planning, 67
scenarios, 155

short-run forecast, 154
supply forecasting. See human resources supply; supply forecasting
time horizons, 154–155
time-series models, 159
transaction-based forecasting, 147
trend analysis, 66
workforce planning activities, 148
HR Lafarge Canada, 235
HR planning
competency-based analysis, 92–93
competency-based approaches, 92–93
contingency plan, 335
and differentiation strategy, 58
due diligence, 335–336
forecasting. See HR forecasting
HR educational training programs, 92–93
and information technology (IT), 123–130
see also information technology (IT)
and job analysis, 96–97
see also job analysis
and low-cost-provider strategy, 55–56
mergers, 335–337
replacement charts, 127
skills inventories, 126
strategic international HR planning, 298
see also strategic international HRM
succession management, 127
see also succession management
transition team, 336–337, 338
workforce planning activities, 148
HR publications, 64
HR role assessment survey, 376
HR scorecard, 370–371, 389–390
HR supply. See human resources supply
HR surplus, 160–161
HR system implementation, 150
HRM strategy
see also strategic HRM
characteristics of effective strategy, 46–48

HRM strategy (continued)
concurrent strategy formulation, 40–41
corporate strategy leads to HR strategy, 39
by division, 45–46
HR competencies lead to business strategy, 39–40
linking HR processes to strategy, 38–43
meaning of, 35–36
purpose of, 46
strategic partnering, 43
Huber, George P., 124
Hudson Institute, 65
Hudson's Bay Company (HBC), 4, 239, 322
human capital, 34
human capital management, 129
human capital theory, 34–35
human resources demand
see also demand forecasting
defined, 150
determination of, 155–157
Human Resources Development Canada (HRDC), 73
human resources information system (HRIS), 128
human resources management (HRM)
see also strategic HRM
analysis of external environment, 63
described, 30
downsizing issues, 280–285
employee potential, identification of, 236
environmental factors, 71–81
environmental scanning, 62–65, 67–71
evaluation. See evaluation of HRM
forecasting methods, 66–67
high involvement human resource management, 283
mega trends, 68–70
mergers, impact of, 333–342
Human Resources Professionals Association of Ontario, 65
human resources supply
see also supply forecasting
defined, 150
determination of, 157–158
and early retirement, 226
Hurricane Katrina, 145–147
Husky Injection Molding Systems Ltd., 69
Hy's, 18

**I**

IBI Income Fund, 323
IBM Corp., 4, 62, 243, 334, 353
IHRM, 297
see also strategic international HRM
illnesses, 380–381
impact analysis, 67
implementation of HR technology, 131–133
incremental growth, 10
index/trend analysis, 169–170
India, 73
Indigo, 323
indirect costs, 385
indirect observation, 101
Industrial Revolution, 72–73
informal feedback, 375–376
information gaps, 336–337
information overload, 394
information technology (IT)
see also technology
areas for IT application, 125
business process re-engineering, 132
competitive advantage, 135
data security, 132–133
different solutions for different needs, 128–130
e-learning, 135
emerging HR technology solutions, 134–135
enterprise portals, 135
enterprise resource planning (ERP), 129–130
evaluation of HR technology, 133–134
and HR planning, 123–130
human resources information system (HRIS), 128
implementation of, 131–133
knowledge management, 135
marketplace exploration, 130–131
needs analysis, 130
outsourcing, 124
and performance appraisals, 124
properties of advanced information technologies, 125
replacement charts, 127
request for proposal (RFP), 131
selection of HRM technology solutions, 130–131
self-service, 134
skills inventories, 126
specialty products, 128–129
succession management, 127
vendor and product evaluation, 131
web-based HR, 134–135
inplacement, 267
insignificant trends, 70–71
institution of HR programs, 160–161
intangible assets, 18
integration, 331
integrative IHRM approach, 301
integrative linkage, 43–45
intended strategy, 7
interactional justice, 271
internal candidates, 229
internal fit, 47, 299
internal labour market, 204
internal supply, 157
international growth, 10
international HRM. See strategic international HRM
International Human Resource Management (IHRM) systems, 297
see also strategic international HRM
international M&A, 331
Internet
see also Web links
e-learning, 135
e-recruiting, 179
interviews, 101
ithink model, 156
Ito, Jack, 243

**J**

Japan, 331, 332
JASR approach, 98
Jazz, 9
Jet Form, 239
job, 93
job analysis
compensable factors, 95
competency models, 110–111
contamination and deficiency, 97–98
costs of, 98–99
current job descriptions and specifications, 102–107
defined, 93
diaries, 102
direct observation, 101
as foundation of HR activities, 94
history of, 95–96
and HR planning, 96–97
indirect observation, 101
interviews, 101

job description, 94
job specification, 94
journals, 102
maintenance of new
    techniques, 106
observation, 101
out of date or non-reviewed, 97
output and production
    analysis, 102
problems associated with, 97–99
process of, 99–107
questionnaires, 101–102
recorded data, 103–104
techniques. See job analysis
    techniques
360° evaluation, 101
time required for, 98–99
videotaping, 101
written outcomes of process, 94
"Job Analysis at the Speed of
    Reality" approach, 98
job analysis process, 99–107
job analysis techniques
    Behaviourally Anchored Rating
        Scales (BARS), 108
    competency-based approaches,
        109–112
    critical incidents
        technique, 107–108
    functional job analysis
        (FJA), 109
    Hay system, 109
    Position Analysis Questionnaire
        (PAQ), 108
job-based approach, 231
job description
    see also job analysis
    defined, 94
    downloading of, 104
    information in, 105
    infrequent use of, 106
    job-focused nature of, 105
    vague, 97
Job Diagnostic Survey, 101
job insecurity, 269, 272
job loss adjustments, 269–270
job rotations, 238–239
job satisfaction, 275
job security, 79
job sharing, 160
job specification
    see also job analysis
    defined, 94
    information in, 105
    person-focused nature of, 105
    vague, 97

Johnson & Johnson, 247
journals, 102
judgmental models, 159
justice, 271

K
K-Mart Canada, 4, 239
KFC, 325
kickbacks, 75
Kimberly-Clark, 13
knowledge, skills and abilities.
    See KSAs
knowledge management, 135
knowledge revolution, 72–73
KnowledgePoint, 104
Kronos, 128
KSAs
    analysis of, and HR supply,
        157–158
    defined, 94
    evaluation of, and M&As, 336
    inventory of, after merger, 341
    specific international
        assignments, 303
    storage of information, 236

L
labour, 34
labour hoarding, 39
labour market, 73, 74
labour relations
    see also unions
    differentiation strategy, 59
    and downsizing, 284–285
    low-cost-provider strategy, 57
    mergers, 341–342
    strategic international HRM,
        313–314
labour shortage, 212–213, 226
larger organizations, 79
late downsizers, 275
Lee Enterprises, 124
legislation, 297–298
legislative factors, 74–75
Leiba-O'Sullivan, Sharon, 295
linear programming, 203–204
linear relationships, 204
liquidation, 10
London Life, 322
long-run forecast, 154
long-term succession, 196
Lotus, 334
low-cost provider strategy, 17,
    55–57
Lufthansa, 325
Lumenon, 187

M
MacMillan Bloedel, 15
macro business forecasting process,
    149–150
Magna International, 225
maintenance strategies, 11
management development
    methods
    coaching, 241–243
    described, 237–238
    formal training and development,
        240–241
    job rotations, 238–239
    mentors, 241–243
    promotion, 238
    special assignments, 239–240
management inventory, 195
management needs, and mergers,
    326–327
managerial competencies, 232
managerial perceptions of
    effectiveness, 383–385
managerial personnel,
    151–152
mandatory retirement,
    192–194
Manulife Financial
    Corp., 243
Maple Leaf Foods, 243
Maritime Life Insurance, 238
market niche strategy, 18
Markov chains, 201–202
Markov models, 200–203
M&As. See mergers
McCain's, 225
McCormick, Earnest, 108
McDonald's, 9, 55, 56, 57, 73
"McJobs," 73
McKenzie & Co., 322, 328
McKinsey, 235
MDS, 234, 247
Meade, James G., 130, 131
measurement of effectiveness.
    See evaluation of HRM
medium-run forecast, 154
mega trends, 68–70
mentors, 241–243
Mercedes-Benz, 57
Merchant, James, 357
mergers
    advisory firms, 329
    asset purchase, 335
    biggest IT merger in
        Canada, 322
    Canadian mergers, studies of,
        328–329

mergers *(continued)*
compensation, 340
conglomerate merger, 323
consolidation, 323
contingency plan, 335
cultural due diligence
checklist, 334
cultural issues, 330–333
defined, 11
development, 341
due diligence, 335–336
employee productivity,
loss of, 329–330
financial benefits, 325–326
financial impact, 328–329
goals of mergers, and achievement
rates, 329
horizontal integration, 325
horizontal mergers, 322–323
HR issues, 333–342
HR planning, 335–337
impact on human resources,
329–330
international, 331
labour relations, 341–342
management needs, 326–327
methods, 327
motives for, 324–327
operating synergy, 324
performance appraisal, 341
post-merger integration practices,
332–333
process, 331–332
real costs, 329
selection, 338–340
share purchase, 335
and size, 328
strategic benefits, 324–325
stress, 337, 341
success rates, 327–328
survivors, 340
takeover, 324
task forces, 332
terms, 322–324
training, 341
transition team, 336–337, 338
vertical integration, 325
vertical merger, 323
metrics, 68–69, 389
Metro Inc., 325
Mexico, 331
Microsoft, 73
Minacs Worldwide Inc., 11
minimum wage, 74–75
Mintzberg, Henry, 5–6, 322
Mintzberg's five P's of strategy, 5–6

mission, 15
mission statements, 15
monitoring, 63
monitoring succession management,
243–244
Morgan's, 4
movement analysis, 204–208
multidomestic strategy, 299–300
multinational corporations
(MNCs), 298
*see also* strategic international
HRM
multinational strategy, 300
multiorganizational career, 281
multiple internal labour markets, 204
multiplier effect, 202

**N**
Nagin, Ray, 147
Nardoni Strategic Solutions, 127
National Film Board of Canada
(NFB), 122–123
National Foreign Trade Council
(NFTC), 304, 309
National Occupational Classification
(NOC), 99, 100–101, 104
National Steel, 384
NCR, 247
needs analysis, 130
Nesbitt Burns, 331
Nestlé, 73
net HR demand, 156–157
net HR requirements, 155–161
"new deal" in employment, 281
New York Fire Department, 224
Newfoundland Minister of Natural
Resources, 270
Newman, Paul, 9
NOC. *See* National Occupational
Classification (NOC)
nominal group technique, 84–85,
174–176
Nortel Networks, 187, 325, 330
The North West Company, 4
Nova Corp., 330
Novell, 331

**O**
objectives
development of, 15–17
of downsizing, 265*f*
methods of accomplishing, 20
observation, 101
Occupational Information Network
(O*Net), 99
occupational injuries, 380–381

on-the-job training, 308
Ontario, 77
Ontario Confederation of University
Faculty Associations (OCUFA),
218–219
Ontario Hydro, 227–228
openness to experience, 305
operating synergy, 324
Organisation for Economic
Co-operation and Development
(OECD), 194
organizational change, 264*f*
organizational culture. *See* culture
organizational factors affecting HR
forecasting, 153
organizational flexibility, 149
organizational politics, 358
organizational size, 79
outplacement, 267
output analysis, 102
outsourcing
advanced technology, 357
contract negotiation, 361–362
core competencies, 356
defined, 124
described, 352–353
and employee morale, 359–360
evaluation team, 361
examples, 353
financial savings, 355–356
HR functions, 353
improved service, 357
larger organizations, and HR
functions, 353–354
management of, 360–363
monitoring the arrangement, 363
organizational politics, 358
payroll outsourcing, 125
projected *versus* actual
benefits, 358
rationale for, 355
and reduced value, 360
request for proposal (RFP),
360–361
risks and limitations, 358
service risks, 359
small businesses, 353, 354
specialized expertise, 357–358
strategic focus, 356–357
vendor selection, 360–361

**P**
Pac-Man defensive manoeuvre, 327
Packard, David, 40
parent-country nationals
(PCNs), 301

Parfitt, Joanna, 296
Parmalat, 322
Pathfinder software, 127, 128
payroll outsourcing, 125
people management, 152
PepsiCo, 30, 243, 252–253, 325
perceptions of justice, 271
performance
    downsizing, and financial
        performance, 273–274
    evaluation of. *See* performance
        evaluation
    improvement of, through strategic
        HRM, 36–37
    measure, 385
performance appraisal. *See*
    performance evaluation
performance evaluation
    differentiation strategy, 59
    employee potential, assessment
        of, 236
    global assignments, 310–312
    information technology
        (IT) and, 124
    low-cost-provider strategy, 56–57
    mergers, 341
    of strategy, 20
performance potential matrix, 236*t*
PERSIM model, 156
personal characteristics, 305–306
personality, 303–304
personnel analyses, 151–153
perspective, 6
Petro Canada, 243
Pfizer, 324
Pillsbury, 332, 333
Pizza Hut, 325
plan
    described, 5
    strategy as, 6
ploy, 6
poison pills, 327
political factors, 74–75
Polo Ralph Lauren, 57
Polo Ralph Lauren Canada, 78
Porter, Michael, 17, 31, 44
position, 6, 93
Position Analysis Questionnaire
    (PAQ), 101, 108
Position Description
    Questionnaire, 101
post-assignment activities
    career development, 310
    compensation, 312–313
    performance appraisal, 310–312
    repatriation, 308–310

Power Financial, 322
Pratt & Whitney Canada, 353
pre-assignment training, 306–308
prediction, 154
PricewaterhouseCoopers, 219, 296,
    328, 332–333
proactive approach, 71
probabilistic models, 201
procedural justice, 271
process-based forecasting, 147
Procter & Gamble, 10, 57
production analysis, 102
professional affiliations, 377
professional associations, 65
professional consultants, 65
professional personnel, 151
profitable personnel, 152
profits, 383
projection, 154
promotion, 238
province of Ontario, 77
province of Saskatchewan, 180
psychological contract
    accommodation, 281–282
    altering, 281–282
    defined, 280
    managing change in, 280–281
    transformation, 282
the public, 79
Public Service Commission
    of Canada, 233
publications, 64
purpose
    described, 5
    strategy as, 6

**Q**
quality improvement, 357
questionnaires, 101–102

**R**
Rand Corporation, 172
rating system, 229–230
rearview-mirror methods, 67
recorded data, 103–104
recruitment
    e-recruiting, 179
    in international context, 301–303
    opportunistic, in succession
        management, 234–235
    recommendations, 215
    strategic advantages and
        disadvantages of key
        options, 302
recruits, 152
redesign. *See* work redesign

regression analysis, 180–183
relational database, 129
renewal model, 208–211
reorientation strategy, 275
repatriation, 308–310
replacement charts, 127, 233
replacement needs, 159
replacement planning, 196–200,
    226–230
*Report on Business,* 322
reputation for corporate social
    performance (RCSP), 274–275
request for proposal
    (RFP), 131, 360–361
*Research, Measurement and Evaluation
    of Human Resources,* 391
resource-based perspective, 31–32
resource constraint, 150
respect, 214
restructuring, 262–263, 264*f*
    *see also* downsizing
restructuring strategies
    bankruptcy, 10
    described, 8–9
    divestiture, 9
    turnaround strategy, 9
results focus, 48
retention of key employees, 69–70
retention programs, 212–213
reverse culture shock, 309
review/react linkage, 43
rightsizing, 262, 276
ripple effects, 199
Riverside County Human Resources
    Department, 134
Robinson's, 4
ROE (return on equity), 383
ROI (return on investments), 383, 384
role competencies, 111
Rolex, 57
rotations, 238–239
Royal Dutch Shell Group, 67, 296

**S**
SAP, 129
Sarbanes Oxley requirements, 372
SAS, 325
Saskatchewan, 180
SaskTel, 214
scarcity, 150
scenario forecasting, 178
scenario planning, 67
scenarios, 155
Schwinn, 359
scientific management, 95–96
scripted demos, 131

Sears, 37
selection
  bias, 248
  differentiation strategy, 58
  in international context, 303–305
  low-cost-provider strategy, 56
  mergers, 338–340
  personal characteristics, 305–306
  personality, 303–304
  trainability, 304–305
  vendor, 360–361
self-evaluations, 101
self-service, 134
seminars, 65
separation, 331
separation of cause and effect, 393
September 11 events, 227
sequencing model, 208–211
serial downsizers, 275
share purchase, 335
shareholders, 78
short-run forecast, 154
short-term emergency
    replacement, 196
shorter-term planning, 6–7
SHRM Global Forum, 304
Siemens Rolm Communications, 41
Silicon Valley, 39
Sim, Howard, 284
Simon Fraser University, 204
simple regression prediction
    model, 18
Simpsons, 4
Singapore Technologies Ltd., 136
situational contexts, 204
size of organization, 79
skillpower™, 126
"skills determine strategy"
    outlook, 40
skills inventory, 126, 195
skills shortage, 212
SkillView Technologies, 127
smile sheets, 240
Smith, Coleen, 310
SmithBooks, 322
smoking, costs of, 381
social factors, 77
Society for Human Resources
    Management, 66, 372
soft goals, 15–17
Southwest Airline, 19, 20, 31, 69, 234
special assignments, 239–240
specialist personnel, 151
specialty products, 128–129
specific competencies, 111
Sperry, 323

staffing table, 177, 178
stakeholders
  client satisfaction, 375
  customers, 78
  defined, 78
  employees, 80
  governments, 79
  the public, 79
  shareholders, 78
  suppliers, 78–79
  unions, 79–80
Star Alliance, 325
stars, 326
Statistics Canada, 80, 171, 264
stewardship role, 70
stochastic models, 201
strategic downsizing, 277–278
strategic HRM
  see also HRM strategy
  defined, 30
  downsizing and competitive
      advantage, 283
  importance of, 36
  improved goal attainment, 36–37
  need for, 4–5
  and performance, 36–37
  planning model, 48
  see also strategic planning process
  risks of, 37–38
  role of, 21–22
  versus traditional, 44
  two-way approach, 40
strategic HRM theories
  behavioural perspective, 32–34
  human capital theory, 34–35
  resource-based view, 31–32
strategic international HR
    planning, 298
strategic international HRM
  adaptive IHRM approach, 300
  career development, 310
  compensation, 312–313
  and corporate international
      business strategies, 299–301
  defined, 299
  domestic strategy, 299
  dual-career couples, 296, 297
  eight developmental goals of
      global competence, 303
  employment legislation, 297–298
  exportive IHRM approach, 300
  external fit, 299
  flexibility, 298
  global strategy, 300–301
  integrative IHRM approach, 301
  internal fit, 299

  key challenges, 297–298
  key HR practices and processes,
      301–306
  labour relations, 313–314
  multidomestic strategy, 299–300
  multinational strategy, 300
  on-the-job training, 308
  performance appraisal, 310–312
  personal characteristics, 305–306
  post-assignment activities,
      308–313
  pre-assignment training, 306–308
  recruitment, 301–303
  repatriation, 308–310
  role of HR function, 298
  selection, 303–305
  strategic international
      HR planning, 298
  workforce diversity, 297
strategic partnering, 43
strategic planning process
  benefits of strategy
      formulation, 20–21
  competitive advantage, 18–20
  competitive position, 17–18
  establishment of mission, vision
      and values, 13–15
  executive team membership, 43
  external environment,
      analysis of, 17
  integrative linkage, 43–45
  involvement in, 43–45
  model of, 13, 21f
  objectives, development of, 15–17
  objectives, methods of
      accomplishing, 20
  performance, evaluation of, 20
  review/react linkage, 43
strategic replacement, 233–234
strategies (types)
  acquisitions, 11
  bankruptcy, 10
  best-cost provider strategy, 18
  broad differentiation
      strategy, 17–18
  business strategy, 11–13
  corporate strategies, 8
  differentiation strategy, 57–59
  divestiture, 9
  domestic strategy, 299
  downsizing strategies. See
      downsizing strategies
  focused niche strategy, 18
  global strategy, 300–301
  growth strategies, 10–11
  harvest strategy, 11

incremental growth, 10
international growth, 10
liquidation, 10
low-cost provider strategy, 17,
    55–57
maintenance strategies, 11
market niche strategy, 18
mergers, 11
multidomestic strategy, 299–300
multinational strategy, 300
reorientation strategy, 275
restructuring strategies, 8–10
turnaround strategy, 9
strategy
    see also strategies (types)
    benefits of strategy formulation,
        20–21
    defined, 5
    as dynamic process, 7
    emergent strategy, 7
    execution of, 6–7
    five Ps of, 5–6
    framework for understanding, 5–6
    and HR deliverables, 390f
    HRM strategy. See HRM strategy
    intended strategy, 7
    linking HR processes to, 38–43
    multiple strategies, 12
    as plan, 6
    as purpose, 6
    reality of the strategic process, 7f
    realized strategy, 7
    shorter-term planning, 6–7
    strategy-making hierarchy, 14f
    succession management,
        alignment of, 230–231
strategy-making hierarchy, 14f
stress, 337, 341
succession management
    broader focus of, 227–228
    challenges to implementation,
        246–249
    defined, 224
    elitism, 246–247
    employee role, 244–246
    evolution of, 226–227
    external candidates, 229
    family businesses, 198, 225
    importance of, 196, 224–226
    and information
        technology (IT), 127
    internal candidates, 229
    long-term succession, 196
    monitoring succession
        management, 243–244
    rating system, 229–230

reasons for, 226
risk of spotlight, 247–248
selection bias, 248
short-term emergency
    replacement, 196
succession readiness code, 199
succession/replacement
    analysis, 196–200
succession/replacement charts
    and tables, 197–200, 198t
talent pools, 228–229
time horizon, 228
versus traditional planning,
    227–230
unpredictable futures, 248–249
succession management process
    alignment with strategy, 230–231
    coaching, 241–243
    competency-based approaches,
        231–232
    described, 230
    developmental opportunities
        and experiences, 237–243
    formal training and development,
        240–241
    high-potential employees,
        identification of, 232–236
    identification of required skills
        and competencies, 231–232
    job-based approach, 231
    job rotations, 238–239
    management development
        methods, 237–243
    mentors, 241–243
    monitoring succession
        management, 243–244
    promotion, 238
    special assignments, 239–240
succession planning. See succession
    management
Succession Pulse™, 127
succession readiness code, 199
succession/replacement analysis,
    196–200
Sumitomo Metals, 58
Sun Life Financial, 224
Sun Microsystems, 39, 164–165
suppliers, 78–79
supply forecasting
    employee retention programs,
        212–213
    linear programming, 203–204
    management inventory, 195
    mandatory retirement, 192–194
    Markov models, 200–203
    movement analysis, 204–208

renewal model, 208–211
sequencing model, 208–211
skills inventory, 195
succession/replacement analysis,
    196–200
vacancy model, 208–211
Surrey Metro Savings Credit
    Union, 43
surveys, 376
survival, 382–383
survivor, 260, 270–271, 271–272, 340
survivor syndrome, 270
Swiss Chalet, 12
SWOT analysis, 17, 24–26
Syncrude Canada Ltd., 235
synergy, 324–325
systematic change, 262

T
Taco Bell, 325
Taiwanese Ministry of
    Communications, 202
takeover
    defined, 324
    hostile takeover, 324, 327
    merger methods, 327
    tax advantages, 326
talent management culture, 234
The Talent Network, 186–187
talent pools, 228–229
talent segmentation, 229
tangible assets, 18
task forces, 332
Taylor, Fred, 95, 103
TD Bank, 17
technical personnel, 151
technological factors, 75
technology
    see also information
        technology (IT)
    acceptance, 133
    impact of, 76
    and outsourcing, 357
    sample technology effectiveness
        items, 133
    trends, 68
technology acceptance, 133
Telus, 325
temporal contexts, 204
temporary replacements, 233
termination, 340
Thai Airways, 325
third-country nationals (TCNs), 301
Thomson, David, 225
Thomson, Ken, 225
Thomson, Roy, 225

Thomson Corporation, 225, 322
3E Model, 242
360° evaluation, 101, 127
3M, 13, 58, 69, 242
time horizon, 228
time-series models, 159
Time Warner, 340
Timex, 55
top management, 80–81
Toronto, 5, 345–347, 359–360
Toronto Blue Jays, 237
Towers/Bonimart, 4
Toyota Motor Co., 55
Toys R Us (Canada) Ltd., 237
trackability, 394
traditional HR
    planning models, 35
    *versus* strategic HR, 44
trainability, 304–305
training
    cross-cultural training, 304,
        306, 310
    differentiation strategy, 58–59
    low-cost-provider strategy, 56
    management development,
        240–241
    mergers, 341
    on-the-job training, 308
    pre-assignment training, 306–308
transaction-based forecasting, 147
TransCanada Pipelines Ltd., 330
transformation, 282
transition team, 335, 336–337, 338
transitional probabilities, 201
trend analysis, 66
trends, 68–70
Trenton Car Works, 284
trust, 214
turnaround strategy, 9
turnover, 41, 46, 212, 380–381
two-way approach, 40

**U**
unions
    *see also* labour relations
    and benefits, 77

and international HR strategy,
    313–314
interventionist response,
    284–285
pragmatic response, 285
and restructuring efforts, 284–285
as stakeholder, 79–80
UNISYS, 323
United Airlines, 325
United Church of Canada, 353
United Food and Commercial
    Workers (UFCW), 56
United Parcel Service (UPS), 45
University of Sheffield Effectiveness
    Program, 152
University of Toronto, 193
unpredictable futures, 248–249
upward mobility rate, 211
urgency, 336
utility analysis, 386

**V**
vacancy model, 208–211
value proposition, 17
values, 15, 16
Vancouver health region, 69
vendor selection, 131,
    360–361
vertical integration, 325
vertical merger, 323
Viasystems Canada, 5
videotaping, 101
violence in the workplace, 77
VIP, 128
vision, 13–15
"Voices of Survivors: Words that
    Downsizing CEOs Should
    Hear" (O'Neill and Lenn), 272

**W**
Wagar, Terry H., 259
Wal-Mart, 4, 13, 72, 78, 243
Wang, Xiaoyun, 295
Wardair, 330
Warner-Lambert, 308, 324
web-based HR, 134–135

Web links
    alignment of HR with strategy, 49
    demand forecasting, 184
    downsizing, 286
    environmental influences, 82
    evaluation of HRM, 395
    HR forecasting, 162
    information technology, 137
    job analysis, 113
    mergers and acquisitions, 343
    outsourcing, 363
    strategic international HRM, 315
    strategic management, 22
    succession management, 249
    supply forecasting, 216
Wedgbury, Mia, 267
Wells Fargo, 398–399
Wendy's Restaurants, 325
Whale, Elliot, 237
white-collar employees, and job
    insecurity, 272
white knights, 327
Williams, Danny, 270
Windham International
    GMAC GRS, 304
Woodward's, 4, 225, 239
work-life family balance, 85–86
work redesign, 262, 278
workforce diversity, 77, 297
workforce planning activities, 148
workforce reduction, 262,
    263, 269f, 276
    *see also* downsizing
Workplace and Employee
    Survey, 264
WorldatWork, 309

**Y**
Yamaha, 326

**Z**
Zellers, 4, 55, 239